D1269782

Holy Gītā

Ready Reference

A compendium of questions and answers with an alphabetical index of the pādas

and

Gītā Aṣṭottaraśata Nāmāvalī

Chinmaya International Foundation
Adi Sankara Nilayam
Veliyanad

First Edition	December 2005	-	2000 copies
Reprint	June 2006	-	2000 copies
Reprint	October 2007	-	5000 copies

Publisher

CHINMAYA INTERNATIONAL FOUNDATION
Adi Sankara Nilayam,Veliyanad
Ernakulam District – 682319, Kerala, INDIA
Tel: 91-484-2747307/2747104
Fax: 91-484-2749729
Email: chinfo@md2.vsnl.net.in
Website: www.chinfo.org

Distribution Centre in India

CHINMAYA INTERNATIONAL FOUNDATION
and
CENTRAL CHINMAYA MISSION TRUST
Sandeepany Sadhanalaya
Saki Vihar Road, Mumbai – 400 072. INDIA
Tel: 91-22-28572367/28575806
Fax: 91-22-28573065
Email: ccmt@vsnl.com
Website: www.chinmayamission.com

Distribution Centre in USA

CHINMAYA MISSION WEST
Publications Division
560 Bridgetown Pike
Langhorne, PA 19053, USA
Tel: (215) 396-0390
Fax: (215) 396-9710
Email: publications@chinmaya.org
Website: www.chinmayapublications.org

Printed in India at
Thomson Press Ltd., Mumbai

Price: Rs. 250/-

ISBN 81-903728-0-7

Dedicated to the latent
Yogeśvara Kṛṣṇa and Dhanurdhara Arjuna

in every individual

॥ गीता सुगीता कर्तव्या किमन्यैः शास्त्रविस्तरैः ॥

gītā sugītā kartavyā kimanyaiḥ śāstravistaraiḥ

"The Bhagavad Gītā needs to be mastered; what is the need for a pile of scriptures?" — ***Mahābhārata 6.43.1***

॥ नमो नमस्ते ॥

Bhagavad Gītā – a class all by itself

The Bhagavad Gītā is a piece of art of strange beauty and it stands apart from everything else, in a class all by itself. It is liquid poetry expounding solid philosophy. In the lucidity of its metre it crystallises some of the rarest gems of moral and spiritual values. Its breezy discourses have a firm style. The fluidity of its eloquence falls like merciful rain upon every broken personality, making it whole by its magic touch. It is not a book of science, and yet, it is very scientific in its approach to the theme. It has not the airy nothingness of familiar philosophical discourses, and yet, all philosophies seem to meet within its ample stretch.

Swami Chinmayananda

Veda Vyāsa – an all-round genius

The versatile genius of Vyāsa has never left anything that he has touched without raising it to the most sublime heights of perfection. With an unimaginable capacity for composing incomparable poetry; unique prose-diction; chaste descriptions; artistic, literary designs; original innovations both in thought and form—a brilliant philosopher, a man of consummate wisdom, a genius in worldly knowledge, at one time in the palace, at another time in the battle-field, at still another time among the silent snow peaks—strode the colossus, Śrī Vyāsa, as an embodiment of what is best in the Hindu tradition. Such an all-round genius has not yet been reported ever to have been born, lived or achieved so much in the history of this globe, at any other time!

Swami Chinmayananda

Foreword

Pujya Gurudev Swami Chinmayanandaji devoted his entire life to spiritual renaissance. For almost half a century, he toured the length and breadth of the world on 'wings and wheels' carrying the message of the Upaniṣads and the Bhagavad Gītā to vast audiences and individuals alike. The global Chinmaya Mission is a testimony to his noble work as well as the gratitude of the many who have benefited by his presence and teachings.

Pujya Gurudev was the 'Geetacharya' of modern times. His discourses on the Bhagavad Gītā held listeners enthralled and transformed millions. His lectures on the Gītā were soon edited and compiled, and thus was born the 'Holy Gītā' – an exhaustive commentary on the Bhagavad Gītā by Swami Chinmayanandaji. This commentary was unique in many ways: the explanations were logical, well elucidated with day-to-day examples, interspersed with humour, abundant with many original interpretations and had a universal appeal. Just as a photo would capture an individual's mood, Pujya Gurudev's multifaceted personality stands wholly revealed in his Holy Gītā. The Holy Gītā is not only a commentary on the Bhagavad Gītā, but is also a thorough presentation of the Vedāntic Philosophy and an unfailing guide to all seekers of Truth.

I am very happy to note that the Chinmaya International Foundation (CIF) has brought out this elegant and student-friendly Ready Reference book on the Holy Gītā. This work is sure to benefit all sincere students of Vedānta, and the Bhagavad Gītā in particular. I am also pleased to see the re-publication of the alphabetical index of all the pādas of the Bhagavad Gītā first compiled by the late Sri C. Madhava Rao. Our profound thanks to Sri D.C. Rao for enthusiastically sponsoring the entire project.

Swami Tejomayananda
Chairman, CIF

Sandeepany Sadhanalaya,
Mumbai, India
Gītā Jayanti and Tapovan Jayanti,
Dec' 11, 2005.

Genesis and Acknowledgements

The Golden Jubilee of the Chinmaya Mission was celebrated in 2001 with the 'Chinmaya Visva Sammelan'. More than 10,000 people from all over the world from the various Chinmaya Mission Centres congregated at Mumbai, India and many unique programmes were conducted and the 'Holy Gītā Quiz' was one among them. For conducting the Holy Gītā Quiz, all the questions and answers had to be first compiled. You could very well say that that compilation of about 250 brief questions and answers gave the first impetus to this book. Once the Chinmaya Visva Sammelan Celebrations were over, the Gītā quiz questions and answers were filed away.

Two years had almost gone by. It was then that Dr. D.C. Rao showed us the book prepared by his late father Sri C. Madhava Rao: the 'pādānukramaṇikā' of the Bhagavad Gītā i.e., an alphabetical arrangement of all quarters of the Bhagavad Gīta verses. He explored whether Chinmaya International Foundation (CIF) would be willing to republish this work. This book published by his father, almost 20 years back, was like a ready reckoner to the Bhagavad Gītā verses. While all regular indices of the Gītā contain only the first pāda, or sometimes the words found in the Gītā, this book was unique—it had all the four pādas (quarters) arranged in alphabetical order. You could, with the help of this book, track with ease any verse of the Gītā. It then struck me that a student friendly book could be prepared with the 'quiz material' as well as the 'pādānukramaṇikā'. Pujya Guruji Swami Tejomayanandaji, Head of the Chinmaya Mission, approved and blessed the project and work started. Sri D.C. Rao, who was keen on this work, came forward to sponsor the entire project.

Little did we realise the magnitude of the effort required to re-create this book. We had imagined that all that was necessary was to retype the originals and publish a book! We had not taken into account two factors—(1) the 'Quiz Material' alone cannot form a complete book and that (2) the 'pādānukramaṇikā' needed a full revision.

- The 'Quiz Material' though adequate to serve its then explicit purpose was incomplete and inadequate to be re-christened a 'compendium of questions and answers of the Bhagavad Gītā'. A compendium had to contain more than just 'quiz-type' brief questions and answers. It had to incorporate elaborations on all the terms, definitions, thoughts and concepts found in the Bhagavad Gītā and highlight the unique interpretations given by Gurudev Swami Chinmayanandaji to certain verses. We also wanted it to contain a section on the important verses of the Gītā to be remembered. To make the book complete and useful to the student, it appeared there was a lot more work pending.

- While checking the 'pādānukramaṇikā', notwithstanding the hard work of the compiler Sri C. Madhava Rao, we entered into difficulties in placing alphabetically words containing anusvāra and visarga. What would be the placement of anusvāra and visarga – which are not regular alphabets – in the Sanskrit alphabetical order? While arranging them we had to keep in mind that the order should be logical yet student-friendly so that a verse could be tracked with ease. Thus started our study of the extant literature on how Sanskrit dictionaries arrange words, including pathbreaking works such as that of Vedic Concordance of Maurice Bloomfield. But as these earlier arrangements were non-student-friendly and would defeat the very purpose of our endeavour, we evolved our own system to arrange the pādas.

Work started in right earnest – in eight months both these were complete.

Br. Pranipata Chaitanya helped in the typing of the Bhagavad Gītā Quiz material. Meera Seth, Dr. D.C. Rao and Br. Rishi Chaitanya edited and proofread the initial 'Quiz material'.

Swamini Niranjanananda, Dr. Kanshi Ram and Swamini Vimalananda, with their constructive criticisms, by just saying -"this won't do" - facilitated the quantum leap from a partial 'Quiz-type-collection' to a complete 'Reference Compendium'. Dr. Kanshi Ram also helped us whenever we had difficulty with Sanskrit grammar. The CIF staff—Smt. Sarala Suresh, Kumari Jaya and Smt. Radhika Manoj—typed, proofread and worked continually for many months at stretch. They worked patiently with full zest.

And when the book required its 'right finish' – help arrived from the Lord Himself – Smt. Padma Narayanan and Smt. Sandhya Sundar joined the team and pooled in their editing talents. Smt. Sandhya Sundar's exceptional editing skills have given this book its well deserved finesse.

As far as the 'pādānukramaṇikā' is concerned, we have followed the footsteps of Sri. C. Madhava Rao, who undertook this daunting task of preparing and publishing an index of all the pādas of the Bhagavad Gītā as a means of "tracing the context of any pāda of profound significance which may haunt one and otherwise would require a taxing search to trace it." We believe that an index of all the pādas is considerably more useful to students of the Bhagavad Gītā than a mere index of the first pāda alone. Using Sri Madhava Rao's pioneering work as a starting point, we have edited and revised the presentation of the pādānukramaṇikā. Sri Madhava Rao's son Dr. D.C Rao, Br. Vedanta Chaitanya, Smt. Sarala Suresh, Kumari Jaya and Smt. Rajalekshmi prepared the revised draft and spent many months in perfecting it to ensure that the coverage of the pādas is complete and accurate. The hard work of Br. Vedanta Chaitanya who revised and re-revised this work almost a dozen times is highly commendable. His persistence enabled us to evolve the logic for the present alphabetical arrangement of the pādānukramaṇikā.

Pujya Guruji Swami Tejomayanandaji permitted us to incorporate his composition of the Bhagavad Gītā Aṣṭottaraśatanamāvalī.

On the whole this work was a 'yajña' in the true sense of the term. Help, advice, guidance, as well as funds flowed freely from everywhere - literally speaking from 'Washington to Moscow'!

Our special thanks to Sri. D.C. Rao of Chinmaya Mission, Washington, who not only has sponsored the entire project but also helped in editing and preparing this work. We are also indebted to Central Chinmaya Mission Trust, Mumbai, the apex body of the Chinmaya Mission – Worldwide, who permitted us to use the Holy Gītā – the very source of the 'Bhagavad Gītā Question and Answer Bank'. Our indebtedness to 'Omkarananda Ashram', Himalayas, whose software Itranslator 99 (freeware) has been of great help in preparing this book. Our thanks to Sri Sreekumar, CIF Administrator, who helped in all the administrative matters with respect to the publishing. Our thanks also to the S.T. Reddiar & Sons for giving an excellent finish to the book.

But for Śrī Kṛṣṇa where is the Bhagavad Gītā? Without Pujya Gurudev Swami Chinmayanandaji there would be no Holy Gītā. Bereft of the grace of Pujya Guruji Swami Tejomayanandaji - the underlying blessing factor of this project - you would not be holding this book in your hand!

Saying just 'thanks' to the Lord and Guru feels so incomplete and unfulfilling.

Swami Advayananda
Acharya, CIF

Adi Sankara Nilayam,
Veliyanad, Ernakulam District,
Pin: 682 319.
Gītā Jayanti and Tapovan Jayanti,
Dec' 11, 2005.

Preface to the Third Reprint

The growing demand for the Holy Gītā Ready Reference has necessitated this third reprint within two years. In this reprint we have improved the quality of the paper and the total finishing of the book. We hope this has made the book more handy and attractive.

We thank Pujya Swami Dheerananda, Acharya, Chinmaya Mission, Washington Regional Center, USA for arranging the sponsorship for this reprint. The major portion of the sponsorship, Rs. 4 lacs, has been offered by the Balakrishnan family: Ramaswamy, Janaki, Karthik and Aparna of Maryland, USA. Dr. D.C. Rao, Washington, USA, who had sponsored the entire first edition of this book, has offered Rs. 1 lac for this fresh reprint. Chinmaya International Foundation is thankful to them for their kind support.

May the immortal message of Śrī Kṛṣṇa inspire us to follow the Gītā way of life.

Dr. K.H. Subramanian,
Director, CIF

Adi Sankara Nilayam,
Veliyanad, Ernakulam District,
Pin: 682 319.
Hanuman Mastakabhisheka at Sidhbari,
October 10, 2007.

Book Arrangement

The book is divided and arranged into the following broad sections:

1. **Bhagavad Gītā Praśnottarī** – a compendium of questions and answers from 'The Holy Gītā'. Every chapter is divided into the following sub-sections:
    - Terms and Definitions
    - Thoughts and Concepts
    - Selections for Reflection
    - Verses for Memorisation

    All these sub-sections are from the Holy Gītā, the commentary on the Bhagavad Gītā by Pujya Gurudev Swami Chinmayanandaji.

2. **Bhagavad Gītā Pādānukramaṇikā** – an alphabetical index to all the quarters of the Bhagavad Gītā.

3. **Bhagavad Gītā Aṣṭottaraśatanāmāvalī** – 108 worshipful glories of the Bhagavad Gītā composed by Pujya Guruji Swami Tejomayanandaji.

Contents

Bhagavad Gītā Praśnottarī

A compendium of questions and answers from the Holy Gītā

Read this first

The Bhagavad Gītā Praśnottarī is designed to be of help to the serious student of the Bhagavad Gītā in general and the 'Holy Gītā' - the commentary of Gurudev Swami Chinmayanandaji - in particular. Don't be cheated by the deceptive semblance this book has with 'school or college guidebooks'.

If you are interested to know what the Bhagavad Gītā is all about: Open any page, any section—read regularly for an hour daily for one week, and pass the book on to others.

If you seek clarifications on some concepts in Vedānta or a chapter of Bhagavad Gītā: Open the concerned chapter and look for a question that voices your doubt. An index of the questions provided at the end of the book will be useful for the 'search operation' you would like to do on questions related to your doubt. Some questions have been answered in more ways than one.

If you want to study the Bhagavad Gītā thoroughly: There are two ways you could use this book for the above purpose: read this book first and then the 'Holy Gītā' or vice versa. Both ways have their own individual benefits. The first one gives ease to your study and the second tests your comprehension.

Tips for best Results:

- Go chapter by chapter, question by question
- Be regular in your study
- If you are not satisfied with the answer or your comprehension of it, make a note of it and move forward
- Revisit your doubts after you complete the whole book—chances are that your doubts have been clarified
- This is a companion-book to the Holy Gītā and a tool for its study—in case you want to have a full understanding refer back to the concerned chapter in the Holy Gītā

Note:

- The term 'Gurudev' - when used in the text - refers to Swami Chinmayananda.
- Throughout the book we have used male terminology 'man, his, him', to follow convention and for ease of reading: it is rather inelegant to use his/her, s/he in every sentence. The term 'man', of course, encompasses all seekers, male and female.
- Any compilation has to be necessarily subjective. This book covers only those questions and answers that the compilers have thought important to be covered in a span of nearly 400 pages.
- This compilation could be used by teachers to teach Bhagavad Gītā in colleges and schools as well.

The Gītā as Others See It

"The Gītā is the universal mother. She turns away nobody. Her door is wide open to anyone who knocks. A true votary of the Gītā does not know what disappointment is.......... When disappointment stares me in the face and all alone I see not one ray of light, I go back to the Bhagavad Gītā. I find a verse here and a verse there, and I immediately begin to smile in the midst of overwhelming tragedies—and my life has been full of external tragedies—and if they have left no visible, no indelible scar on me, I owe it all to the teaching of the Bhagavad Gītā."

- Mahatma Gandhi

"The Gītā was not preached either as a pastime for persons tired out after living a worldly life in the pursuit of selfish motives, nor as a preparatory lesson for living such worldly life, but in order to give philosophical advice as to how one should live one's worldly life with an eye to Release, Mokṣa, and as to the true duty of human beings in worldly life. My last prayer to everyone, therefore, is that one should not fail to thoroughly understand this ancient science of the life of a householder, or of worldly life, as early as possible in one's life."

- Lokamanya Tilak

"Moderation is therefore the key-note of the Gītā and the harmonizing of all the constituents of man, till they vibrate in perfect attunement with the One, the Supreme Self."

"Have no personal interest in the event; carry out the duty imposed by the position in life, realize that Īśvara, at once Lord and Law, is the doer, working out the mighty evolution that ends in Bliss and Peace; be identified with Him by devotion, and then perform duty as duty, fighting without passion or desire, without anger or hatred; thus activity forges no bonds, Yoga is accomplished, and the soul is free."

- Dr. Annie Besant

"The Gītā is a bouquet composed of the beautiful flowers of spiritual truths collected from the Upaniṣads."

- Swami Vivekananda

"To my knowledge, there is no book in the whole range of the world's literature so high above all as the Bhagavad Gītā, which is a treasure-house of Dharma not only for Hindus but for all mankind."

- Madan Mohan Malaviya

"The Gītā is one of the clearest and most comprehensive summaries of the Perennial Philosophy ever to have been done. Hence its enduring value, not only for Indians, but for all mankind."

- Aldous Huxley

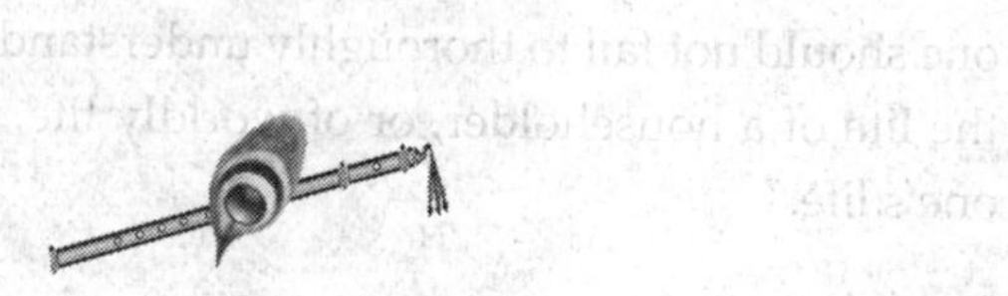

General Introduction to Bhagavad Gītā

If the Upaniṣads are the textbooks of philosophical principles discussing man, world and God, the Gītā is a handbook of instructions as to how every human being can come to live the subtle philosophical principles of Vedānta in the actual work-a-day world.

Thoughts and Concepts

1. What were the causes for Arjuna's emotional repressions?

The causes for Arjuna's emotional repressions are as follows:

(1) Arjuna, a great hero, confident of his own strength, was made to live amidst the unjust tyranny of his cousins. At the same time Arjuna could not give vent to his nature because of the righteous policy of 'peace at all costs' of his eldest brother Yudhiṣṭhira.

(2) During the last year of their lives incognito, the Pāṇḍava family had to serve as menials in the palace of the Rāja of Virāṭa. The carping injustice and the cruel indignities of the situation caused a lot of repression in Arjuna's mind.

(3) After their long and strenuous trials, when the Pāṇḍavas at last reached their native kingdom, their tyrant cousin Duryodhana denied them not only their right to half the kingdom, but also refused all terms of conciliation.

2. Arjuna's arguments for not wanting to fight the Kauravas reflected the earlier suggestions of ____________.

Dhṛtarāṣṭra[1]

1. The shrewd, blind Dhṛtarāṣṭra, father of the Kauravas, probably understood the psychological condition of the great warrior, Arjuna, and on the day previous to the great war sent Sañjaya, his emissary, to Arjuna with a secret message.

3. Differentiate the objective mind (manas) from the subjective mind (buddhi).

The mind, for the purposes of our study and understanding, may be considered as constituted of two distinct sides—one facing the world of stimuli that reach it from the objects of the world and the other facing 'within' which reacts to the stimuli received. The outer mind facing the object is called the 'objective mind'—in Sanskrit it is called the 'manas'—and the inner mind is called the 'subjective mind'—in Sanskrit, the 'buddhi'.

4. The split in the individual between the subjective and objective aspects of the mind is created by the layer of ___________.

Egoistic desires

5.What is the 'Yoga' pointed out in the Gītā?

To bring the subjective and the objective aspects of the mind together into a happy marriage where the objective mind is well disciplined to act faithfully as per the guidance of the subjective is the 'Yoga' pointed out in the Gītā.

6. How can we vitalise the mind?

The mind can be vitalised by reducing the vāsanās.

7. ___________ would result in inner purification.

Selfless activity

8. ___________ is philosophy in action.

Religion

Selections for Reflection

1. Mind is man. As the mind, so is the individual. If the mind is disturbed, the individual is disturbed. If the mind is good, the individual is good.

2. We find Śrī Kṛṣṇa repeatedly goading his friend with the words, "Get up and fight." This does not mean that the Gītā is a war-mongering scripture of the ruling-class. It is a call to each one of us to get up and fight the battle of our own life, according to our own 'svadharma' so that we may exhaust them and thus gain inner purity.

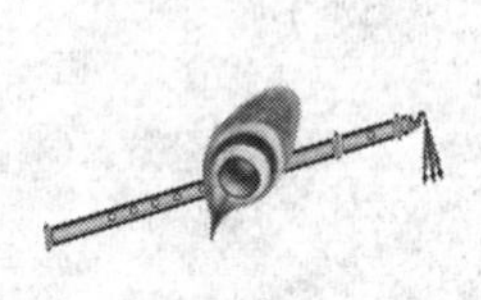

1

Arjunaviṣāda Yoga

The Yoga of Arjuna's Grief

'Active resistance to evil' is the central idea in the doctrine expounded by Śrī Kṛṣṇa in the Gītā. (1.39)

Arjuna's condition of utter despair is the auspicious mental attitude wherein the Gītā-seeds are to be sown and the flowers of Kṛṣṇa-perfection gathered. Be it in an individual or a society, in a community or a nation, religion and philosophy will be in demand only when the heart has come to experience the 'Arjuna-grief'. For learning and living the Gītā, the 'Arjuna-condition' is the initial sādhana.

☙❧

Terms and Definitions

1. Who is a 'Mahāratha'?

He who can single-handedly fight ten thousand archers and is proficient in the science of arms is known as a 'Mahāratha'[1]. (1.4)

2. How does Duryodhana address his teacher?

'Dvijottama' - 'the best among the twice born' (1.7)

3. What are the two ways of interpreting the term 'Hṛṣīkeśa'?

(1) 'Hṛṣīkeśa' is the name of Lord Kṛṣṇa and it has often been translated as 'Lord of the senses'. But this is according to an old derivation: 'hṛṣīka+īśa' = 'Lord of the senses'.

(2) But the word 'hṛṣīka' being an obscure one, modern commentators prefer to explain it as 'hṛṣ+keśa' = 'Having short hair'. (1.15)

4. What does the word 'Pārtha' mean?

'Pārtha' means 'Son of Pṛthā'. It is one of Arjuna's names, 'Pṛthā' being another name for Kuntī. The Sanskrit term Pārtha also carries a flavour of the term 'Pārthiva' meaning 'clay-made', 'earth-formed'. The suggestive implication of this term is very striking, as it connotes that the Gītā is the Song of Truth told by the Immortal to the mortal Arjuna, man's all-time representative. (1.25)

1. He who can fight innumerable but less than ten thousand archers is spoken of as an 'atiratha'. And a 'ratha' is one who can fight against one thousand warriors; he who is lesser than a 'ratha' is called an 'ardha-ratha'.

5. Who is an 'Ātatāyin'?

'Ātatāyin', meaning 'felon' in the Artha Śāstra, is one who deserves to be killed[2]. (1.36)

6. What is 'kula-dharma' (family-dharma)?

'Kula-dharma' is the rules of living, thinking and acting in a united, well-planned family. (1.42)

7. The word 'Dharma' is derived from the Sanskrit root ____________ which means to ________.

'Dhṛ', meaning: to uphold, to sustain, to support (Introduction)

8. What is the meaning of the word 'Upaniṣad'?

'Upaniṣad' is a word indicating a literature that is to be studied by sitting (sad) near (upa) a teacher, in a spirit of receptive meekness and surrender (ni). (Epilogue)

9. Define the term 'Yoga Śāstra'.

The portion of the scriptures that explains the technique of living philosophy and coming to a subjective experience of it is called 'Yoga Śāstra'. (Epilogue)

10. Upaniṣads teach ________.

'Knowledge of Brahman' - 'Brahmavidyā' (Epilogue)

Thoughts and Concepts

1. 'Duryodhana unsettled, runs to his teacher Droṇa'. How does Gurudev compare this?

A child running to its parents in fright (1.2)

2. Why does Duryodhana enumerate the names of the distinguished heroes in his own army?

2. One who sets a house on fire, one who poisons another, one brandishing a sword, one who is a stealer of wealth, a stealer of another's land and wife—these are the six felons (Vasiṣṭha Smṛti, 3.19).

A weak man, to escape from his own mental fears, will whistle to himself in the dark. The guilty conscience of the tyrant king Duryodhana had undermined all his mental strength. The more he realised the combined strength of the great personalities arrayed in the opposite enemy camp, the more abjectly nervous he felt, in spite of the fact that his own army was also manned by highly competent heroes. In order to revive himself, he wanted to hear words of encouragement from his teachers and elders. But when Duryodhana met Droṇa, the Ācārya chose to remain silent, and the helpless king had to find for himself new means of encouragement to revive his own drooping enthusiasm. Therefore, he starts enumerating the great leaders in his own army. (1.7)

3. How does Duryodhana display his vanity?

The incorrigible vanity of the dictatorial tyrant Duryodhana is amply clear when he arrogates to himself the stupendous honour that the vast array of heroes had come ready to lay down their lives for 'his sake'. (1.9)

4. What are the two ways the following verse has been interpreted?

अपर्याप्तं तदस्माकं बलं भीष्माभिरक्षितम् ।
पर्याप्तं त्विदमेतेषां बलं भीमाभिरक्षितम् ॥

aparyāptaṁ tadasmākaṁ balaṁ bhīṣmābhirakṣitam,
paryāptaṁ tvidameteṣāṁ balaṁ bhīmābhirakṣitam.

This verse can be interpreted in the following two ways:

(1) This army of ours defended by Bhīṣma is insufficient, whereas that army of theirs defended by Bhīma is sufficient.

(2) This army of ours protected by Bhīṣma is unlimited, whereas that army of theirs protected by Bhīma is limited. (1.10)

5. Why did Bhīṣma sound his conch?

तस्य सञ्जनयन्हर्षं कुरुवृद्धः पितामहः ।
सिंहनादं विनद्योच्चैः शङ्खं दध्मौ प्रतापवान् ॥

tasya sañjanayanharṣaṁ kuruvṛddhaḥ pitāmahaḥ,
siṁhanādaṁ vinadyoccaiḥ śaṅkhaṁ dadhmau pratāpavān.

Bhīṣma, the oldest of the Kauravas', gave a lion's roar and blew his conch to cheer Duryodhana. (1.12)

6. Gurudev likens the 'sounding of Bhīṣma's conch' to __________ of modern warfare.

The first bullet shot (1.12)

7. What did Arjuna see from his chariot stationed between the two armies?

तत्रापश्यत्स्थितान्पार्थः पितॄनथ पितामहान् ।
आचार्यान्मातुलान्भ्रातॄन्पुत्रान्पौत्रान्सखींस्तथा ॥

tatrāpaśyatsthitānpārthaḥ pitṝnatha pitāmahān,
ācāryānmātulānbhrātṝnputrānpautrānsakhīṁstathā.

श्वशुरान्सुहृदश्चैव सेनयोरुभयोरपि ।
तान्समीक्ष्य स कौन्तेयः सर्वान्बन्धूनवस्थितान् ॥

śvaśurānsuhṛdaścaiva senayorubhayorapi,
tānsamīkṣya sa kaunteyaḥ sarvānbandhūnavasthitān.

Stationed in between both the armies, Arjuna saw fathers, grandfathers, teachers, maternal uncles, brothers, sons, grandsons, fathers-in-law and friends in both armies. (1.26-27)

8. The textbooks of modern psychology would label Arjuna's mental condition as ________.

'Anxiety-state-neurosis' (1.29)

9. What are the physical symptoms displayed by Arjuna in his neurotic condition?

Limbs fail, the mouth is parched, the body quivers, his hair stands on end, the Gāṇḍīva-bow slips from his hand, the skin burns, he is unable to stand and his mind is in a whirl. (1.29-30)

10. What is 'sin'?

'Sin' is only a mistake committed by an ignorant individual ego against its own Divine Nature as the Eternal Soul. To act as the body or the mind or the intellect is to not own up to the responsibilities of a man but to behave under the impulses of an animal nature. All those acts performed and motives entertained are called 'sins' that create gross mental impressions and, thereby, reinforce the walls between us and our cognition of the Divine Spark in us. (1.36)

11. Define 'brāhmaṇa', 'kṣatriya', 'vaiśya' and 'śūdra'.

Those who were intellectuals and had a passion for research and study were styled 'brāhmaṇas'; those who had political ambitions for leadership and took upon themselves the risky art of maintaining peace and plenty and saving the country from internal and external aggressions were called the 'kṣatriyas'; those who served the community through agriculture and trade were the 'vaiśyas'; and lastly, all those who did not fall in any of the above categories were styled as 'śūdras', whose duties in society were service and labour. (1.41)

12. What is meant by 'varṇa-saṅkara' or 'admixture of the castes'?

'Admixture of castes' means people undertaking work incompatible with their inherent vāsanās. E.g. An engineer in charge of a hospital, a doctor in charge of a hydro-electric scheme, etc. (1.41)

13. What were the primary causes of Arjuna's 'anxiety-state-neurosis'?

(1) Anxiety for the fruit of his action (victory in battle) demoralised Arjuna and he got himself into an 'anxiety-state-neurosis'. (1.46)

(2) When the two armies representing the will of the people have marshalled themselves, Arjuna had no individual right to accept any personal honour or dishonour, or to insist on any respect or disrespect, in meeting the individuals who were champions of the wrong side. Without taking this total viewpoint of the situation, Arjuna made the mistake of arrogating to himself the vanities of an individual ego and observed the problem through the glasses of his ego. He recognised himself to be the disciple of Droṇa and the grandson of Bhīṣma. The very same teacher and grandsire were also seeing Arjuna in the opposite camp, but they felt no compunction, because they had no such egoistic misconceptions. They drowned their individuality in the cause they were championing. In short, Arjuna's egoism was the

cause for his terrible moral confusions and misconceptions. (2.4)

These were the primary causes for Arjuna's 'anxiety-state-neurosis'.

14. Every chapter of the Bhagavad Gītā is called 'Upaniṣad'. Why?

Each chapter of the Bhagavad Gītā is called 'Upaniṣad' because each has declarations of such deep significance that a hasty reader will miss their full import unless he does long and intense meditation over the wealth of suggestive meaning that lies concealed behind the simple-looking stanzas. As in the Upaniṣads, here also we need the help of a sympathetic teacher who can train us in the art of opening the seven hundred lockers in the treasure chamber of the Gītā. (Epilogue)

15. The Kauravas and Pāṇḍavas represent ___________.

The negative and divine tendencies, respectively, in human beings (Introduction)

16. Dhṛtarāṣṭra represents ___________.

A mind that is born blind to the Truth (Introduction)

17. Gāndhārī represents ___________.

An intellect that has assumed blindness (Introduction)

18. Kurukṣetra represents ___________.

The spiritual field of self-development (Introduction)

19. On the basis of its first and last words, the contents of the Bhagavad Gītā can be summarised as ___________.

'My Dharma'—'*Mama Dharma*' (Introduction)

20. 'Dharma' can be best translated as ___________.

That which makes a thing or being what it is (Introduction)

21. Explain how Arjuna's condition of dejection symbolises the seeker's mental condition.

The Kauravas, hundred in number, represent the innumerable

ungodly forces of negative tendencies within man, and the Pāṇḍavas, no doubt, represent the divine impulses in him. A constant Mahābhārata war is being waged within every one of us at all our crucial moments of action; and in all cases the negative forces in each one of us are larger in number and usually mightier in their effectiveness, while the inner divine army is ever lesser in number and, apparently, comparatively weaker in efficiency. Therefore, every individual, at the moment of his inward checking up, must necessarily feel the desperations of Arjuna.

The story of the Mahābhārata sounds an optimistic note of hope to man that, even though the divine impulses are seemingly fewer in number, if they are organised fully and brought under the guidance of the Supreme Lord Kṛṣṇa, the Self, then, under His guidance, can easily be ushered into a true and permanent victory over the outnumbering forces of lust and greed.

The Kauravas, representing the negative tendencies and the sinful motives in a man's heart, are born as children to the old king, Dhṛtarāṣṭra, born-blind prince, wedded to Gāndhārī, who had voluntarily blinded herself by putting bandages over her eyes! Commentators are tempted to see in this a very appropriate significance. Mind is born-blind to truth, and when it is wedded to an intellect which also has assumed blindness, the negative instincts yoked with low motives can only beget a hundred criminalities and sins!

When, upon the spiritual field of self-development within (Dharmakṣetra), the lower instincts and the higher ideals array themselves, ready to fight, a true seeker (the captain of the latter), under the guidance of his divine discriminative intellect, takes himself to a point on no-man's land between the two forces for the purpose of reviewing the enemy lines, without identifying himself with either the good or the evil within him. And, at that moment of his introspective meditations, the egoistic entity comes to feel a morbid desperation, unable to undertake the great spiritual adventure of fighting his inner war with any hope of victory.

This peculiar mental condition of a seeker is beautifully represented in the vivid picture of Arjuna's dejection in the opening chapter. (Introduction)

22. Write a short note on 'Dharma'.

The term 'Dharma' is one of the most intractable terms in Hindu philosophy. Derived from the Sanskrit root *'dhṛ'* to uphold, sustain, support—it denotes 'that which holds together the different aspects and qualities of an object into a whole'. Ordinarily, Dharma has been translated as religious code, as righteousness, as a system of morality, as duty, as charity, etc. But the original Sanskrit term has a special connotation of its own which is not captured by any one of these renderings. The best rendering of this term Dharma is 'the Law of Being' meaning 'that which makes a thing or being what it is'. For example, it is the Dharma of the fire to burn, of the sun to shine, etc.

Dharma means, therefore, not merely righteousness or goodness; it indicates the essential nature of anything, without which it cannot retain its independent existence. For example, a cold dark sun is impossible, as heat and light are the Dharmas of the sun. Similarly, if we are to live as truly dynamic men in the world, we can only do so by being faithful to our true nature, and the Gītā explains 'to me my Dharma'. (Introduction)

Selections for Reflection

1. The Upaniṣads were recorded in the form of conversations between the teacher and the taught, in the quiet atmosphere of the silent and peaceful Himalayan valleys. In the Gītā, however, the highest and the best in Hindu philosophy has been reiterated in a more elaborate and detailed dramatic environment, amidst the din and roar of a total war. (Introduction)
2. When our motives are impure and our cause unjust, however well-equipped we may be, our minds inevitably feel restless and

agitated. This is the mental condition of all tyrants and lusty dictators. (1.2)

3. When we are not ourselves pure, we will project our own weaknesses and impurities on others who are working with us as our subordinates. (1.7)

4. The endeavour in chapter 1 of the Gītā is to give the complete 'case-history' of a patient suffering from the typical 'Arjuna-disease'. The Bhagavad Gītā gives an extremely efficient 'Kṛṣṇa-cure' for this soul-killing 'Arjuna-disease'. (1.27)

5. More than deliberate blasphemers of a scripture, the unconscious misinterpreters of a sacred text are the innocent criminals who bring about the wretched downfall of its philosophy. (1.37)

6. Each generation passes down the torch of its culture to the next generation, its children. It is for us to preserve, tend and nourish that torch and hand it over carefully to the succeeding generation, if not more, at least no less bright, than when we got it. (1.42)

7. When the unity of home-life is shattered and when purity of living and sanctity of thought are destroyed within the family, the generation that has caused such a shattering is ordering for itself and for others a melancholy era of hellish sorrows and sufferings. (1.44)

8. Arjuna's unhealthy mental weakness drains off his heroism and he desperately tries to put a paper-crown upon his cowardice, to make it look divine and angelic, and to parade it as 'pity'. Thus, he deliberately misconstrues the very aim of the war and imputes a low motive to the righteous war simply because he wants to justify his pacifist idea, which does not instinctively gurgle out from his known strength, but which oozes out from his ulcerated mind. (1.45)

Verses for Memorisation

धर्मक्षेत्रे कुरुक्षेत्रे समवेता युयुत्सवः ।
मामकाः पाण्डवाश्चैव किमकुर्वत सञ्जय ॥

dharmakṣetre kurukṣetre samavetā yuyutsavaḥ,
māmakāḥ pāṇḍavāścaiva kimakurvata sañjaya.

What did the sons of Pāṇḍu and also my people do when, desirous to fight, they assembled together on the holy plain of Kurukṣetra, O Sañjaya? (1.1)

हृषीकेशं तथा वाक्यमिदमाह महीपते ।
सेनयोरुभयोर्मध्ये रथं स्थापय मेऽच्युत ॥

hṛṣīkeśaṁ tathā vākyamidamāha mahīpate,
senayorubhayormadhye rathaṁ sthāpaya me'cyuta.

Arjuna said these words to Kṛṣṇa (Hṛṣīkeśa), O Lord of the Earth! In the midst of the two armies, place my chariot, O Acyuta. (1.21)

सीदन्ति मम गात्राणि मुखं च परिशुष्यति ।
वेपथुश्च शरीरे मे रोमहर्षश्च जायते ॥

sīdanti mama gātrāṇi mukhaṁ ca pariśuṣyati,
vepathuśca śarīre me romaharṣaśca jāyate.

My limbs fail, and my mouth is parched, my body quivers and my hair stands on end. (1.29)

गाण्डीवं स्रंसते हस्तात्त्वक्चैव परिदह्यते ।
न च शक्नोम्यवस्थातुं भ्रमतीव च मे मनः ॥

gāṇḍīvaṁ sraṁsate hastāttvakcaiva paridahyate,
na ca śaknomyavasthātuṁ bhramatīva ca me manaḥ.

The Gāṇḍīva-bow slips from my hand, and my skin burns all over; I am also unable to stand and my mind is in a whirl, as it were. (1.30)

2

Sāṅkhya Yoga

Yoga of Knowledge

'Sāṅkhya' is the logic of reasoning by which the true nature of the Absolute Reality is comprehended. (2.39)

In this chapter entitled 'Sāṅkhya Yoga', we get an exhaustive summary of the whole philosophical content of the Gītā. The first ten stanzas explain the circumstances under which Arjuna totally surrenders to the 'Kṛṣṇa-influence'. From stanza 11 to stanza 46 we have a digest of the Sāṅkhya, a word denoting 'the logic of thought in a philosophy'. From stanzas 47 to 60 is a sketch of the 'Yoga of Action' (Karma Yoga) as expounded in the entire Gītā. Stanzas 61 to 70 outline the path of Love (Bhakti Yoga) and 71 and 72, the Path of Renunciation (Saṁnyāsa Yoga). Thus, the second chapter of the Gītā can be taken as an epitome of the entire Gītā.

Terms and Definitions

1. What does the word 'Madhusūdana' mean?

Slayer of the demon Madhu (2.1)

2. If a warrior dies fighting in battle for a righteous cause, he is said to reach _______ svarga[1].

Vīra (2.2)

3. What does the term 'Guḍākeśa' mean?

'Conqueror of sleep' or 'knotted-haired' (2.9)

4. What does the appellation 'Govinda' mean?

Winner of the world (2.9)

5. Define 'unreal'.

That which was not in the past and which will not be in the future, but that which seemingly exists only in the present is called the

1. It is believed by the Hindus that to die fighting for righteousness is the duty of one born in a family of kings and by so sacrificing his life on the battle-field for a noble cause, he reaches and enjoys the 'Heaven of the Heroes' (Vīra Svarga).

'unreal'. (2.16)

6. Define 'Real'.

'Real' is that which defies all changes and remains the same in all the periods of time—past, present and future. (2.16)

7. Enumerate the six changes common to all beings.

The six changes are: existence, birth, growth, decay, disease and death. (2.20)

8. Differentiate between 'manifest' and 'unmanifest'.

A thing is called 'manifest' when we can perceive it through one or the other of our sense organs. That which is beyond all five sense organs is called 'unmanifest'. (2.25)

9. What is the meaning of the word 'Mahābāhu'?

'Having long hands'—signifies a hero (2.26)

10. What is 'śravaṇa', 'manana' and 'nididhyāsana'?

To make repeated attempts at listening is 'śravaṇa', continuous reflection is 'manana' and long contemplation is 'nididhyāsana'. (2.29)

11. What are the three 'pairs of opposites'?

The three pairs of opposites are:

(1) Pain and pleasure at an intellectual level

(2) Gain and loss at a mental level

(3) Conquest and defeat at the physical level. (2.38)

12. Define 'pratyavāya'.

The sin accrued through the non-performance, or imperfect performance, of enjoined acts (niyata karma-compulsory duties) is termed 'pratyavāya'. (2.40)

13. What is the meaning of the word 'Kurunandana'?

Joy of the Kurus (2.41)

14. Define 'yoga' and 'kṣema'.

'Yoga' and 'kṣema' in their meaning include all the activities of every living being in the universe. These are the two urges which goad every one in all of one's activities. 'Yoga' means 'to acquire' for purposes of possessing; and 'kṣema' means 'all efforts at preserving the acquired'. Thus the two terms 'yoga' and 'kṣema' encompass all our egocentric activities motivated by selfish desires to acquire and, compelled by equally selfish wishes, to hoard and preserve what has been acquired. (2.45)

15. What is meant by 'Buddhi Yoga'?

To keep the mind perfectly under the control of the discriminative intellect and to live thus as a master of the inner and outer world is called 'Buddhi Yoga'. (2.49)

16. Who is a 'buddhi-yuktaḥ'?

'Buddhi-yuktaḥ' is one whose actions are all guided by a clear vision of his higher and diviner Goal. (2.50)

17. What are the two definitions of Yoga given by Śrī Kṛṣṇa in the second chapter?

समत्वं योग उच्यते ॥

samatvaṁ yoga ucyate.

Evenness of mind is called Yoga (2.48)

योगः कर्मसु कौशलम् ॥

yogaḥ karmasu kauśalam.

Skill in action is Yoga (2.50)

18. What are the two expressions of māyā?

At the intellectual level, māyā expresses itself as a film of doubt and hesitation in our understanding or experiencing of the Self within us. This expression of māyā is the 'veiling power' (āvaraṇa-śakti).

Due to this mist of ignorance that envelops the intellect when it is unconscious of the Spiritual Reality behind it, the mind starts projecting forth the world of the 'not-self' and creates two firm ideas that: (a) 'the world is true' (satyatva), and (b) that 'I am nothing other than the projected world '(anātmabuddhi). This is māyā's expression as 'projecting-power' (vikṣepa-śakti). (2.52)

19. What does the term 'sthitaprajña' mean?

Man of steady Wisdom (2.54)

20. The nature of 'sthitaprajña' is described from verse _____ to verse _____ in the second chapter of the Bhagavad Gītā.

(2.55 to 2.72)

21. What are the three types of calamities?

The three types of calamities are:

(1) Those arising from disorders within the body (ādhyātmika)

(2) Those arising from external objects or beings (ādhibhautika)

(3) Those arising from unseen causes such as the cosmic forces causing rains, storms and so on (ādhidaivika). (2.56)

22. What is 'pratyāhāra' in Yoga Śāstra?

The capacity in an individual to withdraw his senses at will from the fields of objects is called 'pratyāhāra' in Yoga Śāstra. (2.58)

23. What is the equivalent of 'pratyāhāra' in Vedāntic terminology?

Uparati (2.58)

24. Define 'conscience'.

'Conscience' is that knowledge acquired for differentiating the good from the evil and with which one often forms a standard in oneself. Whenever it can, the conscience warns the mind against its lustful sensuousness and animalism. Once this conscience is dulled, man becomes a two-legged animal. (2.63)

25. What is 'prasāda'?

When a mind is trained in these two aspects: (a) to live in self-control, and (b) to move among the sense objects, with neither attachment for nor aversion to them, the disturbances and agitations in the mind caused by the sense-enchantments are all immediately brought under control. This condition of the mind is called 'prasāda' or 'peace' (tranquillity). (2.64)

26. Define 'brāhmī-sthitiḥ'.

When the ego has ended, the Consciousness is not known to be anything other than the Eternal and, as such, the Knower of Truth, in a brilliant experience of the Self, becomes the Self. This state is called 'Self-hood' (brāhmī sthitiḥ). (2.72)

Thoughts and Concepts

1. Who is capable of living in perfect morality?

The more we identify ourselves with the little 'I' in us, the more our problems and confusions in life. When we expand ourselves through our larger identifications—with an army, a cause or principle, or a nation or an age—we shall find our moral confusions dwindling into almost nothingness. Perfect morality can be declared and lived only by him who has sought to live and discover his real identity with the Self, which is one without a second and everywhere in all beings and forms. (2.4)

2. When do sentiments cloud one's understanding?

Once we misread a situation, sentiments cloud our understanding. (2.5)

3. Distinguish between the functions of the mind and the intellect.

The mind, functioning as an efficient 'receiving and despatching clerk' receives the information of the perceptions conveyed to it by the sense organs, and after arranging these perceptions in order, conveys them to the intellect for its judgement. The intellect, with reference to its own stored-up memories of similar experiences in the past, takes final decisions which are conveyed to the mind for execution; and the mind in its turn issues the necessary orders for the organs-of-action to act upon. (2.6)

4. In which verse of the second chapter do we find Arjuna explicitly surrendering to Śrī Kṛṣṇa?

कार्पण्यदोषोपहतस्वभावः
पृच्छामि त्वां धर्मसम्मूढचेताः ।
यच्छ्रेयः स्यान्निश्चितं ब्रूहि तन्मे

शिष्यस्तेऽहं शाधि मां त्वां प्रपन्नम् ॥

kārpaṇyadoṣopahatasvabhāvaḥ
pṛcchāmi tvāṁ dharmasammūḍhacetāḥ,
yacchreyaḥ syānniścitaṁ brūhi tanme
śiṣyaste'haṁ śādhi māṁ tvāṁ prapannam.

My heart is overpowered by the taint of pity; my mind is confused as to duty. I ask Thee. Tell me decisively what is good for me. I am Thy disciple. Instruct me, who have taken refuge in Thee.

Arjuna admits the psychological shattering felt and lived by him in the core of his being. He has instinctively diagnosed his condition correctly, even the cause of it to be 'an uncontrollable amount of overwhelming pity'. Of course, Arjuna does not realise that it is his misplaced compassion; but, whatever it be, the patient is now under the mental stress of extreme confusion and bewilderment. In this stanza, when Arjuna has completely realised the helpless impotency in himself to come to any decision, he surrenders totally to Lord Kṛṣṇa. (2.7)

5. What is the symbolism behind the Mahābhārata battle scene?

Standing between the two forces, the good and the bad, arrayed for a battle to death, Arjuna (the jīva) surrenders completely to the Lord (the subtler discriminative intellect), his charioteer, who holds the five horses (the five senses) yoked to his chariot (body) under perfect control. When the stunned and confused ego—Arjuna—totally surrenders to Kṛṣṇa, the Lord, with a smile, reassures the jīva of its final victory, and declares the entire message of spiritual redemption, the Gītā.

When the ego (Arjuna) in its dejection sits back in the body (chariot), throwing down all instruments of egocentric activities (Gāṇḍīva), and when the sense organs (the white horses) are held back, well under control, by the pulled-reins (the mind), then the charioteer (the pure intellect) shall lend the ego a divine strength and guide it to the ultimate victory over the forces of adharma (Kauravas) with the help of the dynamism of dharma (Pāṇḍavas), even though the former may seem much stronger in force than the simple-looking dynamism in the latter.

[Arjuna—jīva (ego); Śrī Kṛṣṇa—discriminative intellect; horses—five senses; body—chariot; Gāṇḍīva—egocentric activities; Kauravas—forces of adharma; Pāṇḍavas— forces of dharma] (2.10)

6. What is the cause of Arjuna's delusory attachments?

The 'egocentric-idea' that he is conditioned by his own body, mind and intellect is the true seed of Arjuna's delusory attachments to his relations and the consequent deep compassion that has risen in him to make him so impotent and helpless. (2.11)

7. What is the 'ego'?

The Self, getting reflected in the intellect, the body and the senses is the 'ego'. It is the ego which is a victim of the world of objects, feelings and ideas. To this ego belong all the sad destinies of life as well as its fleeting thrills of acquisition and possession. (2.11)

8. From which verse of the second chapter does the teaching of the Bhagavad Gītā actually start?

अशोच्यानन्वशोचस्त्वं प्रज्ञावादांश्च भाषसे ।
गतासूनगतासूंश्च नानुशोचन्ति पण्डिताः ॥

aśocyānanvaśocastvaṁ prajñāvādāṁśca bhāṣase,
gatāsūnagatāsūṁśca nānuśocanti paṇḍitāḥ.

You have grieved for those that should not be grieved for; yet, you speak words of wisdom. The wise grieve neither for the living nor for the dead. (2.11)

9. The misapprehension of Reality takes place due to__________.

Non-apprehension of Reality (2.11)

10. The ego rises when the _______ is not recognised.

Pure Self (2.11)

11. Who is fit for attaining 'Immortality'?

यं हि न व्यथयन्त्येते पुरुषं पुरुषर्षभ ।
समदुःखसुखं धीरं सोऽमृतत्वाय कल्पते ॥

yaṁ hi na vyathayantyete puruṣaṁ puruṣarṣabha,
samaduḥkhasukhaṁ dhīraṁ so'mṛtatvāya kalpate.

That firm man whom, surely, these afflict not, O chief among men, to whom pleasure and pain are the same, is fit for realising the Immortality of the Self.

Lord Kṛṣṇa explains that one who has found in himself a mental equipoise, wherein he is not afflicted or disturbed by circumstances of pain and pleasure is alone fit for attaining 'Immortality'. (2.15)

12. The Self is described as 'unknowable' (aprameya). Does that mean that the Self ever remains unknown?

By qualifying the Self as 'unknowable' it is not, in any sense, intended to indicate that the Supreme Self is 'unknown'. The term 'unknowable' is only meant to express that it is not knowable through the usual organs of perception. (2.18)

13. Which Upaniṣad do the following verses echo?

य एनं वेत्ति हन्तारं यश्चैनं मन्यते हतम् ।
उभौ तौ न विजानीतो नायं हन्ति न हन्यते ॥

ya enaṁ vetti hantāraṁ yaścainaṁ manyate hatam,
ubhau tau na vijānīto nāyaṁ hanti na hanyate.

He who takes the Self to be the slayer and he who thinks He is slain, neither of these knows. He slays not, nor is He slain. (2.19)

न जायते म्रियते वा कदाचित्
नायं भूत्वा भविता वा न भूयः ।
अजो नित्यः शाश्वतोऽयं पुराणो
न हन्यते हन्यमाने शरीरे ॥

na jāyate mriyate vā kadācit
nāyaṁ bhūtvā bhavitā vā na bhūyaḥ,
ajo nityaḥ śāśvato'yaṁ purāṇo
na hanyate hanyamāne śarīre.

He is not born, nor does He ever die; after having been, He again ceases not to be; unborn, eternal, changeless and ancient, He is not killed when the body is killed. (2.20)

The above verses echo the thoughts of Kaṭhopaniṣad[2].

14. What is the analogy used in the Bhagavad Gītā to explain 'transmigration'?

वासांसि जीर्णानि यथा विहाय
नवानि गृह्णाति नरोऽपराणि ।
तथा शरीराणि विहाय जीर्णा-
न्यन्यानि संयाति नवानि देही ॥

vāsāṁsi jīrṇāni yathā vihāya
navāni gṛhṇāti naro'parāṇi,
tathā śarīrāṇi vihāya jīrṇāni
anyāni saṁyāti navāni dehī.

Just as a man casts off his worn out clothes and puts on new ones, so also the embodied-self casts off its worn out bodies and enters others which are new. (2.22)

15. List some of the qualities of the Self as enumerated in the second chapter.

अच्छेद्योऽयमदाह्योऽयमक्लेद्योऽशोष्य एव च ।
नित्यः सर्वगतः स्थाणुरचलोऽयं सनातनः ॥

acchedyo'yamadāhyo'yamakledyo'śoṣya eva ca,
nityaḥ sarvagataḥ sthāṇuracalo'yaṁ sanātanaḥ.

This Self cannot be cut, nor burnt, nor moistened, nor dried up. It is eternal, all-pervading, stable, immovable and ancient. (2.24)

अव्यक्तोऽयमचिन्त्योऽयमविकार्योऽयमुच्यते ।
तस्मादेवं विदित्वैनं नानुशोचितुमर्हसि ॥

avyakto'yamacintyo'yamavikāryo'yamucyate,
tasmādevaṁ viditvainaṁ nānuśocitumarhasi.

This (Self) is said to be unmanifest, unthinkable and unchangeable. Therefore, knowing This to be such, you should not grieve. (2.25)

16. What is 'svadharma'?

The bundle of vāsanās with which an individual has arrived into a particular incarnation is called his 'personal call-of-character' or 'svadharma'. (2.33)

2. Vide verses 1.2.18 and 1.2.19 of Kaṭhopaniṣad.

17. Define 'sin'.

Sin is 'a mistake of the mind in which it acts contrary to its essential nature as the Self'. Any act of sensuousness which the mind craves in the world of objects, hoping to get thereby joy and satisfaction, creates necessarily within itself more and more agitations. This type of a mistake of the mind is called 'sin'. (2.33)

18. How can one live a life of inspired achievement?

A balanced life, wherein we live as an unaffected witness of even our own mind and intellect, is the 'realm of self-forgetfulness', where, instead of becoming inefficient, our profession gathers the scintillating glow of a new dawn. This extra aura in any achievement is that which raises an ordinary success to an 'inspired achievement'. (2.38)

19. What is the secret of success? What is the cause of failure?

With a single-pointed mind, if an individual can entertain any single resolute-determination and act consistently towards its success, achievement must certainly result. But invariably, man, victimised by his ego, entertains hundreds of desires, often mutually contradictory, and therefore, comes to play upon these fields with an impoverished and exhausted mental strength. When this 'self-cancellation of thoughts' comes to plague the mental zone, it exhausts all the potentialities of man and loots all his chances of success. (2.41)

20. What is the purpose of the practice of rituals?

The practice of rituals (karma-kāṇḍa) makes the mind single-pointed when it is pursued without specific desires (niṣkāma); such a prepared mind alone is fit for steady contemplation over the Upaniṣadic declarations. (2.44)

21. How does one always remain established in purity (nitya-sattvastha)?

'Sattva', the subtlest of the guṇas, often becomes impure by its contact with attachments and the consequent agitations (rajas) that attack the intellect with delusion and grief, and veil it from the right cognition of the real nature of things (tamas). To be always established in purity (sattva) would therefore mean keeping ourselves least agitated, and so, least deluded in our perceptions of things and beings and in our estimation of their true nature. (2.45)

22. "Thy right is to work only, but never to its fruits." Explain.

The fruit of an action, when one understands properly, is not anything different from the action itself. An action in the present when conditioned by a future-time appears as the fruit of the action. In fact, the action ends or fulfils itself only in its reaction, and the reaction is not anything different from the action; an action in the present defined in terms of a future moment is its reaction. Therefore, to worry over and get ourselves preoccupied with the anxieties for the rewards of actions is to escape from the dynamic present and to live in a future that is not yet born! In short, the Lord's advice here is a call to man not to waste his present moment in fruitless dreams and fears, but to bring his best—all the best in him—to the present and vitally live every moment, the promise being that the future shall take care of itself and shall provide the Karma Yogin with achievements divine and accomplishments supreme. (2.47)

23. Who is a real Karma Yogī?

A real Karma Yogī is one who understands: (a) that his concern is with action alone; (b) that he has no concern with results; (c) that he should not entertain the motive of gaining a fixed fruit for a given action and (d) that these ideas do not mean that he should sit back courting inaction. (2.47)

24. What does 'giving up attachments' mean?

To 'give up attachments' means renouncing wrong imaginations, false expectations, day-dreams about the fruits of actions, anxieties for the results and fears for future calamities. (2.48)

25. Briefly explain the theory of perception.

In the Vedāntic theory of perception, the mind, bearing the consciousness, goes out through the sense organs to the sense objects, and there it takes, as it were, the shape of the sense objects, and so comes to gain knowledge of the objects perceived. (2.58)

26. When is one said to have attained 'Yoga'?

श्रुतिविप्रतिपन्ना ते यदा स्थास्यति निश्चला ।
समाधावचला बुद्धिस्तदा योगमवाप्स्यसि ॥

śrutivipratipannā te yadā sthāsyati niścalā,
samādhāvacalā buddhistadā yogamavāpsyasi.

When your intellect, though perplexed by what you have heard, shall stand immovable and steady in the Self; then you shall attain Self-Realisation.

The mind gets agitated mainly due to the flooding in of the ever-new rush of stimuli from the outer world. Sense organs are the antennae through which the world's tickling signals creep in and disturb the mental-pool. One is considered as having attained Yoga only when one, even in the midst of enjoying sensuous pleasures, and even while the sense organs are letting in a flood of stimuli, does not get at all disturbed in one's inner serenity and equipoise. (2.53)

27. Arjuna requests Śrī Kṛṣṇa for a description of the 'Man of steady Wisdom'. Quote the relevant verse.

स्थितप्रज्ञस्य का भाषा समाधिस्थस्य केशव ।
स्थितधीः किं प्रभाषेत किमासीत व्रजेत किम् ॥

sthitaprajñasya kā bhāṣā samādhisthasya keśava,
sthitadhīḥ kiṁ prabhāṣeta kimāsīta vrajeta kim.

What, O Keśava, is the description of him who has steady Wisdom and who is merged in the Superconscious state? How does one of steady Wisdom speak? How does he sit? How does he walk? (2.54)

28. Why does the 'Man of steady Wisdom' become desireless?

An intellect, contaminated by ignorance becomes the breeding-ground of desires, and he who has relieved himself of this 'ignorance' through 'right knowledge' gained by right perception, naturally, becomes 'desireless'.

In one's ignorance, when one conceives of oneself as the ego, one has a burning desire for sense objects, a binding attachment with emotions and a jealous preference for one's pet ideas. But when the ego is transcended, when ignorance, like a mist, has lifted and when the finite ego stands face to face with the Divine Reality within, it melts away to become one with the Infinite. The 'Man of steady Wisdom', satisfied in the Self, can no more entertain any desire or have any appetite for the paltry objects of the body, mind, or intellect. He becomes the very source of all Bliss. (2.55)

29. What is 'anger'?

When an object has charmed one to a point of deep attachment, and when fear of its loss has started coming up in waves to disturb the individual, then, such an individual's attitude towards those that come between him and the object of his attachment is called 'anger'. Anger is thus nothing but a feeling that rises in us towards an obstacle between ourselves and the object of our attachment; the anger thus arising within is directly proportional to the amount of fear one entertains on the score of the obstacle holding one back from winning one's object of love. Anger, therefore, is only our attachment (rāga) for an object, expressed at an obstacle that has come between us and the object of our desire. (2.56)

30. The simile of a tortoise withdrawing its limbs is used to describe ______.

A wise person withdrawing his sense organs from sense objects (2.58)

31. How does a Vedāntin gain 'sense-withdrawal' (pratyāhāra or uparati)?

To a Vedāntin, 'pratyāhāra' (uparati or sense-withdrawal) comes from his well-developed and sharpened discriminative faculty, with which his intellect makes his mind understand the futility of licking the crumbs of joy and happiness in the wayside ditches of sensuousness, while he, in his Real Nature, is the Lord of the very store of Bliss Infinite. (2.58)

32. Cite the verses which show the 'ladder of fall' resulting from

our wrong attitude toward objects.

ध्यायतो विषयान्पुंसः सङ्गस्तेषूपजायते ।
सङ्गात्सञ्जायते कामः कामात्क्रोधोऽभिजायते ॥

dhyāyato viṣayānpuṁsaḥ saṅgasteṣūpajāyate,
saṅgātsañjāyate kāmaḥ kāmātkrodho'bhijāyate.

When a man thinks of objects, 'attachment' for them arises; from attachment 'desire' is born; from desire arises 'anger'. (2.62)

क्रोधाद्भवति सम्मोहः सम्मोहात्स्मृतिविभ्रमः ।
स्मृतिभ्रंशाद् बुद्धिनाशो बुद्धिनाशात्प्रणश्यति ॥

krodhādbhavati sammohaḥ sammohātsmṛtivibhramaḥ,
smṛtibhraṁśād buddhināśo buddhināśātpraṇaśyati.

From anger comes 'delusion'; from delusion 'loss of memory'; from loss of memory the 'destruction of discrimination'; from destruction of discrimination, he 'perishes'. (2.63)

33. Elucidating which concept does Śrī Kṛṣṇa use the example of the 'wind carrying away a boat'?

Śrī Kṛṣṇa uses the example of the 'wind carrying away a boat' to elucidate the 'mind carrying away one's discrimination' when it is overpowered by the senses. (2.67)

34. Why should the senses be kept in control?

As a ship with sails up and helmsman dead would be completely at the mercy of the fitful storms and reckless waves and will not reach any definite harbour, but is destroyed by the very tossings of the waves, so too, life gets capsized and the individual drowns if his mind is unanchored and left to be carried hither and thither by the uncertain buffets of passionate sense-storms. Therefore, the senses are to be controlled if man is to live a better and more purposeful life, designed and planned for enduring success. (2.67)

35. Describe an effective strategy to increase one's happiness.

The joy or happiness, at any given time, is a quotient when the 'number of desires fulfilled' is divided by the 'total number of desires entertained'. Along with an attempt to increase the numerator of this quotient, one must, at the same time, control the number of desires entertained. (2.70)

36. Who attains peace?

विहाय कामान्यः सर्वान्पुमांश्चरति निःस्पृहः ।
निर्ममो निरहङ्कारः स शान्तिमधिगच्छति ॥

vihāya kāmānyaḥ sarvānpumāṁścarati niḥspṛhaḥ,
nirmamo nirahaṅkāraḥ sa śāntimadhigacchati.

That man attains peace who, abandoning all desires, moves about without longing, without the sense of 'I-ness' and 'my-ness'. (2.71)

37. Define 'saṁnyāsa'.

'Saṁnyāsa' means sacrifice. To live in a spirit of sacrifice after renouncing completely one's ego and its desires is true saṁnyāsa, wherein an individual comes to live in constant awareness of his fuller and ampler Divinity. He alone is a 'saṁnyāsin' who has learnt the art of living his life in constant inspiration, which is gained through an intelligent renunciation of his egocentric misconceptions. (2.71)

Selections for Reflection

1. To get ourselves overwhelmed by life's circumstances is to ensure disastrous failure on all occasions. (2.1)
2. When life is courted properly, even the ugliest situation can be transformed into a charming smile of success. (2.2)
3. In the tradition of religious devotion, it is very truly said and firmly believed all over the world, that the Lord, in His high seat, keeps mum and is almost deaf so long as we are arguing and asserting our maturity as intellectual beings. But when we come down to live and act as emotional beings, when tears of desperation trickle down the cheeks of true devotees, then, unasked, the 'Lord of Compassion' rushes forward to reach the

lost souls and guides them out of their inward darkness to the resplendent 'Light of Wisdom'. (2.3)

4. Grief and dejection are the price that delusion demands from its victim. (2.11)

5. The embodied Self in every one is set on a great pilgrimage in which It comes to identify Itself with varied forms temporarily to gain a limited but determined set of experiences. (2.12)

6. Since every situation 'of its own nature' must keep on changing, it would be foolish to get upset at every change. It is wisdom to suffer them meekly, with the comfort and consolation of the knowledge of their finite nature. It is the attitude of the wise to go through life, both in joy and sorrow, in success and failure, in pain and joy, with the constant awareness: 'Even this will pass away'. (2.14)

7. To endure meekly, with magnanimous joy, the little pinpricks of life—heat and cold, success and failure, pain and joy—is the highest training that life can provide to all of us. (2.15)

8. Evolution and change are all for the mind and intellect and not for the Self. The Self is perfect and changeless and needs no evolution. (2.22)

9. Kṛṣṇa's life is 'on the whole' a message of cheer and joy. His doctrine of life is an insistence upon: 'to weep is folly and to smile is wisdom'. 'Keep smiling' seems to be Kṛṣṇa's philosophy put in two words. (2.27)

10. True Knowledge makes a man realise that he is a 'Soul with a body', but now in his ignorance, he thinks that he is a 'body with a Soul'. (2.29)

11. Equanimity of the mind alone can bring out the beam of inspiration and give to one's achievements the glow of a real success. (2.38)

12. Every challenge should be estimated from the spiritual standpoint, from the intellectual standpoint of reason, from the emotional level of ethics and morality and from the physical level of tradition and custom. If all these considerations, without any contradiction, indicate a solitary truth, then that is surely the Divine Path that one should pursue at all costs. (2.38)

13. Unselfish work, performed in a spirit of dedication and ego-less surrender, is the secret method of exhausting our vāsanā-store. Such a mind alone, purged clean, can reflect the Self clearly and come to discover the eternal God-hood. (2.49)

14. Man is the supreme creature in the kingdom of the living, because of the rational capacities of his discriminative intellect. As long as man does not utilise this special equipment that he possesses he cannot claim his heritage as man. (2.50)

15. Life, by its very nature, is a mixture of both good and bad and to live, ever adjusting ourselves—avoiding the bad and striving to linger in the experience of the good—is to live unintelligently. The perfect one experiences the best and the worst in life with equal detachment because he is ever established in the True and the Eternal, which is the very Self. (2.57)

16. Even though the sense objects may temporarily seem to turn away from him who is abstinent, the deep taste for them ingrained in his mind is very difficult to erase completely. (2.59)

17. To expose the mind to the quiet atmosphere of meditation upon the All-perfect Being is to heal its ulcers. (2.61)

18. By running away from the sense objects, nobody can assure for himself any inner peace; because the inner disturbance depends not upon the presence or the absence of the sense objects in the outer world, but essentially upon the mind's agitations for procuring desirable objects or for getting rid of the undesirable ones. (2.64)

19. Life in self-control alone is life worth living, if we demand from life anything more than tears, sobs, sighs and groans. (2.68)

ଓଃ ୫୬

Verses for Memorisation

क्लैब्यं मा स्म गमः पार्थ नैतत्त्वय्युपपद्यते ।
क्षुद्रं हृदयदौर्बल्यं त्यक्त्वोत्तिष्ठ परन्तप ॥

klaibyaṁ mā sma gamaḥ pārtha naitattvayyupapadyate,
kṣudraṁ hṛdayadaurbalyaṁ tyaktvottiṣṭha parantapa.

Yield not to impotence, O Pārtha! It does not befit thee. Cast off this mean weakness of heart! Stand up, O Parantapa (O scorcher of foes)! (2.3)

कार्पण्यदोषोपहतस्वभावः
पृच्छामि त्वां धर्मसम्मूढचेताः ।
यच्छ्रेयः स्यान्निश्चितं ब्रूहि तन्मे
शिष्यस्तेऽहं शाधि मां त्वां प्रपन्नम् ॥

kārpaṇyadoṣopahatasvabhāvaḥ
pṛcchāmi tvāṁ dharmasammūḍhacetāḥ,
yacchreyaḥ syānniścitaṁ brūhi tanme
śiṣyaste'haṁ śādhi māṁ tvāṁ prapannam.

My heart is overpowered by the taint of pity; my mind is confused as to duty. I ask Thee. Tell me decisively what is good for me. I am Thy disciple. Instruct me, who have taken refuge in Thee. (2.7)

अशोच्यानन्वशोचस्त्वं प्रज्ञावादांश्च भाषसे ।
गतासूनगतासूंश्च नानुशोचन्ति पण्डिताः ॥

aśocyānanvaśocastvaṁ prajñāvādāṁśca bhāṣase,
gatāsūnagatāsūṁśca nānuśocanti paṇḍitāḥ.

You grieve for those that should not be grieved for; yet, you speak words of wisdom. The wise grieve neither for the living nor for the dead. (2.11)

मात्रास्पर्शास्तु कौन्तेय शीतोष्णसुखदुःखदाः ।

आगमापायिनोऽनित्यास्तांस्तितिक्षस्व भारत ॥

mātrāsparśāstu kaunteya śītoṣṇasukhaduḥkhadāḥ,

āgamāpāyino'nityāstāṁstitikṣasva bhārata.

The contact of the senses with objects, O son of Kuntī, which cause heat and cold, pleasure and pain, have a beginning and an end; they are impermanent; endure them bravely, O descendant of Bhārata. (2.14)

नासतो विद्यते भावो नाभावो विद्यते सतः ।
उभयोरपि दृष्टोऽन्तस्त्वनयोस्तत्त्वदर्शिभिः ॥

nāsato vidyate bhāvo nābhāvo vidyate sataḥ,

ubhayorapi dṛṣṭo'ntastvanayostattvadarśibhiḥ.

The unreal has no being; there is no non-being of the Real; the truth about both has been seen by the knowers of the Truth. (2.16)

य एनं वेत्ति हन्तारं यश्चैनं मन्यते हतम् ।
उभौ तौ न विजानीतो नायं हन्ति न हन्यते ॥

ya enaṁ vetti hantāraṁ yaścainaṁ manyate hatam,

ubhau tau na vijānīto nāyaṁ hanti na hanyate.

He who takes the Self to be the slayer and he who thinks He is slain, neither of these knows. He slays not, nor is He slain. (2.19)

न जायते म्रियते वा कदाचित्
नायं भूत्वा भविता वा न भूयः ।
अजो नित्यः शाश्वतोऽयं पुराणो
न हन्यते हन्यमाने शरीरे ॥

na jāyate mriyate vā kadācit
nāyaṁ bhūtvā bhavitā vā na bhūyaḥ,
ajo nityaḥ śāśvato'yaṁ purāṇo
na hanyate hanyamāne śarīre.

He is not born, nor does He ever die; after having been, He again ceases not to be; unborn, eternal, changeless and ancient, He is not killed when the body is killed. (2.20)

वासांसि जीर्णानि यथा विहाय
नवानि गृह्णाति नरोऽपराणि ।

तथा शरीराणि विहाय जीर्णानि
अन्यानि संयाति नवानि देही ॥

vāsāṁsi jīrṇāni yathā vihāya
navāni gṛhṇāti naro'parāṇi,
tathā śarīrāṇi vihāya jīrṇāni
anyāni saṁyāti navāni dehī.

Just as a man casts off his worn out clothes and puts on new ones, so also the embodied-self casts off its worn out bodies and enters others which are new. (2.22)

आश्चर्यवत्पश्यति कश्चिदेनम्
आश्चर्यवद्वदति तथैव चान्यः ।
आश्चर्यवच्चैनमन्यः शृणोति
श्रुत्वाऽप्येनं वेद न चैव कश्चित् ॥

āścaryavatpaśyati kaścidenam
āścaryavadvadati tathaiva cānyaḥ,
āścaryavaccainamanyaḥ śṛṇoti
śrutvā'pyenaṁ veda na caiva kaścit.

One sees This as a wonder; another speaks of This as a wonder; another hears of This as a wonder: yet, having heard, none understands This at all. (2.29)

नेहाभिक्रमनाशोऽस्ति प्रत्यवायो न विद्यते ।
स्वल्पमप्यस्य धर्मस्य त्रायते महतो भयात् ॥

nehābhikramanāśo'sti pratyavāyo na vidyate,
svalpamapyasya dharmasya trāyate mahato bhayāt.

In this there is no loss of effort, nor is there any harm (production of contrary results). Even a little of this knowledge, even a little practice of this Yoga, protects one from the great fear. (2.40)

त्रैगुण्यविषया वेदा निस्त्रैगुण्यो भवार्जुन ।
निर्द्वन्द्वो नित्यसत्त्वस्थो निर्योगक्षेम आत्मवान् ॥

traiguṇyaviṣayā vedā nistraiguṇyo bhavārjuna,
nirdvandvo nityasattvastho niryogakṣema ātmavān.

The Vedas deal with the three attributes (guṇas); be you above these three attributes. O Arjuna, free yourself from the pairs of opposites, and ever remain in the sattva (goodness), freed from all thoughts of acquisition and preservation, and be established in the Self. (2.45)

कर्मण्येवाधिकारस्ते मा फलेषु कदाचन ।
मा कर्मफलहेतुर्भूर्मा ते सङ्गोऽस्त्वकर्मणि ॥

karmaṇyevādhikāraste mā phaleṣu kadācana,
mā karmaphalaheturbhūrmā te saṅgo'stvakarmaṇi.

Thy right is to work only, but never to its fruits; let not the fruit of action be thy motive, nor let thy attachment be to inaction. (2.47)

योगस्थः कुरु कर्माणि सङ्गं त्यक्त्वा धनञ्जय ।
सिद्ध्यसिद्ध्योः समो भूत्वा समत्वं योग उच्यते ॥

yogasthaḥ kuru karmāṇi saṅgaṁ tyaktvā dhanañjaya,
siddhyasiddhyoḥ samo bhūtvā samatvaṁ yoga ucyate.

Perform action, O Dhanañjaya, abandoning attachment, being steadfast in Yoga and balanced in success and failure. Evenness of mind is called Yoga. (2.48)

बुद्धियुक्तो जहातीह उभे सुकृतदुष्कृते ।
तस्माद्योगाय युज्यस्व योगः कर्मसु कौशलम् ॥

buddhiyukto jahātīha ubhe sukṛtaduṣkṛte,
tasmādyogāya yujyasva yogaḥ karmasu kauśalam.

Endowed with the Wisdom of evenness of mind, one casts off in this life both good deeds and evil deeds; therefore, devote yourself to Yoga. Skill in action is Yoga. (2.50)

स्थितप्रज्ञस्य का भाषा समाधिस्थस्य केशव ।
स्थितधीः किं प्रभाषेत किमासीत व्रजेत किम् ॥

sthitaprajñasya kā bhāṣā samādhisthasya keśava,
sthitadhīḥ kiṁ prabhāṣeta kimāsīta vrajeta kim.

What, O Keśava, is the description of him who has steady Wisdom and who is merged in the Superconscious state? How does one of steady Wisdom speak? How does he sit? How does he walk? (2.54)

प्रजहाति यदा कामान्सर्वान्पार्थ मनोगतान् ।
आत्मन्येवात्मना तुष्टः स्थितप्रज्ञस्तदोच्यते ॥

prajahāti yadā kāmānsarvānpārtha manogatān,

ātmanyevātmanā tuṣṭaḥ sthitaprajñastadocyate.

When a man completely casts off, O Pārtha, all the desires of the mind and is satisfied in the Self by the Self, then is he said to be one of steady Wisdom. (2.55)

दुःखेष्वनुद्विग्नमनाः सुखेषु विगतस्पृहः ।
वीतरागभयक्रोधः स्थितधीर्मुनिरुच्यते ॥

duḥkheṣvanudvignamanāḥ sukheṣu vigataspṛhaḥ,
vītarāgabhayakrodhaḥ sthitadhīrmunirucyate.

He whose mind is not shaken by adversity, and who in prosperity does not hanker after pleasure, who is free from attachment, fear and anger is called a Sage of steady Wisdom. (2.56)

यदा संहरते चायं कूर्मोऽङ्गानीव सर्वशः ।
इन्द्रियाणीन्द्रियार्थेभ्यस्तस्य प्रज्ञा प्रतिष्ठिता ॥

yadā saṁharate cāyaṁ kūrmo'ṅgānīva sarvaśaḥ,
indriyāṇīndriyārthebhyastasya prajñā pratiṣṭhitā.

When, like the tortoise which withdraws its limbs from all sides, he withdraws his senses from the sense objects, then his Wisdom becomes steady. (2.58)

विषया विनिवर्तन्ते निराहारस्य देहिनः ।
रसवर्जं रसोऽप्यस्य परं दृष्ट्वा निवर्तते ॥

viṣayā vinivartante nirāhārasya dehinaḥ,
rasavarjaṁ raso'pyasya paraṁ dṛṣṭvā nivartate.

The objects of the senses turn away from the abstinent man leaving the longing (behind); but his longing also leaves him on seeing the Supreme. (2.59)

ध्यायतो विषयान्पुंसः सङ्गस्तेषूपजायते ।
सङ्गात्सञ्जायते कामः कामात्क्रोधोऽभिजायते ॥

dhyāyato viṣayānpuṁsaḥ saṅgasteṣūpajāyate,
saṅgātsañjāyate kāmaḥ kāmātkrodho'bhijāyate.

When a man thinks of objects, 'attachment' for them arises; from attachment 'desire' is born; from desire arises 'anger'. (2.62)

क्रोधाद्भवति सम्मोहः सम्मोहात्स्मृतिविभ्रमः ।
स्मृतिभ्रंशाद् बुद्धिनाशो बुद्धिनाशात्प्रणश्यति ॥
krodhādbhavati sammohaḥ sammohātsmṛtivibhramaḥ,
smṛtibhraṁśād buddhināśo buddhināśātpraṇaśyati.
From anger comes 'delusion'; from delusion 'loss of memory'; from loss of memory the 'destruction of discrimination'; from destruction of discrimination, he 'perishes'. (2.63)

इन्द्रियाणां हि चरतां यन्मनोऽनुविधीयते ।
तदस्य हरति प्रज्ञां वायुर्नावमिवाम्भसि ॥
indriyāṇāṁ hi caratāṁ yanmano'nuvidhīyate,
tadasya harati prajñāṁ vāyurnāvamivāmbhasi.
For the mind, which follows in the wake of the wandering senses, carries away his discrimination, as the wind carries away a boat on the waters. (2.67)

या निशा सर्वभूतानां तस्यां जागर्ति संयमी ।
यस्यां जाग्रति भूतानि सा निशा पश्यतो मुनेः ॥
yā niśā sarvabhūtānāṁ tasyāṁ jāgarti saṁyamī,
yasyāṁ jāgrati bhūtāni sā niśā paśyato muneḥ.
The Self-controlled man keeps awake during that which is night for all creatures. That during which creatures keep awake, it is night to the seeing sage. (2.69)

आपूर्यमाणमचलप्रतिष्ठं
समुद्रमापः प्रविशन्ति यद्वत् ।
तद्वत्कामा यं प्रविशन्ति सर्वे
स शान्तिमाप्नोति न कामकामी ॥
āpūryamāṇamacalapratiṣṭhaṁ
samudramāpaḥ praviśanti yadvat,
tadvatkāmā yaṁ praviśanti sarve
sa śāntimāpnoti na kāmakāmī.
He attains peace into whom all desires enter as waters enter the ocean, which, filled from all sides, remains unmoved; not the 'desirer of desires'. (2.70)

विहाय कामान्यः सर्वान्पुमांश्चरति निःस्पृहः ।
निर्ममो निरहङ्कारः स शान्तिमधिगच्छति ॥

vihāya kāmānyaḥ sarvānpumāṁścarati niḥspṛhaḥ,
nirmamo nirahaṅkāraḥ sa śāntimadhigacchati.

That man attains peace who, abandoning all desires, moves about without longing, without the sense of 'I-ness' and 'my-ness'. (2.71)

3

Karma Yoga

The Yoga of Action

Actions which are performed without ego, egocentric desires and anxiety for its fruits, with an attitude of offering unto the Lord, become Karma Yoga. (Introduction)

Action has a natural tendency to create fresh vāsanās (impressions) which again generate impulses that force one to act more vigorously. In order to avoid creation of new vāsanās, even while acting for the purpose of vāsanā-exhaustion, Śrī Kṛṣṇa advises Karma Yoga. The training in Karma Yoga prepares us for the greater fights that we must fight on life's battle-fields.

Terms and Definitions

1. What is the twofold path?

The twofold path is the 'Path of Knowledge' of the Sāṅkhyans and the 'Path of Action' of the Karma Yogins.

लोकेऽस्मिन् द्विविधा निष्ठा पुरा प्रोक्ता मयानघ ।
ज्ञानयोगेन साङ्ख्यानां कर्मयोगेन योगिनाम् ॥

loke'smindvividhā niṣṭhā purā proktā mayānagha,
jñānayogena sāṅkhyānāṁ karmayogena yogināṁ.

In this world there is a twofold path, as I said before, O sinless one; the 'Path of Knowledge' of the Sāṅkhyans and the 'Path of Action' of the Yogins. (3.3)

2. Who is a 'hypocrite'?

कर्मेन्द्रियाणि संयम्य य आस्ते मनसा स्मरन् ।
इन्द्रियार्थान्विमूढात्मा मिथ्याचारः स उच्यते ॥

karmendriyāṇi saṁyamya ya āste manasā smaran,
indriyārthānvimūḍhātmā mithyācāraḥ sa ucyate.

He who, restraining the organs of action, sits thinking in his mind of the sense objects, he, of deluded understanding, is called a hypocrite.

To make outwardly a show of morality and ethics, while mentally living a shameless life of low motives and foul sentiments, is the occupation of a man who is not a seeker of spiritual fulfilment, but, as is termed here, a self-deluded hypocrite! (3.6)

3. What is meant by 'niyataṁ karma'?

'Niyataṁ karma', or 'Nitya-karma, means 'bounden duty'. Thus, it includes all 'obligatory actions' of an individual in his home, office and society. (3.8)

4. Who is a 'thief'?

इष्टान्भोगान्हि वो देवा दास्यन्ते यज्ञभाविताः ।
तैर्दत्तानप्रदायैभ्यो यो भुङ्क्ते स्तेन एव सः ॥

iṣṭānbhogānhi vo devā dāsyante yajñabhāvitāḥ,
tairdattānapradāyaibhyo yo bhuṅkte stena eva saḥ.

"The devas, nourished by sacrifice, will give you the desired objects". Indeed, he who enjoys objects given by the devas without making offerings (in return) to them, is verily a thief. (3.12)

5. The appellation 'Vārṣṇeya' (one of the names of Lord Kṛṣṇa) means____________.

One born in the family of the Vṛṣṇis (3.36)

Thoughts and Concepts

1. Action and renunciation are not to be practised together, but to be practised ________________.

Serially (Introduction)

2. What prompted Arjuna to ask the following question in the beginning of the third chapter?

ज्यायसी चेत्कर्मणस्ते मता बुद्धिर्जनार्दन ।
तत्किं कर्माणि घोरे मां नियोजयसि केशव ॥

jyāyasī cetkarmaṇaste matā buddhirjanārdana,
tatkiṁ karmaṇi ghore māṁ niyojayasi keśava.

If it be thought by you that 'Knowledge' is superior to 'action', O Janārdana, why then, do you, O Keśava, engage me in this terrible action? (3.1)

Śrī Kṛṣṇa vehemently argued against Arjuna's decision not to fight but to renounce the glory of success and retire to the quietude of the jungle to live there the life of a monk seeking the Divine. In his arguments, at one moment, the Lord advised Arjuna that it was his duty to work without getting himself preoccupied with its result. Śrī Kṛṣṇa had also warned him, 'let not thy attachment be toward inaction'. Later on, the chapter concluded (verses 2.55-2.72) with the inspired advocacy of the path of knowledge. Naturally, Arjuna felt confused as to which of the paths he was to follow for his self-development.

In fact, the arguments raised by Lord Kṛṣṇa in his discourse create a grave doubt as to which exactly is the path that will take a seeker easily to the Realisation of the Absolute in Him. Is it: (a) Knowledge, (b) Action, (c) both together practised in a synthesis, or lastly, (d) is it the total renunciation of both? It is this which prompts Arjuna to ask the above question. (Introduction)

3. Why is it not possible to prescribe a single spiritual path for all people?

People fit for spiritual discipline fall under two distinct categories: the active and the contemplative. Temperamentally, these two classes fall so widely apart, that to prescribe for both of them one and the same technique for individual development would be to discourage one section and ignore its spiritual progress. (3.3)

4. How does ignorance express itself?

Ignorance (avidyā), when it functions in the intellect, expresses itself as desires. When the desires, which are nothing other than the 'ignorance', function in the mental zone, they express themselves as thoughts. These thoughts, when they express in the outer world, become actions. (3.4)

5. Why does the Bhagavad Gītā advise a man to act vigorously?

Man is ever agitated under the influence of the triple tendencies of unactivity (sattva), activity (rajas) and inactivity (tamas). Even for a single moment he cannot remain totally inactive. Total inactivity is the character of utterly insentient matter. Even if we are physically at rest, mentally and intellectually we are active all the time, except during the state of deep sleep. So long as we are under the influence of these three mental tendencies (guṇas), we are helplessly prompted to labour and to act.

Therefore, not to act at all is to disobey the laws of nature, which will bring about a cultural deterioration within us. A person who remains inactive physically will get dissipated in his thoughts. Therefore, the Gītā advises him to act vigorously, with the right attitude of mind, so that he may avoid all internal waste of energy and learn to grow in himself. (3.5)

6. Why does the Lord advise us to act without attachment?

When a camera is loaded with a piece of plain white paper, however long we may keep the lenses open against any well-lit object, no impression of the object concerned can dirty the paper! On the other hand, if that very same sheet of paper is sensitised, then, even a slight exposure will leave the impressions of the object upon it. Similarly, a mind plastered with attachment soon gathers on to itself impressions (vāsanās) during its contacts in the external fields of activity. The Lord advises us to act without attachment, so that, instead of gathering new impressions, we may make use of our activities for the exhaustion of the existing vāsanā-dirt in our mental equipment. (3.7)

7. How does Karma Yoga become a technique of Self-Liberation?

By withdrawing the organs of perception from their unprofitable fields of activity, we save on the inner energy which would otherwise be spent through the organs of activity. Further, because of our inner attitude of non-attachment while working, no new vāsanās are gathered by our mind; on the contrary, the mind gets burnished by the removal of the existing mental dirt. The very field of activity which ordinarily becomes a snare to capture and imprison a soaring soul, itself becomes the exact art of Self-Liberation. (3.7)

8. What is 'yajña'?

Any self-sacrificing work undertaken in a spirit of dedication, for the blessing of all, is 'yajña'. Also any social, communal, national, or personal activity into which the individual is ready to pour himself forth entirely in a spirit of service and dedication is 'yajña'. (3.9)

9. How does Pujya Gurudev interpret the word 'deva' in the following verse?

देवान्भावयतानेन ते देवा भावयन्तु वः ।
परस्परं भावयन्तः श्रेयः परमवाप्स्यथ ॥

devānbhāvayatānena te devā bhāvayantu vaḥ,
parasparaṁ bhāvayantaḥ śreyaḥ paramavāpsyatha.

With this do you nourish the gods and may those devas nourish you; thus nourishing one another, you shall attain the highest Good.

'Deva' is the 'presiding deity' in any field of activity, who blesses the worker in that field with his profit. The 'deity' that blesses the worker in a field of activity can be nothing other than the 'productive potential' in that given field. Productivity that is dormant in any situation can be invoked only by man's sincere efforts. When we apply in any situation our true and sincere work, the efforts and sacrifices so made, as it were, invoke the 'productive potential' in that situation, which come to manifest and bless the worker. (3.11)

10. How does Śrī Kṛṣṇa describe those who eat the 'remnants of the sacrifices' and those who 'cook food only for their own sake'?

यज्ञशिष्टाशिनः सन्तो मुच्यन्ते सर्वकिल्बिषैः ।
भुञ्जते ते त्वघं पापा ये पचन्त्यात्मकारणात् ॥

yajñaśiṣṭāśinaḥ santo mucyante sarvakilbiṣaiḥ,
bhuñjate te tvaghaṁ pāpā ye pacantyātmakāraṇāt.

The righteous, who eat the 'remnants of the sacrifices' are freed from all sins; but those sinful ones, who cook food (only) for their own sake, verily eat but sin.

As a contrast to social criminals, who feed themselves upon the social wealth in producing which they have not brought in any effort, in this stanza we have the description of the good, who eat the 'remnants of the sacrifices', i.e. they receive their 'share' after sweating hard in sincere yajña-activities. Such people, as explained here, 'go beyond all sins'.

But those who 'cook food for themselves alone', Śrī Kṛṣṇa says, 'eat but sin'. The Lord is against the principle of arrogation of wealth and of hoarding the same, motivated by lust of lucre, meant mainly for selfish enjoyment, utterly regardless of the privations and poverty of the unfortunate folks in the community. It is said that such hoarders of wealth 'eat but sin'. (3.13)

11. How does Pujya Gurudev interpret the words 'yajña', 'rain' and 'food' in the following verse?

अन्नाद्भवन्ति भूतानि पर्जन्यादन्नसम्भवः ।
यज्ञाद्भवति पर्जन्यो यज्ञः कर्मसमुद्भवः ॥

annādbhavanti bhūtāni parjanyādannasambhavaḥ,
yajñādbhavati parjanyo yajñaḥ karmasamudbhavaḥ.

From food come forth beings; from rain food is produced; from sacrifice arises rain, and sacrifice is born of action.

In this stanza, the familiar terms of the Vedic period have been charged with new meaning and significance. 'Rain' is the essential condition for the conversion of the mineral-raw-material into enjoyable and nutritive food. Similarly, in all fields of activity there is 'an enjoyable profit' which can be gathered only when the fields come under 'conditions favourable' for them to produce those profits. 'Self-dedicated activities' (yajña), when performed in any given field of endeavour, will be creating therein 'conditions necessary for the field to smile forth' (rain) in a luxurious 'crop of profit' (annam) enjoyed by the society. (3.14)

[Yajña: dedicated activity; Rain: conditions necessary for the field to smile forth; Food: profit.]

12. What is the 'Cosmic wheel of co-operation'?

The 'Cosmic wheel of co-operation' has been described in the following two verses of the Bhagavad Gītā:

अन्नाद्भवन्ति भूतानि पर्जन्यादन्नसम्भवः ।
यज्ञाद्भवति पर्जन्यो यज्ञः कर्मसमुद्भवः ॥

annādbhavanti bhūtāni parjanyādannasambhavaḥ,
yajñādbhavati parjanyo yajñaḥ karmasamudbhavaḥ.

From food come forth beings; from rain food is produced; from sacrifice arises rain, and sacrifice is born of action. (3.14)

कर्म ब्रह्मोद्भवं विद्धि ब्रह्माक्षरसमुद्भवम्।
तस्मात्सर्वगतं ब्रह्म नित्यं यज्ञे प्रतिष्ठितम्॥

karma brahmodbhavaṁ viddhi brahmākṣarasamudbhavam,
tasmātsarvagataṁ brahma nityaṁ yajñe pratiṣṭhitam.

Know you that action comes from Brahma (the creator) and Brahma comes from the Imperishable. Therefore, the all-pervading Brahman (God-principle) ever rests in sacrifice. (3.15)

13. Śrī Kṛṣṇa declares 'seekers of the senses' (indriyārāma) as 'living in sin' and 'living in vain'. Why?

A community is made up of its individuals. If the individuals are perfect, the community works smoothly. But, if the units are wrongly composed, then the entire structure of the community collapses. The individual's negative existence starts with his pre-occupation with his senses. In his limited recognition that he is nothing more than the body, he becomes pre-occupied with its nourishment and fattening. As a body, he cannot perceive the higher 'ways of life' nor can he entertain any goal other than seeking satisfaction for his mere animal passions.

In such a situation, nobody would come forward to work in the redeeming noble yajña-spirit, without which no 'favourable circumstances' can be created for the 'productive potentials' (devas) to manifest themselves as 'nourishing joy'. 'Seekers of senses' (indriyārāma), they compete among themselves, each seeking with lustful greed his own selfish happiness and bringing about a discordant rhythm in the 'wheel-of-action'. Such people are considered by the Gītā as 'living in sin' and the Gītā asserts, 'they live in vain'. (3.16)

14. _____________ and _____________ are the two wheels of the life-chariot.

Satisfaction and contentment (3.17)

15. Who is free from duties?

यस्त्वात्मरतिरेव स्यादात्मतृप्तश्च मानवः ।
आत्मन्येव च सन्तुष्टस्तस्य कार्यं न विद्यते ॥

yastvātmaratireva syādātmatṛptaśca mānavaḥ,
ātmanyeva ca santuṣṭastasya kāryaṁ na vidyate.

But the man who rejoices only in the Self, who is satisfied with the Self, who is content in the Self alone, for Him verily there is nothing (more) to be done.

An ordinary man is whipped into action either because of his anxiety to gain profit or because of his fear that by not doing work he will be incurring a loss. But an individual, who has the subjective experience of the spiritual stature within him, who has discovered an eternal satisfaction in his own Self and who has reached perfect contentment therein, will have no more action to perform for he has nothing more to gain through activity, nor will he have fear of losing anything in the world due to non-performance of any action. (3.17)

16. How does Pujya Gurudev mathematically define attachment?

Attachment = Ego + Egocentric desires (3.19)

17. Why does the moral rejuvenation of a society depend on the leader of the society?

Man is essentially an imitating animal. This is a psychological truth. Students can be disciplined only when teachers are well-behaved. The minor officials of a country cannot be kind and honest when the rulers are corrupt tyrants. Children's behaviour depends entirely upon, and is ever controlled by, the standard of purity and culture set by their parents. The moral rejuvenation of a society in any period of history can take place only because of the example set by the leaders of that nation. This idea is made amply clear in the following verse:

यद्यदाचरति श्रेष्ठस्तत्तदेवेतरो जनः ।
स यत्प्रमाणं कुरुते लोकस्तदनुवर्तते ॥

yadyadācarati śreṣṭhastattadevetaro janaḥ,
sa yatpramāṇaṁ kurute lokastadanuvartate.

Whatever a great man does, that other men also do (imitate); whatever he sets up as the standard, that the world (people) follows. (3.21)

18. Why does the Lord work? What would be the loss if He were not to work at all?

The Lord explains the reason for his continued action in the following two verses:

यदि ह्यहं न वर्तेयं जातु कर्मण्यतन्द्रितः ।
मम वर्त्मानुवर्तन्ते मनुष्याः पार्थ सर्वशः ॥

yadi hyahaṁ na varteyaṁ jātu karmaṇyatandritaḥ,
mama vartmānuvartante manuṣyāḥ pārtha sarvaśaḥ.

For, should I not ever engage Myself in action, without relaxation, men would in every way follow My path, O son of Pṛthā. (3.23)

उत्सीदेयुरिमे लोका न कुर्यां कर्म चेदहम् ।
सङ्करस्य च कर्ता स्यामुपहन्यामिमाः प्रजाः ॥

utsīdeyurime lokā na kuryāṁ karma cedaham,
saṅkarasya ca kartā syāmupahanyāmimāḥ prajāḥ.

These worlds would perish if I did not perform action; I would be the author of confusion of caste, and would destroy these beings. (3.24)

19. What is the difference between the activities of the 'wise' and the 'ignorant'?

Everybody works in their own given fields of activity with enthusiasm and deep interest, all day through, every day of the year and through their entire life-time. Man is seen to wear himself out in the strain of constant activity. Irrespective of his health, careless of the severity of seasons, through joy and sorrow, man constantly strives to earn and to hoard, to gain and to enjoy.

A Man of Self-Realisation also works in the world with as much diligence and sincerity, tireless enthusiasm and energising joy, burning hopes and scalding fears as any ordinary man striving in the competition of the market-place. The only difference between the two is that whereas the ignorant acts and is motivated by his attachment and anxiety for the fruits, a Man of Perfection will work in the world, without attachment, only for the purpose of the redemption of the world. (3.25)

20. When does attachment become a cure for one's imperfections?

Attachment becomes a clog or a painful chain only when it is extremely egocentric. To the extent we work for larger schemes to bless a vaster section of humanity, to that extent the attachment loses its poison and comes to bless the age. Many poisons serve as medicines in their diluted form, while the same in a concentrated form can bring instantaneous death!

The ego and its egocentric desires bind and destroy man, but to the extent that he can lift his identifications to include and accommodate in it larger sections of the living world, to that extent the attachment gathers an ethical halo, a divine glow, and becomes a cure for our subjective pains and imperfections. (3.25)

21. How should a 'wise man' guide his generation?

न बुद्धिभेदं जनयेदज्ञानां कर्मसङ्गिनाम् ।
जोषयेत्सर्वकर्माणि विद्वान्युक्तः समाचरन् ॥

na buddhibhedaṁ janayedajñānāṁ karmasaṅginām,
joṣayetsarvakarmāṇi vidvānyuktaḥ samācaran.

Let no 'wise man' unsettle the minds of ignorant people, who are attached to action; he should engage them in all actions, himself fulfilling his duties with devotion.

No 'wise man' should unsettle his generation's firm faith in action. He must himself diligently perform the ordinary actions in a diviner and better fashion, and he must make himself an example to the world, so that lesser folk may automatically imitate him and learn to follow his unfaltering footsteps. (3.26)

22. What is the notion of the ignorant man while acting?

All actions are performed by the guṇas. The ignorant man deluded by egoism thinks "I am the doer".

प्रकृतेः क्रियमाणानि गुणैः कर्माणि सर्वशः ।

अहङ्कारविमूढात्मा कर्ताहमिति मन्यते ॥

prakṛteḥ kriyamāṇāni guṇaiḥ karmāṇi sarvaśaḥ,
ahaṅkāravimūḍhātmā kartāhamiti manyate.

All actions are performed, in all cases, merely by the 'qualities in nature' (guṇas). He whose mind is deluded by egoism thinks "I am the doer." (3.27)

23. Explain how ignorance of the Self manifests in the intellectual and mental zones.

Ignorance of the Self expresses itself at the intellectual level as 'desires', which again, in the mental zone, manifests as 'thoughts'. (3.27)

24. Why is the 'wise man' not bound by actions and their results?

तत्त्ववित्तु महाबाहो गुणकर्मविभागयोः ।
गुणा गुणेषु वर्तन्त इति मत्वा न सज्जते ॥

tattvavittu mahābāho guṇakarmavibhāgayoḥ,
guṇā guṇeṣu vartanta iti matvā na sajjate.

But he—who knows the Truth, O mighty-armed, about the divisions of the qualities and (their) functions, and he who knows that guṇas-as-senses move amidst guṇas-as-objects, is not attached. (3.28)

25. What is hope?

Hope is the expectation of a happening that is yet to manifest and mature in a future period of time. Whatever be the hope it refers to a period of time not yet born. (3.30)

26. What is the meaning of 'vigatajvara' in the following verse?

मयि सर्वाणि कर्माणि संन्यस्याध्यात्मचेतसा ।
निराशीर्निर्ममो भूत्वा युध्यस्व विगतज्वरः ॥

mayi sarvāṇi karmāṇi saṁnyasyādhyātmacetasā,
nirāśīrnirmamo bhūtvā yudhyasva vigatajvaraḥ.

Renouncing all actions in Me, with the mind centred on the Self, free from hope and egoism, free from (mental) fever, do you fight.

The term 'vigatajvara' means the 'absence of feverish anxiety about the results of one's action in the present'. (3.30)

27. Why is the ego considered to be 'the shadow of the past'?

Our egocentric concept of ourselves is nothing but a bundle of our happenings and achievements which took place, or were gained in the past. Ego is therefore 'the shadow of the past'. (3.30)

28. What is 'faith'?

'Faith' is the ability to digest mentally, and comprehend intellectually, the full import of the advice of the saints and the declarations of the scriptures. (3.31)

29. How does the term 'worklessness' indicate the 'State of Self-hood'?

Ignorance of our spiritual nature gives rise to desires, which in turn cause thought-agitations. Work is nothing other than thoughts fulfilled among the sense objects. Thus, the 'state of worklessness' is itself the 'state of thoughtlessness', which indicates the 'condition of desirelessness'. Absence of all desires can come only when we rediscover the all-full nature of the Self. In short, with the Knowledge of the Self, when spiritual 'ignorance' is terminated, desires can no more arise. Thus the term 'state of worklessness' indicates the state beyond ignorance or the 'State of Self-hood'. (3.31)

30. Who are doomed to destruction?

ये त्वेतदभ्यसूयन्तो नानुतिष्ठन्ति मे मतम्।
सर्वज्ञानविमूढांस्तान्विद्धि नष्टानचेतसः ॥

ye tvetadabhyasūyanto nānutiṣṭhanti me matam,
sarvajñānavimūḍhāṁstānviddhi naṣṭānacetasaḥ.

But those who carp at My teaching (of Karma Yoga) and do not practise it, deluded in all knowledge, and devoid of discrimination, know them to be doomed to destruction. (3.32)

31. "*Sadṛśaṁ ceṣṭate svasyāḥ prakṛterjñānavānapi*—Even a 'man of knowledge' acts in accordance with his own nature." Explain.

Even the 'man of knowledge' acts in conformity with his own nature, which is determined by the pattern of thoughts that arise in him. At any given instant of time, each one of us is determined by the thoughts that are in us at that moment; and the thoughts in us always get patternised by the channels of thinking, designed by the thoughts which we had entertained in the past. The nature of each individual is decided by the style of thinking which each is capable of.

The 'man of knowledge' mentioned here indicates one who has read and understood thoroughly the technique of action as explained in this chapter. Even when he knows the technique, the Lord says that it is not easy for him to follow it, because his mind is designed to carry his thoughts through egocentric and selfish channels, ever panting to gain some desires. Because of these past impressions (vāsanās), even an honest student finds it hard to practise this simple-looking technique of action in his life. (3.33)

32. Explain the significance of Śrī Kṛṣṇa's question *'nigrahaḥ kiṁ kariṣyati*—what can restraint do'?

What can restraint do is not a cry of despair but it is the honest all-seeing vision of the philosopher in Kṛṣṇa, who recognises that the higher ways of living are not meant for all. Men crowding on the lowest rung of the evolutionary ladder, overwhelmed by their own animal passions, find themselves incapable of renouncing them, and are, therefore, incapacitated to walk the 'path of action'. It is only a slightly evolved person, full of enthusiasm, activity and a passion for progress who can follow this sacred 'path' and benefit himself. (3.33)

33. What are one's internal foes that prevent one from right living?

Attachment and aversion for objects are the internal forces that loot away the joys of right living.

इन्द्रियस्येन्द्रियस्यार्थे रागद्वेषौ व्यवस्थितौ ।
तयोर्न वशमागच्छेत्तौ ह्यस्य परिपन्थिनौ ॥

indriyasyendriyasyārthe rāgadveṣau vyavasthitau,
tayorna vaśamāgacchettau hyasya paripanthinau.

Attachment and aversion for the objects of the senses abide in the senses; let none come under their sway; for they are his foes. (3.34)

34. What is the relation between vāsanās, mind and ego?

Vāsanās create the mind; where the mind is, there revels the ego. To the extent the vāsanās have been reduced, to that extent the mind has become non-existent. Where the mind has ended, there the reflection of the consciousness called the 'ego' has also ended. (3.34)

35. Man's texture of thoughts is determined by his _______.

Vāsanās (3.35)

36. Distinguish 'svadharma' from 'paradharma'.

'Svadharma' (one's own duty) is not the duty which accrues to an individual because of his 'caste', which is ever a sheer accident of birth. In its right import 'svadharma' means the type of vāsanās that one discovers in one's own mind. To act according to one's own taste, inborn and natural, is the only known method of living in peace and joy, in success and satisfaction. To act against the grain of one's own vāsanās would be acting in terms of 'paradharma' (duty of another) and this is fraught with danger. (3.35)

37. What impels man to commit sin even against his wishes?

Desire and anger impel man to commit sin even against his wishes.

काम एष क्रोध एष रजोगुणसमुद्भवः ।
महाशनो महापाप्मा विद्ध्येनमिह वैरिणम् ॥

kāma eṣa krodha eṣa rajoguṇasamudbhavaḥ,
mahāśano mahāpāpmā viddhyenamiha vairiṇam.

It is desire, it is anger born of the 'active', all-devouring, all-sinful; know this as the foe here (in this world). (3.37)

38. Define 'desire'.

A constant agitation of the mind, expressing as an uncontrollable impatience to gain something, is called 'desire'. (3.37)

39. "Desire itself, under certain circumstances, gains expression as anger." Explain.

Whenever emotions for acquisition and possession of an object flow incessantly towards that object, the bundle of thoughts so flowing is called 'desire'; while the same desire, when it gets obstructed from reaching its desired objects and gets refracted at an intermediate obstacle is called 'anger'. (3.37)

40. Śrī Kṛṣṇa uses three examples to illustrate the manner in which desire and anger veil one's reason and discrimination. What are the three examples and explain their significance.

धूमेनाव्रियते वह्निर्यथादर्शो मलेन च ।
यथोल्बेनावृतो गर्भस्तथा तेनेदमावृतम् ॥

dhūmenāvriyate vahniryathādarśo malena ca,
yatholbenāvṛto garbhastathā tenedamāvṛtam.

As fire is enveloped by smoke, as a mirror by dust, as an embryo by the womb, so this (wisdom) is enveloped by that (desire and anger).

Desires fall under three categories according to the quality of the attachment—inert (tāmasic), or active (rājasic), or noble and divine (sāttvic). All the three types of desires veil one's wisdom. These different types of qualities (guṇas) are indicated by the following three different examples:

(1) '**Fire enveloped by smoke**'—signifies wisdom enveloped by sattva. A passing breeze or slight effort is sufficient to remove the smoke. So too a little effort is sufficient to remove sāttvic desires that cloud our wisdom.

(2) '**A mirror covered by dust**'—indicates wisdom covered by rajas. Just as an effort of wiping is required to remove the dust, so too one needs to put in a little more effort to remove rājasic desires.

(3) '**The embryo covered by the womb**'—indicates wisdom covered by tamas. Effort alone is incapable of freeing the baby from the womb. It takes time and patience to be free of tāmasic desires. (3.38)

41. What are the three seats of desire?

Senses, mind and intellect are the three seats of desire.

इन्द्रियाणि मनो बुद्धिरस्याधिष्ठानमुच्यते ।
एतैर्विमोहयत्येष ज्ञानमावृत्य देहिनम् ॥

indriyāṇi mano buddhirasyādhiṣṭhānamucyate,
etairvimohayatyeṣa jñānamāvṛtya dehinam.

The senses, the mind, and the intellect are said to be its seat; through these, it deludes the embodied by veiling his wisdom.

The sense organs, functioning without restraint in the world of sense objects, are a very convenient theatre for 'desire' to function in. When the external stimuli reach the mind through the sense organs, the mind also becomes a breeding centre of sorrows created by 'desire'. Lastly, the intellect, working and playing with the memories of the sense-enjoyments it had lived, and of the mental attachments it had entertained, becomes yet another safe den for 'desire' to function from.

The deluded ego, foolishly identifying with the body, desires sense-enjoyments. Thoughtlessly identifying with the mind, it thirsts to experience more and more emotional satisfactions. And lastly, identifying with the intellect, it plans to re-live the remembered experiences of sense-enjoyments and mental-joys. (3.40)

42. How is desire conquered?

Desire is conquered by the Knowledge of the Self. This is made clear in the following verse:

एवं बुद्धेः परं बुद्ध्वा संस्तभ्यात्मानमात्मना ।
जहि शत्रुं महाबाहो कामरूपं दुरासदम् ॥

evaṁ buddheḥ paraṁ buddhvā saṁstabhyātmānamātmanā,
jahi śatruṁ mahābāho kāmarūpaṁ durāsadam.

Thus knowing Him, who is superior to intellect, and restraining the self by the Self, slay you, O mighty-armed, the enemy in the form of 'desire', no doubt hard indeed to conquer. (3.43)

Selections for Reflection

1. Vedānta being a complete and exhaustive science of religion, the great Ṛṣis never by-passed the intellect of their disciples by appealing to their blind faith or insisting upon their abject devotion. The Masters of old encouraged doubts and invited discussions. It is during these discussions that the student wrestled with the teacher in the arena of the intellect, and in this exercise he became spiritually stronger and perfectly agile. (Introduction)

2. The Gītā was written as an answer to an urgent demand in the time of Vyāsa. The old traditional thoughts became stereotyped and lifeless. Dead phrases and cliches cannot nourish a culture. Thus, through the Gītā, Śrī Kṛṣṇa is made to give out a re-interpretation of the Vedic truths in the context of His time, and in the language of the world in which He Himself happened to live. (Introduction)

3. Any action can be a glorious 'worship' (yajña) if only it is undertaken with the required purity of motive, with a spirit of surrender, and with the deep emotion of love. (Introduction)

4. Arjuna cannot have any individual personality in an army. It was a war. In a war when two armies fight they represent the clash of two ideologies. The Pāṇḍavas were convinced of the moral purity, the spiritual worth and the divine glory of their standpoint. But unfortunately, Arjuna could not sink his egoism, and see himself totally identified with the army, championing the cause of the good. To the degree he could not identify himself with the cause, to that extent he nourished a self-centred egoistic vanity, and, therefore, his moral puritanism in fighting the war. (3.1)

5. To consider the 'path of action' and the 'path of knowledge' as competitive is to understand neither of them. They, being complementary, are to be practised serially one after the other. Selfless activity gives a chance to the mind to exhaust many of its existing mental impressions. Thus purified, the mind gains such a flight and ethereal poise that it can steadily soar into the subtlest realms of meditation, and finally come to gain the experience of the transcendental Absolute. (3.3)

6. As the desires in us, so are our thoughts; thoughts are the disturbances created in our mental zone by our desires. At every moment, the texture and quality of our thoughts are directly conditioned and controlled by our desires. Thoughts in an individual, expressed in the outer world of objects, become his

actions; actions are nothing other than the actor's thoughts projected and expressed in the world. Thus, in this 'chain of ignorance' constituted of desires, thoughts and actions, each one of us is caught and bound. (3.4)

7. Life is dynamic. Nobody can sit idle. Even the idler contributes to the general activity. In this ever-surging onward rush of life's full impetuosity, if there be a foolish guide who would plunge himself in the mid-stream and stand with upraised hands, howling to the generation to halt, he would certainly be pulverized by the ever-moving flood of life and its endless activities. (3.26)

8. A serpent is dangerous only as long as its fangs are not removed. The moment these are taken out, even the most poisonous reptile becomes a tame creature incapable of harming anyone. Similarly, action gives rise to bondage only when it is performed with a heart laden with selfish-desires. Actions performed without desires are not actions at all, inasmuch as they are incapable of producing any painful reactions. (3.30)

9. Prescribing a medicine which is not available is not the art of healing. It is the philosopher's duty not only to indicate the weaknesses in our present life and the 'State of Perfection', but he must also show us ways and means by which we can transport ourselves from our weaknesses into this ideal 'State of Perfection'. Then, and then alone, can the philosopher bless his generation. (3.34)

Verses for Memorisation

ज्यायसी चेत्कर्मणस्ते मता बुद्धिर्जनार्दन ।
तत्किं कर्मणि घोरे मां नियोजयसि केशव ॥

jyāyasī cetkarmaṇaste matā buddhirjanārdana,
tatkiṁ karmaṇi ghore māṁ niyojayasi keśava.

If it be thought by you that 'knowledge' is superior to 'action', O

Janārdana, why then, do you, O Keśava, engage me in this terrible action? (3.1)

न हि कश्चित्क्षणमपि जातु तिष्ठत्यकर्मकृत्।
कार्यते ह्यवशः कर्म सर्वः प्रकृतिजैर्गुणैः॥

na hi kaścitkṣaṇamapi jātu tiṣṭhatyakarmakṛt,
kāryate hyavaśaḥ karma sarvaḥ prakṛtijairguṇaiḥ.

Verily, none can ever remain, even for a moment, without performing action; for, everyone is made to act helplessly, indeed, by the qualities born of prakṛti. (3.5)

सक्ताः कर्मण्यविद्वांसो यथा कुर्वन्ति भारत।
कुर्याद्विद्वांस्तथाऽसक्तश्चिकीर्षुर्लोकसङ्ग्रहम्॥

saktāḥ karmaṇyavidvāṁso yathā kurvanti bhārata,
kuryādvidvāṁstathā'saktaścikīrṣurlokasaṅgraham.

As the 'ignorant' men act from attachment to action, O Bhārata, so should the 'wise' men act without attachment, wishing for the welfare of the world. (3.25)

मयि सर्वाणि कर्माणि संन्यस्याध्यात्मचेतसा।
निराशीर्निर्ममो भूत्वा युध्यस्व विगतज्वरः॥

mayi sarvāṇi karmāṇi saṁnyasyādhyātmacetasā,
nirāśīrnirmamo bhūtvā yudhyasva vigatajvaraḥ.

Renouncing all actions in Me, with the mind centred on the Self, free from hope and egoism, free from (mental) fever, do you fight. (3.30)

श्रेयान्स्वधर्मो विगुणः परधर्मात्स्वनुष्ठितात्।
स्वधर्मे निधनं श्रेयः परधर्मो भयावहः॥

śreyānsvadharmo viguṇaḥ paradharmātsvanuṣṭhitāt,
svadharme nidhanaṁ śreyaḥ paradharmo bhayāvahaḥ.

Better one's own 'duty' though devoid of merit, than the 'duty' of another well discharged. Better is death in one's own 'duty'; the 'duty' of another is fraught with fear (is productive of positive danger). (3.35)

आवृतं ज्ञानमेतेन ज्ञानिनो नित्यवैरिणा।
कामरूपेण कौन्तेय दुष्पूरेणानलेन च॥

āvṛtaṁ jñānametena jñānino nityavairiṇā,
kāmarūpeṇa kaunteya duṣpūreṇānalena ca.
Enveloped, O son of Kuntī, is 'wisdom' by this constant enemy of the wise in the form of 'desire' which is difficult to appease, like fire. (3.39)

4

Jñāna Karma Saṁnyāsa Yoga

The Yoga of Renunciation of Action in Knowledge

An egoless Man of Perfection is the 'wonder instrument' through which the divine orchestra plays, faithfully singing the song of the Lord's Will. (4.21)

ॐ

In the third chapter, Śrī Kṛṣṇa had propounded a revolutionary idea in the form of Karma Yoga which had sounded as though it was a novel intellectual theory. Arjuna would not willingly accept it unless his teacher gave an endorsement that what he had lectured upon was nothing other than an intelligent reinterpretation of the ancient sacred Vedic Science. In this chapter, an all-out effort is made by Śrī Kṛṣṇa to bring home to Arjuna that He had been asserting the same old Truth and nothing new.

Again, whenever a teacher, in his inspiration, emphasises a particular stage of self-development, chances are that seekers may misunderstand the import of the words and conclude that the partial-path explained is the entire-route to the Infinite. In order to remove this misunderstanding, the fourth chapter indicates the greater path of Jñāna Yoga, the 'Path of Knowledge', which is the main archway through which all pilgrims must pass in order to reach the Temple of the Self. Up to this archway, seekers living in different psychological and intellectual domains may walk their own paths, but the main gate is Jñāna Yoga through which all must pass to have Darśana at the glorious Altar.

To Arjuna, Lord Kṛṣṇa was only a friend, the cowherd boy of Vṛndāvana. Familiarity, if it does not breed contempt, is at least sure to pull down the familiar in our estimation of its importance and sanctity. This chapter is also intended to invoke in Arjuna's mind the necessary amount of reverence and respect towards his Charioteer. In short, Kṛṣṇa is here divesting himself of his work-a-day clothes and is putting on, for the first time, His complete Divine apparel of

Omnipotence and Omniscience, descended upon the earth.

ଓଃ

Terms and Definitions

1. What does the term 'Parantapa' mean?

'Scorcher of foes'—Śrī Kṛṣṇa uses it as an appellation for Arjuna. (4.5)

2. Define 'Jñāna Tapas'.

A study of the theory of Vedānta and all our attempts to live the life of tranquillity and love indicated therein together constitute 'Jñāna Tapas'. (4.10)

3. Who is a 'kavi'?

The word 'kavi', now-a-days mainly used for poets, was the name for Ṛṣis, the seers of Upaniṣadic declarations. Any inspired man, recognising and expressing a truth that was noble and immortal, was called a 'kavi'. (4.16)

4. Differentiate between 'karma' and 'vikarma'.

Constructive activities that contribute towards the evolution of the individual are termed 'karma'. Karma can be of three kinds: nitya—constant duties, naimittika—special duties on special occasions, and kāmya—work purposeful and self-determined for winning a desirable result or reward. Destructive activities (niṣiddha) are those that are totally condemned by the śāstras, because they tend to de-evolve the individual, and are termed 'vikarma'. (4.17)

5. What is 'akarma' (unactivity)?

A true and diligent man can discover and recognise that even in physical inaction there can be an intense mental and intellectual activity. Also, even in these most intense activities, he can recognise himself to be an observer of all the activities and thus revel in 'unactivity' (akarma). This 'akarma' is the maximum sāttvic state, the state of sāttvic peace and joy. This ability to stand constantly apart from himself and observe 'the activity in inactivity' and 'complete inactivity even in the highest activity' is called 'unactivity' or 'akarma'. (4.18)

6. Who is a 'paṇḍita' (sage)?

यस्य सर्वे समारम्भाः कामसङ्कल्पवर्जिताः ।
ज्ञानाग्निदग्धकर्माणं तमाहुः पण्डितं बुधाः ॥

yasya sarve samārambhāḥ kāmasaṅkalpavarjitāḥ,
jñānāgnidagdhakarmāṇaṁ tamāhuḥ paṇḍitaṁ budhāḥ.

Whose undertakings are all devoid of desires and purposes, and whose actions have been burnt by the fire of Knowledge, him the wise call a 'paṇḍita' (sage). (4.19)

7. Define the terms 'Brahman' and 'Ātman'.

The infinite Reality, which is the changeless substratum behind and beneath the changing panorama of the world, is termed 'Brahman'. The very same infinite Reality when functioning in and through the body is called 'Ātman'. But though the Eternal Truth has been thus indicated by two different terms, Vedānta roars that "the Ātman is Brahman". (4.24)

8. What is 'ātma-saṁyama-yoga'?

Yoga of self-restraint (4.27)

9. Define the terms 'pūraka', 'kumbhaka' and 'recaka'.

In the technique of prāṇāyāma, the process of filling in air is 'pūraka', the process of blowing out is 'recaka' and holding the breath for some time within or without is called 'kumbhaka'. (4.29)

10. What is prāṇa? What are the five types of prāṇa?

The term 'prāṇa' indicates the various physiological functions in a living body.

The five types of prāṇa are:

(1) the function of respiration (prāṇa)
(2) the function of excretion (apāna)
(3) the function of digestion and assimilation (samāna)
(4) the function of blood-circulation (vyāna)

(5) the function of involuntary reverse actions (like vomiting, etc.) as well as the capacity in a living creature to improve himself in his mental outlook and intellectual life (udāna). (4.29)

11. What are the twelve yajñas (sacrifices) mentioned in the fourth chapter?

The twelve yajñas are:

(1) Daiva-yajña (4.25)
(2) Brahma-yajña (4.25)
(3) Yajña of sense-control (4.26)
(4) Yajña of mind-control (4.26)
(5) Yajña of self-restraint (4.27)
(6) Dravya-yajña (4.28)
(7) Tapo-yajña (4.28)
(8) Yoga-yajña (4.28)
(9) Svādhyāya-yajña (4.28)
(10) Jñāna-yajña (4.28)
(11) Prāṇāyāma-yajña (4.29)
(12) Niyatāhāra-yajña (4.30)

12. What are three classifications of karma-phala (fruits of action)?

Karma-phala has been classified into three groups. They are:

(1) 'Not yet operative'—'sañcita'
(2) 'Operative'—'prārabdha'
(3) 'To be operative in future'—'āgāmī'. (4.37)

Thoughts and Concepts

1.What is the 'guru-śiṣya-paramparā' (lineage of teacher and taught) pointed out by Śrī Kṛṣṇa?

इमं विवस्वते योगं प्रोक्तवानहमव्ययम्।
विवस्वान्मनवे प्राह मनुरिक्ष्वाकवेऽब्रवीत्॥

imaṁ vivasvate yogaṁ proktavānahamavyayam,
vivasvānmanave prāha manurikṣvākave'bravīt.

I taught this Imperishable Yoga to Vivasvān; Vivasvān taught it to Manu; Manu taught it to Ikṣvāku.

The Lord declares that He Himself, at the very beginning of creation, imparted the Knowledge of the Vedas to the Sun (Vivasvān), and later on, the Sun-god conveyed it to his son, Manu, the ancient law-giver of India. Manu, in turn, declared it to Ikṣvāku, the ancestor of the Solar dynasty that ruled over Ayodhya for a long period of time. (4.1)

2. What is the meaning of the word 'Veda'?

The word 'Veda' is derived from the root *'vid'*, 'to know'; 'Veda', therefore, means 'Knowledge'. The Knowledge of divinity lurking in man and the technique by which it can be brought out to full manifestation are the themes of the Veda textbooks. (4.1)

3. Why should spiritual lessons be directly heard from a true master?

The theme of Vedic literature being the subjective Divinity, language fails to express it completely. No deep experience can be exhaustively expressed in words. Therefore, a study of the scriptures by oneself is apt to create misunderstanding rather than a right appreciation of it. Thus it is a time-honored tradition in India that spiritual lessons are directly heard from a true Master, who has had vivid inner experiences in the realm of the Spirit. (4.1)

4. Why is the 'Science of Truth' called the 'supreme secret'?

The 'Science of Truth' being described as the 'supreme secret' only indicates that a man, however wise he might be, may not come to suspect the existence of the Ātman in himself without being so advised by a Man of Experience. The Self being that which is beyond the intellect, the reasoning capacity in a man cannot come to suspect the existence of the eternal and changeless Conscious Principle which is subtler than the intellect. Hence, this 'Science of Truth' is called the 'supreme secret'. (4.3)

5. "A jīva becomes victimised by his avidyā, while the Lord is Master

of His māyā." Explain.

A driver is bound by his duty to the vehicle, while the owner of the vehicle is Lord of it. He uses the vehicle for his purposes, and whenever he reaches his destination, he leaves the vehicle with all freedom, and enjoys his own independent activities. But the poor driver, bound to the vehicle, will have to guard it against intruders and serve the vehicle as its servant.

The Lord uses the matter envelopments and their limitations as a convenience and as a set of necessary tools in His game of protecting creation. Thus, though the Lord is Unborn and Changeless in His Nature and ever a Lord of matter, yet, keeping His māyā perfectly under His own control, He comes into the world through His own free will. All the time He is fully conscious of His own divine status and unchallenged prerogative. He does not come into being as others do, compelled by His past karma, to live here in the world under the thraldom of Nature. He is not bound by His mental temperaments but He is ever free from the mischiefs of His own māyā. On the other hand, the jīva is ignorant of his true Nature and is ever compelled by his past karma. He is bound by his mental temperaments and is under the clutches of avidyā (ignorance). (4.6)

6. When does the Lord take an 'avatāra' (incarnation)?

The following verse provides the answer to the above question:

यदा यदा हि धर्मस्य ग्लानिर्भवति भारत ।
अभ्युत्थानमधर्मस्य तदात्मानं सृजाम्यहम् ॥

yadā yadā hi dharmasya glānirbhavati bhārata,
abhyutthānamadharmasya tadātmānaṁ sṛjāmyaham.

Whenever there is a decay of righteousness, O Bhārata, and a rise of unrighteousness, then I manifest myself. (4.7)

7. Why does the Lord take 'avatāra'?

The following verse answers the above question:

परित्राणाय साधूनां विनाशाय च दुष्कृताम् ।
धर्मसंस्थापनार्थाय सम्भवामि युगे युगे ॥

paritrāṇāya sādhūnāṁ vināśāya ca duṣkṛtām,

dharmasaṁsthāpanārthāya sambhavāmi yuge yuge.

For the protection of the good, for the destruction of the wicked and for the establishment of righteousness, I am born in every age. (4.8)

8. What are the three constituents in the technique of self-development?

The following three together constitute the technique of self-development:

(1) Study of the scriptures at the feet of a Master

(2) Independent analysis of Vedāntic truths by oneself in an attempt to understand their real import and

(3) Slow and steady attempts at balancing oneself in single-pointed meditation (4.10)

9. Indicate how all the three paths of action, devotion and knowledge find their mention in the following verse.

वीतरागभयक्रोधा मन्मया मामुपाश्रिताः ।

बहवो ज्ञानतपसा पूता मद्भावमागताः ॥

vītarāgabhayakrodhā manmayā māmupāśritāḥ,

bahavo jñānatapasā pūtā madbhāvamāgatāḥ.

Freed from attachment, fear and anger, absorbed in Me, taking refuge in Me, purified by the Fire-of-Knowledge, many have attained My Being.

The Path of Action is indicated in the first-half of the first line '*vītarāgabhayakrodhaḥ*—freed from attachment, fear and anger'. For unless one trains oneself in the field of activity, detachment from desires, fear and anger cannot be gained. The second-half, '*manmayāmāmupāśritāḥ*—absorbed in me and taking refuge in me' indicates the Path of Devotion, wherein the devotee, binding himself with love to the Lord of his heart lives his life, taking refuge in nothing other than the Lord. The Path of Knowledge is indicated by the discriminative analysis and the constant and continued attempts at identification with the Self (Jñāna Tapas). The import is that seekers walking all the seemingly different paths reach but the same supreme Goal. (4.10)

10. The Lord says, "I lend my power to all without any partiality and in whatever form they invoke me, in that form I serve them." Explain.

An electric plug in the house can be used to hear a song over the radio, to cool ourselves with the breeze of a fan, to boil water, to cook or to warm the room with a heater; it all depends upon what instrument we plug into it. It is never possible that electricity flowing through the fan, of its own accord, can start emitting fire or light. Similarly, the unmanifest eternal force of life can be invoked, and it shall fulfil all 'desires' through us according to the type of our invocations. This is the significance of the Lord's statement, "I lend my power to all without any partiality and in whatever form they invoke me, in that form I serve them." (4.11)

11. If the Ātmic-force guides us on both the path of good and on the path of evil, then how is it that we see but a rare few who are honestly trying to travel the path of righteousness, while the majority are pursuing the road of evil?

Whether the mind wants to pursue an extrovert life or live the introvert joys, it can do so only by borrowing its capacity and capability from the omnipotency of the Ātman; but the mind ever chooses an extrovert career because it is easy to gain cheap pleasures by satisfying the sensuous ticklings of nerve-tips. The quickest results are gained when our sense organs come in contact with their desired objects as the result of deliberate actions. Since a sensuous life is a life of least resistance the majority of men, in their keen appetite for joy and peace, waste their strength in hunting after, procuring and enjoying the fleeting pleasures of sense objects. (4.12)

12. The fourfold-castes are based on ________ and ________.

Guṇa and karma.

The following stanza makes this clear:

चातुर्वर्ण्यं मया सृष्टं गुणकर्मविभागशः ।
तस्य कर्तारमपि मां विद्ध्यकर्तारमव्ययम् ॥

cāturvarṇyaṁ mayā sṛṣṭaṁ guṇakarmavibhāgaśaḥ,
tasya kartāramapi māṁ viddhyakartāramavyayam.

The fourfold-caste has been created by Me according to the differentiation of guṇa and karma; though I am the author thereof, know Me as non-doer and immutable. (4.13)

13. Explain the concept of 'varṇa'.

'Varṇa' literally means different shades of texture or colour. In the Yoga Śāstra, they attribute some definite colours to the triple 'guṇas' or 'the mental temperaments'. Thus, sattva is considered white, rajas red, and tamas black. Man is essentially the thoughts that he entertains. From individual to individual, even when the thoughts are superficially the same, there are clear distinctions recognisable from their temperaments. On the basis of these temperamental distinctions, the entire mankind has been, for the purpose of spiritual study, classified into four 'castes' or 'varṇas'. Just as, in a metropolis, on the basis of trade or professions, we divide people into groups as doctors, advocates, professors, traders, politicians, tongawalas, etc., so too on the basis of the different textures of thoughts entertained, the four 'castes' had been labelled in the past. From the standpoint of the State, a doctor and a tongawala are as important as an advocate and a mechanic. So too, for the perfectly healthy life of a society, 'castes' should not be competitive but co-operative units, each being complementary to the others, never competing among themselves.

This complete definition of the 'varṇa' not only removes the present misunderstanding but also provides us with some data to understand its true significance. Not by birth is man a brāhmaṇa (brāhmin); by cultivating good intentions and noble thoughts alone can we ever aspire to brāhmaṇahood; nor can we pose as brāhmaṇa merely because of our external physical marks, or bodily actions in the outer world. The definition insists that he alone is a brāhmaṇa, whose thoughts are as sāttvic as his actions. Those who have a commercial attitude are vaiśyas. A kṣatriya is one who is rājasic in his thoughts and actions. A śūdra is not only one whose thoughts are tāmasic but also he who lives a life of low endeavours, for satisfying his base animal passions and flesh-appetites. (4.13)

14. Who is not bound by his actions?

The following verse provides the reply to the above question:

न मां कर्माणि लिम्पन्ति न मे कर्मफले स्पृहा ।
इति मां योऽभिजानाति कर्मभिर्न स बध्यते ॥

na māṁ karmāṇi limpanti na me karmaphale spṛhā,
iti māṁ yo'bhijānāti karmabhirna sa badhyate.

Actions do not taint Me, nor have I any desire for the fruits of actions. He who knows Me thus is not bound by his actions. (4.14)

15. "What is action? What is inaction? As to this even the 'wise' are deluded." Explain.

'Action' commonly means movement of the limbs with relation to things in the outer world, and 'inaction' means a state of existence wherein there is a total cessation of such vigorous and conscious movements. This is the popular definition of 'action' and 'inaction' which, no doubt, is quite acceptable as far as the everyday activities of life are concerned. But from the philosophical standpoint, the concept and features of both 'action' and 'inaction' change.

For purposes of self-development, when we consider 'action', it is not to be valued merely by observing its manifested qualities, but we must also take into consideration the unmanifested but subtly-working motives behind the very same action. An action in itself cannot be considered either good or bad. It is the motive behind it which determines the quality of the action. Just as the beauty of a fruit is not the last word for its edibility but depends upon its contents, so too a beautiful action in itself could be a poisonous act of criminality if the motive behind it is low and vicious.

Therefore, it is said that in discriminating between what is 'action' and what is 'inaction' 'even the poet-seers of old are confused'. (4.16)

16. "Physical inactivity is no criterion to call one an idler." Explain.

When we are intensely thinking—whenever we are in a state of creative thinking—we are invariably quiet and inactive physically. Therefore, in the physical inactivity of one we can detect intense activity in his deep 'within'. A Buddha under the fig-tree, an artist at his easel, a musician at his instrument, a writer at his desk—all of them punctuate their activities with 'still moments of intense inactivity—called 'unactivity'—and they bend forward to pour out their artistic and literary creations. All these physical moments of cessation are not mere inactivity but they are the necessary quietude and silence when the mind and intellect function with the highest velocity. (4.18)

17. Who is the individual who is actionless inspite of his external action?

त्यक्त्वा कर्मफलासङ्गं नित्यतृप्तो निराश्रयः ।
कर्मण्यभिप्रवृत्तोऽपि नैव किञ्चित्करोति सः ॥

tyaktvā karmaphalāsaṅgaṁ nityatṛpto nirāśrayaḥ,
karmaṇyabhipravṛtto'pi naiva kiñcitkaroti saḥ.

Having abandoned attachment to the fruits of action, ever content, depending on nothing, he does not do anything, though engaged in actions. (4.20)

18. Who is not bound even while acting?

यदृच्छालाभसन्तुष्टो द्वन्द्वातीतो विमत्सरः ।
समः सिद्धावसिद्धौ च कृत्वापि न निबध्यते ॥

yadṛcchālābhasantuṣṭo dvandvātīto vimatsaraḥ,
samaḥ siddhāvasiddhau ca kṛtvāpi na nibadhyate.

Content with what comes to him without effort, free from the pairs of opposites and envy, even-minded in success and failure, though acting he is not bound. (4.22)

19. Explain the concept of 'yajña'.

'Yajña' is an activity performed with full personal dedication in a spirit of service to the many. All actions performed without ego, and not motivated by one's egocentric desires, are termed 'yajña'. (4.23)

20. Whose actions are 'dissolved'?

गतसङ्गस्य मुक्तस्य ज्ञानावस्थितचेतसः ।
यज्ञायाचरतः कर्म समग्रं प्रविलीयते ॥

gatasaṅgasya muktasya jñānāvasthitacetasaḥ,
yajñāyācarataḥ karma samagraṁ pravilīyate.

Of one who is devoid of attachment, who is liberated, whose mind is established in knowledge, who acts for the sake of sacrifice, all his actions are 'dissolved'.

When a sage performs actions in a spirit of yajña, they dissolve without leaving any impression upon his mind, just as the rainbow disappears when the thin shower falling against the sunlight ends. (4.23)

21. _____________makes every act a yajña.

Right knowledge (bhāvanā). (4.24)

22. What are the four essential factors of yajña?

In every yajña there are four essential factors:

(1) Deity invoked to whom the oblations are offered

(2) Fire in which the offerings are poured

(3) Material things that constitute the offerings

(4) Individual who is performing the yajña. (4.24)

23. What is the significance of chanting the following verse before taking food?

ब्रह्मार्पणं ब्रह्म हविर्ब्रह्माग्नौ ब्रह्मणा हुतम् ।
ब्रह्मैव तेन गन्तव्यं ब्रह्मकर्मसमाधिना ॥

brahmārpaṇaṁ brahma havirbrahmāgnau brahmaṇā hutam,
brahmaiva tena gantavyaṁ brahmakarmasamādhinā.

Brahman is the oblation; Brahman is the clarified butter etc., constituting the offerings; by Brahman is the oblation poured into the fire of Brahman, Brahman verily shall be reached by him who always sees Brahman in all actions.

To live we must eat. Food is necessary for existence. Whatever be the type of food, when one is hungry one will enjoy one's meals. The suggestion is that even at this moment of natural enjoyment, we are not to forget the great Truth that it is Brahman eating Brahman, and that during our meals we are offering to Brahman the food that is Brahman invoking nothing but the grace of Brahman. To keep this idea constantly in the mind is to get perfectly detached from the enjoyment and raise ourselves to a greater and endless beatitude. Hence, this stanza is chanted as a prayer in all Hindu traditional households before taking food. (4.24)

24. What does the word 'deva' mean? From the subjective viewpoint what are the 'devas'?

The word 'deva' comes from the Sanskrit verbal root '*div*' meaning 'illumination'. Subjectively viewed, the greatest 'devas' are the five sense organs: eyes illumining forms and colours, ears illumining sounds, the nose illumining smells, and the tongue and the skin illumining tastes and touch respectively. (4.25)

25. What is 'dravya-yajña'?

'Dravya-yajña' is 'sacrifice of wealth'. Charity and distribution of honestly acquired wealth, in a sincere spirit of service to an individual or the community, is called 'dravya-yajña'. This includes more than a mere offering of money or food. The word 'dravya' includes everything that we possess, not only in the world outside but also in our worlds of emotions and ideas. To pursue thus a life of charity, serving the world as best as we can, with all that we possess physically, mentally and intellectually is the noble sacrifice called 'dravya-yajña'. (4.28)

26. What is 'svādhyāya-yajña'?

The daily deep study of the scriptures is called 'svādhyāya'. Without a complete study of the scriptures we will not be in a position to know the logic of what we are doing in the name of spiritual practice, and without this knowledge our practices cannot gain the edge and the depth that are essential for sure progress. Even after Self-Realisation, we find that the Sages spend all their spare-time reading and contemplating upon the inexhaustible wealth of details and suggestions in the scriptures.

'Svādhyāya' also includes the art of introspection pursued for understanding our own inner weaknesses. If, in the case of a seeker, 'svādhyāya-yajña' is a technique of estimating his own spiritual progress, in the case of a Seer, it will be for revelling in his own Self. (4.28)

27. What is 'jñāna-yajña'?

'Jñāna-yajña' is the term given to that activity in man by which he renounces all his ignorance into the 'fire of knowledge' kindled by him, in himself. This is constituted of two aspects: (1) negation of the false and (2) assertion of the real nature of the Self and are effectively undertaken during the seeker's meditation. (4.28)

28. What is meditation?

Meditation is the path in which the ego learns to withdraw its false evaluations of itself in particular, and of life in general, and comes to the final experience of its own Divine nature. (4.30)

29. 'Jñāna-yajña' is superior to 'dravya-yajña'. Explain.

Śrī Kṛṣṇa compares 'dravya-yajña' - the sacrifice of material oblations with 'jñāna-yajña' and declares that, for self-development , jñāna-yajña is any day nobler and divine than mere formalistic ritualism with material offerings (dravya-yajña).

The Lord explains how and why He considers 'the sacrifice of ignorance in Knowledge' (jñāna-yajña) as greater and nobler than the sacrifice of 'food and other materials in the sacred fire' (dravya-yajña). Ritualistic karmas produce results to enjoy which the individual ego has to take up new manifestations wherein, again, he has to undertake and perform more activities. Karma never ends karma and, therefore, action cannot be a complete fulfilment in itself. On the other hand, Right-Knowledge (jñāna) ends all karmas once and for all, inasmuch as the deluded ego destroys itself in the light of Self Knowledge. Since it is the jñāna-yajña that directly destroys ignorance and not dravya-yajña, jñāna-yajña is superior to dravya-yajña. (4.33)

30. How should one approach the Guru?

तद्विद्धि प्रणिपातेन परिप्रश्नेन सेवया ।
उपदेक्ष्यन्ति ते ज्ञानं ज्ञानिनस्तत्त्वदर्शिनः ॥

tadviddhi praṇipātena paripraśnena sevayā,

upadekṣyanti te jñānaṁ jñāninastattvadarśinaḥ.

Know That (Self-Knowledge) by long prostration, by question and service, the 'wise' who have realised the Truth will instruct you in (that) 'Knowledge'.

Prostrating yourself—The student must have an intellectual attitude of surrender and meekness, respect and obedience when he approaches the teacher who has to instruct him upon the secret-of-life.

By questions—By raising doubts to the teacher we are opening up the treasure chest of 'Knowledge' locked in the Master. A perfect Guru immediately detects from the questions the false line of thinking in the student, and while removing the very doubt, imperceptibly orders and reorganises the right way of thinking in the inner thought-life of the student. When this intellectual wrestling has been practised for a long time, the fragrance of perfection in the teacher, as it were, gets transferred to the student's life!

By service—True service to the teacher lies in the attempt of the student to attune himself to the principles of life advocated by and as advised by the Master. To live the life indicated by the Ṛṣis is the greatest seva that an imperfect mortal can offer to the Man of Perfection. (4.34)

31. What are the qualifications of a teacher?

The two main qualifications essential for a fully useful teacher of the spiritual path are (1) perfect knowledge of scriptural literature and (2) complete subjective experience of the Infinite Reality. (4.34)

32. What is true Wisdom?

To rediscover that in reality the ego is nothing other than the Self in us, and to live thereafter as the Self of all is called true Wisdom. (4.36)

33. "The fire of Knowledge reduces all actions to ashes." Explain.

Whatever be the quality, shape, condition, colour, etc., of the fuel pieces, when all of them are taken to the fire-place and digested by the fire, they become one homogeneous mass of ash! In the samples of ash left in the hearth we cannot recognise the ash of a particular twig as different from that of another. Similarly, all karmas, it is said—good, bad, or indifferent—get burnt up in the 'Fire of Knowledge' and will become something altogether different from what they were in their 'cause and effect condition' in weight, smell, etc. Pieces of kindling, for instance, become almost weightless, with no specific colour except a light-greyness, when they come to the final state of ash.

Actions leave reactions (results). The reactions mature at different periods of time depending upon the quality and intensity of the actions. From beginningless time, in our different manifestations we have been, at every moment, acting in our egocentric vanity and individuality. All those actions must have left their residual impressions and they have to be lived through. This entire karma has been considered as falling under three classifications. They are called 'not yet operative' (sañcita) 'operative' (prārabdha) and 'to be operative in future' (āgāmī). When in the Gītā it is said that all karmas are burnt down, the Lord means the entire sañcita and āgāmī. (4.37)

34. What is the greatest purifier?

Knowledge of the Self is the greatest purifier. This is made clear in the following verse:

न हि ज्ञानेन सदृशं पवित्रमिह विद्यते ।
तत्स्वयं योगसंसिद्धः कालेनात्मनि विन्दति ॥

na hi jñānena sadṛśaṁ pavitramiha vidyate,
tatsvayaṁ yogasaṁsiddhaḥ kālenātmani vindati.

Certainly, there is no purifier in this world like 'Knowledge'. He who is himself perfected in Yoga finds it in the Self in time. (4.38)

35. Which verses in the fourth chapter describe the glory of Knowledge?

अपि चेदसि पापेभ्यः सर्वेभ्यः पापकृत्तमः ।
सर्वं ज्ञानप्लवेनैव वृजिनं सन्तरिष्यसि ॥

api cedasi pāpebhyaḥ sarvebhyaḥ pāpakṛttamaḥ,
sarvaṁ jñānaplavenaiva vṛjinaṁ santariṣyasi.
Even if you are the most sinful of all sinners, yet you shall verily cross all sins by the raft of 'Knowledge'. (4.36)
यथैधांसि समिद्धोऽग्निर्भस्मसात्कुरुतेऽर्जुन ।
ज्ञानाग्निः सर्वकर्माणि भस्मसात्कुरुते तथा ॥
yathaidhāṁsi samiddho'gnirbhasmasātkurute'rjuna,
jñānāgniḥ sarvakarmāṇi bhasmasātkurute tathā.
As the blazing fire reduces fuel to ashes, O Arjuna, so does the Fire of Knowledge reduce all actions to ashes. (4.37)
न हि ज्ञानेन सदृशं पवित्रमिह विद्यते ।
तत्स्वयं योगसंसिद्धः कालेनात्मनि विन्दति ॥
na hi jñānena sadṛśaṁ pavitramiha vidyate,
tatsvayaṁ yogasaṁsiddhaḥ kālenātmani vindati.
Certainly, there is no purifier in this world like 'Knowledge'. He who is himself perfected in Yoga finds it in the Self in time. (4.38)

36. What are the three categories of persons who get destroyed?

The ignorant, faithless and the doubting-self fail in the spiritual path.
अज्ञश्चाश्रद्दधानश्च संशयात्मा विनश्यति ।
नायं लोकोऽस्ति न परो न सुखं संशयात्मनः ॥
ajñaścāśraddadhānaśca saṁśayātmā vinaśyati,
nāyaṁ loko'sti na paro na sukhaṁ saṁśayātmanaḥ.
The ignorant, the faithless, the doubting-self goes to destruction; there is neither this world nor the other nor happiness for the doubter. (4.40)

37. By what means can one destroy doubt about the Self?

With the sword of Knowledge
तस्मादज्ञानसम्भूतं हृत्स्थं ज्ञानासिनात्मनः ।
छित्त्वैनं संशयं योगमातिष्ठोत्तिष्ठ भारत ॥
tasmādajñānasambhūtaṁ hṛtsthaṁ jñānāsinātmanaḥ,
chittvainaṁ saṁśayaṁ yogamātiṣṭhottiṣṭha bhārata.
Therefore with the sword of Knowledge, cut asunder the doubt

about the Self, born of 'ignorance', residing in your heart, and take refuge in Yoga. Arise O Bhārata. (4.42)

38. What does the term 'heart' mean in spiritual literature?

It is the traditional belief in Vedānta that 'the intellect is seated in the heart' wherein the term 'heart' does not mean the fleshy pumping instrument in the human body. The term 'heart' is used not in its physiological meaning but in its literary usage, where heart means the source of all love and sympathy—of all noble human emotions. (4.42)

Selections for Reflection

1. At certain periods of history, this Knowledge (Brahma-vidyā) seems to be readily available for the service of mankind, but at certain other periods of history it falls into disuse and becomes, as it were, defunct. The golden era of spirituality dies down to inaugurate the dark ages of undivine life. At such periods of monstrous materialism, the generation is not left in neglect to suffer and groan under its own negative values. For, at that time, some great Master appears on the horizon to inspire, to encourage and to lead the generation away from the ruts of sorrow onto the highroads of cultural revival. (4.2)

2. To the Lord, His 'ignorance' is but a pose assumed, not a fact lived. (4.6)

3. The divinest of all 'desires' is, indeed, a selfless thirst to serve the world; but all the same it is a desire. (4.8)

4. Whatever be the path pursued and whatever be the type to which seekers belong, the ultimate experience of Spiritual Perfection gained by every one of them at the moment of illumination is one and the same. This is an incontrovertible fact, for the mystical literature of the world reads as though every saint has borrowed and copied from all the earlier Masters across the world! (4.10)

5. The sun reflected in bowl of water is entirely dependent upon the condition of the water. The reflected-sun is shaken when the water in the bowl is disturbed and it appears to be dim when the water is muddy. Neither the dimness nor the agitations of the reflection have caused any change at all in the original object—the sun in the heavens. Similarly, the ego suffers the evil tendencies and such other taints of the mind and also gets disturbed due to its 'desires' for the fruits of its actions. The Self, in Its pure Consciousnature, is not at all affected by these delusory disturbances of Its own reflection in the mental pool. (4.14)

6. Life means activity. Where activity has ended death has entered. In active life alone can we progress or deteriorate. A stagnant pool of water decays and soon gets putrefied, whereas the flowing water of a river ever keeps itself fresh, pure and clean. Life being dynamic, it cannot even for a moment cease to function. Complete cessation from activities is impossible so long as life exists. Activity, therefore, is the very corner-stone of life. (4.17)

7. Right action undertaken with a sense of devotion and dedication creates in the student a sense of complete detachment, as though he himself is a disinterested observer of all that is happening within him and without. When thus an individual detaches himself and observes his own activities as part and parcel of the world of activities around, he gains in himself an indescribable poise which is essential for the practice of meditation. (4.18)

8. The train runs but not the steam. The fan moves but not the electricity. The fuel burns but not the fire. The body, mind and intellect function and act but not the Self, the Life in them! (4.18)

9. The ego draws its sustenance from the 'hopes of the future' and from the 'satisfaction of its present' possessions. (4.21)

10. We are self-exiled from ourselves due to our attachments with the finite world of objects. (4.23)

11. When an individual's sense organs of perception and action are to function and act—not for his own egocentric, selfish satisfactions but for the sake of serving the society or the world—then even if such an individual lives in the world of objects he will not be enslaved by his attachments to his possessions. (4.25)

12. The more we try to satisfy the sense organs the more riotous they become and loot our inner joy. By self-control alone can the sense-organs be fully controlled and mastered. (4.26)

13. Vedānta is not a philosophy that heartlessly keeps sinners out of its halls of Wisdom. It does not believe that there is any lost soul who will ever wander faithless and who can only be redeemed if he enters the portals of Vedānta! Ever-tolerant, Vedānta declares the Truth and nothing but the Truth. The all-pervading Divine manifests everywhere and therefore, there is no sinner who cannot, through his endeavour, come to claim his own heritage of Absolute Perfection. (4.36)

14. Just as to a drowning man there is nothing more precious than a life-belt, so too to the deluded ego there cannot be a greater possession and a nobler endeavour than the acquisition of 'Knowledge' of its own Real Nature. (4.38)

15. To walk the Path-Divine is to get out of the gutter of sensuousness. Excessive sense-life and Absolute God-life are antitheses to each other; where the one is, the other cannot be. Where the light of inward serenity and deeper peace have come, the darkness created by sense passions and animal appetites must depart. (4.39)

16. He whose teeth have become septic must constantly poison the food that he is taking; so too, those who have the tendency to doubt everything will never be able to accommodate themselves to any situation, however perfect and just it might be. (4.40)

Verses for Memorisation

अजोऽपि सन्नव्ययात्मा भूतानामीश्वरोऽपि सन्।
प्रकृतिं स्वामधिष्ठाय सम्भवाम्यात्ममायया॥

ajo'pi sannavyayātmā bhūtānāmīśvaro'pi san,
prakṛtiṁ svāmadhiṣṭhāya sambhavāmyātmamāyayā.

Though I am unborn and am of imperishable naure, and though I am the Lord of all beings, yet, ruling over My own Nature, I take birth by my own māyā. (4.6)

यदा यदा हि धर्मस्य ग्लानिर्भवति भारत।
अभ्युत्थानमधर्मस्य तदात्मानं सृजाम्यहम्॥

yadā yadā hi dharmasya glānirbhavati bhārata,
abhyutthānamadharmasya tadātmānaṁ sṛjāmyaham.

Whenever there is a decay of righteousness, O Bhārata, and a rise of unrighteousness, then I manifest Myself. (4.7)

परित्राणाय साधूनां विनाशाय च दुष्कृताम्।
धर्मसंस्थापनार्थाय सम्भवामि युगे युगे॥

paritrāṇāya sādhūnāṁ vināśāya ca duṣkṛtām,
dharmasaṁsthāpanārthāya sambhavāmi yuge yuge.

For the protection of the good, for the destruction of the wicked and for the establishment of righteousness, I am born in every age. (4.8)

चातुर्वर्ण्यं मया सृष्टं गुणकर्मविभागशः।
तस्य कर्तारमपि मां विद्ध्यकर्तारमव्ययम्॥

cāturvarṇyaṁ mayā sṛṣṭaṁ guṇakarmavibhāgaśaḥ,
tasya kartāramapi māṁ viddhyakartāramavyayam.

The fourfold-caste has been created by Me according to the differentiation of guṇa and karma; though I am the author thereof know Me as non-doer and immutable. (4.13)

न मां कर्माणि लिम्पन्ति न मे कर्मफले स्पृहा।
इति मां योऽभिजानाति कर्मभिर्न स बध्यते॥

na māṁ karmāṇi limpanti na me karmaphale spṛhā,
iti māṁ yo'bhijānāti karmabhirna sa badhyate.

Actions do not taint Me, nor have I any desire for the fruits of actions. He who knows Me thus is not bound by his actions. (4.14)

कर्मण्यकर्म यः पश्येदकर्मणि च कर्म यः।
स बुद्धिमान्मनुष्येषु स युक्तः कृत्स्नकर्मकृत्॥

karmaṇyakarma yaḥ paśyedakarmaṇi ca karma yaḥ,
sa buddhimānmanuṣyeṣu sa yuktaḥ kṛtsnakarmakṛt.

He who recognises inaction in action and action in inaction is wise among men; he is a Yogi and a true performer of all actions. (4.18)

यस्य सर्वे समारम्भाः कामसङ्कल्पवर्जिताः।
ज्ञानाग्निदग्धकर्माणं तमाहुः पण्डितं बुधाः॥

yasya sarve samārambhāḥ kāmasaṅkalpavarjitāḥ,
jñānāgnidagdhakarmāṇaṁ tamāhuḥ paṇḍitaṁ budhāḥ.

Whose undertakings are all devoid of desires and purposes, and whose actions have been burnt by the Fire of Knowledge, him the 'wise' call a sage. (4.19)

यदृच्छालाभसन्तुष्टो द्वन्द्वातीतो विमत्सरः।
समः सिद्धावसिद्धौ च कृत्वापि न निबध्यते॥

yadṛcchālābhasantuṣṭo dvandvātīto vimatsaraḥ,
samaḥ siddhāvasiddhau ca kṛtvāpi na nibadhyate.

Content with what comes to him without effort, free from the pairs of opposites and envy, even minded in success and failure, though acting he is not bound. (4.22)

ब्रह्मार्पणं ब्रह्म हविर्ब्रह्माग्नौ ब्रह्मणा हुतम्।
ब्रह्मैव तेन गन्तव्यं ब्रह्मकर्मसमाधिना॥

brahmārpaṇaṁ brahma havirbrahmāgnau brahmaṇā hutam,
brahmaiva tena gantavyaṁ brahmakarmasamādhinā.

Brahman is the oblation; Brahman is the clarified butter, etc., constituting the offerings; by Brahman is the oblation poured into the fire of Brahman; Brahman verily shall be reached by him who always sees Brahman in all actions. (4.24)

श्रेयान्द्रव्यमयाद्यज्ञाज्ज्ञानयज्ञः परन्तप।
सर्वं कर्माखिलं पार्थ ज्ञाने परिसमाप्यते॥

śreyāndravyamayādyajñājjñānayajñaḥ parantapa,
sarvaṁ karmākhilaṁ pārtha jñāne parisamāpyate.
Superior is 'Knowledge-sacrifice' to 'Sacrifice with objects', O Parantapa. All actions in their entirety, O Pārtha, culminate in Knowledge. (4.33)

तद्विद्धि प्रणिपातेन परिप्रश्नेन सेवया ।
उपदेक्ष्यन्ति ते ज्ञानं ज्ञानिनस्तत्त्वदर्शिनः ॥
tadviddhi praṇipātena paripraśnena sevayā,
upadekṣyanti te jñānaṁ jñāninastattvadarśinaḥ.
Know that by long prostration, by question and service, the 'wise' who have realised the Truth will instruct you in (that) 'Knowledge'. (4.34)

अपि चेदसि पापेभ्यः सर्वेभ्यः पापकृत्तमः ।
सर्वं ज्ञानप्लवेनैव वृजिनं सन्तरिष्यसि ॥
api cedasi pāpebhyaḥ sarvebhyaḥ pāpakṛttamaḥ,
sarvaṁ jñānaplavenaiva vṛjinaṁ santariṣyasi.
Even if you are the most sinful of all sinners, yet you shall verily cross all sins by the raft of 'Knowledge'. (4.36)

यथैधांसि समिद्धोऽग्निर्भस्मसात्कुरुतेऽर्जुन ।
ज्ञानाग्निः सर्वकर्माणि भस्मसात्कुरुते तथा ॥
yathaidhāṁsi samiddho'gnirbhasmasātkurute'rjuna,
jñānāgniḥ sarvakarmāṇi bhasmasātkurute tathā.
As the blazing fire reduces fuel to ashes, O Arjuna, so does the fire of Knowledge reduce all actions to ashes. (4.37)

न हि ज्ञानेन सदृशं पवित्रमिह विद्यते ।
तत्स्वयं योगसंसिद्धः कालेनात्मनि विन्दति ॥
na hi jñānena sadṛśaṁ pavitramiha vidyate,
tatsvayaṁ yogasaṁsiddhaḥ kālenātmani vindati.
Certainly, there is no purifier in this world like 'Knowledge'. He who is himself perfected in Yoga finds it in the Self in time. (4.38)

श्रद्धावाँल्लभते ज्ञानं तत्परः संयतेन्द्रियः ।
ज्ञानं लब्ध्वा परां शान्तिमचिरेणाधिगच्छति ॥

śraddhāvāṁllabhate jñānaṁ tatparaḥ saṁyatendriyaḥ,
jñānaṁ labdhvā parāṁ śāntimacireṇādhigacchati.
The man who is full of faith, who is devoted to It, and who has subdued the senses, obtains (this) 'Knowledge'; and having obtained 'Knowledge' ere long he goes to the Supreme Peace. (4.39)

अज्ञश्चाश्रद्दधानश्च संशयात्मा विनश्यति ।
नायं लोकोऽस्ति न परो न सुखं संशयात्मनः ॥
ajñaścāśraddadhānaśca saṁśayātmā vinaśyati,
nāyaṁ loko'sti na paro na sukhaṁ saṁśayātmanaḥ.
The ignorant, the faithless, the doubting-self goes to destruction; there is neither this world, nor the other, nor happiness for the doubter. (4.40)

5

Karma Saṁnyāsa Yoga

Yoga of True Renunciation

We are 'ego-realised Souls'. The Gītā's call to man is to become 'Soul-realised egos'. (5.10)

What is the spirit of renunciation? How can the 'Yoga of Renunciation of Action' be practised? What would be the result of acting in this special mental attitude, and how far could this contribute to the inward development and growth of the human personality? All these topics are discussed in the fifth chapter, which stands as a bridge between Karma Yoga and Pure Meditation.

Terms and Definitions

1.What are the mantra, brāhmaṇa and āraṇyaka divisions of the Vedas?

The 'mantra' portion of the Vedas expresses an all-absorbing sense of wonderment of the deluded at the sight of Nature's vastness in strength and beauty. The 'brāhmaṇa' portion prescribes ways and means by which ritualistic activities can be undertaken for the satisfaction of one's material desires. After the 'brāhmaṇa' portion, there is, in all the textbooks of Vedas, a separate section called the 'āraṇyaka', which prescribes varieties of worship-methods called the 'upāsanās', which are to be undertaken by pure minds uncontaminated by any desire. (Introduction)

2. Who is the perpetual (true) saṁnyāsī?

One who neither hates nor desires is a perpetual saṁnyāsī.

ज्ञेयः स नित्यसंन्यासी यो न द्वेष्टि न काङ्क्षति ।
निर्द्वन्द्वो हि महाबाहो सुखं बन्धात्प्रमुच्यते ॥

jñeyaḥ sa nityasaṁnyāsī yo na dveṣṭi na kāṅkṣati,
nirdvandvo hi mahābāho sukhaṁ bandhātpramucyate.

He should be known as a perpetual saṁnyāsī who neither hates nor desires; for, free from the pairs of opposites, O Mighty-armed, he is easily set free from bondage.

While defining a saṁnyāsī, Śrī Kṛṣṇa's revolutionary statement cleanses the idea of renunciation from all its external embellishments.

He gives more importance to the internal mental condition than to the external uniform. According to the Lord, he is a true saṁnyāsī who 'neither likes nor dislikes'. (5.3)

3. What do the terms 'sāṅkhya' and 'yoga' denote in the fifth chapter?

Two methods are indicated for turning an ordinary act into a divine action of dedication and worship. It can either be done by (1) the renunciation of the concept of agency in every action or (2) a consistent refusal to get dissipated by our unintelligent preoccupation with our anxieties for the fruits of our action. The former is called the 'sāṅkhya' and the latter is called 'yoga'. (5.4)

4. What is 'sākṣibhāva'?

Witness-attitude (5.11)

5. What is the 'city of nine gates'?

Body (5.13)

6. What are the 'nine gates'?

The body is considered a fortress city, having nine main gates, which are the nine apertures in the physical structure, seven of them on the face (two eyes, two nostrils, two ears and one mouth) and the two apertures on the trunk—the genital organ and the excretory organ. (5.13)

7. Who lives in the 'city of nine gates'?

Ātman (5.13)

8. What is 'svabhāva'?

'Nature' or 'māyā' is termed 'svabhāva'. (5.14)

9. What does the term 'vibhu' mean?

The term 'vibhu' means 'all-pervading'. (5.15)

10. Define desire and anger.

'Desire' is the avalanche of thoughts sweeping down from the pinnacles of our intellect, along the valleys of our heart, towards an object of desire in the outer world.

When this avalanche of thought is barricaded on its sweep by a substantial obstacle before it reaches its destination, the blast with which it shatters itself on that obstacle is called 'anger'. (5.23)

ଔ ଓ

Thoughts and Concepts

1. How does Arjuna's question in the third chapter differ from that of the fifth chapter?

The fifth chapter opens with a doubt raised by Arjuna. It is almost similar to but not the same as the one he raised at the beginning of the third chapter. At the end of Śrī Kṛṣṇa's discourses in chapter two, the disturbed mind of Arjuna could not come to a definite decision whether action had any place at all in the life of Spiritual-seeking, and hence his question on knowledge versus action at the beginning of the third chapter. But in the fifth chapter, the Pāṇḍava Prince only asks which of the two—renunciation of action or participation in action—is the nobler and the greater. (Introduction)

2. What is Arjuna's question at the beginning of chapter five?

संन्यासं कर्मणां कृष्ण पुनर्योगं च शंससि ।
यच्छ्रेय एतयोरेकं तन्मे ब्रूहि सुनिश्चितम् ॥

saṁnyāsaṁ karmaṇāṁ kṛṣṇa punaryogaṁ ca śaṁsasi,
yacchreya etayorekaṁ tanme brūhi suniścitam.

Renunciation of actions, O Kṛṣṇa, you praise and again Yoga, performance of actions. Tell me conclusively that which is the better of the two. (5.1)

3. Renunciation of action and full participation in action are two different exercises to be practised ______ and not ______.

Serially and not simultaneously (5.1)

4. What are three stages in the spiritual process of self-evolution?

The spiritual process of self-evolution falls into three stages:

(1) Desire-prompted activity

(2) Selfless dedicated activity

(3) Quiet meditation.

Man is essentially prone to be inert. If left to themselves, the majority of men would demand in life only food to eat, with the least amount of exertion and plenty of idle hours. From this unproductive inertia, the first stage of man's growth is his being awakened to activity, and this is most easily and efficiently done when the individual's desires are whipped up. Thus, in the first stage of his evolution, desire-prompted activity takes man out of his mental and intellectual inertia to vigorous activity.

In the second stage of his growth, he becomes tired of the desire-motivated activities, and feels energetic when advised to spend at least a few hours in a noble field, with a spirit of dedication and service. Such activities are generally undertaken in the service of others, where the individual works with the least ego.

When an individual in this second stage of self-development works with his ego subdued, in a spirit of devotion and dedication, he comes to exhaust his vāsanās. Thus unloaded, his mind and intellect develop the wings of meditation and become capable of taking longer flights into the subtle realms of joy and peace. This is the third stage in the seeker's self-evolution. (5.2)

5. "To go beyond the pairs of opposites is to transcend the mind." Explain.

Likes and dislikes, success and failure, joy and sorrow and such other pairs of opposites are the wheels on which the mind rolls forward earning the experience of life. Our intellect can register a situation or a condition only with reference to the comparative estimate of its opposite. Thus, I can understand light only with reference to my knowledge of darkness. Comparison is the only way of understanding given to man. If there is no contrast for a thing, we cannot gain knowledge of that thing.

If comparison and contrast are the methods 'of knowing' then to renounce them is to renounce the vehicle. In the field of plurality where comparison and contrast are possible, I can use the vehicle of the intellect and mind. To go beyond the perception of contrast is the means to transcend the inner instrument of mind and intellect. (5.3)

6. Why does the Lord insist that only childish minds can find Sāṅkhya and Yoga contradictory?

Two methods are indicated for turning an ordinary act into a divine action of dedication and worship. It can either be done by Sāṅkhya—the renunciation of the concept of agency in every action or by Yoga—a consistent refusal to get dissipated by our unintelligent preoccupation with our anxieties for the fruits of our action.

The first method i.e., the Sāṅkhya technique is not available to everyone, since the 'renunciation of agency' is not easy unless the practitioner is highly evolved and has in himself a capacity to see the collective universe in action. Only when we see the total logic of things can we really come to feel the insignificance of our individual ego in all our achievements in our successes.

Whether we practise the renunciation of our agency-idea (Sāṅkhya) or live a life of detachment from the fruits of our actions (Yoga), if as seekers we consistently persevere in our chosen path, we shall come to the Goal, which is the same whether we follow the one path or the other. Therefore, the Lord insists that only undeveloped, childish minds can find a contradiction between these two methods, whereas wise men who have lived either of the paths will vouchsafe for the equal effectiveness of both. (5.4)

7. Explain how Karma Yoga through purification of mind makes a seeker fit for meditation and Realisation.

Through Karma Yoga i.e., action when it is selfless and without anxiety for the fruits, the practitioner exhausts his existing vāsanās. When the inner equipment is swept clean of its desire-waves, it must necessarily become more and more quiet and peaceful. When once the intellect is purified—rendered immune to desire-disturbances—the mind cannot have any disturbances. The sentimental and emotional life of one who has controlled the floodgates of desires automatically becomes tame and equanimous.

When, through Karma Yoga, a man has gained inward peace, both at the mental and intellectual levels, it becomes child's play for him to deny and to restrain, to control and to guide his sense organs and their never-ending appetites. A seeker who has thus controlled his body, mind and intellect is best fitted for the highest meditation. In fact, all obstacles in meditation are nothing other than the milestones of sensuous appetites, emotional agitations and desire-problems. Once these chains are snapped, he comes to the natural condition of deep meditation, wherein the re-discovery of the Self is instantaneous and complete. (5.7)

8. What is the attitude of the sage while acting?

Even while acting the sage maintains a 'Witness-attitude' of 'I do nothing at all'. To explain: Just as the ocean were it conscious could watch and observe its own waves rising and setting upon its own surface, declaring its own glory, so too from the infinite depths of his own personality, the Master watches the actions performed by the various layers of matter in him. A sage can, once having entered the innermost sanctum of his Self, ever afterwards watch the inert matter entities in him get thrilled with activity in a thousand channels of independent pre-occupations. He is unconcerned; he is unperturbed; from the bottomless depths of his own Being he watches on, in perfect detachment born of his realised Knowledge and he is ever confident that 'I do nothing at all'. This is made amply clear by the following verses:

नैव किञ्चित्करोमीति युक्तो मन्येत तत्त्ववित् ।
पश्यञ्शृण्वन्स्पृशञ्जिघ्रन्नश्नन्गच्छन्स्वपञ्श्वसन् ॥

naiva kiñcitkaromīti yukto manyeta tattvavit,
paśyañśṛṇvanspṛśañjighrannaśnangacchansvapanśvasan.

"I do nothing at all", thus would be the harmonised knower of Truth while thinking, seeing, hearing, touching, smelling, eating, going, sleeping, breathing… (5.8)

प्रलपन्विसृजन्गृह्णन्नुन्मिषन्निमिषन्नपि ।
इन्द्रियाणीन्द्रियार्थेषु वर्तन्त इति धारयन् ॥

pralapanvisṛjangṛhṇannunmiṣannimiṣannapi,

indriyāṇīndriyārtheṣu vartanta iti dhārayan.

Speaking, letting go, seizing, opening and closing the eyes—convinced that the senses move among the sense objects. (5.9)

9. Who is not tainted by sin?

ब्रह्मण्याधाय कर्माणि सङ्गं त्यक्त्वा करोति यः ।
लिप्यते न स पापेन पद्मपत्रमिवाम्भसा ॥

brahmaṇyādhāya karmāṇi saṅgaṁ tyaktvā karoti yaḥ,

lipyate na sa pāpena padmapatramivāmbhasā.

He who offers his actions to Brahman, abandoning attachment, is not tainted by sin, just as a lotus leaf remains unaffected by the water on it. (5.10)

10. Why does a Karma Yogī perform actions?

कायेन मनसा बुद्ध्या केवलैरिन्द्रियैरपि ।
योगिनः कर्म कुर्वन्ति सङ्गं त्यक्त्वात्मशुद्धये ॥

kāyena manasā buddhyā kevalairindriyairapi,

yoginaḥ karma kurvanti saṅgaṁ tyaktvātmaśuddhaye.

Karma Yogis, having abandoned attachment, perform actions merely by the body, mind, intellect and senses merely for the purification of the ego. (5.11)

11. Who is the Observer in oneself?

The Observer is 'Truth standing on the open balcony of the intellect'. All actions belong to the instruments of action and not to the detached Observer in one. The Observer himself is not the Truth, but is illumined by Consciousness. (5.11)

12. Who attains eternal peace and who becomes bound?

युक्तः कर्मफलं त्यक्त्वा शान्तिमाप्नोति नैष्ठिकीम् ।
अयुक्तः कामकारेण फले सक्तो निबध्यते ॥

yuktaḥ karmaphalaṁ tyaktvā śāntimāpnoti naiṣṭhikīm,

ayuktaḥ kāmakāreṇa phale sakto nibadhyate.

The 'Yukta' (the well-poised or the harmonised), having abandoned the fruit of action, attains Eternal Peace; the 'ayukta' (the unsteady or the unbalanced), impelled by desire and attached to the fruit, is bound. (5.12)

13. "Knowledge reveals the supreme Brahman like the sun." Explain.

It is the experience of all that during the monsoon we do not see the sun for days together, and we, in our hasty conclusions, cry out: "The sun has been covered by clouds."

When we reconsider this statement, it is not very difficult for us to understand that the sun cannot be covered by a tiny bit of a cloud. Also, the region of the cloud is far removed from the centre of the Universe where the sun, in its infinite glory, revels as the one without a second. Minute humans observing from the surface of the globe with their tiny eyes experience that the glorious orb of the sun is being veiled because of a wisp of cloud. Even a mighty mountain can be veiled from our vision if we put our tiny little finger very near our eyes!

Similarly, the ego (jīva) looking up to the Ātman finds that ignorance is enveloping the infinite. This ignorance is not in Truth, just as the clouds are never in the sun. The finite ignorance is certainly a limited factor compared with the infinitude of Reality. And yet, the mist of Self-forgetfulness that hangs in the chambers of the heart gives the ego the false notion that the Spiritual Reality is enveloped by ignorance. When this ignorance is removed, the Self becomes manifest, just as when the cloud has moved away, the sun becomes manifest.

Also, to see the sun we need no other light; to experience the Self we need no other experience. The Self is Awareness. It is Consciousness. To become conscious of Consciousness, we need no separate consciousness; to know knowledge we need no knowledge other than Knowledge; Knowledge is the very faculty of knowing. Similarly, when the ego rediscovers the Self, it becomes the Self. (5.16)

14. What is the hallmark of Realisation?

विद्याविनयसम्पन्ने ब्राह्मणे गवि हस्तिनि ।
शुनि चैव श्वपाके च पण्डिताः समदर्शिनः ॥

vidyāvinayasampanne brāhmaṇe gavi hastini,
śuni caiva śvapāke ca paṇḍitāḥ samadarśinaḥ.

Sages look with an equal eye upon a Brāhmaṇa endowed with learning and humility, on a cow, on an elephant, and even on a dog and eater of dog's meat.

Equal vision is the hallmark of Realisation. The Perfected cannot make distinctions based upon likes and dislikes. In and through all forms and situations, he sees the expressions of the same dynamic Truth which he experiences as his own Self. (5.18)

15. "Brahman is even and ever-perfect." Explain.

Brahman is homogeneous and All-pervading. Everything happens because of It, and yet, nothing happens to It. Thus, the Truth remains changeless and ever the same, just as the river-bed ever remains motionless, although the units of water flowing in it are ever-changing. It is the quality of the substratum to remain changeless; all manifestations and superimpositions by their very nature must change. An individual in his identifications with his body etc., becomes a changing factor, a victim of every passing disturbance; but the substratum, the Self, ever remains the same. (5.19)

16. "The wise do not revel in sense pleasures." What is the reason?

ये हि संस्पर्शजाः भोगा दुःखयोनय एव ते ।
आद्यन्तवन्तः कौन्तेय न तेषु रमते बुधः ॥

ye hi saṁsparśajāḥ bhogā duḥkhayonaya eva te,
ādyantavantaḥ kaunteya na teṣu ramate budhaḥ.

The enjoyments that are born of contacts are only generators of pain, for they have a beginning and an end. O son of Kuntī, the wise do not rejoice in them.

Even an average intelligent man, if he cares to investigate his own experiences with the outer world, will discover, all by himself, that joy-hunting among finite objects is no profitable preoccupation. The law of diminishing returns works in all our experiences and the very thing that gave a certain unit of joy in the beginning, itself soon becomes a stinking putrefying pit of sorrow.

Finite things can only torture us with hopes of getting a more satisfactory joy and whip us along the path of sensuousness, making us pant is sheer exhaustion. Man, if he is wise, is satisfied only with the infinite and refuses to revel in sense-pleasures. The more chaste, full, divine joy is gained only when we come to experience the Self. (5.22)

17. Who is a happy man?

A happy man is one who can withstand the impulse of desire and anger.

शक्नोतीहैव यः सोढुं प्राक्शरीरविमोक्षणात् ।
कामक्रोधोद्भवं वेगं स युक्तः स सुखी नरः ॥

śaknotīhaiva yaḥ soḍhuṁ prākśarīravimokṣaṇāt,
kāmakrodhodbhavaṁ vegaṁ sa yuktaḥ sa sukhī naraḥ.

He who is able while still here (in this world) to withstand, before the liberation from the body (death), the impulse born out of desire and anger, he is a Yogin, he is a happy man. (5.23)

18. Who attains Nirvāṇa?

The following three verses explain the qualifications required for an individual to attain Nirvāṇa:

योऽन्तःसुखोऽन्तरारामस्तथान्तर्ज्योतिरेव यः ।
स योगी ब्रह्मनिर्वाणं ब्रह्मभूतोऽधिगच्छति ॥

yo'ntaḥsukho'ntarārāmastathāntarjyotireva yaḥ,
sa yogī brahmanirvāṇaṁ brahmabhūto'dhigacchati.

He who is happy within, who rejoices within, who is illuminated within, that Yogī attains absolute freedom (Nirvāṇa), himself becoming Brahman. (5.24)

लभन्ते ब्रह्मनिर्वाणमृषयः क्षीणकल्मषाः ।
छिन्नद्वैधा यतात्मानः सर्वभूतहिते रताः ॥

labhante brahmanirvāṇamṛṣayaḥ kṣīṇakalmaṣāḥ,
chinnadvaidhā yatātmānaḥ sarvabhūtahite ratāḥ.

Those Ṛṣis obtain Absolute freedom (Nirvāṇa) whose sins have been destroyed, whose dualities are torn asunder, who are self-controlled and intent on the welfare of all beings. (5.25)

कामक्रोधवियुक्तानां यतीनां यतचेतसाम् ।
अभितो ब्रह्मनिर्वाणं वर्तते विदितात्मनाम् ॥

kāmakrodhaviyuktānāṁ yatīnāṁ yatacetasām,
abhito brahmanirvāṇaṁ vartate viditātmanām.

Absolute Freedom (Nirvāṇa) exists on all sides for those self-controlled ascetics who are free from desire and anger, who have controlled their thoughts and who have realised the Self. (5.26)

19. Which are the two aphoristic stanzas in the fifth chapter that give the summary of the entire sixth chapter?

स्पर्शान्कृत्वा बहिर्बाह्यांश्चक्षुश्चैवान्तरे भ्रुवोः ।
प्राणापानौ समौ कृत्वा नासाभ्यन्तरचारिणौ ॥

sparśānkṛtvā bahirbāhyāṁścakṣuścaivāntare bhruvoḥ,
prāṇāpānau samau kṛtvā nāsābhyantaracāriṇau.

Shutting out (all) external contacts and fixing the gaze (as though) between the eyebrows, equalising the outgoing and incoming breath moving within the nostrils,

यतेन्द्रियमनोबुद्धिर्मुनिर्मोक्षपरायणः ।
विगतेच्छाभयक्रोधो यः सदा मुक्त एव सः ॥

yatendriyamanobuddhirmunirmokṣaparāyaṇaḥ,
vigatecchābhayakrodho yaḥ sadā mukta eva saḥ.

With senses, mind and intellect (ever) controlled, having Liberation as his Supreme Goal, free from desire, fear and anger—the sage is verily liberated for ever.

The above two verses give the summary of the entire sixth chapter. (5.27, 28)

20. What is the relationship between desire, fear and anger?

There is an intimate relationship between desire, fear and anger. 'Desire' is that pattern of thought in which the mind runs constantly towards a given object with an anxious expectation of procuring and possessing it. Where there is desire, there we come to experience 'fear'. And it is very well known that when we desire a thing so much as to live ever in the fear of losing it, maddening 'anger' can exhibit itself at any moment against any threat of an obstacle between ourselves and our object of desire. When these three emotions—desire, fear and anger—are controlled, we have controlled almost all the mad impulses of our intellect. (5.28)

21. When does one discover the necessary tranquillity to start meditation?

The external world of objects cannot by itself bring any disturbance to any one of us. It is only when we are in contact with the world of objects that we suffer. So long as we are standing on the bank of a river or on the seashore, the waves cannot buffet us. It is only when we are in contact with them that we will be tossed hither and thither. Forms, sounds, tastes, smells and touches constantly bring their objects to agitate the mind, but we get agitated by them only when we identify with our mental conditions. If we, therefore, shut out the external objects—not by physical methods such as plugging the ears, but by a discreet intellectual detachment from our mental reactions to the external world of objects—we shall discover in ourselves the necessary tranquillity to start meditation. (5.28)

22. Explain the significance of Śrī Kṛṣṇa advising the meditator to fix his gaze between the eyebrows.

It is a great mistake that seekers often take the instruction of fixing the gaze between the eyebrows too literally. They converge their eyeballs and gaze towards the space between the eyebrows for the purpose of meditation. This is not what is meant, though it faithfully follows the instruction laid down here. It is to be understood, as Ādi Śaṅkara says, "to gaze as it were towards the point between the two eyebrows." It is psychologically very true that when we are looking 'as it were towards the brow', our gaze would be turned upward at about forty-five degrees to the vertical backbone. In that attitude of upward gaze, the human mind is held uplifted and it becomes the right vehicle for higher contemplation. (5.28)

23. Why does Śrī Kṛṣṇa advise the meditator to make the flow of breath even?

There is an intimate relationship between the rhythm of the flow of breath in us and our own mental thought conditions. The more agitated the mind is, the more spasmodic and uncertain becomes the rhythm of our breathing. Therefore, the instructions here to control one's breath-flow and make it even becomes a conducive physical practice for coaxing the mind to become relatively quiet. (5.28)

24. What does the term 'tapas' mean?

'Tapas' includes all practices of self-denial and self-control which the ego undertakes in order to integrate and revive its own capacities to seek its real identity with the Eternal. (5.29)

25. Why is the Self termed 'Sarva-loka-maheśvara'?

The Self is certainly the 'Maheśvara' –The Lord of all lords, the God of all gods. Here 'Īśvara' is to be understood as the controller of all fields of activities of perception and action. Each field of activity is presided over by various faculties, and these faculties are termed 'devas', meaning 'illuminators'. The faculty of seeing illumines the field of the eyes and thus gives the knowledge of forms and colours; the faculty of hearing illumines the field of the ears and thus provides the knowledge of sound and so on. The Self is in fact the Lord of all these individual lords governing, controlling and ruling over the various fields. Therefore, the term 'Sarva-loka-maheśvara' is used as an appellation for the Self. (5.29)

26. Who attains peace?

भोक्तारं यज्ञतपसां सर्वलोकमहेश्वरम् ।
सुहृदं सर्वभूतानां ज्ञात्वा मां शान्तिमृच्छति ॥

bhoktāraṁ yajñatapasāṁ sarvalokamaheśvaram,
suhṛdaṁ sarvabhūtānāṁ jñātvā māṁ śāntimṛcchati.

He attains peace who knows Me as the enjoyer of sacrifices and austerities, the Great Lord of all worlds and the friend of all beings. (5.29)

Selections for Reflection

1. The secret wealth of the Vedas, which was enjoyed by only a choice few, was 'nationalised' to become a free heritage to be enjoyed by all seekers among mankind. With this subtle missionary work, Śrī Kṛṣṇa brought Hinduism and its scientific methods within the reach of every man living in the world. (Introduction)

2. Desireless activities (yajñas) make fine adjustments in the mind and intellect equipment of seekers and provide them with a pair of wings with which they can fly across the finite straight into the realms of the Infinite. (Introduction)

3. To free oneself from the pairs of opposites is to be free from all the limitations of mortal existence among finite objects. (5.3)

4. In synthesising both Sāṅkhya and Karma, it is not meant that they together form an alloy; they both must be practised serially. We can consider them as one and the same inasmuch as Karma Yoga purifies the intellect and gives a greater poise for meditation (Sāṅkhya) through which alone the final Experience is achieved. Thus, a combination of these two is possible serially and not simultaneously. This is to be very carefully noted by all sincere students. (5.5)

5. Reactions of actions can be claimed and arrogated only by the ego, and since after God-Realisation there is no sense of ego left in the God-man, his actions can thereafter leave no impression upon him. Like a signature upon running waters, nothing can ever stay in him to leave behind a vāsanā. (5.7)

6. Total detachment is impossible for the human mind and that is exactly what spiritual seekers often fail to understand. As long as there is a mind it has to attach itself to something. Therefore, detachment from the false can be successful only when we attach ourselves to the Real. (5.10)

7. When the frequency of our thoughts upon the Lord becomes as high as the frequency with which we now remember the ego-idea, we shall come to realise the Brahman-ideal as intimately as we now know our own ego. (5.10)

8. Peace is not a product manufactured by any economic condition or cooked up by any political set-up. It cannot be ordered by constitution-making bodies or international assemblies. It is the mental condition in the individual when his inner world is not agitated by any mad storms of disturbing thoughts. Peace is an unbroken sense of joy and it is the fragrance of an integrated personality. (5.12)

9. The Eternal-Principle underlying life's activities cannot be conceived of as taking any active note of or interest in the finite creation. From the Infinite standpoint, the finite exists not. (5.15)

10. The unveiling of Truth is a process of the removal of ignorance and not a creation of knowledge and, therefore, it is only an act of re-discovery and not a creative achievement. (5.15)

11. God-Realisation is the last stage of growth. To be the Supreme is the goal of all evolutionary struggles, to achieve which the ego, in its self-evolution, roamed about so long in its self-created world of finitude and imperfections. (5.17)

12. The wise cannot but see and recognise the presence of the one Divinity everywhere. The ocean has no difference in feeling for different waves. Gold cannot recognise itself as different in different pieces of ornaments. From the standpoint of mud, all mud pots are the same. Similarly, an egoless man, having recognised himself to be God, can find in no way any distinction in the outer world of names and forms. (5.18)

13. Where the thought-flow, which creates unequal and spasmodic mental fluctuations, is arrested, there the mind ends. Where the mind ends, it being the equipment through which Life expresses

itself as the limited ego, this sense of separate existence also ends. When the ego has ended, the egocentric thraldom of saṁsāra also ends. The ego, thus undressed of its saṁsāric sorrows, rediscovers itself to be nothing other than the Self Itself. (5.19)

14. A reed on the waves will be tossed up and down by the waves, but a light house built upon firm rock always remains upright and changeless, allowing even the stormy waves to exhaust their anger at its feet. The one who can maintain his equanimity under all conditions is indeed one who has contacted the Divine and the Eternal in Himself. He indeed rests in Brahman. (5.19)

15. My great-grandfather was a great violinist. His violin was preserved and worshipped in my house till now. I too have gained now a preliminary nodding acquaintance with music. Suddenly an idea struck me: "Why not take my great-grandfather's instrument and play upon it and thus become overnight a great musician?" If I play directly upon that ancient and faithful instrument, I will be forced to break it to pieces, for that violin, in that condition, cannot give me perfect music. It needs general cleaning and dusting; perhaps re-stringing and a lot of tuning up. When these adjustments are made, then only can it faithfully sound all the notes, implicitly obeying the strokes of my bow and the ticklings of my finger. In the same fashion, our mind and intellect, the instruments with which to sing the song of Perfection and neglected from beginningless time, need a lot of re-adjustments before they can gurgle forth their laughter and joy. (5.23)

16. Where there is no desire, hatred is an unknown, alien factor. (5.23)

17. Just as a doctor working among the unhealthy and the suffering is not himself contaminated by the diseases or the sorrows, so too the Man of Wisdom working amongst the wretched and the lustful, the passionate and the sensuous, the false and the low, is

not in any sense of the term touched, even by a passing breeze, of the stink around him. (5.26)

Verses for Memorisation

ज्ञेयः स नित्यसंन्यासी यो न द्वेष्टि न काङ्क्षति ।
निर्द्वन्द्वो हि महाबाहो सुखं बन्धात्प्रमुच्यते ॥

jñeyaḥ sa nityasaṁnyāsī yo na dveṣṭi na kāṅkṣati,
nirdvandvo hi mahābāho sukhaṁ bandhātpramucyate.

He should be known as a perpetual saṁnyāsi who neither hates nor desires; for, free from the pairs of opposites, O Mighty-armed, he is easily set free from bondage. (5.3)

यत्साङ्ख्यैः प्राप्यते स्थानं तद्योगैरपि गम्यते ।
एकं साङ्ख्यं च योगं च यः पश्यति स पश्यति ॥

yatsāṅkhyaiḥ prāpyate sthānaṁ tadyogairapi gamyate,
ekaṁ sāṅkhyaṁ ca yogaṁ ca yaḥ paśyati sa paśyati.

That place which is reached by the Sāṅkhyas (Jñānis) is also reached by the Yogins (Karma Yogins). He 'sees' who 'sees' Sāṅkhya and Yoga as one. (5.5)

नैव किञ्चित्करोमीति युक्तो मन्येत तत्त्ववित् ।
पश्यञ्शृण्वन्स्पृशञ्जिघ्रन्नश्नन्गच्छन्स्वपन्श्वसन् ॥

naiva kiñcitkaromīti yukto manyeta tattvavit,
paśyañśṛṇvanspṛśañjighrannaśnangacchansvapanśvasan.

"I do nothing at all", thus would be the harmonised knower of Truth while thinking, seeing, hearing, touching, smelling, eating, going, sleeping, breathing… (5.8)

प्रलपन्विसृजन्गृह्णन्नुन्मिषन्निमिषन्नपि ।
इन्द्रियाणीन्द्रियार्थेषु वर्तन्त इति धारयन् ॥

pralapanvisṛjangṛhṇannunmiṣannimiṣannapi,
indriyāṇīndriyārtheṣu vartanta iti dhārayan.

Speaking, letting go, seizing, opening and closing the eyes—convinced that the senses move among the sense objects. (5.9)

ब्रह्मण्याधाय कर्माणि सङ्गं त्यक्त्वा करोति यः ।
लिप्यते न स पापेन पद्मपत्रमिवाम्भसा ॥

brahmaṇyādhāya karmāṇi saṅgaṁ tyaktvā karoti yaḥ,
lipyate na sa pāpena padmapatramivāmbhasā.

He who offers his actions to Brahman, abandoning attachment, is not tainted by sin, just as a lotus leaf remains unaffected by the water on it. (5.10)

कायेन मनसा बुद्ध्या केवलैरिन्द्रियैरपि ।
योगिनः कर्म कुर्वन्ति सङ्गं त्यक्त्वात्मशुद्धये ॥

kāyena manasā buddhyā kevalairindriyairapi,
yoginaḥ karma kurvanti saṅgaṁ tyaktvātmaśuddhaye.

Karma Yogis, having abandoned attachment, perform actions by the body, mind, intellect and senses merely for the purification of the ego. (5.11)

युक्तः कर्मफलं त्यक्त्वा शान्तिमाप्नोति नैष्ठिकीम् ।
अयुक्तः कामकारेण फले सक्तो निबध्यते ॥

yuktaḥ karmaphalaṁ tyaktvā śāntimāpnoti naiṣṭhikīm,
ayuktaḥ kāmakāreṇa phale sakto nibadhyate.

The 'Yukta' (the well-poised or the harmonised), having abandoned the fruit of action, attains Eternal Peace; the 'ayukta' (the unsteady or the unbalanced), impelled by desire and attached to the fruit, is bound. (5.12)

सर्वकर्माणि मनसा संन्यस्यास्ते सुखं वशी ।
नवद्वारे पुरे देही नैव कुर्वन्न कारयन् ॥

sarvakarmāṇi manasā saṁnyasyāste sukhaṁ vaśī,
navadvāre pure dehī naiva kurvanna kārayan.

Mentally renouncing all actions and fully self-controlled, the 'embodied' one rests happily in the nine-gated city, neither acting nor causing others (body and senses) to act. (5.13)

न कर्तृत्वं न कर्माणि लोकस्य सृजति प्रभुः ।
न कर्मफलसंयोगं स्वभावस्तु प्रवर्तते ॥

na kartṛtvaṁ na karmāṇi lokasya sṛjati prabhuḥ,

na karmaphalasaṁyogaṁ svabhāvastu pravartate.
Neither agency nor actions does the Lord create for the world, nor union with the fruits of actions. It is Nature that acts. (5.14)

नादत्ते कस्यचित्पापं न चैव सुकृतं विभुः ।
अज्ञानेनावृतं ज्ञानं तेन मुह्यन्ति जन्तवः ॥
nādatte kasyacitpāpaṁ na caiva sukṛtaṁ vibhuḥ,
ajñānenāvṛtaṁ jñānaṁ tena muhyanti jantavaḥ.
The Lord takes neither the demerit not even the merit of any. Knowledge is enveloped by ignorance, thereby beings are deluded. (5.15)

तद्बुद्धयस्तदात्मानस्तन्निष्ठास्तत्परायणाः ।
गच्छन्त्यपुनरावृत्तिं ज्ञाननिर्धूतकल्मषाः ॥
tadbuddhayastadātmānastanniṣṭhāstatparāyaṇāḥ,
gacchantyapunarāvṛttiṁ jñānanirdhūtakalmaṣāḥ.
Intellect absorbed in That, their Self being That, established in That, with That for their Supreme Goal, they go whence there is no return, their sins dispelled by Knowledge. (5.17)

विद्याविनयसम्पन्ने ब्राह्मणे गवि हस्तिनि ।
शुनि चैव श्वपाके च पण्डिताः समदर्शिनः ॥
vidyāvinayasampanne brāhmaṇe gavi hastini,
śuni caiva śvapāke ca paṇḍitāḥ samadarśinaḥ.
Sages look with an equal eye upon a Brāhmaṇa endowed with learning and humility, on a cow, on an elephant, and even on a dog and eater of dog's meat. (5.18)

इहैव तैर्जितः सर्गो येषां साम्ये स्थितं मनः ।
निर्दोषं हि समं ब्रह्म तस्माद्ब्रह्मणि ते स्थिताः ॥
ihaiva tairjitaḥ sargo yeṣāṁ sāmye sthitaṁ manaḥ,
nirdoṣaṁ hi samaṁ brahma tasmādbrahmaṇi te sthitāḥ.
Even here (in this world), birth (everything) is overcome by those whose minds rest in equality; Brahman is spotless indeed and equal; therefore they are established in Brahman. (5.19)

ये हि संस्पर्शजाः भोगा दुःखयोनय एव ते ।
आद्यन्तवन्तः कौन्तेय न तेषु रमते बुधः ॥

ye hi saṁsparśajāḥ bhogā duḥkhayonaya eva te,
ādyantavantaḥ kaunteya na teṣu ramate budhaḥ.

The enjoyments that are born of contacts are only generators of pain, for they have a beginning and an end. O son of Kuntī, the wise do not rejoice in them. (5.22)

शक्नोतीहैव यः सोढुं प्राक्शरीरविमोक्षणात् ।
कामक्रोधोद्भवं वेगं स युक्तः स सुखी नरः ॥

śaknotīhaiva yaḥ soḍhuṁ prākśarīravimokṣaṇāt,
kāmakrodhodbhavaṁ vegaṁ sa yuktaḥ sa sukhī naraḥ.

He who is able while still here (in this world) to withstand, before the liberation from the body (death), the impulse born out of desire and anger, he is a Yogin, he is a happy man. (5.23)

भोक्तारं यज्ञतपसां सर्वलोकमहेश्वरम् ।
सुहृदं सर्वभूतानां ज्ञात्वा मां शान्तिमृच्छति ॥

bhoktāraṁ yajñatapasāṁ sarvalokamaheśvaram,
suhṛdaṁ sarvabhūtānāṁ jñātvā māṁ śāntimṛcchati.

He attains peace who knows Me as the enjoyer of sacrifices and austerities, the Great Lord of all worlds and the friend of all beings. (5.29)

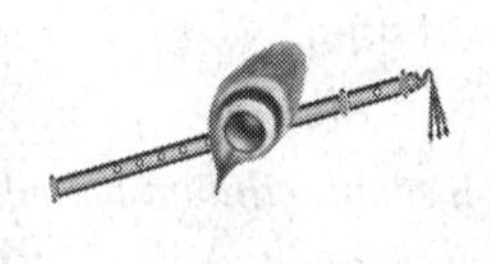

No scripture fails to hint at the Path of Meditation as the way to reach the highest possibilities in life; and yet, nowhere have we, among our reported and compiled heritage of sacred books, such a vivid discussion of the entire path as in the Bhagavad Gītā. To a true seeker, indeed, a thorough study of the sixth chapter is ample direction and guidance to reach the highest through meditation. It is therefore but proper that this chapter is titled 'The Yoga of Meditation'.

Terms and Definitions

1. Karma Yoga forms an ___________ to Dhyāna Yoga.

External aid (bahiraṅga-sādhana) (6.2)

2. Who is a 'Yogārūḍha'?

The 'Yogārūḍha' is one who has achieved mastery over his senses and mind. The following verse defines a 'Yogārūḍha'.

यदा हि नेन्द्रियार्थेषु न कर्मस्वनुषज्जते ।
सर्वसङ्कल्पसंन्यासी योगारूढस्तदोच्यते ॥

yadā hi nendriyārtheṣu na karmasvanuṣajjate,
sarvasaṅkalpasaṁnyāsī yogārūḍhastadocyate.

When a man is not attached to sense objects or to actions, having renounced all thoughts, then he is said to be a 'Yogārūḍha'. (6.4)

3. What is 'introspection'?

Realising our own weaknesses, rejecting the false, asserting the better and trying to live as best we can the higher way of life is the process of 'introspection'. (6.5)

4. Differentiate between 'jñāna' and 'Vijñāna'.

'Jñāna' is 'knowledge' gained through the study of the scriptures and 'Vijñāna' is 'Wisdom' gained through direct Realisation. (6.8)

5. What does the term 'kūṭastha' mean?

'Kūṭastha' means 'unchanging' or 'immutable'. This is the term used to describe the Eternal Self. Its expressiveness becomes apparent when we understand that the term 'kūṭa' in Sanskrit means the 'anvil'. The anvil is that upon which the blacksmith places his red-hot iron and bits and hammers them into the required shapes. In spite of the hammerings nothing happens to the anvil. The anvil resists all modifications and change, but allows all other things to get changed upon it. Thus, the term 'kūṭastha' means that which 'remains anvil-like' and though it makes others change, itself suffers no change. (6.8)

6. When does a meditator become a 'yukta' (united or steadfast in meditation)?

'Yukta' is one who has become steadfast in his meditation after having attained Nirvikalpa-samādhi. The following two verses describe his state of perfection:

ज्ञानविज्ञानतृप्तात्मा कूटस्थो विजितेन्द्रियः ।
युक्त इत्युच्यते योगी समलोष्टाश्मकाञ्चनः ॥

jñānavijñānatṛptātmā kūṭastho vijitendriyaḥ,
yukta ityucyate yogī samaloṣṭāśmakāñcanaḥ.

The Yogī who is satisfied with knowledge and wisdom, who remains unshaken, who has conquered the senses, to whom a lump of earth, a stone and gold are the same, is said to be a 'yukta' – 'united'. (6.8)

यदा विनियतं चित्तमात्मन्येवावतिष्ठते ।
निःस्पृहः सर्वकामेभ्यो युक्त इत्युच्यते तदा ॥

yadā viniyataṁ cittamātmanyevāvatiṣṭhate,
niḥspṛhaḥ sarvakāmebhyo yukta ityucyate tadā.

When the perfectly controlled mind rests in the Self alone, free from longing for all objects of desire, then it is said: 'he is united' (yukta). (6.18)

7. How is 'Yoga' defined in the sixth chapter of the Gītā?

"Let it be known that the severence from the union-with-pain is

Yoga—*taṁ vidyād duḥkhasaṁyogaviyogaṁ yogasaṁjñitam.*" (6.23)[1]

8. Who is the highest Yogī?

आत्मौपम्येन सर्वत्र समं पश्यति योऽर्जुन ।
सुखं वा यदि वा दुःखं स योगी परमो मतः ॥

ātmaupamyena sarvatra samaṁ paśyati yo'rjuna,
sukhaṁ vā yadi vā duḥkhaṁ sa yogī paramo mataḥ.

He who, through the likeness (sameness) of the Self, O Arjuna, sees equality everywhere, be it pleasure or pain, he is regarded as the highest Yogī.

The highest Yogī, according to the Gītā, is one who feels the pains and joys of others as intimately as if they were his own. (6.32)

9. What does the word 'Kṛṣṇa' mean?

The word 'Kṛṣṇa' comes from the Sanskrit verbal root *'kṛṣ'*—'to scrape'. The term 'Kṛṣṇa' is applicable to the Self because, on Realisation of the Truth, the threats of the delusory mind and the consequent vāsanās will all be scraped away from our cognition. (6.34)

10. Define 'abhyāsa'.

'Abhyāsa' (practice) is 'constant repetition of an idea regarding a single object of thought'. (6.35)

11. Who is a 'Yogabhraṣṭa'?

A sincere seeker, faithfully treading the path of self-control to rediscover the Self, may get lost, if (1) death were to rob him on his way or (2) for want of complete self-control. Such a seeker who has 'fallen' from his spiritual pursuit is termed 'Yogabhraṣṭa' (fallen Yogī). (6.38)

12. Explain the term 'śabdabrahma' in the following verse?

पूर्वाभ्यासेन तेनैव ह्रियते ह्यवशोऽपि सः ।
जिज्ञासुरपि योगस्य शब्दब्रह्मातिवर्तते ॥

pūrvābhyāsena tenaiva hriyate hyavaśo'pi saḥ,

1. See Q 25 of 'Thoughts and Concepts' for a full explanation.

jijñāsurapi yogasya śabdabrahmātivartate.

By that very former practice he is borne on in spite of himself. Even he who merely wishes to know Yoga goes beyond the śabda-brahma.

The term 'śabdabrahma' in the verse denotes 'the words in the Veda', wherein the word 'Veda' indicates only the 'ritualistic portion'[2]. (6.44)

Thoughts and Concepts

1. How are the chapters of the Bhagavad Gītā divided on the basis of the Mahāvākya 'Tat Tvam Asi'?

The eighteen chapters of the Gītā fall into three definite sections and they group themselves to expound the implications and significances of the sacred Vedic statement (Mahāvākya) 'Tat Tvam Asi—That Thou Art.' The first six chapters (1-6) together constitute an explanation of the philosophical significance indicated by the word 'Thou' (Tvam); the next six chapters (7-12) explain 'Tat'; and the last six chapters (13-18) are devoted to 'Asi'. (Introduction)

2. Explain the thought flow and inter-connection of chapters two to six.

Chapter Two: Lord Kṛṣṇa paints herein the philosophical perfection which is the theme of all the Upaniṣads. He concludes the chapter with a vivid and expressive picture of a Saint of Perfection and his mental equipoise. Naturally, Arjuna's interest is aroused, and he seeks to find means and methods by which he too can grow within to reach these divine heights of self-control and equipoise.

Chapter Three: Śrī Kṛṣṇa, as a true teacher, understands Arjuna's mental debilities and intellectual incompetency at that particular moment to start right away upon the arduous lines of pure meditation and clear detached thinking. In order to bring him to the level of

2. For a full explanation see Q 34 in 'Thoughts and Concepts'.

Perfection, various lower methods of self-integration had to be prescribed. Hence, in chapter three, Śrī Kṛṣṇa provides an exhaustive, scientific treatment of Karma Yoga—the Path of Action.

Chapter Four: Activities in the outer world, however noble they may be in their motive, cannot but leave deep ulcerations and painful restlessness in the seeker. To mitigate the 'reactions of actions' (karma-phala) and as a balm to soothe the bleeding mental wounds, new methods of maintaining the mind in quietude and ease are expounded in chapter four under the title 'Renunciation of Action in Knowledge'.

Chapter Five: Arjuna's limited intellect gets extremely confused, since the teacher argues in the beginning of chapter four for 'action', and in the conclusion for 'the renunciation of action'. In chapter five, therefore, the 'Way of Renunciation' is explained and the technique of guaranteeing to our mind immunity from reactions, even while it is engaged in activity, is expounded. This 'Way of Renunciation' is explained under two different categories: (a) renunciation of our sense of agency in activities and (b) renunciation of our unintelligent anxieties arising out of our thoughtless preoccupations with the fruits of our action. The chapter exhaustively explains these two techniques and shows how, by the renunciation of agency or by the renunciation of our attachment to the fruits of actions, we can come to gain a release from the vāsanā bondages which generally shackle our personality when we act.

Chapter Six: A seeker who has faithfully followed the technique so far unravelled by the Lord, would have come to a condition wherein his insentient and inert mind has been stirred into a field of intense activity. A mind developed through this training is taught to come under the intelligent will of the seeker. The mind thus gathered and trained is certainly a better-equipped instrument for the higher purposes of Self-contemplation and Self-unfoldment. How this is done through the technique of meditation is, in a nutshell, the theme of chapter six. (Introduction)

3. Explain why no achievement can be gained so long as one has

not destroyed the 'unbridled saṅkalpa-śakti'.

Man cannot ordinarily remain without imagining and constantly creating. And in his imagination he invariably tries to pull down the beautiful veil thrown over the face of the future. Ripping open this veil over the unknown, every one of us, on all occasions, in our imaginations, fix for ourselves a goal to be fulfilled by us in the near future. Having fixed the temporary goal, our mind plans and creates a method for achieving that hazy goal. But before we execute our plans and enter into the field of effort to carve out a success for ourselves, the never-tiring, ever-active power of imagination in us would already have wiped clean the goal fixed earlier, and would have rewritten a modified destination to be gained in the future. By the time we prepare ourselves mentally and start executing our ideas in life, our mischievous fancy would again have wiped the distant goal clean. Thus, each time the goal remains only so long as we have not started our pilgrimage to it; and the moment we start the pilgrimage, the goal fades away from our vision!

In short, when we have a goal, we have not yet started acting, and the moment we start the strife, we seem to have no goal to reach! The subtle force in our inner composition which unconsciously creates this lunatic temperament in us is called the 'unbridled saṅkalpa-śakti'. This is the inner saboteur of all achievements and as long as one has not arrested and destroyed this, no achievement is possible. (6.2)

4. For whom does the Gītā prescribe action as the means for spiritual progress and for whom does it prescribe inaction (śama)?

आरुरुक्षोर्मुनेर्योगं कर्म कारणमुच्यते ।
योगारूढस्य तस्यैव शमः कारणमुच्यते ॥

āruruk ṣormuneryogaṁ karma kāraṇamucyate,
yogārūḍhasya tasyaiva śamaḥ kāraṇamucyate.

For a muni or sage who 'wishes to attain to Yoga', action is said to be the means; for the same sage who has 'attained to Yoga', inaction (quiescence) is said to be the means.

An individual desiring to bring the mind under his control and rise over it (āruruksa) takes upon work without the ego and ego-centric desires. Such desireless activities, undertaken in the spirit of Karma Yoga, cleanse the mind of its past impressions and integrate the entire inner equipment. An individual whose mind has been thus conquered and whose agitations well-controlled by the practice of Karma Yoga is termed as 'having mounted the steed of the mind' (Yoga-ārūḍha). To such an individual, in that state of mental equipoise and self-application, 'inaction' (śama or quiescience) is the means for gaining higher perfection and self-growth. He has to stop his activities slowly and apply himself more and more to live in deeper meditation. (6.3)

5. When is the Self one's friend and when is It one's enemy?

The following verse answers the above question:

बन्धुरात्मात्मनस्तस्य येनात्मैवात्मना जितः ।
अनात्मनस्तु शत्रुत्वे वर्तेतात्मैव शत्रुवत् ॥

bandhurātmātmanastasya yenātmaivātmanā jitaḥ,
anātmanastu śatrutve vartetātmaiva śatruvat.

The Self is the friend of the self for him who has conquered himself by the Self, but to the unconquered self, the Self stands in the position of an enemy like the (external) foe.

The Divine in us becomes a friend when, under Its influence, the ego in us gets converted. To the extent the lower ego withdraws itself from its identifications with the body and the sense organs, feelings and ideas relating to the extrovert life, to that extent the ego has come under the salutory influence of the nobler and the Diviner. To such an ego, available for corrective proselytisation, the Self is a friend. But where the little self remains a constant rebel against the Higher, to that unconquered-self, the Diviner Self is as if inimical in Its attitude.

In short, the higher Self becomes a friend to the lower self (ego) which is available for and which allows itself to be conquered by the Higher influence; and the Diviner becomes inimical to the undivine when the lower limited ego remains unconquered by the higher aspirations in us. (6.6)

6. What is the test of spiritual evolution?

Equanimity of mind in profit and loss is the litmus test to show that the individual has spiritually evolved. To him, no gain can bring any extra joy, nor loss any sorrow. (6.8)

7. "A Man of Perfection regards all relationships with equal love and consideration." Explain.

A Man of Perfection regards all relationships with equal love and consideration, be they friends or foes, indifferent or neutral, hateful or not. In his equal vision, all of them are equally important and he embraces, in his Infinitude, all of them with the same warmth and ardour. His love knows no distinction between the righteous and the unrighteous, the good and the bad. To him a sinner is but an ego living in its misunderstandings, since sin is only a mistake of the soul and not a positive blasphemy against itself.

In the right understanding of his own Self and the resulting Realisation of his own Self, he becomes the Self everywhere. He discovers a unity in the perceived diversity and a subtle rhythm in the obvious discord in the world outside. To him, who has realised himself to be the Self which is all pervading, the entire universe becomes his own Self, and therefore, his relationship with every other part of the universe is equal and same. (6.9)

8. Differentiate between the terms 'nirāśī' and 'aparigraha' in the following verse.

योगी युञ्जीत सततमात्मानं रहसि स्थितः ।
एकाकी यतचित्तात्मा निराशीरपरिग्रहः ॥

yogī yuñjīta satatamātmānaṁ rahasi sthitaḥ,
ekākī yatacittātmā nirāśīraparigrahaḥ.

Let the Yogī try constantly to keep the mind steady, remaining in solitude, alone, with the mind and body controlled, free from hope and greed.

Self-control is not possible unless we know how to free ourselves from the 'eagerness to possess' and the 'anxiety to hoard'. To renounce our preoccupations with our endless plans for possessing more is indicated here by the term 'free from hope' (nirāśi). And the term 'free from possessions' (aparigraha) indicates the absence of anxieties in saving, hoarding and protecting what we possess. (6.10)

9. Śrī Kṛṣṇa enjoins on the seeker to sit in solitude (*rahasi sthitaḥ*) and meditate. What does 'sitting in solitude' mean?

Sitting in solitude does not mean that meditation can be practised only in the jungles and in the solitude of caves. It only means that the seeker should try to withdraw himself from his mental and physical preoccupations. Solitude can be gained only when there is a mental withdrawal from the world outside. One who is full of desires and constantly meditating upon the sense objects cannot hope to gain any solitude even in a virgin forest.

The word 'solitude' (rahasi) also suggests a meaning of secretiveness, indicating that religion should not be a broadcast of self-advertisement, but must be a set of true values of life, secretly practised within the heart, ordering our way of thinking and encouraging our pursuit of the nobler values in life. (6.10)

10. Why should the seat of meditation be neither too high nor too low?

If the seat of meditation is too high there will be a sense of insecurity in the meditator, created as a result of the instinct of self-preservation, and he will find it difficult to extricate himself from his outer-world-consciousness and plunge himself into the inner. The seat should not be too low also. This is to avoid the mistake of meditating in any damp under-ground cellar, where perchance, the seeker may develop rheumatic pains in his body. During meditation, the heart-action becomes relatively slow and, to the extent we are withdrawn into ourselves, even the blood pressure falls. At such a time of low resistance, if the place be damp, there is a great chance of a seeker developing pains in his joints. (6.11)

11. What is the importance of Śrī Kṛṣṇa's advice to a seeker to 'sit in a clean place' for meditation?

'Sitting in a clean place' is important inasmuch as the external conditions have a direct bearing upon the human mind. In a clean place there is more chance for the seeker to maintain a cleaner mental condition. The place should be free of mosquitoes, house-flies, bugs, ants and such other creatures that may disturb the beginner's mental concentration when he is trying to turn inward. (6.11)

12. "The seat (āsana) for meditation is made of a cloth, a skin and kuśa-grass one over the other." Explain.

A mattress of kuśa-grass on the ground, with a deer-skin covered with a piece of cloth on top of it, is the perfect seat for long meditations. Dampness is avoided by kuśa-grass which keeps the seat warm during winter. In summer the skin becomes too hot and some seekers are allergic to the animal skin, especially when their skin has become slightly moist with perspiration. This contingency is being avoided by spreading over the skin a piece of clean cloth. (6.11)

13. When does the mind naturally become single-pointed?

Single-pointedness is a very potent nature of the mind. But the mind gets stunned by its own silence, confused and even mad when it gets dynamised by either the inner forces of its own surging imaginations or the outward pull exerted by the hallucinations of the sense organs. If these two avenues of dissipation are blocked, instantaneously the mind becomes, by its own nature, single-pointed. (6.12)

14. What are the initial preparations and adjustments to be made regarding the 'seat' (āsana) and 'body-posture' for meditation?

The following two verses explain the initial preparations and adjustments regarding the seat (āsana) and 'body-posture' for meditation:

शुचौ देशे प्रतिष्ठाप्य स्थिरमासनमात्मनः ।
नात्युच्छ्रितं नातिनीचं चैलाजिनकुशोत्तरम् ॥

śucau deśe pratiṣṭhāpya sthiramāsanamātmanaḥ,
nātyucchritaṁ nātinīcaṁ cailājinakuśottaram.

Having, in a clean spot, established a firm seat of his own, neither too high nor too low, made of a cloth, a skin and kuśa grass, one over the other... (6.11)

समं कायशिरोग्रीवं धारयन्नचलं स्थिरः ।
सम्प्रेक्ष्य नासिकाग्रं स्वं दिशश्चानवलोकयन् ॥

samaṁ kāyaśirogrīvaṁ dhārayannacalaṁ sthiraḥ,
samprekṣya nāsikāgraṁ svaṁ diśaścānavalokayan.

Let him firmly hold his body, head and neck erect and still, gazing at the tip of his nose, without looking around. (6.13)

15. The meditator is asked to gaze at the tip of the nose. What does this instruction signify?

'Gaze at the tip of the nose' does not mean that an individual should, with half-opened eyes, deliberately turn his eye-balls towards the 'tip of his own nose'. There are many seekers who have come to suffer physical discomforts, such as headaches, giddiness, exhaustion, tensions, etc., because they have tried to follow this instruction too literally. This instruction only means that the meditator should have his attention 'as though turned towards the tip of his own nose' so that his concentration may not be dissipated and his mind may not wander all around. (6.13)

16. "Renouncing fear the seeker should meditate", is the instruction of Śrī Kṛṣṇa. What is the 'fear' spoken of here?

A meditator invariably finds it difficult to scale into the higher realms of experience due to sheer psychological fear-complex. As the Yogī slowly and steadily gets unwound from his sensuous vāsanās, he gets released, as it were, from the cruel embrace of his own mental octopus. At this moment of transcendence, the unprepared seeker feels mortally afraid of the thought that he is getting himself dissolved into 'nothingness'. This sense of fear is the death-knell of all spiritual progress. Even if progress were to reach such an individual, he would be compelled to reject it, because of the rising storm of his subjective fear. (6.14)

17. What is 'brahmacarya'?

'Brahmacarya', generally translated as 'celibacy', has also a wider and a more general implication. Brahmacarya is not only the control of the sex-impulses but is also the practice of self-control in all avenues of sense-impulses and sense-satisfactions.

'Brahmacarya,' is a term that can be dissolved in Sanskrit to mean wandering in 'Brahma-vicāra'. To engage our mind in the contemplation of the Self, the Supreme Reality, is the saving factor that can really help us in withdrawing the mind from external objects. This is the deeper implication of the term 'Brahmacarya'. (6.14)

18. "Yoga is not possible for him who eats too much nor for him who does not eat at all." Explain.

This is the golden rule of diet for a successful meditator: Do not indulge or demand tasty food. Eat without creating unnecessary destruction to the living kingdom just for your personal existence, and intelligently consume a quantity which does not load the stomach.

Further the term 'eat' should be understood in its comprehensive meaning as including all sense enjoyments, mental feelings and intellectual perceptions. It is not only the process of consuming things through the mouth; it includes the enjoyments gained through all the avenues of sense perceptions and inward experiences. (6.16)

19. "Intelligent moderation is the golden rule for successful meditation." Quote the relevant verses and explain the importance of moderation.

नात्यश्नतस्तु योगोऽस्ति न चैकान्तमनश्नतः ।
न चातिस्वप्नशीलस्य जाग्रतो नैव चार्जुन ॥

nātyaśnatastu yogo'sti na caikāntamanaśnataḥ,
na cātisvapnaśīlasya jāgrato naiva cārjuna.

Verily, Yoga is not possible for him who eats too much, nor for him who does not eat at all; nor for him who sleeps too much, nor for him who is (always) awake, O Arjuna. (6.16)

युक्ताहारविहारस्य युक्तचेष्टस्य कर्मसु ।
युक्तस्वप्नावबोधस्य योगो भवति दुःखहा ॥

yuktāhāravihārasya yuktaceṣṭasya karmasu,
yuktasvapnāvabodhasya yogo bhavati duḥkhahā.

Yoga becomes the destroyer of pain for him who is moderate in eating and recreation, who is moderate in his exertion during his actions, who is moderate in sleep and wakefulness. (6.17)

Moderation in indulgence and activities at all levels of one's personality is an imperative requisite, which alone can assure true success in meditation. Intemperance in food, sleep and recreation would bring discordant and riotous agitations in the various matter layers of the personality, shattering the harmonious melody of integration. Hence the importance of moderation.

20. Differentiate between an 'uncontrolled mind' and a 'controlled mind'?

An 'uncontrolled mind' is one that frantically gallops on, seeking satisfaction among the sense objects. A mind that is fully controlled is a mind that has lost itself, as it were, in the steady and continuous contemplation upon the Self. (6.18)

21. Differentiate 'kāma' (desires) from 'spṛhā' (longing after desires)?

There is an ocean of difference between 'kāma' (desires) and 'spṛhā' (longing after desires). Desires in themselves are not unhealthy, nor can they actually bring any sorrow to us. But the disproportionate fervour with which we cling to our desires is a cancer of the mind that brings mortal agony into our lives. For example: desire for wealth is healthy, inasmuch as it encourages the mind to act and to accomplish, to acquire and to keep, to earn and to save. But when desire 'possesses' an individual in such a way that he becomes almost hysterical with over-anxiety, it makes him incompetent to put forth any substantial creative effort and accomplish glories worthy of the dignity of man.

A desire (kāma) in itself cannot and does not bring about storms in the mind as our longing (spṛhā) after those very same desires does. (6.18)

22. What is the simile used to describe a Yogī's self-controlled mind?

The Bhagavad Gītā uses the following simile to describe the Yogī's self-controlled mind:

यथा दीपो निवातस्थो नेङ्गते सोपमा स्मृता ।
योगिनो यतचित्तस्य युञ्जतो योगमात्मनः ॥

yathā dīpo nivātastho neṅgate sopamā smṛtā,
yogino yatacittasya yuñjato yogamātmanaḥ.

'As a lamp placed in a windless place does not flicker'—is the simile used to describe the Yogī of controlled-mind, practising Yoga of the Self (or absorbed in the Yoga of the Self).

The above stanza explains the mind of the Yogī of collected thoughts, who is absorbed in Yoga. This explanation is given with the help of a famous simile: 'as a lamp in a spot sheltered from the wind does not flicker'. The example is quite appropriate, as the mind is fickle and as unsteady as the tip of a flame. Thoughts appear in the mind every second, in a continuous stream, and these constant thought disturbances—each dying, yielding its place to a new one—give us the apprehension of a solid factor called the 'mind'. Similarly, the tip of a flame also is never steady, but the flickering is so fast, that it gives us an illusion of a definite shape and solidity.

When this flame is well protected from the breeze, it becomes steady in its upward flight. In the same fashion, the flame of the mind, flickering at the whims and fancies of passing sensuous desires, when arrested in meditation, becomes steadily brilliant and is employed in the contemplation of the Self by a constant flow of Brahmākāravṛtti (thoughts of Brahman). (6.19)

23. Cite the four verses that give a complete picture of the state of Yoga?

The following four verses give a complete picture of the state of Yoga:

यत्रोपरमते चित्तं निरुद्धं योगसेवया ।
यत्र चैवात्मनात्मानं पश्यन्नात्मनि तुष्यति ॥

yatroparamate cittaṁ niruddhaṁ yogasevayā,
yatra caivātmanātmānaṁ paśyannātmani tuṣyati.

When the mind, restrained by the practice of Yoga, attains quietude and when seeing the Self by the self, he is satisfied in his own Self; (6.20)

सुखमात्यन्तिकं यत्तद् बुद्धिग्राह्यमतीन्द्रियम् ।
वेत्ति यत्र न चैवायं स्थितश्चलति तत्त्वतः ॥

sukhamātyantikaṁ yattad buddhigrāhyamatīndriyam,
vetti yatra na caivāyaṁ sthitaścalati tattvataḥ.

When the Yogī feels that Infinite Bliss—which can be grasped by the (pure) intellect and which transcends the senses—wherein established he never moves from the Reality; (6.21)

यं लब्ध्वा चापरं लाभं मन्यते नाधिकं ततः ।
यस्मिन्स्थितो न दुःखेन गुरुणापि विचाल्यते ॥

yaṁ labdhvā cāparaṁ lābhaṁ manyate nādhikaṁ tataḥ,
yasminsthito na duḥkhena guruṇāpi vicālyate.

Which, having obtained, he thinks there is no other gain superior to it; wherein established, he is not moved even by heavy sorrow. (6.22)

तं विद्याद् दुःखसंयोगवियोगं योगसंज्ञितम् ।
स निश्चयेन योक्तव्यो योगोऽनिर्विण्णचेतसा ॥

taṁ vidyād duḥkhasaṁyogaviyogaṁ yogasaṁjñitam,
sa niścayena yoktavyo yogo'nirviṇṇacetasā.

Let it be known: the severance from the union-with-pain is Yoga. This Yoga should be practised with determination and with a mind steady and undespairing. (6.23)

24. The Self is pointed out as being perceivable only through the pure intellect. Explain.

The intellect that is purified of its rajoguṇa and tamoguṇa is called in Vedānta the 'pure intellect'. Tamas and rajas respectively create in man the 'veiling of Truth' (āvaraṇa) and the consequent 'agitations' (vikṣepa). When both of them are to a degree removed, to that degree the percentage of sattva increases in the intellect. The sāttvic intellect is termed 'pure intellect'. When the intellect comes under the influence of pure sattva, it ends in an experience of Infinite tranquillity, and the Self is thus experienced on transcending the intellect. Since the Self is experienced on transcending the sāttvic intellect alone, the Self is described as perceivable through the pure intellect. (6.21)

25. Explain how Śrī Kṛṣṇa defines and reinterprets Yoga?

Śrī Kṛṣṇa defines Yoga as *'duḥkha-saṁyoga-viyoga*—a state of disunion from every union with pain'. This re-interpretation of Yoga not only provides us with a striking definition but, at the same time, it is couched in such a clapping language of contradiction that it arrests the attention of every student and makes him think for himself.

The term 'Yoga' means 'contact'. Today, man in his imperfection has contacts with only the world of finite objects and, therefore, he ekes out of life only finite joys. These objects of the world are contacted through the instruments of man's body, mind and intellect. Joy ended is the birth of sorrow. Therefore, life experienced through the matter vestures is the life of 'pain-yoga' (*duḥkha-saṁyoga*).

Detachment from this 'pain-yoga' is naturally a process in which we disconnect (viyoga) ourselves from the fields of objects and their experiences. A total or even a partial divorce from the perceptions of the world of objects is not possible, as long as we are using the mechanism of perception, the organ of feeling and the instrument of thinking. To get detached from the mechanism of perceptions, feelings and thoughts would naturally be the 'total detachment from the pain-yoga'—*'duḥkha-saṁyoga-viyoga'*.

Existence of the mind is possible only through its attachment; the mind can never live without attaching itself to some object or other. Detachment from one object is possible for the mind only when it has attached itself to another. For the mind, detachment from pain caused by the unreal is possible only when it gets attached to the Bliss, that is the Nature of the Real. In this sense, the true Yoga—which is the seeking and establishing an enduring attachment with the Real—is gained only when the seeker cries a halt in his onward march towards pain, and deliberately takes a 'right about turn' to proceed towards the Real and the Permanent in himself. This wonderful idea has been most expressively brought out in the phrase which the Lord employs here, as a definition of Yoga—*'duḥkha-saṁyoga-viyoga'*. (6.23)

26. Cite the relevant verses that explain the art of making the mind

single-pointed in meditation.

सङ्कल्पप्रभवान्कामांस्त्यक्त्वा सर्वानशेषतः ।
मनसैवेन्द्रियग्रामं विनियम्य समन्ततः ॥

saṅkalpaprabhavānkāmāṁstyaktvā sarvānaśeṣataḥ,
manasaivendriyagrāmaṁ viniyamya samantataḥ.

Abandoning without reserve all desires born of saṅkalpa, and completely restraining the whole group of senses by the mind from all sides... (6.24)

शनैः शनैरुपरमेद् बुद्ध्या धृतिगृहीतया ।
आत्मसंस्थं मनः कृत्वा न किञ्चिदपि चिन्तयेत् ॥

śanaiḥ śanairuparamed buddhyā dhṛtigṛhītayā,
ātmasaṁsthaṁ manaḥ kṛtvā na kiñcidapi cintayet.

Little by little, let him attain quietude by his intellect held firm; having made the mind established in the Self, let him not think of anything. (6.25)

27. "The Man of Wisdom beholds the Self in all beings and equally beholds all beings in the Self." Explain.

The pluralistic phenomenon is a manifestation of and a projection upon the Self. The essence in all names and forms, thus, is the same transcendental Self. The perfect Man of God-Realisation is not merely one who has realised his own Divinity, but is also the one who has equally understood and has come to live in an intimate Knowledge and Experience of the Divinity inherent in all creatures, without any distinction whatsoever. The Awareness in us is the Awareness everywhere in all forms and names, and this Divine Awareness is the very essence in the entire world of perceptions and experience. To contact the Infinite in us, is to contact the Eternal everywhere.

When an individual transcends his intellect, he rediscovers his own Divine Nature, and from that Spiritual Centre, when he looks out, he finds the Self pervading everywhere. The meditator, on transcending his intellect, becomes the Self; and to the Self there is nothing but the Self everywhere. (6.29)

28. Should a Man of Realisation necessarily withdraw from the

world to maintain his Divine Consciousness?

The Man of Realisation need not necessarily retire to some secret cave in some remote valley of the Himalayas, but can maintain his Divine Consciousness in all states of existence, in all conditions of life, and under all happy or unhappy circumstances.

When a man is ill, he has to withdraw from the fields of activities, strains, and exhausting recreations, and go to a hospital to recuperate. Having regained his natural health, he need not thereafter live forever in the sanatorium. On the other hand, he should come back to his old fields of work and live, perhaps, a more active life than ever before. Similarly, a disintegrated man of unhealthy temperament is, in spiritual life, treated through meditation, and when he regains his Godly strength and vitality, he can certainly re-enter the fields of his earlier activity, and yet maintain in himself the spiritual Knowledge that he has gained. (6.31)

29.The mind is described by Arjuna as being ever turbulent, strong and unyielding. Explain.

Arjuna voices the experience of all meditators when he describes the mind to be 'turbulent', 'strong' and 'unyielding'. These terms are quite pregnant in their own import:

(1) 'Turbulence' shows not only the speed in the flow of thoughts but also their restlessness and agitations, causing undulating waves rising on the surface.

(2) Not only does the flood of thoughts flow fast and rough, but having reached its destination at some sense object or the other, it gets so powerfully attached to it, that it becomes 'strong' in its new roots.

(3) When the mind has flown into any new channel of its choice, for the moment, it is 'unyielding' and so it is impossible for the individual to pull it back from its flight and persuade it to stay at any chosen point of concentration. (6.34)

30. How can the mind be brought under control?

The mind can be brought under control through (1) 'practice' (adhyāsa) and (2) 'dispassion' (vairāgya). This two-pronged method is made explicit in the following verse:

असंशयं महाबाहो मनो दुर्निग्रहं चलम्।
अभ्यासेन तु कौन्तेय वैराग्येण च गृह्यते॥

asaṁśayaṁ mahābāho mano durnigrahaṁ calam,
abhyāsena tu kaunteya vairāgyeṇa ca gṛhyate.

Undoubtedly, O mighty-armed one, the mind is difficult to control and is restless; but, by practice, O son of Kuntī, and by dispassion, it is restrained.

'Dispassion' (vairāgya) is the giving up of (1) all clinging attachments to the objects of the world and (2) lingering expectations for the fruits of action. These two are the main causes for the agitation of thoughts, which thicken the flood of the thought flow and make the mind uncontrollable. 'Practice' (abhyāsa) is the constant repetition of an idea regarding one and the same object of thought. From the moment we start trying to become aware of our own lives, we are in the realm of 'practice' (abhyāsa). As a result of this, the detachment that comes automatically to us is the true and enduring 'detachment' (vairāgya). Vairāgya born out of abhyāsa alone is the charter for spiritual growth. (6.35)

31. Śrī Kṛṣṇa gives 'practice' (abhyāsa) and 'detachment' (vairāgya) as the twofold means to control the mind. What is the significance of listing 'practice' as the prior means of mind-control?

In scriptural textbooks, the arrangement of words is to be carefully noted, for, in all cases, the words are arranged in a descending order of importance. While enumerating the two methods—'practice' (abhyāsa) and 'detachment' (vairāgya)—Śrī Kṛṣṇa mentions 'practice' as the prior means.

To every seeker the question comes at one time or the other, whether he should wait for the 'spirit of detachment' (vairāgya) arriving in his mind of its own accord, or he should start his 'practice' (abhyāsa). The majority wait in vain for the accidental arrival of the moment of vairāgya before they start their abhyāsa. The Gītā, in this stanza, by putting the word 'practice' (abhyāsa) before the word 'detachment' (vairāgya) clearly declares that such an expectation is as ridiculous as waiting for the harvest of the crops that we have never sowed! From the moment we start trying to become aware of our own lives, we are in the realm of 'practice' (abhyāsa). As a result of this, the detachment that comes automatically to us is the true and enduring 'vairāgya'. Vairāgya born out of abhyāsa alone is the charter for spiritual growth.

Practice (abhyāsa) strengthens renunciation (vairāgya), which, in turn, deepens the practice of meditation (abhyāsa). Hand in hand, each strengthening the other control of the mind is achieved. (6.35)

32. Cite and explain the verses wherein Arjuna questions the Lord about the fate of a Yogabhraṣṭa (fallen Yogī).

अयतिः श्रद्धयोपेतो योगाच्चलितमानसः ।
अप्राप्य योगसंसिद्धिं कां गतिं कृष्ण गच्छति ॥

ayatiḥ śraddhayopeto yogāccalitamānasaḥ,
aprāpya yogasaṁsiddhiṁ kāṁ gatiṁ kṛṣṇa gacchati.

He who, though possessed of faith, is unable to control himself, whose mind wanders away from Yoga, to what end does he, having failed to attain perfection in Yoga go, O Kṛṣṇa. (6.37)

कच्चिन्नोभयविभ्रष्टश्छिन्नाभ्रमिव नश्यति ।
अप्रतिष्ठो महाबाहो विमूढो ब्रह्मणः पथि ॥

kaccinnobhayavibhraṣṭaśchinnābhramiva naśyati,
apratiṣṭho mahābāho vimūḍho brahmaṇaḥ pathi.

Fallen from both, does he not, O mighty-armed, perish like a rent cloud, supportless and deluded in the path of Brahman? (6.38)

एतन्मे संशयं कृष्ण छेत्तुमर्हस्यशेषतः ।
त्वदन्यः संशयस्यास्य छेत्ता न ह्युपपद्यते ॥

etanme saṁśayaṁ kṛṣṇa chettumarhasyaśeṣataḥ,
tvadanyaḥ saṁśayasyāsya chettā na hyupapadyate.

This doubt of mine, O Kṛṣṇa, please dispel completely; because it is not possible for anyone but You to dispel this doubt. (6.39)

Arjuna asks as to what will happen to a Yogabhraṣṭa (fallen Yogī)—the one who strives with deep faith (śraddhā) but fails to accomplish complete self-control during his life-time due to untimely death or due to lack of sufficient self-control.

The doubt is that such an individual may thereby come to lose both the little joys of the sense objects and the Absolute Bliss in the hereafter. A seeker, striving all his life to live in self-control, will be consciously avoiding all the finite joy-temptations in the gross world here. But, if the uncertain factor – death – were to clip the thread of his life, he would lose his chances of gaining the Absolute Beatitude. The secret import of the question is that those who faithfully follow Śrī Kṛṣṇa's theory may come to lose both the chances of experiencing the finite and the Infinite joy.

Again, suppose that a seeker, due to lack of self-control, falls from Yoga. To win in Yoga, no doubt, is a great victory, a gain par excellence. But if, in the race, one were to get knocked down by the stealthy club of sensuousness, one would stand to lose both here and hereafter. Naturally, Arjuna wants some guidance from Śrī Kṛṣṇa as to what will happen to such an individual.

The striking example with which this doubt is voiced by Arjuna is one of the most brilliant poetic strokes in the entire Gītā. In summer, mushroom-shaped floating castles of clouds arise from behind the mountains to peep into the valleys below. At the touch of some strong current of wind the mass takes to flight, leaving along its trail, small bits of fleecy cloudlets. Those little ones, torn away from the parental bulk, get knocked about and are at the mercy of every puff of breeze. They get tossed hither and thither without any haven for themselves. "Like the rent cloud," Arjuna asks, "will not the seeker be forced to roam about and ultimately get lost in the vast amphitheatre of the universe?"

33. What are the two possible destinies of a Yogabhraṣṭa?

The following are the two possible destinies of a Yogabhraṣṭa (fallen Yogī):

(1) Those who were engaged in the worship of the Lord (upāsanās) with inner unfulfilled desires will, after their death, reach those

planes of consciousness (heavens) that are conducive for exhausting all such desires and, having exhausted these desires therein, they will take birth again, in this world, in the houses of the pure and the prosperous to continue their spiritual journey.

(2) The desireless who pursue selfless upāsanās, thereby gain more and more inner integration and, as a result of it, they become dynamic minds capable of the highest meditation. Such individuals—as soon as they leave one embodiment—are immediately born in a conducive atmosphere in a family of wise men of meditation, where they can continue their pilgrimage without any obstruction.

These two destinies of a Yogabhraṣṭa have been indicated by Śrī Kṛṣṇa in the following two verses:

प्राप्य पुण्यकृतां लोकानुषित्वा शाश्वतीः समाः ।
शुचीनां श्रीमतां गेहे योगभ्रष्टोऽभिजायते ॥

prāpya puṇyakṛtāṁ lokānuṣitvā śāśvatīḥ samāḥ,
śucīnāṁ śrīmatāṁ gehe yogabhraṣṭo'bhijāyate.

Having attained to the worlds of the righteous, and having dwelt there for everlasting (long) years, he who had fallen from Yoga is born again in the house of the pure and the wealthy. (6.41)

अथवा योगिनामेव कुले भवति धीमताम् ।
एतद्धि दुर्लभतरं लोके जन्म यदीदृशम् ॥

athavā yogināmeva kule bhavati dhīmatām,
etaddhi durlabhataraṁ loke janma yadīdṛśam.

Or, he is even born in the family of the wise Yogis, verily, a birth like this is very difficult to obtain in this world. (6.42)

34. Explain the significance of Śrī Kṛṣṇa's statement—"By that very former practice the Yogabhraṣṭa is borne on inspite of himself."

An individual who has been in Yoga in his past life, will be, 'by that very former practice, borne on in spite of himself'. A man who had in the past lived the life of self-control, study and practice gathers to himself those cultural traits and he, in this life, in spite of himself and regardless of all his adverse circumstances, environments and conditions of life cannot but instinctively come to exhibit—in his attitudes to life, and in his behaviour towards the things and beings in the world—a tranquillity and a balance, which are a surprise even to himself.

When an individual, who was a fallen Yogī in the past, is reborn, 'in spite of himself' he is drawn towards a life of meditation and quietude, of seeking and striving, of self-control and discipline. Let him be put on the throne of a kingdom, or in the bustle of a market-place, or in the ignominy of the gutters, he cannot but express his nobility of heart and his philosophical bent of mind. All the wealth in the world brought under command, unquestioned might and power gained, love and respect given…yet he cannot be dissuaded from his path Divine. "By that previous practice alone is he borne on in spite of himself." (6.44)

35. Who is the most devout of the Yogins?

योगिनामपि सर्वेषां मद्गतेनान्तरात्मना ।
श्रद्धावान्भजते यो मां स मे युक्ततमो मतः ॥

yogināmapi sarveṣāṁ madgatenāntarātmanā,
śraddhāvānbhajate yo māṁ sa me yuktatamo mataḥ.

And among all Yogins, he who, full of faith, with his inner-self merged in Me, worships Me, is, according to Me, the most devout Yogin.

In this concluding stanza of the sixth chapter, the Lord declares that of all the meditators, the one who has merged his inner-self (mind and intellect) in the Self, and endowed with śraddhā (faith) devotes himself to the Self, is the most devout of the Yogins. (6.47)

36. What is 'bhajana'?

'Bhajana' is the attempt of the ego to pour itself out in an act of devoted dedication towards the Principle of Reality, whereby the devoted personality successfully invokes the experience that lies beyond the noisy shores of the mind-intellect equipment. (6.47)

Selections for Reflection

1. By constantly maintaining in the mind the awareness of the Greater Principle that presides over all human endeavours, the seeker can, even in the thick of activities, maintain a healthy and well-ventilated inner life. (Introduction)

2. The 'Yajña-spirit'—the spirit of dedicated activity for the benefit of the larger majority and not for any self-arrogating profit—is the antidote that Śrī Kṛṣṇa prescribes for a mind and intellect that are to work in the world. (Introduction)

3. To escape from the buzz of life in our present state of unpreparedness into the quiet atmosphere of the banks of the Ganges, is only the fall of an average good man to the level of the insentient stone in the very Ganges. (6.1)

4. First, 'work without self' is the means, afterwards 'work on self' is the means; and the process is continued until, working or not working, through meditation, it is realised that the Self alone is the only reality. (6.3)

5. If the mind is kept engaged in the contemplation of a great Truth, providing a glow reflecting the ample joy within, it will no more go hunting for bits of joy in the gutters of sensuality. A well-fed pet dog will not seek the public dust-bins for its food. (6.4)

6. Intellectually we may have a clear and vivid picture of what we should be, but mentally and physically we behave as though we were the opposites of our own ideal concepts. The gulf between the 'ideal me' and the 'actual me' is the measure of man's fall from his perfection. (6.5)

7. 'Alone to the alone all alone' is the way. No guru can take the responsibility; no scripture can promise this redemption; no altar can, with its divine blessings, make the lower the higher. The lower must necessarily be trained slowly and steadily to accept and come under the influence of the discipline of the higher. In

this process, the teacher, the scripture and the houses of God, all have their proper appointed duties and limited influences. But the actual happening depends upon how far we by our own efforts learn to haul ourselves out from the gutters of misunderstanding in ourselves. (6.5)

8. Agitations in the mind are its impurities. A purified mind is that which has no agitations. (6.12)

9. Not only must we be temperate—discriminately careful in choosing the right field of activity—but we must also see that the efforts that we put into that activity are moderate. Having selected a divine work, if we get bound and enslaved in its programme of effort, the chances are that the work, instead of redeeming us from our existing vāsanās, will create in us more and more new tendencies and in the exhaustion created by the work we will slowly sink into agitations. (6.17)

10. The mind cannot be restrained except by fixing its entire attention on one idea to the total exclusion of all other ideas. The mind is 'thought flow' and, as such, the constant thought of the nature of the Self is the exercise by which the mind should be restrained by the intellect. A mind that has merged in the steady contemplation of the Self becomes still, and a divine quietude comes to pervade its very substance. (6.25)

11. During practice, even though the seeker has brought his sense organs to a large extent under his control, still the mind, disturbed by the memories of its past experiences, will shoot out in search of sense objects. These are the moments of dejection and despair for the seekers. These wanderings of the mind may be due to very many reasons: the memory of the past, the vicinity of some tempting objects, the association of ideas, some attachment or aversion, or may be, even the very spiritual aspiration of the seeker. Śrī Kṛṣṇa's instruction in this regard is very categorical and all-embracing. He says 'whatever be the reason because of which the restless

and the unsteady mind wanders away', the seeker is not to despair, but should understand that it is the nature of the mind to wander, and that the very process of meditation is only a technique to stop this wandering. (6.26)

12. When the meditator keeps his mind undisturbed in the roaring silence within, in the white-heat of meditation, his mind gets purified, like a piece of iron in the smithy furnace. This is the frontier-line upto which human-effort (puruṣārtha) can raise the mind. There it ends itself, just as a balloon, as it goes higher and higher, blasts itself in the rarefied atmosphere of higher altitudes and drops down, merging the balloon-space with the space outside. Similarly, the mind too, at the pinnacle of meditation, shatters itself, drops the ego down and merges with the Supreme. Just as the space in the balloon automatically merges with the space outside when it has exploded, so too, when the finite mind has ended, the individual Self becomes one with Brahman. (6.28)

13. Misguided God is a man. Rightly guided, a man rediscovers himself to be nothing other than the Supreme. (6.30)

14. There is a deeper significance in the fact that Śrī Kṛṣṇa, the Perfect, is exposing Himself, perhaps, more to the dangers of the battle than Prince Arjuna himself. A charioteer meets the arrows earlier than the warrior who stands behind him! Entering the battlefield, armed with nothing but His irresistible smile, He, in effect, almost becomes the Lord of the battlefield, wherein the entire war, as it were, comes to revolve round Him, the central personality. This means that a Man of Realisation will in all conditions be able to enter into any activity, and still maintain in himself the unbroken awareness of the Divine that he is. (6.31)

15. A Seer of Self-Realisation instinctively becomes a divinely compassionate man, producing in society more than what he consumes, and creating in the community much more than what he destroys during his lifetime. Love is his very breath, kindness his very

sustenance. (6.32)

16. It is no glory for a warrior to claim that he has plucked half-a-dozen flowers from a bush in his own courtyard. The mind is, no doubt, a great enemy—but, the greater the enemy, the nobler the victory. To achieve the impossible and the difficult is the job of the mighty. (6.35)

17. Even in ordinary life, when a person wants to achieve something of true value, he will have to live, to a large extent, a life of self-denial. The life of a candidate during election time, that of a student before examinations, or of an actor or a dancer before his first performance…are all examples wherein we find that the individuals deny themselves all their idle preoccupations in their anxiety for success in their respective fields. If, for material gains and flimsy ephemeral glories, we have to deny ourselves, how much more should we deny ourselves the joys of the world outside in order to win the glories of the Eternal and the Permanent, the Infinite and the Absolute Bliss of the Self. (6.36)

18. None, striving on the Path Divine, can ever be destroyed; and whatever he accomplishes will be faithfully carried over, as a legacy, by the individualised-self in its pursuit here and in the hereafter. Each today is an added link in the endless chain of the dead and gone yesterdays. The chain continues growing, by adding to itself, link after link, all the yesterdays. Death is only one of the incidents in a human existence and the tomorrow has no accidental or arbitrary beginning, but it is only a perfect continuation of yesterday, modified by the thoughts and actions of today. (6.37)

19. The present is the product of the past and thought by thought, action by action, knowledge by knowledge, we are creating for ourselves in the present the blue-print of our future. One who acts rightly in the present can come to no grief in the future, because the future is but a product of the past and the present. (6.40)

20. Knowledge without practice is a dull, dreary load upon the shoulders of a seeker. (6.43)

21. No cultured man can successfully imitate the idiot for a long time; so too, no rascal can act the part of the noble for any length of time. Both will, sooner or later, be compelled, in spite of themselves, to exhibit unconsciously their true nature through their words, ideas and actions. (6.44)

22. Spiritual evolution is not a drama played out during an afternoon, but it is the slow revelation of the history of progress through endless aeons. (6.45)

23. The one who has the proper temperament to seek life, the anxiety to realise the Perfection, the capacity to understand the hollowness of sense-life, the daring to follow the narrow foot-prints of the Seers of the world, the appetite for Infinite peace and tranquillity, the courage to live the moral and the ethical values, the heroism to barter one's all to achieve the Highest…such a one is not a 'mineral-man' nor a 'vegetable-specimen' nor an 'animal-man', but he is the noblest creation under the sun, a perfect 'man-man', standing right in front of the doors of Truth, demanding as a God-man his admission into the Sanctum Sanctorum. (6.45)

Verses for Memorisation

अनाश्रितः कर्मफलं कार्यं कर्म करोति यः ।
स संन्यासी च योगी च न निरग्निर्न चाक्रियः ॥

anāśritaḥ karmaphalaṁ kāryaṁ karma karoti yaḥ,
sa saṁnyāsī ca yogī ca na niragnirna cākriyaḥ.

He who performs his bounden duty without depending on the fruits of actions—he is a saṁnyāsin and a yogin; not he who (has renounced) is without fire and without action. (6.1)

आरुरुक्षोर्मुनेर्योगं कर्म कारणमुच्यते ।
योगारूढस्य तस्यैव शमः कारणमुच्यते ॥

āruruksormuneryogaṁ karma kāraṇamucyate,
yogārūḍhasya tasyaiva śamaḥ kāraṇamucyate.

For a muni or sage who 'wishes to attain to Yoga', action is said to be the means; for the same sage who has 'attained to Yoga', inaction (quiescence) is said to be the means. (6.3)

यदा हि नेन्द्रियार्थेषु न कर्मस्वनुषज्जते ।
सर्वसङ्कल्पसंन्यासी योगारूढस्तदोच्यते ॥

yadā hi nendriyārtheṣu na karmasvanuṣajjate,
sarvasaṅkalpasaṁnyāsī yogārūḍhastadocyate.

When a man is not attached to sense objects or to actions, having renounced all thoughts, then he is said to have attained to Yoga. (6.4)

उद्धरेदात्मनात्मानं नात्मानमवसादयेत् ।
आत्मैव ह्यात्मनो बन्धुरात्मैव रिपुरात्मनः ॥

uddharedātmanātmānaṁ nātmānamavasādayet,
ātmaiva hyātmano bandhurātmaiva ripurātmanaḥ.

Let a man lift himself by his own Self alone, and let him not lower himself; for, this Self alone is one's friend and this Self alone the enemy. (6.5)

बन्धुरात्मात्मनस्तस्य येनात्मैवात्मना जितः ।
अनात्मनस्तु शत्रुत्वे वर्तेतात्मैव शत्रुवत् ॥

bandhurātmātmanastasya yenātmaivātmanā jitaḥ,
anātmanastu śatrutve vartetātmaiva śatruvat.

The Self is the friend of the self for him who has conquered himself by the Self, but to the unconquered self, the Self stands in the position of an enemy like the (external) foe. (6.6)

ज्ञानविज्ञानतृप्तात्मा कूटस्थो विजितेन्द्रियः ।
युक्त इत्युच्यते योगी समलोष्टाश्मकाञ्चनः ॥

jñānavijñānatṛptātmā kūṭastho vijitendriyaḥ,
yukta ityucyate yogī samaloṣṭāśmakāñcanaḥ.

The Yogī who is satisfied with knowledge and wisdom, who remains unshaken, who has conquered the senses, to whom a lump of earth, a stone and gold are the same, is said to be a 'yukta'. (6.8)

सुहृन्मित्रार्युदासीनमध्यस्थद्वेष्यबन्धुषु ।
साधुष्वपि च पापेषु समबुद्धिर्विशिष्यते ॥

suhṛnmitrāryudāsīnamadhyasthadveṣyabandhuṣu,
sādhuṣvapi ca pāpeṣu samabuddhirviśiṣyate.

He who is of the same mind to the good-hearted, friends, enemies, the indifferent, the neutral, the hateful, relatives, the righteous and the unrighteous, he excels. (6.9)

युक्ताहारविहारस्य युक्तचेष्टस्य कर्मसु ।
युक्तस्वप्नावबोधस्य योगो भवति दुःखहा ॥

yuktāhāravihārasya yuktaceṣṭasya karmasu,
yuktasvapnāvabodhasya yogo bhavati duḥkhahā.

'Yoga' becomes the destroyer of pain for him who is moderate in eating and recreation, who is moderate in his exertion during his actions, who is moderate in sleep and wakefulness. (6.17)

यदा विनियतं चित्तमात्मन्येवावतिष्ठते ।
निःस्पृहः सर्वकामेभ्यो युक्त इत्युच्यते तदा ॥

yadā viniyataṁ cittamātmanyevāvatiṣṭhate,
niḥspṛhaḥ sarvakāmebhyo yukta ityucyate tadā.

When the perfectly controlled mind rests in the Self only, free from longing for all (objects of) desire, then it is said: "he is united" (yukta). (6.18)

यथा दीपो निवातस्थो नेङ्गते सोपमा स्मृता ।
योगिनो यतचित्तस्य युञ्जतो योगमात्मनः ॥

yathā dīpo nivātastho neṅgate sopamā smṛtā,
yogino yatacittasya yuñjato yogamātmanaḥ.

'As a lamp placed in a windless place does not flicker'—is a simile used to describe the Yogī of controlled-mind, practising yoga of the Self (or absorbed in the Yoga of the Self). (6.19)

यं लब्ध्वा चापरं लाभं मन्यते नाधिकं ततः ।
यस्मिन्स्थितो न दुःखेन गुरुणापि विचाल्यते ॥

yaṁ labdhvā cāparaṁ lābhaṁ manyate nādhikaṁ tataḥ,
yasminsthito na duḥkhena guruṇāpi vicālyate.

Which, having obtained, he thinks there is no other gain superior to it; wherein established, he is not moved even by heavy sorrow. (6.22)

तं विद्याद् दुःखसंयोगवियोगं योगसंज्ञितम्।
स निश्चयेन योक्तव्यो योगोऽनिर्विण्णचेतसा ॥

taṁ vidyād duḥkhasaṁyogaviyogaṁ yogasaṁjñitam,
sa niścayena yoktavyo yogo'nirviṇṇacetasā.

Let it be known: the severance from the union-with-pain is Yoga. This Yoga should be practised with determination and with a mind steady and undespairing. (6.23)

शनैः शनैरुपरमेद् बुद्ध्या धृतिगृहीतया।
आत्मसंस्थं मनः कृत्वा न किञ्चिदपि चिन्तयेत्॥

śanaiḥ śanairuparamed buddhyā dhṛtigṛhītayā,
ātmasaṁsthaṁ manaḥ kṛtvā na kiñcidapi cintayet.

Little by little, let him attain quietude by his intellect held firm; having made the mind established in the Self, let him not think of anything. (6.25)

यतो यतो निश्चरति मनश्चञ्चलमस्थिरम्।
ततस्ततो नियम्यैतदात्मन्येव वशं नयेत्॥

yato yato niścarati manaścañcalamasthiram,
tatastato niyamyaitadātmanyeva vaśaṁ nayet.

From whatever cause the restless and the unsteady mind wanders away, from that let him restrain it, and bring it back under the control of the Self alone. (6.26)

यो मां पश्यति सर्वत्र सर्वं च मयि पश्यति।
तस्याहं न प्रणश्यामि स च मे न प्रणश्यति॥

yo māṁ paśyati sarvatra sarvaṁ ca mayi paśyati,
tasyāhaṁ na praṇaśyāmi sa ca me na praṇaśyati.

He who sees Me everywhere, and sees everything in Me, he never gets separated from Me, nor do I get separated from him. (6.30)

आत्मौपम्येन सर्वत्र समं पश्यति योऽर्जुन।
सुखं वा यदि वा दुःखं स योगी परमो मतः॥

ātmaupamyena sarvatra samaṁ paśyati yo'rjuna,
sukhaṁ vā yadi vā duḥkhaṁ sa yogī paramo mataḥ.
He who, through the likeness (sameness) of the Self, O Arjuna, sees equality everywhere, be it pleasure or pain, he is regarded as the highest Yogī. (6.32)

चञ्चलं हि मनः कृष्ण प्रमाथि बलवद् दृढम् ।
तस्याहं निग्रहं मन्ये वायोरिव सुदुष्करम् ॥
cañcalaṁ hi manaḥ kṛṣṇa pramāthi balavad dṛḍham,
tasyāhaṁ nigrahaṁ manye vāyoriva suduṣkaram.
The mind verily is, O Kṛṣṇa, restless, turbulent, strong and unyielding; I deem it quite as difficult to control as the wind. (6.34)

असंशयं महाबाहो मनो दुर्निग्रहं चलम् ।
अभ्यासेन तु कौन्तेय वैराग्येण च गृह्यते ॥
asaṁśayaṁ mahābāho mano durnigrahaṁ calam,
abhyāsena tu kaunteya vairāgyeṇa ca gṛhyate.
Undoubtedly, O mighty-armed one, the mind is difficult to control and is restless; but, by practice, O son of Kuntī, and by dispassion, it is restrained. (6.35)

अयतिः श्रद्धयोपेतो योगाच्चलितमानसः ।
अप्राप्य योगसंसिद्धिं कां गतिं कृष्ण गच्छति ॥
ayatiḥ śraddhayopeto yogāccalitamānasaḥ,
aprāpya yogasaṁsiddhiṁ kāṁ gatiṁ kṛṣṇa gacchati.
He who, though possessed of faith, is unable to control himself, whose mind wanders away from Yoga, to what end does he, having failed to attain perfection in Yoga go, O Kṛṣṇa? (6.37)

पार्थ नैवेह नामुत्र विनाशस्तस्य विद्यते ।
न हि कल्याणकृत्कश्चिद् दुर्गतिं तात गच्छति ॥
pārtha naiveha nāmutra vināśastasya vidyate,
na hi kalyāṇakṛtkaścid durgatiṁ tāta gacchati.
O Pārtha, neither in this world nor in the next is there destruction for him; none, verily, who strives to be good, O My son, ever comes to grief. (6.40)

प्राप्य पुण्यकृतां लोकानुषित्वा शाश्वतीः समाः ।
शुचीनां श्रीमतां गेहे योगभ्रष्टोऽभिजायते ॥

prāpya puṇyakṛtāṁ lokānuṣitvā śāśvatīḥ samāḥ,
śucīnāṁ śrīmatāṁ gehe yogabhraṣṭo'bhijāyate.

Having attained to the worlds of the righteous, and having dwelt there for everlasting (long) years, he who had fallen from Yoga is born again in the house of the pure and the wealthy. (6.41)

अथवा योगिनामेव कुले भवति धीमताम् ।
एतद्धि दुर्लभतरं लोके जन्म यदीदृशम् ॥

athavā yogināmeva kule bhavati dhīmatām,
etaddhi durlabhataraṁ loke janma yadīdṛśam.

Or, he is even born in the family of the wise Yogis, verily, a birth like this is very difficult to obtain in this world. (6.42)

तत्र तं बुद्धिसंयोगं लभते पौर्वदेहिकम् ।
यतते च ततो भूयः संसिद्धौ कुरुनन्दन ॥

tatra taṁ buddhisaṁyogaṁ labhate paurvadehikam,
yatate ca tato bhūyaḥ saṁsiddhau kurunandana.

There he comes to be united with the knowledge acquired in his former body and strives more than before for Perfection, O son of the Kurus. (6.43)

7

Jñāna Vijñāna Yoga

The Yoga of Knowledge and Wisdom

The only way we can come to rediscover our equipoise and tranquillity as the Eternal Self is to arrest, control and win over the agitations of the mind. (7.27)

At the end of the sixth chapter, the Lord declared that the greatest Yogī is one who worships Him with absolute faith and single-pointed concentration. But this kind of faith and concentration is possible only by knowing the nature of the Lord – His all-pervasive and all-including infinity. Hence, in this chapter, the Lord explains the Self's excellence, supremacy and all-pervasiveness.

Terms and Definitions

1. Define 'Mahāvākya'. What are the four Mahāvākyas?

Upaniṣadic statements that indicate the identity between the inner-Self and Brahman - the supreme Reality, are called Mahāvākyas. The four important Mahāvākyas are:

1. *Prajñānaṁ brahma* (Consciousness is Brahman)
2. *Tat tvam asi* (That Thou Art)
3. *Ayam ātmā brahma* (This Ātman is Brahman)
4. *Ahaṁ brahma asmi* (I am Brahman). (Introduction)

2. Differentiate 'jñāna' from 'Vijñāna'.

Speculative knowledge is 'jñāna', and actual Experience of the Self is 'Vijñāna'. (7.2)

3. Define 'jīva'.

The Spirit identifying with matter, and sharing the destinies of the inert equipment, is called the 'jīva' (ego). (7.4)

4. Define parā-prakṛti and aparā-prakṛti.

Aparā-prakṛti (lower nature) consists of the five elements, mind, intellect and egoism. Parā-prakṛti (higher nature) is the very Life-element or consciousness by which this world of aparā-prakṛti is nourished and upheld. The following two verses define aparā-prakṛti and parā-prakṛti:

भूमिरापोऽनलो वायुः खं मनो बुद्धिरेव च।
अहङ्कार इतीयं मे भिन्ना प्रकृतिरष्टधा॥

bhūmirāpo'nalo vāyuḥ khaṁ mano buddhireva ca,
ahaṅkāra itīyaṁ me bhinnā prakṛtiraṣṭadhā.

Earth, water, fire, air, ether, mind, intellect, egoism—these are My eightfold prakṛti. (7.4)

अपरेयमितस्त्वन्यां प्रकृतिं विद्धि मे पराम्।
जीवभूतां महाबाहो ययेदं धार्यते जगत्॥

apareyamitastvanyāṁ prakṛtiṁ viddhi me parām,
jīvabhūtāṁ mahābāho yayedaṁ dhāryate jagat.

This is the 'lower' prakṛti; different from it, know thou, O mighty-armed, My 'Higher' prakṛti, the very Life-element, by which this world is upheld. (7.5)

5. What does the term 'jagat' (world) mean?

The term 'jagat' (world) means not only the world of objects perceived by us through our sense organs, but also includes in its concept the world experienced through and interpreted by the mind and intellect. Thus the world of objects, the world of feelings and the world of ideas that we experience, together, in their totality, constitute the 'jagat'. (7.5)

6. Differentiate between 'kāma' (desire) and 'rāga' (attachment).

'Kāma' is desire for what is absent at present in the scheme of our life, and 'rāga' is affection or attachment for what one already has. (7.11)

7. What are the four categories of devotees?

The four categories of devotees are:

(1) Ārta (dissatisfied)

(2) Jijñāsu (seeker of knowledge)

(3) Arthārthin (seeker of wealth) and

(4) Jñānin (wise)

These four categories of devotees are enumerated by the Lord in the following verse:

चतुर्विधा भजन्ते मां जनाः सुकृतिनोऽर्जुन ।
आर्तो जिज्ञासुरर्थार्थी ज्ञानी च भरतर्षभ ॥

caturvidhā bhajante māṁ janāḥ sukṛtino'rjuna,
ārto jijñāsurarthārthī jñānī ca bharatarṣabha.

Four kinds of virtuous men worship Me, O Arjuna: the dissatisfied, the seeker of (systematized) knowledge, the seeker of wealth and the wise, O best among the Bharatas[1]. (7.16)

8. Differentiate 'māyā' from 'avidyā'.

'Māyā' is the collective conditioning through which the non-dual Truth expresses Itself. It is through māyā that the One Reality seems to spring forth as the spectrum of the multiple universe. The principle of māyā when functioning in the individual is termed 'avidyā' (ignorance). In short, māyā is the conditioning of 'Īśvara' (Lord) and 'avidyā' the conditioning of 'jīva' (individual). (7.25)

9. Define Īśvara.

Īśvara is Brahman (Pure consciousness) with the conditioning of māyā wherein there is a predominance of sattva. (7.26)

Thoughts and Concepts

1. How is it that Self-Realised masters are so rare in the world?

Vedāntic Realisation and knowledge can be experienced by only a rare few. Vedānta being a subjective science, it is not sufficient that we know how to eradicate our weaknesses and cultivate inward strength; we must also live up to those ideals and try to bring about the necessary readjustments in ourselves. Very few can discover in themselves this urge to evolve. Of the thousands that hear intelligently, and perhaps understand all the theory and text of Vedānta, only a few sincerely apply themselves to live fully the Vedāntic way of life. Even among a thousand such sincere seekers, only a rare few actually experience the Self. Hence, the rarity of Self-Realised masters. (7.3)

1. See also Q. 9 in the section 'Thoughts and Concepts'.

2. Elucidate how the Self alone supports the entire world?

The Self alone supports the entire world. This fact can be logically corroborated as follows: I am standing on the floor of my house; the house is supported by my piece of land; the land is supported by the city, the city is supported by the country; and the country is supported by the world; the world is supported by water—the waters of the ocean; water is held in position by the atmosphere, and the atmosphere is a part of the planetary system! The Universe stays in space, and this space rests upon the 'concept of space' that is in our mind! The mind gets its support from the judgement of the intellect. Since the decision of the intellect is known and realised by the Consciousness in us, this Self is, indeed, the ultimate support for the entire world of change (jagat). (7.5)

3. Explain the significance of the example – 'clusters of gems on a string' in the following verse.

मत्तः परतरं नान्यत्किञ्चिदस्ति धनञ्जय ।
मयि सर्वमिदं प्रोतं सूत्रे मणिगणा इव ॥

mattaḥ parataraṁ nānyatkiñcidasti dhanañjaya,
mayi sarvamidaṁ protaṁ sūtre maṇigaṇā iva.

There is nothing whatsoever higher than Me, O Dhanañjaya. All this is strung in Me, as clusters of gems on a string.

To show that the Self is one and the same in all forms, it has been said here that the Lord is the common factor in all forms in the universe. He holds them all intact as 'the string holds all the pearls in a necklace'. These words have deep significance.

The pearls in the necklace are not necessarily uniform and homogeneous, and its thread, which is generally unseen, passes through the central core of every pearl, and holds them all, the big and the small, as a harmonious ornament of beauty. Again, the substance of which the pearls are made is totally different from the constituents that go to make the thread. Similarly, the world is constituted of an infinite variety of names and forms, which are all held together by the Spiritual Truth into a complete whole. Even in an individual, the mind, the intellect, the body, each different from the other, can work harmoniously and unitedly, playing the music of life for him because the same Conscious Principle works through all those different and varying matter-envelopments. (7.7)

4. Cite the verses that declare the Lord's omnipresence?

The following verses declare the Lord's omnipresence:

रसोऽहमप्सु कौन्तेय प्रभास्मि शशिसूर्ययोः ।
प्रणवः सर्ववेदेषु शब्दः खे पौरुषं नृषु ॥

raso'hamapsu kaunteya prabhāsmi śaśisūryayoḥ,
praṇavaḥ sarvavedeṣu śabdaḥ khe pauruṣaṁ nṛṣu.

I am the sapidity in water, O son of Kuntī. I am the light in the moon and the sun; I am the syllable OM in all the Vedas, sound in ether, and virility in men; (7.8)

पुण्यो गन्धः पृथिव्यां च तेजश्चास्मि विभावसौ ।
जीवनं सर्वभूतेषु तपश्चास्मि तपस्विषु ॥

puṇyo gandhaḥ pṛthivyāṁ ca tejaścāsmi vibhāvasau,
jīvanaṁ sarvabhūteṣu tapaścāsmi tapasviṣu.

I am the sweet fragrance in earth and the brilliance in fire, the life in all beings, and I am austerity in the austere. (7.9)

बीजं मां सर्वभूतानां विद्धि पार्थ सनातनम् ।
बुद्धिर्बुद्धिमतामस्मि तेजस्तेजस्विनामहम् ॥

bījaṁ māṁ sarvabhūtānāṁ viddhi pārtha sanātanam,
buddhirbuddhimatāmasmi tejastejasvināmaham.

Know Me, O Pārtha, as the eternal seed of all beings; I am the intelligence of the intelligent; the splendour of the splendid (things and beings) am I. (7.10)

बलं बलवतां चाहं कामरागविवर्जितम् ।
धर्माविरुद्धो भूतेषु कामोऽस्मि भरतर्षभ ॥

balaṁ balavatāṁ cāhaṁ kāmarāgavivarjitam,
dharmāviruddho bhūteṣu kāmo'smi bharatarṣabha.

Of the strong, I am the strength—devoid of desire and attachment, and in (all) beings, I am the desire—unopposed to Dharma, O best among the Bharatas. (7.11)

ये चैव सात्त्विका भावा राजसास्तामसाश्च ये।
मत्त एवेति तान्विद्धि न त्वहं तेषु ते मयि॥

ye caiva sāttvikā bhāvā rājasāstāmasāśca ye,
matta eveti tānviddhi na tvahaṁ teṣu te mayi.

Whatever beings (and objects) that are pure, active and inert, know them to proceed from Me; yet, I am not in them, they are in Me. (7.12)

5. Differentiate 'dharma' from 'adharma'.

All actions, thoughts and ideas entertained by an individual, which are not opposed to his essential Divine Nature constitute 'dharma' (righteous action). All actions and thoughts that hasten the evolution of man to rediscover his essential Divine Nature are considered righteous action; whereas all activities of the mind and intellect that take him away from his true Divine Nature and make him behave like an animal and degrade him in his evolutionary status are called 'adharma' (unrighteous action). (7.12)

6. Explain the Lord's declaration *"na tvahaṁ teṣu te mayi*—I am not in them, they are in me."

The statement of Śrī Kṛṣṇa that 'I am not in them, they are in me' means that even though matter depends entirely for its existence upon the Conscious Principle, yet the Divine Spark is in no way constrained by matter. Matter ekes out its existence from the Spirit; but the Spirit is—in no way, at no time, howsoever little—controlled, contaminated, or shackled by the sad lot of the finite, imperfect matter. (7.12)

7. Why does an individual find it difficult to realise his own Self?

त्रिभिर्गुणमयैर्भावैरेभिः सर्वमिदं जगत्।
मोहितं नाभिजानाति मामेभ्यः परमव्ययम्॥

tribhirguṇamayairbhāvairebhiḥ sarvamidaṁ jagat,
mohitaṁ nābhijānāti māmebhyaḥ paramavyayam.

Deluded by these natures (states or things) composed of the three guṇas (of prakṛti), all the world knows Me not as Immutable and distinct from them.

Deluded by the modifications of the three guṇas—sattva, rajas and tamas, living creatures become blind to the divine possibilities in themselves, and live totally a life of mere identification with the matter-envelopments. Further, identifying with the Māyā-products, one comes to play the tragic role of the ego, and the ego, preoccupied and obsessed with the outer-world, finds itself incapable of knowing its own true nature. (7.13)

8. Who crosses over māyā?

Those who devote themselves to the Lord alone shall cross over their subjective delusion (māyā). The following verse makes this clear:

दैवी ह्येषा गुणमयी मम माया दुरत्यया ।
मामेव ये प्रपद्यन्ते मायामेतां तरन्ति ते ॥

daivī hyeṣā guṇamayī mama māyā duratyayā,
māmeva ye prapadyante māyāmetāṁ taranti te.

Verily, this divine illusion of Mine, made up of guṇas (caused by the qualities) is difficult to cross over; those who take refuge in Me, they alone cross over this illusion. (7.14)

9. Define Ārta, Jijñāsu, Arthārthin and Jñānin.

Ārta, Jijñāsu, Arthārthin and Jñānin are the four categories of devotees enumerated by the Lord.

Ārta: Men who are dissatisfied with even the best in life approach the Lord to fight against and gain total relief from the spiritual distress that threatens them from within. They are called 'Ārta'.

Jijñāsu: These are seekers of knowledge and understanding who, from a mere idle curiosity to study and know the Lord's nature, ever invoke His grace.

Arthārthī: Almost all men, throughout their lifetime, spend themselves irresistibly in some field of activity or the other, under the whip of their desires. Fulfilment of desires is the urge under which every member of the living kingdom acts restlessly, all through his lifetime. Those who turn to the Lord for the fulfilment of their desires are called 'Arthārthī'.

Jñānī: A rare few approach the sanctum sanctorum of the temple of the Spirit, demanding nothing, expecting nothing, carrying with them only themselves as their offerings. They are the 'Jñānis'. They offer themselves as an oblation in a pure spirit of love-inspired total surrender. The only cry in their heart is that the Lord should end their sense of separation and accept them back into the embrace, to be made one with Him. (7.16)

10. Of these four types of devotees - Ārta, Jijñāsu, Arthārthī and Jñānī—which is the highest?

The Jñānī (wise) is the highest type of devotee. This is made clear in the following verse:

तेषां ज्ञानी नित्ययुक्त एकभक्तिर्विशिष्यते ।
प्रियो हि ज्ञानिनोऽत्यर्थमहं स च मम प्रियः ॥

teṣāṁ jñānī nityayukta ekabhaktirviśiṣyate,
priyo hi jñānino'tyarthamahaṁ sa ca mama priyaḥ.

Of them the Jñānī (wise), ever steadfast and devoted to the One, excels; for I am exceedingly dear to the Jñānī and he is dear to Me. (7.17)

11. What is 'ekabhakti'?

The unbroken and all-out aspiration of the seeker to reach his own Real Nature, the Self, is called 'ekabhakti' (single-pointed-devotion). This is possible only when one withdraws oneself totally from all other extrovert demands of the lower nature. (7.17)

12. The Lord declares that He regards the Jñānī as His own Self. Explain.

A Man of Knowledge (Jñānī) is one who, courting Truth in a spirit of total identification with It, successfully attains the total transcendence of his individual mind and intellect, whereby his ego rediscovers itself to be nothing other than the Self. He becomes one with It. Such a Jñānī, thereafter, ever remains identified with the Self. Hence the Lord declares that the Jñānī is His very Self. (7.18)

13. Why is the Self termed 'unmanifest' (avyakta)?

The 'manifest' (vyakta) is available either for the perceptions of the sense organs, or for the feelings of the mind, or for the understanding of the intellect. That which is not available for any one of these instruments of cognition, feeling or understanding is considered as the 'unmanifest' (avyakta).

The Self is considered as unmanifest, for it is the vitality behind the sense organs, the feeler-potential in the mind, the very light that illumines the intellect and, therefore, ever remains beyond the ken of the senses, mind and intellect. (7.24)

14. Cite and explain the verse that declares the Lord's omniscience.

The following verse declares the Lord's omniscience:

वेदाहं समतीतानि वर्तमानानि चार्जुन ।
भविष्याणि च भूतानि मां तु वेद न कश्चन ॥

vedāhaṁ samatītāni vartamānāni cārjuna,
bhaviṣyāṇi ca bhūtāni māṁ tu veda na kaścana.

I know, O Arjuna, the beings of the past, the present and the future, but no one knows Me.

To be aware of a thing is to know that thing; and to know is to illumine. Just as the sun can be considered as the 'eye of the world', inasmuch as without the sun all organs of vision will be blind apertures, so too, the Self can be considered as the knower of everything, in everyone, at all times and in all places. This omniscience of the Lord is vivid when He declares, "I know the beings of the past, of the present and of the future."

The eternal Self is not only the Awareness that lights up all life at this present moment, but It was the Awareness that illumined the objects, feelings and thoughts in all from the beginningless beginning of creation and it shall be the same principle behind every knower that knows anything in all the future generations till the endless end of time. The Lord is thus omniscient, as He is the knower of everything in all the three periods of time. (7.26)

15. Explain why the 'knower-hood' status of the Self is not absolutely true.

According to the strictest Vedāntic philosophy, the Self is not a 'knower', just as in the strictest logic of thought it would not be correct to say that the sun 'illumines' the world. From our standpoint, contrasting with the hours of night when things are not illumined, we may rightly attribute the function of illuminating things during the day to the 'principle of light' called the sun. However, from the standpoint of the sun, which is ever brilliant, there is no moment when he is not blessing the objects with his shining touch. Therefore, it is as meaningless to say that the sun 'illumines' the objects, as to say, "I am too busy breathing these days"!

'Knower-hood' is only the status gained by the Self when It functions through the equipment of māyā; bereft of māyā, the Self cannot be called even a 'knower'. (7.26)

16. What is the source of 'pairs of opposites' (dvandva)?

Attachment (rāga) and aversion (dveṣa) are the source of pairs of opposites (dvandva). (7.27)

Selections for Reflection

1. The more an individual misunderstands himself to be only a mere mass of flesh, and continuously pants for self-gratification through sense indulgences, the more is he considered a 'sinner'. (7.15)

2. Self-surrender is the tune in which the song of love is truly sung. Selflessness is the key in which the duet of love is played. (7.17)

3. Love, with no strings attached to it, can not only order its own fulfilment, but can also convert even the base into the noble by its silent persuasions and mysterious charms. If we can give the required dose of pure and sincere love, unmotivated by any desire or selfishness, it is a law that even the bitterest enemies, with their hearts full of hatred, can be forced to reflect nothing but love towards us. (7.17)

4. Śrī Kṛṣṇa declares the sacred truth that in all Churches, Mosques, and Temples, in public places, or in private institutions, in the open, or on the sly, in the quiet huts, and in the silent caves—wherever and in whatsoever form, any devotee seeks to worship, "his faith do I make unwavering." A faithful follower of the Gītā can never be contaminated by sectarianism or intolerance. At the foot of every altar, it is Śrī Kṛṣṇa, the Self, that constantly supplies more and more faith to water the expanding fields of devotion in sincere devotees. (7.21)

5. Seekers of happiness in the world of sense objects, as a result of their strife and struggle, gain their insignificant success in the field of sense enjoyments. If the same effort is applied by them in the right life of constructive living, they can come to discover their identity with the Eternal Absolute, the Self. (7.23)

6. The 'point of concentration' (upāsya) is to be considered, no doubt, as the symbol of the Truth that the devotee is seeking, but it cannot in itself be the Truth. Idol worship is only a convenience for gathering true concentration, for getting an initial momentum for the final flight into themselves, to reach the Self and discover therein their own oneness with it. (7.24)

7. When the Self in anyone beams out through the steadied and purified mind and intellect completely sublimating his lower nature (aparā-prakṛti), he becomes a Prophet, a Sage. Kṛṣṇa, Rāma, Christ, Mohammed, Buddha, Mahāvīra are some of the examples. These Men of Realisation, discovering their Self, understood and lived every moment of their lives in the Self, as the Self of all. To mistake their physical structure, or the lingering traces of their mind, or the film of their intellectual personality for the very Essence of Truth, which these God-men were, is to make as miserable a mistake as taking the waves to be the ocean! (7.24)

8. The three guṇas – sattva, rajas and tamas – provide a prism, viewed through which the kaleidoscopic world seems to dance,

flashing its infinite patterns. (7.25)

9. In the tug-of-war between the two forces of desire and aversion, the hapless ego gets torn asunder and comes to suffer the agonising pain of lynching tensions within. (7.27)

10. He is called a sinful-person in whom his body makes the heaviest calls on his time and attention. In such a person, the body becomes the dominant partner and it 'enslaves' the Self. (7.28)

11. Knowledge can be imparted, but Wisdom cannot be given. (Conclusion)

Verses for Memorisation

मनुष्याणां सहस्रेषु कश्चिद्यतति सिद्धये ।
यततामपि सिद्धानां कश्चिन्मां वेत्ति तत्त्वतः ॥

manuṣyāṇāṁ sahasreṣu kaścidyatati siddhaye,
yatatāmapi siddhānāṁ kaścinmāṁ vetti tattvataḥ.

Among thousands of men, one perchance strives for perfection; even among those successful strivers, only one perchance knows Me in essence. (7.3)

भूमिरापोऽनलो वायुः खं मनो बुद्धिरेव च ।
अहङ्कार इतीयं मे भिन्ना प्रकृतिरष्टधा ॥

bhūmirāpo'nalo vāyuḥ khaṁ mano buddhireva ca,
ahaṅkāra itīyaṁ me bhinnā prakṛtiraṣṭadhā.

Earth, water, fire, air, ether, mind, intellect, egoism—these are My eightfold prakṛti. (7.4)

अपरेयमितस्त्वन्यां प्रकृतिं विद्धि मे पराम् ।
जीवभूतां महाबाहो ययेदं धार्यते जगत् ॥

apareyamitastvanyāṁ prakṛtiṁ viddhi me parām,
jīvabhūtāṁ mahābāho yayedaṁ dhāryate jagat.

This is the 'lower' prakṛti; different from it, know thou, O mighty-armed, My 'Higher' prakṛti, the very Life-element, by which this world is upheld. (7.5)

मत्तः परतरं नान्यत्किञ्चिदस्ति धनञ्जय ।
मयि सर्वमिदं प्रोतं सूत्रे मणिगणा इव ॥

mattaḥ parataraṁ nānyatkiñcidasti dhanañjaya,
mayi sarvamidaṁ protaṁ sūtre maṇigaṇā iva.

There is nothing whatsoever higher than Me, O Dhanañjaya. All this is strung in Me, as clusters of gems on a string. (7.7)

बलं बलवतां चाहं कामरागविवर्जितम् ।
धर्माविरुद्धो भूतेषु कामोऽस्मि भरतर्षभ ॥

balaṁ balavatāṁ cāhaṁ kāmarāgavivarjitam,
dharmāviruddho bhūteṣu kāmo'smi bharatarṣabha.

Of the strong, I am the strength—devoid of desire and attachment, and in (all) beings, I am the desire—unopposed to Dharma, O best among the Bharatas. (7.11)

ये चैव सात्त्विका भावा राजसास्तामसाश्च ये ।
मत्त एवेति तान्विद्धि न त्वहं तेषु ते मयि ॥

ye caiva sāttvikā bhāvā rājasāstāmasāśca ye,
matta eveti tānviddhi na tvahaṁ teṣu te mayi.

Whatever beings (and objects) that are pure, active and inert, know them to proceed from Me; yet, I am not in them, they are in Me. (7.12)

दैवी ह्येषा गुणमयी मम माया दुरत्यया ।
मामेव ये प्रपद्यन्ते मायामेतां तरन्ति ते ॥

daivī hyeṣā guṇamayī mama māyā duratyayā,
māmeva ye prapadyante māyāmetāṁ taranti te.

Verily, this divine illusion of Mine, made up of guṇas (caused by the qualities) is difficult to cross over; those who take refuge in Me, they alone cross over this illusion. (7.14)

चतुर्विधा भजन्ते मां जनाः सुकृतिनोऽर्जुन ।
आर्तो जिज्ञासुरर्थार्थी ज्ञानी च भरतर्षभ ॥

caturvidhā bhajante māṁ janāḥ sukṛtino'rjuna,
ārto jijñāsurarthārthī jñānī ca bharatarṣabha.

Four kinds of virtuous men worship Me, O Arjuna, the dissatisfied, the seeker of (systematised) knowledge, the seeker of wealth and the wise, O best among the Bharatas. (7.16)

तेषां ज्ञानी नित्ययुक्त एकभक्तिर्विशिष्यते।
प्रियो हि ज्ञानिनोऽत्यर्थमहं स च मम प्रियः॥

teṣāṁ jñānī nityayukta ekabhaktirviśiṣyate,
priyo hi jñānino'tyarthamahaṁ sa ca mama priyaḥ.
Of them the Jñānī (wise), ever steadfast and devoted to the One, excels; for, I am exceedingly dear to the Jñānī, and he is dear to Me. (7.17)

उदाराः सर्व एवैते ज्ञानी त्वात्मैव मे मतम्।
आस्थितः स हि युक्तात्मा मामेवानुत्तमां गतिम्॥

udārāḥ sarva evaite jñānī tvātmaiva me matam,
āsthitaḥ sa hi yuktātmā māmevānuttamāṁ gatim.
Noble indeed are all these, but the wise man, I deem, as My very Self; for, steadfast in mind he is established in Me alone as the Supreme Goal. (7.18)

बहूनां जन्मनामन्ते ज्ञानवान्मां प्रपद्यते।
वासुदेवः सर्वमिति स महात्मा सुदुर्लभः॥

bahūnāṁ janmanāmante jñānavānmāṁ prapadyate,
vāsudevaḥ sarvamiti sa mahātmā sudurlabhaḥ.
At the end of many births, the wise man comes to Me, realising that all this is Vāsudeva (the innermost Self); such a great soul (Mahātmā) is very hard to find. (7.19)

यो यो यां यां तनुं भक्तः श्रद्धयार्चितुमिच्छति।
तस्य तस्याचलां श्रद्धां तामेव विदधाम्यहम्॥

yo yo yāṁ yāṁ tanuṁ bhaktaḥ śraddhayārcitumicchati,
tasya tasyācalāṁ śraddhāṁ tāmeva vidadhāmyaham.
Whatsoever form any devotee desires to worship with faith—that (same) faith of his I make (firm and) unflinching. (7.21)

8

Akṣara Brahma Yoga

The Yoga of Imperishable Brahman

Pure Awareness, poured into the moulds of vāsanās, when frozen with ignorance becomes the world of names and forms. (8.22)

The aim of Vedānta is to carve out of ordinary folks blissful Men of Wisdom. In the earlier chapter a vivid description of both knowledge and Wisdom was elaborately given. Continuing the idea contained in the previous chapter, Śrī Kṛṣṇa starts with the glorification of the Man of Wisdom and declares that he is perfect not only because of his special Knowledge and Experience of the Self, but also because he becomes thereby a well-integrated personality at all levels of his existence and contacts with the world.

In the preceding chapter (chapter seven), a mere mention was made that there is a practical aspect of Vedānta, apart from its theoretical literature, but no definite technique for carving out the Vedāntic ideals in practice was given there. In this chapter, however, the technique has been completely and fully explained, and the relationship between the Eternal Spirit and the delusory realm of names and forms – the lower prakṛti – has been clearly indicated. Exemplary definitions indicating the Absolute Truth are found in this chapter.

The previous chapter concluded with a statement that the Man of Wisdom not only realises the Absolute Essence that sustains the world, but that he also, at once, comes to master the world of objects, the organs of perception and action and the instruments of comprehension, so that he proves himself to be a dynamic doer, ever carving out enduring successes all along, everywhere. In this chapter, this idea has been made more clear by Lord Kṛṣṇa, with His explanations.

Terms and Definitions

1. What are the seven questions and answers with which the 8th chapter begins?

(1) What is 'Brahman'?

The imperishable Supreme Being is Brahman. The term 'Brahman' indicates the one changeless and imperishable subjective Essence behind the entire phenomenal world.

(2) What is 'adhyātma'?

'Svabhāva', the principle that graces all bodies as the Self, is termed 'Adhyātma'. Though the Self is formless and subtle, and therefore all-pervading, Its glory, might, power and grace are felt and lived by each physical structure. This Self, expressing Itself through a given embodiment, as though conditioned by it, is called the 'adhyātma'.

(3) What is 'karma'?

The creative urge and subtle spiritual strength that is behind every active intellect, which ultimately fulfils itself in the creation of things and beings is called 'karma' (action).

(4) What is 'adhibhūta'?

'Adhibhūta' is the world of elements and constitutes the Lord's perishable nature.

(5) What is 'adhidaiva'?

The 'Indweller' is the 'adhidaiva'. This term is used to indicate the 'special faculty' that presides over the instruments of knowledge and action in living creatures. The presiding deities of the sense organs, of the mind and of the intellect are called 'devatās', which are nothing other than the faculty of vision in the eyes, the faculty of audition in the ears, the power of smelling in the nose and so on.

(6) What is 'adhiyajña'?

The Lord alone is the 'adhiyajña'. 'Yajña' here means the 'act of perception, feeling or thought'. As in the Yajña, here also when the sense objects (oblations) are poured into the sense organs (Yajña-altar) and when the particular faculty in it (devatā) gets propitiated and invoked, we gain as a blessing from it the fruit thereof, viz., the knowledge of the perception. In this subjective Yajña-act of perception, 'adhiyajña' is the Self, the one Vital Factor and Principle of Life that dominates the entire field of knowledge and action.

(7) In what manner is the Lord known by the self-controlled at the time of death?

The Lord is known by the individual who remembering Him alone at the time of his death gives up his physical body.

By giving these definitions, the Lord is on the whole suggesting, with a subtle undercurrent of implications, that the Eternal Self alone is the Real, and that all else are delusory superimpositions upon it. (8.1-8.5)

2. Define 'meditation'.

Thoughts of the same species made to run towards one fixed ideal or goal, in an unbroken flow, is called 'meditation'. (8.8)

3. What is 'Bhakti'?

Selfless love, seeking fulfillment in itself, when directed towards the Divine with firm faith and an all-out belief, is called 'Bhakti'. (8.10)

4. What does the term 'heart' (hṛd) in the Vedāntic context mean?

The term 'heart' (Sanskrit – *'hṛd'* or *'hṛdayam'*) in Vedānta is not the pumping-organ that maintains the circulatory system in a physical structure. 'Heart' is a conceptual centre in the mind from where all positive and noble thoughts of love and tenderness, kindness and charity, devotion and surrender constantly spring up. (8.12)

5. Explain the concept of 'krama-mukti'.

The 'theory of gradual liberation' (krama-mukti) says that ritualism (karma), accompanied by contemplation (upāsanā), takes the ego to the realm of the Creator (Brahmaloka) where, at the end of the kalpa (the cycle of creation and dissolution), it merges with the Supreme.

Even in Brahmaloka it is necessary that the ego must, through self-effort, live strictly by all the spiritual directions of the Creator, and through constant contemplation upon the Self (Ātma-vicāra) come to deserve total Liberation ending all its connections with ignorance. (8.16)

6. Define the term 'Mahāyuga'.

The four yugas viz. Satya (1,728,000 years), Tretā (1,296,000 years), Dvāpara (864,000 years) and Kali (432,000 years) total to 4,320,000 years. This is called 'Mahāyuga'. (8.17)

7. How many Mahāyugas constitute one day of Brahma?

A thousand Mahāyugas constitute the daytime of Brahma, the Creator. Another 1,000 Mahāyugas constitute his night-time. Thus 2000 Mahāyugas constitute a single day of the creator Brahma. (8.17)

8. What are the two possible paths described as being available to individuals after their death?

The two paths available to an individual after death are:

(1) **The Path of Return (punarāvṛtti)** – also called the Pitṛyāna (Path of Ancestors) or the Path of Darkness. Those who leave the world after spending their lifetime in doing good and performing rituals (karmas) unaccompanied by any worship (upāsanās) take this path and reach heaven. After their puṇyas (merits) are exhausted they are born again. This is the path leading to saṁsāra (bondage).

(2) **The Path of No-return (apunarāvṛtti)** – also called Devayāna (Path of the Gods) or the Path of Light. This path is taken by those who die after spending their lifetime doing good, and performing the specified rituals (karmas) accompanied by worship (upāsanās). They reach the world of the Creator (Brahma) and attain gradual liberation (karma-mukti). This is the path leading to Mokṣa (Liberation). (8.23-26)

9. What are the presiding deities of the 'Path of No-return'?

The following verse mentions the various deities associated with the 'Path of No-return'.

अग्निर्ज्योतिरहः शुक्लः षण्मासा उत्तरायणम् ।
तत्र प्रयाता गच्छन्ति ब्रह्म ब्रह्मविदो जनाः ॥

agnirjyotirahaḥ śuklaḥ ṣaṇmāsā uttarāyaṇam,
tatra prayātā gacchanti brahma brahmavido janāḥ.

Fire, light, daytime, the bright fortnight, the six months of the northern solstice; following this path, men who know Brahman, go to Brahman.

The presiding deities of the 'Path of No-return' are thus: (1) Fire (2) Light (3) Daytime (4) The bright fortnight and (5) The six months of the northern solstice. (8.24)

10. What are the presiding deities of the 'Path of Return'?

The following verse mentions the various deities associated with the 'Path of Return'.

धूमो रात्रिस्तथा कृष्णः षण्मासा दक्षिणायनम् ।
तत्र चान्द्रमसं ज्योतिर्योगी प्राप्य निवर्तते ॥

dhūmo rātristathā kṛṣṇaḥ ṣaṇmāsā dakṣiṇāyanam,
tatra cāndramasaṁ jyotiryogī prāpya nivartate.

Smoke, night-time, the dark fortnight, also six months of the southern solstice, attaining by these to the Moon, the lunar light, the Yogī returns.

The presiding deities of the 'Path of Return' are thus: (1) Smoke (2) Night-time (3) The dark fortnight and (4) The six months of southern solstice. (8.25)

Thoughts and Concepts

1. "Whatever object one remembers while leaving the body, that alone is reached by him." Explain.

'As you think so you become'. Thoughts guide all actions, and at any given moment the run of thoughts in an individual is governed and ordered by the channel of thinking that he himself has ploughed with his conscious and wilful thoughts and actions in the past. The time of death, when the occupant of the body has packed up to quit, is not the moment to decide or to plan the travel. At such a moment, instinctively, thoughts will run through its habitual channels, and the flight of thoughts at that moment determines the direction of the ego's pilgrimage. (8.6)

2. Would not the Lord's instruction of remembering Him while working hamper the success of both?

Hardly ever is man's mind totally invested where his hands function. Ordinarily, a major portion of the mind, all the time, wanders into the jungles of dreadful fears, or into the caves of jealousies or into the deserts of imaginary possibilities of failures. Instead of thus wasting the total mental energy and dynamism, Śrī Kṛṣṇa advises us that a truly successful man, striving to achieve the highest, both in the outer world of plurality, and in the realms within, should rest his mind at the gracious and peaceful feet of Truth. He can then pour out the entire wealth of his capacities into the work in his hand, and thereby assure for himself the highest laurels both here and in the hereafter. (8.7)

3. Is it practical to remember our Divine Nature (Lord) even while acting in the world?

An actor, playing the part of a king in a drama, can never completely forget that he has a wife and a child in his own house on the outskirts of the city. He is efficient as the actor because he constantly remembers his own real identity. Similarly, even with continuous cognition of our Divine Nature, we can act in the world without any hindrance, and thereby add a glow to our achievements, and soften the reactions of any disappointments that we might meet with in life's pilgrimage. (8.7)

4. What are the attributes of the Supreme Puruṣa upon whom the seeker is directed to constantly meditate?

The attributes of the Supreme Puruṣa upon whom the seeker is directed to meditate are: (1) Omniscient (2) Ancient (3) Ruler (of the whole world) (4) Minuter than the atom (5) Supporter of all (6) Of inconceivable form (7) Effulgent like the sun and (8) Beyond the darkness of ignorance. (8.9)

5. Why is the Self described to be 'kavi' (omniscient)?

The Conscious Principle, serving as the Soul in an embodiment, is that which illumines all the thought waves that rise in that particular mind, functioning in that given embodiment. The infinite Self being one everywhere, it is the same Principle that illumines all the different embodiments and thought-experiences at all times. Just as the sun is said to be 'seeing everything' because it illumines all the objects on the globe, so too, is the Divine Principle of Awareness—the factor without which no knowledge is ever possible. Thus, the Self is considered as 'kavi' (omniscient)—the Supreme Knower who knows everything, and without whom no knowledge is ever possible. (8.9)

6. The Self is described as 'the most ancient' (purāṇa). Why?

The Self is considered as the 'most ancient' because the Eternal Truth is that which was before all creation, which remains the same all through the ages of existence, and which shall ever remain the same even after the projections of plurality have ended. To indicate that the One Self ever remains the same everywhere, providing a substratum even for the concept of time, It is described as the 'most ancient' (purāṇa). (8.9)

7. Explain the significance of the Self being described as 'minuter than an atom' (aṇoraṇīyān).

The subtlest and the smallest particle of any element which still maintains the specific properties of that element is called its 'atom'. By describing the Self to be 'minuter than an atom' the Self is indicated to be 'subtlest of the subtle'. The subtler a thing, the greater is its pervasiveness. Water is considered subtler than a block of ice, and the steam issuing when water is boiled is considered subtler than the water itself. In all these stages, pervasiveness is the measuring rod of their comparative subtleties. Thus the description that the Self as 'minuter than an atom' signifies that the Self pervades all and nothing pervades It. (8.9)

8. Why is the Self described as 'luminous like the sun'?

In order to see the sun, no other light is necessary, as the sun is the source of all light and the one illuminator that illumines everything else. Just as in the physical world, the sun, in its self-effulgence, is self-evident, so too, in the spiritual realm, to know the Knowledge Absolute no other knowing-principle is needed. The dreamer can never know the waker, for, while knowing the waking-state the dreamer himself ends to become the waker. To awaken oneself from the dream is to know the waker; to know the waker is to become the waker. So too, on ending the egocentric existence in a flash of spiritual awakening, the misguided ego ends itself in the rediscovery that it has been nothing but the Self, at all times. This vast suggestion is cramped into a mystic word-picture of the Self being 'luminous like the sun'. (8.9)

9. Who reaches the supreme resplendent Puruṣa?

The following two verses specify the requirements for reaching the Puruṣa:

कविं पुराणमनुशासितारं
अणोरणीयांसमनुस्मरेद्यः ।
सर्वस्य धातारमचिन्त्यरूपं
आदित्यवर्णं तमसः परस्तात् ॥

kavim purāṇamanuśāsitāram
aṇoraṇīyāṁsamanusmaredyaḥ,
sarvasya dhātāramacintyarūpam
ādityavarṇam tamasaḥ parastāt.

Whosoever, meditates upon the supreme Puruṣa described as Omniscient, Ancient, Ruler (of the whole world), Minuter than the atom, the Supporter of all, of Form inconceivable, Effulgent like the sun and Beyond the darkness of ignorance. (8.9)

प्रयाणकाले मनसाऽचलेन
भक्त्या युक्तो योगबलेन चैव ।
भ्रुवोर्मध्ये प्राणमावेश्य सम्यक्
स तं परं पुरुषमुपैति दिव्यम् ॥

prayāṇakāle manasā'calena
bhaktyā yukto yogabalena caiva,
bhruvormadhye prāṇamāveśya samyak
sa taṁ paraṁ puruṣamupaiti divyam.

At the time of death, with an unshaken mind full of devotion, by the power of Yoga fixing the whole prāṇa (breath) between the two eyebrows, he (the seeker) reaches the supreme resplendent Puruṣa. (8.10)

10. What is 'yoga-bala'?

The strength acquired by a meditator, when he meditates upon the Supreme regularly for a long period of time, is the 'yoga-bala' (power of Yoga). This is nothing other than the inward strength, the inward fire, that grows when the mind is withdrawn from its endless agitations and the intellect is peacefully rested in its contemplations upon the infinite qualities of the Absolute. (8.10)

11. What are the three conditions for the practice of meditation?

The following are the three necessary conditions for the practice of meditation:

(1) Controlling all the senses: The sense organs—skin, ear, nose, eyes and the tongue are the five main gates through which the external stimuli reach the mental zone to agitate it. To shut these five doors through discrimination and detachment is the first process, before the meditator can ever hope to enter the field of meditation. These are the five inlets through which not only does the external world storm in and agitate the mind, but the mind also runs out to wander among sensuous realms. When once these tunnels of disturbance are closed, the new flow of disturbances is shut out.

(2) Confining the mind in the heart: Even though the mind is not now directly open for any onslaught by fresh contingents of sense stimuli, it is capable of getting disturbed due to the previous impressions that it might have gathered in its past experiences in the finite world of change and pleasure. Therefore, we are advised to confine the mind, the instrument of emotion and feeling, in the 'heart'. The 'heart' is a conceptual centre in the mind from where all positive and noble thoughts of love and tenderness, kindness and charity, devotion and surrender constantly spring up. When once the gross stimuli are held back from entering the mind, the seeker is advised not to choke his faculty of emotion and feeling but to divinise it.

(3) Withdrawing the prāṇas into the intellect and engaging it in the yoga-dhāraṇā: This implies the total withdrawal of the intellect from all its identifications with the lower by dissociating ourselves from all our perceptions. This is accomplished through a process of totally engaging the mind-intellect in the contemplation of the Self. When the meditator's mind, drawn away from the sense-disturbances, is purified in the realm of divine thoughts, and when such a mind is perfectly controlled and held steady by an intellect gushing out towards the contemplation of the Self, the existing mental condition is said to be engaged in the practice of concentration (yoga-dhāraṇā). (8.12,13)

12. For whom is the Lord easy to attain?

The following verse describes the qualities required for one to easily attain the Lord:

अनन्यचेताः सततं यो मां स्मरति नित्यशः ।
तस्याहं सुलभः पार्थ नित्ययुक्तस्य योगिनः ॥

ananyacetāḥ satataṁ yo māṁ smarati nityaśaḥ,
tasyāhaṁ sulabhaḥ pārtha nityayuktasya yoginaḥ.

I am easily attainable for that ever-steadfast Yogī who constantly remembers Me daily, not thinking of anything else, O Pārtha.

To the one who is ever-steadfast in the Life Divine and remembers the Lord, always and daily, with a single-pointed mind, to him the Lord is easily attainable. (8.14)

13. What is 'creation' in the Vedāntic context?

In the worldly sense of the term, 'creation' is generally understood as the production of something new. Philosophically viewed, 'creation' has a subtler significance. A pot-maker creates pots out of mud. The act of 'creation' is only the production of a name and form, with some specific qualities, out of a raw material in which the name, form and qualities are already existing in an unmanifest condition. Hence, in Vedānta creation is nothing but a crystallisation of the unmanifest dormant names, forms and qualities into their manifest forms of existence. (8.18)

14. After Liberation why should there be no-returning to bondage?

The question of why there should be no-returning to bondage after Liberation, though natural, cannot stand even a moment's scrutiny. Generally, cause-hunting is for things that happen and not for things that do not happen! Nobody anxiously enquires why I am not in a hospital but an intelligent enquirer has every right to enquire why I have gone to the hospital. We may enquire why the Infinite has become the 'finite'; but the question does not arise at all why the Infinite should not fall again into the finite. This question is as absurd as my enquiring why you are not yet in jail. For not going to jail, no cause-hunting is necessary. And if you have actually gone to jail, there is certainly a justification to ask and enquire what is the exact crime for which you have been sent to jail. (8.21)

Selections for Reflection

1. To know the Self is to know everything and having known the Eternal as one's own Real Nature, one is free to act or not to act in any of the fields of the not-Self. (8.4)

2. The last thoughts of a dying man order his future embodiment and environment. The one who leaves the physical structure with his mind completely turned towards the Self will reach the Eternal and the Immortal, the Supreme Abode, reaching which there is no return. (8.5)

3. Even while living through the turmoils of existence, a true seeker

must learn to keep his mind continuously upon the awareness of his Real Nature and the Substratum of the world in one vast embrace of blissful homogeneity. This is not difficult, nor is it impractical. (8.7)

4. As long as man identifies with his limiting adjuncts, he lives in the external world of his self-projected delusory multiplicity, wherein the Self is 'inconceivable' and 'inexperiencable'. (8.9)

5. The entire Gītā is a 'Song of Renunciation'; not a dull-witted and un-creative renunciation, but a healthy detachment through right knowledge, which is the harbinger of all progress and development everywhere. (8.11)

6. Renunciation is not a sad and melancholy self-denial or self-punishment. It has to spring up from the fertile lands of efficient discrimination. (8.11)

7. A meditator's success depends upon his mental dynamism, and the only wealth that can ease the rigours of the journey is his own mental equipoise and inward peace. (8.11)

8. Prayer is no insecticide to be sprayed now and then; nor should the Divine Altar be considered as a bath-room, where one enters dirty and walks out clean! (8.14)

9. Just as sleep is not the end of life, but only a refreshing pause between two spans of activity, so too death is not an end, but often only a restful pause in the unmanifested condition, that comes between two successive manifested existences in different embodiments. (8.21)

10. Even in an elderly sādhaka (seeker), who has been on the path for years, the existing vāsanās in him may now and then come up to insist upon his extroversion. At such moments of inner revolt, the sādhaka need not at all get flabbergasted because aspirations for the higher-life and temptations for the lower existence are the

two opposing forces that are eternally at tug-of-war with each other. (8.26)

ଔଷ

Verses for Memorisation

अक्षरं ब्रह्म परमं स्वभावोऽध्यात्ममुच्यते ।
भूतभावोद्भवकरो विसर्गः कर्मसंज्ञितः ॥

akṣaraṁ brahma paramaṁ svabhāvo'dhyātmamucyate,
bhūtabhāvodbhavakaro visargaḥ karmasaṁjñitaḥ.

Brahman is Imperishable, the Supreme; His essential nature is called Self Knowledge, the creative force that causes beings to spring into manifestation is called 'work'. (8.3)

अधिभूतं क्षरो भावः पुरुषश्चाधिदैवतम् ।
अधियज्ञोऽहमेवात्र देहे देहभृतां वर ॥

adhibhūtaṁ kṣaro bhāvaḥ puruṣaścādhidaivatam,
adhiyajño'hamevātra dehe dehabhṛtāṁ vara.

Adhibhūta (or elements) constitutes My perishable nature, and the Indweller (or the essence) is the adhidaivata; I alone am the adhiyajña here, in this body, O best of the embodied. (8.4)

अन्तकाले च मामेव स्मरन्मुक्त्वा कलेवरम् ।
यः प्रयाति स मद्भावं याति नास्त्यत्र संशयः ॥

antakāle ca māmeva smaranmuktvā kalevaram,
yaḥ prayāti sa madbhāvaṁ yāti nāstyatra saṁśayaḥ.

And whosoever, leaving the body, goes forth remembering Me alone, at the time of his death, he attains My being; there is no doubt about this. (8.5)

यं यं वाऽपि स्मरन्भावं त्यजत्यन्ते कलेवरम् ।
तं तमेवैति कौन्तेय सदा तद्भावभावितः ॥

yaṁ yaṁ vā'pi smaranbhāvaṁ tyajatyante kalevaram,
taṁ tamevaiti kaunteya sadā tadbhāvabhāvitaḥ.

Whosoever, at the end, leaves the body, thinking of any being, to that being only he goes, O Kaunteya (O son of Kuntī) because of his constant thought of that being. (8.6)

तस्मात्सर्वेषु कालेषु मामनुस्मर युध्य च।
मय्यर्पितमनोबुद्धिर्मामेवैष्यस्यसंशयः॥

tasmātsarveṣu kāleṣu māmanusmara yudhya ca,
mayyarpitamanobuddhirmāmevaiṣyasyasaṁśayaḥ.

Therefore, at all times, remember Me and fight, with mind and intellect fixed (or absorbed) in Me; you shall doubtless come to Me alone. (8.7)

कविं पुराणमनुशासितारं
अणोरणीयांसमनुस्मरेद्यः।
सर्वस्य धातारमचिन्त्यरूपं
आदित्यवर्णं तमसः परस्तात्॥

kaviṁ purāṇamanuśāsitāraṁ
aṇoraṇīyāṁsamanusmaredyaḥ,
sarvasya dhātāramacintyarūpaṁ
ādityavarṇaṁ tamasaḥ parastāt.

Whosoever meditates upon the Omniscient, the Ancient, the Ruler (of the whole world), Minuter than the atom, the Supporter of all, of Form inconceivable, Effulgent like the Sun and Beyond the darkness (of ignorance). . . (8.9)

प्रयाणकाले मनसाऽचलेन
भक्त्या युक्तो योगबलेन चैव।
भ्रुवोर्मध्ये प्राणमावेश्य सम्यक्
स तं परं पुरुषमुपैति दिव्यम्॥

prayāṇakāle manasā'calena
bhaktyā yukto yogabalena caiva,
bhruvormadhye prāṇamāveśya samyak
sa taṁ paraṁ puruṣamupaiti divyam.

At the time of death, with all unshaken mind full of devotion, by the power of Yoga fixing the whole prāṇa (breath) between the two eye-brows, he (the seeker) reaches the supreme resplendent 'Puruṣa'. (8.10)

ओमित्येकाक्षरं ब्रह्म व्याहरन्मामनुस्मरन्।
यः प्रयाति त्यजन्देहं स याति परमां गतिम्॥

omityekākṣaraṁ brahma vyāharanmāmanusmaran,
yaḥ prayāti tyajandehaṁ sa yāti paramāṁ gatim.
Uttering the one-syllabled 'OM'—the (symbol of) Brahman—and remembering Me he who departs, leaving the body, attains the Supreme Goal. (8.13)

आब्रह्मभुवनाल्लोकाः पुनरावर्तिनोऽर्जुन।
मामुपेत्य तु कौन्तेय पुनर्जन्म न विद्यते॥
ābrahmabhuvanāllokāḥ punarāvartino'rjuna,
māmupetya tu kaunteya punarjanma na vidyate.
Worlds upto the 'world of Brahma' are subject to rebirth, O Arjuna; but he who reaches Me, O Kaunteya, has no birth. (8.16)

पुरुषः स परः पार्थ भक्त्या लभ्यस्त्वनन्यया।
यस्यान्तःस्थानि भूतानि येन सर्वमिदं ततम्॥
puruṣaḥ sa paraḥ pārtha bhaktyā labhyastvananyayā,
yasyāntaḥsthāni bhūtāni yena sarvamidaṁ tatam.
That highest 'Puruṣa', O Pārtha, is attainable by unswerving devotion to Him alone within whom all beings dwell and by whom all this is pervaded. (8.22)

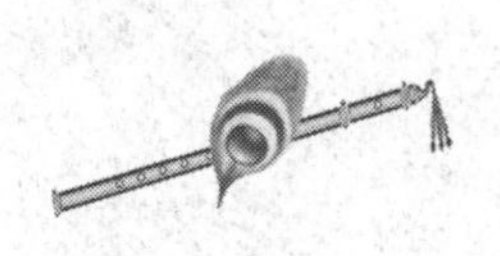

9

Rājavidyā Rājaguhya Yoga

The Yoga of Royal Knowledge and Royal Secret

A still mind is an open window through which man peeps out to see himself reflected in the mirror of Truth. (9.31)

The word 'rājan' (king) connotes 'supremacy'. Thus 'rāja-vidyā' indicates 'royal knowledge' and 'rāja-guhyam' means 'royal secret'. The Self-Knowledge that is declared in this chapter is verily the 'supreme knowledge' and the 'supreme secret.' Hence the title of this chapter—'Rājavidyā Rājaguhya Yoga'. This chapter is a continuation of the ideas stated by the Lord in the eighth chapter while answering the seven questions put forth by Arjuna. Herein we find a detailed explanation of Self-Knowledge.

Terms and Definitions

1. What is 'death'?

The world of names and forms is finite and ever changing. At every moment, every object is living through a process of change. According to Vedānta, each change is death to the previous state of existence of the object. (9.3)

2. Subtlety of a thing is measured in terms of its _________.

Pervasiveness (9.4)

3. Differentiate 'Īśvara' from 'jīva'.

The Eternal Brahman functioning through the equipment of the total mind is 'Īśvara' (God-principle) and the same Absolute Brahman functioning through the limited individual mind and intellect is the individualised Self, the 'jīva' (ego). (9.7)

4. How does Śrī Kṛṣṇa describe men of 'rākṣasic' and 'āsuric' temperaments?

मोघाशा मोघकर्माणो मोघज्ञाना विचेतसः।
राक्षसीमासुरीं चैव प्रकृतिं मोहिनीं श्रिताः॥

moghāśā moghakarmāṇo moghajñānā vicetasaḥ,
rākṣasīmāsurīṁ caiva prakṛtiṁ mohinīṁ śritāḥ.

Of vain hopes, of vain actions, of vain knowledge, and senseless, they verily are possessed of the delusive nature of rākṣasas and asuras.

Deluded by false desires and wearied with false activities to fulfil those wrong desires, some become confused in intellect and totally confounded in their reasoning. Such people lose all divine perspective and become monstrous in their activities, expressing nothing but their demoniac sensuous nature at all times. Such men are called here as 'rākṣasas' and 'asuras'. (9.12)

5. Describe men of divine temperament.

महात्मानस्तु मां पार्थ दैवीं प्रकृतिमाश्रिताः ।
भजन्त्यनन्यमनसो ज्ञात्वा भूतादिमव्ययम् ॥

mahātmānastu māṁ pārtha daivīṁ prakṛtimāśritāḥ,
bhajantyananyamanaso jñātvā bhūtādimavyayam.

But the mahātmas (great-souls) O Pārtha, partaking of My divine nature, worship Me with a single mind (with a mind devoted to nothing else), knowing Me as the Imperishable Source of all beings. (9.13)

सततं कीर्तयन्तो मां यतन्तश्च दृढव्रताः ।
नमस्यन्तश्च मां भक्त्या नित्ययुक्ता उपासते ॥

satataṁ kīrtayanto māṁ yatantaśca dṛḍhavratāḥ,
namasyantaśca māṁ bhaktyā nityayuktā upāsate.

Always glorifying Me, striving, firm in vows, prostrating before Me, and always steadfast, they worship Me with devotion. (9.14)

6. What is 'Jñāna-yajña'?

Jñāna-yajña has no rituals. It is a constant attempt on the part of the performer to see, in and through the experienced names and forms, the expression and vitality of the One Conscious Principle, the Self. The seeker practising Jñāna-yajña understands the significance of the Vedāntic assertion that the Immutable Self pervades all, penetrating everything, and in Its homogenous web of existence, It holds together the phenomenal multiplicity and their variegated interactions. (9.15)

7. What is 'svadhā'?

Food offerings made to ancestors is 'svadhā'. (9.16)

8. What is the 'Turīya-state'?

Life is conceived of as the flow of waking, dream and deep-sleep states. The substratum for these superimposed three states and their experiences must be something other than these three for the substratum has to be different from the superimposition upon it. This substratum is conceived of as the 'Fourth State' or 'Turīya', and it supports and embraces the three ordinary states of consciousness. (9.17)

9. What is 'Soma'?

'Soma' is the milky juice of a creeper-plant (perhaps, belonging to the group *ephedra* or *periploca*) that was used in Vedic rituals and drunk in very small quantities at the end of the rituals. (9.21)

10. Differentiate 'yoga' from 'kṣema'.

Securing that which we do not already possess is 'yoga' and preserving that which is already in our possession is 'kṣema'. (9.22)

11. What is 'Saṁnyāsa'?

Saṁnyāsa or renunciation is not the physical rejection of the world but is the renunciation of: (a) all egocentric activities and (b) all anxieties or cravings for the fruits of action. (9.28)

12. Who is a 'Rājarṣi'?

A king who, having enjoyed intelligently his power and wealth, is satiated, and who, out of his growing inner discrimination, comes to experience the peace of true contemplation upon the Self—such a 'Man of Perfection' is termed a 'Rājarṣi'. (9.33)

Thoughts and Concepts

1. Who is marked out for victory in life?

An individual becomes incapable of facing the challenges of life and meeting its rising demands because, in his false estimation of things and beings, he comes to play out of tune with the whole orchestra of life. To understand oursleves and the world is to know the secret of keeping a healthy and happy relationship with the world outside. He who is capable of tuning himself up thus to be in harmony with the Whole is the one marked for sure success and victory. (9.1)

2. What is the nature of Self-Knowledge?

The nature and glory of Self-Knowledge is described in the following verse:

राजविद्या राजगुह्यं पवित्रमिदमुत्तमम्।
प्रत्यक्षावगमं धर्म्यं सुसुखं कर्तुमव्ययम्॥

rājavidyā rājaguhyaṁ pavitramidamuttamam,
pratyakṣāvagamaṁ dharmyaṁ susukhaṁ kartumavyayam.

Royal Science, Royal Secret, the Supreme Purifier is this (Self-Knowledge), realisable by direct intuitive Knowledge, according to the Dharma, very easy to perform, Imperishable. (9.2)

3. Cite and explain the relevant statement of the Gītā that proclaims the 'relationless-relationship' between the Real and the unreal.

The statement of Śrī Kṛṣṇa: "*matsthāni sarvabhūtāni na cāhaṁ teṣvavasthitaḥ*—All beings exist in me but I don't dwell in them" is a classic description of the 'relationless-relationship' between the Real and unreal. This can be understood using the theory of superimposition. To explain: a traveller comes upon a post and mistakes it for a ghost. He superimposes a vision of the unreal ghost upon a real post. And what exactly is the relationship between the ghost and the post from the standpoint of the post? "The ghost", the post would say, "is no doubt in me, but I am not in the ghost; and therefore, I have never frightened any deluded traveller at any time." In the same fashion, the Lord says, "I, in my unmanifest nature, am the substratum for all the manifested names and forms, but neither in their joys nor in their sorrows, neither in their births nor in their deaths, do I share their destinies, because I do not dwell in them." (9.4)

4. Explain the significance of the Lord's statement "*na ca matsthāni*

***bhūtāni*—Nor do beings exist (in reality) in Me."**

In the example of the post and the ghost this statement of the Lord is equivalent to the post declaring that, "in me, the post, never has a ghost existed." In Pure Awareness, in Its Infinite Nature of sheer Knowledge, there never was, never is and can never be any world of pluralistic embodiment, just as for the awake, the pleasures of the dream world are never available. At the time of the direct subjective Experience of the Self, there is no cognition of the pluralistic world, which is born out of an individual's forgetfulness of the Infinite. This is the significance of the Lord's statement "Beings don't exist in reality in Me." (9.5)

5. Cite and explain the verse wherein the Lord gives a simile to explain his 'relationless-relationship' with the finite.

यथाकाशस्थितो नित्यं वायुः सर्वत्रगो महान् ।
तथा सर्वाणि भूतानि मत्स्थानीत्युपधारय ॥

yathākāśasthito nityaṁ vāyuḥ sarvatrago mahān,
tathā sarvāṇi bhūtāni matsthānītyupadhāraya.

As the mighty wind, moving everywhere, rests always in space even so, know you, all beings rest in Me.

The gross (sthūla) can never condition the subtle (sūkṣma). The wind curls and swirls and whirls around everywhere in subtle space; space supports and envelopes it everywhere, and yet, the wind does not ever limit space. Similarly, the Real supports the unreal; the unreal seemingly lives through its history of misery and sorrows, fleeting joys and passing pleasures in the Real and yet, the unreal can never condition the Real. When the wind is moving, space need never move. None of the qualities of the wind is the quality of space (ākāśa). Compared to the expanse of infinite space, atmospheric disturbances occur only upto a height of a few miles off the surface of the globe. In the infinite vastness of the Real, the arena of disturbances caused by Its flirtations with Its own assumed self-ignorance, is only a negligible area…and even there, the relationship between the false and the Real is the relationship between the fickle breeze and infinite space. (9.6)

6. How does the Lord declare His detachment to the activities of prakṛti?

न च मां तानि कर्माणि निबध्नन्ति धनञ्जय ।
उदासीनवदासीनमसक्तं तेषु कर्मसु ॥

na ca māṁ tāni karmāṇi nibadhnanti dhanañjaya,
udāsīnavadāsīnamasaktaṁ teṣu karmasu.

Sitting like one indifferent, and unattached to these acts, Dhanañjaya, these acts do not bind Me.

However tragic and murderous the play, however tearful and sad the story, however rainy and stormy the scene, the white screen in the cinema hall at the end of the play carries neither the marks of the blood spilt, nor the stains of the tears shed, nor the wear and tear of the storm that raged. Yet, but for the changeless screen, the story could never have been unravelled through the medium of light and shade.

In the same fashion, the ever-pure Infinite, as the Self, becomes the enduring platform for the drama of sorrow that is expressed in the language of plurality, ceaselessly enacted by the infinite number of egos, helplessly repeating the parts ordered by their vāsanās, gathered by them in the past. The Self, as Pure Consciousness, illumines the vāsanās and lends them the capacity to project out, be it for their damnation or glorification. 'Sitting like one indifferent and unattached to these acts' the Self revels in the realm of Its lower nature (prakṛti). (9.9)

7. "*Mayādhyakṣeṇa prakṛtiḥ sūyate sacarācaram*—Under Me as her Supervisor, prakṛti (nature) produces the whole world of the moving and the unmoving." Explain.

The Ātman, merely by Its 'presence' illumines the mind and intellect and creates for the expression of vāsanās an entire field of the world of objects and the instruments of experience, constituted of the organs of perception and the organs of action. The continued dance of the world of plurality to the rhythm of change and death is maintained in the 'presence' of the Self.

In the final analysis, the Self does nothing. It is prakṛti that projects and executes; prakṛti that gets animated in the proximity of the Self. It is the Light of the Self that vitalises prakṛti and makes her exist and act. (9.10)

8. What is 'true worship'?

To keep in the mind an alert and vigilant flow of thoughts in our adoration for the Self, the Substratum of the entire Universe and the Essence in all beings, is the truest worship that can open up the buds of our egocentric lives into blossoms of God-men wafting their fragrance of Perfection around. (9.14)

9. How does the Lord declare that men worship Him in various ways?

ज्ञानयज्ञेन चाप्यन्ये यजन्तो मामुपासते ।
एकत्वेन पृथक्त्वेन बहुधा विश्वतोमुखम् ॥

jñānayajñena cāpyanye yajanto māmupāsate,
ekatvena pṛthaktvena bahudhā viśvatomukham.

Others also, offering the 'wisdom-sacrifice' worship Me, regarding Me as One, as distinct, as manifold—Me, who is in all forms, faces, everywhere. (9.15)

10. What is 'Īśvara-darśana' (Vision of the Lord)?

A Man of Realisation moves about the world, seeing the Self expressed through every movement and action, word and thought that clusters around him at all times. Just as one light in the midst of a thousand mirrors comes to provide crores of reflections everywhere, so too, the one centred in the Self, when he walks out into the world, sees everywhere the Self dancing, shooting glances at him from all around at once, thrilling him always with the homogeneous ecstasy of perfection and bliss.

In the sparkle of the eyes, in the smile of a friend, in the grin of an enemy, in the harsh words of jealousy and in the soft tones of love, in heat and in cold, in success and in failure—among men, among animals, amidst the trees and in the company of the inert, everywhere, he successfully gains the auspicious vision of the Supreme, either as Existence Pure, Knowledge Absolute or Bliss Infinite. This is the meaning of 'Īśvara-darśana' or the 'Vision of the Lord', which is sung so gloriously in all the scriptures of the world. (9.15)

11. Cite the verses that declare the Lord's universal presence.

The following verses declare the Lord's universal presence:

अहं क्रतुरहं यज्ञः स्वधाहमहमौषधम् ।
मन्त्रोऽहमहमेवाज्यमहमग्निरहं हुतम् ॥

ahaṁ kraturahaṁ yajñaḥ svadhāhamahamauṣadham,
mantro'hamahamevājyamahamagnirahaṁ hutam.

I am the 'kratu'; I am the sacrifice; I am the offering (food) to pitṛs (or ancestors); I am the medicinal herb, and all plants; I am the mantra; I am also the clarified butter; I am the fire; I am the oblation. (9.16)

पिताहमस्य जगतो माता धाता पितामहः ।
वेद्यं पवित्रमोङ्कार ऋक्साम यजुरेव च ॥

pitāhamasya jagato mātā dhātā pitāmahaḥ,
vedyaṁ pavitramoṅkāra ṛksāma yajureva ca.

I am the father of this world, the mother, the supporter and the grandsire; the (one) thing to be known, the purifier, (the syllable) OM, and also the Ṛk, the Sāma and the Yajus. (9.17)

गतिर्भर्ता प्रभुः साक्षी निवासः शरणं सुहृत् ।
प्रभवः प्रलयः स्थानं निधानं बीजमव्ययम् ॥

gatirbhartā prabhuḥ sākṣī nivāsaḥ śaraṇaṁ suhṛt,
prabhavaḥ pralayaḥ sthānaṁ nidhānaṁ bījamavyayam.

I am the goal, the supporter, the lord, the witness, the abode, the shelter, the friend, the origin, the dissolution, the foundation, the treasure-house and the seed imperishable. (9.18)

तपाम्यहमहं वर्षं निगृह्णाम्युत्सृजामि च ।
अमृतं चैव मृत्युश्च सदसच्चाहमर्जुन ॥

tapāmyahamahaṁ varṣaṁ nigṛhṇāmyutsṛjāmi ca,
amṛtaṁ caiva mṛtyuśca sadasaccāhamarjuna.

(As the sun) I give heat; I withhold and send forth the rain; I am immortality and also death, both existence and non-existence, O Arjuna. (9.19)

12. What is the significance of the Lord's description of Himself being the 'immutable seed'?

All seeds perish when they germinate and produce trees. The Self is no doubt the origin of the 'Tree of Saṁsāra', but in the production of this tree, the Self is not transformed, It being ever immutable. By declaring that He is the 'immutable seed' the Lord clarifies His indestructible nature even while being the cause of the world. (9.18)

13. Cite the relevant verse wherein the Lord declares that He fulfils all the needs of His true devotee.

The following verse declares that the Lord fulfils all the needs of His true devotee:

अनन्याश्चिन्तयन्तो मां ये जनाः पर्युपासते ।
तेषां नित्याभियुक्तानां योगक्षेमं वहाम्यहम् ॥

ananyāścintayanto māṁ ye janāḥ paryupāsate,
teṣāṁ nityābhiyuktānāṁ yogakṣemaṁ vahāmyaham.

To those men who worship Me alone, thinking of no other, to those ever self-controlled, I secure for them that which is not already possessed (yoga) by them, and preserve for them what they already possess (kṣema). (9.22)

14. Who is dead to the world of sorrows?

All conflicts and contests, all struggles and sorrows, whatever be the form in which they appear, though different from individual to individual, from place to place and from time to time, all of them fall into two distinct groups: (a) the struggle to gain, and (b) the effort to guard what has been gained by one's struggle. These two tensions tear to bits the joy and tranquillity of life. He who is without these two preoccupations is the luckiest, in the sense that he has gained all that is to be gained; and when these two factors are totally blotted out from one's life, one is dead to the world of sorrows. (9.22)

15. What are the three factors that enable success in life?

The three constituent factors for success in life are:
(1) Consistency of will and thought
(2) Singleness of purpose and resolve in facing situations
(3) Self-control. (9.22)

16. "Even those devotees who, endowed with faith, worship other devas, worship Me alone, O son of Kuntī (but) by the wrong method." What does the Lord mean by the phrase 'wrong method' (*avidhipūrvakam*)?

The various devas (deities such as Indra, Vāyu, Agni, Rāhu, Śani and so on) confer different rewards such as health and wealth, children and prosperity in worldly life but the worship of the Supreme confers the highest reward of Liberation.

The phrase 'by the wrong method' (*avidhipūrvakam*) only indicates that ultimately, worship of the devas for fruits leads seekers to the well of dejection and sorrow that lies in the darkness of the not-Self, instead of leading to the Bliss of Perfection that is the nature of the Self.

Further, it is the Lord in one form or another, expressing some special power, who forms the different devas (deities), invoked by the various sacrifices performed by the seekers of their grace. The Lord says 'I am the Immutable Reality' behind all the deities that are invoked during every sacrifice with faith and devotion. But because the seekers invoke the 'limited potential of the Lord' (deva) they do not come to realise the Lord's Infinite Glory revelling as their Self and, therefore, jumping from one worship to another, they slip down to fall into delusory confusions and endless entanglements. (9.24)

17. What do the terms 'devavrata', 'pitṛvrata' and 'bhūtejya' connote in the following verse?

यान्ति देवव्रता देवान्पितॄन्यान्ति पितृव्रताः ।
भूतानि यान्ति भूतेज्या यान्ति मद्याजिनोऽपि माम् ॥

yānti devavratā devānpitṝnyānti pitṛvratāḥ,
bhūtāni yānti bhūtejyā yānti madyājino'pi mām.

The worshippers of the devas or gods go to the devas; to the pitṛs or ancestors go the ancestor-worshippers; to the bhūtas or the elements go worshippers of the bhūtas; but My worshippers come unto Me.

Devavrata: Devas represent the various sense organs through which we experience the world. To indicate the work done, by the term denoting the instrument with which the work is executed, is quite common in life. To axe, to scissor, to knife, to hammer, to steer, to pen, etc., are examples wherein the name of the instrument is employed to indicate the work done with it. Similarly, the plural noun 'devas' may here be taken to mean 'the entire field of all physical experiences'. Those who court the external world of joys and successes consistently and with the required amount of devotion are termed 'devavrata' and they come to gain that field of demanded experiences.

Pitṛvrata: The term 'pitṛ' denotes the 'ancestors'. 'Pitṛvrata' means 'votaries of ancestors' and indicates persons who are enthusiastically alive to the cultural purity and tradition of their ancients, and strive to live up to those ideals. Such an individual, who constantly endeavours to live up to the ancient cultural tradition of spiritual India, as a result of his constant self-application, comes to gain the beauty and the shine of the exquisite life of purity and perfection.

Bhūtejya: The active quest in the field of 'objective-sciences' is a part of man's hunt for knowledge, and therefore, the 'bhūtejya' or 'worshippers of the bhūtas' are the secular scientists who try to observe, codify and systematize the observed knowledge of physical nature and behaviour of things and beings as is now done under such classifications as Physics, Chemistry, Biology, Zoology, Botany, Engineering, Agriculture, Politics, Sociology, Geography, History, Geology, and so on—an endless array of specialised lines of investigation, adopted, pursued and accepted by the modern world. A large portion of the Atharvaṇa Veda gives us the accepted theories of nature and its behaviour, as conceived of by the Ṛṣis of that time. (9.25)

18. The Lord accepts any little thing offered to Him with devotion.

Cite the relevant verse.

पत्रं पुष्पं फलं तोयं यो मे भक्त्या प्रयच्छति ।
तदहं भक्त्युपहृतमश्नामि प्रयतात्मनः ॥

patraṁ puṣpaṁ phalaṁ toyaṁ yo me bhaktyā prayacchati,
tadahaṁ bhaktyupahṛtamaśnāmi prayatātmanaḥ.

Whoever offers Me with devotion a leaf, a flower, a fruit, water, that I accept, offered by the pure-minded with devotion. (9.26)

19. What are the two pre-requisites for a true offering unto the Lord?

An offering unto the Lord can be true only when it is accompanied by these two conditions: (a) It is offered with devotion and (b) The worshipper is endowed with a pure mind. Such an offering serves as a good vehicle for a man to tread the spiritual path of self-development. (9.26)

20. Cite the verse wherein the Lord goads us to offer all our actions to Him as worship?

यत्करोषि यदश्नासि यज्जुहोषि ददासि यत् ।
यत्तपस्यसि कौन्तेय तत्कुरुष्व मदर्पणम् ॥

yatkaroṣi yadaśnāsi yajjuhoṣi dadāsi yat,
yattapasyasi kaunteya tatkuruṣva madarpaṇam.

Whatever you do, whatever you eat, whatever you offer in sacrifice, whatever you give, whatever you practise as austerity, O Kaunteya, do it as an offering to Me. (9.27)

21. What would be the result of living life in the pure spirit of dedicated offering?

The fruit of a life of dedication unto the Lord is Liberation. This is pointed out in the following verse:

शुभाशुभफलैरेवं मोक्ष्यसे कर्मबन्धनैः ।
संन्यासयोगयुक्तात्मा विमुक्तो मामुपैष्यसि ॥

śubhāśubhaphalairevaṁ mokṣyase karmabandhanaiḥ,
saṁnyāsayogayuktātmā vimukto māmupaiṣyasi.

Thus shall you be freed from the bonds of actions yielding good and evil fruits; with the mind steadfast in the Yoga of renunciation, and liberated, you shall come unto Me.

When actions are undertaken without ego, as an offering unto the Lord the reactions of those actions (vāsanās), whether good or bad, cannot reach us.

Since the reactions (vāsanās) arising from fresh actions do not add their impressions onto the mind, and since the existing impressions (vāsanās) get wiped out during the mind's activities in the world outside, slowly and steadily, the mind gets almost a total purgation of all its existing vāsanās and becomes more and more purified. A purified mind has more concentration and single-pointedness.

The next stage of evolution is that such a purified mind, discovering in itself more and more discrimination, learns to live a life of 'Saṁnyāsa' and 'Yoga'. Such a seeker comes to attain Liberation. (9.28)

22. If the Lord is impartial to all beings, how is it that some people show a greater manifestation of divinity?

Even though the same sunlight reflects upon the different types of objects in the world, the quality and the nature of the reflecting surface will determine the clarity and the intensity of the light reflected. On a dull piece of rough stone the least amount of light will be reflected, while in a bright clean and polished mirror there will be maximum reflection. Because of this difference, sunlight cannot be accused of having a special love for the mirror, or disgust for the rough stone.

Applying the analogy to the subjective life, it becomes clear that if the spiritual strength and beauty reflect more from the golden-hearts of the rare few and not at all from the stone-hearts of the many, it is not because the Self entertains any preference for or any prejudice against anyone, but it is only a natural phenomenon, happening in perfect obedience to the law of the universe. (9.29)

23. What is 'worship'?

'Worship' is a technique by which the entire 'thought-forces' in the worshipper are mobilised and turned to flow towards the Divine, ever seeking a total identity with the Truth so meditated upon. When this is done in a spirit of devotion or love the worshipper comes to realise his total oneness with his 'Object of Worship'. (9.29)

24. Why should even the most sinful person be regarded as 'righteous' if he has taken a strong right resolution to be good?

Right resolution is more important than mere routine. The majority of seekers only plod on their path—a melancholy brood. He who steadily walks the path with an iron-heart of resolution, open-eyed and enthusiastic, cheerful and heroic, he alone is marked for sure success and therefore, the rightly resolved man of evil ways is to be considered, from the moment of his noble decision, as one especially marked out to be soon a successful Man of Perfection. Hence, even the most sinful person is to be regarded as 'righteous' the very moment he has rightly resolved. (9.30)

25. Explain the terms 'strī', 'vaiśya' and 'śūdra' in the following verse.

मां हि पार्थ व्यपाश्रित्य येऽपि स्युः पापयोनयः ।
स्त्रियो वैश्यास्तथा शूद्रास्तेऽपि यान्ति परां गतिम् ॥

māṁ hi pārtha vyapāśritya ye'pi syuḥ pāpayonayaḥ,
striyo vaiśyāstathā śūdrāste'pi yānti parāṁ gatim.

For, taking refuge in Me, they also, who, O Pārtha, may be of a 'sinful birth' – women, vaiśyas as well as śūdras – even they attain the supreme goal.

These terms – 'strī', 'vaiśya' and 'śūdra' – are used by Śrī Kṛṣṇa to indicate special types of mind-intellect equipments.

Strī: By 'strī', is meant a feminine mind and not a woman. The 'feminine-minds' (striyaḥ) are those that have a larger share of deep affections and binding attachments.

Vaiśya: By traders (vaiśyas) are meant those who have a 'commercial attitude' in all their thoughts and actions, ever calculating the profits that would accrue from all their investments. Such a calculating mind, ever looking for the profits that could be raised, is not fit for easily evolving through the 'Path of Meditation'. To surrender all fruits of actions is the secret of holding the mind still.

Thus, when the Science of Spirit-development condemns the 'traders', it is only a denunciation of the 'particular commercial tendency' of the mind. Those who fall, psychologically, under the group of 'traders', cannot hope to progress on the Path Divine.

Śūdra: Those with mental attitudes of slumber and sloth are indicated by the term 'śūdras'. (9.32)

ᗧ ᗤ

Selections for Reflection

1. Blind belief can have a compelling charm only in the early history of a people, and when they grow and become stalwart in their reason, the impetuosity of the generation can no more be tamed and kept within the bounds of barren belief. It demands and expects walls of unshakeable logic and reason to support the assertions of philosophy. (Introduction)

2. Wherever and whenever an egocentric action, whipped by selfish desire, is undertaken, gross and painful reactions (vāsanās) must necessarily ensue. (9.9)

3. Chocolates made by different firms, irrespective of their shapes and colours, flavours and prices, are all chocolates and therefore their essential nature of sweetness is common to all of them and the child who is seeking the sweetness of the chocolates will enjoy them, whatever be their shape, size or packing. Similarly, a seeker of the Self watches for, observes and detects the expression of the Self in all forms and names, in all situations and conditions. (9.15)

4. Just as I permeate, exist, enjoy and experience in and through every little portion of my body, all through my waking hours, at one and the same time, so too the Man of Realisation realises that at all times his own Self permeates the entire universe. (9.15)

5. To know the Self is to destroy the consciousness of imperfection,

the existence finite, the sorrows poignant. To live in the ego as a mere embodied self is to live self-exiled from all the Divine potentialities that one is heir to. (9.17)

6. Delusion breeds sorrows, Knowledge produces joy. The universe is pain-ridden because it is delusion-projected. (9.18)

7. Complete happiness and satisfaction, perfect contentment and peace, lie only in the innermost precincts of the heart and not in the extrovert fields of profit and success, glory and fame. Unmindful of this enduring profit that lies within themselves, men, bitten by a thousand scorpions of desire, run amuck—bringing about chaos and sorrows not only to themselves but to others walking the same road. (9.24)

8. A devotee who can constantly remember the Divine in all his contacts in life is alone the one who can give to life the respect and reverence that it deserves. It is a law of life that as you give unto life, so shall life give unto you. Smile at life and life smiles; frown at life and life frowns at you; approach life with due reverence and respect, born out of the cognition of the Divine essence in it, and life shall respect and revere you. (9.27)

9. The condition of the mind declares whether the individual is confused or clear, bound or redeemed. A mind that is turned outward, rushing out and panting to gain its satisfactions in the world of objects, gets bound to the finite and comes to groan with pain and disappointment; while the same mind when turned inward, away from the objects, seeking the Self, comes to rediscover its own identity with the Spiritual Centre. (9.29)

10. Never does the Gītā, at any point, encourage man's surrender to circumstances or to his own debilities and incompetencies. As a scripture of activity and optimistic endeavour, the Gītā unmistakably emphasizes the ultimate supremacy of man over his weaknesses and even over his circumstances. (9.29)

11. The Vedas condemn the sin, not the sinner. The evil ways of the sinner are but expressions of the evil thoughts in his mind, and so if the texture of the thoughts flowing in his mind could be changed, the texture of his behaviour would also be transformed. He who has come to keep consistently in his mind thoughts of the Lord accomplishes, in the warmth of his growing devotion, so total a rehabilitation of the mental life that he cannot thereafter carry on his career in sin. (9.30)

12. The perfection indicated in religion lies only as far away from us as our waking state is from our dream. (9.31)

13. Of all the spiritual practices (sādhana), the most efficient is the constant remembrance of the Lord with a heart overflowing with love and devotion (upāsanā). (9.32)

Verses for Memorisation

राजविद्या राजगुह्यं पवित्रमिदमुत्तमम् ।
प्रत्यक्षावगमं धर्म्यं सुसुखं कर्तुमव्ययम् ॥

rājavidyā rājaguhyaṁ pavitramidamuttamam,
pratyakṣāvagamaṁ dharmyaṁ susukhaṁ kartumavyayam.

Royal Science, Royal Secret, the Supreme Purifier is this (Self-Knowledge), realisable by direct intuitive Knowledge, according to the Dharma, very easy to perform, Imperishable. (9.2)

मया ततमिदं सर्वं जगदव्यक्तमूर्तिना ।
मत्स्थानि सर्वभूतानि न चाहं तेष्ववस्थितः ॥

mayā tatamidaṁ sarvaṁ jagadavyaktamūrtinā,
matsthāni sarvabhūtāni na cāhaṁ teṣvavasthitaḥ.

All this world is pervaded by Me in My unmanifest form (aspect); all beings exist in Me, but I do not dwell in them. (9.4)

न च मत्स्थानि भूतानि पश्य मे योगमैश्वरम् ।
भूतभृन्न च भूतस्थो ममात्मा भूतभावनः ॥

na ca matsthāni bhūtāni paśya me yogamaiśvaram,
bhūtabhṛnna ca bhūtastho mamātmā bhūtabhāvanaḥ.
Nor do beings exist (in reality) in Me—behold My Divine Yoga; supporting all beings but not dwelling in them I remain the 'efficient-cause' of all beings. (9.5)

न च मां तानि कर्माणि निबध्नन्ति धनञ्जय।
उदासीनवदासीनमसक्तं तेषु कर्मसु॥
na ca māṁ tāni karmāṇi nibadhnanti dhanañjaya,
udāsīnavadāsīnamasaktaṁ teṣu karmasu.
Sitting like one indifferent, and unattached to these acts, Dhanañjaya, these acts do not bind Me. (9.9)

मयाध्यक्षेण प्रकृतिः सूयते सचराचरम्।
हेतुनानेन कौन्तेय जगद्विपरिवर्तते॥
mayādhyakṣeṇa prakṛtiḥ sūyate sacarācaram,
hetunānena kaunteya jagadviparivartate.
Under Me as her Supervisor, Prakṛti (nature) produces the moving and the unmoving; because of this, O Kaunteya, the world revolves. (9.10)

मोघाशा मोघकर्माणो मोघज्ञाना विचेतसः।
राक्षसीमासुरीं चैव प्रकृतिं मोहिनीं श्रिताः॥
moghāśā moghakarmāṇo moghajñānā vicetasaḥ,
rākṣasīmāsurīṁ caiva prakṛtiṁ mohinīṁ śritāḥ.
Of vain hopes, of vain actions, of vain knowledge, and senseless, they verily are possessed of the delusive nature of rākṣasas and asuras. (9.12)

महात्मानस्तु मां पार्थ दैवीं प्रकृतिमाश्रिताः।
भजन्त्यनन्यमनसो ज्ञात्वा भूतादिमव्ययम्॥
mahātmānastu māṁ pārtha daivīṁ prakṛtimāśritāḥ,
bhajantyananyamanaso jñātvā bhūtādimavyayam.
But the Mahātmas (great-souls) O Pārtha, partaking of My Divine nature, worship Me with a single mind (with a mind devoted to nothing else), knowing Me as the Imperishable Source of all beings. (9.13)

सततं कीर्तयन्तो मां यतन्तश्च दृढव्रताः ।
नमस्यन्तश्च मां भक्त्या नित्ययुक्ता उपासते ॥

satataṁ kīrtayanto māṁ yatantaśca dṛḍhavratāḥ,
namasyantaśca māṁ bhaktyā nityayuktā upāsate.

Always glorifying Me, striving, firm in vows, prostrating before Me, and always steadfast, they worship Me with devotion. (9.14)

ज्ञानयज्ञेन चाप्यन्ये यजन्तो मामुपासते ।
एकत्वेन पृथक्त्वेन बहुधा विश्वतोमुखम् ॥

jñānayajñena cāpyanye yajanto māmupāsate,
ekatvena pṛthaktvena bahudhā viśvatomukham.

Others also, offering the 'wisdom-sacrifice' worship Me, regarding Me as One, as distinct, as manifold—Me, who in all forms, faces everywhere. (9.15)

गतिर्भर्ता प्रभुः साक्षी निवासः शरणं सुहृत् ।
प्रभवः प्रलयः स्थानं निधानं बीजमव्ययम् ॥

gatirbhartā prabhuḥ sākṣī nivāsaḥ śaraṇaṁ suhṛt,
prabhavaḥ pralayaḥ sthānaṁ nidhānaṁ bījamavyayam.

I am the Goal, the Supporter, the Lord, the Witness, the Abode, the Shelter, the Friend, the Origin, the Dissolution, the Foundation, the Treasure-house and the Seed Imperishable. (9.18)

ते तं भुक्त्वा स्वर्गलोकं विशालं
क्षीणे पुण्ये मर्त्यलोकं विशन्ति ।
एवं त्रयीधर्ममनुप्रपन्ना
गतागतं कामकामा लभन्ते ॥

te taṁ bhuktvā svargalokaṁ viśālaṁ
kṣīṇe puṇye martyalokaṁ viśanti,
evaṁ trayīdharmamanuprapannā
gatāgataṁ kāmakāmā labhante.

They, having enjoyed the vast heaven-world, when their merits are exhausted enter the world of the mortals; thus abiding by the injunctions of the three (Vedas), desiring (objects of) desires, they attain to the state of 'going and returning'. (9.21)

अनन्याश्चिन्तयन्तो मां ये जनाः पर्युपासते ।
तेषां नित्याभियुक्तानां योगक्षेमं वहाम्यहम् ॥
ananyāścintayanto māṁ ye janāḥ paryupāsate,
teṣāṁ nityābhiyuktānāṁ yogakṣemaṁ vahāmyaham.
To those men who worship Me alone, thinking of no other, to those ever self-controlled, I secure for them that which is not already possessed (yoga) by them, and preserve for them what they already possess (kṣema). (9.22)

येऽप्यन्यदेवता भक्ता यजन्ते श्रद्धयान्विताः ।
तेऽपि मामेव कौन्तेय यजन्त्यविधिपूर्वकम् ॥
ye'pyanyadevatā bhaktā yajante śraddhayānvitāḥ,
te'pi māmeva kaunteya yajantyavidhipūrvakam.
Even those devotees, who endowed with faith worship other gods, worship Me alone, O son of Kuntī, (but) by the wrong method. (9.23)

पत्रं पुष्पं फलं तोयं यो मे भक्त्या प्रयच्छति ।
तदहं भक्त्युपहृतमश्नामि प्रयतात्मनः ॥
patraṁ puṣpaṁ phalaṁ toyaṁ yo me bhaktyā prayacchati,
tadahaṁ bhaktyupahṛtamaśnāmi prayatātmanaḥ.
Whoever offers Me with devotion a leaf, a flower, a fruit, water, that I accept, offered by the pure-minded with devotion. (9.26)

यत्करोषि यदश्नासि यज्जुहोषि ददासि यत् ।
यत्तपस्यसि कौन्तेय तत्कुरुष्व मदर्पणम् ॥
yatkaroṣi yadaśnāsi yajjuhoṣi dadāsi yat,
yattapasyasi kaunteya tatkuruṣva madarpaṇam.
Whatever you do, whatever you eat, whatever you offer in sacrifice, whatever you give, whatever you practise as austerity, O Kaunteya, do it as an offering to Me. (9.27)

समोऽहं सर्वभूतेषु न मे द्वेष्योऽस्ति न प्रियः ।
ये भजन्ति तु मां भक्त्या मयि ते तेषु चाप्यहम् ॥
samo'haṁ sarvabhūteṣu na me dveṣyo'sti na priyaḥ,
ye bhajanti tu māṁ bhaktyā mayi te teṣu cāpyaham.
The same am I to all beings; to Me there is none hateful nor dear; but

those who worship Me with devotion are in Me and I am also in them. (9.29)

अपि चेत्सुदुराचारो भजते मामनन्यभाक् ।
साधुरेव स मन्तव्यः सम्यग्व्यवसितो हि सः ॥

api cetsudurācāro bhajate māmananyabhāk,
sādhureva sa mantavyaḥ samyagvyavasito hi saḥ.

Even if the most sinful worships Me, with devotion to none else, (or with single-pointedness), he too should indeed be regarded as 'righteous', for he has rightly resolved. (9.30)

क्षिप्रं भवति धर्मात्मा शश्वच्छान्तिं निगच्छति ।
कौन्तेय प्रतिजानीहि न मे भक्तः प्रणश्यति ॥

kṣipraṁ bhavati dharmātmā śaśvacchāntiṁ nigacchati,
kaunteya pratijānīhi na me bhaktaḥ praṇaśyati.

Soon he becomes righteous and attains Eternal Peace, O Kaunteya, know for certain that My devotees never perish. (9.31)

मन्मना भव मद्भक्तो मद्याजी मां नमस्कुरु ।
मामेवैष्यसि युक्त्वैवमात्मानं मत्परायणः ॥

manmanā bhava madbhakto madyājī māṁ namaskuru,
māmevaiṣyasi yuktvaivamātmānaṁ matparāyaṇaḥ.

Fix your mind on Me, be devoted to Me, sacrifice to Me, bow down to Me; having thus united your (whole) Self with Me, taking Me as the Supreme Goal, you shall come to Me. (9.34)

10

Vibhūti Yoga

The Yoga of Divine Glories

The world outside is only the Infinite misinterpreted by the finite mind. (10.20)

The tenth chapter is called the 'Vibhūti Yoga' inasmuch as it describes (a) the Power or Lordship and (b) the Pervasiveness or Immanence of the Self. The Self is the Essence in the world of plurality. Therefore, we find Śrī Kṛṣṇa herein indicating Himself both as the most prominent and Chief Factor in all classes of beings and as the Supreme Factor without which specimens belonging to each class cannot maintain themselves as existent beings. In this chapter, Arjuna wants to know how one can constantly keep in touch with the Eternal aspect of Truth, even while perceiving the pluralistic world and transacting with its objects. As an answer to this particular question, the chapter is packed with indications of the joyous Infinite among the joyless finite objects.

Terms and Definitions

1. Distinguish 'jīva' from 'Īśvara'.

In Vedānta, the Self seemingly conditioned by or reflected in or functioning through the individual mind and intellect is the 'jīva' (ego), limited and thwarted by its own imperfections; whereas the same eternal Self conditioned by or reflected in or functioning through the total mind and intellect is the 'Īśvara' (God-principle), unlimited and ever a Master of its own Perfection. (Introduction)

2. Define 'tanmātra'.

When the Infinite is seemingly identified with the Total-intellect or Cosmic-intellect (mahat) and develops thereby an egocentric personality of Its own (ahaṅkāra), It projects Itself, for Its own joy-transactions, as the world of sense objects. These sense objects are called the five tanmātras. These are nothing but the qualities that predominate in each of the five elements; in Ether—the Sound, in

Air—the Touch, in Fire—the Form, in Water—the Taste—and in Earth—the Smell. (10.2)

3. What is 'Avikampa Yoga' (unwavering or steady Yoga)?

The permanent and steady establishment in the experience of the Self is 'Avikampa Yoga' (unwavering Yoga). (10.7)

4. What is 'Buddhi Yoga'?

'Buddhi Yoga' is the right knowledge gained through meditation upon the infinite nature of the Self. (10.10)

5. What does the term 'Keśava' mean?

The term 'Keśava' means one who removes all sorrows of those who have surrendered to Him. (10.14)

6. Who are the 'Maruts'?

'Maruts' are the sons of Rudra and represent the presiding deities of the storms, wind and breeze. Marīci is the chief among the Maruts. (10.21)

7. What is the etymology of the word 'Śaṅkara'?

'Śaṁ karoti iti śaṅkaraḥ—He who does 'kalyāṇa' (śaṁ-welfare) is 'Śaṅkara'. (10.23)

8. What is 'jalpa', 'vitaṇḍa' and 'vāda'?

Jalpa, vitaṇḍa and vāda are the three types of approaches used in all discussions. In 'jalpa', the attempt is to smother the opposition and its arguments by vehement criticism and bitter rejoinders, spoken with an overbearing arrogance in assertions. In the case of 'vitaṇḍa', the champion of discussion mercilessly criticises the arguments of the opposition, exposing by means fair or foul, both the real and the imaginary fallacies in their line of argument the aim being to destroy the edifice built by the other. The third, 'vāda', is the technique of discussion by which the one arguing is trying to read the letter and the verse as directly as possible with the object of coming directly to truth, without indulging in any hair-splitting arguments. Both the former techniques (jalpa and vitaṇḍa) are only strategies to weaken the enemies, while the actual thrust into the enemy lines and the ultimate real conquest is only through 'vāda'. (10.32)

9. What does the term 'kavi' mean?

In the Upaniṣads, the term 'kavi' means a 'seer of the Vedic mantras'. Men of inspiration declaring their experiences without egocentric awareness were called 'kavis'. (10.37)

10. What do the terms 'yoga' and 'vibhūti' mean?

'Yoga' signifies the Lord's expression in the individual. 'Vibhūti' is the description of the Lord's glory as the 'Cosmic Man'. (10.42)

Thoughts and Concepts

1. Explain how the world is a projection of the Total-mind.

I create my world with my mind; you create your world with your mind; and a third person creates his world with his mind. No doubt, into the pool of my world certain aspects and portions of the world of others creep in to overlap for varying periods of time. Philosophically viewed, therefore, the total world of forms and beings is created, sustained and destroyed by the number of minds totally available to cognize and to experience this whole Universe. This Total-mind includes even the rudimentary perceptions of a mind in the plant kingdom, the relatively better-developed minds and intellects of the animal kingdom and also the well-developed mind of man. (Introduction)

2. What does the term 'Sapta Ṛṣi' (Seven Ṛṣis) symbolize?

When the Infinite is seemingly identified with the Cosmic-intellect (mahat) and develops thereby an egocentric personality of Its own (ahaṅkāra), It projects Itself, for Its own joy-transactions, as a world of sense objects. These sense objects are called the five tanmātras. The 'mahat', the 'ahaṅkāra' and the five 'tanmātras' together constitute the 'Sapta Ṛṣi' (Seven Ṛṣis) personified in the Purāṇas. (10.2)

3. What does the term 'deva' signify?

The word 'deva' rises from its root, *'div'*, meaning 'to illumine'. The 'devas', therefore, are the sense organs which illumine for us the world of objects for our innumerable experiences. (10.2)

4. Who is undeluded and liberated from all sins?

The following verse answers the above question:

यो मामजमनादिं च वेत्ति लोकमहेश्वरम् ।
असम्मूढः स मर्त्येषु सर्वपापैः प्रमुच्यते ॥

yo māmajamanādiṁ ca vetti lokamaheśvaram,
asammūḍhaḥ sa martyeṣu sarvapāpaiḥ pramucyate.

He who amongst the mortals knows Me as unborn and beginningless, as the great Lord of the worlds, is undeluded and is liberated from all sins. (10.3)

5. Why is the Self described as 'unborn' and 'beginningless'?

The world of matter is the realm of finitude, where each being or thing or experience has a beginning and an end, a birth and a death. The Infinite cannot ever be born, inasmuch as It never expresses as Itself in any of the finite manifestations. To explain: the ghost is born and therefore it must also die; but it cannot be said either that the post, which is the substratum of the superimposed ghost, has given birth to the ghost or that the post has come to be born out of the ghost. The post was, is and shall ever be.

The Self is Eternal and therefore It is birthless; everything else is born in the Self, exists in the Self, and when all things are totally destroyed, they end in the Self. The waves are born out of the ocean but the ocean is birthless. Every wave, every manifestation, has a beginning, an existence and an end. But the substratum cannot have a beginning and therefore the Self is described as 'unborn' and 'beginningless'. (10.3)

6. What is 'loka'?

The term 'loka' (world) is one of the Sanskrit words that has a vast range of implications. 'Loka' comes from a root meaning 'to experience' and, therefore, the word in its full import means 'a field for experiencing'. In this sense, we make use of the word 'loka' even in ordinary, everyday usage: 'the world of the rich', 'the world of the underdog', 'the world of the poet', etc. In its ampler meaning, the universe, indicated by the word 'loka', is not only the physical world experienced by our physical equipment, but also the world of feelings and the world of ideas recognised, reacted upon and experienced by all of us in our lives. Thus 'my loka' is the 'field of experiences' that I revel in at all levels of my body, mind and intellect. (10.3)

7. Who becomes the 'Lord of the worlds' (*sarva-loka-maheśvara*)?

The moment an individual understands and lives in the Realisation that the Self is unborn and beginningless, and that It is not concerned with decaying and perishable matter, he has gained all that has to be gained and known all that has to be known. Such an individual of true Realisation becomes himself the 'Lord of the worlds'. (10.3)

8. Cite the relevant verses to elucidate that the Lord is the source of all our mental and intellectual abilities.

The Lord being the material cause of the universe is ever the source of all our mental and intellectual abilities. The following verses make explicit mention of this:

बुद्धिर्ज्ञानमसम्मोहः क्षमा सत्यं दमः शमः ।
सुखं दुःखं भवोऽभावो भयं चाभयमेव च ॥

buddhirjñānamasammohaḥ kṣamā satyaṁ damaḥ śamaḥ,
sukhaṁ duḥkhaṁ bhavo'bhāvo bhayaṁ cābhayameva ca.

Intellect, wisdom, non-illusion, forgiveness, truth, self-restraint, calmness, happiness, pain, birth or death, fear and also fearlessness. (10.4)

अहिंसा समता तुष्टिस्तपो दानं यशोऽयशः ।
भवन्ति भावा भूतानां मत्त एव पृथग्विधाः ॥

ahiṁsā samatā tuṣṭistapo dānaṁ yaśo'yaśaḥ,
bhavanti bhāvā bhūtānāṁ matta eva pṛthagvidhāḥ.

Non-injury, equanimity, contentment, austerity, beneficence, fame, infamy – all these different kinds of 'qualities of beings' arise from Me alone. (10.5)

9. What do the four 'Sanatkumāras' symbolize?

It is described in the Purāṇas that Brahma, the Creator, at the very beginning of creation, produced out of his own mind four eternal boys (Kumāras): Sanatkumāra, Sanaka, Sanātana and Sanandana. The Creator in us is the life in us functioning through an 'urge to create' in any field. Whenever the creative urge expresses itself, immediately the factors constituting the subtle-body (antaḥkaraṇa) express themselves and function with full vigour. When the creator of the whole universe comes under the 'urge to express', he has to maintain a constant saṅkalpa, which immediately produces a channel of 'constant thoughts' creating the stuff for the 'inner-instruments'. This 'bundle of thoughts', flowing constantly, functions as the mind, intellect, memory and ego. These four factors, comprising the total inner instrument are represented by the Sanatkumāras (Eternal Boys of Wisdom), born out of the mind of the Creator, at the very beginning of his creative activity. (10.6)

10. Who becomes established in the Supreme Awareness through Avikampa Yoga (unwavering Yoga)?

The following verse answers this question:

एतां विभूतिं योगं च मम यो वेत्ति तत्त्वतः ।
सोऽविकम्पेन योगेन युज्यते नात्र संशयः ॥

etāṁ vibhūtiṁ yogaṁ ca mama yo vetti tattvataḥ,
so'vikampena yogena yujyate nātra saṁśayaḥ.

He who in truth knows these manifold manifestations of my being (Macrocosm) and (this) Yoga-power of Mine (Microcosm) becomes established in the 'unwavering Yoga'; there is no doubt about it.

The difference between the microcosm and the macrocosm is the difference in the equipment through which the same Truth, the Eternal and the All-perfect, expresses. When Life surges through the Cosmic-Mind, It comes to project out the entire Universe of plurality and when the same Infinite expresses through an individual-mind, It projects out the individual world. In both these manifestations—the God-principle (Īśvara) and the individual ego (jīva)—the Essence is one and the same. In Pure Self, in its Essential Nature, there is neither the God-principle nor the ego. He who realises this 'in reality' will become established in the Supreme Awareness through the 'unwavering Yoga'. (10.7)

11. When is devotion fulfilled?

Love or devotion is measured by the capacity of the lover to identify himself with the beloved. In short, love is fulfilled when identification is complete and when the devotee is capable of experiencing in himself that he is none other than the Infinite Self which, functioning through the Cosmic-mind, plays the part of the Īśvara, the Creator, and which, when functioning through an individual mind and intellect equipment, behaves as though It is the jīva, the limited ego. (10.8)

12. Who is a true seeker?

A true seeker is he who maintains in himself a constant remembrance of the Conscious Principle in him—whatever be the activities of the mind or of the sense organs. He maintains this channel of thinking steadily through mutual discussions with fellow seekers and a constant seeking of the Ātman. (10.9)

13. Explain the secret of successful detachment.

Withdrawal of one's identifications with the perceived world of objects or the world of thoughts or the world of ideas can be successful only when one has discovered in oneself some other all-consuming thought to serve as an efficient substitute, yielding a satisfactory quota of absorbing happiness. The Self, which is of the nature of Bliss Absolute, has enough captivating charm to engage the human attention entirely and therefore to the extent to which an individual gets attached to the Truth, to that extent he gains detachment from the painful embrace of the false. (10.10)

14. Cite the relevant verses wherein the Lord declares that He bestows Ātma-jñāna (Self-Knowledge) to his devotees.

In the following two verses the Lord declares that He bestows Self-Knowledge to those who are steadfast in devotion unto Him:

तेषां सततयुक्तानां भजतां प्रीतिपूर्वकम् ।
ददामि बुद्धियोगं तं येन मामुपयान्ति ते ॥

teṣāṁ satatayuktānāṁ bhajatāṁ prītipūrvakam,
dadāmi buddhiyogaṁ taṁ yena māmupayānti te.
To the ever-steadfast, worshipping Me with love, I give the 'Buddhi Yoga' by which they come to Me. (10.10)

तेषामेवानुकम्पार्थमहमज्ञानजं तमः ।
नाशयाम्यात्मभावस्थो ज्ञानदीपेन भास्वता ॥
teṣāmevānukampārthamahamajñānajaṁ tamaḥ,
nāśayāmyātmabhāvastho jñānadīpena bhāsvatā.
Out of mere compassion for them, I, dwelling within their hearts, destroy the darkness born of ignorance by the luminous Lamp of Knowledge. (10.11)

15. Explain the Lord's declaration that He reveals Himself to His devotees out of compassion.

Up to the Savikalpa Samādhi alone is the realm of conscious self-effort, and Realisation comes not as a result of any deliberate action but is a spontaneous revelation when the density of the mist between the ego and the Self is thinned.

When the darkness of ignorance is destroyed by the 'Luminous Lamp of Knowledge', the Self stands revealed in Its own glory as the One without a second, All-pervading and All-full. This act of Self-revelation is undertaken and performed by the Lord, the Self, who ever abides in the heart of his very devotees. This kindly act of revealing the Self is undertaken in a spirit of compassion—in fact, towards Itself. When I am tired of walking, I sit on the roadside in my pilgrimage—out of compassion for myself. (10.11)

16. What are the four requests made by Arjuna to the Lord in the tenth chapter?

Arjuna makes the following four requests to the Lord:
(1) Tell me about Your Divine Glories through which You exist, pervading all these worlds.
(2) How shall I, ever-meditating, know You?
(3) In what aspects or things are You to be thought of by me?
(4) Tell me in detail Your 'yoga-power' and immanent glory.

The following three verses enumerate these four requests of Arjuna:

वक्तुमर्हस्यशेषेण दिव्या ह्यात्मविभूतयः ।
याभिर्विभूतिभिर्लोकानिमांस्त्वं व्याप्य तिष्ठसि ॥

vaktumarhasyaśeṣeṇa divyā hyātmavibhūtayaḥ,
yābhirvibhūtibhirlokānimāṁstvaṁ vyāpya tiṣṭhasi.

You should indeed, without reserve, tell me of Your Divine glories by which You exist, pervading all these worlds. (10.16)

कथं विद्यामहं योगिंस्त्वां सदा परिचिन्तयन् ।
केषु केषु च भावेषु चिन्त्योऽसि भगवन्मया ॥

kathaṁ vidyāmahaṁ yogiṁstvāṁ sadā paricintayan,
keṣu keṣu ca bhāveṣu cintyo'si bhagavanmayā.

How shall I, ever-meditating, know You, O Yogin? In what aspects or things, O Blessed Lord, are You to be thought of by me? (10.17)

विस्तरेणात्मनो योगं विभूतिं च जनार्दन ।
भूयः कथय तृप्तिर्हि शृण्वतो नास्ति मेऽमृतम् ॥

vistareṇātmano yogaṁ vibhūtiṁ ca janārdana,
bhūyaḥ kathaya tṛptirhi śṛṇvato nāsti me'mṛtam.

Tell me again, in detail, O Janārdana, of Your 'yoga-power' and immanent glory; for I do not feel satisfied by hearing Your (life-giving) nectar-like speech. (10.18)

17. Enumerate the 75 Vibhūtis of the Lord.

Verses 21 to 38 of the tenth chapter enumerate the 75 Vibhūtis of the Lord. Herein, Lord Kṛṣṇa provides 75 thoughts to help seekers who are on the path of knowledge, to meditate upon and intensify their integration and sharpen their single-pointedness. These are 75 independent exercises in meditation. (The first person pronoun 'I' herein refers to the Lord).

(1) Among the twelve Ādityas I am Viṣṇu. (10.21)
(2) Among luminaries I am the radiant Sun. (10.21)
(3) Among the Maruts I am Marīci. (10.21)
(4) Among asterisms I am the moon. (10.21)
(5) Among the Vedas I am the Sāma Veda. (10.22)
(6) Among the gods I am Vāsava (Indra). (10.22)

(7) Among the senses I am the mind. (10.22)
(8) Among living beings I am intelligence. (10.22)
(9) Among the Rudras I am Śaṅkara. (10.23)
(10) Among the Yakṣas and Rākṣasas I am Kubera. (10.23)
(11) Among the Vasus I am Agni. (10.23)
(12) Among the mountains I am Meru. (10.23)
(13) Among the household priests, I am Bṛhaspati. (10.24)
(14) Among generals I am Skanda. (10.24)
(15) Among lakes I am the ocean. (10.24)
(16) Among the Maharṣis I am Bṛgu. (10.25)
(17) Among words I am the one-syllabled 'OM'. (10.25)
(18) Among sacrifices I am the sacrifice of silent repetition (Japa Yajña). (10.25)
(19) Among immovable things I am the Himalayas. (10.25)
(20) Among trees I am the Aśvattha-tree. (10.26)
(21) Among the Devarṣis I am Nārada. (10.26)
(22) Among Gandharvas I am Citraratha. (10.26)
(23) Among Siddhas I am Kapila Muni. (10.26)
(24) Among horses I am Ucchaiśravas. (10.27)
(25) Among lordly elephants I am Airāvata. (10.27)
(26) Among men I am the King. (10.27)
(27) Among weapons I am the Vajra (thunderbolt). (10.28)
(28) Among cows I am Kāmadhuk. (10.28)
(29) I am Kandarpa the cause for offspring. (10.28)
(30) Among serpents I am Vāsukī. (10.28)
(31) Among Nāgas I am Ananta. (10.29)
(32) Among water deities I am Varuṇa. (10.29)
(33) Among the ancestors I am Aryamā. (10.29)
(34) Among 'controllers' I am Yama. (10.29)
(35) Among Daityas I am Prahlāda. (10.30)
(36) Among reckoners I am 'Time'. (10.30)
(37) Among animals I am the Lion. (10.30)
(38) Among birds I am Vainateya (Garuḍa). (10.30)
(39) Among purifiers I am the wind. (10.31)

(40) Among warriors I am Rāma. (10.31)
(41) Among fishes I am the shark. (10.31)
(42) Among rivers I am the Ganges. (10.31)
(43) I am the beginning, the middle and the end of creation. (10.32)
(44) Among sciences I am the 'Science of the Self'. (10.32)
(45) I am the logic in all arguments. (10.32)
(46) Among letters I am 'A'. (10.33)
(47) Among all compounds I am the dual. (10.33)
(48) I am inexhaustible time. (10.33)
(49) I am the Dispenser of the fruits of actions. (10.33)
(50) I am all-devouring Death. (10.34)
(51) I am the prosperity of those who are to become prosperous[1]. (10.34)
(52) Among the feminine qualities I am fame. (10.34)
(53) (Among the feminine qualities) I am prosperity. (10.34)
(54) (Among the feminine qualities) I am speech. (10.34)
(55) (Among the feminine qualities) I am memory. (10.34)
(56) (Among the feminine qualities) I am intelligence. (10.34)
(57) (Among the feminine qualities) I am steadfastness. (10.34)
(58) (Among the feminine qualities) I am forgiveness. (10.34)
(59) Among hymns I am the Bṛhatsāman. (10.35)
(60) Among the metres I am Gāyatrī. (10.35)
(61) Among months I am Mārgaśīrṣa (parts of December-January). (10.35)
(62) Among seasons I am the 'flowery spring'. (10.35)
(63) I am the gambling of the fraudulent. (10.36)
(64) I am the splendour of the splendid. (10.36)
(65) I am victory in the victorious. (10.36)
(66) I am industry in the determined. (10.36)
(67) I am the goodness in the good. (10.36)
(68) Among the Vṛṣṇis I am Vāsudeva. (10.37)
(69) Among Pāṇḍavas I am Dhanañjaya. (10.37)
(70) Among the Munis I am Vyāsa. (10.37)

1. 'Also translated as "I am the source of all that is to be."

(71) Among the poets I am Uśanas. (10.37)
(72) Among punishers I am the 'Sceptre'. (10.38)
(73) Among those who seek victory I am 'Statesmanship'. (10.38)
(74) Among secrets I am 'Silence'. (10.38)
(75) Among knowers I am 'Knowledge'. (10.38)

18. Why is 'Śaṅkara' (Lord of destruction) respected and adored?

Destruction is a necessary precedent to every subsequent construction. The flower must die to yield its place to the fruit. The fruit must perish for the seeds to come out. The seeds must rot to bring forth the seedling. Thus, in every progress there is a continuous stream of constructive destruction. The Ṛṣis recognised this and in their full understanding they fearlessly respected and adored the blessed deity of creative destruction—'Śaṅkara'. (10.23)

19. What is the subjective meaning of 'Kāmadhenu'?

Subjectively, 'Kāmadhenu' is nothing other than the saṅkalpa śakti that automatically rises in an individual as he increases the powers of his concentration and gains progress in his inward integration. (10.28)

20. Explain how annihilation is Death's creative art.

The 'Principle of Death' is the governing factor that controls and regulates life, and, at every moment, prepares a field for creative development everywhere. Childhood must die before youth can express itself. One must leave high school in order to enter college. Step by step, one dies in order to be born into the next step. Progress in itself is a partial picture of life; it is only a squint-eyed vision of life's total dynamism. Every development is preceded by destruction. Annihilation, thus contributing to progress, is called 'Death's own creative art'. (10.29)

21. The Lord declares that among all letters He is the letter 'A'. What is the importance of this alphabet 'A'?

Without the help of vowels, words cannot be pronounced. Sanskrit is an extremely sweet language because of the preponderance of the 'A' sound in it. In fact, every letter in its combination is to be pronounced in Sanskrit with the sound of 'A' added to it to lengthen it to its full sweetness. This, as it were, lubricates the words and consequently the language has no back-firing disturbances of rattling nuisance or disgusting hoarseness. Because of this smooth run of the 'A' sound in every letter, there is a melody even between words and a lingering echo between sentences. In fact, after a long chanting of a Sanskrit text in a hall, there is, for the sensitive, a perceptible atmosphere of soothing music in the air that can lull all the agitations of the human mind.

The sound 'A' is not only the essence in each letter of a word—not only does it transcend or overflow the sentences and flood the very atmosphere—but it has itself the first place among the alphabets in all the languages. Realising these implications, the Upaniṣads declare that the 'A' sound is the essence in all speech (*akāro vai sarvā vāk*). (10.33)

22. Explain why of all secret things, the Lord is the deep unbroken 'Silence'.

Secrecy is maintained in and nourished by silence. When a secret is ventilated in open discussions, it is no longer a secret. Thus the very essence of a secret lies in silence. So too, it may be noted that the Knowledge of the Self is described in our textbooks as 'the secret of secrets', because it is not generally known. This great secret is also experienced, and the divine experience is maintained and enjoyed, sustained and nourished, as well as fed and grown, only upon the deep inner silence. Of all secret things, the Lord is the deep and unbroken Silence! (10.38)

23. What is the philosophical significance of the term 'jagat' (world)?

In philosophical usage, the term 'jagat' (world) means all the fields of experience which man has—as a physical body, as a psychological being and as an intellectual entity. This would mean that the 'jagat' is the sum-total of the world perceived by my senses, plus the world of my emotions and sentiments, plus the world of my ideas and ideologies. The entire 'field' that is comprehended by the sense organs, the mind and the intellect is to be understood in its totality as 'jagat'. Literally, 'jagat' means 'that which is ever-changing'. In short, this term embraces in its meaning and import the entire 'realm of objects'. (10.42)

Selections for Reflection

1. Consciousness, being the very Subjective Truth in us, can never become an object of perception for the sense organs or an object of feeling for the mind or an object of knowing for the intellect. (10.2)

2. When one wanders away from one's own Real Nature as the Self, identifies oneself with the happenings of the world and behaves as a mass of repulsive flesh or a bundle of throbbing emotions or a pack of ideas, one is in a manner dishonouring one's Godly dignity and Divine status. Such acts and thoughts chain a person down to a pursuit of the low pleasures only, never allowing him to rise above and climb the higher peaks of real Perfection. (10.3)

3. To the extent the ego identifies with the Self, to that extent is one a devotee of the Truth and when one becomes steadfast in It, one comes really to invoke the Divinity that is now dormant within. (10.10)

4. The self-effulgent Truth, when hidden behind the fumes of ignorance, may, for the time being, appear as though non-existent. When the enveloping ignorance is removed, Its own Self-effulgence is sufficient to illumine it! (10.11)

5. Satsaṅga has a chastening effect upon all intelligent and interested listeners. This intoxication vicariously experienced by the students when a true teacher discourses upon the Truth is only a temporary exhilaration, a passing mood of false peace, which

cannot stand in good stead when the student is left all alone by himself. However volatile it may be, it can enchant the new initiates and some may become addicted to it. Though this is not the end this is a good beginning no doubt, and those who feel a fulfilment in the study of philosophy are certainly much more noble than the thousands who cannot even stand a philosophical discourse discussing the nature of the Divine! (10.18)

6. Unlike anywhere else in the world, in India, the Himalayas have the secret peaks where man sat to thrust his thoughts even beyond the frontiers of his intellect. He did it successfully, as was never before done by any living creature from the beginningless history of the world. (10.25)

7. In India, we worship the terrible, the sad and the tragic also, because to us God is the Substratum for both the good and the bad, for the pleasant and the unpleasant. We are not satisfied by any theory of compromise by which we reject God's association with what we do not like. (10.29)

8. Death, the leveller, brings even the sceptre and the crown to the level of the begging bowl and the staff. After death, the wise and the fool, the good and the bad, the strong and the weak, the ruler and the ruled—all come to dust, levelled into a uniformity that recognises no distinction within itself. (10.34)

Verses for Memorisation

एतां विभूतिं योगं च मम यो वेत्ति तत्त्वतः ।
सोऽविकम्पेन योगेन युज्यते नात्र संशयः ॥

etāṁ vibhūtiṁ yogaṁ ca mama yo vetti tattvataḥ,
so'vikampena yogena yujyate nātra saṁśayaḥ.

He who in truth knows these manifold manifestations of my being (Macrocosm) and (this) Yoga-power of Mine (Microcosm) becomes established in the 'unwavering Yoga'; there is no doubt about it. (10.7)

मच्चित्ता मद्गतप्राणा बोधयन्तः परस्परम् ।
कथयन्तश्च मां नित्यं तुष्यन्ति च रमन्ति च ॥

maccittā madgataprāṇā bodhayantaḥ parasparam,
kathayantaśca māṁ nityaṁ tuṣyanti ca ramanti ca.

With their minds wholly resting in Me, with their senses absorbed in Me, enlightening one another and ever speaking of Me, they are satisfied and delighted. (10.9)

तेषां सततयुक्तानां भजतां प्रीतिपूर्वकम् ।
ददामि बुद्धियोगं तं येन मामुपयान्ति ते ॥

teṣāṁ satatayuktānāṁ bhajatāṁ prītipūrvakam,
dadāmi buddhiyogaṁ taṁ yena māmupayānti te.

To the ever-steadfast, worshipping Me with love, I give the 'Buddhi Yoga' by which they come to Me. (10.10)

तेषामेवानुकम्पार्थमहमज्ञानजं तमः ।
नाशयाम्यात्मभावस्थो ज्ञानदीपेन भास्वता ॥

teṣāmevānukampārthamahamajñānajaṁ tamaḥ,
nāśayāmyātmabhāvastho jñānadīpena bhāsvatā.

Out of mere compassion for them, I, dwelling within their hearts, destroy the darkness born of ignorance by the luminous Lamp of Knowledge. (10.11)

अहमात्मा गुडाकेश सर्वभूताशयस्थितः ।
अहमादिश्च मध्यं च भूतानामन्त एव च ॥

ahamātmā guḍākeśa sarvabhūtāśayasthitaḥ,
ahamādiśca madhyaṁ ca bhūtānāmanta eva ca.

I am the Self, O Guḍākeśa, seated in the hearts of all beings; I am the Beginning, the Middle and also the End of all beings. (10.20)

सर्गाणामादिरन्तश्च मध्यं चैवाहमर्जुन ।
अध्यात्मविद्या विद्यानां वादः प्रवदतामहम् ॥

sargāṇāmādirantaśca madhyaṁ caivāhamarjuna,
adhyātmavidyā vidyānāṁ vādaḥ pravadatāmaham.

Among creations, I am the beginning, the middle and also the end, O Arjuna; among sciences I am the Science of the Self and I am the logic in all arguments. (10.32)

यद्यद्विभूतिमत्सत्त्वं श्रीमदूर्जितमेव वा ।
तत्तदेवावगच्छ त्वं मम तेजोंशसम्भवम् ॥

yadyadvibhūtimatsattvaṁ śrīmadūrjitameva vā,
tattadevāvagaccha tvaṁ mama tejoṁśasambhavam.

Whatever it is that is glorious, prosperous or powerful in any being, know that to be a manifestation of a part of My splendour. (10.41)

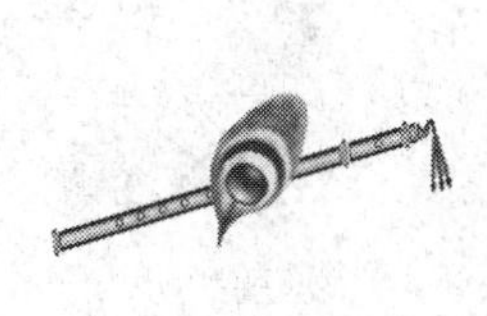

11

Viśvarūpa Darśana Yoga

The Yoga of the Vision of the Universal Form

To Realise the unity in the diversity is to get an inoculation against the sorrows of plurality. (11.1)

The tenth chapter has supplied enough data to prove that the Self is the substratum for the multiple world. In the 11th chapter, the attempt is to supply Arjuna with a practical demonstration that everything does exist only in the Self. The Lord shows Arjuna a vision wherein he sees in the Kṛṣṇa-form the entire Universe compressed and packed. Having seen the form, Arjuna gets completely converted both in his faith and in his understanding.

In this chapter, we find how the exquisite dramatist in Vyāsa has squeezed the Sanskrit language dry to feed the beauty of his literary masterpiece. Apart from the chosen words and the mellifluous phrases, every metrical dexterity is being employed here, as an effective strategy to heighten the dramatic situation and to paint clearly the emotions of wonderment, amazement, fear, reverence, devotion, etc., in Arjuna. Altogether, in the dignity of concept, in the beauty of diction, in the artistry of its depiction and in its inner stream of drama, this chapter has been rightly upheld by all as one of the highest philosophical poems in the world's treasure-house of Sacred Books.

Terms and Definitions

1. What are the characteristic features of Īśvara, the God-principle?

The characteristic features of the Īśvara (God-principle) are omnipotence, infinite wisdom, strength, virtue and splendour. (11.3)

2. What does the term 'Viṣṇu' signify?

The term 'Viṣṇu' appears in Vedic literature, where it is used in its etymological meaning as 'one having long strides'. The measure between the two feet when one walks is called the 'stride' (or reach).

The stride of a child is short, when compared with the stride of a man. The All-pervading Infinite, if it were to take its longest stride, would be from the 'beginningless' to the 'endless'. Thus, the term 'Viṣṇu' has the implication 'the All-pervading, the All-reaching'. (11.24)

3. Differentiate 'sat' from 'asat'.

The entire world of things and beings that exist can fall under two categories: 'manifest' (sat) and 'unmanifest' (asat). 'Sat' or the 'manifest' is that which can become objects of experience for the organs of perception, for the instrument of feeling and the equipment of thought. Thus all perceptions, feelings and thoughts fall under the category of 'sat' or 'manifest'. The 'asat' or the 'unmanifest' is the vāsanās, which causes the perceptions, feelings and thoughts. (11.37)

4. What does the term 'viśva' mean?

The Sanskrit term 'viśva' includes not only the physical universe but also the entire world of perceptions, the whole field of emotions and the total realms of thought. This totality of the world of experience through the body, mind and intellect together is indicated by the term 'viśva'. (11.38)

5. What does the term 'śaśāṇka' signify?

'Śaśāṇka'—literally means the 'hare-marked'. This name has been coined for the 'moon' as a rabbit-like-form is seen as a patch on the moon's face. (11.39)

6. Why does the term 'Viśva-rūpa' indicate 'Virāṭ-rūpa'?

'Viśva', in Vedānta, is the Self which identifies with the individual physical body and comes to experience the waking state. When the same Self identifies Itself with the total physical gross bodies of the Universe, it is called the Cosmic Virāṭa. The Lord showed His 'Cosmic Form' or 'Virāṭ-rūpa' to Arjuna. Thus the term 'Viśva-rūpa' used in the eleventh chapter is actually what in Vedānta is termed the 'Virāṭ-rūpa'. (Epilogue)

Thoughts and Concepts

1. Describe briefly the concept of the Cosmic Man.

That which separates one object from another and one individual from another individual is the intervening space. Thus it is the concept of space that divides the physical structures into independent islands. If the concept of space is totally blotted out, all objects will immediately come together into a happy embrace and will represent themselves as one congenial, homogeneous whole. And, in this mass of things, there must be all the shapes and forms of all the things of this world at one and the same place and time. This is the concept of the Cosmic Man: the vision of the world, when viewed by a mind in which the concept of time and space has dried up! (Introduction)

2. Cite the relevant verse wherein the Lord bestows Arjuna with the 'divya-cakṣu' (divine-eye).

In the following verse we have the mention of the Lord bestowing Arjuna with the 'divya-cakṣu':

न तु मां शक्यसे द्रष्टुमनेनैव स्वचक्षुषा ।
दिव्यं ददामि ते चक्षुः पश्य मे योगमैश्वरम् ॥

na tu māṁ śakyase draṣṭumanenaiva svacakṣuṣā,
divyaṁ dadāmi te cakṣuḥ paśya me yogamaiśvaram.

But you are not able to behold Me with these your own eyes; I give you the divine-eye; behold My lordly Yoga. (11.8)

3. Explain the term 'divya-cakṣu' (divine-eye).

It is relatively easy to see the one cause as the very core of all individual effects of names and forms; but the reverse of it—'to discover the many in the one', is the work of a subtle intellect functioning through right philosophical understanding. To see 'the one in the many' is the work of a 'heart' soaked with faith; but to perceive 'the many in the one', besides the 'heart', an educated 'intellect' that has learnt to see for itself the logic of the philosophers is required. This 'vision of the intellect' to comprehend 'the many in the one' is termed 'divya-cakṣu' or 'divine eye'. (11.8)

4. How does Sañjaya describe to Dhṛtarāṣṭra the wonderful glory of the Cosmic Form?

In the following verses Sañjaya describes to Dhṛtarāṣṭra the glory of the Cosmic Form:

अनेकवक्त्रनयनमनेकाद्भुतदर्शनम् ।
अनेकदिव्याभरणं दिव्यानेकोद्यतायुधम् ॥

anekavaktranayanamanekādbhutadarśanam,
anekadivyābharaṇaṁ divyānekodyatāyudham.

With numerous mouths and eyes, with numerous wonderful sights, with numerous divine ornaments, with numerous divine weapons uplifted (such a form He showed). (11.10)

दिव्यमाल्याम्बरधरं दिव्यगन्धानुलेपनम् ।
सर्वाश्चर्यमयं देवमनन्तं विश्वतोमुखम् ॥

divyamālyāmbaradharaṁ divyagandhānulepanam,
sarvāścaryamayaṁ devamanantaṁ viśvatomukham.

Wearing divine garlands (necklaces) and apparel, anointed with divine unguents, the All-wonderful, Resplendent, Endless, facing all sides. (11.11)

दिवि सूर्यसहस्रस्य भवेद्युगपदुत्थिता ।
यदि भाः सदृशी सा स्याद्भासस्तस्य महात्मनः ॥

divi sūryasahasrasya bhavedyugapadutthitā,
yadi bhāḥ sadṛśī sā syādbhāsastasya mahātmanaḥ.

If the splendour of a thousand suns were to blaze all at once (simultaneously) in the sky, that would be like the splendour of that Mighty Being. (11.12)

5. What do the conch, discus, club and lotus in Lord Viṣṇu's hands symbolise?

The four-armed Viṣṇu carries in his hands the Conch, the Discus, the Club and the Lotus. The Lotus represents 'peace and joy, auspiciousness and happiness'. The Conch blows and calls man to duty; and if there be a generation of men who listen not to the Higher-call in themselves – restlessness, war, pestilence, famine, storms and chaotic social and communal disturbances visit them – the Club descends to hammer the generation to shape and discipline. Even after this punishment, if there be a generation so totally dissipated that it cannot improve, then comes the Discus—the sharp-toothed wheel, ever revolving, the Whirling of Time (kāla-cakra) to annihilate the irredeemable generation. (11.17)

6. Explain why the Infinite is described by Arjuna as being endowed with endless arms and of having the sun and the moon as Its eyes?

The term 'infinite arms' means that the Supreme Self, as the dynamic life, is the one essential strength behind every hand that acts and achieves.

The 'principle of light' is the very 'principle' in the eye. If the 'principle of light' were not to bless the objects of form, the instruments of cognition – the eyes – could not have functioned at all. The 'principle of light' is described as the pair of eyes in the Cosmic Form of the Lord. The sun and the moon represent this 'principle of light'. Therefore, in the technical language of Vedānta, it has been aptly described that the sun and the moon are the Lord's eyes. (11.19)

7. The entire human world can be brought under three heads: the 'sub-normal' the 'normal' and the 'super-normal'. Explain these three categories.

The 'sub-normal' are so miserably unaware of the very process of death that they do not at all revolt against it. They are the victims of death and they unconsciously die away.

The 'normal' dread when they intelligently observe and become aware of the process of decay and death. They become apprehensive of their own fate, and failing to realise that nothing is lost by death, they, in their ignorance, shudder at the inescapable lot of all living names and forms.

When bubbles are broken, there is no occasion to regret for those who know what they are and how they are born. The 'super-normal' men have sufficient apprehension of the Totality and Its behaviour, and are not at all perturbed by the thought that death will visit them also one day. (11.21)

8. What qualifies as 'complete philosophy'?

The world is a combination of the beautiful and the ugly, the good and the bad, the soft and the hard, the sweet and the bitter. The Lord has Himself become all these and, therefore, no adoration of the Lord or estimate of the Reality will be complete, if, according to our taste, we recognise only His beautiful, good, soft and sweet aspects. An unprejudiced and detached mind will have to recognise Him as the ugly and the bad, the hard and the bitter also. That philosophy alone is complete which points out that the Supreme is, in fact, in Its Absolute Nature, beyond all these qualities. (11.27)

9. Explain the following verse which uses the analogy of torrential rivers gushing towards the ocean to describe the many heroes of the war entering the Lord's flaming mouth.

यथा नदीनां बहवोऽम्बुवेगाः
समुद्रमेवाभिमुखा द्रवन्ति ।
तथा तवामी नरलोकवीरा
विशन्ति वक्त्राण्यभिविज्वलन्ति ॥

yathā nadīnāṁ bahavo'mbuvegāḥ
samudramevābhimukhā dravanti,
tathā tavāmī naralokavīrā
viśanti vaktrāṇyabhivijvalanti.

Verily, as many torrents of rivers flow towards the ocean, so these heroes in the world of men enter Your flaming mouths.

Each river has its own distinct personality, gathered from the nature and condition of the terrain through which it has flowed. However, all rivers reach the one ocean. At no point does any river pause or hesitate to gush forward. An observer with limited powers of understanding may say that each drop of water in its flow in the river is moving towards a known point down on its way; but, to a true observer, all rivers flow towards the ocean and they cannot, and will not, stop until they reach the ocean, having reached which, all distinctions end. Each drop of water in the river comes from the ocean—in the form of a cloud it reached the mountains, and there in the form of rain it manifested. Watering the lands on the banks and supplying life and nourishment to the fields, rivers gush down in their torrential haste to the very basin from which they took off on this 'mercy flight'. Similarly, from the 'Totality' individuals have come to serve and nourish the culture and to contribute to the beauty of the world…and yet, on their pilgrimage none of them can pause even for a moment en route. All must rush towards the Source from which they arose. The river loses nothing by reaching the ocean. So too individuals are fulfilled when they become one with the Infinite. (11.28)

10. Why does Arjuna use the additional analogy of 'moths rushing hurriedly into a blazing fire' after giving the analogy of 'rivers rushing towards the ocean'?

The essential oneness between the manifest that has come out of the Unmanifest, and the very Unmanifest which is the womb of every manifestation, has been beautifully brought out by the picture of the river that has risen from the ocean and is, in all haste, rushing down only to lose its very name and form and become one with the ocean. But the picture of the river does not show any intrinsic conscious effort on the part of the river to reach the ocean. One may doubt that the living kingdom, with its own free discrimination, would act as the inert waters of the river. To show that even sentient beings are irresistibly drawn towards the mouth of their own destruction, by the whipping hand of instinct, the example of 'the moths precipitately rushing into the blazing fire to perish' is given. (11.29)

11. Why does Śrī Kṛṣṇa show Arjuna the vision of destruction of warriors?

Arjuna's mental tension was mainly created by his hasty evaluation of the enormous destruction he would be causing in the battle-field of Kurukṣetra. Śrī Kṛṣṇa had to cure him, by lifting him to heights from which he could witness and realise, in one sweeping gaze, the unavoidable phenomenon of death. As the river hastens to the ocean, as the moths into the fire, so too all names and forms must, and most irresistibly do, rush towards the unmanifest. With this realisation, Arjuna's apprehension that he would be the cause of everyone's death is allayed. (11.29)

12. Explain how the perception of 'continuity of existence' is an illusion.

In a cinema show, the various frames of the film are made to run on in front of the arc-lights, and each picture that has passed away from the arc-light may be considered dead, and those reaching the arc-light as those that are born. The continuity in these two series of happenings of births and deaths, or constructions and destructions, gives us the hallucination of a logical sequence in the theme revealed on the screen. Conditioned by 'place and time', things and beings, happenings and circumstances come and go in the plane of our experiences and their continuity – what we experience as 'existence' – is a mere illusion. (11.30)

13. In the following verse Śrī Kṛṣṇa mentions specifically that Droṇa, Bhīṣma, Karṇa and Jayadratha—as having been already killed by him. Why is a special mention made of these four warriors?

द्रोणं च भीष्मं च जयद्रथं च
कर्णं तथान्यानपि योधवीरान्।
मया हतांस्त्वं जहि मा व्यथिष्ठा
युध्यस्व जेतासि रणे सपत्नान्॥

droṇaṁ ca bhīṣmaṁ ca jayadrathaṁ ca
karṇaṁ tathānyānapi yodhavīrān,
mayā hatāṁstvaṁ jahi mā vyathiṣṭhā
yudhyasva jetāsi raṇe sapatnān.

Droṇa, Bhīṣma, Jayadratha, Karṇa and other brave warriors – those have already been slain by Me; you do kill; be not distressed with fear; fight and you shall conquer your enemies in battle.

Droṇa was Arjuna's teacher who taught him the art of archery. The Ācārya had with him some special weapons and he was particularly revered and respected by Arjuna. The grandsire Bhīṣma had his death at his command, and he too had very powerful celestial weapons. Once in the past Bhīṣma had defeated even the great Paraśurāma. Jayadratha was invincible; for his father, who was engaged in austerity, had firmly resolved that whoever causes his son's head to drop down on earth, his head too shall fall. Karṇa also had a powerful missile given to him by Indra. These four names are particularly enumerated by the Lord in the list of personalities that Time had already devastated, for Arjuna had reason to be particularly afraid of them. (11.34)

14. Cite the verses of the 11th chapter that constitute the universal prayer.

Stanzas 36 to 44 represent the perfect universal prayer that we have in all the religious literature of the world. There cannot be any creed or caste which has any objection to these, inasmuch as they summarise the entire galaxy of philosophic thoughts regarding the Eternal.

स्थाने हृषीकेश तव प्रकीर्त्या
जगत्प्रहृष्यत्यनुरज्यते च ।
रक्षांसि भीतानि दिशो द्रवन्ति
सर्वे नमस्यन्ति च सिद्धसङ्घाः ॥

sthāne hṛṣīkeśa tava prakīrtyā
jagatprahṛṣyatyanurajyate ca,
rakṣāṁsi bhītāni diśo dravanti
sarve namasyanti ca siddhasaṅghāḥ.

It is but meet, O Hṛṣīkeśa (Śrī Kṛṣṇa), that the world delights and rejoices in Thy praise; Rākṣasas fly in fear to all quarters, and all hosts of Siddhas bow to Thee. (11.36)

कस्माच्च ते न नमेरन्महात्मन्
गरीयसे ब्रह्मणोऽप्यादिकर्त्रे ।
अनन्त देवेश जगन्निवास
त्वमक्षरं सदसत्तत्परं यत् ॥

kasmācca te na nameranmahātman
garīyase brahmaṇo'pyādikartre,
ananta deveśa jagannivāsa
tvamakṣaraṁ sadasattatparaṁ yat.

And why should they not, O Great-souled One, bow to Thee, greater (than all else), the Primal Cause even of Brahma, O Infinite Being, O Lord of Lords, O Abode of the Universe, You are the Imperishable, that which is beyond both the manifest and the unmanifest. (11.37)

त्वमादिदेवः पुरुषः पुराणः
त्वमस्य विश्वस्य परं निधानम् ।
वेत्तासि वेद्यं च परं च धाम
त्वया ततं विश्वमनन्तरूप ॥

tvamādidevaḥ puruṣaḥ purāṇaḥ
tvamasya viśvasya paraṁ nidhānam,
vettāsi vedyaṁ ca paraṁ ca dhāma
tvayā tataṁ viśvamanantarūpa.

You are the Primal God, the Ancient Puruṣa; You are the Supreme Refuge of this universe. You are the knower, the knowable, and the Abode-Supreme. By Thee is the universe pervaded, O Being of Infinite forms. (11.38)

वायुर्यमोऽग्निर्वरुणः शशाङ्कः
प्रजापतिस्त्वं प्रपितामहश्च ।
नमो नमस्तेऽस्तु सहस्रकृत्वः
पुनश्च भूयोऽपि नमो नमस्ते ॥

vāyuryamo'gnirvaruṇaḥ śaśāṅkaḥ
prajāpatistvaṁ prapitāmahaśca,
namo namaste'stu sahasrakṛtvaḥ
punaśca bhūyo'pi namo namaste.

You are Vāyu, Yama, Agni, Varuṇa, the Moon, Prajāpati and the great-grandfather of all. Salutations! Salutations unto You a thousand times and again Salutations unto You! (11.39)

नमः पुरस्तादथ पृष्ठतस्ते
नमोऽस्तु ते सर्वत एव सर्व ।
अनन्तवीर्यामितविक्रमस्त्वं
सर्वं समाप्नोषि ततोऽसि सर्वः ॥

namaḥ purastādatha pṛṣṭhataste
namo'stu te sarvata eva sarva,
anantavīryāmitavikramastvaṁ
sarvaṁ samāpnoṣi tato'si sarvaḥ.

Salutations to You, before and behind! Salutations to You on every side! O All! You, Infinite in Power and Infinite in Prowess, pervade all; wherefore You are the All. (11.40)

सखेति मत्वा प्रसभं यदुक्तं
हे कृष्ण हे यादव हे सखेति ।
अजानता महिमानं तवेदं
मया प्रमादात्प्रणयेन वापि ॥

sakheti matvā prasabhaṁ yaduktaṁ
he kṛṣṇa he yādava he sakheti,
ajānatā mahimānaṁ tavedaṁ
mayā pramādātpraṇayena vāpi.

Whatever I have rashly said from carelessness or love, addressing You as "O Kṛṣṇa, O Yādava, O Friend", and regarding You merely as a friend, unknowing of this Your greatness. (11.41)

यच्चावहासार्थमसत्कृतोऽसि
विहारशय्यासनभोजनेषु ।
एकोऽथवाप्यच्युत तत्समक्षं
तत्क्षामये त्वामहमप्रमेयम् ॥

yaccāvahāsārthamasatkṛto'si
vihāraśayyāsanabhojaneṣu,
eko'thavāpyacyuta tatsamakṣaṁ
tatkṣāmaye tvāmahamaprameyam.

In whatever way I may have insulted You for the sake of fun, while at play, reposing or sitting, or at meals, when alone (with You), O Acyuta, or in company—that, O Immeasurable One, I implore You to forgive. (11.42)

पितासि लोकस्य चराचरस्य
त्वमस्य पूज्यश्च गुरुर्गरीयान् ।
न त्वत्समोऽस्त्यभ्यधिकः कुतोऽन्यो
लोकत्रयेऽप्यप्रतिमप्रभाव ॥

pitāsi lokasya carācarasya
tvamasya pūjyaśca gururgarīyān,
na tvatsamo'styabhyadhikaḥ kuto'nyo
lokatraye'pyapratimaprabhāva.

You are the Father of this world, moving and unmoving. You are to be adored by this world. You are the greatest Guru, (for) there exists none who is equal to You; how can there be then another, superior to You in the three worlds, O Being of unequalled power? (11.43)

तस्मात्प्रणम्य प्रणिधाय कायं
प्रसादये त्वामहमीशमीड्यम् ।
पितेव पुत्रस्य सखेव सख्युः
प्रियः प्रियायार्हसि देव सोढुम् ॥

tasmātpraṇamya praṇidhāya kāyaṁ
prasādaye tvāmahamīśamīḍyam,
piteva putrasya sakheva sakhyuḥ
priyaḥ priyāyārhasi deva soḍhum.

Therefore, bowing down, prostrating my body, I crave your forgiveness, adorable Lord. As a father forgives his son, a friend his friend, a lover his beloved, even so should You forgive me, O Deva. (11.44)

15. How is the Self the Primal God?

The Self is the Supreme Creator. The Pure Consciousness is the womb from which even the Creator has risen. This Pure Consciousness, the Self, conditioned by Its own creative urge, plays the part of the Creator, the 'Primal God'. (11.38)

16. Explain the symbolism of Lord Viṣṇu's form and his various physical attributes.

The four hands of the God-form represent the four facets of the 'inner-instrument' in man: mind (manas), intellect (buddhi), memory (citta) and the ego-sense (ahaṅkāra).

The Lord Himself, the Self, who wields these four hands is represented everywhere as blue in colour, and clothed in yellow. Blue is the colour of the Infinite; the measureless always appears as blue, just as the summer-sky or the deep-ocean. Yellow is the colour of the earth. Thus the Infinite, clothed in the finite, playing the game of life through the four 'inner-instruments' is the symbolism behind Lord Viṣṇu.

The concept of God in every religion is the same inasmuch as He is the Supreme-most with every power and all knowledge. Man achieves things by the strength of His hands and the Lord, who is all-powerful, can therefore be symbolised only by showing that He has four hands.

The four symbolic instruments which the Lord is represented as carrying in His four hands are the club, the discus, the conch and the lotus. The call of the Divine comes to everyone when He blows His conch, and if man were not to listen to the call of the Higher dictates in himself, the club follows to punch him; in spite of that, if man continues his own mistakes, the discus chops him down. In case the roar of the 'conch' is obeyed implicitly, then he gains the lotus, a flower that represents peace, prosperity and spiritual perfection. (11.46)

17. What is the form in which Arjuna wants the Lord to appear after having the vision of the 'Universal Form'?

The following verse answers the question:

किरीटिनं गदिनं चक्रहस्तं
इच्छामि त्वां द्रष्टुमहं तथैव ।
तेनैव रूपेण चतुर्भुजेन
सहस्रबाहो भव विश्वमूर्ते ॥

kirīṭinaṁ gadinaṁ cakrahastaṁ
icchāmi tvāṁ draṣṭumahaṁ tathaiva,
tenaiva rūpeṇa caturbhujena
sahasrabāho bhava viśvamūrte.

I desire to see You as before, crowned, bearing a mace, with a discus in hand, in Your Former Form only, having four arms, O Thousand-armed, O Universal Form[1]. (11.46)

18. What does Śrī Kṛṣṇa's declaration that His Universal Form has not been seen by anybody else other than Arjuna mean?

The Lord's declaration that His Universal Form has not been seen by anybody else means that the intellectual realisation of the Universal Oneness has not been gained by anyone placed in the same

1. A question arises in this verse: when Arjuna says, *"tenaiva rūpeṇa caturbhujena"*, it is implied that he has seen the Lord having four arms before. If so, when did he see this form? This can be reconciled in the following way:

circumstances as those of Arjuna in the war-front. Mentally shattered, physically worn-out, emotionally upset—the miserable condition of Arjuna and this Arjuna-state of utter despondency are, in fact, far removed from the favourable conditions for a single-pointed intellectual quest, without which the underlying Principle of Oneness in the multiplicity of the gross world cannot easily be comprehended. But Śrī Kṛṣṇa had, due to his tremendous powers, given the required 'eye of wisdom' to Arjuna and made him realise, in a chance moment of mental pause, the vision of the Cosmic Form. (11.47)

19. Cite the relevant verse wherein Lord Kṛṣṇa declares that His Cosmic Form can be known only by those with single-minded devotion.

The following verse declares that the Cosmic Form of the Lord can only be see by those endowed with single-minded devotion:

भक्त्या त्वनन्यया शक्य अहमेवंविधोऽर्जुन ।
ज्ञातुं द्रष्टुं च तत्त्वेन प्रवेष्टुं च परन्तप ॥

bhaktyā tvananyayā śakya ahamevaṁvidho'rjuna,
jñātuṁ draṣṭuṁ ca tattvena praveṣṭuṁ ca parantapa.

But, by single-minded devotion can I, of this form, be known and seen in reality and also entered into, O Parantapa (O scorcher of your foes)! (11.54)

20. What are the three stages in which Realisation dawns?

The three stages in which Realisation of Truth comes to man are indicated when the Lord says: 'to know, to see and to enter'. A definite intellectual knowledge of the goal and the path is the beginning of a

(1) Before the Lord revealed His Cosmic-Form, He should have shown the four-armed form of Viṣṇu. In the 50th verse, it is said that the Lord appeared again in His normal form, (*bhūyaḥ svakaṁ rūpaṁ darśayāmāsa*) and also that the Lord appeared in His gentle form (*punaḥ saumyavapurmahātmā*). Thus we come to know that the Lord had shown the four-armed form of Viṣṇu just before he assumed the Viśvarūpa.

(2) Arjuna might have heard that when the Lord was born to Devaki, He appeared with the four-armed form of Viṣṇu with Discus, Conch and Crown, etc.

(3) By seeing the Cosmic Form, Arjuna realises that He is none other than the Supreme Lord Viṣṇu.

seeker's pilgrimage—'to know'. Next comes the seeker's attempt to ruminate over the ideas intellectually understood through his personal reflections, based upon the information he has already gathered—'to see'. Having thus 'known' and 'seen' the goal, thereafter, the seeker, through a process of detachment from the false and attachment to the Real, comes to experience the Truth as no object other than himself—'to enter'. The term 'entering' also indicates that the fulfilled seeker becomes the very essence of the sought. The dreamer, suffering from the sorrows of the dream, ends it all when he no more 'knows' or 'sees', but 'enters' the waking-state, himself to become the waker. (11.54)

21. What are the conditions required for a seeker to attain the Lord?

The conditions required of a seeker to attain the Lord are:

(1) dedicating all work unto the Lord

(2) keeping the Lord as one's goal

(3) being a devotee of the Lord

(4) being free from all attachments and

(5) being devoid of all sense of enmity towards anyone.

These conditions are made amply clear in the following verse:

मत्कर्मकृन्मत्परमो मद्भक्तः सङ्गवर्जितः ।
निर्वैरः सर्वभूतेषु यः स मामेति पाण्डव ॥

matkarmakṛnmatparamo madbhaktaḥ saṅgavarjitaḥ,
nirvairaḥ sarvabhūteṣu yaḥ sa māmeti pāṇḍava.

He who does actions for Me, who looks upon Me as the Supreme, who is devoted to Me, who is free from attachment, who bears enmity towards none, he comes to Me, O Pāṇḍava (11.55)

Selections for Reflection

1. Śrī Kṛṣṇa did not transform Himself into His Cosmic Form, but He only helped Arjuna to make the necessary inward adjustments so that he could perceive what was there evidently in Śrī Kṛṣṇa. (11.5)

2. The concept of the Cosmic Man is the vision of the Universe through a mind that has ceased to act with the concept of time or space. This vision of 'the many in one' is not so much a physical perception as an intellectual comprehension. (11.13)

3. No authority or effectiveness in life is possible unless the man in power has self-control and self-mastery. No man can live a happy and mighty life unless he has conquered his passions and crowned himself with kingship over himself. (11.17)

4. The eternal Truth is one and the same, everywhere, at all times; only Its manifestations are varied and the degree of Divinity sparkling from each differs according to the grossness or subtlety of the equipment through which the same Infinite Reality expresses Itself. (11.17)

5. Each man sees the world as he himself is. We look at the world through the windows of our mind; as our mind is, so is the world to us. (11.20)

6. When man is threatened with a sure mishap, and when he knows of no remedy or defence against it, he in his despair, always turns to prayer. (11.21)

7. In a condition of extreme wonderment, the astounded mortal comes to realise that his physical might, his mental capacities and his intellectual subtleties are all, both individually and in their aggregate, unimportant vehicles indeed. The little ego drops its veil of vanity and its armour of false strength and stands naked, meekly surrendering itself to the influence of the Cosmic Power. Prayer is the only resort of the individual, who has thus fully realised the emptiness of his vanities in the presence of the Mighty-Total and the Supreme-Divine. (11.25)

8. That terrible-looking monstrous happening called 'death', when approached in a correct perspective and with true understanding, unmasks itself to reveal a gladdening cheerful face. (11.29)

9. To every thinking man, the truth is obvious that in life he is at best only an instrument in His hands. However, we are not generally ready to accept this proposition because the self-arrogating ego-sense in us will not easily retire, so as to allow the Divine in us to play out in all its omnipotence. (11.34)

10. The world overwhelms the ego. To the extent the ego is surrendered in the awareness of the greater and the nobler, to that extent, the entire world and achievements therein become a game of simple and sure success everywhere. (11.34)

11. Wherever there is an incentive to act, or a capacity to achieve, it is all a ray of His infinite potentiality. (11.40)

12. The bed of peace and tranquillity upon which the inner personality of man can revive and grow into its fuller stature is the glorious Form of the Lord. (11.46)

13. Love for all and hatred for none can be considered the Gītā 'touch-stone' to know the quality of Realisation and intensity of experience a seeker has gained through his sādhana. (11.55)

Verses for Memorisation

न तु मां शक्यसे द्रष्टुमनेनैव स्वचक्षुषा ।
दिव्यं ददामि ते चक्षुः पश्य मे योगमैश्वरम् ॥

na tu māṁ śakyase draṣṭumanenaiva svacakṣuṣā,
divyaṁ dadāmi te cakṣuḥ paśya me yogamaiśvaram.

But you are not able to behold Me with these your own eyes; I give you the divine-eye; behold My lordly Yoga. (11.8)

दिवि सूर्यसहस्रस्य भवेद्युगपदुत्थिता ।
यदि भाः सदृशी सा स्याद्भासस्तस्य महात्मनः ॥

divi sūryasahasrasya bhavedyugapadutthitā,
yadi bhāḥ sadṛśī sā syādbhāsastasya mahātmanaḥ.

If the splendour of a thousand suns was to blaze all at once (simultaneously) in the sky, that would be like the splendour of that Mighty Being. (11.12)

तत्रैकस्थं जगत्कृत्स्नं प्रविभक्तमनेकधा ।
अपश्यद्देवदेवस्य शरीरे पाण्डवस्तदा ॥

tatraikastham jagatkṛtsnam pravibhaktamanekadhā,
apaśyaddevadevasya śarīre pāṇḍavastadā.

There, in the body of the God of gods, the Pāṇḍava (Son of Pāṇḍu) then saw the whole Universe resting in one, with all its infinite parts. (11.13)

अनेकबाहूदरवक्त्रनेत्रं
पश्यामि त्वां सर्वतोऽनन्तरूपम् ।
नान्तं न मध्यं न पुनस्तवादिं
पश्यामि विश्वेश्वर विश्वरूप ॥

anekabāhūdaravaktranetraṁ
paśyāmi tvāṁ sarvato'nantarūpam,
nāntaṁ na madhyaṁ na punastavādiṁ
paśyāmi viśveśvara viśvarūpa.

I see Thee of boundless form on every side, with manifold arms, stomachs, mouths and eyes; neither the end nor the middle nor also the beginning do I see; O, Lord of the Universe, O, Cosmic Form. (11.16)

त्वमक्षरं परमं वेदितव्यं
त्वमस्य विश्वस्य परं निधानम् ।
त्वमव्ययः शाश्वतधर्मगोप्ता
सनातनस्त्वं पुरुषो मतो मे ॥

tvamakṣaraṁ paramaṁ veditavyaṁ
tvamasya viśvasya paraṁ nidhānam,
tvamavyayaḥ śāśvatadharmagoptā
sanātanastvaṁ puruṣo mato me.

You are the Imperishable, the Supreme Being worthy to be known. You are the great treasure-house of this universe. You are the imperishable Protector of the Eternal Dharma. In my opinion, You are the ancient Puruṣa. (11.18)

यथा नदीनां बहवोऽम्बुवेगाः
समुद्रमेवाभिमुखा द्रवन्ति ।
तथा तवामी नरलोकवीरा
विशन्ति वक्त्राण्यभिविज्वलन्ति ॥

yathā nadīnāṁ bahavo'mbuvegāḥ
samudramevābhimukhā dravanti,
tathā tavāmī naralokavīrā
viśanti vaktrāṇyabhivijvalanti.

Verily, as many torrents of rivers flow towards the ocean, so these heroes in the world of men enter Your flaming mouths. (11.28)

यथा प्रदीप्तं ज्वलनं पतङ्गा
विशन्ति नाशाय समृद्धवेगाः ।
तथैव नाशाय विशन्ति लोकाः
तवापि वक्त्राणि समृद्धवेगाः ॥

yathā pradīptaṁ jvalanaṁ pataṅgā
viśanti nāśāya samṛddhavegāḥ,
tathaiva nāśāya viśanti lokāḥ
tavāpi vaktrāṇi samṛddhavegāḥ.

As moths rush hurriedly into a blazing fire for their own destruction, so also these creatures hastily rush into Your mouths for destruction. (11.29)

कालोऽस्मि लोकक्षयकृत्प्रवृद्धो
लोकान्समाहर्तुमिह प्रवृत्तः ।
ऋतेऽपि त्वां न भविष्यन्ति सर्वे
येऽवस्थिताः प्रत्यनीकेषु योधाः ॥

kālo'smi lokakṣayakṛtpravṛddho
lokānsamāhartumiha pravṛttaḥ,
ṛte'pi tvāṁ na bhaviṣyanti sarve
ye'vasthitāḥ pratyanīkeṣu yodhāḥ.

I am the mighty world-destroying Time, now engaged in destroying the worlds. Even without You, none of the warriors arrayed in hostile armies shall live. (11.32)

तस्मात्त्वमुत्तिष्ठ यशो लभस्व

जित्वा शत्रून् भुङ्क्ष्व राज्यं समृद्धम् ।
मयैवैते निहताः पूर्वमेव
निमित्तमात्रं भव सव्यसाचिन् ॥

tasmāttvamuttiṣṭha yaśo labhasva
jitvā śatrūn bhuṅkṣva rājyaṁ samṛddham,
mayaivaite nihatāḥ pūrvameva
nimittamātraṁ bhava savyasācin.

Therefore, stand up, and obtain fame. Conquer the enemies and enjoy the flourishing kingdom. Verily by Myself they have already been slain; be you a mere instrument, O left-handed archer. (11.33)

त्वमादिदेवः पुरुषः पुराणः
त्वमस्य विश्वस्य परं निधानम् ।
वेत्तासि वेद्यं च परं च धाम
त्वया ततं विश्वमनन्तरूप ॥

tvamādidevaḥ puruṣaḥ purāṇaḥ
tvamasya viśvasya paraṁ nidhānam,
vettāsi vedyaṁ ca paraṁ ca dhāma
tvayā tataṁ viśvamanantarūpa.

You are the Primal God, the Ancient Puruṣa; You are the Supreme Refuge of this universe. You are the knower, the knowable, and the Abode-Supreme. By Thee is the universe pervaded, O Being of Infinite forms. (11.38)

सखेति मत्वा प्रसभं यदुक्तं
हे कृष्ण हे यादव हे सखेति ।
अजानता महिमानं तवेदं
मया प्रमादात्प्रणयेन वापि ॥

sakheti matvā prasabhaṁ yaduktaṁ
he kṛṣṇa he yādava he sakheti,
ajānatā mahimānaṁ tavedaṁ
mayā pramādātpraṇayena vāpi.

Whatever I have rashly said from carelessness or love, addressing You as "O Kṛṣṇa, O Yādava, O Friend", and regarding You merely as a friend, unknowing of this Your greatness. (11.41)

यच्चावहासार्थमसत्कृतोऽसि
  विहारशय्यासनभोजनेषु।
एकोऽथवाप्यच्युत तत्समक्षं
  तत्क्षामये त्वामहमप्रमेयम्॥

yaccāvahāsārthamasatkṛto'si
vihāraśayyāsanabhojaneṣu,
eko'thavāpyacyuta tatsamakṣaṁ
tatkṣāmaye tvāmahamaprameyam.

In whatever way I may have insulted You for the sake of fun, while at play, reposing or sitting, or at meals, when alone (with You), O Acyuta, or in company—that, O Immeasurable One, I implore You to forgive. (11.42)

पितासि लोकस्य चराचरस्य
  त्वमस्य पूज्यश्च गुरुर्गरीयान्।
न त्वत्समोऽस्त्यभ्यधिकः कुतोऽन्यो
  लोकत्रयेऽप्यप्रतिमप्रभाव॥

pitāsi lokasya carācarasya
tvamasya pūjyaśca gururgarīyān,
na tvatsamo'styabhyadhikaḥ kuto'nyo
lokatraye'pyapratimaprabhāva.

You are the Father of this world, moving and unmoving. You are to be adored by this world. You are the greatest Guru, (for) there exists none who is equal to You; how can there be then another, superior to You in the three worlds, O Being of unequalled power? (11.43)

तस्मात्प्रणम्य प्रणिधाय कायं
  प्रसादये त्वामहमीशमीड्यम्।
पितेव पुत्रस्य सखेव सख्युः
  प्रियः प्रियायार्हसि देव सोढुम्॥

tasmātpraṇamya praṇidhāya kāyaṁ
prasādaye tvāmahamīśamīḍyam,
piteva putrasya sakheva sakhyuḥ
priyaḥ priyāyārhasi deva soḍhum.

Therefore, bowing down, prostrating my body, I crave your

forgiveness, adorable Lord. As a father forgives his son, a friend his friend, a lover his beloved, even so should You forgive me, O Deva. (11.44)

न वेद यज्ञाध्ययनैर्न दानैः
  न च क्रियाभिर्न तपोभिरुग्रैः ।
एवंरूपः शक्य अहं नृलोके
  द्रष्टुं त्वदन्येन कुरुप्रवीर ॥

na veda yajñādhyayanairna dānaiḥ
  na ca kriyābhirna tapobhirugraiḥ,
evaṁrūpaḥ śakya ahaṁ nṛloke
  draṣṭuṁ tvadanyena kurupravīra.

Neither by the study of the Vedas and sacrifices, nor by rituals, nor by severe austerities, can I be seen in this form in the world of men by any other than yourself, O great hero among the Kurus. (11.48)

नाहं वेदैर्न तपसा न दानेन न चेज्यया ।
शक्य एवंविधो द्रष्टुं दृष्टवानसि मां यथा ॥

nāhaṁ vedairna tapasā na dānena na cejyayā,
śakya evaṁvidho draṣṭuṁ dṛṣṭavānasi māṁ yathā.

Neither by the Vedas, nor by austerity, nor by gift, nor by sacrifices can I be seen in this Form as you have seen Me (in your present mental condition). (11.53)

भक्त्या त्वनन्यया शक्य अहमेवंविधोऽर्जुन ।
ज्ञातुं द्रष्टुं च तत्त्वेन प्रवेष्टुं च परन्तप ॥

bhaktyā tvananyayā śakya ahamevaṁvidho'rjuna,
  jñātuṁ draṣṭuṁ ca tattvena praveṣṭuṁ ca parantapa.

But, by single-minded devotion can I, of this form, be known and seen in reality and also entered into, O Parantapa (O scorcher of your foes)! (11.54)

मत्कर्मकृन्मत्परमो मद्भक्तः सङ्गवर्जितः ।
निर्वैरः सर्वभूतेषु यः स मामेति पाण्डव ॥

matkarmakṛnmatparamo madbhaktaḥ saṅgavarjitaḥ,
nirvairaḥ sarvabhūteṣu yaḥ sa māmeti pāṇḍava.

He who does actions for Me, who looks upon Me as the Supreme, who is devoted to Me, who is free from attachment, who bears enmity towards none, he comes to Me, O Pāṇḍava (11.55)

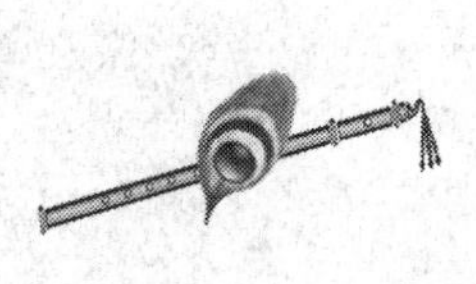

12

Bhakti Yoga

The Yoga of Devotion

A real devotee is completely independent of the world outside and he draws his inspiration, equanimity and joyous ecstasy from the Source, deep within himself. (12.16)

This chapter expounds the principles of Bhakti (devotion). The nature of devotion, the qualities of a devotee and the various methods of spiritual practice are all elaborated herein. Since this chapter is a thorough exposition on devotion, it is rightly named 'Bhakti Yoga' or 'Yoga of Devotion.'

Terms and Definitions

1. What is 'śraddhā'?

'Śraddhā' is belief in something which one does not know, so that one may come to know what one believes in. (12.2)

2. What is true upāsanā (worship)?

True upāsanā (worship) is an inward act of attunement with the Higher principle so as to get oneself completely merged with It. (12.2)

3. What is the meaning of the expression 'Ananya Yoga'?

To lift our minds from its present agitations and wasteful tendencies towards a greater goal of ampler joy and fuller wisdom is 'Yoga'. Ordinarily, our goal keeps on changing, and we reach nowhere even though our struggle is consistent. 'Anya' means 'other'; 'Ananya' means 'without otherness'; 'Ananya Yoga' means 'Yoga in which the goal is ever steady'. (12.6)

4. Explain the terms – rejoice, hate, grieve and desire – occurring in the following verse.

यो न हृष्यति न द्वेष्टि न शोचति न काङ्क्षति ।
शुभाशुभपरित्यागी भक्तिमान्यः स मे प्रियः ॥

yo na hṛṣyati na dveṣṭi na śocati na kāṅkṣati,
śubhāśubhaparityāgī bhaktimānyaḥ sa me priyaḥ.

He who neither rejoices nor hates nor grieves nor desires, renouncing good and evil, full of devotion, is dear to Me.

Rejoice: This is the feeling of satisfaction and fulfilment that comes to an individual on attaining a desired object that is extremely desirable and at the same time difficult to realise.

Hate: The sense of revulsion that comes towards undesirable things and circumstances is called 'hatred'.

Grief: This is the mental state experienced while parting from a beloved object.

Desire: This is the yearning to possess something which is unattained at present.

All these are absent in the Lord's devotee. (12.17)

Thoughts and Concepts

1. How is chapter 12 connected with the earlier chapters?

Chapter 10 and 11 had completely satisfied the sceptic in Arjuna through discussion (chapter 10) and actual demonstration (chapter 11) of the Lord's Cosmic Form. Arjuna now feels an irresistible urge to conquer the Kingdom Divine within himself. The secret strategy for achieving this was also indicated in the concluding stanza of the 11th chapter. Devotion and consistency of self-application, free from all egocentric attachment to the world of objects were pointed out as the way. As a man of action, Arjuna was impatient to achieve his Goal, and in the 12th chapter the Lord explains in detail the actual methods to achieve It.

Further, from the 2nd chapter up to the 11th chapter, the Lord had explained in some places the knowledge of the unmanifest Brahman (nirguṇa) and again He has presented His manifested form (saguṇa) in the 10th and 11th chapters. Arjuna wants to know whether it is more profitable to meditate upon the Truth as unmanifest or as manifest and the chapter begins with his question in this regard. (Introduction)

2. What is Arjuna's question at the beginning of the 12th chapter?

In the world there are two types of seekers seeking one and the same goal. Some meditate upon the manifested form (saguṇa) of the Infinite and others contemplate upon the unmanifested Supreme (nirguṇa). Both of them are sincere and both progress onwards. The question of Arjuna is as to which out of these two types of seekers is better versed in Yoga.

एवं सततयुक्ता ये भक्तास्त्वां पर्युपासते ।
ये चाप्यक्षरमव्यक्तं तेषां के योगवित्तमाः ॥

evaṁ satatayuktā ye bhaktāstvāṁ paryupāsate,
ye cāpyakṣaramavyaktaṁ teṣāṁ ke yogavittamāḥ.

Those devotees who, ever steadfast, thus worship You, and also those who worship the Imperishable, the Unmanifested—which of them are better versed in Yoga? (12.1)

3. What does the term 'āveśya' mean in the following verse? What is its importance?

मय्यावेश्य मनो ये मां नित्ययुक्ता उपासते ।
श्रद्धया परयोपेताः ते मे युक्ततमा मताः ॥

mayyāveśya mano ye māṁ nityayuktā upāsate,
śraddhayā parayopetāḥ te me yuktatamā matāḥ.

Those who, fixing their mind on Me, worship Me, ever steadfast and endowed with Supreme faith, these, in my opinion, are the best in Yoga.

Thought is the content of our subtle body. Both the mind and intellect are nothing but thoughts. It is not sufficient if they leisurely wander around the concept of the Lord, but they have actually to penetrate, delve into, merge and ultimately dissolve themselves to become the very ideal perfection which the Lord represents. The word 'āveśya' being used in the stanza indicates not merely 'thought-contact' but actual 'thought-penetration'. Human thought takes the form of, gathers the fragrance of and even puts on the glow of the qualities in the object of its contemplation. Thus, when a devotee's thoughts gush forward in sincerity, in a newly found urge of irrepressible love towards the Lord, the devotee as a personality ends for the time being and himself acquires the glow and beauty of the Lord of his heart. (12.2)

4. What are the three essential conditions for one to become a true devotee?

The three essential conditions for one to become a true devotee are:

(1) Fixing the mind on the Lord

(2) Worshipping the Lord with steadfastness

(3) Being endowed with supreme faith. (12.2)

5. Explain the terms (1)Akṣara (Imperishable) (2) Anirdeśya (Indefinable) (3) Sarvatraga (All-pervading) (4) Acintya (Unthinkable) (5) Kūṭastha (Unchanging) (6) Acala (Immovable) (7) Dhruva (Eternal) which are used in the following verse to describe the formless Brahman.

ये त्वक्षरमनिर्देश्यमव्यक्तं पर्युपासते।
सर्वत्रगमचिन्त्यं च कूटस्थमचलं ध्रुवम्॥

ye tvakṣaramanirdeśyamavyaktaṁ paryupāsate,
sarvatragamacintyaṁ ca kūṭasthamacalaṁ dhruvam.

Those who worship the Imperishable, the Indefinable, the Unmanifest, the Omnipresent, the Immovable and the Eternal, Unchangeable, Unthinkable.

(1)**Akṣara (Imperishable):** All those that have forms and qualities are substances and all substances are perishable. The Imperishable is, therefore, that which has no qualities and can't be destroyed. Further, qualities alone can be perceived, and the term 'Imperishable' therefore implies that sense organs cannot perceive It.

(2)**Anirdeśya (Indefinable):** Definitions are always in terms of what is perceived and when a thing not perceivable, it cannot be defined and distinguished from other things.

(3)**Sarvatraga (All-pervading):** If the Supreme can be indicated as existing in a particular place alone, then the Supreme will have a particular shape and that which has a shape will necessarily perish!

(4)**Acintya (Unthinkable):** That which can be conceived of by a human mind will immediately become the object of feelings and thoughts. The Supreme Brahman being beyond the concept of the mind is necessarily Inconceivable, Incomprehensible and Unthinkable.

(5) **Kūṭastha (Unchanging):** The Self, the Consciousness, remains unchanged even though it is the Substratum on which all changes constantly take place. 'Kūṭa' in Sanskrit is an 'anvil'. Just as the iron block in a smithy, without itself undergoing any change, allows other pieces of iron to be beaten out on it and changed into any shape, so too the Consciousness, the substratum of all our personalities, allows our personalities to change without Itself undergoing any modification.

(6) **Acala (Immovable):** Motion is change in the time-space system. A thing can never move in itself; it can do so only to a point in space and time where it is not already. The Infinite is All-pervading and there is no point in space or time where It is not and, therefore, the Infinite cannot move. It is here, there and everywhere; It has the past, the present and the future in It.

(7) **Dhruva (Eternal):** That which is conditioned by time and space is subject to change. But the Supreme, the Substratum of all, at all times and in all places, is the One that supports the very play of time and space, and therefore time and space cannot condition the Infinite. Consciousness, which is the Infinite Self in us, is the same everywhere and at all times: in our childhood, youth and old age, in all places and at all times and in all conditions of joy and sorrow or success and failure. The Supreme is unconditioned by Time; It is the ruler of Time. It is Eternal. (12.3)

6. Why should the seeker cultivate the habit of restraining the senses?

To dissipate one's energies through the sense organs is the hobby of the thoughtless mortal. A seeker, who is aspiring to reach the summit of perfection, must necessarily curtail such dissipations and redirect the energies so conserved towards the higher flight. The sense organs are the real gateways through which the disturbing world of plurality steals in, to storm the seeker's inner citadel and plunge him into destruction. It is again through the organs of action that the mind gushes out into the world of objects. These two transactions break up the seeker's harmonious equipoise and steady balance. Therefore, if a seeker is to succeed in the spiritual path he must cultivate a habit of living with his senses in control. (12.4)

7. Explain the term 'samabuddhi' (equanimity).

The things of the world in themselves and in their patterns keep on changing. In such a kaleidoscope design of existence, it is indeed unintelligent to expect any desirable system to remain changeless. Therefore, in the world of change a seeker must discover his own balance and equipoise, by controlling his intellectual evaluations, mental attachments and physical contacts with the world outside.

The intelligent relationship maintained by a seeker towards the world outside, whereby he experiences a uniform steadiness in himself, in spite of the mad revelry of things and beings around him, is called 'samabuddhi'—the condition of equanimity. An individual who has developed this 'samabuddhi', can easily watch for and see the Golden Chord of Beauty that holds together all that is enchanting and grotesque constituting the outer world. (12.4)

8. Cite the relevant verse which states the difficult nature of worshipping the unmanifest and formless Brahman.

The following verse declares that it is difficult for the 'embodied' to worship the unmanifest and formless Brahman:

क्लेशोऽधिकतरस्तेषां अव्यक्तासक्तचेतसाम् ।
अव्यक्ताहि गतिर्दुःखं देहवद्भिरवाप्यते ॥

kleśo'dhikatarasteṣām avyaktāsaktacetasām,
avyaktāhi gatirduḥkhaṁ dehavadbhiravāpyate.

Greater is their trouble whose minds are set on the 'Unmanifest'; for the goal, the 'Unmanifest', is very hard for the embodied to reach. (12.5)

9. Śrī Kṛṣṇa says that the 'avyakta' (unmanifest) is very hard for the 'embodied' to reach. What is the meaning of the expression 'embodied' (dehavat)?

The term'embodied' (dehavat) refers to 'those who are attached to their bodies'. If an individual lives only a life of sensuality and satisfaction of one's body-cravings, he will find it very difficult to steadily meditate upon the subtle Formless Brahman. (12.5)

10. What are the levels of spiritual practices advocated by Śrī Kṛṣṇa?

The levels of spiritual practices advocated by the Lord are:

(1) Fixing the mind and intellect on the Lord alone.

(2) If one is unable to accomplish that, by 'Abhyāsa Yoga' one should train the mind to focus on the Lord.

(3) If one is unable to do that, such a person should be intent on performing actions for the Lord's sake.

(4) If it is not possible to do even that, then one should renounce the fruits of all actions and live fully in the present.

These four-levels of spiritual practices are expounded by the Lord in the following verses:

मय्येव मन आधत्स्व मयि बुद्धिं निवेशय ।
निवसिष्यसि मय्येव अत ऊर्ध्वं न संशयः ॥

mayyeva mana ādhatsva mayi buddhiṁ niveśaya,
nivasiṣyasi mayyeva ata ūrdhvaṁ na saṁśayaḥ.

Fix your mind on Me only, place your intellect in Me; then, (thereafter) you shall, no doubt, live in Me alone. (12.8)

अथ चित्तं समाधातुं न शक्नोषि मयि स्थिरम् ।
अभ्यासयोगेन ततो मामिच्छाप्तुं धनञ्जय ॥

atha cittaṁ samādhātuṁ na śaknoṣi mayi sthiram,
abhyāsayogena tato māmicchāptuṁ dhanañjaya.

If you are unable to fix your mind steadily upon Me, then by Abhyāsa Yoga (the Yoga of constant practice), seek to reach Me, O Dhanañjaya. (12.9)

अभ्यासेऽप्यसमर्थोऽसि मत्कर्मपरमो भव ।
मदर्थमपि कर्माणि कुर्वन्सिद्धिमवाप्स्यसि ॥

abhyāse'pyasamartho'si matkarmaparamo bhava,
madarthamapi karmāṇi kurvansiddhimavāpsyasi.

If you are unable even to practise Abhyāsa Yoga, be you intent on performing actions for My sake; even by doing actions for My sake, you shall attain perfection. (12.10)

अथैतदप्यशक्तोऽसि कर्तुं मद्योगमाश्रितः ।
सर्वकर्मफलत्यागं ततः कुरु यतात्मवान् ॥

athaitadapyaśakto'si kartuṁ madyogamāśritaḥ,
sarvakarmaphalatyāgaṁ tataḥ kuru yatātmavān.

If you are unable to do even this, then taking refuge in Me, self-controlled, renounce the fruits of all actions. (12.11)

11. What is the technique for controlling the mind?

In order to gather the dissipated and riotous mental rays and to focus them at the point of concentration, the meditator must develop a capacity to stand by himself and in himself, apart from his wandering mind. If we identify ourselves with the mind, wherever the mind takes us, we also must go. Therefore, in order to control the mind, the meditator must stand apart from the mind, identifying himself with that power in him which possesses the ability to rule over and direct his mental energies. (12.9)

12. How does the Lord extol 'karma-phala-tyāga'?

The following verse glorifies 'karma-phala-tyāga' (renunciation of the fruits of action) by stating that peace is immediately attained by the one who renounces the fruits of all actions.

श्रेयो हि ज्ञानमभ्यासाज्ज्ञानाद्ध्यानं विशिष्यते ।
ध्यानात्कर्मफलत्यागस्त्यागाच्छान्तिरनन्तरम् ॥

śreyo hi jñānamabhyāsājjñānāddhyānaṁ viśiṣyate,
dhyānātkarmaphalatyāgastyāgācchāntiranantaram.

'Knowledge' is indeed better than 'practice'; 'meditation' is better than 'knowledge'; 'renunciation of the fruits of actions' is better than 'meditation'; peace immediately follows (this) renunciation. (12.12)

13. Why is 'knowledge' (jñāna) superior to 'practice' (abhyāsa)?

The inner personality cannot be persuaded to toe the line with the physical acts of devotion (abhyāsa) unless the practitioner has a correct grasp of what he is doing. An intellectual conversion born out of knowledge (jñāna) is a pre-requisite to force the mind to act in the right spirit and to gain a perfect attunement with the physical act (abhyāsa). A correct and exhaustive knowledge of what we are doing and why we are doing it is an unavoidable pre-condition for making our Yoga fruitful. Therefore, it is said here that knowledge (jñāna) of the psychological, intellectual and spiritual implications of our practices is greater in importance than the very external 'devotional performances' (abhyāsa). (12.12)

14. Why is 'meditation' (dhyāna) superior to knowledge (jñāna)?

More important than mere theoretical 'knowledge' (jñāna) is 'meditation' (dhyāna) upon the 'knowledge' one has attained. The technical explanation—of the why and the wherefore of religious practices—can be more easily learnt than understood. To convert our learning into our understanding and self-transformation, there must necessarily be a process of intellectual assimilation and absorption. This cannot be accomplished by a mere factual learning of the word-meanings. The student will have to delve, with hearty enthusiasm, into the very meaning of the śāstra (scripture), and this is possible only through long, subjective, independent pondering over the significant terms in the śāstras. This process of inward assimilation of knowledge can take place only through 'meditation' (dhyāna). Hence, in the hierarchy of importance, 'meditation' (dhyāna) has been given a greater place than the 'knowledge of the technique' (jñāna). (12.12)

15. Why does the Lord give greater importance to 'renunciation of fruits of action' (karma-phala-tyāga) – and place it even higher than meditation (dhyāna) – in the hierarchy of spiritual practices?

Meditation (dhyāna) can never be possible for an individual in whom all energy and steadiness of mind are shattered by the agitation created by his own ruinous imagination of the future. Anxiety for the future depletes ones vitality to face the present. All fruits of action belong to the future and to be over-anxious about them is to invite a lot of idle agitation. Stormed by agitation, one loses all equipoise and such an individual has no ability to meditate upon and assimilate the significance of the scriptures. Therefore, Śrī Kṛṣṇa gives a greater place of importance in his ladder-of-ideas to the renunciation of the fruits of action (karma-phala-tyāga).

Renunciation of our anxiety for the future immediately brings about a healthy condition of peace within oneself. As a result of this renunciation, a dynamic quietude comes to pervade within; the intellect can now meditate upon the knowledge of the śāstras (scriptures) and thereby understand the ways of self-development as explained therein. And when with this knowledge one meditates one is assured of definite success and steady progress.

It is because of this reason that the Lord gives greater importance to 'renunciation of the results of action' (karma-phala-tyāga) and places it even higher than meditation (dhyāna). (12.12)

16. Cite the verses that describe the attributes of a devotee and enumerate the attributes.

In the following seven stanzas (12.13-19) Śrī Kṛṣṇa enumerates the 36 characteristic features of a true devotee, and thereby prescribes the correct mode of conduct and the way of life for all seekers.

अद्वेष्टा सर्वभूतानां मैत्रः करुण एव च ।
निर्ममो निरहङ्कारः समदुःखसुखः क्षमी ॥

adveṣṭā sarvabhūtānāṁ maitraḥ karuṇa eva ca,
nirmamo nirahaṅkāraḥ samaduḥkhasukhaḥ kṣamī.

He who hates no creature, who is friendly and compassionate to all, who is free from attachment and egoism, balanced in pleasure and pain, and forgiving, (12.13)

सन्तुष्टः सततं योगी यतात्मा दृढनिश्चयः ।
मय्यर्पितमनोबुद्धिर्यो मद्भक्तः स मे प्रियः ॥

santuṣṭaḥ satataṁ yogī yatātmā dṛḍhaniścayaḥ,
mayyarpitamanobuddhiryo madbhaktaḥ sa me priyaḥ.

Ever content, steady in meditation, self-controlled, possessed of firm conviction, with the mind and intellect dedicated to Me, he, My devotee, is dear to Me. (12.14)

यस्मान्नोद्विजते लोको लोकान्नोद्विजते च यः ।
हर्षामर्षभयोद्वेगैर्मुक्तो यः स च मे प्रियः ॥

yasmānnodvijate loko lokānnodvijate ca yaḥ,
harṣāmarṣabhayodvegairmukto yaḥ sa ca me priyaḥ.

He by whom the world is not agitated (affected) and who cannot be agitated by the world, who is freed from joy, envy, fear and anxiety—he is dear to Me. (12.15)

अनपेक्षः शुचिर्दक्ष उदासीनो गतव्यथः ।
सर्वारम्भपरित्यागी यो मद्भक्तः स मे प्रियः ॥

anapekṣaḥ śucirdakṣa udāsīno gatavyathaḥ,
sarvārambhaparityāgī yo madbhaktaḥ sa me priyaḥ.

He who is free from wants, pure, alert, unconcerned, untroubled, renouncing all undertakings (or commencements)—he who is (thus) devoted to Me, is dear to Me. (12.16)

यो न हृष्यति न द्वेष्टि न शोचति न काङ्क्षति ।
शुभाशुभपरित्यागी भक्तिमान्यः स मे प्रियः ॥

yo na hṛṣyati na dveṣṭi na śocati na kāṅkṣati,
śubhāśubhaparityāgī bhaktimānyaḥ sa me priyaḥ.

He who neither rejoices, nor hates, nor grieves, nor desires, renouncing good and evil, full of devotion, is dear to Me. (12.17)

समः शत्रौ च मित्रे च तथा मानापमानयोः ।
शीतोष्णसुखदुःखेषु समः सङ्गविवर्जितः ॥

samaḥ śatrau ca mitre ca tathā mānāpamānayoḥ,
śītoṣṇasukhaduḥkheṣu samaḥ saṅgavivarjitaḥ.

He who is the same to foe and friend, and also in honour and dishonour, who is the same in cold and heat and in pleasure and pain, who is free from attachment, (12.18)

तुल्यनिन्दास्तुतिर्मौनी सन्तुष्टो येन केनचित् ।
अनिकेतः स्थिरमतिर्भक्तिमान्मे प्रियो नरः ॥

tulyanindāstutirmaunī santuṣṭo yena kenacit,
aniketaḥ sthiramatirbhaktimānme priyo naraḥ.

To whom censure and praise are equal, who is silent, content with anything, homeless, steady-minded, full of devotion—that man is dear to Me. (12.19)

The 36 qualities of a true devotee that are mentioned in the above verses are:

(1) Absence of hatred towards all beings
(2) Friendliness
(3) Compassion
(4) The absence of 'My-ness'
(5) Absence of egoism
(6) Equanimity in joy and sorrow
(7) Forbearance
(8) Contentment
(9) Self-control
(10) Firm determination
(11) Surrendering the mind and intellect to God
(12) The world not being agitated by him
(13) He being unagitated by the world
(14) Absence of joy, envy, fear and anxiety
(15) Desirelessness
(16) Purity
(17) Competence in action
(18) Indifference
(19) Freedom from anxiety
(20) Renunciation of the fruits of action
(21) Absence of elation
(22) Absence of hatred
(23) Absence of fear
(24) Absence of desire
(25) Renunciation of good and evil
(26) Equal-mindedness towards friends and enemies
(27) Equanimity in honour and dishonour
(28) Equanimity in heat and cold
(29) Equanimity in joy and sorrow
(30) Non-attachment
(31) Equal-mindedness in praise and blame
(32) Silence

(33) Contentment with what-so-ever obtained by chance
(34) Absence of attachment to home
(35) Firmness of decision
(36) Devotion to God

17. A true devotee is one "by whom the world is not agitated and one who cannot be agitated by the world." Explain.

A true devotee is one who will not create any agitations in the world around him. Where there is the sun, there cannot be any darkness; where the peaceful Master of Equanimity and Perfection dwells, he, by the intrinsic Divinity in him, creates, as it were, an atmosphere of serene joy and endless peace around him and even those who are agitated in the world will suffer no more from such agitations when they approach such a Master-mind, and enjoy peace in themselves.

Not only does a true devotee quieten the very world around him into a dynamic peace, but also the world, however chaotic, revolting, boisterous and vengeful it may be, cannot create any agitations in him. The world of objects will almost always be in a state of flux, and its maddening death dance cannot bring even a whiff of its storms to disturb the calm serenity of the Saint. In and through the battling circumstances, he perceives the Changeless Ground—he hears the harmony that runs through the various discordant notes in life around. Since he is not attached to the superficial conditions of matter and its playful magic, any amount of wild agitations outside cannot bring any disturbance to his inner equipoise. (12.15)

18. Explain why the one who does not entertain any desire for objects is free from joy, envy, fear and anxiety.

When a desired object is gained, there is joy; if it is not gained, there is envy of those who have it. When we possess what we desire, there is fear of losing it; and when the desired object is missing, there is anxiety. All these are not in one who has no desire for objects. (12.15)

19. Why does a true devotee consider himself as only an instrument of the Lord?

No undertaking in our life is a new act that has an independent beginning or end. All actions in the world are in an eternal pattern of the total world movements. If correctly analysed, our undertakings are controlled, regulated, governed and ordered by the available world of things and situations. Apart from them all, no independent action is undertaken or can be fulfilled by anyone. A devotee of Truth is ever conscious of this oneness of the Universe and, therefore, he will always work in the world only as an instrument of the Lord and not as an independent agent in any undertaking. (12.16)

20. What does the description of the 'Man of Realisation' as 'Aniketa' (homeless) signify?

'Home' (niketa) is that which provides shelter from the external inclemencies of weather for the resident who is dwelling under its roof. Living under a roof, in itself, does not make the place a 'home'. To spend a night on a railway station, or in the retiring room at an airport, does not make the place the traveller's own home. It is only along with a sense of possession, reinforced with a sense of happiness and comfort, that the place under a roof becomes a 'home'. A true devotee has for himself a satisfactory shelter only at the seat of the All-Pervading and, therefore, his mental condition is indicated by the simple pertinent term 'aniketa' (homeless). (12.19)

21. Explain the deeper significance of the Lord's description that a "true devotee is equal to foe and friend, honour and dishonour and heat and cold."

The estimation of our relationship with another as foe or friend is generally our own mental reaction towards another. A true devotee is one who does not identify with his mental estimation of things and, therefore, he is equanimous and maintains a uniformity of attitude towards his friends and foes.

A situation is judged by the intellect as honourable or dis-honourable with reference to its own existing values and cultivated habits of thinking. That which is ordinarily considered dishonourable can itself come to be estimated by the same person as honourable in a new pattern of circumstances ordered by a change in time and place. These are all different tides in the intellect. A true devotee lives in a realm higher than the intellect and is unaffected by them.

Heat and cold are only the experiences of the body and affect only the body. A true devotee of the Lord in his identification with the Lord stands above the body and is unaffected by the experiences at the body level.

Thus, the Lord's declaration that a true devotee is equal to foe and friend, honour and dishonour and heat and cold signifies that he does not identfy with the matter vestures of body, mind and intellect. (12.19)

22. Why should one place no importance on censure and praise?

He who has been praised today will be censured by society tomorrow, and yesterday's censured man becomes the praiseworthy leader of today! Praise and censure are in themselves nothing more than the passing fancy of those who express them. Hence one should not give importance to either censure or praise. (12.19)

23. What is the importance of contentment in spiritual life?

The motto of all serious seekers of inward growth should be contentment with anything that might reach him accidentally, unasked and unexpected. To entertain the demands of the mind and to strive forth to satisfy them would be an unending game, as the mind has a knack of breeding its own demands very fast. The policy of contentment is the only intelligent attitude to be taken up by all sincere seekers or else there will be no time to seek, to strive for and to achieve the Divine Goal of life. (12.19)

24. Who is exceedingly dear to the Lord?

ये तु धर्म्यामृतमिदं यथोक्तं पर्युपासते ।
श्रद्दधाना मत्परमा भक्तास्तेऽतीव मे प्रियाः ॥

ye tu dharmyāmṛtamidaṁ yathoktaṁ paryupāsate,

śraddadhānā matparamā bhaktāste'tīva me priyāḥ.
They, indeed, who follow this 'Immortal Dharma' (Law of Life) as described above, endowed with faith, regarding Me as their Supreme Goal—such devotees are exceedingly dear to Me.

By the term 'Immortal Dharma' (*dharmyāmṛtam*) is meant all the 36 qualities (refer verses 12.13-19) of a true devotee – an accomplished Man of Realisation. A seeker who strives to imbibe these qualities in his life is exceedingly dear to the Lord. (12.20)

Selections for Reflection

1. Every individual wants to become and live what he is convinced of. And one who is convinced is a greater seeker than a man of blind faith jogging along the thorny path of time-worn habits. (Introduction)

2. My child may be dirty at one moment, mischievous at another; screaming in the morning, laughing in the noon; bullying in the evening and wild at night! Yet, through all such conditions, the father in me sees but one and the same son, and therefore, I give my love equally in all these different manifestations of my own son. This is a loving father's 'samabuddhi' (equanimity). In the same way, a true seeker learns to recognise the Lord of his heart in the grim tragedies, in the pleasant comedies, in the tremendous successes, in the sighing sorrows and in the disappointing failures in his own day-to-day life and he becomes equanimous. (12.4)

3. Whether the devotee is seeking his spiritual unfoldment through meditation upon a personal or an impersonal God, the result achieved remains the same if the disciplines required of him are all fully and faithfully followed. (12.4)

4. An old man whose vision is lost and whose hands are shaky may find it very difficult to thread a needle; so too a mind and intellect agitated, panting and restless, suffering from desire-plays, are

not vehicles that can successfully fly beyond the frontiers of names and forms to the endless Spiritual Glory. (12.5)

5. To the majority of us, meditation upon the Lord, as expressed in the Universe, is easier and more profitable. Man can worship the myriad forms through service undertaken in a spirit of worship and divine dedication. By doing so, the body-attachments and sense-appetites get purged from his inner make-up and his mind becomes subtle enough to conceive and contemplate upon the Formless and the Imperishable Unmanifest. (12.5)

6. When a devotee of the Infinite Lord surrenders himself totally at His feet and acts as a messenger or as a representative of the Will of the Lord, he becomes not only divinely dynamic, but in and through his own activities becomes aware of the Presence and Grace of the Universal Spirit. (12.6)

7. It is the mind that gives us the hallucination of our egocentric limitations and again it is the mind that rediscovers the Infinitude. Bondage and liberation are both of the mind. The Self is ever free, ever liberated and never bound. (12.7)

8. That the mind runs away into a wild wool-gathering is not in itself such a tragedy as that when the meditator himself gets abducted by the mind and unconsciously follows it into the fields of ready distractions. (12.9)

9. The inner personality is a million times more delicate than an unopened flower-bud and to hasten its unfoldment is to ruin for ever its beauty and fragrance. (12.10)

10. The fruit of an action is the action of the present-moment maturing itself in a future-period of time. (12.11)

11. An intellectual conversion is a pre-requisite to force the mind to act in the right spirit and to gain a perfect attunement with the physical act. (12.12)

12. Moral rules and ethical codes of behaviour are in Hinduism not arbitrary commandments thrust upon its followers. These rules of conduct are copied from the behaviour of God-men who had attained the Spiritual Perfection and had actually lived among us. Seekers are those who are striving hard to attain the spiritual experience of those saints and seers. A devotee who is trying to attune himself with these Masters of Yoga should necessarily start at least copying their external behaviour and mental beauties, which constitute the moral and ethical rules prescribed in our religion. (12.14)

13. To be alert always becomes the second nature of an integrated person. He is mentally agile and intellectually vigorous. Since there is no dissipation in him, he is ever on his toes to spring forward to activity, once he determines to shoulder any endeavour. (12.16)

14. In human life, small difficulties, simple illnesses, discomforts, wants etc., are but natural. To exaggerate their importance and strive to escape from them all is to enter into a life-long struggle of adjustments. In all such instances, the seeker is warned not to squander away his mental energies but to conserve them by overlooking these little pin-pricks of life in an attitude of utter indifference towards them. (12.16)

15. Attachment to and identification with the matter equipments – body, mind and intellect – is the cause by which we are helplessly made to dance to the mad tunes that chance happenings dictate. One who is detached from these equipments is the one who is a master over them all. (12.18)

16. Keeping physical silence but letting the mind loose to talk results in repression. Be truly silent and understand how really silent silence can be! (12.18,19)

17. The Path of Devotion is not a mere sentimental explosion or an excessive emotional display. It is not a mere frivolous hysteria. It

is the blossoming of the human personality through the surrender of all our limitations and by acquiring new vitality during the inspired moments of deep contemplation. (Epilogue)

ঙঙ ঙ৩

Verses for Memorisation

मय्यावेश्य मनो ये मां नित्ययुक्ता उपासते।
श्रद्धया परयोपेताः ते मे युक्ततमा मताः॥

mayyāveśya mano ye māṁ nityayuktā upāsate,
śraddhayā parayopetāḥ te me yuktatamā matāḥ.

Those who, fixing their mind on Me, worship Me, ever steadfast and endowed with Supreme faith, these, in my opinion, are the best in Yoga. (12.2)

क्लेशोऽधिकतरस्तेषां अव्यक्तासक्तचेतसाम्।
अव्यक्ताहि गतिर्दुःखं देहवद्भिरवाप्यते॥

kleśo'dhikatarasteṣām avyaktāsaktacetasām,
avyaktāhi gatirduḥkhaṁ dehavadbhiravāpyate.

Greater is their trouble whose minds are set on the 'Unmanifest'; for the goal, the 'Unmanifest', is very hard for the embodied to reach. (12.5)

ये तु सर्वाणि कर्माणि मयि संन्यस्य मत्परः।
अनन्येनैव योगेन मां ध्यायन्त उपासते॥

ye tu sarvāṇi karmāṇi mayi saṁnyasya matparaḥ,
ananyenaiva yogena māṁ dhyāyanta upāsate.

But those who worship Me, renouncing all actions in Me, regarding Me as the Supreme Goal, meditating on Me with single-minded devotion, (12.6)

तेषामहं समुद्धर्ता मृत्युसंसारसागरात्।
भवामि न चिरात्पार्थ मय्यावेशितचेतसाम्॥

teṣāmahaṁ samuddhartā mṛtyusaṁsārasāgarāt,
bhavāmi na cirātpārtha mayyāveśitacetasām.

For them whose minds are set on Me, verily I become, ere-long, O

Pārtha, the Saviour, (to save them) out of the ocean of finite experiences, the Saṁsāra. (12.7)

मय्येव मन आधत्स्व मयि बुद्धिं निवेशय ।
निवसिष्यसि मय्येव अत ऊर्ध्वं न संशयः ॥

mayyeva mana ādhatsva mayi buddhiṁ niveśaya,
nivasiṣyasi mayyeva ata ūrdhvaṁ na saṁśayaḥ.

Fix your mind on Me only, place your intellect in Me; then, (thereafter) you shall, no doubt, live in Me alone. (12.8)

अथ चित्तं समाधातुं न शक्नोषि मयि स्थिरम् ।
अभ्यासयोगेन ततो मामिच्छाप्तुं धनञ्जय ॥

atha cittaṁ samādhātuṁ na śaknoṣi mayi sthiram,
abhyāsayogena tato māmicchāptuṁ dhanañjaya.

If you are unable to fix your mind steadily upon Me, then by Abhyāsa Yoga (the Yoga of constant practice), seek to reach Me, O Dhanañjaya. (12.9)

अभ्यासेऽप्यसमर्थोऽसि मत्कर्मपरमो भव ।
मदर्थमपि कर्माणि कुर्वन्सिद्धिमवाप्स्यसि ॥

abhyāse'pyasamartho'si matkarmaparamo bhava,
madarthamapi karmāṇi kurvansiddhimavāpsyasi.

If you are unable even to practise Abhyāsa Yoga, be you intent on performing actions for My sake; even by doing actions for My sake, you shall attain perfection. (12.10)

अथैतदप्यशक्तोऽसि कर्तुं मद्योगमाश्रितः ।
सर्वकर्मफलत्यागं ततः कुरु यतात्मवान् ॥

athaitadapyaśakto'si kartuṁ madyogamāśritaḥ,
sarvakarmaphalatyāgaṁ tataḥ kuru yatātmavān.

If you are unable to do even this, then taking refuge in Me, self-controlled, renounce the fruits of all actions. (12.11)

श्रेयो हि ज्ञानमभ्यासाज्ज्ञानाद्ध्यानं विशिष्यते ।
ध्यानात्कर्मफलत्यागस्त्यागाच्छान्तिरनन्तरम् ॥

śreyo hi jñānamabhyāsājjñānāddhyānaṁ viśiṣyate,
dhyānātkarmaphalatyāgastyāgācchāntiranantaram.

'Knowledge' is indeed better than 'practice'; 'meditation' is better than 'knowledge'; 'renunciation of the fruits of actions' is better than 'meditation'; peace immediately follows (this) renunciation. (12.12)

अद्वेष्टा सर्वभूतानां मैत्रः करुण एव च ।
निर्ममो निरहङ्कारः समदुःखसुखः क्षमी ॥

adveṣṭā sarvabhūtānāṁ maitraḥ karuṇa eva ca,
nirmamo nirahaṅkāraḥ samaduḥkhasukhaḥ kṣamī.

He who hates no creature, who is friendly and compassionate to all, who is free from attachment and egoism, balanced in pleasure and pain, and forgiving, (12.13)

यस्मान्नोद्विजते लोको लोकान्नोद्विजते च यः ।
हर्षामर्षभयोद्वेगैर्मुक्तो यः स च मे प्रियः ॥

yasmānnodvijate loko lokānnodvijate ca yaḥ,
harṣāmarṣabhayodvegairmukto yaḥ sa ca me priyaḥ.

He by whom the world is not agitated (affected) and who cannot be agitated by the world, who is freed from joy, envy, fear and anxiety—he is dear to Me. (12.15)

यो न हृष्यति न द्वेष्टि न शोचति न काङ्क्षति ।
शुभाशुभपरित्यागी भक्तिमान्यः स मे प्रियः ॥

yo na hṛṣyati na dveṣṭi na śocati na kāṅkṣati,
śubhāśubhaparityāgī bhaktimānyaḥ sa me priyaḥ.

He who neither rejoices, nor hates, nor grieves, nor desires, renouncing good and evil, full of devotion, is dear to Me. (12.17)

तुल्यनिन्दास्तुतिर्मौनी सन्तुष्टो येन केनचित् ।
अनिकेतः स्थिरमतिर्भक्तिमान्मे प्रियो नरः ॥

tulyanindāstutirmaunī santuṣṭo yena kenacit,
aniketaḥ sthiramatirbhaktimānme priyo naraḥ.

To whom censure and praise are equal, who is silent, content with anything, homeless, steady-minded, full of devotion—that man is dear to Me. (12.19)

ये तु धर्म्यामृतमिदं यथोक्तं पर्युपासते ।
श्रद्दधाना मत्परमा भक्तास्तेऽतीव मे प्रियाः ॥

ye tu dharmyāmṛtamidaṁ yathoktaṁ paryupāsate,
śraddadhānā matparamā bhaktāste'tīva me priyāḥ.

They, indeed, who follow this 'Immortal Dharma' (Law of Life) as described above, endowed with faith, regarding Me as their Supreme Goal—such devotees are exceedingly dear to Me.

13

Kṣetra Kṣetrajña Vibhāga Yoga

The Yoga of the Field and its Knower

Mathematically, 'Knowledge' in a 'field of known' things and happenings, becomes the 'Knower', which suffers the imperfections of the known. The 'Knower', minus the 'field of the known' becomes Pure Knowledge, ever perfect and joyous. (Introduction)

ॐ

This chapter gives the student a direct explanation for, and almost a personal experience of, the Subject in him, the Self. Herein, we also have an exhaustive exposition of how to meditate directly upon the Imperishable Formless Spirit. In the 12th chapter, the Lord taught Arjuna the worship of the manifest Brahman (saguṇa) and the qualities of the devotee (bhakta), but had not fully touched upon the nature of the unmanifest Brahman (nirguṇa) or the Knowledge (Jñāna) of It. The Lord explains in the 13th chapter the subject of Knowledge and the Man of Knowledge.

Spirit functioning through matter-envelopments is the living organism. 'That' dressed up in matter is the vain 'Thou' (tvam). Therefore, man, undressed of matter, is the Eternal and the Infinite Spirit. To undress and thereby to get rid of matter we must have a precise knowledge of all that constitutes matter. This discrimination between the inert matter equipment and the vibrant Spark of Life, the Spirit, is presented in this chapter, which is rightly called the 'Kṣetra Kṣetrajña Vibhāga Yoga'—'Yoga of the Field and the Knower of the Field'.

Terms and Definitions

1. Differentiate 'prakṛti' from 'Puruṣa'.

The Ācāryas of the Sāṅkhyan philosophy have used prakṛti to indicate the inert-equipment and Puruṣa to indicate the vital sentient Truth that sets the entire assemblage of matter in action. In short prakṛti is matter and Puruṣa is the Spirit. (13.1)

2. Define 'ego' in terms of 'kṣetra' (field) and 'Kṣetrajña' (Knower of the field).

The 'Kṣetrajña' (Principle of Knowing) functioning in the kṣetra (field) is the 'enjoyer of the field', the 'knower'. It is this 'knower' that is commonly known as the 'ego'. (13.2)

3. Differentiate 'kṣetra' (field) from 'Kṣetrajña' (Knower of the field).

Verse two of the 13th chapter declares the 'body' to be the 'kṣetra' (field) and the Principle that knows the body as 'Kṣetrajña' (Knower of the field). 'Kṣetra' is the 'field of matter', which is constituted of the various equipments of perception and the vast fields of the perceived. 'Kṣetrajña' is the subject that enjoys the activities of the instruments of perception and the world perceived by them. In a word, the entire world of 'knowable' together in a bunch can be labelled as the 'kṣetra' (field), and the Knowing-Principle, seemingly functioning as the 'subject' or 'Knower' is the 'Kṣetrajña'. (13.2,3,7)

4. What are the 'mahābhūtas' (five great elements)?

The 'mahābhūtas' or the 'five great elements' are space, air, fire, water and earth. They are the rudimentary elements (tanmātras) that combine to form the perceptible grosser elements (indriya-gocarāḥ). (13.6)

5. What is 'ahaṅkāra' (egoism)?

'Ahaṅkāra' (egoism) is the sense of 'I-ness' and 'My-ness' that arises due to the identification with the matter equipments of body, mind and intellect. It is this that is the 'perceiver' and 'enjoyer' of this world, who enjoys and suffers the joys and sorrows of his own world of likes and dislikes, loves and hatreds, and ever weeps because of his innumerable attachments to the world outside. (13.6)

6. Define 'buddhi' (intellect).

The 'determining faculty' which rationally thinks and comes to its own conclusions and judges good and bad in every experience of a living man is called the 'buddhi' (intellect). (13.6)

7. What is the 'avyakta' (unmanifest)?

Mental capacities, intellectual decisions and aptitudes in each are ordered by the type of impressions (vāsanās) left over in his subtle body as a result of his previous egocentric existence amidst the world of objects. This source of all individual activities is the residual vāsanās in the individual. Naturally therefore, in its macrocosmic aspect, the total universe of men and things and their behaviours must spring from the total vāsanās of all living beings. The 'avyakta' or 'unmanifest' is this unseen cause – the total vāsanās – that has manifested as the 'seen' the world of objects. (13.6)

8. What is 'mūla-prakṛti' or 'māyā'?

The source of all individual activities is the residual vāsanās in the individual. In its macrocosmic aspect, the total universe of men and things and their behaviours springs from the total vāsanās of all living beings. The Sāṅkhyans term this totality of vāsanās as 'mūla-prakṛti', and the Vedāntins call this very same total vāsanās 'māyā'. (13.6)

9. Distinguish between 'Īśvara' and 'jīva'.

The Supreme functioning through māyā (mūla-prakṛti) is the 'Īśvara' (Lord) of the total universe; and the same Supreme functioning through the vāsanā-layers in the individual (avidyā) is the creator, sustainer and destroyer of the individual life, the 'jīva' (ego). (13.7)

10. What are the 24 tattvas of Sāṅkhyan philosophy?

The five great elements (space, air, fire, water and earth), ego, intellect, the unmanifest, the 10 organs (five organs of knowledge and five organs of action), mind, and the five sense objects (sound, touch, form, taste and smell) are the 24 tattvas (principles) of the Sāṅkhyan philosophy. (13.7)

11. Matter and Spirit are the two aspects of ______.

Īśvara (Lord) (13.20)

12. The term 'Puruṣa' is used synonymously with the terms ______, ______ and ______.

Jīva (Ego), Kṣetrajña (Knower of the field) and Bhoktṛ (Enjoyer) (13.21)

13. What are the various appellations of Puruṣa?

The following verse enumerates the various appellations of Puruṣa:

उपद्रष्टानुमन्ता च भर्ता भोक्ता महेश्वरः ।
परमात्मेति चाप्युक्तो देहेऽस्मिन्पुरुषः परः ॥

upadraṣṭānumantā ca bhartā bhoktā maheśvaraḥ,
paramātmeti cāpyukto dehe'sminpuruṣaḥ paraḥ.

The supreme Puruṣa in this body is also called the Spectator, the Permitter, the Supporter, the Enjoyer, the great Lord and the Supreme Self. (13.23)

14. What is 'meditation'?

'Meditation' consists in withdrawing, by concentration, all the sense organs away from their respective sense objects into the mind, and then withdrawing the mind into the inner intelligence, and then contemplating upon the Highest. It is a continuous and unbroken thought-flow, like a stream of flowing oil. In order to pursue this path, the individual must have a dynamic head and heart—both least disturbed by their own subjective defects. (13.25)

15. What is 'mutual superimposition' (anyonya-adhyāsa)?

In every superimposition, like the ghost in the post, a delusion is projected upon a substratum. Not only the form and all attributes of the ghost come to be projected upon the post, but the post also lends its existence to the non-existent ghost. As a result of their mutual exhange, we find that the non-existent ghost comes to exist in our experience while the existing post becomes a non-existent ghost with illusions of physical limbs and ghastly behaviour. This process, a trick of the human mind, is called 'mutual superimposition' (anyonya-adhyāsa). (13.27)

Thoughts and Concepts

1. Cite the relevant verse wherein the Lord declares that He is the Kṣetrajña in all kṣetras.

In the following verse the Lord declares that He is the 'Kṣetrajña' (Knower of the field) in all kṣetras (fields).

क्षेत्रज्ञं चापि मां विद्धि सर्वक्षेत्रेषु भारत ।
क्षेत्रक्षेत्रज्ञयोर्ज्ञानं यत्तज्ज्ञानं मतं मम ॥

kṣetrajñaṁ cāpi māṁ viddhi sarvakṣetreṣu bhārata,
kṣetrakṣetrajñayorjñānaṁ yattajjñānaṁ mataṁ mama.

Know Me as the 'Knower of the field' in all 'fields' O Bhārata; Knowledge of the 'field' as also of the 'Knower of the field' is considered by Me to be My Knowledge. (13.3)

2. How does the Lord eulogise the knowledge of kṣetra and Kṣetrajña?

Śrī Kṛṣṇa glorifies the 'knowledge of kṣetra and Kṣetrajña' in the following verse:

ऋषिभिर्बहुधा गीतं छन्दोभिर्विविधैः पृथक् ।
ब्रह्मसूत्रपदैश्चैव हेतुमद्भिर्विनिश्चितैः ॥

ṛṣibhirbahudhā gītaṁ chandobhirvividhaiḥ pṛthak,
brahmasūtrapadaiścaiva hetumadbhirviniścitaiḥ.

Ṛṣis have sung (about the 'field' and the 'Knower of the field) in many ways, in various distinctive chants and also in the suggestive words indicative of Brahman, full of reason and decision. (13.5)

3. What does the term 'ekam' (one) mean in the expression: *'indriyāṇi daśaikaṁ ca*—the ten senses and the *one*'?

The five organs of perception and the five organs of action are the vehicles by which each individual perceives stimuli and responds to them. The term 'one' in this context stands for the mind. Even though the sense organs are many, the faculty in us that receives all the stimuli from all the five avenues of perception is one and the same, the mind. Not only does the mind receive the stimuli but it also executes the judgement of the intellect and sends forth responses to the outer world. It is again the only outlet for the individual personality to express through. The term 'one' thus indicates the mind. (13.6)

4. Why are mental modifications such as desire, hatred, pleasure, pain, etc., also included in kṣetra (field)?

The entire world of objects i.e., the 'field' (kṣetra) is indicated by the phrase 'this body' (*idaṁ śarīram*). Since everything other than the subject belongs to the world of objects and can be perceived as an object, mental modifications like desire, hatred, pain, etc., are also the objects of our knowledge, and therefore, they are also classified under 'kṣetra'. (13.7)

5. What are the various factors that constitute the 'kṣetra'?

The following two verses describe the kṣetra (field):

महाभूतान्यहङ्कारो बुद्धिरव्यक्तमेव च ।
इन्द्रियाणि दशैकं च पञ्च चेन्द्रियगोचराः ॥

mahābhūtānyahaṅkāro buddhiravyaktameva ca,
indriyāṇi daśaikaṁ ca pañca cendriyagocarāḥ.

The great elements, egoism, intellect and also the unmanifested (mūla-prakṛti), the 10 senses and the one (the mind) and the five objects of the senses,... (13.6)

इच्छा द्वेषः सुखं दुःखं सङ्घातश्चेतना धृतिः ।
एतत्क्षेत्रं समासेन सविकारमुदाहृतम् ॥

icchā dveṣaḥ sukhaṁ duḥkhaṁ saṅghātaścetanā dhṛtiḥ,
etatkṣetraṁ samāsena savikāramudāhṛtam.

Desire, hatred, pleasure, pain, aggregate (body), intelligence, fortitude—this is kṣetra and it has been thus briefly described with its modifications. (13.7)

Kṣetra is thus:

(1) The five great elements
(2) Egoism
(3) Intellect
(4) Mūla-prakṛti
(5) The 10 senses (organs of knowledge and action) and the mind
(6) The five sense objects
(7) Desire

(8) Hatred
(9) Pleasure
(10) Pain
(11) The aggregate (of the matter vestures of body, mind, prāṇas and so on)
(12) Intelligence
(13) Fortitude

6. What are the twenty qualities of Jñāna (Knowledge)? Cite the verses that enumerate them.

The twenty qualities of Jñāna (Knowledge) enumerated in the Gītā are certain mental and emotional attributes, moral attitudes and ethical principles that are essential pre-requisites for a seeker who is desirous of experiencing the Infinite Self. They are as follows:

(1) Humility
(2) Unpretentiousness
(3) Non-injury
(4) Forgiveness
(5) Uprightness
(6) Service to the teacher
(7) Purity
(8) Steadfastness
(9) Self-control
(10) Indifference to the objects of the senses
(11) Absence of egoism
(12) Perception of evil in birth, death, old age, sickness and pain
(13) Non-attachment
(14) Non-identification of Self with son, spouse, home and the rest
(15) Constant even-mindedness on the attainment of desirable and undesirable objects
(16) Unswerving devotion unto the Lord by the Yoga of non-separation
(17) Resorting to solitary places
(18) Distaste for the society of people
(19) Constancy in Self-Knowledge

(20) Perception of the goal of true Knowledge.

The following five verses (verses 8-12) enumerate these 20 qualities of Jñāna (Knowledge):

अमानित्वमदम्भित्वमहिंसा क्षान्तिरार्जवम् ।
आचार्योपासनं शौचं स्थैर्यमात्मविनिग्रहः ॥

amānitvamadambhitvamahiṁsā kṣāntirārjavam,
ācāryopāsanaṁ śaucaṁ sthairyamātmavinigrahaḥ.

Humility, unpretentiousness, non-injury, forgiveness, uprightness, service to the teacher, purity, steadfastness, self-control... (13.8)

इन्द्रियार्थेषु वैराग्यमनहङ्कार एव च ।
जन्ममृत्युजराव्याधिदुःखदोषानुदर्शनम् ॥

indriyārtheṣu vairāgyamanahaṅkāra eva ca,
janmamṛtyujarāvyādhiduḥkhadoṣānudarśanam.

Indifference to the objects of the senses, and also absence of egoism, perception of (or reflection upon) evil in birth, death, old age, sickness and pain... (13.9)

असक्तिरनभिष्वङ्गः पुत्रदारगृहादिषु ।
नित्यं च समचित्तत्वमिष्टानिष्टोपपत्तिषु ॥

asaktiranabhiṣvaṅgaḥ putradāragṛhādiṣu,
nityaṁ ca samacittatvamiṣṭāniṣṭopapattiṣu.

Non-attachment, non-identification of Self with son, spouse, home and the rest; and constant even-mindedness on the attainment of the desirable and the undesirable... (13.10)

मयि चानन्ययोगेन भक्तिरव्यभिचारिणी ।
विविक्तदेशसेवित्वमरतिर्जनसंसदि ॥

mayi cānanyayogena bhaktiravyabhicāriṇī,
viviktadeśasevitvamaratirjanasaṁsadi.

Unswerving devotion unto Me by the Yoga of non-separation, resorting to solitary places, distaste for the society of people... (13.11)

अध्यात्मज्ञाननित्यत्वं तत्त्वज्ञानार्थदर्शनम् ।
एतज्ज्ञानमिति प्रोक्तमज्ञानं यदतोऽन्यथा ॥

adhyātmajñānanityatvaṁ tattvajñānārthadarśanam,
etajjñānamiti proktamajñānaṁ yadato'nyathā.

Constancy in Self-Knowledge, perception of the goal of true Knowledge—this is declared to be Knowledge and what is opposed to it is 'ignorance'. (13.12)

7. What is the importance of perception of the evil in birth, death, old age, sickness and pain?

Unless a seeker is constantly conscious of the evil of the pain in his present stage of existence, he will not discover the necessary spiritual urge, intellectual dynamism, emotional enthusiasm or physical courage to seek, to fight for, to win and to possess the Divine Fields of Perfection. Birth, growth, decay, disease and death are the tragic destinies of all living equipment. Every physical body in the world goes through these modifications. And each one of them is an inlet for fresh sources of sorrow. In all these stages of our metamorphosis, to constantly recognise pain is to feel an impatience with it. This sense of revolt against pain is the fuel that drives the seeker faster and faster into a search for the Peaks of Perfection. (13.9)

8. What is 'concentration'?

'Concentration' is the art of focussing the mind upon a particular point to the exclusion of all mental excitement and agitation. This steadiness in concentration may be destroyed by causes arising at two different points—either in the individual's own mind or in the object contemplated upon. Unless both are steady, concentration cannot be successful. (13.11)

9. What is the importance of ever keeping in mind one's goal of true Knowledge?

Liberation (Mokṣa) from all our imperfections and limitations is the goal striven for by all spiritual seekers. To remember constantly the goal of our endeavour is to add more enthusiasm to our activities. Sincerity of purpose in and undying devotion to any endeavour can be had only if the seeker is thrilled by the vision of the goal that he has to reach. Hence the importance of always keeping in mind one's goal of true Knowledge. (13.12)

10. Why are the various attributes starting from 'humility' to 'perception of the goal' (verses 8-12) declared to be Knowledge itself when they are only attributes to be cultivated for gaining Knowledge?

The attributes from 'humility' to 'perception of the goal' are declared to be 'Knowledge' because they are conducive to the final Realisation of the Self. A train in full steam waiting for the signal at a platform is generally described as "Chennai is ready to leave now." In the language of the railways, it is usual to say—"Delhi is expected", "Calcutta is late", "Bombay has left", etc. In each of these cases only the train leaving for or coming from these various cities is meant. Similarly here, the qualities which are the means for Knowledge are called 'Knowledge' (Jñāna) because once these qualities have been fully developed, it is easier to reach the goal, the Pure knowledge of the Self. (13.12)

11. Why is Brahman neither 'sat' nor 'asat'?

The terms 'sat' and 'asat' in this context mean 'existent' and 'non-existent' respectively. These two concepts of 'sat' (existent) and 'asat' (non-existent) are judgements of the human intellect. The Consciousness that illumines these judgements is the Self. The illuminator and the illumined cannot be one and the same. Therefore, the one Subject, the Brahman, as opposed to all 'objects' can neither be 'sat' (existent) nor 'asat' (non-existent), because 'sat' and 'asat' are two types of thought waves alone, and the Self illumines them both. (13.13)

12. Why is the Self described as 'seeming to possess the function of all senses and yet devoid of all senses'?

Electricity is not the light in the bulb, nor the heat in the heater; yet while functioning through the bulb or the heater and conditioned by them, the same electricity looks as though it is light or fire. The Self in us, while functioning through the equipment, the sense organs, and conditioned by them, looks as though It has all the sense organs. But the sense organs are material and they decay and perish, while the Consciousness—functioning in and through them and providing each of them with its own individual faculty is Itself Eternal and

Changeless. The Truth, while functioning through the sense organs, looks as though It possesses them. But in fact, It has Itself none of these sense faculties. Hence the description of the Self as 'seeming to possess the function of all senses and yet devoid of all senses'. (13.15)

13. Explain why the Self is described as possessing 'incomprehensible subtlety'.

The grosser the thing the more perceptible it is. Earth can be smelt, can be tasted, can be seen, can be heard. Water cannot be smelt. Fire cannot be tasted. Air cannot be seen. Space has only sound as its property. Cause is always subtler than effect. Space itself being a gross product, it must have a cause. That which is the cause for space is the Eternal Substratum, from which all the elements have arisen. Consciousness being thus the 'subtlest of the subtle', pervading even space, It is incomprehensible to the gross equipment of thought, feeling and perception. (13.16)

14. Why is the Self described as 'far as well as near'?

Limited and conditioned things can be defined by their location in space as 'here' or 'there'. And with reference to their distance from the observer, we can say they are 'near' or 'far'. But that which is All-pervading must be at once 'here' and 'there'. And, therefore, it is 'near as well as far'. This phrase has also been sometimes interpreted as 'far and yet near'. 'Far'—in its Transcendental Absolute nature the Truth is far away from all the hallucinations of names and forms that in their aggregate constitute the Universe, but at the same time, as Existence It exists in every name and form and is hence 'near'. (13.16)

15. What is the nature of the 'Jñeyam' (Brahman)?

The nature of the Jñeyam (Brahman) is described in the following verses (verses 13-18):

ज्ञेयं यत्तत्प्रवक्ष्यामि यज्ज्ञात्वाऽमृतमश्नुते ।
अनादिमत्परं ब्रह्म न सत्तन्नासदुच्यते ॥

jñeyaṁ yattatpravakṣyāmi yajjñātvā'mṛtamaśnute,
anādimatparaṁ brahma na sattannāsaducyate.

I will declare that which has to be 'Known', knowing which one attains Immortality—the beginningless Supreme Brahman, called neither 'being' nor 'non-being'. (13.13)

सर्वतः पाणिपादं तत्सर्वतोऽक्षिशिरोमुखम् ।
सर्वतः श्रुतिमल्लोके सर्वमावृत्य तिष्ठति ॥

sarvataḥ pāṇipādaṁ tatsarvato'kṣiśiromukham,
sarvataḥ śrutimalloke sarvamāvṛtya tiṣṭhati.

With hands and feet everywhere, with eyes, heads and mouths everywhere, with ears everywhere, He exists in the world, enveloping all... (13.14)

सर्वेन्द्रियगुणाभासं सर्वेन्द्रियविवर्जितम् ।
असक्तं सर्वभृच्चैव निर्गुणं गुणभोक्तृ च ॥

sarvendriyaguṇābhāsaṁ sarvendriyavivarjitam,
asaktaṁ sarvabhṛccaiva nirguṇaṁ guṇabhoktṛ ca.

Shining by the functions of all senses, yet without the senses; unattached, yet supporting all; devoid of qualities, yet their experiencer... (13.15)

बहिरन्तश्च भूतानामचरं चरमेव च ।
सूक्ष्मत्वात्तदविज्ञेयं दूरस्थं चान्तिके च तत् ॥

bahirantaśca bhūtānāmacaraṁ carameva ca,
sūkṣmatvāttadavijñeyaṁ dūrasthaṁ cāntike ca tat.

Without and within (all) beings, the 'unmoving' and also the 'moving'; because of its subtlety unknowable; and the near and far away—is That. (13.16)

अविभक्तं च भूतेषु विभक्तमिव च स्थितम् ।
भूतभर्तृ च तज्ज्ञेयं ग्रसिष्णु प्रभविष्णु च ॥

avibhaktaṁ ca bhūteṣu vibhaktamiva ca sthitam,
bhūtabhartṛ ca tajjñeyaṁ grasiṣṇu prabhaviṣṇu ca.

And undivided, yet He exists as if divided in beings; That is to be known as the Supporter of Beings; He is worthy to be known; He devours and He generates. (13.17)

ज्योतिषामपि तज्ज्योतिस्तमसः परमुच्यते ।
ज्ञानं ज्ञेयं ज्ञानगम्यं हृदि सर्वस्य विष्ठितम् ॥

jyotiṣāmapi tajjyotistamasaḥ paramucyate,
jñānaṁ jñeyaṁ jñānagamyaṁ hṛdi sarvasya viṣṭhitam.

That (Brahman), the Light of all lights, is said to be beyond darkness; (It is) Knowledge, the Object of Knowledge, seated in the hearts of all, to be reached by Knowledge. (13.18)

The following is the enumeration of the nature of Jñeyam (Brahman) as described in the above verses:

(1) Beginningless
(2) Neither 'being' nor 'non-being'
(3) Having hands, feet, eyes, head, mouth, heads everywhere and enveloping all
(4) Shining by the functions of all the senses
(5) Without senses
(6) Unattached
(7) Supporting all
(8) Without the three qualities of sattva, rajas and tamas
(9) The experiencer of the qualities
(10) Existing within and without all beings
(11) Unmoving
(12) Moving
(13) Unknowable to ignorant because of its subtlety
(14) Far away
(15) Near
(16) Indivisible but existing as if divided in beings
(17) Supporter of beings
(18) Worthy to be known
(19) Destroyer and also that which generates
(20) Light of all shining objects like the sun, the moon and the fire
(21) Beyond ignorance
(22) Knowledge, the Knowable and the goal of Knowledge
(23) Seated in the heart of all beings

16. Why is Brahman compared with light and often even called 'Light'?

Brahman, the illuminator in all, is the One Consciousness by which everything is known intellectually, realised intuitively and experienced spiritually. Since the Consciousness in us brings various experiences within our understanding and knowledge, it is generally compared with light. Further, by the 'Light' of Consciousness, every thought is brilliantly lit in the awareness of our life. Thus, it has become a spiritual tradition to often call Consciousness (Brahman) 'Light'. (13.18)

17. What do the terms 'jñānam', 'jñeyam' and 'jñāna-gamyam' mean?

'Jñānam' is 'knowledge' and stands for the 20 values enumerated from verses 8-12. 'Jñeyam' is the Self that is to be known. This has been described in verses 13-18. The Self, the 'Jñeyam', which is to be known by 'jñānam', i.e., the 20 values enumerated is alone termed 'jñāna-gamyam'. This 're-terming' is done in order to explicitly state that 'Jñānam' (knowledge) alone is the method of knowing the Self. (13.18)

18. Cite the verse which declares that both prakṛti (matter) and Puruṣa (spirit) are beginningless.

The following verse declares that both prakṛti and Puruṣa are beginningless (anādi):

प्रकृतिं पुरुषं चैव विद्ध्यनादि उभावपि ।
विकारांश्च गुणांश्चैव विद्धि प्रकृतिसम्भवान् ॥

prakṛtiṁ puruṣaṁ caiva viddhyanādi ubhāvapi,
vikārāṁśca guṇāṁścaiva viddhi prakṛtisambhavān.

Know that matter and Spirit are both beginningless, and know also that all modifications and qualities are born of Prakṛti.

Matter (prakṛti) and Spirit (Puruṣa) are both beginningless. Matter and Spirit are the two aspects of Īśvara, the Lord. As the Lord is Eternal, it is but natural that His nature – matter and Spirit – should also be beginningless. (13.20)

19. What are the effects of prakṛti and Puruṣa?

The following verse mentions the specific effects of both prakṛti and Puruṣa:

कार्यकरणकर्तृत्वे हेतुः प्रकृतिरुच्यते ।
पुरुषः सुखदुःखानां भोक्तृत्वे हेतुरुच्यते ॥

kāryakaraṇakartṛtve hetuḥ prakṛtirucyate,
puruṣaḥ sukhaduḥkhānāṁ bhoktṛtve heturucyate.

In the production of the effect and the cause, prakṛti is said to be the cause; in the experience of pleasure and pain, Puruṣa is said to be the cause.

By 'kārya' (effect) is meant the body. By 'karaṇa' (means) is meant the five great elements, five senses, mind, intellect and ego. Both these constitute the world of matter and are produced by prakṛti.

Puruṣa is said to be the cause of pleasure and pain. Pleasure and pain are the reactions in the intellect. When desirable objects in a conducive pattern reach our life, the experience is called 'pleasure'. And the opposite sensation produced by undesirable objects is called 'pain'. Every experience, in its final analysis, is judged either as pain or as pleasure. The Awareness in us illumines these. It would be impossible to be conscious of the flow of experiences without the grace of the Consciousness. Therefore, the Spirit (Puruṣa) is explained as the cause for one's experiences in life. (13.21)

20. What is the cause for the rebirth of the Puruṣa (Kṣetrajña)?

In truth, the Puruṣa (Spirit) has no saṁsāra (transmigration). But when It identifies Itself with the body and the senses, i.e., the 'field' (prakṛti), It becomes the 'experiencer'. The sensations arising out of the matter envelopment (prakṛti) such as pleasure and pain, heat and cold, success and failure, etc., constitute the painful shackles on the 'Knower of the field' (Puruṣa or Kṣetrajña).

Thus, the destinies of matter become the tragic experiences of the Spirit, not because they are in the Spirit, but because the Spirit makes an unhealthy contact, through its own identification, with the realm of sorrow. The Puruṣa then not only experiences the joys and sorrows in life but also develops a blind attachment to them and this is 'the cause for its birth in good or evil wombs'.

To reiterate: while living in the world the Puruṣa experiences the pleasures and joys interpreted by the world of matter and gets attached to them, and thereby develops residual impressions (vāsanās), and to exhaust these impressions it takes conducive fields of birth where it can eke out its cherished satisfaction through various experiences.

This idea is expressed in the following verse:

पुरुषः प्रकृतिस्थो हि भुङ्क्ते प्रकृतिजान्गुणान् ।
कारणं गुणसङ्गोऽस्य सदसद्योनिजन्मसु ॥

puruṣaḥ prakṛtistho hi bhuṅkte prakṛtijānguṇān,
kāraṇaṁ guṇasaṅgo'sya sadasadyonijanmasu.

The Puruṣa, seated in prakṛti, experiences the qualities born of prakṛti; attachment to the qualities is the cause of His birth in good and evil wombs. (13.22)

21. The Supreme Self has been termed as Upadraṣṭā, Anumantā, Bhartā, Bhoktā and Maheśvara in the following verse. Explain these terms.

उपद्रष्टानुमन्ता च भर्ता भोक्ता महेश्वरः ।
परमात्मेति चाप्युक्तो देहेऽस्मिन्पुरुषः परः ॥

upadraṣṭānumantā ca bhartā bhoktā maheśvaraḥ,
paramātmeti cāpyukto dehe'sminpuruṣaḥ paraḥ.

The supreme Puruṣa in this body is also called the Spectator, the Permitter, the Supporter, the Enjoyer, the great Lord and the Supreme Self.

Upadraṣṭā: When an individual is completely deluded and totally unconscious of the Self, in and through him the Infinite Divine expresses Himself as though He is only an 'onlooker' (upadraṣṭā). To explain with an example: when a person murders an innocent victim, the Lord expresses through that criminal's vehicle only as a silent spectator of it all (upadraṣṭā).

Anumantā: When the individual is not totally forgetful of the Self and undertakes right actions, in such an individual, the Supreme expresses Himself as a 'Permitter' (anumantā).

Bhartā: When right actions are done with full consciousness of the Self and in a spirit of total surrender to the Lord, the Lord is the 'fulfiller' (bhartā). Such actions are filled with success by His grace.

Bhoktā: When, with entire dedication unto Him, the individual is completely a yoga-yuktaḥ (united) in His Eternal Conscious nature (nitya-caitanya-svarūpa), the Self seems to be the very 'enjoyer' (bhoktā).

Maheśvara: The great Īśvara, the Lord of Lords (Maheśvara) is the Higher Self in this very body. (13.23)

22. Who becomes a 'Man of Wisdom'?

He who has realised in himself (1) the nature of matter (2) the nature of the Spirit (3) how the Spirit, deluded by its own pre-occupations, gets identified with matter and behaves as a 'Knower of the Field' and also (4) the mysteries of the guṇas, under the influences of which the equipments function—becomes a Man of Wisdom. (13.24)

23. Cite and explain the verses wherein the Lord declares that seekers attain Liberation in various ways.

The Realisation of the Self is the final goal of all spiritual seeking, and there are more 'paths' than one prescribed for this Divine Achievement. Seekers can realise the Self by (1) Dhyāna Yoga (2) Sāṅkhya Yoga (3) Karma Yoga and (4) By hearing from others and worshipping according to instructions (even if they are not able to practise the other paths).

These four paths are indicated in the following two verses:

ध्यानेनात्मनि पश्यन्ति केचिदात्मानमात्मना ।
अन्ये साङ्ख्येन योगेन कर्मयोगेन चापरे ॥

dhyānenātmani paśyanti kecidātmānamātmanā,
anye sāṅkhyena yogena karmayogena cāpare.

Some, by meditation, behold the Self in the Self by the Self; others by the Yoga of Knowledge (Sāṅkhya Yoga); and others by Karma Yoga. (13.25)

अन्ये त्वेवमजानन्तः श्रुत्वान्येभ्य उपासते ।
तेऽपि चातितरन्त्येव मृत्युं श्रुतिपरायणाः ॥

anye tvevamajānantaḥ śrutvānyebhya upāsate,
te'pi cātitarantyeva mṛtyuṁ śrutiparāyaṇāḥ.

Others also, not knowing this, worship, having heard of It from others; they too cross beyond death if they would regard what they have heard as their supreme refuge. (13.26)

(1) Dhyāna Yoga: This path of quietening the mind, steadying the intellect and, with an integrated mind and intellect, contemplating steadily upon the transcendental Self is not a 'path' that is available to all, as it calls for certain mental and intellectual perfections which are not commonly seen in everyone. Those who have these qualifications are considered as the highest type of aspirants. The seekers of the best type—who have developed in themselves a sufficient detachment (vairāgya) from the sense objects, and a ready discrimination to distinguish the permanent from the impermanent (viveka)—alone can steadily walk this Highest 'path'.

(2) Sāṅkhya Yoga: In the case of those who have not the required amount of steadiness in mind and intellect—not because of any lack of aspiration but for want of right understanding of the Goal (viveka)—their sense of detachment (vairāgya) waxes and wanes. Sometimes they are good at meditation, and at other times they experience a tremendous amount of restlessness and agitation. For such seekers, the only remedy is the enthusiastic study of the śāstras. The term 'Sāṅkhya' means 'the sequence of logical thought through which we reach a definite philosophical conclusion that is unassailable by any doubts. This deep study and reflection (vicāra) provides the seeker with a better understanding of the text, and therefore, a deeper conviction of the goal. This will discover for him a very healthy and steady self-application and a divine equipoise in his meditation.

(3) Karma Yoga: There are still other types of seekers for whom even study of the śāstra and effective reflections upon it become almost impossible because their inward personality is sullied by the existing hosts of sensuous vāsanās. They are in a state of mental agitation in which no dynamic and effective meditation is possible. For them, selfless activity in a spirit of Yajña is prescribed. When this Karma Yoga is pursued for a time, the existing vāsanās exhaust themselves and more and more quietude and tranquillity are experienced by the seeker. A mind, thus steadied, is fit for delving into the deeper significances of the scriptures, and when the conviction of the goal is intensified in the individual, as a result of these reflections, he becomes fit for meditation.

(4) Worshipping after hearing from others: If a person does not possess the capacity to follow any of the three Yogas described above, he need not be disheartened. He can hear of God and the ways of God, the path to reach Him from experienced elders and act accor-dingly. That is enough to take him across saṁsāra—if he has faith in their words and worships with devotion.

24. Why is the 'Ātman' described as the 'object recognised' (ātmānam) 'instrument of cognition' (ātmanā) as well as 'recognising subject ' (ātmani)?

In the final Realisation, it is experienced that the intellect – the instrument of cognition, the seeker – the cognising subject, as well as the Subject – the object of cognition are all in fact nothing other than the One Self. It is for this reason that the 'Ātman' is described as the 'cognised object' (ātmānam), the instrument of cognition (ātmanā) as well as the 'subject cognising It' (ātmani). (13.25)

25. Cite and explain the verse which asserts that every being is the union of kṣetra and Kṣetrajña.

The following verse explicitly states that all beings are born from the union of kṣetra and Kṣetrajña:

यावत्सञ्जायते किञ्चित्सत्त्वं स्थावरजङ्गमम् ।
क्षेत्रक्षेत्रज्ञसंयोगात्तद्विद्धि भरतर्षभ ॥

yāvatsañjāyate kiñcitsattvaṁ sthāvarajaṅgamam,
kṣetrakṣetrajñasaṁyogāttadviddhi bharatarṣabha.

Whenever any being is born, the unmoving or the moving, know you, O best of the Bharatas, that it is from the union between the 'Field' and the 'Knower of the Field'.

All things in the world that are born – both the world of inert matter (unmoving) and the world of conscious beings (moving) – arise neither from the 'field' (kṣetra or prakṛti) nor from the 'Knower of the field (Kṣetrajña or Puruṣa). The source is from the marriage of prakṛti and Puruṣa. The spirit plays in the 'field' (prakṛti) and becomes the 'Knower of the Field' (Puruṣa) and when this Puruṣa works in prakṛti the combination breeds the entire phenomenal universe. (13.27)

26. Explain the Lord's declaration that "he who sees the Supreme Lord existing equally in all beings, the Unperishing within the perishing, alone sees."

He who is capable of recognising the Supreme Lord (Parameśvara), who revels everywhere as the Pure Spirit, in all names and forms, who changes not, while the outer equipments change, he alone is the one who sees what is really to be seen. Everybody sees, but not the Real. Therefore, the Lord asserts that he who recognises this harmony of the one Truth, this thread of Reality that holds all experiences together, which is one in all beings, experiences the Truth to be realised in the world. Others see, and yet do not see; he alone sees who realises this Supreme Lord, which is the Imperishable. (13.28)

27. Cite the two verses wherein the following expression is found: "He who sees, verily sees" (*yaḥ paśyati sa paśyati*).

समं सर्वेषु भूतेषु तिष्ठन्तं परमेश्वरम् ।
विनश्यत्स्वविनश्यन्तं यः पश्यति स पश्यति ॥

samaṁ sarveṣu bhūteṣu tiṣṭhantaṁ parameśvaram,
vinaśyatsvavinaśyantaṁ yaḥ paśyati sa paśyati.

He sees who sees the Supreme Lord existing equally in all beings, the unperishing within the perishing. (13.28)

प्रकृत्यैव च कर्माणि क्रियमाणानि सर्वशः ।
यः पश्यति तथात्मानमकर्तारं स पश्यति ॥

prakṛtyaiva ca karmāṇi kriyamāṇāni sarvaśaḥ,
yaḥ paśyati tathātmānamakartāraṁ sa paśyati.

He sees who sees that all actions are performed by prakṛti alone, and the Self is actionless. (13.30)

28. Who attains the Highest Goal (*parāṁ gatim*)?

The one who sees the one Lord pervading equally everywhere alone attains the Higher Goal. This is stated in the following verse:

समं पश्यन्हि सर्वत्र समवस्थितमीश्वरम् ।
न हिनस्त्यात्मनात्मानं ततो याति परां गतिम् ॥

samaṁ paśyanhi sarvatra samavasthitamīśvaram,
na hinastyātmanātmānaṁ tato yāti parāṁ gatim.

Indeed, he who sees the same Lord everywhere equally dwelling destroys not the Self by the Self; therefore, he goes to the Highest Goal. (13.29)

29. Explain the Lord's declaration that the person who sees that the Lord exists equally in all does not destroy the Self by the Self (*na hinasti ātmanā ātmānam*).

The wise man who realises that the Ātman or Lord exists in all does not destroy the Self with the self. What is meant is that the ignorant man destroys the Self by identifying himself with the body. In fact this amounts to suicide (ātmahatya). The ignorant man, thinking of himself as the non-Self, destroys his true Self. He sees the body and the world externally and thinks that he is the body. In this case the true Self is as good as having been destroyed, because Its existence is not realised. The Man of Wisdom sees and realises the all-pervading true Self; and so he is described as not having destroyed the all-pervading pure Self by the limited understanding of the Self. (13.29)

30. Explain the Lord's declaration in the following verse: "he alone sees who sees the Self as actionless."

प्रकृत्यैव च कर्माणि क्रियमाणानि सर्वशः ।
यः पश्यति तथात्मानमकर्तारं स पश्यति ॥

prakṛtyaiva ca karmāṇi kriyamāṇāni sarvaśaḥ,
yaḥ paśyati tathātmānamakartāraṁ sa paśyati.

He sees who sees that all actions are performed by prakṛti alone, and that the Self is actionless. (13.30)

Prakṛti alone performs all actions. Matter is the equipment that orders the types of action that should manifest. The Self is All-pervading, Perfect and, as such, there is no desire in It. He who recognises how his own 'vehicles' function and realises that the Self in him is ever actionless is alone the right perceiver. This is indicated by the Lord's declaration that "he alone sees who sees the Self as actionless." (13.30)

31. When has one 'become' Brahman?

Having understood the ocean, one realises how the numberless waves rise from that one ocean; so too a Man of Knowledge also realises the expansion of plurality from the one Brahman alone. Such moments of complete understanding, wherein the Man of Wisdom experiences the One Self within and without – enveloping and embracing, penetrating and nourishing not only the depthless and the measureless Infinite, but also the superficial world of pluralistic names and forms – are the sacred moments when he has 'become' Brahman. The following verse states this explicitly:

यदा भूतपृथग्भावमेकस्थमनुपश्यति ।
तत एव च विस्तारं ब्रह्म सम्पद्यते तदा ॥

yadā bhūtapṛthagbhāvamekasthamanupaśyati,
tata eva ca vistāraṁ brahma sampadyate tadā.

When he sees the whole variety of beings as resting in the One and spreading forth from That (One) alone, he then becomes Brahman. (13.31)

32. Who is a person of 'True Wisdom' and 'Right Perception'?

He who recognises the one homogeneous Self, he who experiences that the Consciousness in him is one with the homogeneous mass of Consciousness everywhere, and he who also understands how on his coming into the body awareness, the world of plurality throws the mantle of its magic upon the fair face of the Infinite and makes It look ugly with all its perishable names and forms—such a person possesses 'True Wisdom' and 'Right Perception'. (13.31)

33. Cite the verse wherein the Lord declares that though dwelling in the body the Self does not act.

अनादित्वान्निर्गुणत्वात्परमात्मायमव्ययः ।
शरीरस्थोऽपि कौन्तेय न करोति न लिप्यते ॥

anāditvānnirguṇatvātparamātmāyamavyayaḥ,
śarīrastho'pi kaunteya na karoti na lipyate.

Being without beginning and devoid of qualities, the Supreme Self, the Imperishable, though dwelling in the body, O Kaunteya, neither acts nor is tainted. (13.32)

34. What is the analogy that Śrī Kṛṣṇa uses to explain the Self's untainted nature.

Śrī Kṛṣṇa uses the analogy of space being unaffected to explain the untainted nature of Brahman:

यथा सर्वगतं सौक्ष्म्यादाकाशं नोपलिप्यते ।
सर्वत्रावस्थितो देहे तथात्मा नोपलिप्यते ॥

yathā sarvagataṁ saukṣmyādākāśaṁ nopalipyate,
sarvatrāvasthito dehe tathātmā nopalipyate.

As the all-pervading ether is not tainted because of its subtlety, so too the Self, seated everywhere in the body, is not tainted.

Space, being subtle, it allows everything to remain in it, yet nothing that it contains can contaminate it. Similarly, the Supreme Self, which is the very cause for the space itself and, therefore, subtler than it, cannot be contaminated by anything that exists or happens in the world of plurality. (13.33)

35. Why is the Self not contaminated by the realm of matter (prakṛti)?

Superimpositions do not really taint their substratums. For example: murders committed in the dream cannot soil the hands of the waker! The bloody garb of the ghost cannot leave its marks on the post. The mirage waters cannot wet even a grain of sand in the desert. These are examples of hallucinations and are delusory superimpositions. The world of plurality being nothing but misapprehensions of Reality arising out of the non-apprehension of the Real, the realm of matter (prakṛti) and its activities cannot contaminate and soil the Perfect and the Eternal. (13.33)

36. The Lord gives the example of the 'sun illumining the world' in the following verse to explain the concept of Kṣetrajña illumining the kṣetra. Explain this analogy.

यथा प्रकाशयत्येकः कृत्स्नं लोकमिमं रविः ।
क्षेत्रं क्षेत्री तथा कृत्स्नं प्रकाशयति भारत ॥

yathā prakāśayatyekaḥ kṛtsnaṁ lokamimaṁ raviḥ,
kṣetraṁ kṣetrī tathā kṛtsnaṁ prakāśayati bhārata.

Just as the one sun illumines the whole world, so also the 'Lord of the Field' (Paramātman) illumines the whole 'Field', O Bhārata.

This example of 'sun illumining the world' helps one to comprehend the exact relationship of the Consciousness, the Eternal Principle of Life, with reference to the various worlds of matter and their expressions. Just as the one Sun illumines the entire universe from afar, and at all times, so too the Consciousness merely illumines the world of objects, the body, the mind and the intellect.

Though in our everyday talks we attribute the activity of lighting up the world to the sun, we find on close examination that we cannot attribute any such activity to the sun. An action is that which has a beginning and an end and it is generally undertaken to fulfil a deep desire, or a silent purpose. The sun does not illumine the world in this sense of the term. On the other hand, 'light' itself is the nature of the sun, and in its presence everything gets illumined. Similarly, Consciousness is of the nature of Awareness and in Its presence everything becomes known—illumined.

Further, in the world there is only one sun and it illumines everything, good and bad, the vicious and the virtuous, the ugly and the beautiful. And yet the sun is not sullied by the ugly, the vicious and the bad, nor is it blessed by the good, the virtuous or the beautiful. So too, in our inner life, the Ever-perfect and Joyous Consciousness functions through the equipments and illumines them, but It never gets contaminated by the sins of the mind, by the perversions of the intellect, or by the crimes of the physical body. It only illumines. (13.34)

37. What is the 'jñānacakṣu' (eye of wisdom)?

Lord Kṛṣṇa advocates that man's life is fulfilled only when he, in his subtle discrimination, successfully meditates upon and realises the constitution, behaviour and relationship among the 'Field', 'the Knower of the Field' – the 'Supreme Self' in himself. This can be done only with a well-integrated instrument, a combination of a fully developed head and heart, which alone can apprehend the Invisible and Imperishable Self. The faculty that comes to experience this Divine Infinitude is often termed 'intuition', and in the language of the Hindu scriptures, it is called the 'jñānacakṣu' or 'eye of wisdom'. (13.35)

Selections for Reflection

1. To distinguish the world of the Subject from the world of objects is the salutary Knowledge that can redeem us from the confusions and sorrows from which we suffer today as individualised egos. (13.3)

2. To close our eyes to the causes that create our present problems is not to solve the problems. To know the nature of all matter envelopments—their play, and how they behave under given sets of circumstances—is to know the 'Field' where we have to battle for Release and win our Victory. (13.4)

3. When a truth is declared along with logical reasoning the conclusions arrived at are acceptable to any intelligent student by the sheer force of its appeal. (13.5)

4. To build a wall of discrimination around our inner personality and to keep such disturbances away is to discover the equipoise in ourselves—without which no progress or growth is ever possible. (13.10)

5. Wild imaginations and futile day-dreaming are the preoccupations of only a disintegrated mind. (13.11)

6. The more integrated the personality grows and the more maddening becomes its enthusiasm for the quest of that which is dear to its heart, the more it automatically lives alone in itself away from the noisy crowd. Whenever the mind is fascinated by an enchanting ideal, it loses all its contact with other preoccupations and becomes wedded faithfully to its own all-absorbing theme of interest. (13.11)

7. One of the ways of defining the indefinable Supreme, the Subject in the seeker himself, is to indicate It in a language of contradiction, which, without confusing the intellect, tickles it to a special kind of activity thereby facilitating the Realisation of the Eternal. The language of contradiction is the characteristic feature of all scriptural textbooks. (13.15)

8. The Consciousness functioning in the seeker's mind and intellect, if lived and experienced by Itself, must give the experience of the Infinite, just as by knowing the composition of a minute particle of salt, the world of sodium chloride is understood. (13.18)

9. The difference between the various seekers is the difference in their mental equanimity and intellectual equipoise. Each path is the fittest for the one who is walking it. No path can be said to be nobler than the other. In a pharmacy there are different medicines; each one serves a definite type of patient and the medicine prescribed for a given disease is the fittest medicine for that patient. (13.25)

10. The 'lesser paths' are mainly meant for purifying the inner equipments, and when the mind becomes steady and concentrated, when the intellect is redeemed from its wasteful habits of wrong imaginations, then the equipments are ready for Higher flights through the 'Path of Meditation'. (13.25)

11. Ordinarily I am a quiet man. But sometimes my heart's passion is endless. When I identify myself with the passion in my heart, I play in the world as the passionate man and perform deeds for which I myself might later on regret! Now in this example, the regret, and the regretting person, the passion and passionate entity—all of them revel in me. They all belong to me but I am not they! Yet, when I identify myself with them, I become the perpetrator of the regrettable actions and the passionate actor in me comes to brood over what has happened, and so it suffers. Similarly, the Self contains matter possibilities—the Self being 'paripūrṇa' (complete). To project matter and to identify with it is to become

Puruṣa, and the Puruṣa maintaining Itself in the 'field of matter' so projected becomes the source of the entire saṁsāra. To analyse closely with discrimination, to detach courageously with vitality, to carefully and heroically live as an observer of all that is happening within, not allowing ourselves to be misled by our own imaginations—is the method of Realising the Perfection in ourselves. (13.28)

12. Erroneous perception of the Reality through maladjusted equipments is the perception of the world, which, in its turn is throttling the individual perceiving it. When the Pure Consciousness looks upon Itself through the refracting medium of matter envelopments, It perceives, as it were, a world of plurality, and the pluralistic world grins and dances, whistles, shrieks and howls—ever ugly, stinking and sweating—according to the maddening changes that take place in the very equipments (field) through which the ego (Knower of the field) happens to gaze. (13.29)

Verses for Memorisation

इदं शरीरं कौन्तेय क्षेत्रमित्यभिधीयते ।
एतद्यो वेत्ति तं प्राहुः क्षेत्रज्ञ इति तद्विदः ॥

idaṁ śarīraṁ kaunteya kṣetramityabhidhīyate,
etadyo vetti taṁ prāhuḥ kṣetrajña iti tadvidaḥ.

This body, O Kaunteya, is called the 'kṣetra' (field), and He who knows it is called 'Kṣetrajña' (the Knower of the field) by those who know them (sages). (13.2)

क्षेत्रज्ञं चापि मां विद्धि सर्वक्षेत्रेषु भारत ।
क्षेत्रक्षेत्रज्ञयोर्ज्ञानं यत्तज्ज्ञानं मतं मम ॥

kṣetrajñaṁ cāpi māṁ viddhi sarvakṣetreṣu bhārata,
kṣetrakṣetrajñayorjñānaṁ yattajjñānaṁ mataṁ mama.

Know Me as the 'Knower of the field' in all 'fields' O Bhārata; Knowledge of the 'field' as also of the 'Knower of the field' is considered by Me to be My Knowledge. (13.3)

महाभूतान्यहङ्कारो बुद्धिरव्यक्तमेव च ।
इन्द्रियाणि दशैकं च पञ्च चेन्द्रियगोचराः ॥
mahābhūtānyahaṅkāro buddhiravyaktameva ca,
indriyāṇi daśaikaṁ ca pañca cendriyagocarāḥ.
The great elements, egoism, intellect and also the unmanifested (mūla-prakṛti), the ten senses and the one (the mind) and the five objects of the senses,... (13.6)

इच्छा द्वेषः सुखं दुःखं सङ्घातश्चेतना धृतिः ।
एतत्क्षेत्रं समासेन सविकारमुदाहृतम् ॥
icchā dveṣaḥ sukhaṁ duḥkhaṁ saṅghātaścetanā dhṛtiḥ,
etatkṣetraṁ samāsena savikāramudāhṛtam.
Desire, hatred, pleasure, pain, aggregate (body), intelligence, fortitude—this is kṣetra and it has been thus briefly described with its modifications. (13.7)

अमानित्वमदम्भित्वमहिंसा क्षान्तिरार्जवम् ।
आचार्योपासनं शौचं स्थैर्यमात्मविनिग्रहः ॥
amānitvamadambhitvamahiṁsā kṣāntirārjavam,
ācāryopāsanaṁ śaucaṁ sthairyamātmavinigrahaḥ.
Humility, unpretentiousness, non-injury, forgiveness, uprightness, service to the teacher, purity, steadfastness, self-control... (13.8)

इन्द्रियार्थेषु वैराग्यमनहङ्कार एव च ।
जन्ममृत्युजराव्याधिदुःखदोषानुदर्शनम् ॥
indriyārtheṣu vairāgyamanahaṅkāra eva ca,
janmamṛtyujarāvyādhiduḥkhadoṣānudarśanam.
Indifference to the objects of the senses, and also absence of egoism, perception of (or reflection upon) evil in birth, death, old age, sickness and pain... (13.9)

असक्तिरनभिष्वङ्गः पुत्रदारगृहादिषु ।
नित्यं च समचित्तत्वमिष्टानिष्टोपपत्तिषु ॥
asaktiranabhiṣvaṅgaḥ putradāragṛhādiṣu,
nityaṁ ca samacittatvamiṣṭāniṣṭopapattiṣu.
Non-attachment, non-identification of Self with son, spouse, home

and the rest; and constant even-mindedness on the attainment of the desirable and the undesirable... (13.10)

मयि चानन्ययोगेन भक्तिरव्यभिचारिणी ।
विविक्तदेशसेवित्वमरतिर्जनसंसदि ॥

mayi cānanyayogena bhaktiravyabhicāriṇī,
viviktadeśasevitvamaratirjanasaṁsadi.

Unswerving devotion unto Me by the Yoga of non-separation, resorting to solitary places, distaste for the society of people... (13.11)

अध्यात्मज्ञाननित्यत्वं तत्त्वज्ञानार्थदर्शनम् ।
एतज्ज्ञानमिति प्रोक्तमज्ञानं यदतोऽन्यथा ॥

adhyātmajñānanityatvaṁ tattvajñānārthadarśanam,
etajjñānamiti proktamajñānaṁ yadato'nyathā.

Constancy in Self-Knowledge, perception of the goal of true Knowledge—this is declared to be Knowledge and what is opposed to it is 'ignorance'. (13.12)

सर्वेन्द्रियगुणाभासं सर्वेन्द्रियविवर्जितम् ।
असक्तं सर्वभृच्चैव निर्गुणं गुणभोक्तृ च ॥

sarvendriyaguṇābhāsaṁ sarvendriyavivarjitam,
asaktaṁ sarvabhṛccaiva nirguṇaṁ guṇabhoktṛ ca.

Shining by the functions of all senses, yet without the senses; unattached, yet supporting all; devoid of qualities, yet their experiencer... (13.15)

प्रकृतिं पुरुषं चैव विद्ध्यनादि उभावपि ।
विकारांश्च गुणांश्चैव विद्धि प्रकृतिसम्भवान् ॥

prakṛtiṁ puruṣaṁ caiva viddhyanādi ubhāvapi,
vikārāṁśca guṇāṁścaiva viddhi prakṛtisambhavān.

Know that matter and Spirit are both beginningless, and know also that all modifications and qualities are born of Prakṛti. (13.20)

कार्यकरणकर्तृत्वे हेतुः प्रकृतिरुच्यते ।
पुरुषः सुखदुःखानां भोक्तृत्वे हेतुरुच्यते ॥

kāryakaraṇakartṛtve hetuḥ prakṛtirucyate,
puruṣaḥ sukhaduḥkhānāṁ bhoktṛtve heturucyate.

In the production of the effect and the cause, prakṛti is said to be the cause; in the experience of pleasure and pain, Puruṣa is said to be the cause. (13.21)

पुरुषः प्रकृतिस्थो हि भुङ्क्ते प्रकृतिजान्गुणान् ।
कारणं गुणसङ्गोऽस्य सदसद्योनिजन्मसु ॥

puruṣaḥ prakṛtistho hi bhuṅkte prakṛtijānguṇān,
kāraṇaṁ guṇasaṅgo'sya sadasadyonijanmasu.

The Puruṣa, seated in prakṛti, experiences the qualities born of prakṛti; attachment to the qualities is the cause of His birth in good and evil wombs. (13.22)

उपद्रष्टानुमन्ता च भर्ता भोक्ता महेश्वरः ।
परमात्मेति चाप्युक्तो देहेऽस्मिन्पुरुषः परः ॥

upadraṣṭānumantā ca bhartā bhoktā maheśvaraḥ,
paramātmeti cāpyukto dehe'sminpuruṣaḥ paraḥ.

The supreme Puruṣa in this body is also called the Spectator, the Permitter, the Supporter, the Enjoyer, the great Lord and the Supreme Self. (13.23)

ध्यानेनात्मनि पश्यन्ति केचिदात्मानमात्मना ।
अन्ये साङ्ख्येन योगेन कर्मयोगेन चापरे ॥

dhyānenātmani paśyanti kecidātmānamātmanā,
anye sāṅkhyena yogena karmayogena cāpare.

Some, by meditation, behold the Self in the Self by the Self; others by the Yoga of Knowledge (Sāṅkhya Yoga); and others by Karma Yoga. (13.25)

यावत्सञ्जायते किञ्चित्सत्त्वं स्थावरजङ्गमम् ।
क्षेत्रक्षेत्रज्ञसंयोगात्तद्विद्धि भरतर्षभ ॥

yāvatsañjāyate kiñcitsattvaṁ sthāvarajaṅgamam,
kṣetrakṣetrajñasaṁyogāttadviddhi bharatarṣabha.

Whenever any being is born, the unmoving or the moving, know you, O best of the Bharatas, that it is from the union between the 'Field' and the 'Knower of the Field'. (13.27)

समं सर्वेषु भूतेषु तिष्ठन्तं परमेश्वरम् ।
विनश्यत्स्वविनश्यन्तं यः पश्यति स पश्यति ॥

samaṁ sarveṣu bhūteṣu tiṣṭhantaṁ parameśvaram,
vinaśyatsvavinaśyantaṁ yaḥ paśyati sa paśyati.

He sees who sees the Supreme Lord existing equally in all beings, the unperishing within the perishing. (13.28)

समं पश्यन्हि सर्वत्र समवस्थितमीश्वरम् ।
न हिनस्त्यात्मनात्मानं ततो याति परां गतिम् ॥

samaṁ paśyanhi sarvatra samavasthitamīśvaram,
na hinastyātmanātmānaṁ tato yāti parāṁ gatim.

Indeed, he who sees the same Lord everywhere equally dwelling destroys not the Self by the Self; therefore, he goes to the Highest Goal. (13.29)

प्रकृत्यैव च कर्माणि क्रियमाणानि सर्वशः ।
यः पश्यति तथात्मानमकर्तारं स पश्यति ॥

prakṛtyaiva ca karmāṇi kriyamāṇāni sarvaśaḥ,
yaḥ paśyati tathātmānamakartāraṁ sa paśyati.

He sees who sees that all actions are performed by prakṛti alone, and the Self is actionless. (13.30)

यदा भूतपृथग्भावमेकस्थमनुपश्यति ।
तत एव च विस्तारं ब्रह्म सम्पद्यते तदा ॥

yadā bhūtapṛthagbhāvamekasthamanupaśyati,
tata eva ca vistāraṁ brahma sampadyate tadā.

When he sees the whole variety of beings as resting in the One and spreading forth from That (One) alone, he then becomes Brahman. (13.31)

अनादित्वान्निर्गुणत्वात्परमात्मायमव्ययः ।
शरीरस्थोऽपि कौन्तेय न करोति न लिप्यते ।

anāditvānnirguṇatvātparamātmāyamavyayaḥ,
śarīrastho'pi kaunteya na karoti na lipyate.

Being without beginning and devoid of qualities, the Supreme Self, the Imperishable, though dwelling in the body, O Kaunteya, neither acts nor is tainted. (13.32)

यथा प्रकाशयत्येकः कृत्स्नं लोकमिमं रविः ।
क्षेत्रं क्षेत्री तथा कृत्स्नं प्रकाशयति भारत ॥

yathā prakāśayatyekaḥ kṛtsnaṁ lokamimaṁ raviḥ,
kṣetraṁ kṣetrī tathā kṛtsnaṁ prakāśayati bhārata.

Just as the one sun illumines the whole world, so also the 'Lord of the Field' (Paramātman) illumines the whole 'Field', O Bhārata. (13.34)

14

Guṇa Traya Vibhāga Yoga

The Yoga of the Three Guṇas

Can there be even a single cup of sweet-water in the entire expanse of the saline-waters of the ocean? In a world of change and pain, how can there be constant joy, or even one instance of perfect happiness? (14.17)

There are evident distinctions in nature between the kingdom of plants, that of animals and the world of man. Even within each species we observe a variety of specimens; no two species express the same features, either physical or mental. This chapter gives an elaborate explanation for the observed variety that has been merely indicated in the earlier chapter (13.22): "The Puruṣa, seated in matter, experiences the guṇas born of matter." The Lord has also declared that the guṇas are the cause of man's birth in good and evil wombs. Naturally, one would be eager to know what these guṇas are, how they affect man's life, and how man could rise above them. Hence the Lord, in this chapter, even without any particular question from Arjuna, proceeds to speak of the three guṇas and the way to go beyond them.

Terms and Definitions

1. Explain the term 'guṇa'.

The term 'guṇa', used in the Bhagavad Gītā, indicates not the 'properties' of a material but the 'attitude' with which the mind functions. It indicates the three different 'climatic conditions' that influence the psychological being in us. The three guṇas are sattva (unactivity), rajas (activity) and tamas (inactivity).

These three guṇas, in different proportions, influence the mental and the intellectual calibre of every individual and these influences provide the distinct flavour in each personality. All three are always present in every person but from individual to individual their proportion slightly differs; hence the distinct aroma in the character, conduct and behaviour of each individual.

The term 'guṇa' also means 'rope', suggesting that the spiritual beauty of Life in us is tied down to the inert and insentient matter vestures by these three guṇas. (Introduction)

2. Who is a 'muni'?

A man of reflection and contemplation (*manana-śīlavān*) is termed 'muni'. (14.1).

3. Define 'Hiraṇyagarbha'.

The Supreme identified with the total mind-intellect (cosmic subtle body) is termed 'Hiraṇyagarbha'. (14.3)

4. Define 'prakṛti'.

The total potential factor from which the world of matter emerges is termed 'prakṛti' (nature). (14.3)

5. Differentiate 'desire' (tṛṣṇā) from 'attachment' (rāga).

'Desire' (tṛṣṇā) is our mental relationship with 'objects' which have not yet been acquired by us and 'attachment' (rāga) is the mental slavishness binding us to the objects so acquired. (14.7)

6. What is 'greed' (lobha)?

'Greed' (lobha) is the inexhaustible desire and an appetite for more and more, which has the tendency to grow in volume as we keep satisfying it. (14.12)

7. What is 'dullness of the intellect' (aprakāśa)?

'Dullness of the intellect' (aprakāśa) is the condition wherein the intellect is incapable of arriving at any decision. It is a state of 'drowsiness' that veils the potentialities of one's intelligence and makes it impossible for one to differentiate the right from the wrong. (14.13)

8. Define 'idleness' (apravṛtti).

The tendency to escape all responsibilities, the sense of incapacity to undertake any endeavour and the lack of enthusiasm to strive for and achieve anything is described as the 'state of idleness' (apravṛtti). (14.13)

9. What is death?

Death is the total divorce of the subtle-body from its physical structure. It occurs when I, as my subtle-body, move out of the present physical structure when I have exhausted my purpose with the present body. (14.13)

☙❧

Thoughts and Concepts

1. Explain the importance of the study of the 14th chapter in one's spiritual pursuit.

A careful study of the 14th chapter provides us with the capacity to detect within ourselves the most powerful tendency that rises up to rule our mental life at any given moment. A seeker, who is sensitive enough to recognise the various influences under which he is forced to function from time to time in the world outside, will be able to discard all wrong impulses, immoral tendencies, unethical urges and animal passions, and keep himself safely balanced in righteous living, in self-control and in serene purity. A knowledge of this chapter thus assures us of steady progress on our path, as it introduces us to the secret methods of the mind on all occasions. This chapter is an exhaustive handbook of instructions explaining the working of the subtle body and providing us with some tips as to how we can re-adjust ourselves when the inner mechanism gets choked up and starts misfiring. Hence the importance of the study of the 14th chapter for all seekers of Truth. (Introduction)

2. How can one explain the cause for the endless variety of individuals, if it is the one Eternal Principle alone that expresses through all matter equipments?

This question can be answered with the help of an example: when the same Ganges water is poured into a hundred different bottles each one will look different from the other, not because the waters are different but because of the shape and colour of each bottle. When the same sacred water is seen through the coloured bottles, the properties of the bottles get superimposed upon the contents: the blue-water, the yellow-water, the red-water, the green-water, etc. Similarly, the One Eternal Principle expressing Itself in the various matter equipment appears as different individuals. (Introduction)

3. Explain how creation is a trick of the mind.

Creation is a trick of the mind for when one is no more expressing through the mind and, therefore, no longer conditioned by it, one cannot have the experience of any creation. The tricks of the mind consist in projecting a world of creation, thought by thought, and in feeling oneself irredeemably conditioned by one's own imagination. As long as one is drowned in the mind, the storms of the mind must necessarily toss one about. On transcending the mind, one realises the Self and its Infinite Nature and there is no experience of creation. (14.2)

4. Explain the inter-relation between 'vāsanā', 'guṇa', 'māyā', 'avidyā', 'jīva' and 'Īśvara'.

The world of 'vāsanās', of ideas, of thoughts and of actions, together constituting all 'nature' (prakṛti), is ever controlled and directed by the guṇas and, therefore, the three 'guṇas' are together called in Vedānta 'māyā', the 'cause of the universe'. Māyā expressed in the individual is called 'avidyā' (ignorance). 'Avidyā' is, therefore, the microcosmic expression of māyā, and the total 'ignorance', in its macrocosmic expression, is 'māyā'. A jīva or individualised ego is under the control of avidyā, while māyā is under the control of Īśvara. (14.3)

5. What is the nature of the bondage produced by sattva?

Sattva binds the Infinite to matter through the attachment to 'knowledge' and 'happiness'. When once one has experienced the thrilling joys of creative thinking and the inspiring life of goodness and wisdom one gets so attached to them that one will thereafter sacrifice anything in order to live constantly that subtle joy. A true scientist, working self-dedicatedly in his laboratory; a painter working at his canvas in his shabby studio, pale with hunger and weak with disease; a poet hunted out from society, living in public parks, seeking his own joys in his own visions and words; martyrs facing cruel persecutions; politicians, suffering long years of exile; mountaineers embracing death—are all examples of how, having known the subtler thrills of a higher joy, when the mind is inspired with sattva, the individual becomes as much bound with attachment to them as others are to their own material joys and possessions.

This bondage caused by sattva is explained in the following verse:

तत्र सत्त्वं निर्मलत्वात्प्रकाशकमनामयम् ।
सुखसङ्गेन बध्नाति ज्ञानसङ्गेन चानघ ॥

tatra sattvaṁ nirmalatvātprakāśakamanāmayam,
sukhasaṅgena badhnāti jñānasaṅgena cānagha.

Of these 'sattva' which, because of its stainlessness, is luminous and healthy, binds by attachment to 'happiness' and by attachment to 'knowledge', O sinless one. (14.6)

6. Describe the bondage caused by rajas in an individual.

When once an individual has come under the influence of rajas, he expresses innumerable desires, and bound in his own attachments, he lives on in the world manifesting a variety of passions. Such a passionate being—goaded by his desires for things not yet acquired and crushed under the weight and responsibility of his attachments to things that he possesses—can never keep quiet but must necessarily act on endlessly earning and spending, saving and procuring, procreating and protecting, and yet thirsting for more and more. Anxious to have more, fearing to lose, he is whipped from action to action. Restlessly rushing, he becomes entangled in the joys of successes, involved in the pangs of his failures, and lives as an 'embodied one' chained by his own actions. Though the Self is not an agent (actor) rajas makes It act with the idea 'I am the doer'.

The following verse explains the bondage caused by rajas:

रजो रागात्मकं विद्धि तृष्णासङ्गसमुद्भवम् ।
तन्निबध्नाति कौन्तेय कर्मसङ्गेन देहिनम् ॥

rajo rāgātmakaṁ viddhi tṛṣṇāsaṅgasamudbhavam,
tannibadhnāti kaunteya karmasaṅgena dehinam.

Know thou 'rajas' to be of the nature of passion, the source of thirst and attachment; it binds fast, O Kaunteya, the embodied one, by attachment to action. (14.7)

7. Explain the significance of 'desire' being termed 'tṛṣṇā' (thirst) in Sanskrit.

When an individual is thirsty, nothing, for the time being, is of as much importance as water, which alone can satisfy his thirst. Just as a thirsty man would struggle and suffer, wanting nothing but water to relieve his pangs, so too a human personality thirsts for the satisfaction of every desire that burns him down. Hence, 'desire' is termed 'thirst' (tṛṣṇā) in Sanskrit. (14.7)

8. Explain the bondage caused by tamas.

Under the influence of tamas man's intellectual capacity to discriminate between right and wrong gets veiled and he starts acting as if under some hallucination or stupefaction. Tamas binds the individual to his lower nature by providing him with endless misconceptions and miscomprehensions of the true divine purpose of life, which, naturally, forces one in that condition to live in indolence and heedless of the higher purposes. One thereafter lives ever asleep to the nobler and the diviner aspirations of life. There is no consistency of purpose, brilliance of thought, tenderness of emotion, or nobility of action in an individual who comes under the contamination of the tamoguṇa-influences.

The nature of the bondage produced by tamas is explained in the following verse:

तमस्त्वज्ञानजं विद्धि मोहनं सर्वदेहिनाम् ।
प्रमादालस्यनिद्राभिस्तन्निबध्नाति भारत ॥

tamastvajñānajaṁ viddhi mohanaṁ sarvadehinām,
pramādālasyanidrābhistannibadhnāti bhārata.

But know that tamas is born of ignorance. Deluding all embodied beings, it binds fast, O Bhārata, by heedlessness, indolence and sleep. (14.8)

9. Cite the verse which in a nutshell gives the different types of bondage produced by sattva, rajas and tamas.

The following verse gives an overall view of the different types of bondage caused by sattva, rajas and tamas:

सत्त्वं सुखे सञ्जयति रजः कर्मणि भारत ।
ज्ञानमावृत्य तु तमः प्रमादे सञ्जयत्युत ॥

sattvaṁ sukhe sañjayati rajaḥ karmaṇi bhārata,
jñānamāvṛtya tu tamaḥ pramāde sañjayatyuta.

Sattva attaches one to happiness, rajas to action, O Bhārata, while tamas, verily, shrouding knowledge, attaches one to heedlessness. (14.9)

10. Explain how the guṇas dominate one another and cite the relevant verse.

At any given moment, a human personality, if analysed, can be found to work under the influence of one predominating guṇa, wherein the other two guṇas though not totally absent are only of secondary importance. When we say that one is under the influence of sattva, it means that rajas and tamas in him are, at that given moment, not quite prominent to contribute enough of their particular nature. Thus, when sattva predominates over rajas and tamas, it produces, at that time, its own nature of happiness and knowledge. When rajas predominates over sattva and tamas, it expresses its own nature of passions and desires, attachments and actions. When tamas predominates over sattva and rajas, it produces its own effects of shrouding knowledge and making the personality heedless of its nobler duties.

The following verse make this idea clear:

रजस्तमश्चाभिभूय सत्त्वं भवति भारत ।
रजः सत्त्वं तमश्चैव तमः सत्त्वं रजस्तथा ॥

rajastamaścābhibhūya sattvaṁ bhavati bhārata,
rajaḥ sattvaṁ tamaścaiva tamaḥ sattvaṁ rajastathā.

Now sattva rises (prevails), O Bhārata, having overpowered rajas and tamas (inertia); now rajas, having overpowered sattva and tamas; and tamas, having overpowered sattva and rajas. (14.10)

11. How can one recognise that one is under the influence of sattva?

When sattva predominates, the senses and mind are filled with the light of knowledge and one's conduct is balanced and one experiences a lot of peace. The individual's speech is soft and pleasing. He walks steadily, he thinks nobly and peacefully, he reads good books, and keeps the company of the wise. The intellect (buddhi) is then sharp and clear. He sees things as they are, and is not perturbed or troubled by the happenings around him. Such balanced conduct is the quality of sattva.

The following verse explains the above idea:

सर्वद्वारेषु देहेऽस्मिन्प्रकाश उपजायते ।
ज्ञानं यदा तदा विद्याद्विवृद्धं सत्त्वमित्युत ॥

sarvadvāreṣu dehe'sminprakāśa upajāyate,
jñānaṁ yadā tadā vidyādvivṛddhaṁ sattvamityuta.

When through every gate (sense) in this body the light of intelligence shines, then it may be known that 'sattva' is predominant. (14.11)

12. What are the characteristics that indicate the predominance of rajas?

Under the contagion of rajas, the mind-intellect gets extremely persecuted by its own restlessness, endless plans, exhausting actions, agonising desires, painful longings, maddening greed and oppressive restlessness. When rajoguṇa dominates, man burdens himself with a hundred kinds of activities. The result is he is restless. Greed and longing urge him to undertake many actions for the fulfilment of his selfish desires. Longing for objects drives him into acts of evil and sin. He employs tricks and stratagems to realise his ambitions. He has no regard to truth. His mind is extroverted and he lacks intros-pection. His words are harsh and proud. His mind being full of desires, he lives a life of passion, and does not know what is peace and real joy. When such an individual works in society, his sorrows do not rest with himself—they spread, like contagion, to many thousands around him.

The following verse explains this:

लोभः प्रवृत्तिरारम्भः कर्मणामशमः स्पृहा ।
रजस्येतानि जायन्ते विवृद्धे भरतर्षभ ॥

lobhaḥ pravṛttirārambhaḥ karmaṇāmaśamaḥ spṛhā,
rajasyetāni jāyante vivṛddhe bharatarṣabha.

Greed, activity, undertaking of actions, restlessness, longing—these arise when rajas is predominant, O best in the Bharata family. (14.12)

13. When tamas predominates what exactly are the symptoms?

When tamas predominates all ambitions are sapped. Energy is dormant, capacity is gone and, thereafter, eating and sleeping alone become the individual's main occupations in life. The natural effect on the personality of a man who is living such a life is that as an individual he becomes heedless of the higher calls within himself. He not only becomes incapable of responding to the good or the bad in him, but also slowly sinks into delusions. He miscalculates the world around him, misinterprets his own possibilities and always makes mistakes in determining his relationship with the world around.

The following verse states the above-mentioned thoughts:

अप्रकाशोऽप्रवृत्तिश्च प्रमादो मोह एव च ।
तमस्येतानि जायन्ते विवृद्धे कुरुनन्दन ॥

aprakāśo'pravṛttiśca pramādo moha eva ca,
tamasyetāni jāyante vivṛddhe kurunandana.

Darkness, inertness, heedlessness and delusion—these arise when 'tamas' is predominant, O descendant of Kuru. (14.13)

14. Cite the verses wherein the Lord declares the future life of an individual based on the predominance of the guṇas at the moment of death.

The following two verses state the various types of births attained by individuals occasioned by the predominance of the guṇas at the time of death:

यदा सत्त्वे प्रवृद्धे तु प्रलयं याति देहभृत् ।
तदोत्तमविदां लोकानमलान्प्रतिपद्यते ॥

yadā sattve pravṛddhe tu pralayaṁ yāti dehabhṛt,
tadottamavidāṁ lokānamalānpratipadyate.
If the embodied one meets death when sattva is predominant, then he attains to the spotless worlds of the 'knowers of the Highest'. (14.14)

रजसि प्रलयं गत्वा कर्मसङ्गिषु जायते ।
तथा प्रलीनस्तमसि मूढयोनिषु जायते ॥

rajasi pralayaṁ gatvā karmasaṅgiṣu jāyate,
tathā pralīnastamasi mūḍhayoniṣu jāyate.
Meeting death in rajas, he is born among those attached to action; and dying in tamas, he is born in the womb of the senseless. (14.15)

15. Explain how the thoughts entertained during one's life time will determine the thoughts at the moment of death when one departs from the body.

There is continuity of thought in an individual's lifetime. To explain: A doctor cannot, all of a sudden one fine morning, start thinking of and solving a subtle architectural problem. The doctor has trained his mind to think about medicines. At any given moment, the mind of a doctor will be thinking of medicines alone, in conformity with his education and the type of thoughts his mind is trained to entertain. Thus, there is a continuity of thought-life in this embodiment; this year's thoughts have continuity with our last year's thoughts; this month's thoughts are determined by the last month's thoughts; this week's thoughts are an extension of last week's thoughts; today's thoughts are continued tomorrow. And every moment is an extension of the previous moment's thoughts. If, thus, there is unbroken continuity of thoughts connecting the past, the present, and the future, then there is no reason why, at the time of death, this continuity should suddenly end. Therefore, the type of thoughts entertained during our lifetime will determine the type of thoughts we will have at the time of death and even after our departure from this physical body. (14.14)

16. What is the fruit of sattva, rajas and tamas?

The following verse gives the answer to the above question:

कर्मणः सुकृतस्याहुः सात्त्विकं निर्मलं फलम्।
रजसस्तु फलं दुःखमज्ञानं तमसः फलम्॥

karmaṇaḥ sukṛtasyāhuḥ sāttvikaṁ nirmalaṁ phalam,
rajasastu phalaṁ duḥkhamajñānaṁ tamasaḥ phalam.

The fruit of good action, they say, is sāttvic and pure; verily, the fruit of rajas is pain, and the fruit of tamas is ignorance. (14.16)

17. How does one start becoming 'good'?

All religions, the world over, answer this question in their injunction and insistence that seekers of Truth, devotees of the Lord, votaries of culture—all must strive to live ethically a pure, moral and noble life. No doubt, disciplining the mind and changing the quality of thoughts are not easy jobs; but to change the type of actions and to discipline our external movements is relatively easy. Therefore, to practise goodness, to discipline our behaviour, to act the good Samaritan, are all the beginning of this great scheme of self-revival. When noble action is undertaken soon it becomes a habit and this external habit of discipline tends to discipline the mind. Passions and agitations are the impurities in the mind; bad actions increase them; good actions, by their very nature, quieten the mind and sap its passions. (14.16)

18. What are the effects of sattva, rajas and tamas?

The following verse gives a brief summary of the effects of sattva, rajas and tamas:

सत्त्वात्सञ्जायते ज्ञानं रजसो लोभ एव च।
प्रमादमोहौ तमसो भवतोऽज्ञानमेव च॥

sattvātsañjāyate jñānaṁ rajaso lobha eva ca,
pramādamohau tamaso bhavato'jñānameva ca.

Knowledge arises from sattva, greed from rajas, heedlessness, delusion and also ignorance arise from tamas. (14.17)

19. Write a short note on 'evolution' as conceived in the Hindu philosophy. Explain the position that man holds in the ladder of evolution.

'Evolution' means a greater awareness of experience, a lesser amount of agitations and a sharper power of intelligence. The yard-stick used to measure evolution is the quantity of joy or happiness, peace or bliss, experienced by the being. In this measurement of evolution, the stone-life is of zero evolution, inasmuch as it has no awareness at all of the world. The plant life comes next, wherein consciousness has dimly started expressing Itself. In the animal kingdom, this awareness has become clearer and more vivid. Of the animals, man is, no doubt, the greatest being with the fullest consciousness and the sharpest intellect. But, man also has his own limitations, and functions only within a limited field of time and space. The ample possibilities reached when once these limitations of man are broken down are indicated as the state of existence enjoyed by beings of a still higher evolution, and they are called the 'denizens of heaven'.

The unique position that man holds in this ladder of evolution can be explained with an example: consider a double-storeyed house with its staircase. Invariably, after climbing a few steps, there is a landing from which we turn and climb up the rest of the stairs to reach the rooms on the first floor. Those who are standing on the lower flight of steps are considered of a lower evolution. Those who are standing on the landing are of the middle type and those who are standing on the top-flights are of the highest evolution. The vegetable and the animal kingdoms stand on the lower rungs. Man stands on the landing and the higher beings (denizens of heaven) on the upper flights of steps. Man has the freedom either to go up or to go down. This is the concept of evolution as conceived by Hindu philosophy wherein the evolution of life is always measured by the degree of Consciousness unveiled through matter. (14.18)

20. How can one be free from the thraldom of thought-entanglements?

As long as one is travelling on the train, the movement of the train is also one's movement. But the moment one alights and stands on the platform the train alone moves. So too, the Spirit identifying Itself with and, therefore, riding on the mind-intellect equipment, dances to the moods of the mind determined by the three guṇas. To stand apart from the mind by ending all our identifications with it is to get complete freedom from the thraldom of thought-entanglements. (14.19)

21. When does one attain oneness with the Lord and gain Liberation?

The following two verses answer the above question:

नान्यं गुणेभ्यः कर्तारं यदा द्रष्टानुपश्यति ।
गुणेभ्यश्च परं वेत्ति मद्भावं सोऽधिगच्छति ॥

nānyaṁ guṇebhyaḥ kartāraṁ yadā draṣṭānupaśyati,
guṇebhyaśca paraṁ vetti madbhāvaṁ so'dhigacchati.

When the seer beholds no agent other than the guṇas and knows that which is higher than the guṇas, he attains to My being. (14.19)

गुणानेतानतीत्य त्रीन्देही देहसमुद्भवान् ।
जन्ममृत्युजरादुःखैर्विमुक्तोऽमृतमश्नुते ॥

guṇānetānatītya trīndehī dehasamudbhavān,
janmamṛtyujarāduḥkhairvimukto'mṛtamaśnute.

The embodied one, having crossed beyond these three guṇas out of which the body is evolved, is freed from birth, death, decay and pain and attains to Immortality. (14.20)

22. What are the three questions of Arjuna about the individual who has 'transcended the three guṇas' (guṇātīta)?

The three questions of Arjuna are:

(1) What are the marks by which a man who has gone beyond the influences of these three guṇas can be recognised?

(2) What would be, in that State of Perfection, his relationship with the world outside and how is his behaviour among those who are still under the persecution of the three guṇas?

(3) How does such a Man of Perfection conquer his inner confusions and entanglements and attain spiritual glory?

These three questions of Arjuna are evident in the following verse:

कैर्लिङ्गैस्त्रीन्गुणानेतानतीतो भवति प्रभो ।
किमाचारः कथं चैतांस्त्रीन्गुणानतिवर्तते ॥

kairliṅgaistrīnguṇānetānatīto bhavati prabho,
kimācāraḥ kathaṁ caitāṁstrīnguṇānativartate.
What are the marks of him who has crossed over the three guṇas, O Lord? What is his conduct, and how does he go beyond these three guṇas? (14.21)

23. Who is a 'Guṇātīta'? Cite the verses that describe the 'Guṇātīta'.

The term 'Guṇātīta' signifies the individual who has transcended the three guṇas. Such an individual who has risen above the guṇas is unaffected by the effects of the three guṇas when they are present in his inner life; nor does he long for them when they have disappeared. Equanimity is the essence of perfection and a Guṇātīta is ever in perfect balance. He craves for nothing, nor does he strive to acquire anything new. To have and not to have—both are equal to him, because he is beyond both, living a life of inward peace which is totally independent of all environments.

The following verses describe the nature of a Guṇātīta:
प्रकाशं च प्रवृत्तिं च मोहमेव च पाण्डव ।
न द्वेष्टि सम्प्रवृत्तानि न निवृत्तानि काङ्क्षति ॥
prakāśaṁ ca pravṛttiṁ ca mohameva ca pāṇḍava,
na dveṣṭi sampravṛttāni na nivṛttāni kāṅkṣati.
Light, activity and delusion, when present, O Pāṇḍava, he hates not, nor longs for them when absent. (14.22)
उदासीनवदासीनो गुणैर्यो न विचाल्यते ।
गुणा वर्तन्त इत्येव योऽवतिष्ठति नेङ्गते ॥
udāsīnavadāsīno guṇairyo na vicālyate,
guṇā vartanta ityeva yo'vatiṣṭhati neṅgate.
He who, seated like one unconcerned, is not moved by the 'guṇas', who, knowing that the 'guṇas' operate, is self-centred and swerves not... (14.23)
समदुःखसुखः स्वस्थः समलोष्टाश्मकाञ्चनः ।
तुल्यप्रियाप्रियो धीरस्तुल्यनिन्दात्मसंस्तुतिः ॥
samaduḥkhasukhaḥ svasthaḥ samaloṣṭāśmakāñcanaḥ,
tulyapriyāpriyo dhīrastulyanindātmasaṁstutiḥ.

Alike in pleasure and pain; who dwells in the Self; to whom a clod of earth, precious stone and gold are alike; to whom the dear and the not-dear are the same; firm; the same in censure and self-praise... (14.24)

मानापमानयोस्तुल्यस्तुल्यो मित्रारिपक्षयोः ।
सर्वारम्भपरित्यागी गुणातीतः स उच्यते ॥

mānāpamānayostulyastulyo mitrāripakṣayoḥ,
sarvārambhaparityāgī guṇātītaḥ sa ucyate.

The same in honour and dishonour; the same to friend and foe; abandoning all undertakings—he is said to have crossed beyond the guṇas. (14.25)

24. Why is the 'Guṇātīta' unaffected by the play of the guṇas in his mind?

The 'Guṇātīta' is established in his Pure Spiritual Nature and he is able to observe detachedly and enjoy the play of the guṇas in himself and in the world around him. An observer of a street fight, looking down from his balcony, is not affected by what he observes; so too the Man of Wisdom, awakened to the Spiritual Consciousness, swerves not from his consummate equilibrium when he witnesses the play of the guṇas in himself, and ever remains established in his own Divine Nature. (14.23)

25. How does the 'Guṇātīta' remain alike in pleasure and pain?

To come in contact with the outside world through sense perceptions, to evaluate them in terms of similar experiences in the past and to experience pleasure or pain is a trick of the mind. The worlds of stimuli march into us and we respond to them, and these responses can fall under two categories: pleasure and pain. That which is pleasurable to one is bound to be painful to another. If the things of the world were in their own nature either pleasurable or painful, they would have certainly caused the same uniform reactions in all of us. But the things of the world do not produce reactions in everyone in the same way and, therefore, pleasure and pain are interpretations of our mind and intellect, which is coloured by our own past experiences. The 'Guṇātīta' who is not looking at the world through the coloured goggles of the mind and intellect is therefore alike in pleasure and pain. (14.24)

26. Why is a 'Guṇātīta' free of hankering for worldly possessions?

Children collect peacock feathers, shells, marbles, broken glass-bangles, old stamps, shapely stones, etc., from the roadside or from waste-paper baskets, and with extreme possessiveness, keep them as their precious possessions. But as they grow, without a regret they throw them away and the younger ones in the family accept them with gratitude, as a precious inheritance from their elders. Similarly, a man living his egocentric life of desire for possessions may value his worldly goods as precious but to the Awakened Soul, in his sense of Infinitude, these limited possessions, hugged on to by lesser minds, have no charm at all. (14.24)

27. Why does the Lord describe the 'Guṇātīta' as 'one who is free of all enterprise' (*sarvārambhaparityāgī*).

Desire-motivated activities, undertaken with an anxiety to earn and to acquire, to possess and to hoard, to aggrandise and to claim ownership are indicated by the term 'enterprise' (ārambha). All these are possible only when the ego is there. The 'Guṇātīta' living in God-consciousness has no more ego in him, nor is he pestered by the endless egocentric desires that are the sorrows of life. When the limited ego-sense has volatilised in the Realisation of the Infinite, all 'enterprise' (ārambha), i.e., ego-motivated activities also end. There-after, the God-inspired Guṇātīta works in the world as a God-man devoid of ego and selfishness. (14.25)

28. Give a bird's eye view of the three guṇas—sattva, rajas and tamas—as presented in the 14th chapter.

The following tabular column gives an overall picture of the three guṇas as discussed in the 14th chapter of the Gītā:

	Sattva	**Rajas**	**Tamas**
Representative Colour (14.5)	White	Red	Black
Nature (14.6-8)	Stainless, luminous sorrowless	Passion, thirst and attachment	Ignorance
Effects (14.6-8)	Binds the individual to happiness and knowledge	Binds the individual to action	Binds the individual to heedlessness, indolence and sleep
Characteristic signs (14.11-13)	The light of understanding shines through all the senses	The individual is overcome by greed, activity, desire, restlessness and longing for worldly enjoyments	The individual exhibits dullness, inertness, heedlessness and delusion
Future life (14.14, 15, 18)	Born in higher and purer worlds	Born among men attached to action	Born among the lower realms of beings such as the animal and the vegetable kingdom
Fruit (14.16)	Pure joy	Suffering	Ignorance
Effect (14.17)	Wisdom	Greed	Heedlessness, forgetfulness, delusion and ignorance

Selections for Reflection

1. A knowledge of the strategy of our enemies is an essential pre-requisite to plan our attacks successfully. In order to conquer the mind, a seeker must know very clearly the tricks by which the mind generally hoodwinks him. (14.2)

2. We call that an evil whereby we try to satisfy the appetites of the flesh, the selfish agitations of the mind and the egocentric desires of our head. Egocentric self gratification is the womb from which all evils are born. (14.6)

3. A gold-chain, if sufficiently strong, can also bind as any iron-chain. 'Goodness' though it gives us freedom from all vulgarities can also shackle us within its own limitations! A perfect one, absolutely free, is bound neither by goodness nor by evil. (14.6)

4. Desire for the acquisition of things and the creation of situations that are expected to yield a certain quota of personal happiness, and the sense of clinging attachment to things already so acquired—are the volcanoes that constantly throw up their molten lava to scorch and raze the smiling fields of life. (14.7)

5. Even to be bad, it needs a good amount of enthusiasm and an endless spirit of activity! (14.13)

6. When an individual fails to understand rightly, himself, the world outside, and his own right relationship with the world, then life becomes an error—his very existence, a sad mistake. (14.13)

7. Whatever life is obtained after death is caused by the quality and quantity of desires and attachments; and the nature and number of desires and attachments are determined by the 'guṇas'. (14.13)

8. To a teetotaller, a drinking booth is nothing but a den of sorrow and death; but to the drunkard the same is his haven of joy and harbour of happiness. To the tāmasic, to be born in the animal kingdom is a wonderful chance to exhaust their appetites and to express fully their nature. (14.15)

9. Thought is the father of all action. Thoughts are the seeds sown, and actions the harvest gathered. Seeds of weeds cannot but produce weeds; bad thoughts can manifest only as bad actions. And the negative actions in the outside world fatten the wrong tendencies of the mind and thus multiply the inward agitations. (14.16)

10. A patient is suffering from high temperature, excruciating headache and back pain. All three are symptoms of his illness. When the fever is down the patient is still suffering. We can say the patient has fully recovered not when these three symptoms have ended, but only when the patient has also regained his old health and energy. Similarly, the three guṇas may be present in each of us in different proportions, but the true release comes not only when all chains have been snapped—meaning all the guṇas are transcended—but when we are also established in the Spiritual Experience. (14.18)

11. If the art in me is to be expressed in colours, I need the canvas and the brush. If I am a musician, I need musical instruments and accompaniments to express my art. Each artist employs the appropriate instruments to express himself. A violin in the hands of a painter, and a brush with colour and canvas in the hands of a musician are both useless because they are not the media of expression for them. If my thoughts are dull and animalistic, it would be sorrow for me to bear the physical body of man. Thus, each body—plant, animal or man—is the exact instrument given for the full expression of its subtle body. (14.20)

12. The sun may illumine floods, famine, war, pestilence, funerals, marriages and a million varieties of happenings and yet, none of them is in the sun. Similarly, the Consciousness in us illumines the various changes in our matter envelopments, but they do not appertain to the Spirit. (14.20)

13. Every disciple has the full freedom to seek and first of all, to

understand properly the logic of the philosophy. Understanding alone can give rise to a true appreciation, and unless we appreciate an idea, we will never be able to live it day after day. (14.21)

14. To a millionaire, it is immaterial whether or not he gets, by chance, a 25-paise coin on the roadside. He may stoop down and pick it up but he would never congratulate himself for it as much as a poor man would do under the same circumstances. Thus, he who has extricated himself from the entanglements of the guṇas has transcended fully the equipment of the mind and intellect and lives the infinite joys of the Self. To him, the ordinary vehicles of joys and sorrows can no more supply any special quota of experiences. Ever steady and balanced, he lives beyond all storms and clouds in a realm of unbroken peace and brilliance. He conquers the world of Pure Awareness—attains the State of Godhood. (14.22)

15. A man's culture may be a false mask. Many of us can act the part of God-man as long as the situations around us are not too tempting. A man may not be a tyrant as long as he has no power; he may live a quiet life, as long as he is poor; he may be above corruption, as long as he has no seducing chances. Thus, many good qualities which we attribute to many people around are all a falsely painted, superficial beauty, concealing behind its artifice a weak and unhealthy personality. Potential devils stalk about in the world in the borrowed garb of artificial raiment! (14.23)

16. The real test of a Perfect One is not in the jungle or in a cave, but in the market-place where he is teased by the mischiefs of the world. Christ was never so great as when he was nailed to the cross! The true nature in us will come out only when we are crushed, the fragrance of *chandana* (sandal) emerges only when rubbed; *tulasi* (ocimum) leaves leave their fragrance on the very fingers that crush them! (14.23)

17. Spirit, conditioned by matter, behaves like a reed upon the tumultuous surface of an ever-agitated mind. Always disturbed by the constant storms of love and hate, likes and dislikes, this unhappy sense of individuality suffers its shattering agitations and endless sorrows. To withdraw, therefore, from this chaotic field of desires and attachments into the shelter of the Self is to release the more divine possibilities in ourselves. The dreamer dies to be reborn as the waker; the individual sense of the ego dies to release the infinite glories of the Self. (14.24)

18. Rooted in his own firm Experience of Divinity, a Man of Vision is not afraid of life and its rewards, because such a Perfect One looks at things and happenings from his own special angle. It is only the egoistic evaluation of life that tends to respect honour and shun dishonour. To one who has transcended the ordinary planes of egoism and vanity, both are the same, a crown of thorns is as welcome as a crown of roses! (14.25)

Verses for Memorisation

सत्त्वं रजस्तम इति गुणाः प्रकृतिसम्भवाः ।
निबध्नन्ति महाबाहो देहे देहिनमव्ययम् ॥

sattvaṁ rajastama iti guṇāḥ prakṛtisambhavāḥ,
nibadhnanti mahābāho dehe dehinamavyayam.

Purity, passion and inertia—these 'guṇas', O mighty-armed, born of 'prakṛti', bind fast in the body the Embodied, the Indestructible. (14.5)

तत्र सत्त्वं निर्मलत्वात्प्रकाशकमनामयम् ।
सुखसङ्गेन बध्नाति ज्ञानसङ्गेन चानघ ॥

tatra sattvaṁ nirmalatvātprakāśakamanāmayam,
sukhasaṅgena badhnāti jñānasaṅgena cānagha.

Of these, 'sattva' which, because of its stainlessness, is luminous and healthy, binds by attachment to 'happiness' and by attachment to 'knowledge', O sinless one. (14.6)

रजो रागात्मकं विद्धि तृष्णासङ्गसमुद्भवम् ।
तन्निबध्नाति कौन्तेय कर्मसङ्गेन देहिनम् ॥

rajo rāgātmakaṁ viddhi tṛṣṇāsaṅgasamudbhavam,
tannibadhnāti kaunteya karmasaṅgena dehinam.

Know thou 'rajas' (to be) of the nature of passion, the source of thirst and attachment; it binds fast the embodied one, O Kaunteya, by attachment to action. (14.7)

तमस्त्वज्ञानजं विद्धि मोहनं सर्वदेहिनाम् ।
प्रमादालस्यनिद्राभिस्तन्निबध्नाति भारत ॥

tamastvajñānajaṁ viddhi mohanaṁ sarvadehinām,
pramādālasyanidrābhistannibadhnāti bhārata.

But know that tamas is born of ignorance. Deluding all embodied beings, it binds fast, O Bhārata, by heedlessness, indolence and sleep. (14.8)

सर्वद्वारेषु देहेऽस्मिन्प्रकाश उपजायते ।
ज्ञानं यदा तदा विद्याद्विवृद्धं सत्त्वमित्युत ॥

sarvadvāreṣu dehe'sminprakāśa upajāyate,
jñānaṁ yadā tadā vidyādvivṛddhaṁ sattvamityuta.

When through every gate (sense) in this body the light of intelligence shines, then it may be known that 'sattva' is predominant. (14.11)

ऊर्ध्वं गच्छन्ति सत्त्वस्था मध्ये तिष्ठन्ति राजसाः ।
जघन्यगुणवृत्तिस्था अधो गच्छन्ति तामसाः ॥

ūrdhvaṁ gacchanti sattvasthā madhye tiṣṭhanti rājasāḥ,
jaghanyaguṇavṛttisthā adho gacchanti tāmasāḥ.

Those who are abiding in sattva go upwards; the rājasic dwell in the middle; and the tāmasic, abiding in the function of the lowest guṇa, go downwards. (14.18)

नान्यं गुणेभ्यः कर्तारं यदा द्रष्टानुपश्यति ।
गुणेभ्यश्च परं वेत्ति मद्भावं सोऽधिगच्छति ॥

nānyaṁ guṇebhyaḥ kartāraṁ yadā draṣṭānupaśyati,
guṇebhyaśca paraṁ vetti madbhāvaṁ so'dhigacchati.

When the seer beholds no agent other than the guṇas and knows that which is higher than the guṇas, he attains to My being. (14.19)

प्रकाशं च प्रवृत्तिं च मोहमेव च पाण्डव ।
न द्वेष्टि सम्प्रवृत्तानि न निवृत्तानि काङ्क्षति ॥

prakāśaṁ ca pravṛttiṁ ca mohameva ca pāṇḍava,
na dveṣṭi sampravṛttāni na nivṛttāni kāṅkṣati.

Light, activity and delusion, when present, O Pāṇḍava, he hates not, nor longs for them when absent. (14.22)

उदासीनवदासीनो गुणैर्यो न विचाल्यते ।
गुणा वर्तन्त इत्येव योऽवतिष्ठति नेङ्गते ॥

udāsīnavadāsīno guṇairyo na vicālyate,
guṇā vartanta ityeva yo'vatiṣṭhati neṅgate.

He who seated like one unconcerned is not moved by the 'guṇas', who, knowing that the 'guṇas' operate, is Self-centred and swerves not... (14.23)

मानापमानयोस्तुल्यस्तुल्यो मित्रारिपक्षयोः ।
सर्वारम्भपरित्यागी गुणातीतः स उच्यते ॥

mānāpamānayostulyastulyo mitrāripakṣayoḥ,
sarvārambhaparityāgī guṇātītaḥ sa ucyate.

The same in honour and dishonour; the same to friend and foe; abandoning all undertakings—he is said to have crossed beyond the guṇas. (14.25)

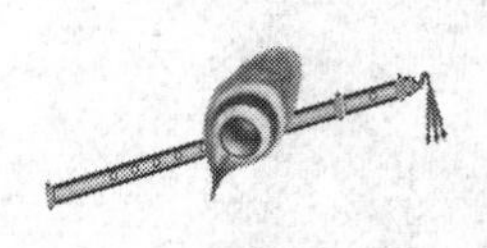

15

Puruṣottama Yoga

The Yoga of the Supreme Spirit

The 'tree of saṁsāra' springs from the ignorance of Reality, ends on the Realisation of the Self, and it exists only so long as the mental demands and desires function. (Introduction)

The field of experience (kṣetra) and the knower of the field (Kṣetrajña) were described in the 13th chapter and it was shown that the 'Knower of the field' minus the 'field of experience' is the Pure Awareness, at once infinite and permanent. In this chapter, the Lord discusses the nature of the Pure Awareness with all its implications.

This chapter is one of the rarest pieces of literature available in the world that so directly indicates the Infinite. For the beauty and brevity of the stanzas in this chapter, no other portion even in the Bhagavad Gītā can stand a favourable comparison. In India, from the ancient days onwards, this chapter has been recited as a prayer before taking food.

Terms and Definitions

1. What is the aśvattha tree?

The aśvattha tree used as a metaphor in the 15th chapter, whose botanical name is *Ficus religiosa,* is the 'pippala' or the 'pipal' tree, which has heart-shaped leaves and does not have hanging adventitious roots. This tree is not to be confused with the banyan tree or 'vaṭa', which has adventitious roots growing down from its branches and whose botanical name is *'Ficus benghalensis'*. Both the *Ficus religiosa* (pipal tree) and *Ficus benghalensis* (banyan tree) belong to the 'Ficus' or 'Fig' genus of trees along with the popular *Ficus carica,* which is commonly called the 'fig tree' and is widely cultivated in the Middle East and Western Africa for its edible fig fruits. (15.1)

2. The metaphor of the aśvattha tree echoes the thoughts of _______Upaniṣad.

Kaṭhopaniṣad[1] (15.1)

3. What are the leaves of saṁsāra-vṛkṣa (tree of saṁsāra)?

Vedas (15.1)

4. What are the buds of saṁsāra-vṛkṣa?

Sense objects (15.2)

5. What are the roots of saṁsāra-vṛkṣa?

Attachment to action (15.2)

6. What is 'mysticism'?

Taking any convenient object of the world and describing it in such a poetic style so as to express some of the subtler philosophical truths and thereby to convey some deeper religious message is called 'mysticism'. (15.2)

7. What does the metaphor of the aśvattha tree signify?

The metaphor of the aśvattha tree is given to describe the 'tree of life'. The 'tree of life' represents the entire field of manifested life. The subtle Principle of Life manifests through an individual, in different planes and in a variety of forms: as perceptions of the body, as emotions and feelings of the mind, as ideals and thoughts of the intellect and as mere non-apprehension of the causal-body. All these vehicles and their experiences, manifesting in the Infinite Life, in their totality constitute the aśvattha tree spreading out into all quarters. (15.3)

8. What are the four categories into which the human diet is classified in Sanskrit literature?

The entire variety of human diet—vegetarian and non-vegetarian, prepared and unprepared, raw and ripe—is classified under four

---

1. ऊर्ध्वमूलोऽवाक्शाख एषोऽश्वत्थः सनातनः।
तदेव शुक्रं तद्ब्रह्म तदेवामृतमुच्यते।
तस्मिन् लोकाः श्रिताः सर्वे तदु नात्येति कश्चन। एतद् वै तत्॥

This is the ancient aśvattha tree whose roots are above and whose branches (spread) below. That is verily the Pure that is Brahman and that is also called the Immortal. In that rest all the worlds, and none can transcend It. Verily this is That. (2.3.1) heads as food that should be (1) masticated (bhojyam) (2) swallowed (bhakṣyam) (3) sucked (coṣyam) and (4) licked (lehyam). (15.14)

9. What does the term 'vaiśvānara' mean?

The term 'vaiśvānara' means the 'digestive fire'. It is popularly called 'jaṭharāgni'. (15.14)

10. Why is the Life Principle termed 'Puruṣa'?

The Life Principle is called 'Puruṣa' because it dwells in the 'city of the physical body' (*puri śayāt*). (15.16)

11. What is sin?

'Sin' means an act, a feeling, or a thought, which having been perpetrated, entertained, or thought of comes back after a time to agitate us with its insulting taunts and helpless regrets. 'Sin' is thus the result of the past that comes to demean one's self-esteem and creates in one a lot of mental storm and consequent dissipation. (15.20)

Thoughts and Concepts

1. Cite the verses that describe the metaphor of the aśvattha tree.

ऊर्ध्वमूलमधःशाखमश्वत्थं प्राहुरव्ययम्।
छन्दांसि यस्य पर्णानि यस्तं वेद स वेदवित्॥

ūrdhvamūlamadhaḥśākhamaśvatthaṁ prāhuravyayam,
chandāṁsi yasya parṇāni yastaṁ veda sa vedavit.

They (wise people) speak of the indestructible aśvattha tree as having its roots above and branches below, whose leaves are the Vedas; he who knows it is alone a Veda-knower. (15.1)

अधश्चोर्ध्वं प्रसृतास्तस्य शाखा
गुणप्रवृद्धा विषयप्रवालाः।
अधश्च मूलान्यनुसन्ततानि
कर्मानुबन्धीनि मनुष्यलोके॥

adhaścordhvaṁ prasṛtāstasya śākhā
guṇapravṛddhā viṣayapravālāḥ,
adhaśca mūlānyanusantatāni

karmānubandhīni manuṣyaloke.

Below and above are spread its branches, nourished by the guṇas; sense objects are its buds; and below, in the world of men, stretch forth the roots, originating in action. (15.2)

न रूपमस्येह तथोपलभ्यते
नान्तो न चादिर्न च सम्प्रतिष्ठा ।
अश्वत्थमेनं सुविरूढमूलं
असङ्गशस्त्रेण दृढेन छित्त्वा ॥

na rūpamasyeha tathopalabhyate
nānto na cādirna ca sampratiṣṭhā,
aśvatthamenaṁ suvirūḍhamūlaṁ
asaṅgaśastreṇa dṛḍhena chittvā.

Its form is not perceived here as such, neither its end, nor its origin, nor its foundation, nor its resting-place; having cut asunder this firm-rooted 'aśvattha'... (15.3)

2 Why has the aśvattha tree (pipal tree) been chosen to represent the entire cosmos?

The aśvattha tree (pipal tree) has been chosen to represent the entire cosmos because of its derivative meaning—'śva' means 'tomorrow'; 'stha' means 'that which remains'; therefore 'aśvattha' is 'that which will not remain the same till tomorrow'. The term 'aśvattha' thus indicates the ephemeral and ever-changing world of the phenomena. (15.1)

3. Why has saṁsāra been represented as a 'vṛkṣa' (tree)?

Saṁsāra is represented as a tree (vṛkṣa) because of the etymological meaning of the Sanskrit term 'vṛkṣa'—'that which can be cut down'. The experiences of change and sorrow that the world of plurality gives us can be totally ended through detachment. The 'tree of saṁsāra' that has seemingly sprung forth from the Infinite Consciousness Divine, can be cut down by shifting our attention from the tree to the Divine. It is thus for the purpose of indicating that saṁsāra can be ended that it has been represented as a 'vṛkṣa' (tree). (15.1)

4. Why is the 'tree of saṁsāra' described as having its roots (primary

root) up?

The 'tree of saṁsāra' has its roots 'up' in the Divine Consciousness. A tree holds itself up and gets nourished by its roots; similarly, the 'experiences of change' and the 'experiencer of change' are all established in the Infinite and draw their sustenance from the Divine Consciousness alone.

The word 'up' (ūrdhva) is used in the same connotation as we use the term 'up' in our everyday expressions, like 'high-command', 'higher-officials', 'top-men', 'upper-class', 'high-class jewellery', etc. In all these cases, by the term 'high' or 'up' or 'top', no geometrical elevation is indicated, but it indicates a superiority, a greater nobility, or value. Psychologically, it is natural for man to concede to the subtler and the more divine a 'higher' place of reverence and to consider the gross and the devilish as belonging to a 'lower' status. The Perfect is the Highest Consciousness, illumined and vitalised by which alone can the 'body-mind-intellect' experience its world of 'perception-emotion-thought'. Naturally, therefore, the world of plurality is allegorically pictured here as the pipal tree arising from and sustained by the roots of Higher Consciousness, the Reality, and hence the description of the roots of the saṁsāra-tree as being 'up'. (15.1)

5. Explain why the leaves are compared to the Vedas themselves.

'Veda' means 'knowledge'. Knowledge brings forth a greater spurt of dynamism of life into the world. To compare Veda—knowledge, to the leaves of the 'tree of saṁsāra' is quite appropriate, for just as the leaves nourish the tree so too knowledge (Veda) nourishes life. The larger the number of branches and leaves, the greater is the tree's dimension and growth. Cut down the leaves of a tree and its growth is immediately stunted. Where there is greater knowledge, there we are sure to find a greater flare of manifest-life. Hence the comparison of the leaves with Veda (knowledge). (15.1)

6. Explain the Lord's declaration that he who knows the entire aśvattha tree is alone the 'knower of the entire Veda'—(*Vedavit*).

The individual who has realised that the aśvattha-tree represents the 'tree of saṁsāra'—along with its 'roots', the Higher Consciousness, from which the 'tree' derives its existence—is the one whose knoweldge of the Vedas is complete.

The Vedas indicate the One Eternal Principle from which all the realms of experience have sprung. Knowledge is perfect only when we know of the here and the hereafter, of the finite and the Infinite, of the created and the Creator. Mere pursuit of the knowledge of the finite, however spectacular it might be, is at best only a one-sided view of the whole Truth. The 'Man of Wisdom', as conceived by the Vedas, is the knower of both the 'perishable' and the 'Imperishable'. This 'Man of Perfection' alone is recognised by the Lord as the '*Vedavit*'—'knower of the Vedas'. (15.1)

7. Why are the branches of the 'tree of saṁsāra' described as growing both 'upwards and downwards'?

The flow of life in the individual as well as in the world is sometimes towards the higher evolutionary purposes, but more often it tends to cater to the lower animal nature. These two tendencies are spoken of here when it is said that the branches of the 'tree of life' grow both 'upwards and downwards'. (15.2)

8. Why are the secondary roots of the 'tree of saṁsāra' described as extending even downwards?

The secondary roots signify the vāsanās (thought-channels), which propel an individual towards his own typical actions and reactions in the world and bind him firmly to saṁsāra. If the primary tap root of the tree of saṁsāra is lost in the Absolute Reality high above, the 'secondary roots' that spring from the primary root spread all around, and grow even 'downwards'—'into the world of man, initiating all actions'. Just as the main tap root, while spreading its secondary roots, claws the earth through them and gets the plant well-rooted, so too, these vāsanās – both good and evil – bind the individuals fast to the earthly plane of likes and dislikes, of profits and losses, of earning and spending. The earthly plane is spoken of here as 'down' and since the vāsanās – here compared to the secondary roots – bind the individual to this lower plane, the secondary roots of the 'tree of saṁsāra' are described as extending even downwards. (15.2)

9. How can one cut the 'tree of saṁsāra'?

The world of the tree of saṁsāra is to be cut asunder with the strong axe of detachment to the objective world (*asaṅgaśastreṇa dṛḍhena cittvā*). (15.3)

10. What is 'detachment' (asaṅga)?

The nature of detachment can be explained with an example: as long as the wheels of a car are geared on to the machine, the vehicle moves. In case we can clutch the motive-power off from the moving wheels, the vehicle must necessarily come to a halt. Similarly, if Consciousness is withdrawn from the body-mind-intellect vehicle, its play of perception-emotion-thought must necessarily halt. This clutching off of Consciousness from inert matter vehicles is verily 'detachment'(asaṅga). (15.3)

11. Cite the verse wherein the Lord declares the qualities that are required to attain the Paramātman.

The following verse declares the qualities required for those who wish to attain the Supreme Self:

निर्मानमोहा जितसङ्गदोषा
अध्यात्मनित्या विनिवृत्तकामाः ।
द्वन्द्वैर्विमुक्ताः सुखदुःखसञ्ज्ञैः
गच्छन्त्यमूढाः पदमव्ययं तत् ॥

nirmānamohā jitasaṅgadoṣā
adhyātmanityā vinivṛttakāmāḥ,
dvandvairvimuktāḥ sukhaduḥkhasaṁjñaiḥ
gacchantyamūḍhāḥ padamavyayaṁ tat.

Free from pride and delusion, victorious over the evil of attachment, dwelling constantly in the Self, their desires having completely retired, freed from the pairs of opposites – such as pleasure and pain – the wise reach that Goal Eternal. (15.5)

The qualities enumerated in the above verse are:

(1) Freedom from pride and delusion

(2) Conquest of attachment
(3) Dwelling constantly in the Self
(4) Absence of desires
(5) Freedom from the pairs of opposites like pleasure and pain

An individual who possesses these qualities attains the Self.

12. What are pride and delusion?

An erroneous estimate of one's own importance is called 'pride'. It call for an acceptance of enormous responsibility upon oneself just to maintain it. There is no time thereafter to cultivate oneself, or to seek knowledge, or to get truly educated.

Error in judgement regarding things and beings, happenings and situations in the world outside is called 'delusion'. It makes us live in a false world of our own imagination without actually facing the immediate problems around us, as they really are. (15.5)

13. What is the secret of cultivating 'detachment'?

Detachment from the world of objects is never possible without attaching ourselves to something nobler and more divine. The human mind and intellect equipment can exist only in the positive contemplation of some object. It cannot remain in a void of not contemplating anything. For example, from the next day onwards, if one were to determine not to think of a bald-headed man so to say, as soon as one wakes up the following morning, it is absolutely certain that the very first thing that one will remember will be a bald-head! But supposing we give the mind a positive point to contemplate upon – 'Nārāyaṇa-Nārāyaṇa' – we shall find that the mind has totally avoided the thought of the 'bald-head'. In the same way, in order that the mind may not have evil attachments, it should attach to the Self and live in a spirit of contemplation upon It. (15.5)

14. Explain why the external sources of effulgence like the sun, moon and fire cannot illumine the Supreme Self.

The inner Light of Consciousness cannot be illumined by the gross sources of light available in the world outside, such as the sun, the moon or the fire. In fact, the very light of the sun or the moon or the fire is an object of our Consciousness for we are constantly conscious of it. An object of perception cannot illumine the subject that perceives it because the subject and the object cannot be at any time one and the same. Hence the description that the external sources of effulgence like the sun, moon, fire etc., cannot illumine the Supreme Self. (15.6)

15. Explain the logic behind the Lord's assertion that the Supreme Abode is that 'to which having gone none returns' (*yad gatvā na nivartante*).

When one has mastered a knowledge, it is almost impossible to make any mistakes in it. To explain: for a great musician to sing deliberately out of tune in disharmonious notes is as difficult as it is for a beginner to sing correctly. Having known a language, to talk ungrammatically is as difficult as it is for the illiterate to talk correctly. If, in the imperfect world of imperfect knowledge, a cultured man, educated and artistic, cannot easily fall back to the levels of the uncivilised and the illiterate, how much more must it be an impossible act for the Perfect to come back and fall into the earlier confusions created by ignorance! Hence the Lord's description of the Supreme Abode as that having reached which there is no return. (15.6)

16. If the Infinite Consciousness, the Lord, has no parts (niraṁśa), how can it be said that the 'jīva' is a part (aṁśa) of the Lord?

The Infinite has no parts. It can suffer no division within Itself, and yet, just as with reference to the four walls of a room we consider the 'room-space' as different from the 'outer-space', so too with reference to a given mind-intellect, the Infinite Consciousness appears to the ignorant as being limited by the conditioning of the mind-intellect equipment. It is this seemingly 'conditioned Consciousness' – termed 'jīva' (individual) – that is called 'part of the Lord'. (15.7)

17. What is rebirth of the jīva (individual)?

When the Lord acquires a body, meaning when the Infinite deludes Itself that It is conditioned by the mind-intellect, It becomes the jīva; and the jīva takes to itself various bodies from time to time and incarnates in different environments, which are ordered by its own burning desires and aspirations, and which are most suited for exhausting and fulfilling all its demands. From the moment the jīva enters a particular gross body till it leaves it, the jīva keeps the sense faculties and mental impressions at all times with itself.

At death, the jīva permanently departs from the 'gross-body' which is left inert. The jīva moves off gathering unto itself all the sense faculties, 'even as the wind takes scents from their resting places' (flowers and so on). Just as an officer, on receiving his transfer orders from the Government, packs up his belongings and moves out of his residence and, having reached the new seat of appointment, unpacks and spreads out his furniture for his comforts, so too, at the time of departing from the body, the jīva packs up the sense faculties, gathers itself from the physical body and on reaching the new physical body spreads itself out again to use its sense faculties through that new 'house of experience'. (15.8)

18. What is 'Jñāna Cakṣu' (Eye of Wisdom)?

An average man is so preoccupied with the details of experiences that he, clinging to his desires to enjoy the outer beauty of things and situations, comes to overlook and fails to recognise the steady Light of Consciousness within him, in the presence of which alone can any experience be ever possible. Those who have got the necessary detachment from the minor details of the outer field of experience alone come to perceive and live the joys of the Pure Self—the Subject. This special perception or vision available to the Man of Perfection to perceive the Self is called the 'Jñāna Cakṣu' or 'Eye of Wisdom'. It only represents an extra faculty with which he comes to perceive the one Self in the superficially chaotic play of plurality. (15.10)

19. What are the two essential conditions for meditation to lead one to Liberation?

The two unavoidable conditions for meditation to ultimately yield its promised result of Liberation are:

(1) The purification of the mind—generally defined as the removal of agitations (vikṣepa) created by one's false egocentric attachment to sense objects

(2) Tuning the intellect to a correct understanding of the Self through study, reflection and practice, which alone removes the doubts of the mind (āvaraṇa) that veil its right perception. (15.11)

20. Explain and cite the verse wherein the Lord declares that mere effort without purity of heart cannot lead one to Liberation.

All those who mechanically put in plenty of self-effort (Yoga) do not necessarily succeed. Hundreds are those who complain that though they were regular in their spiritual programme for years, no appreciable amount of self-development has come to them. Only those who are successful in their attempts at stilling their mind and cleansing their intellect of its disturbing attachments and desires come to recognise the glory of the Self and experience Its Infinite Beatitude.

Those whose minds have not been properly regenerated through practice of self-control of the senses, and who have not renounced and abandoned their evil ways of looking at things from the limited egocentric standpoint, whose pride has not yet been subdued—such seekers, however sincerely and ardently they may meditate, have little or no chance of unfolding themselves into their more divine possibilities; they behold Him not. Though the Self is the nearest and, therefore, the most easily perceivable, yet all do not see Him, because of their complete slavery to the enchantments of the sense objects. This idea is stated in the following verse:

यतन्तो योगिनश्चैनं पश्यन्त्यात्मन्यवस्थितम् ।
यतन्तोऽप्यकृतात्मानो नैनं पश्यन्त्यचेतसः ॥

yatanto yoginaścainaṁ paśyantyātmanyavasthitam,
yatanto'pyakṛtātmāno nainaṁ paśyantyacetasaḥ.

The seekers striving (for Perfection) behold Him dwelling in the Self; but the unrefined and unintelligent, even though striving, see Him not. (15.11)

21. Cite the verses wherein the Immanence of the Lord as —(1) the All-illumining Light of Consciousness (2) the All-sustaining Life (3) the subjective warmth of Life in all living organisms and (4) the Self in all the hearts—is described.

(1)Immanence of the Lord as the All-illumining Light of Consciousness:

यदादित्यगतं तेजो जगद्भासयतेऽखिलम् ।
यच्चन्द्रमसि यच्चाग्नौ तत्तेजो विद्धि मामकम् ॥

yadādityagataṁ tejo jagadbhāsayate'khilam,
yaccandramasi yaccāgnau tattejo viddhi māmakam.

That Light which is residing in the sun and which illumines the whole world and that which is in the moon and in the fire—know that Light to be Mine. (15.12)

(2) Immanence of the Lord as the All-sustaining Life:

गामाविश्य च भूतानि धारयाम्यहमोजसा ।
पुष्णामि चौषधीः सर्वाः सोमो भूत्वा रसात्मकः ॥

gāmāviśya ca bhūtāni dhārayāmyahamojasā,
puṣṇāmi cauṣadhīḥ sarvāḥ somo bhūtvā rasātmakaḥ.

Permeating the earth I support all beings by (My) energy; and having become the liquid moon, I nourish all herbs. (15.13)

(3) Immanence of the Lord as the subjective warmth of Life in all living organisms:

अहं वैश्वानरो भूत्वा प्राणिनां देहमाश्रितः ।
प्राणापानसमायुक्तः पचाम्यन्नं चतुर्विधम् ॥

ahaṁ vaiśvānaro bhūtvā prāṇināṁ dehamāśritaḥ,
prāṇāpānasamāyuktaḥ pacāmyannaṁ caturvidham.

Having become (the fire) vaiśvānara, I abide in the body of beings, and associated with prāṇa and apāna, digest the fourfold food. (15.14)

(4) Immanence of the Lord as the Self in all hearts:

सर्वस्य चाहं हृदि सन्निविष्टो
मत्तः स्मृतिर्ज्ञानमपोहनं च ।
वेदैश्च सर्वैरहमेव वेद्यो
वेदान्तकृद्वेदविदेव चाहम् ॥

sarvasya cāhaṁ hṛdi sanniviṣṭo
mattaḥ smṛtirjñānamapohanaṁ ca,
vedaiśca sarvairahameva vedyo
vedāntakṛdvedavideva cāham.

And I am seated in the hearts of all, from Me are memory, knowledge, as well as their absence. I am verily that which has to be known in all the Vedas; I am indeed the author of Vedānta and the 'knower of the Vedas' am I. (15.15)

22. Explain the limitation of science and the pivotal role of philosophy in revealing the Absolute.

Science can move only in a field where it can gather the necessary data to calculate and to prove. But philosophy seeks to satisfy the questionings of the human intellect regarding the Ultimate Source of all things, even if the necessary scientific data for such an attempt is available in the laboratory. There is a definite frontier at which the intellect and its observations, its logic and conclusions, its reasoning and assertions must necessarily exhaust themselves and cry halt. And yet, the question is not fully answered, for we find an honest intellect still left wondering: Why? How?? What??? There science is silent. Where science has fulfilled itself, and from where its light fails to illumine the onward path, there philosophy starts its pilgrimage towards the Absolute Satisfaction. (15.12)

23. How is the effulgence of the sun, moon, fire, etc., that of the Lord alone?

This question can be answered with an example: the light in the bulb, the heat in the furnace, the movement in the fan are all indeed different manifestations of electricity—the difference being caused by the dissimilar equipments of bulb, the furnace and the fan. Similarly, Consciousness expressed through the sun manifests sunlight, expressed through the moon is the moonlight and expressed through dry fuel is the fire—and yet, all of them are, in reality, nothing but the Infinite Itself, in Its varied glorious manifestations. The Infinite manifests Itself in order to create a conducive environment in which alone the world can exist and wherein, as the Lord, He can come to express Himself and play His game of plurality. (15.12)

24. Why is the Lord stated as being seated in the heart of all living beings?

Lord Kṛṣṇa says that He lives in the hearts of all living creatures. Here the term 'heart' does not mean the 'physiological heart' but it is the 'metaphysical heart'. The term 'heart' in philosophy, means 'mind which has been trained to entertain constantly the positive qualities of love, tolerance, mercy, charity, kindness and the like. A peaceful, joyous mind, settled in tranquillity, alert and vigilant to receive higher intimations, is called the 'heart'. The Infinite 'dwells in the heart' means that though He is present everywhere, the Lord is most conspicuously self-evident during meditation in the 'heart' of the meditator. (15.15)

25. Define and explain the terms 'Kṣara Puruṣa' and 'Akṣara Puruṣa'.

The following verse defines the terms 'Kṣara Puruṣa' and 'Akṣara Puruṣa':

द्वाविमौ पुरुषौ लोके क्षरश्चाक्षर एव च ।
क्षरः सर्वाणि भूतानि कूटस्थोऽक्षर उच्यते ॥

dvāvimau puruṣau loke kṣaraścākṣara eva ca,
kṣaraḥ sarvāṇi bhūtāni kūṭastho'kṣara ucyate.

Two Puruṣas are there in this world, the Perishable (Kṣara) and the Imperishable (Akṣara). All beings are the Perishable and the 'Kūṭastha' is called the Imperishable.

When the Infinite Consciousness becomes the light and heat of the sun, the fertility of the earth, the essence in the plant, the Consciousness in the heart, the faculties of knowing and remembering, etc., (as explained in verses 15.12-15) they are all different forms of Consciousness alone. Thus the field of matter is nothing other than the Spirit Itself. The only difference is that the Spirit, when It has assumed the form of matter, looks as though It is subject to change and destruction. Thus the 'realm of matter' is indicated as the Perishable Kṣara Puruṣa.

In the relative field of experience, when we talk with reference to the inert and perishable world of matter (Kṣara), the Spirit is indicated as the Conscious Principle, which is Imperishable (Akṣara). To explain: with reference to one's wife alone is one called a husband; when I have a son I will become a father. Similarly, with reference to the perishable and the changing matter-envelopments (Kṣara), the Consciousness is indicated as the Imperishable Akṣara Puruṣa. (15.16)

26. Define and describe the 'Uttama Puruṣa' (Puruṣottama).

The following two verses describe the 'Uttama Puruṣa':

उत्तमः पुरुषस्त्वन्यः परमात्मेत्युदाहृतः ।
यो लोकत्रयमाविश्य बिभर्त्यव्यय ईश्वरः ॥

uttamaḥ puruṣastvanyaḥ paramātmetyudāhṛtaḥ,
yo lokatrayamāviśya bibhartyavyaya īśvaraḥ.

But distinct is the Supreme Puruṣa (Uttama Puruṣa) called the Highest Self, the Indestructible Lord, who, pervading the three worlds (waking, dream and deep-sleep), sustains them. (15.17)

यस्मात्क्षरमतीतोऽहमक्षरादपि चोत्तमः ।
अतोऽस्मि लोके वेदे च प्रथितः पुरुषोत्तमः ॥

yasmātkṣaramatīto'hamakṣarādapi cottamaḥ,
ato'smi loke vede ca prathitaḥ puruṣottamaḥ.

As I transcend the perishable and am even Higher than the Imperishable, I am declared the 'Puruṣottama' (the Highest Puruṣa) in the world and in the Vedas. (15.18)

Distinct from the 'Kṣara Puruṣa' and 'Akṣara Puruṣa' is the Highest Spirit spoken of as the 'Ultimate Puruṣa' (Uttama Puruṣa) or 'Supreme Self' (Paramātmā). The Imperishable (Akṣara) is a status and a dignity gained by the Spirit only with reference to the field of the perishables (Kṣara) around and about It, through which It manifests as the various expressions of Life. But when the perishable (Kṣara) is transcended, what remains is not Imperishable (Akṣara) but that which played as the 'Perishable Puruṣa' (Kṣara Puruṣa) as well as the 'Imperishable Puruṣa (Akṣara Puruṣa).

This concept can be explained with an example: With reference to my own children alone am I really a father. With reference to my duty or the status I may have yet another name. When my children have died, or I am dismissed from my job, I am no more a father, nor can I any more claim my erstwhile official dignity. But that does not mean that I am, in the absence of children or work, an absolute zero, a total non-entity! No. I will exist in my individual capacity, though devoid of all my special status and dignity born out of my relationship with my profession, or with my children. It is this Pure Spirit (Puruṣa), which pervades and sustains the three worlds of the waking, dream and deep-sleep, that is spoken of as the Supreme Self (Paramātmā) or Highest Self (Uttama Puruṣa or Puruṣottama).

27. Explain how the 'Kṣara Puruṣa', 'Akṣara Puruṣa' and 'Uttama Puruṣa' are the one Consciousness alone.

The Infinite Consciousness is Itself the perishable-field (Kṣara Puruṣa) in another form; and as the 'Knower of the field', the same Consciousness is the Imperishable Reality (Akṣara Puruṣa) in the perishable conditioning (Kṣara Puruṣa). But when this conditioning is transcended, the same Self is experienced as the Supreme Self (Uttama Puruṣa). (15.17)

28. Cite the verse wherein the Lord declares that the individual who recognises Him as Uttama Puruṣa (Supreme Self) alone worships Him with pure devotion.

The following verse states that the one who worships the Lord as the Uttama Puruṣa worships Him with his whole being:

यो मामेवमसम्मूढो जानाति पुरुषोत्तमम् ।
स सर्वविद्भजति मां सर्वभावेन भारत ॥

yo māmevamasammūḍho jānāti puruṣottamam,
sa sarvavidbhajati māṁ sarvabhāvena bhārata.

He who, undeluded, thus knows Me, the Supreme Puruṣa, he all-knowing, worships Me with his whole being, O Bhārata. (15.19)

29. Why is the knower of the Uttama Puruṣa called 'all-knower'?

The Highest Spirit, Puruṣottama, being the Infinite Consciousness, is the 'All-knower', inasmuch as whenever anything is known through perception, feeling, or thought, it is the Principle of Consciousness that illumines it. One who has transcended one's matter-equipment and has successfully sought and discovered one's spiritual nature as the Infinite Consciousness, that individual verily becomes the Infinite Consciousness, the Uttama Puruṣa. Hence, the knower of the Uttama Puruṣa is described as the 'All-knower' (*sarvavit*). (15.19)

30. Why is Brahmavidyā termed 'secret'?

The spiritual science (Brahmavidyā) is termed 'secret' not in the sense that it should not be given out to anybody, but that it is a knowledge which cannot, of its own accord come to anyone, unless one is initiated into it by a Knower of Reality. (15.20)

Selections for Reflection

1. Seekers (sādhakas) who seek the Divine in themselves should learn to withdraw more and more from their usual dissipations of perceptions, feelings and thoughts, and must, in the still moments of meditation, contemplate upon the Higher—the Source from which the aśvattha-tree itself draws its sustenance and nourishment. (15.3)

2. To live in the flesh, seeking our life's fulfilment only in the joy derived from our contact with the sense objects in the world around us, is to live in the outer layer, cheating ourselves entirely of life's deeper possibilities. Such an ignorant fool gets extremely attached to the objects of the world, and once this attachment has grown, all his attentions in life will be irresistibly turned towards those objects. Shackled by them, ever dancing to their rhythm of change and destruction, he comes to lay waste his powers, without ever realising the nobler purpose of the Life-Divine. (15.5)

3. Repetition is a method of emphasis in all scriptural literature. Of course, this method is not used everywhere. Wherever logic is available, ideas are nailed in by logical reasoning. But there are realms into which the teacher alone has admission in the beginning and not the student-class and, therefore, the Ṛṣis had no other go but to repeatedly assert for our acceptance, the nature and condition of the unknown experience of the Infinite. (15.6)

4. The pure Light of Consciousness never illumines any object, because in the Pure Light of the Infinite, there are no objects at all to illumine. It is only the Light of Consciousness reflected in the mind-intellect that becomes the special beam of light, the intelligence, in which alone the sense objects become illumined. (15.9)

5. Everybody can read a great piece of literature, but a man of letters alone can come to comprehend and enjoy fully the vision expressed in and through the artistic design of the piece. Only a jeweller can really estimate the quality and worth of a jewel, even though all can look at it. Everyone can hear music, but only a musician can judge and experience the subtle beauties in a masterly recital. Similarly, every one of us, so long as life resides in us, can perceive, feel and think and yet, it is only the 'wise' man who can come to recognise and live the Infinite Essence of Life Itself. (15.10)

6. Identification with the beloved is the measure of love; the greater the love, the greater is our identification with the object of our love. Therefore, arithmetically, total identification should be the maximum love or devotion. (15.19)

Verses for Memorisation

ऊर्ध्वमूलमधःशाखमश्वत्थं प्राहुरव्ययम् ।
छन्दांसि यस्य पर्णानि यस्तं वेद स वेदवित् ॥

ūrdhvamūlamadhaḥśākhamaśvattham prāhuravyayam,
chandāṁsi yasya parṇāni yastaṁ veda sa vedavit.

They (wise people) speak of the indestructible aśvattha tree as having its roots above and branches below, whose leaves are the Vedas; he who knows it is alone a Veda-knower. (15.1)

अधश्चोर्ध्वं प्रसृतास्तस्य शाखा
गुणप्रवृद्धा विषयप्रवालाः ।

अधश्च मूलान्यनुसन्ततानि
  कर्मानुबन्धीनि मनुष्यलोके ॥

adhaścordhvaṁ prasṛtāstasya śākhā
  guṇapravṛddhā viṣayapravālāḥ,
adhaśca mūlānyanusantatāni
  karmānubandhīni manuṣyaloke.

Below and above are spread its branches, nourished by the guṇas; sense objects are its buds; and below, in the world of men, stretch forth the roots, originating in action. (15.2)

न रूपमस्येह तथोपलभ्यते
  नान्तो न चादिर्न च सम्प्रतिष्ठा ।
अश्वत्थमेनं सुविरूढमूलं
  असङ्गशस्त्रेण दृढेन छित्त्वा ॥

na rūpamasyeha tathopalabhyate
  nānto na cādirna ca sampratiṣṭhā,
aśvatthamenaṁ suvirūḍhamūlaṁ
  asaṅgaśastreṇa dṛḍhena chittvā.

Its form is not perceived here as such, neither its end, nor its origin, nor its foundation, nor its resting-place; having cut asunder this firm-rooted 'aśvattha'... (15.3)

ततः पदं तत्परिमार्गितव्यं
  यस्मिन्गता न निवर्तन्ति भूयः ।
तमेव चाद्यं पुरुषं प्रपद्ये
  यतः प्रवृत्तिः प्रसृता पुराणी ॥

tataḥ padaṁ tatparimārgitavyaṁ
  yasmingatā na nivartanti bhūyaḥ,
tameva cādyaṁ puruṣaṁ prapadye
  yataḥ pravṛttiḥ prasṛtā purāṇī.

Then that Goal should be sought after, where having gone, none returns again. I seek refuge in that 'Primeval Puruṣa' from which streamed forth, from time immemorial, all activity (or energy). (15.4)

निर्मानमोहा जितसङ्गदोषा
  अध्यात्मनित्या विनिवृत्तकामाः ।

द्वन्द्वैर्विमुक्ताः सुखदुःखसंज्ञैः
गच्छन्त्यमूढाः पदमव्ययं तत् ॥

nirmānamohā jitasaṅgadoṣā
adhyātmanityā vinivṛttakāmāḥ,
dvandvairvimuktāḥ sukhaduḥkhasaṁjñaiḥ
gacchantyamūḍhāḥ padamavyayaṁ tat.

Free from pride and delusion, victorious over the evil of attachment, dwelling constantly in the Self, their desires having completely retired, freed from the pairs of opposites – such as pleasure and pain – the wise reach that Goal Eternal. (15.5)

न तद्भासयते सूर्यो न शशाङ्को न पावकः ।
यद्गत्वा न निवर्तन्ते तद्धाम परमं मम ॥

na tadbhāsayate sūryo na śaśāṅko na pāvakaḥ,
yadgatvā na nivartante taddhāma paramaṁ mama.

Nor does the sun shine there, nor the moon, nor fire, to which having gone they return not; that is My Supreme Abode. (15.6)

यतन्तो योगिनश्चैनं पश्यन्त्यात्मन्यवस्थितम् ।
यतन्तोऽप्यकृतात्मानो नैनं पश्यन्त्यचेतसः ॥

yatanto yoginaścainaṁ paśyantyātmanyavasthitam,
yatanto'pyakṛtātmāno nainaṁ paśyantyacetasaḥ.

The seekers striving (for Perfection) behold Him dwelling in the Self; but the unrefined and unintelligent, even though striving, see Him not. (15.11)

अहं वैश्वानरो भूत्वा प्राणिनां देहमाश्रितः ।
प्राणापानसमायुक्तः पचाम्यन्नं चतुर्विधम् ॥

ahaṁ vaiśvānaro bhūtvā prāṇināṁ dehamāśritaḥ,
prāṇāpānasamāyuktaḥ pacāmyannaṁ caturvidham.

Having become (the fire) vaiśvānara, I abide in the body of beings, and associated with prāṇa and apāna, digest the fourfold food. (15.14)

द्वाविमौ पुरुषौ लोके क्षरश्चाक्षर एव च ।
क्षरः सर्वाणि भूतानि कूटस्थोऽक्षर उच्यते ॥

dvāvimau puruṣau loke kṣaraścākṣara eva ca,
kṣaraḥ sarvāṇi bhūtāni kūṭastho'kṣara ucyate.
Two Puruṣas are there in this world, the Perishable (Kṣara) and the Imperishable (Akṣara). All beings are the Perishable and the 'Kūṭastha' is called the Imperishable. (15.16)

उत्तमः पुरुषस्त्वन्यः परमात्मेत्युदाहृतः ।
यो लोकत्रयमाविश्य बिभर्त्यव्यय ईश्वरः ॥
uttamaḥ puruṣastvanyaḥ paramātmetyudāhṛtaḥ,
yo lokatrayamāviśya bibhartyavyaya īśvaraḥ.
But distinct is the Supreme Puruṣa (Uttama Puruṣa) called the Highest Self, the Indestructible Lord, who, pervading the three worlds (waking, dream and deep-sleep) sustains them. (15.17)

यस्मात्क्षरमतीतोऽहमक्षरादपि चोत्तमः ।
अतोऽस्मि लोके वेदे च प्रथितः पुरुषोत्तमः ॥
yasmātkṣaramatīto'hamakṣarādapi cottamaḥ,
ato'smi loke vede ca prathitaḥ puruṣottamaḥ.
As I transcend the perishable and am even Higher than the Imperishable, I am declared the 'Puruṣottama' (the Highest Puruṣa) in the world and in the Vedas. (15.18)

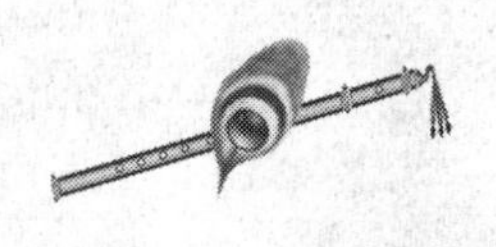

dvāvimau puruṣau loke kṣaraścākṣara eva ca
kṣaraḥ sarvāṇi bhūtāni kūṭastho'kṣara ucyate

Two Purusas are there in this world, the Perishable (Ksara) and the Imperishable (Aksara). All beings are the Perishable and the Kutastha is called the Imperishable. (15.16)

[illegible]

uttamaḥ puruṣastvanyaḥ paramātmetyudāhṛtaḥ
yo lokatrayamāviśya bibhartyavyaya īśvaraḥ

But distinct is the Supreme Purusa (Uttama Purusa) called the Highest Self, the indestructible Lord, who, pervading the three worlds (waking, dream and deep-sleep) sustains them. (15.17)

[illegible]

yasmāt kṣaramatīto'hamakṣarādapi cottamaḥ
ato'smi loke vede ca prathitaḥ puruṣottamaḥ

As I transcend the perishable and am even higher than the imperishable, I am declared as Purusottama (the Highest Purusa) in the world and in the Vedas. (15.18)

16

Daiva Āsura Sampat Vibhāga Yoga

The Yoga of Divine and Devilish Estates

Just as an individual will never have, even in his dream, any idea of injuring himself, a true seeker, in his recognition of the Oneness in all living creatures, must come to feel that to injure anyone is to injure himself. (16.3)

The sequence in the thought development in chapter 16 is from the ideas not yet concluded in chapter seven and nine and from the ideas merely touched upon in the preceding three chapters.

Based on the individual's qualities this chapter classifies the entire mankind, of all times and of all ages, under three types: (1) the divinely good (devas) (2) the diabolically fallen (asuras) and (3) the incorrigibly indifferent (rākṣasas). However, the rākṣasic type is not taken up for discussion in the following stanzas because, for that type, no conscious self-development programme is ever possible unless it be broken, recast and moulded again by the relentless hand of adversity.

The purpose of the Gītā is not merely to classify mankind as good and bad based on their qualities. As a practical instruction manual to life it seeks to help seekers on the path to Realisation. This chapter answers the immediate concern of all seekers as to what qualities to adopt and what qualities to abandon. The main theme of the entire chapter is to call man away from a life of sense-gratification into the ampler fields of desireless action and egoless perfection.

Terms and Definitions

1. What is 'tapas' (asceticism)?

All conscious self-denials at the body level, whereby an individual reduces his indulgences in the world outside, gains more and more energy within himself and applies the new-found energy for the purpose of self-development are called 'tapas' (asceticism). (16.1)

2. What does 'akrodha' (absence of anger) really mean?

'Akrodha' (absence of anger) is the capacity to check at the right time the waves of anger as they mount up so that we do not manifest anger in our actions. It is almost unnatural to expect the mind to become incapable of anger. But no emotion should be allowed to overwhelm us to such a degree as to render us almost ineffective. Anger arises out of an insufferable impatience with others—especially when they, by their thought, word or deed, come to injure our interest or insult our own self-evaluation. In short, 'akrodha' means 'keeping an even temper'. (16.2)

3. What is 'kṣamā' (patience)?

'Kṣamā' is not merely a capacity to patiently live through some minor physical or mental inconvenience when insulted or injured by others. It is also the subtle boldness that is shown by an individual in facing the world around with an unruffled serenity even in the face of the most powerful opposition and provoking situations. (16.3)

4. What does the term 'śāstra' and 'prakaraṇa' mean?

Textbooks discussing the 'Knowledge of Truth' (Brahma Vidyā) and the 'technique of self-perfection' (Yoga) are called śāstras. Other subsidiary books which explain and throw light upon the śāstras are called 'prakaraṇa grantha'. (16.23)

ᴄᴃ ᴕ

Thoughts and Concepts

1. How is the 16th chapter connected with the earlier chapters?

In the seventh and the ninth chapters, the Lord has already referred to people of evil and demonical natures who fail to understand Him and who deny Him:

na mām duṣkṛtino mūḍhāḥ – 7.15
avajānanti mām mūḍhāḥ – 9.11
moghāśā moghakarmāṇaḥ – 9.12

Soon after, the Lord again refers to the great souls who think of

Him and worship Him with faith and devotion:

mahātmanastu mām pārtha – 9.13

satataṁ kīrtayanto mām – 9.14

A fuller explanation of these two hostile forces – the divine and the diabolical – would be helpful to cultivate the qualities of the divine and eschew the qualities of the diabolical. The Lord therefore elaborately describes in this chapter the man of divine qualities and the man of demonical qualities.

Moreover, in the 15th chapter (15.5) the Lord made it clear that the possession of divine qualities is absolutely essential to Realise the Supreme Puruṣa. In this chapter, He continues the very same idea and describes those divine qualities in greater detail.

2. How can an individual attain ethical purity?

Ethical purity at the level of the heart cannot be brought about when the human mind is turned outward to the flesh. Only when the mind is constantly in unison with the Infinite Song of the Soul can it discover in itself the necessary courage to renounce its low appetites, clinging attachments and the consequent foul motives emanating from within itself. A mind that is awakened to the serene joys of the Self will never hang on to sensuous objects and their fleeting joys. Ethical purity is thus a direct result of keeping the mind tuned to the Higher in us. (16.1)

3. List the qualities of the 'divine estate' (daivī sampat) and cite the relevant verses.

Twenty-one qualities are enumerated as those of the 'divine estate' (daivī sampat). This enumeration serves as a guide to all those who thirst to become perfect. To the extent we are able to reorganise our way of life and change our vision of the world around us on these lines, to that extent we shall economise our energies that are often wasted in idle pursuits. To respect and live these 26 values of life completely is to assure ourselves of a right way of living:

(1) Fearlessness

(2) Purity of heart

(3) Steadfastness in the Yoga of knowledge
(4) Charity
(5) Control of the senses
(6) Sacrifice
(7) Study of the scriptures
(8) Asceticism
(9) Straightforwardness
(10) Harmlessness
(11) Truth
(12) Absence of anger
(13) Renunciation
(14) Peacefulness
(15) Absence of crookedness
(16) Compassion to all beings
(17) Non-covetousness
(18) Gentleness
(19) Modesty
(20) Absence of fickle-mindedness
(21) Vigour
(22) Patience
(23) Fortitude
(24) Purity
(25) Absence of hatred
(26) Absence of pride.

The following three verses enumerate the 26 qualities of the 'divine estate' listed above: (16.1-3)

अभयं सत्त्वसंशुद्धिर्ज्ञानयोगव्यवस्थितिः ।
दानं दमश्च यज्ञश्च स्वाध्यायस्तप आर्जवम् ॥

abhayaṁ sattvasaṁśuddhirjñānayogavyavasthitiḥ,
dānaṁ damaśca yajñaśca svādhyāyastapa ārjavam.

Fearlessness, purity of heart, steadfastness in the Yoga of knowledge, charity, control of the senses, sacrifice, study of the śāstras, and straightforwardness… (16.1)

अहिंसा सत्यमक्रोधस्त्यागः शान्तिरपैशुनम् ।

दया भूतेष्वलोलुप्त्वं मार्दवं ह्रीरचापलम् ॥

ahiṁsā satyamakrodhastyāgaḥ śāntirapaiśunam,

dayā bhūteṣvaloluptvaṁ mārdavaṁ hrīracāpalam.

Harmlessness, truth, absence of anger, renunciation, peacefulness, absence of crookedness, compassion to beings, non-covetousness, gentleness, modesty, absence of fickle-mindedness… (16.2)

तेजः क्षमा धृतिः शौचमद्रोहो नातिमानिता ।
भवन्ति सम्पदं दैवीमभिजातस्य भारत ॥

tejaḥ kṣamā dhṛtiḥ śaucamadroho nātimānitā,

bhavanti sampadaṁ daivīmabhijātasya bhārata.

Vigour, forgiveness, fortitude, purity, absence of hatred, absence of pride—these belong to the one born for the Divine Estate, O Bhārata. (16.1-3)

4. In the enumeration of the qualities of the 'divine estate' 'fearlessness' has been placed upfront. Explain the importance of 'fearlessness' in one's spiritual evolution.

Fear is the expression of ignorance. When there is 'Knowledge' there is no fear. By placing this quality of fearlessness at the head of the list, the Lord indicates that the true ethical perfection – that he has started to describe – is directly proportional to the fearlessness attained by the individual. (16.1)

5. What is 'dāna' (charity)?

'Dāna' (charity) consists in sharing with others the objects of the world that one possesses. True charity comes from one's sense of abundance and is born out of the capacity to restrain the instinct of acquisition and aggrandisement and to replace it with the spirit of sacrifice. This spirit of sharing can come only from a sense of oneness —oneness between the giver and the recipient. Unless one is able to identify oneself with others, one will not feel this noble urge to share all that one has.

Charity is also at the level of the heart and the head. To share with others our sympathy and kindness and to distribute one's knowledge are also to be considered as great charities. (16.1)

6. Explain the importance of 'dama' (sense control) in one's spiritual life.

To keep the mind turned up to the Self, a subtle energy is called for, and it will be discovered within ourselves when we control our sense excesses. To give a complete license for indulgence to the sense organs is to waste unproductively the total human vitality. To economise the needless expenditure of energy through the sense organs in the field of sense objects is to discover an extra amount of untapped energy. This energy can be made use of as the motive power behind the mind and intellect on its flight into the higher realms of meditation. (16.1)

7. What is 'svādhyāya' and its importance in the seeker's life?

The term 'svādhyāya' indicates regular study of the scriptures. Study of scriptural literature daily, in measured quantities, will provide the necessary inspiration to live the divine life in our day-to-day existence. 'Svādhyāya' is a very significant term for it suggests that the study of the scriptures should not end in mere intellectual appreciation, but as the student studies the textbooks, he must be able to simultaneously observe, analyse and realise the truth of what he is studying within his own life (sva+adhyāya = self-study). Regular studies coupled with sincere practice will give us the courage to live in self-control which alone in its turn will supply us the steadiness in meditation for Realising the Highest. (16.1)

8. What is the secret of enduring tenderness towards all beings?

It is not reasonable for an individual to expect that all will keep up to the ideal that one oneself entertains. There will be imperfections around. But to recognise in and through those imperfections the Infinite beauty of life expressed is the secret of enduring tenderness that is seen in all Saints and Sages. Love alone can discover an infinite amount of tenderness in us. Unless we train ourselves to see the beauty of life pulsating through even wretched hearts and ugly characters, we will fail to bring forth tenderness to sweeten our life. (16.2)

9. What is the importance of 'dhṛti' (fortitude) in one's life?

When an individual daringly meets life he cannot expect all the time, happy situations, favourable circumstances and a conducive arrangement of chances in his field of activity. Ordinarily, a weak man suddenly feels dejected and is tempted to leave his field of work when it is only half done. Many lose their chances of achieving the highest and desert the field of action almost at the moment when, perhaps, victory is round the corner. In order to 'stick to his guns' man needs a secret energy to nurture and nourish his exhausted and fatigued morale, and this sacred energy welling up in his well-integrated personality is 'fortitude'.

Strength of faith, conviction in the goal, consistency of purpose, vivid perception of the ideal and a bold spirit of sacrifice cultivated diligently—all these form the source from which fortitude gushes down to remove exhaustion, fatigue and despair. (16.3)

10. What are the qualities of the 'demoniac estate' (āsurī sampat)?

The following are the six qualities of the 'demoniac estate' (āsurīi sampat):

(1) Hypocrisy
(2) Arrogance
(3) Conceit
(4) Anger
(5) Harshness
(6) Ignorance

The following verse enumerates the above listed six āsuric qualities:

दम्भो दर्पोऽभिमानश्च क्रोधः पारुष्यमेव च।
अज्ञानं चाभिजातस्य पार्थ सम्पदमासुरीम्॥

dambho darpo'bhimānaśca krodhaḥ pāruṣyameva ca,
ajñānaṁ cābhijātasya pārtha sampadamāsurīm.

Hypocrisy, arrogance and conceit, anger and also harshness and ignorance belong to one who is born, O Pārtha, for a demoniac estate. (16.4)

11. Cite the verses wherein Śrī Kṛṣṇa describes the people of

demoniac traits (āsurī pravṛtti)?

In the following 12 verses, the Lord gives a graphic description of the people endowed with demoniac traits (āsurī pravṛtti) (16.7-18):

प्रवृत्तिं च निवृत्तिं च जना न विदुरासुराः ।
न शौचं नापि चाचारो न सत्यं तेषु विद्यते ॥

pravṛttiṁ ca nivṛttiṁ ca janā na vidurāsurāḥ,
na śaucaṁ nāpi cācāro na satyaṁ teṣu vidyate.

The demoniac know not what to do and what to refrain from; neither purity nor right conduct nor truth is found in them. (16.7)

असत्यमप्रतिष्ठं ते जगदाहुरनीश्वरम् ।
अपरस्परसम्भूतं किमन्यत्कामहैतुकम् ॥

asatyamapratiṣṭhaṁ te jagadāhuranīśvaram,
aparasparasammbhūtaṁ kimanyatkāmahaitukam.

They say, "the universe is without truth, without (moral) basis, without a God; not brought about by any regular causal sequence, with lust for its cause, what else?" (16.8)

एतां दृष्टिमवष्टभ्य नष्टात्मानोऽल्पबुद्धयः ।
प्रभवन्त्युग्रकर्माणः क्षयाय जगतोऽहिताः ॥

etāṁ dṛṣṭimavaṣṭabhya naṣṭātmāno'lpabuddhayaḥ,
prabhavantyugrakarmāṇaḥ kṣayāya jagato'hitāḥ.

Holding this view, these ruined souls of small intellect and fierce deeds come forth as the enemies of the world, for its destruction. (16.9)

काममाश्रित्य दुष्पूरं दम्भमानमदान्विताः ।
मोहाद्गृहीत्वासद्ग्राहान्प्रवर्तन्तेऽशुचिव्रताः ॥

kāmamāśritya duṣpūraṁ dambhamānamadānvitāḥ,
mohādgṛhītvāsadgrāhānpravartante'śucivratāḥ.

Filled with insatiable desires, full of hypocrisy, pride and arrogance, holding evil ideas through delusion, they work with impure resolves. (16.10)

चिन्तामपरिमेयां च प्रलयान्तामुपाश्रिताः ।
कामोपभोगपरमा एतावदिति निश्चिताः ॥

cintāmaparimeyāṁ ca pralayāntāmupāśritāḥ,
kāmopabhogaparamā etāvaditi niścitāḥ.

Giving themselves over to immeasurable cares ending only with death, regarding gratification of lust as their highest aim, and feeling sure that, that is all (that matters). (16.11)

आशापाशशतैर्बद्धाः कामक्रोधपरायणाः ।
ईहन्ते कामभोगार्थमन्यायेनार्थसञ्चयान् ॥

āśāpāśaśatairbaddhāḥ kāmakrodhaparāyaṇāḥ,
īhante kāmabhogārthamanyāyenārthasañcayān.

Bound by a hundred ties of hope, given to lust and anger, they do strive to obtain, by unlawful means, hoards of wealth for sensual enjoyments. (16.12)

इदमद्य मया लब्धमिमं प्राप्स्ये मनोरथम् ।
इदमस्तीदमपि मे भविष्यति पुनर्धनम् ॥

idamadya mayā labdhamimaṁ prāpsye manoratham,
idamastīdamapi me bhaviṣyati punardhanam.

"This has today been gained by me—this desire I shall obtain—this is mine—and this wealth shall also be mine in future." (16.13)

असौ मया हतः शत्रुर्हनिष्ये चापरानपि ।
ईश्वरोऽहमहं भोगी सिद्धोऽहं बलवान्सुखी ॥

asau mayā hataḥ śatrurhaniṣye cāparānapi,
īśvaro'hamahaṁ bhogī siddho'haṁ balavānsukhī.

"That enemy has been slain by me—and others also shall I destroy—I am the Lord—I am the enjoyer—I am perfect, powerful and happy." (16.14)

आढ्योऽभिजनवानस्मि कोऽन्योस्ति सदृशो मया ।
यक्ष्ये दास्यामि मोदिष्य इत्यज्ञानविमोहिताः ॥

āḍhyo'bhijanavānasmi ko'nyosti sadṛśo mayā,
yakṣye dāsyāmi modiṣya ityajñānavimohitāḥ.

"I am rich and well-born—Who else is equal to me?—I will give (alms, money)—I will rejoice." Thus are they, deluded by ignorance. (16.15)

अनेकचित्तविभ्रान्ता मोहजालसमावृताः ।
प्रसक्ताः कामभोगेषु पतन्ति नरकेऽशुचौ ॥

anekacittavibhrāntā mohajālasamāvṛtāḥ,
prasaktāḥ kāmabhogeṣu patanti narake'śucau.

Bewildered by many a fancy, entangled in the snare of delusion, addicted to the gratification of lust, they fall into a foul hell. (16.16)

आत्मसम्भाविताः स्तब्धा धनमानमदान्विताः ।
यजन्ते नामयज्ञैस्ते दम्भेनाविधिपूर्वकम् ॥

ātmasambhāvitāḥ stabdhā dhanamānamadānvitāḥ,
yajante nāmayajñaiste dambhenāvidhipūrvakam.

Self-conceited, stubborn, filled with pride and drunk with wealth, they perform sacrifices in name (only) out of ostentation, contrary to scriptural ordinance. (16.17)

अहङ्कारं बलं दर्पं कामं क्रोधं च संश्रिताः ।
मामात्मपरदेहेषु प्रद्विषन्तोऽभ्यसूयकाः ॥

ahaṅkāraṁ balaṁ darpaṁ kāmaṁ krodhaṁ ca saṁśritāḥ,
māmātmaparadeheṣu pradviṣanto'bhyasūyakāḥ.

Given to egoism, power, haughtiness, lust and anger, these malicious people hate Me in their own bodies and in those of others. (16.18)

12. Why is the 'game of desire' an endless gamble?

The more one possesses the more one is tempted to strive to possess more. Each time a man strives to acquire something, his desire is to feel his full share of satisfaction. But, invariably, his experience is that he is not fully satisfied and, in his disappointment, he thirsts for more and more possessions. The 'game of desire' is thus an endless gamble. (16.13)

13. Why does the Lord declare that the individuals endowed with the diabolical qualities of 'āsurī sampat' as hating the Lord Himself in their own bodies and others?

The consequence of disrespecting cultural values and living an uncultured egocentric existence of passions and desires would be nothing short of total destruction of Life. Persons who entertain the attitudes of āsurī sampat (qualities of the diabolically fallen) would ignore the sanctity of Life and without any compunction whatsoever desecrate It. They will grow malignant and in order to satisfy the low urges of egoism, the Lord declares, they would come to 'hate Him in their own bodies and in those of others'.

This statement of the Lord only indicates that such people do not allow the Sacred Life, the Paramātman to come out and express Its full play because their minds are blanketed by low unethical urges. Ethical values are disciplines whereby a mind so tuned up becomes the right instrument to serve faithfully the Self. Unethical values and immoral intentions choke the great Melody of Life and reduce it to a discordant, purposeless noise, shattering both peace and contentment within oneself and others. (16.18)

14. Cite the verses wherein the Lord declares the fate of those endowed with 'āsurī sampat'.

The following two verses declare the cruel fate of those endowed with the ignoble traits of 'āsurī sampat' (diabolically fallen):

तानहं द्विषतः क्रूरान्संसारेषु नराधमान् ।
क्षिपाम्यजस्रमशुभानासुरीष्वेव योनिषु ॥

tānahaṁ dviṣataḥ krūrānsaṁsāreṣu narādhamān,
kṣipāmyajasramaśubhānāsurīṣveva yoniṣu.

These cruel haters, worst among men in the world, I hurl these evil-doers for ever into the wombs of the demons only. (16.19)

आसुरीं योनिमापन्ना मूढा जन्मनि जन्मनि ।
मामप्राप्यैव कौन्तेय ततो यान्त्यधमां गतिम् ॥

āsurīṁ yonimāpannā mūḍhā janmani janmani,
māmaprāpyaiva kaunteya tato yāntyadhamāṁ gatim.

Entering into demoniacal wombs, and deluded, not attaining to Me birth after birth, they thus fall, O Kaunteya, into a condition still lower than that. (16.20)

An āsuric individual should necessarily discover his fulfilment only in an āsuric environment. Therefore the 'law of action and reaction' orders that such cruel men, again and again, reach similar wombs until the sheer horror of their experiences brings home to them a sudden realisation of the follies and futilities in following such a low tempo of life.

15. What are the three gateways to hell?

The following verse speaks about the three gateways to hell:

त्रिविधं नरकस्येदं द्वारं नाशनमात्मनः ।
कामः क्रोधस्तथा लोभस्तस्मादेतत्त्रयं त्यजेत् ॥

trividhaṁ narakasyedaṁ dvāraṁ nāśanamātmanaḥ,
kāmaḥ krodhastathā lobhastasmādetattrayaṁ tyajet.

These three are the gates of hell, destructive of the Self—desire, anger and greed; therefore, one should abandon these three. (16.21)

16. Describe the inter-relation between desire, anger and greed.

Where there is desire, anger is a natural corollary. The constant flying of an individual's thoughts towards an object of gratification is called 'desire', and when the steady flow of these thoughts of aggrandisement and possession are deflected by some obstacle, the refracted thoughts are called 'anger'.

If anger is thus the thought-storm arising in our mind at the disappointment of a desire, greed is the erosion of our mental strength and inner peace when desires are more and more satiated. Greed is a sense of dissatisfaction constantly pursuing and poisoning the sense of satisfaction that we have already experienced. When a desire gets fulfilled, an insatiable thirst for more and more joy holds the individual, and this endless appetite ruins the mental strength and saps dry the personality-vitality in the individual. (16.21)

17. Cite the verses that persuade an individual to live life in accordance with the declarations of the śāstras (scriptures).

The following two verses describe the importance of the śāstras (scriptures) and advise the seeker to live and act according to its dictates:

यः शास्त्रविधिमुत्सृज्य वर्तते कामकारतः ।
न स सिद्धिमवाप्नोति न सुखं न परां गतिम् ॥

yaḥ śāstravidhimutsṛjya vartate kāmakārataḥ,
na sa siddhimavāpnoti na sukhaṁ na parāṁ gatim.

He who, having cast aside the ordinance of the scriptures, acts under the impulse of desire attains neither perfection nor happiness nor the Supreme Goal. (16.23)

तस्माच्छास्त्रं प्रमाणं ते कार्याकार्यव्यवस्थितौ ।
ज्ञात्वा शास्त्रविधानोक्तं कर्म कर्तुमिहार्हसि ॥

tasmācchāstraṁ pramāṇaṁ te kāryākāryavyavasthitau,
jñātvā śāstravidhānoktaṁ karma kartumihārhasi.

Therefore, let the scriptures be your authority in determining what ought to be done and what ought not to be done. Having known what is said in the commandments of the scriptures, you should act here in this world. (16.24)

18. Why does the Lord advise us to follow the śāstras?

The seeker of an ampler life must necessarily follow the authority of the śāstras (scriptures) in planning his way of life. The right conduct in life can be determined only when the individual has correct knowledge of what is to be pursued and what is to be avoided. The grand road to Truth is the same for all. It cannot be determined by each pilgrim according to his own whims and fancies. Śāstras are declared by those who have travelled the road many a time. And when the Ṛṣis supply us with a road map to Perfection, we, the humble pedestrains, must pursue the path faithfully and come to bless ourselves. (16.24)

Selections for Reflection

1. Without dama and dāna the pilgrimage to Truth is merely a dream. (16.1)

2. Ethical values and moral beauties described in Hinduism are not arbitrary declarations of an imaginative Saint or a melancholy prophet! They are built on the rocky foundations of reason and experience. Ethics in India is not, by itself, a passport to heaven, but is a preparation for a fuller unfoldment of the divine in man. Sincerely pursued and consciously lived, it contributes to a better expression of the divine possibilities that generally lie dormant. (16.1)

3. The ugliness or beauty of the tongue is ordered by the personality behind it. A shattered entity will seek self-gratification in malicious scandal-mongering, and the soft, fleshy tongue can often become more devastating than the most destructive missile. (16.2)

4. A speech with softness of tone, clarity of expression, honesty of conviction, power of bringing a clear picture in the listener's mind with no veiled meaning, overflowing with sincerity, devotion and love, becomes the very quality of the autobiography of the speaker's personality. To develop, therefore, a habit of such speech would be unconsciously training many aspects in ourselves which are all necessary for the perfect disciplining of the inner equipments. (16.2)

5. The brilliance of his intellect, the twinkling joy in his eyes, the thrilling fragrance of peace around, the serene poise in his activities, the dalliance of his love for all, the light of joy that ever shines forth from the innermost depths of his being—these constitute the irresistible attraction of the personality of the Sage who, with abundant energy, serves all and discovers for himself a fulfilment in that service. (16.3)

6. Hypocrisy is one of the cheapest poses assumed by the vicious. To them, all their superficial glow of goodness and purity, of religiosity and sincerity are but attractive hoods to cover their deadly motives and ugly intentions. (16.4)

7. An arrogant man is a lonely creature in the world and his only companions are his own imagined self-importance and dreams of his own glories which none but he can see! (16.4)

8. Ethical virtues are the intelligent ways of reviving man's exhausted energies and fatigued spirit to live. By living healthy values of a righteous life, the individual unshackles his psychological personality from its self-made entanglements. (16.5)

9. To become sentimental and desperate or to exhaust oneself in self-pity or self-condemnation is a psychological malady, and one suffering from it can never discover in oneself, the energising cheer, the sustaining confidence and the steady will that are required for an intelligent self-diagnosis and an effective self-cure. (16.5)

10. The good, contaminated by weakness and ignorance, is the evil. And the evil, when cured of ignorance, itself becomes the good. A looking glass covered with dust cannot reflect light and mirror properly the objects in front of it. This is not because the glass has lost its capacity to reflect, but because its effectiveness has got veiled at present by the accumulated dust, which is essentially something other than the glass. To wipe it clean is to bring forth from it more clarity and light for the reflection. A 'Diabolically Fallen' one has also the same Infinite Light of Pure Wisdom—but alas, extremely dimmed by false values and wrong concepts! (16.5)

11. The contents of the bad mind are all the very same as those of the good, but misapplied under a wrong enthusiasm created as a result of some false evaluations. Virtue poisoned with ignorance is evil; evil treated and cured of its poison, when it regains its health, becomes virtue. (16.5)

12. Outer cleanliness is, to a large measure, a reflection of the inner condition. A disciplined man alone can, in fact, maintain a systematic order and cleanliness around him. (16.7)

13. Desire cannot come to the all-fulfilled. Desire can come only to him who fails to feel his own Infinitude and expresses himself as a limited ego. (16.10)

14. Life's beauty depends upon the beauty of the philosophy upon which it is built. If the foundations are false, the edifice, however strongly built, will prove to be no better than a card-castle. (16.10)

15. "I destroyed one competitor in the market, and now I must destroy the remaining competitors also......In fact, what can those poor

men do to stop me from doing what I want?.....Because there is none equal to me in any respect......I am the Lord. I enjoy, I am the most successful man. I am strong in influence, among political leaders, in my business connections, and in my bank balance. I am strong and healthy." This is the ego's song of success that is ever hummed in the heart of a true materialist. Under the spell of this foolish lullaby, the higher instincts and the divine urges in him go into a sleep of intoxication. (16.14)

16. A man can make a heaven of hell, and a hell of heaven, by the harmony or discord in himself. A subjectively shattered personality cannot find peace or fulfilment in any situation. Even if the environments are conducive, he discovers in himself methods of unsettling them by his own inner sufferings. (16.16)

17. When a man of the 'Diabolically Fallen' type reaches any field of activity, in spite of his vociferous claims of selfless service he is incapable of it, because of the very nature of his personality and character. Such members of society can perform a 'Yajña' (selfless service) in name only. Unconsciously, their actions will be poisoned by their vanity, coloured by their sensuality, distorted by their arrogance and generally polluted by their false philosophy. As a result of all their actions, sorrow alone will be the result. (16.17)

18. Ninety percent of the seekers, perhaps, know the śāstras exhaustively, in all detail, but alas, how few of them discover in themselves the courage to live, the will to pursue and the patience to wait till the Supreme is realised within themselves! (16.24)

Verses for Memorisation

अभयं सत्त्वसंशुद्धिर्ज्ञानयोगव्यवस्थितिः ।
दानं दमश्च यज्ञश्च स्वाध्यायस्तप आर्जवम् ॥

abhayaṁ sattvasaṁśuddhirjñānayogavyavasthitiḥ,

dānaṁ damaśca yajñaśca svādhyāyastapa ārjavam.

Fearlessness, purity of heart, steadfastness in the Yoga of knowledge, charity, control of the senses, sacrifice, study of the śāstras and straightforwardness… (16.1)

अहिंसा सत्यमक्रोधस्त्यागः शान्तिरपैशुनम् ।
दया भूतेष्वलोलुप्त्वं मार्दवं ह्रीरचापलम् ॥

ahiṁsā satyamakrodhastyāgaḥ śāntirapaiśunam,
dayā bhūteṣvaloluptvaṁ mārdavaṁ hrīracāpalam.

Harmlessness, truth, absence of anger, renunciation, peacefulness, absence of crookedness, compassion to beings, non-covetousness, gentleness, modesty, absence of fickle-mindedness… (16.2)

तेजः क्षमा धृतिः शौचमद्रोहो नातिमानिता ।
भवन्ति सम्पदं दैवीमभिजातस्य भारत ॥

tejaḥ kṣamā dhṛtiḥ śaucamadroho nātimānitā,
bhavanti sampadaṁ daivīmabhijātasya bhārata.

Vigour, forgiveness, fortitude, purity, absence of hatred, absence of pride—these belong to the one born for the Divine Estate, O Bhārata. (16.3)

दम्भो दर्पोऽभिमानश्च क्रोधः पारुष्यमेव च ।
अज्ञानं चाभिजातस्य पार्थ सम्पदमासुरीम् ॥

dambho darpo'bhimānaśca krodhaḥ pāruṣyameva ca,
ajñānaṁ cābhijātasya pārtha sampadamāsurīm.

Hypocrisy, arrogance and self-conceit, anger and also harshness and ignorance belong to one who is born, O Pārtha, for a demoniac estate. (16.4)

दैवी सम्पद्विमोक्षाय निबन्धायासुरी मता ।
मा शुचः सम्पदं दैवीमभिजातोऽसि पाण्डव ॥

daivī sampadvimokṣāya nibandhāyāsurī matā,
mā śucaḥ sampadaṁ daivīmabhijāto'si pāṇḍava.

The divine nature is deemed for Liberation, the demoniacal for bondage; grieve not, O Pāṇḍava, you are born with divine qualities. (16.5)

आशापाशशतैर्बद्धाः कामक्रोधपरायणाः ।
ईहन्ते कामभोगार्थमन्यायेनार्थसञ्चयान् ॥
āśāpāśaśatairbaddhāḥ kāmakrodhaparāyaṇāḥ,
īhante kāmabhogārthamanyāyenārthasañcayān.
Bound by a hundred ties of hope, given to lust and anger, they do strive to obtain, by unlawful means, hoards of wealth for sensual enjoyments. (16.12)

आत्मसम्भाविताः स्तब्धा धनमानमदान्विताः ।
यजन्ते नामयज्ञैस्ते दम्भेनाविधिपूर्वकम् ॥
ātmasambhāvitāḥ stabdhā dhanamānamadānvitāḥ,
yajante nāmayajñaiste dambhenāvidhipūrvakam.
Self-conceited, stubborn, filled with pride and drunk with wealth, they perform sacrifices in name (only) out of ostentation, contrary to scriptural ordinance. (16.17)

अहङ्कारं बलं दर्पं कामं क्रोधं च संश्रिताः ।
मामात्मपरदेहेषु प्रद्विषन्तोऽभ्यसूयकाः ॥
ahaṅkāraṁ balaṁ darpaṁ kāmaṁ krodhaṁ ca saṁśritāḥ,
māmātmaparadeheṣu pradviṣanto'bhyasūyakāḥ.
Given to egoism, power, haughtiness, lust and anger, these malicious people hate Me in their own bodies and in those of others. (16.18)

त्रिविधं नरकस्येदं द्वारं नाशनमात्मनः ।
कामः क्रोधस्तथा लोभस्तस्मादेतत्त्रयं त्यजेत् ॥
trividhaṁ narakasyedaṁ dvāraṁ nāśanamātmanaḥ,
kāmaḥ krodhastathā lobhastasmādetattrayaṁ tyajet.
These three are the gates of hell, destructive of the Self—desire, anger, and greed; therefore, one should abandon these three. (16.21)

यः शास्त्रविधिमुत्सृज्य वर्तते कामकारतः ।
न स सिद्धिमवाप्नोति न सुखं न परां गतिम् ॥
yaḥ śāstravidhimutsṛjya vartate kāmakārataḥ,
na sa siddhimavāpnoti na sukhaṁ na parāṁ gatim.
He who having cast aside the ordinance of the scriptures acts under the impulse of desire attains neither perfection nor happiness nor the Supreme Goal. (16.23)

तस्माच्छास्त्रं प्रमाणं ते कार्याकार्यव्यवस्थितौ ।
ज्ञात्वा शास्त्रविधानोक्तं कर्म कर्तुमिहार्हसि ॥

tasmācchāstraṁ pramāṇaṁ te kāryākāryavyavasthitau,
jñātvā śāstravidhānoktaṁ karma kartumihārhasi.

Therefore, let the scriptures be your authority in determining what ought to be done and what ought not to be done. Having known what is said in the commandments of the scriptures, you should act here in this world. (16.24)

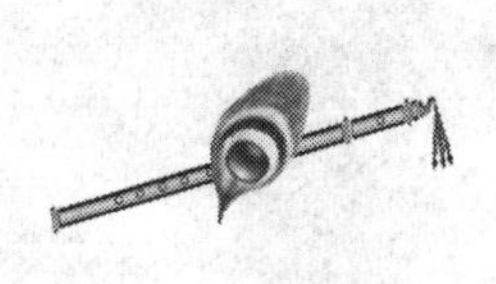

17

Śraddhā Traya Vibhāga Yoga

The Yoga of the Threefold Faith

Faith is the content and the very essence of man's whole being. Faith gives the direction, the dash, and provides a destination for one's determination. (Introduction)

The concluding two verses of the 16th chapter (16.23,24) introduced an idea that the śāstra (scripture) is the final court of appeal in all doubts and a sure guide for an individual to use in all the moment-to-moment judgements. But it is difficult for all to develop the required amount of proficiency in the scriptures. Many people, ignorant of the scriptural injunctions and prohibitions, nevertheless follow a life which they consider noble and they do possess great faith (śraddhā) in it.

This chapter opens with this doubt of Arjuna: Is it sufficient if one lives with faith a life of good conduct and noble aspirations, or is it necessary that one must also know the śāstras (scriptures) and implicitly obey the injunctions laid down by them? Arjuna also seeks to know from the Lord the nature of the faith of these people who try to live a religious life to the best of their knowledge – is it sattva, rajas or tamas? He also questions the Lord as to whether even without the knowledge of the śāstras blind-faith alone can enable a seeker to progress. This doubt of Arjuna is quite natural, for the emphasis and importance given to śraddhā (faith) by the Bhagavad Gītā are almost equal to those given to the śāstra (scripture).

While answering this question, Śrī Kṛṣṇa takes the opportunity to give a thorough exposition of faith as seen in the various fields of man's endeavours—his physical indulgences (āhāra), his dedicated activities (yajña), his self-denials (tapas) and his charities (dāna). He declares that the classification of the faith of these individuals, who are ignorant of the scriptural injunctions and prohibitions, as sattva, rajas and tamas does not merely depend on the firmness of their faith in a particular life style which they consider religious but rather on the object of their faith. Hence the Lord avers that faith is to be classified as sattva, rajas, or tamas based on 'what one believes in rather than how firm it is' and it is the sāttvic faith alone, even if one does not know the scriptures, that leads one to Perfection.

From a close study of this chapter, we can direct our activities away from the influences of the lower urges and guide our spiritual practices consistently on the royal path of sure success.

Terms and Definitions

1. What is 'yāta-yāmam food'?

In the Hindu time calculation, a day is divided into eight yāmas wherein a period of three hours constitutes one 'yāma'. The food cooked a 'yāma' before i.e., three hours earlier and which has, 'gone cold' is considered 'yāta-yāmam'. One is advised to take freshly cooked food and avoid 'yāta-yāmam food'. (17.10)

2. What are the three categories into which the Lord divides the sāttvic tapas (austerity)?

The Lord divides the sāttvic tapas (austerity) into the following three types:

(1) Śārīra tapas - austerity pertaining to the body

(2) Vāṅmaya tapas - austerity pertaining to the speech

(3) Mānasa tapas - austerity pertaining to the mind (17.14-16)

3. What does the term 'dvija' (twice born) mean?

The term 'dvija' or 'twice born' indicates 'Brāhmin', the term which means: 'the one who has Realised the Self'. Born as we are from the wombs of our mothers, we are all born as humans with certain intellectual beauties, no doubt, but also with many moral defects. Born out of the womb all right, but we are still in the 'womb of matter'! To hatch ourselves out of our matter-identifications and to emerge into the joy of Perfection is to grow into Godmen. This is conceived in philosophy as the 'second birth', and the one who has accomplished it is called the 'dvija' (twice born): once born from the womb, and for a second time grown out of all the limitations suffered by the Spirit in its seeming identifications with matter. (17.14)

4. Explain the term 'brahmacarya'.

Constant revelling in the contemplation of the Supreme Brahman is called 'brahmacarya'. This is not possible unless the mind is turned away from the sense objects and is trained to turn inward towards the Spirit. Therefore, all mental disciplines by which an individual comes to develop this introspection are to be together comprehended by the term 'brahmacarya'. (17.14)

5. Define 'svādhyāya'.

'Svādhyāya' is a technical term which is used to indicate the careful study of and deep reflections upon the theme of the scriptures. (17.15)

6. What is 'mouna'?

'Mouna' is the noiseless inner calm that one comes to experience when corroding passions and exhausting desires are no more building up in one's mind. 'Mouna' (silence) can also mean 'the State of Muni', implying the state of constant contemplation. (17.16)

Thoughts and Concepts

1. Cite and explain the significance of Arjuna's question at the beginning of the 17th chapter.

The Lord declares that action contrary to the śāstra-commands cannot lead to Perfection (16.23). But there are many who have not read the śāstras (scriptues), either due to indifference or incompetence or some other reasons, and yet believe in a Higher Power and carry on some form of worship. These men are definitely different from the demoniacal type (āsurī sampat) – described in the earlier 16th chapter – who entirely deny the existence of the Higher power.

These people have faith in the various spiritual practices like worship, sacrifice and so on that they practise, but their practices may not be entirely in conformity with the śāstras (scriptures) because of their ignorance of the śāstra commands. What is their condition? Do they attain Perfection? What is the nature of their worship—is it sāttvic, rājasic or tāmasic? This is Arjuna's question.

The above-mentioned question of Arjuna is enshrined in the following verse:

ये शास्त्रविधिमुत्सृज्य यजन्ते श्रद्धयान्विताः ।
तेषां निष्ठा तु का कृष्ण सत्त्वमाहो रजस्तमः ॥

ye śāstravidhimutsṛjya yajante śraddhayānvitāḥ,
teṣāṁ niṣṭhā tu kā kṛṣṇa sattvamāho rajastamaḥ.

Those who setting aside the ordinance of the scriptures perform sacrifice with faith, what is their condition, O Kṛṣṇa? Is it sattva, rajas or tamas?[1] (17.1)

2. What is the interrelation between 'faith' (śraddhā), 'nature' (sattva or svabhāva) and 'guṇa'?

It is very difficult to say whether one's faith determines one's nature or one's nature determines faith. For, indeed, each is intimately wedded to the other, each obeys the other most faithfully. However, the Gītā declares that it is the 'nature' (svabhāva or sattva) in an individual that rules his 'faith' (śraddhā). In rare cases alone when faith is broken and remoulded at the irresistible compulsion of painful experiences, one's nature (svabhāva) does faithfully obey the new śraddhā. But, generally speaking, the 'faith' (śraddhā) in each individual takes the hue and quality from the nature or predominant temperament in him of his being (svabhāva or sattva).

This nature i.e., disposition or temperament – termed as sattva[2] or

1. The introduction to this chapter explains Arjuna's question and also in brief the Lord's answer.

2. Not to be confused with 'sattva' or 'purity' – one of the three guṇas.

svabhāva – of man is in turn determined by the preponderance of any one of the guṇas over the others. Thus sāttvic guṇa leads to sāttvic nature (svabhāva or sattva) which in turn leads to sāttvic śraddhā (faith).

Thus there is a causal relationship between guṇa, svabhāva (sattva) and śraddhā. (17.3)

3. Cite and explain the verse wherein the Lord describes the worship of the sāttvic, rājasic and tāmasic śraddhā types.

The spirit of devotion in men ever remaining the same, each will select his own altar of devotion according to the type of his 'śraddhā'. The following verse discusses the various altars of worship of the sāttvic, rājasic and tāmasic:

यजन्ते सात्त्विका देवान्यक्षरक्षांसि राजसाः ।
प्रेतान्भूतगणांश्चान्ये यजन्ते तामसा जनाः ॥

yajante sāttvikā devānyakṣarakṣāṁsi rājasāḥ,
pretānbhūtagaṇāṁścānye yajante tāmasā janāḥ.

The sāttvic or pure men worship the gods; the rājasic or the passionate, the yakṣas and the rākṣasas; the others—tāmasic people or the 'dark' folk, worship the ghosts and the hosts of bhūtas or the nature spirits.

Sāttvic: Men of sāttvic temperament, because of their serene composure and tranquil disposition, seek their fulfilment at an altar of divinity indicating the higher impulses and the nobler qualities of their being. Naturally, they seek and come to adore such a divine Godly altar.

Rājasic: Men of 'passionate nature' (rajas) are those who have extreme ambition and are constantly restless in their self-chosen fields of activity. Such passionate type of men feel an admiration for and can appreciate only an equally active and passionate (rājasic) demi-god or deity.

Tāmasic: The dead 'spirits' and such other low and vicious powers are invoked by the men of 'inactivity' (tamas) for the satisfaction of some of their low urges and vicious sense gratifications. (17.4)

4. Why does the Lord condemn the body-mortifying austerities of the āsuric type of men?

In the following two verses the Lord condemns the frightful body-mortifying austerities of the āsuric type of men:

अशास्त्रविहितं घोरं तप्यन्ते ये तपो जनाः ।
दम्भाहङ्कारसंयुक्ताः कामरागबलान्विताः ॥

aśāstravihitaṁ ghoraṁ tapyante ye tapo janāḥ,
dambhāhaṅkārasaṁyuktāḥ kāmarāgabalānvitāḥ.

Those men who practise terrific austerities, not enjoined by the scriptures, given to hyprocrisy and egoism, impelled by the force of lust and attachment... (17.5)

कर्षयन्तः शरीरस्थं भूतग्राममचेतसः ।
मां चैवान्तःशरीरस्थं तान्विद्ध्यासुरनिश्चयान् ॥

karṣayantaḥ śarīrasthaṁ bhūtagrāmamacetasaḥ,
māṁ caivāntaḥśarīrasthaṁ tānviddhyāsuraniścayān.

Senselessly torturing all the elements in the body, and Me also who dwells within the body—you may know these to be of 'demoniacal' resolve. (17.6)

Austerities which are prohibited by the śāstras should not be undertaken. These prohibited austerities fall under tāmasic and rājasic types of tapas. They are frightful and horrid to the very performers of these austerities as well as to other beings. Inhuman forms of austerity show that the individuals performing them are devoid of understanding. The true purpose of tapas is the purification, of the mind and not the torturing of the body. The evil tendencies of the mind should no doubt be burnt up but cruel mortification of the flesh is not sanctioned by the śāstras as a means to self-purification for it does not lead to mental purity. Extreme tapas is stupid and stands condemned by the Lord.

Unintelligent austerities not only oppress the elements constituting the physical frame but also the Sacred and the Divine Lord within. Life gets choked as it were in such an individual and cannot express its full beauty through such a broken form. Since the Lord dwells within the body, torturing the body is verily torturing the Lord Himself. (17.6)

5. Is there any interrelation between food and one's inner nature?

Food does have certain effects upon the eater. Generally, people are, to some extent, conditioned by the type of diet they eat. But this is not to be over-emphasised. For not only is our inner nature built by the type of food consumed, but the inner nature, in its turn, commands our tastes; and we find very often that we have developed an irresistible appetite for certain types of food. Though a sāttvic diet helps to an extent in mind-control, mere change or control of food cannot however bring about thought-discipline. The Gītā rather explains that when the texture of thought improves, the individual finds himself changing his tastes: even his choice of the food that would give him full satisfaction is totally revolutionised. (17.8,9)

6. Cite the verses wherein the Lord declares the food choice of sāttvic, rājasic and tāmasic types.

In the following verses the Lord declares the food choice of the sāttvic, rājasic and tāmasic types:

आयुःसत्त्वबलारोग्यसुखप्रीतिविवर्धनाः ।
रस्याः स्निग्धाः स्थिरा हृद्या आहाराः सात्त्विकप्रियाः ॥

āyuḥsattvabalārogyasukhaprītivivardhanāḥ,
rasyāḥ snigdhāḥ sthirā hṛdyā āhārāḥ sāttvikapriyāḥ.

The food which increases life, purity, strength, health, joy and cheerfulness (good appetite), which are savoury and oleaginous, substantial and agreeable, are dear to the sāttvic (pure). (17.8)

कट्वम्ललवणात्युष्णतीक्ष्णरूक्षविदाहिनः ।
आहारा राजसस्येष्टा दुःखशोकामयप्रदाः ॥

kaṭvamlalavaṇātyuṣṇatīkṣṇarūkṣavidāhinaḥ,
āhārā rājasasyeṣṭā duḥkhaśokāmayapradāḥ.

The foods that are bitter, sour, saline, excessively hot, pungent, dry and burning, are liked by the rājasic, and are productive of pain, grief and disease. (17.9)

यातयामं गतरसं पूति पर्युषितं च यत् ।
उच्छिष्टमपि चामेध्यं भोजनं तामसप्रियम् ॥

yātayāmaṁ gatarasaṁ pūti paryuṣitaṁ ca yat,
ucchiṣṭamapi cāmedhyaṁ bhojanaṁ tāmasapriyam.

That which is stale, tasteless, putrid and rotten, refuse and impure, is the food liked by the tāmasic. (17.10)

7. What are the actions to be avoided and what are the actions to be performed?

Actions in the world fall under four categories, according to ancient Vedic lore. Of them 'desire-ridden' (kāmya) and 'forbidden' acts (niṣiddha) are the two types that are to be studiously avoided. The other two classes: the 'daily duties' (nitya) and the 'special duties' on special occasion (naimittika) are the types of actions that should be most diligently pursued. (17.11)

8. What are the yajña-types (sacrifices) that sāttvic, rājasic and tāmasic classes of men would engage themselves in?

The following three verses describe the choice of sacrifice (yajña) of the sāttvic, rājasic and tāmasic men:

अफलाकाङ्क्षिभिर्यज्ञो विधिदृष्टो य इज्यते ।
यष्टव्यमेवेति मनः समाधाय स सात्त्विकः ॥

aphalākāṅkṣibhiryajño vidhidṛṣṭo ya ijyate,
yaṣṭavyameveti manaḥ samādhāya sa sāttvikaḥ.

That sacrifice which is offered by men without desire for fruit and as enjoined by ordinance, with a firm faith that sacrifice is a duty, is sāttvic (pure). (17.11)

अभिसन्धाय तु फलं दम्भार्थमपि चैव यत् ।
इज्यते भरतश्रेष्ठ तं यज्ञं विद्धि राजसम् ॥

abhisandhāya tu phalaṁ dambhārthamapi caiva yat,
ijyate bharataśreṣṭha taṁ yajñaṁ viddhi rājasam.

The sacrifice which is offered, O best of the Bharatas, seeking for fruit and for ostentation, you may know that to be rājasic. (17.12)

विधिहीनमसृष्टान्नं मन्त्रहीनमदक्षिणम् ।
श्रद्धाविरहितं यज्ञं तामसं परिचक्षते ॥

vidhihīnamasṛṣṭānnaṁ mantrahīnamadakṣiṇam,
śraddhāvirahitaṁ yajñaṁ tāmasaṁ paricakṣate.

They declare that sacrifice to be tāmasic which is contrary to the ordinances, in which no food is distributed, which is devoid of mantras and gifts, and which is devoid of faith. (17.13)

9. What is the nature and purpose of tapas?

Tapas (austerity) is not merely a life of brutal self-denial. On the contrary, it is an intelligent method of living in a right relationship with the world of objects, thereby avoiding all unnecessary dissipations of our vital energies. The energies that are so economised and conserved are thereafter to be directed and employed in creative fields. This scheme of discovering precious new energies, conserving them intelligently and directing them into more profitable fields of spiritual enquiry is termed 'tapas'. (17.14)

10. Cite the verse wherein the Lord describes 'austerity of speech'.

The following verse explains the nature of 'austerity of speech':

अनुद्वेगकरं वाक्यं सत्यं प्रियहितं च यत्।
स्वाध्यायाभ्यसनं चैव वाङ्मयं तप उच्यते ॥

anudvegakaraṁ vākyaṁ satyaṁ priyahitaṁ ca yat,
svādhyāyābhyasanaṁ caiva vāṅmayaṁ tapa ucyate.

Speech which causes no excitement and is truthful, pleasant and beneficial, and the practice of the study of the Vedas—these constitute 'austerity of speech'. (17.15)

11. Explain the importance of speech that is 'satyam' (true), 'priyam' (agreeable) and 'hitam' (beneficial).

Satyam (true): In telling a lie, a lot of energy is wasted. This waste is avoidable if one adopts the policy of truthfulness in expression. Words that harmoniously bring forth the exact shade of ideas in the intellect are truthful expressions, and those that deliberately distort the intentions and meanings of the intellect are called falsehood.

Priyam (agreeable): In the name of truthfulness one can become a disagreeable person. Speech should be truthful as well as agreeable. Words uttered to express the truth in an agreeable style alone constitute right speech. This blesses the listener as well as the speaker. When a truth is disagreeable to others the speaker is required to maintain a discreet silence!

Hitam (beneficial): It is not sufficient that the words in the speech should be honest and agreeable, but they should also be beneficial. Speech should not be wasted. Unprofitable talking is a great drain on man's energies. One should talk only when one wants to express agreeable ideas of permanent value that will be useful to the listeners. (17.15)

12. Describe austerity of the mind.

The following verse explains austerity concerning the mind:

मनःप्रसादः सौम्यत्वं मौनमात्मविनिग्रहः ।
भावसंशुद्धिरित्येतत्तपो मानसमुच्यते ॥

manaḥprasādaḥ saumyatvaṁ maunamātmavinigrahaḥ,
bhāvasaṁśuddhirityetattapo mānasamucyate.

Serenity of mind, good-heartedness, silence, self-control, purity of nature—these together are called 'mental austerity'. (17.16)

13. How can one attain serenity of mind (*manaḥ prasāda*)?

Serenity of mind can be gained only when our relationship with the world at large is put on a healthy basis of understanding, tolerance and love. Further, one who is an uncontrolled sensualist can have little serenity or composure. The mind runs out through the sense organs into the sensual fields to eke out its satisfaction. The driving force that sets the mind on its endless errands is an intellect ever seething with desires. Quietude of the mind can be gained only when it is protected from both the inflow of stimuli from the tempting sense objects of the outer world and the whipping desires that march out from the intellect to drive the mind out into the fields of enjoyment. One who has discovered for himself a divine ideal—in the contemplation of which his mind forgets to run about, or his intellect overlooks to send out new desires—alone can hope to win serenity of the mind (*manaḥ prasāda*). (17.16)

14. Cite the verses that explain the nature of tapas (austerity) performed by the sāttvic, rājasic and tāmasic types of people.

The following verses describe the nature of the tapas performed by the sāttvic, rājasic and tāmasic types:

श्रद्धया परया तप्तं तपस्तत्त्रिविधं नरैः ।

अफलाकाङ्क्षिभिर्युक्तैः सात्त्विकं परिचक्षते ॥
śraddhayā parayā taptaṁ tapastattrividhaṁ naraiḥ,
aphalākāṅkṣibhiryuktaiḥ sāttvikaṁ paricakṣate.
This threefold austerity[3] practised by steadfast men with the utmost faith, desiring no fruit, they call sāttvic. (17.17)

सत्कारमानपूजार्थं तपो दम्भेन चैव यत् ।
क्रियते तदिह प्रोक्तं राजसं चलमध्रुवम् ॥
satkāramānapūjārthaṁ tapo dambhena caiva yat,
kriyate tadiha proktaṁ rājasaṁ calamadhruvam.
The austerity which is practised with the object of gaining good reception, honour and worship, and with hypocrisy, is here said to be rājasic, unstable and transitory. (17.18)

मूढग्राहेणात्मनो यत्पीडया क्रियते तपः ।
परस्योत्सादनार्थं वा तत्तामसमुदाहृतम् ॥
mūḍhagrāheṇātmano yatpīḍayā kriyate tapaḥ,
parasyotsādanārthaṁ vā tattāmasamudāhṛtam.
That austerity which is practised with self-torture, out of some foolish notion, for the purpose of destroying another is declared to be tāmasic. (17.19)

15. Why is the tapas (austerity) of the rājasic type of men described as 'transitory'?

Any intelligent self-effort, ordinarily, has a time-lapse before it can produce its results. Self-application must be constant and continuous in order that it may produce substantial results. When tapas (austerity) is performed with such a low motive as of winning respectability in society, it cannot even gather the necessary amount of intensity and thus, the tapas performed by the rājasic is transitory and merely ends in a lot of unproductive and painful self-denials, without producing any concrete results. (17.18)

16. Cite the verses that enumerate the three kinds of charity.

The following verses describe the sāttvic, rājasic and tāmasic types of charity:

3. The threefold austerity refers to the austerities of the body, speech and mind described from verses 17.14-16.

दातव्यमिति यद्दानं दीयतेऽनुपकारिणे ।
देशे काले च पात्रे च तद्दानं सात्त्विकं स्मृतम् ॥

dātavyamiti yaddānaṁ dīyate'nupakāriṇe,
deśe kāle ca pātre ca taddānaṁ sāttvikaṁ smṛtam.

That gift which is given knowing it to be a duty in a fit time and place, to a worthy person, from whom we expect nothing in return is held to be sāttvic. (17.20)

यत्तु प्रत्युपकारार्थं फलमुद्दिश्य वा पुनः ।
दीयते च परिक्लिष्टं तद्दानं राजसं स्मृतम् ॥

yattu pratyupakārārthaṁ phalamuddiśya vā punaḥ,
dīyate ca parikliṣṭaṁ taddānaṁ rājasaṁ smṛtam.

And that gift which is given with a view to receiving in return or looking for fruit or reluctantly is held to be rājasic. (17.21)

अदेशकाले यद्दानमपात्रेभ्यश्च दीयते ।
असत्कृतमवज्ञातं तत्तामसमुदाहृतम् ॥

adeśakāle yaddānamapātrebhyaśca dīyate,
asatkṛtamavajñātaṁ tattāmasamudāhṛtam.

The gift that is given at a wrong place and time, to unworthy persons, without respect, or with insult, is declared to be tāmasic. (17.22)

17. What is 'nirdeśa'? Why is 'Om Tat Sat' a nirdeśa?

A 'nirdeśa', usually a ritual or a japa, is enjoined on the performer of a Vedic act by the Vedic Ritual Science (Karma Mīmāṁsā) to overcome or render powerless any defect that could have arisen in the performance of the Vedic ritual.

'Om Tat Sat' – a sentence of three words – is pointed out as a 'nirdeśa' as it nullifies the defects that may have arisen due to the improper performance of a sacrifice (yajña), austerity (tapas) or charity (dāna). The logic is this: All the three – Om, Tat and Sat – are indicative of the Supreme Lord. The remembrance of the Lord while performing a sacrifice, austerity or charity purifies one's heart and intentions which in turn purifies the sacrifice, austerity and charity that one has undertaken. Thus the chanting and remembrance of 'Om Tat Sat' is pointed out as a 'nirdeśa'.

The term 'nirdeśa' additionally means 'designation'. Since the words 'Om', 'Tat' and 'Sat' are names of Brahman, even from the point of view of being a 'designation', 'Om Tat Sat' is spoken of as a 'nirdeśa' of Brahman. (17.23)

18. Explain in detail the manner in which 'Om Tat Sat' acts as a nirdeśa.

Each action has its fruit, but the fruit depends not only on the action as such, but also on the purity of the intentions and motives entertained by the performer. Actions performed by all of us may appear similar, but the results thereof would vary from individual to individual, according to the essential quality of their intentions. However diligent the performer of the sacred acts such as yajña (scripture), dāna (charity) and tapas (austerity) may be, if the intentions behind such acts be foul, they are rendered ineffective to yield rich dividends.

The glory of intentions can be heightened by the remembrance of the Lord. To the extent the sacred activity is selfless, to that extent its rewards are pure. To liquidate the ego, the individual must gain the consciousness of his spiritual status.

'Om Tat Sat' is a sentence of three words, and each word denotes an aspect of the Supreme Reality:

(1) 'Om' represents the Transcendental and the pure Self, the absolute and the unborn, which is the infinite substratum upon which the projections of the body, mind and intellect are maintained.

(2) 'Tat' is used in the scriptures to indicate the Eternal Goal, the changeless and the Ever-perfect. Thus, in the Mahāvākya 'Tat Tvam Asi,' the term 'Tat' indicates that from which everything has come, in which everything exists and into which everything merges back in the end.

(3) 'Sat' means 'existence.' The 'Principle of Existence' functioning through all things—perceived, felt and thought of in our everyday life—is called 'Sat'.

Whatever defects may arise in the performance of yajña (sacrifice), dāna (charity) or tapas (austerity) become nullified by an ardent remembrance of the Lord. Thus, to invoke the thoughts of 'Om', which expresses the Transcendental Absolute; or to invoke 'Tat' the Universal Truth; or to cherish the concept of 'Sat' the Reality is to tune up our instruments of action and thereby chasten and purify all our activities in the world outside and render it free of defects. It is thus by invoking the remembrance of the Lord that the sentence 'Om Tat Sat' acts as a 'nirdeśa'. (17.23)

19. Cite and explain the verse which explains the usage of the word 'Om'.

The term 'Om' is uttered while acts of sacrifice, gift and austerity are undertaken. To cherish in our minds the divine awareness and the absolute supremacy of the Infinite as expressed in 'Om' is to add purpose and meaning to all our acts of sacrifice, charity and austerity. To invoke the divine concept of the Absolute is to free our personality from its limited fields of egocentric attachments. When a mind is thus liberated from its limitations, it becomes more efficient in all austerities, more selfless in all yajñas, and more liberal in all charities.

The following verse explains the importance of 'Om' in all Vedic as well as noble actions:

तस्मादोमित्युदाहृत्य यज्ञदानतपःक्रियाः ।
प्रवर्तन्ते विधानोक्ताः सततं ब्रह्मवादिनाम् ॥

tasmādomityudāhṛtya yajñadānatapaḥkriyāḥ,
pravartante vidhānoktāḥ satataṁ brahmavādinām.

Therefore, with the utterance of 'Om' are begun the acts of sacrifice, gifts and austerity as enjoined in the scriptures, always by the students of Brahman. (17.24)

20. Cite and explain the relevant verse wherein the Lord declares the importance of the term 'Tat'.

With the utterance of the 'Tat' alone, the acts of sacrifice, penance and gift are undertaken by the seekers of Freedom, without expectation of any reward. 'Tat' indicates the 'Universal Truth' and it declares 'the oneness of all living creatures'. To work in the field of yajña or dāna or tapas with a mind that is tuned to 'Tat', 'the universal oneness of the Spiritual Truth', is to work with no ego and, consequently, redeem ourselves from the thraldom of the flesh, from all the limitations of matter.

The following verse explains the importance of 'Tat':

तदित्यनभिसन्धाय फलं यज्ञतपःक्रियाः ।
दानक्रियाश्च विविधाः क्रियन्ते मोक्षकाङ्क्षिभिः ॥

tadityanabhisandhāya phalaṁ yajñatapaḥkriyāḥ,
dānakriyāśca vividhāḥ kriyante mokṣakāṅkṣibhiḥ.

Uttering 'Tat' without aiming at the fruits, are the acts of sacrifice and austerity and the various acts of gift performed by the seekers of Liberation. (17.25)

21. Cite the verses which explain the usage of the word 'Sat'.

'Sat' is used to mean both Reality and goodness. It is also used for all praiseworthy actions. The term 'Sat' is used to indicate a man's faith and devotion in sacrifice, austerity and gift.

The following two verses explain these ideas:

सद्भावे साधुभावे च सदित्येतत्प्रयुज्यते ।
प्रशस्ते कर्मणि तथा सच्छब्दः पार्थ युज्यते ॥

sadbhāve sādhubhāve ca sadityetatprayujyate,
praśaste karmaṇi tathā sacchabdaḥ pārtha yujyate.

The word 'Sat' is used in the sense of Reality and of goodness; and also, O Pārtha, the word 'Sat' is used in the sense of an auspicious act. (17.26).

यज्ञे तपसि दाने च स्थितिः सदिति चोच्यते ।
कर्म चैव तदर्थीयं सदित्येवाभिधीयते ॥

yajñe tapasi dāne ca sthitiḥ saditi cocyate,
karma caiva tadarthīyaṁ sadityevābhidhīyate.

Steadfastness in sacrifice, austerity and gift is also called 'Sat' and also action in connection with these (for the sake of the Supreme) is called 'Sat'. (17.27)

22. Explain how even acts of sacrifice, charity and austerity which are not sāttvic in the beginning of their performance can be rendered so by the use of 'Om Tat Sat'.

Even acts of sacrifice, charity and austerity when they are not of the sāttvic type at the beginning of those acts can be rendered good when they are pursued with the required inner attunement with the Divine, which is gained by invoking in the performer's heart the concept of the Supreme (Om), the Universal (Tat) and the Real (Sat) Brahman. If these chantings are undertaken with faith and sincerity, the seeker's mind expands and gives up all its selfishness and arrogance. The fundamental principle is: actions can leave behind only such reactions as are ordered by the type of motives and attitudes of the performer. The vāsanās, the very creators of our psychological imperfections, are overcome by an intelligent and right adjustment of one's mental attitude at work by the remembrance of the infinite Reality as indicated by the three terms 'Om Tat Sat'. (17.27)

23. Explain how sacrifices, austerities and charity done without faith is 'asat'.

'Unreality' or 'non-existence' is called 'asat'. From the unreal, nothing real can ever emerge. Whatever sacrifice is made, whatever penance is performed, or whatever charity is given, it is called 'asat', if it is undertaken 'without faith'. From an unreal activity, no real result can come. Therefore, actions – spiritual or religious – when undertaken without faith, fail to produce any result. By so saying, the Lord is indicating that śraddhā (faith) is unavoidable, and that without it no progress or evolution can ever take place.

The following verse makes this clear:

अश्रद्धया हुतं दत्तं तपस्तप्तं कृतं च यत्।
असदित्युच्यते पार्थ न च तत्प्रेत्य नो इह ॥

aśraddhayā hutaṁ dattaṁ tapastaptaṁ kṛtaṁ ca yat,
asadityucyate pārtha na ca tatpretya no iha.

Whatever is sacrificed, given or performed and whatever austerity is practised without faith, it is called 'asat', O Pārtha; it is not for here or hereafter. (17.28)

24. Give an overall view of the choice of (1) altar of worship (2) āhāra (food) (3) yajña (sacrifice) (4) tapas (austerity) and dāna (charity) of the sāttvic, rājasic and tāmasic types of people.

	Choice of	Sattva	Rajas	Tamas
1.	Altar of worship (17.4)	Gods	Yakṣas and Rākṣasas	Ghosts and Bhūtas
2.	Āhāra - food (17.8-10)	Food which increases vitality, purity, strength, health, joy, cheerfulness, which are savoury, oleaginous, substantial and agreeable.	Food that is bitter, sour, saline, excessively hot, purgent, dry and burning.	Food that is stale, putrid, rotten, refuse and impure.
3.	Yajña - sacrifice (17.11-13)	Sacrifice that is performed without desire for fruit, enjoined by the scriptures, and with a firm faith that the sacrifice is one's duty.	Sacrifice which is offered with desire for fruits and for ostentation.	Sacrifice which is contrary to scriptural injunctions, in which there is no distribution of food or gift and that which is devoid of faith and mantras.
4.	Tapas - austerity (17.17-19)	Performing the triple austerity of body, mind and speech (17.14-16) with steadfastness, faith and desirelessness.	Performed for the sake of gaining good reputation, honour and reverence in society and with hypocrisy. This tapas is unstable and transitory.	Performed with self-torture out of some foolish notion and for the purpose of destroying others.
5.	Dāna - charity (17.20-22)	Gift that is given with a sense of duty, in a fit time and place, to a worthy person without expecting anything in return.	Gift that is given with the expectation of receiving something in return, for reward or given reluctantly.	Gift given at a wrong place and time to unworthy persons without respect or with insult.

Selections for Reflection

1. The help gained from good friends, the protection invoked from the rich and the powerful and the enormous strength gathered from the low thoughtless men of criminal intentions—these are respectively the different types of altars at which men of serenity (sāttvic), of ambition (rājasic), of heedlessness (tāmasic), generally seek their individual satisfaction. From the nature of a man's field of activity, we can, to a large extent, understand to what type he belongs. (17.4)

2. The temperamental influences that govern the mind and its thought-life express themselves in all departments of activity in which the individual employs himself. His choice of food, of friends, of the type of emotions, of the view of life that he entertains are all indicative of the type to which the seeker belongs—sāttvic, rājasic or tāmasic. (17.7)

3. 'Sacrifice is our duty'—this is the motive that propels the good (sāttvic) to act in life. He suffers no dissipation of his inner energies either through anxieties to drive himself to a particular goal or through his restlessness in herding his environment into a pre-planned and pre-conceived system of harmony. His mind is ever at rest in its own native satisfaction. He is consciously happy that he is pursuing a line of action which is most conducive to the welfare of all. (17.11)

4. Unless a seeker diligently practises straightforwardness in his dealings with others he will be developing in himself a split-personality, which will drain away all his composure, tranquillity and mental vitality. (17.14)

5. Speech is the constant activity of all and it is an outlet through which the greatest amount of one's energies are wasted. To control and conserve this unproductive waste of energy would constitute a great inner wealth indeed for the seeker. But, this does not mean that one must keep a self-ruining, disgustingly

irritating, silence (mouna)! The power of speech must also be made use of by the seeker for integrating his personality. (17.15)

6. Without any definite goal in life, without planning our onward march towards the ideal, we are apt to fall a victim to the various temptations enroute and exhaust ourselves in the bylanes of life. To stick constantly on to the grand road to success is to assure for ourselves a happy pilgrimage to Truth. (17.16)

7. Self-torture cannot bring about any unveiling of the true beauty of the Soul; it can only create a ludicrous caricature of the Perfection in us. Twisted and torn into a disfigured personality, perverted in its emotion and unclean in its ideals – this alone can be the outcome of any unintelligent austerity. (17.19)

8. There is a school which believes that charity must be given just as a tree gives its fruits. The fruits on a tree are available to all who come under its shade—irrespective of their race, status or gender. They argue that as the trees do not make any discrimination between one enjoyer and the other, so too man should, without making any discrimination between one recipient and another, share his possessions freely. Many will find it difficult to believe in and live up to this principle. The Bhagavad Gītā insists, and rightly so, that man must use his faculty of discrimination and see whether his charities are reaching the deserving members in the community. (17.20)

9. Charity must come from within, as an expression of an irrepressible urge of one's own heart. Intelligent charity must spring from the abundance felt within the individual. He who feels impoverished by his giving has not done a charity by the mere physical act of giving away. (17.22)

10. Dissociation of oneself from one's matter-envelopments is at once one's awakening and identification with the Lord. (17.23)

11. Without faith, no one can come to shine in any field of activity. No

one can hope to gather any profit at all out of any activity, if he has no faith in it. Both in the secular activities of the market-place and in the sacred performance of religious acts, the factor that determines the quality and quantity of the result is our faith in our efficiency and goodness, in our chosen field of our activity. (17.28)

ଓଃ ଃଠ

Verses for Memorisation

सत्त्वानुरूपा सर्वस्य श्रद्धा भवति भारत।
श्रद्धामयोऽयं पुरुषो यो यच्छ्रद्धः स एव सः॥

sattvānurūpā sarvasya śraddhā bhavati bhārata,
śraddhāmayo'yaṁ puruṣo yo yacchraddhaḥ sa eva saḥ.

The faith of each is in accordance with his own nature, O Bhārata. Man consists of his faith; as a man's faith is, so is he. (17.3)

आयुःसत्त्वबलारोग्यसुखप्रीतिविवर्धनाः।
रस्याः स्निग्धाः स्थिरा हृद्या आहाराः सात्त्विकप्रियाः॥

āyuḥsattvabalārogyasukhaprītivivardhanāḥ,
rasyāḥ snigdhāḥ sthirā hṛdyā āhārāḥ sāttvikapriyāḥ.

The food which increases life, purity, strength, health, joy and cheerfulness (good appetite), which are savoury and oleaginous, substantial and agreeable, are dear to the sāttvic (pure). (17.8)

कट्वम्ललवणात्युष्णतीक्ष्णरूक्षविदाहिनः।
आहारा राजसस्येष्टा दुःखशोकामयप्रदाः॥

kaṭvamlalavaṇātyuṣṇatīkṣṇarūkṣavidāhinaḥ,
āhārā rājasasyeṣṭā duḥkhaśokāmayapradāḥ.

The foods that are bitter, sour, saline, excessively hot, pungent, dry and burning are liked by the rājasic, and are productive of pain, grief and disease. (17.9)

यातयामं गतरसं पूति पर्युषितं च यत्।
उच्छिष्टमपि चामेध्यं भोजनं तामसप्रियम्॥

yātayāmaṁ gatarasaṁ pūti paryuṣitaṁ ca yat,

ucchiṣṭamapi cāmedhyaṁ bhojanaṁ tāmasapriyam.
That which is stale, tasteless, putrid and rotten, refuse and impure is the food liked by the tāmasic. (17.10)

अफलाकाङ्क्षिभिर्यज्ञो विधिदृष्टो य इज्यते ।
यष्टव्यमेवेति मनः समाधाय स सात्त्विकः ॥
aphalākāṅkṣibhiryajño vidhidṛṣṭo ya ijyate,
yaṣṭavyameveti manaḥ samādhāya sa sāttvikaḥ.
That sacrifice which is offered by men without desire for fruit and as enjoined by ordinance, with a firm faith that sacrifice is a duty, is sāttvic (pure). (17.11)

देवद्विजगुरुप्राज्ञपूजनं शौचमार्जवम् ।
ब्रह्मचर्यमहिंसा च शारीरं तप उच्यते ॥
devadvijagurupräjñapūjanaṁ śaucamārjavam,
brahmacaryamahiṁsā ca śārīraṁ tapa ucyate.
Worship of the gods, the twice-born, the teachers and the wise; purity, straightforwardness, celibacy and non-injury; these are called the 'austerities of the body'. (17.14)

अनुद्वेगकरं वाक्यं सत्यं प्रियहितं च यत् ।
स्वाध्यायाभ्यसनं चैव वाङ्मयं तप उच्यते ॥
anudvegakaraṁ vākyaṁ satyaṁ priyahitaṁ ca yat,
svādhyāyābhyasanaṁ caiva vāṅmayaṁ tapa ucyate.
Speech which causes no excitement, and is truthful, pleasant and beneficial, and the practice of the study of the Vedas, these constitute the 'austerities of speech'. (17.15)

मनःप्रसादः सौम्यत्वं मौनमात्मविनिग्रहः ।
भावसंशुद्धिरित्येतत्तपो मानसमुच्यते ॥
manaḥprasādaḥ saumyatvaṁ maunamātmavinigrahaḥ,
bhāvasaṁśuddhirityetattapo mānasamucyate.
Serenity of mind, good-heartedness, silence, self-control, purity of nature—these together are called the 'mental austerities'. (17.16)

सत्कारमानपूजार्थं तपो दम्भेन चैव यत् ।
क्रियते तदिह प्रोक्तं राजसं चलमध्रुवम् ॥

satkāramānapūjārthaṁ tapo dambhena caiva yat,
kriyate tadiha proktaṁ rājasaṁ calamadhruvam.
The austerity that is practised with the object of gaining good reception, honour and worship, and with hypocrisy, is here said to be rājasic, unstable and transitory. (17.18)

दातव्यमिति यद्दानं दीयतेऽनुपकारिणे ।
देशे काले च पात्रे च तद्दानं सात्त्विकं स्मृतम् ॥
dātavyamiti yaddānaṁ dīyate'nupakāriṇe,
deśe kāle ca pātre ca taddānaṁ sāttvikaṁ smṛtam.
That gift which is given, knowing it to be a duty, in a fit time and place to a worthy person, from whom we expect nothing in return, is held to be sāttvic. (17.20)

ॐ तत्सदिति निर्देशो ब्रह्मणस्त्रिविधः स्मृतः ।
ब्राह्मणास्तेन वेदाश्च यज्ञाश्च विहिताः पुरा ॥
om tatsaditi nirdeśo brahmaṇastrividhaḥ smṛtaḥ,
brāhmaṇāstena vedāśca yajñāśca vihitāḥ purā.
'Om Tat Sat'—this has been declared to be the triple designation of Brahman. By that were created formerly the Brāhmaṇas, Vedas and sacrifices. (17.23)

अश्रद्धया हुतं दत्तं तपस्तप्तं कृतं च यत् ।
असदित्युच्यते पार्थ न च तत्प्रेत्य नो इह ॥
aśraddhayā hutaṁ dattaṁ tapastaptaṁ kṛtaṁ ca yat,
asadityucyate pārtha na ca tatpretya no iha.
Whatever is sacrificed, given or performed, and whatever austerity is practised without faith, is called 'asat,' O Pārtha; it is not for here or hereafter. (17.28)

18

Mokṣa Saṁnyāsa Yoga

The Yoga of Liberation through Renunciation

The essence of dispassion is not in our running away from the object; from a truly dispassionate man, the objects run away in inexplicable despair! (18.52)

On the basis of temperaments, the Gītā indicates three types of personalities: the 'good' (sāttvic), the 'passionate' (rājasic) and the 'dull' (tāmasic). In the 18th chapter, we have an elaborate and exhaustive discussion on how these three temperaments, in their variations, create differences among individuals, in sacrifice, in wisdom, in actions, in fortitude and in happiness.

There are two terms in the Bhagavad Gītā: 'renunciation' (saṁnyāsa) and 'abandonment' (tyāga) that are very often used in different contexts with seemingly different import[1]. The terms are defined at the beginning of this chapter in order to remove all the confusions pertaining to these terms. This closing chapter of the Gītā is, in fact, a summary of the entire Song of the Lord. If the second chapter is a summary of the Bhagavad Gītā in anticipation, the 18th chapter is a report on the Bhagavad Gītā in retrospect.

Terms and Definitions

1. Differentiate between the terms 'tyāga' (abandonment) and 'saṁnyāsa' (renunciation).

The giving up of the lower impulses of the 'passionate' (rājasic) and the dull (tāmasic) in our moment-to-moment contacts with life is tyāga (abandonment). This tyāga alone will give one sufficient mastery enabling one to ultimately renounce the very ego-centre which is the root cause of all these lower impulses. It is this final renunciation of the finite ego-centre in the acquired Wisdom of the Infinite that is the fulfilment of life and is indicated by the term 'saṁnyāsa' (renunciation). (Introduction)

1. Refer verses 3.30, 4.20, 4.41, 9.28, 12.6, 12.11, 12.12, 12.16 and 14.25.

2. Why is Śrī Kṛṣṇa called 'Keśiniṣūdana'?

'Keśi' was a daitya (demon) who took the form of a horse and attacked Śrī Kṛṣṇa. The Lord killed him by tearing him into two halves. Hence Śrī Kṛṣṇa is called 'Keśiniṣūdana'. (18.1)

3. What is the mathematical definition of attachment?

The arithmetic of attachment in the Gītā is 'Ego + Egocentric desires = Attachment '. (18.6)

4. What is 'attachment' (asaṅga)?

When an ego strives to fulfil its own burning desires, it comes to live in a certain wrong relationship with the world of things and objects around. This wrong relationship is called 'attachment' (saṅga). (18.6)

5. What is 'medhā śakti'?

The intellect's power to understand, memorise and retain is termed 'medhā śakti'. (18.10)

6. Who is a 'medhāvī'?

A 'medhāvī' is a man of firm understanding and who has a constant memory of:

(1) The constituents of the field of his activity
(2) The instruments through which he contacts the world outside
(3) His own essential Divine nature
(4) His exact relationship with the world of objects when he is contacting it through his senses. (18.10)

7. What are the three types of 'results of actions' (karma-phala)?

The results or the consequence of one's action are of three types:

(1) The disagreeable or the calamitous—meaning those that are positively bad
(2) The agreeable or non-calamitous—meaning those that are positively good
(3) The mixed type or balanced—wherein the results are balanced equally between the good and the bad. (18.12)

8. What does the term 'guṇa' mean? What are the three guṇas?

'Guṇa' is the preponderance of a given type of temperament in one's inner nature. The human mind and intellect function constantly, but they always come to function under the different 'climatic conditions' within our mind. These varying climates of the mind are called the three guṇas: the good (sattva), the passionate (rajas) and the dull (tamas). (18.19)

9. Define 'dhṛti'.

The term 'dhṛti' means 'fortitude' or 'determination'. This is the subtle faculty in man that makes him strive continuously towards a goal. When obstacles come his way it is this faculty of 'dhṛti' that discovers for an individual more and more courage and enthusiasm to face them all and to continue striving towards the same determined goal. This persevering tendency to push oneself on with the work until one reaches the halls of success unmindful of the obstacles one might meet with on the path is called 'dhṛti'. (18.26)

10. What is 'utsāha'?

'Utsāha' is the untiring self-application and dynamic enthusiasm for achieving a chosen goal. (18.26)

11. Who is a 'durmedhā' (fool)?

The one who holds on firmly to sleep, fear, grief, depression and conceit is described by the Lord as a 'durmedhā' (fool). (18.35)

12. What is 'prasāda' (peace)?

The peace and tranquillity, the joy and expansion that the mind and intellect come to experience as a result of their discipline and contemplation on the Self are the true 'prasāda' (peace). (18.37)

13. Define 'śama'.

'Śama' is controlling the mind from running into the world of objects seeking sense enjoyments. Even if one shuts off the world of objects by carrying himself away from the tumults and temptations of life into a quiet, lonely place, even there the same mind could stride forth into the sense fields through the memories of past indulgences.

To control consciously this instinctive flow of the mind towards the sense objects is called 'śama'. (18.42)

14. What is 'dama'?

Controlling the sense organs, which are the gateways through which the external world of stimuli infiltrates into our mental domain and mars our peace, is called 'dama'. A man practising 'dama', even if he be in the midst of sense objects, is not disturbed by them. (18.42)

15. Define 'tapas'.

Conscious physical self-denial in order to economise the expenditure of human energy so lavishly spent in the wrong channels of sense indulgence, and conserving it for reaching the higher unfoldment within is called 'tapas' (austerity). (18.42)

16. What is 'kṣānti' (forbearance)?

To be patient and forgiving and thus to live without struggling even against wrongs done against one is 'kṣānti' (forbearance). (18.42)

17. Define 'ego'.

Mind is the seat of all vanities of agency—"I am the doer" (kartṛtva bhāvanā). The intellect is the seat of all false arrogations that—"I am the enjoyer" (bhoktṛtva bhāvanā). These two – the sense of doership and enjoyership – together make up the ego. (18.49)

18. What is a 'viśuddha buddhi' (pure intellect)?

An intellect that has grown to remain without vāsanās and has purified itself of all its tendencies of joy hunting is indicated as 'viśuddha buddhi' (pure intellect). (18.51)

19. Differentiate the 'sceptic' from the 'atheist'.

A 'sceptic' is one who questions the existing beliefs; he wants to be intellectually convinced of the logical grounds upon which the existing beliefs stand. As a contrast to the sceptic, the 'atheist' is one whose head and heart are not yet awakened to feel the majesty and glory of Life or to think and question the existence of faith and its basis. (18.62)

20. What does the term 'Vāsudeva' mean?

'Vāsudeva' means the lord (deva) of the Vasus; the eight Vasus (aṣṭavasus) together preside over time. Therefore, 'Vāsudeva', in its mystic symbolism, stands for the Consciousness that illumines the time-concept. (18.74)

Thoughts and Concepts

1. What is the purpose served in the 18th chapter analysing the tendencies, urges, emotions etc., of an individual?

The endless minute details given as the 18th chapter analysing and classifying the tendencies, urges, emotions, actions, etc., of the individual are pointers that help each one to understand himself. They are so many 'instruments' on the 'dashboard' of our personality within, which can by their indications give us a true picture of the condition of the personality-mechanism working within us. Just as a driver of a car can understand the condition of the engine and the nature of its performance by watching the play of the 'pointers' in the metres on the dashboard in front of him—heat, pressure, oil, charge, speed, fuel, mileage, ignition and whatnot—a seeker is asked to check up at similar definite 'pointers' within and note their readings. If all are indicating the safe-sign – sāttvic – a smooth life of maximum efficiency and definite progress in cultural evolution is promised. If we can classify ourselves in our tendencies and actions only as rājasic, we are advised to take note and be cautious. If the tendencies declare a definite tāmasic temperament, better halt the vehicle and attend to the 'engine'. (Introduction)

2. What is Arjuna's question at the beginning of the chapter? What is the Lord's reply?

The following two verses indicate Arjuna's question and the reply that the Lord gives to his question:

संन्यासस्य महाबाहो तत्त्वमिच्छामि वेदितुम् ।
त्यागस्य च हृषीकेश पृथक्केशिनिषूदन ॥

saṁnyāsasya mahābāho tattvamicchāmi veditum,
tyāgasya ca hṛṣīkeśa pṛthakkeśiniṣūdana.

I desire to know severally, O mighty-armed, the essence or truth of 'Renunciation', O Hṛṣīkeśa, as also of 'abandonment', O slayer of Keśi. (18.1)

काम्यानां कर्मणां न्यासं संन्यासं कवयो विदुः ।
सर्वकर्मफलत्यागं प्राहुस्त्यागं विचक्षणाः ॥

kāmyānāṁ karmaṇāṁ nyāsaṁ saṁnyāsaṁ kavayo viduḥ,
sarvakarmaphalatyāgaṁ prāhustyāgaṁ vicakṣaṇāḥ.

The Sages understand saṁnyāsa to be 'the renunciation of actions with desire'; the wise declare 'the abandonment of the fruits of all actions' as tyāga. (18.2)

The following is an explanation of Arjuna's question and the import of the Lord's answer: 'totally giving up all desire-prompted activities' is saṁnyāsa (renunciation) and tyāga (abandonment) is 'giving up of all anxieties for enjoying the fruits of action'. Renouncing 'desire-motivated activity' (saṁnyāsa) and 'renouncing our anxiety for the fruit' (tyāga) seem similar at first glance. No doubt, both mean giving up desire. But 'tyāga' (abandonment) is slightly different from 'saṁnyāsa' (renunciation) inspite of its integral relationship with it. The difference between these two: renouncing desire-motivated activity (saṁnyāsa) and renouncing one's anxiety for the fruits of actions (tyāga) is this: 'saṁnyāsa' pertains to the present moment while 'tyāga' pertains to the future. To explain: action is an effort made in the present, which in its own time, it is hoped will fulfil itself into the desired fruit. And the fruit is what we reap in the future as a result of the present action. The 'renunciation of desire-prompted activity' i.e., 'saṁnyāsa' belongs to the present, whereas the 'desire or anxiety' to enjoy the fruit is a disturbance of our mind regarding a future period of time. Therefore, 'saṁnyāsa' (renunciation) belongs to the present moment whereas 'tyāga' (abandonment) pertains to the future.

3. Why is 'tyāga' (abandonment of fruits of action) a pre-requisite

for 'saṁnyāsa' (renunciation of desire-prompted actions)?

The 'abandoning of anxiety for the fruits of action' is termed 'tyāga' while the 'renunciation of desire-prompted activity' is termed 'saṁnyāsa'. As long as one's attention is focused on the fruits or results of action, one's actions will have to be desire-prompted. Thus, 'tyāga' becomes a pre-requisite for saṁnyāsa. 'Renunciation of desire-prompted activity' is the goal to be reached through the process of 'abandonment of our moment-to-moment anxiety to enjoy the fruits'. 'Abandonment' (tyāga) is thus the means to reach the goal of 'renunciation' (saṁnyāsa). (18.3)

4. Cite the verse wherein the Lord declares that 'yajña', 'dāna' and 'tapas' should not be given up.

In the following verse the Lord states that 'yajña', 'dāna' and 'tapas' should not be given up and thus He clearly declares their importance in the spiritual pursuit:

यज्ञदानतपःकर्म न त्याज्यं कार्यमेव तत् ।
यज्ञो दानं तपश्चैव पावनानि मनीषिणाम् ॥

yajñadānatapaḥkarma na tyājyaṁ kāryameva tat,
yajño dānaṁ tapaścaiva pāvanāni manīṣiṇām.

Acts of sacrifice, charity and austerity should not be abandoned, but should be performed; worship, charity and also austerity are the purifiers of even the 'wise'. (18.5)

5. How should 'yajña' (sacrifice), 'dāna' (charity) and 'tapas' (austerity) be performed?

'Sacrifice' (yajña), 'charity' (dāna) and 'austerity' (tapas) should be performed without attachments to their fruits.

एतान्यपि तु कर्माणि सङ्गं त्यक्त्वा फलानि च ।
कर्तव्यानीति मे पार्थ निश्चितं मतमुत्तमम् ॥

etānyapi tu karmāṇi saṅgaṁ tyaktvā phalāni ca,
kartavyānīti me pārtha niścitaṁ matamuttamam.

But even these actions should be performed leaving aside attachment and the fruits. O Pārtha, this is my certain and best belief. (18.6)

6. Cite the verses that explain the three types of tyāga (abandonment).

The following three verses describe the tāmasic, rājasic and sāttvic tyāga (abandonment):

नियतस्य तु संन्यासः कर्मणो नोपपद्यते ।
मोहात्तस्य परित्यागस्तामसः परिकीर्तितः ॥

niyatasya tu saṁnyāsaḥ karmaṇo nopapadyate,
mohāttasya parityāgastāmasaḥ parikīrtitaḥ.

Verily, the renunciation of 'obligatory actions' is not proper; the abandonment of the same from delusion is declared to be tāmasic (dull). (18.7)

दुःखमित्येव यत्कर्म कायक्लेशभयात्त्यजेत् ।
स कृत्वा राजसं त्यागं नैव त्यागफलं लभेत् ॥

duḥkhamityeva yatkarma kāyakleśabhayāttyajet,
sa kṛtvā rājasaṁ tyāgaṁ naiva tyāgaphalaṁ labhet.

He who, from fear of bodily trouble, abandons action because it is painful, thus performing a rājasic (passionate) abandonment, obtains not the fruit of abandonment. (18.8)

कार्यमित्येव यत्कर्म नियतं क्रियतेऽर्जुन ।
सङ्गं त्यक्त्वा फलं चैव स त्यागः सात्त्विको मतः ॥

kāryamityeva yatkarma niyataṁ kriyate'rjuna,
saṅgaṁ tyaktvā phalaṁ caiva sa tyāgaḥ sāttviko mataḥ.

Whatever 'obligatory action' is done, O Arjuna, merely because it ought to be done, abandoning attachment and also fruit, that abandonment is regarded as sāttvic (pure). (18.9)

7. Can an individual be excused for abandoning one's duties out of ignorance?

There is no excuse even if one abandons one's moral duties out of ignorance. For, as in the civil laws of the modern world and in the physical laws of the phenomenal world, so in the spiritual kingdom also ignorance of the law is no excuse. Out of ignorance and lack of proper thinking, if an individual ignores his obligations and refuses to serve the world he is living in, that 'abandonment' is considered 'dull' (tāmasic). Tāmasic abandonment will certainly produce its negative effects. (18.7)

8. What is the nature of tyāga (abandonment) recommended by the Bhagavad Gītā?

Performance of one's obligatory duties is itself the most glorious of all forms of 'tyāga', and it can be considered doubly so when it involves a certain amount of sacrifice of one's own personal con-venience and bodily comfort.

Real tyāga (abandonment) is doing actions with the correct mental attitude. Lord Kṛṣṇa's concept of tyāga condemns abandonment of the world and our duties in it. To the Lord, 'tyāga' is a subjective renunciation of all inner selfishness and desire, which limit the freedom of the individual in his field of activity. Thus, the 'tyāga' (abandonment) of the Bhagavad Gītā is not the abandonment of actions but abandonment of such things within our subjective personality that block the free flow of our own possibilities. Tyāga thus makes an active man a more potent worker in the world. (18.8,9)

9. Describe the nature of the sāttvic tyāgī.

A man established in sāttvic abandonment never hates nor does he ever feel attached. He is not miserable in disagreeable environments nor does he get attached to the circumstances and schemes of things which are agreeable to his taste. He does his duties under all circumstances, agreeable or disagreeable, without feeling elated when he finds himself on the 'peaks' or feeling dejected when he discovers himself in the 'pits' of life. He is overwhelmed neither by extreme joy nor by extreme sorrow; equanimity becomes his essential nature. He stands as a rock, ever at ease, and watches with an unbroken balance of vision, the waves of happenings rising and falling all around him at all times. He is, in short, independent of the activities in the outer world around him.

A man of sāttvic abandonment (tyāgī) readily discovers in himself a secret faculty to abandon his identification with the false, the lower instincts in himself. When, to such a man of sāttvic tyāga, impulses such as jealousy, anger, passion, greed, etc., come, he does not get involved in those impulses and drops them readily. Without becoming a victim of his own mental impressions (vāsanās) he stands ever free and apart from the tumults of his mind. (18.10)

10. Why does the Lord dissuade Arjuna and through Arjuna all of us from actual renunciation of all actions and recommends only the renunciation of the fruits of actions?

Action cannot be completely abandoned by one who is identified with his gross, subtle and causal bodies. Such an individual—Arjuna and most of us at this stage of our evolution fall under this category—is advised by Śrī Kṛṣṇa to abandon the anxiety to enjoy the fruits of actions which are yet to come in a future period of time, and act diligently, entirely and enthusiastically in the present.

The following verse explains this:

न हि देहभृता शक्यं त्यक्तुं कर्माण्यशेषतः ।
यस्तु कर्मफलत्यागी स त्यागीत्यभिधीयते ॥

na hi dehabhṛtā śakyaṁ tyaktuṁ karmāṇyaśeṣataḥ,
yastu karmaphalatyāgī sa tyāgītyabhidhīyate.

Verily, it is not possible for an embodied being to abandon actions entirely, but he who relinquishes 'the fruits of actions' is verily called a 'tyāgī' (relinquisher). (18.11)

11. What is the essence of the Gītā-technique of personality rehabilitation?

The Gītā-technique for rehabilitation of man's personality is:

(1) The seeker first gets detached from the lower sensuous cravings and passions by identifying himself with the nobler ideals of self-control and moral perfection.
(2) The mind so purified develops in itself the required amount of subtle powers of thinking, consistent self-application and steady contemplation.
(3) With this single-pointed mind and steady intellect one comes to Realise the pure Self. (18.12)

12. What are the five constituent factors of all actions? Why does the Lord enumerate these five factors?

The five constituent factors of all actions are enumerated in the following verse:

अधिष्ठानं तथा कर्ता करणं च पृथग्विधम्।
विविधाश्च पृथक्चेष्टा दैवं चैवात्र पञ्चमम्॥

adhiṣṭhānaṁ tathā kartā karaṇaṁ ca pṛthagvidham,
vividhāśca pṛthakceṣṭā daivaṁ caivātra pañcamam.

The 'seat' (body), the doer (ego), the various organs, the different psychological functions and also the presiding deity, the fifth. (18.14)

(1) Adhiṣṭhānam: This term refers to the body. Every work is undertaken with the help of the 'body' (adhiṣṭhānam), for the body is the gateway for the stimuli to enter as well as for the responses to exit.

(2) Kartā: A body in itself can neither receive the world nor react to it unless there is the ego (kartā) functioning in and through it. There must be an intelligent personality, presiding over desires, wanting to fulfil them constantly and seeking the fulfilment through the activities of the body.

(3) Karaṇa: The ego (kartā) sets the body in continuous activity. When an ego, thus riddled with its own desires, seeks its fulfilment in the outside world of objects, it certainly needs various 'instruments' (karaṇa) to contact the field of enjoyment and find satisfaction in it. The instruments are the organs of perception (jñānendriya) and action (karmendriya) as well as the mind and the intellect (antaḥkaraṇa).

(4) Ceṣṭā: Refers to the five prāṇas – prāṇa, apāna, vyāna, udāna and samāna – which govern the physiological activities[2]. The term 'prāṇa' indicates the various physiological functions in a living body[3].

As a result of these prāṇas the health of the body gets toned up and there is vigour and enthusiasm expressed through the organs of action.

2. Another interpretation given for 'ceṣṭā' is the organs of action. In this interpretation, the earlier term 'karaṇa' will take the meaning of the organs of perception.
3. Refer to Question 10 in 'Terms and Definitions' of Chapter 4.

(5) Daiva: The instruments (karaṇa) are presided over by their respective deities, the eye by Sun, the ears by Space, the tongue by Water, the skin by Air and the nose by Earth and so on. These forces are technically called 'devas', and they indicate particular functions and faculties in the sense organs, such as the 'power of vision' of the eye, the 'power of audition' in the ears and so on.

The Lord enumerates these five factors to establish that whatever action an individual performs by his body, speech and mind—whether dhārmic (right) or adhārmic (wrong)—these five alone are its causes and the Self is beyond the pale of action and its results.

This is made clear in the following two verses:

शरीरवाङ्मनोभिर्यत्कर्म प्रारभते नरः ।
न्याय्यं वा विपरीतं वा पञ्चैते तस्य हेतवः ॥

śarīravāṅmanobhiryatkarma prārabhate naraḥ,
nyāyyaṁ vā viparītaṁ vā pañcaite tasya hetavaḥ.

Whatever action a man performs by his body, speech and mind—whether right or the reverse—these five are its causes. (18.15)

तत्रैवं सति कर्तारमात्मानं केवलं तु यः ।
पश्यत्यकृतबुद्धित्वान्न स पश्यति दुर्मतिः ॥

tatraivaṁ sati kartāramātmānaṁ kevalaṁ tu yaḥ,
paśyatyakṛtabuddhitvānna sa paśyati durmatiḥ.

Now, such being the case, verily he who—owing to his untrained understanding—looks upon his Self, which is 'alone', as the 'doer', he, of perverted intelligence, sees not. (18.16)

13. What is the significance of the 'rāsa-krīḍā'?

Even while the gopis are all dancing around Śrī Kṛṣṇa, He remains motionless in the centre of the ring of the dancing crowd, untouched by the gopis moving in their ecstatic trance. The divinely sweet maidens of Vraja, the gopis, dance in thrilled ecstasy because of the maddening music of the Flute-bearer, who by His breath draws out the 'melody of existence'.

The Vedāntic siginificance of the rāsa-krīḍā is this: the gopis represent the thoughts and Śrī Kṛṣṇa the Self seated in the hearts of all. To identify ourselves with the Centre Self is to be the master of the situation; to play among the whirls of the dancing thoughts is to suffer the fatigue and exhaustion, the thrills and sorrows of thoughts. (18.17)

14. List the threefold impulse of action (karmacodanā) and the threefold basis of action (karmasaṅgraha)?

The threefold impulse of action is:

(1) Knowledge (jñānam)

(2) Known (jñeyam)

(3) Knower (parijñātā)

The threefold basis of action is:

(1) Organs (karaṇam)

(2) Action (karma)

(3) Agent (kartā)

The following verse lists both the threefold impulse of action (karmacodanā) and the threefold basis of action (karmasaṅgraha).

ज्ञानं ज्ञेयं परिज्ञाता त्रिविधा कर्मचोदना ।
करणं कर्म कर्तेति त्रिविधः कर्मसङ्ग्रहः ॥

jñānaṁ jñeyaṁ parijñātā trividhā karmacodanā,
karaṇaṁ karma karteti trividhaḥ karmasaṅgrahaḥ.

Knowledge, the known and knower form the threefold 'impulse to action'; the organs, the action and the agent form the threefold 'basis of action'. (18.18)

15. Justify the triad of 'knower' (parijñātā), 'known' (jñeyam) and 'knowledge' (jñānam) together termed as the 'threefold impulse of action' (karmacodanā).

The 'impulse to action' (karmacodanā) can spring from one or many of these following factors alone:

(1) From the experiencer/knower (parijñātā) in the form of desire

(2) From the experienced/known (jñeyam) in the form of temptation

(3) From the experience/knowledge (jñānam) in the form of similar memories of some past enjoyments.

Beyond these three there is no other 'impulse to action' (karmacodanā) and hence it is perfectly justified to term the above-mentioned triad as the 'impulse of action' (karmacodanā). (18.18)

16. Explain the term (1) doer (kartā) (2) instruments (karaṇa) and (3) action (karma). Why are they termed as the 'threefold basis of action (karmasaṅgraha)?

The 'impulse to action' (karmacodanā) when it has arisen must also find a field to act in. This field forms the 'basis for action' (karmasaṅgraha) and is constituted of the:

(1) Agent (kartā)

(2) Instruments (karaṇa)

(3) Result or reaction of the action (karma).

The ego that is suffering from its desires enters the field of activity and assumes to itself the attitude: "I am the doer." This is the 'kartā' (doer). This 'sense of agency' expressed by the ego can maintain itself only as long as it holds a vivid picture of the 'fruit of its action' which it wants to gain. It is this 'fruit' (karmaphala) – meaning the 'profit or the gain that is intended to be gained by the action' – that is indicated by the term 'karma'[4]. When a desirer i.e., the agent (kartā) encouraged by this constant attraction towards a satisfying end or result (karma) wants to achieve it, he must necessarily have the instruments of action (karaṇa). These instruments include not only the organs of perception and action, but also the inner equipments of the mind and the intellect.

An 'agent' (kartā) having a desire and maintaining in his mind a clear picture of the goal (karma) with all the necessary instruments (karaṇa) to act thereupon would be the sum total of any activity (karmasaṅgraha). If any one of the above three items is absent, action cannot take place. These three—karaṇa, kartā, karma—are together designated as the parts of the 'karma-assembly' or 'the basis of all karmas' (karmasaṅgraha). (18.18)

---

4. The Sanskrit term 'karma' can mean both 'action' as well as 'fruit of action'. Here the word 'karma' is used in the latter connotation.

17. Cite the verse that describes the three types of knowledge.

The following three verses describe the nature of sāttvic, rājasic and tāmasic knowledge:

सर्वभूतेषु येनैकं भावमव्ययमीक्षते ।
अविभक्तं विभक्तेषु तज्ज्ञानं विद्धि सात्त्विकम् ॥

sarvabhūteṣu yenaikaṁ bhāvamavyayamīkṣate,
avibhaktaṁ vibhakteṣu tajjñānaṁ viddhi sāttvikam.

That by which one sees the one indestructible Reality in all beings, undivided in the divided, know that 'knowledge' as sāttvic (pure). (18.20)

पृथक्त्वेन तु यज्ज्ञानं नानाभावान्पृथग्विधान् ।
वेत्ति सर्वेषु भूतेषु तज्ज्ञानं विद्धि राजसम् ॥

pṛthaktvẹna tu yajjñānaṁ nānābhāvānpṛthagvidhān,
vetti sarveṣu bhūteṣu tajjñānaṁ viddhi rājasam.

But that 'knowledge' which sees in all beings various entities of distinct kinds, (and) as different from one another, know that knowledge as rājasic (passionate). (18.21)

यत्तु कृत्स्नवदेकस्मिन्कार्ये सक्तमहैतुकम् ।
अतत्त्वार्थवदल्पं च तत्तामसमुदाहृतम् ॥

yattu kṛtsnavadekasminkārye saktamahaitukam,
atattvārthavadalpaṁ ca tattāmasamudāhṛtam.

But that 'knowledge', which clings to one single effect, as if it were the whole, without reason, without foundation in truth, and narrow, that is declared to be tāmasic (dull). (18.22)

18. Explain the Lord's assertion that 'to see the one undivided in the many' is 'sāttvic knowledge' (sāttvikaṁ jñānam).

This can be explained with the following examples: even if there are a hundred different pots, of different shapes and colour, and of different sizes, the 'space' is the one undivided factor in all these different pots. Bulbs are different, but the current that is expressing through them all is the one electricity. Waves are different, and yet the same ocean is the reality and the substance in all the waves.

Similarly, the one Life throbs in all, expressing itself differently as

Its manifestations, because of the different constitution in the matter-arrangements. The Knowledge that can recognise the play (vilāsa) of this One Principle of Consciousness in and through all the different equipments, is fully sāttvic. (18.20)

19. Describe the nature of rājasic knowledge (rājasaṁ jñānam).

The 'knowledge' that recognises plurality on the basis of separateness is 'rājasic' in its texture. The knowledge of the 'passionate' (rājasic), ever restless in its energy considers various entities as different from one another; to the rājasic knowledge, the world is an assortment of innumerable types of different varieties; the intellect of such an individual perceives distinctions among the living creatures, and divides them into different classes—as the animal, the vegetable and the human kingdoms—as men of different castes, creeds, races, nationalities, etc. It is this rājasic knowledge that is the cause of all strife and dissension. (18.21)

20. Briefly explain the nature of tāmasic knowledge (tāmasaṁ jñānam).

An intellect under the dulling effects of extreme tamas clings to one single 'effect' as though it were the whole, never enquiring into its 'cause'. Those with tāmasic knowledge are generally fanatic in their faith and in their devotion, in their views and values in life. They never enquire into and try to discover the cause of things and happenings; they are unreasonable (ahaitukam). Looking through such a confused intellect loaded with fixed ideas, tāmasic individuals not only fail to see things as they are, but invariably project their own ideas upon the world and judge it all wrong.

Further, an individual of tāmasic intellect views the world as if it is meant for him and his pleasures alone. He totally ignores the Divine Presence, the Infinite Consciousness. The knowledge of the dull is thus circumscribed by its own concept of self-importance, and thus his vision becomes narrow and limited (alpam). (18.22)

21. Cite the verses which describe the three types of action.

The following three verses describe the sāttvic, rājasic and tāmasic types of action:

नियतं सङ्गरहितमरागद्वेषतः कृतम् ।
अफलप्रेप्सुना कर्म यत्तत्सात्त्विकमुच्यते ॥

niyataṁ saṅgarahitamarāgadveṣataḥ kṛtam,
aphalaprepsunā karma yattatsāttvikamucyate.

An action which is ordained, which is free from attachment, which is done without love or hatred, by one who is not desirous of the fruit, that action is declared 'sāttvic' (pure). (18.23)

यत्तु कामेप्सुना कर्म साहङ्कारेण वा पुनः ।
क्रियते बहुलायासं तद्राजसमुदाहृतम् ॥

yattu kāmepsunā karma sāhaṅkāreṇa vā punaḥ,
kriyate bahulāyāsaṁ tadrājasamudāhṛtam.

But that action which is done by one, longing for desires, or gain, done with egoism, or with much effort, is declared to be rājasic (passionate). (18.24)

अनुबन्धं क्षयं हिंसामनपेक्ष्य च पौरुषम् ।
मोहादारभ्यते कर्म यत्तत्तामसमुच्यते ॥

anubandhaṁ kṣayaṁ hiṁsāmanapekṣya ca pauruṣam,
mohādārabhyate karma yattattāmasamucyate.

That action, which is undertaken from delusion, without regard for the consequence, loss, injury and ability is declared 'tāmasic' (dull). (18.25)

22. Why does an individual with sāttvic intellect serve the whole world with love and joy?

This can be answered with an example: as soon as, say, one's left toe strikes against some furniture and gets wounded, the entire body bends down to nurse it. Herein, there is neither any special love for the left leg nor any particular extra attachment for it, as compared with other parts of the body. To an individual the whole body is himself, and all parts are equally important; he pervades his whole body. In the same fashion, an individual with sāttvic intellect who has recognised the All-pervading one lives in the consciousness of the one Reality that permeates the whole universe and, therefore, to him the leper and the prince, the sick and the healthy, the rich and the poor are so many different parts of his own spiritual personality only. Such an individual serves the world in a sense of self-fulfilment and inspired joy. (18.23)

23. Briefly describe the action of a rājasic nature.

The action of the 'rājasic' (passionate) nature is that which is undertaken to win one's desires with an extremely insistent 'I-act' mentality. These undertakings are works of heavy toil involving great strain and all the consequent physical fatigue and mental exhaustion. The individual is impelled to act and struggle by a well-defined and extremely arrogant ego-sense. He works, generally under tension and strain, since he comes to believe that he alone can perform it and nobody else will ever help him. All the time he is exhausted with his own anxieties and fears at the thought whether his goal will ever be achieved. When an individual works thus with an arrogant ego, and with all its selfcentredness, he becomes restless enough to make himself totally exhausted and completely shattered. Such actions belong to the category of the 'rājasic' (passionate). (18.24)

24. Why does a 'sāttvic kartā' remain non-egoistic (anahaṁvādin)?

A sāttvic kartā (doer) is absolutely non-egoistic because he sincerely feels that he has not done anything spectacular even when he has actually done the greatest good to mankind, because he surrenders his egocentric individuality to the Lord, through his perfect attunement with the Infinite. He realises that in all his actions, his body, mind and intellect come into play and serve the world only because the Spirit, the Infinite, is in contact with them. (18.26)

25. Why is a 'tāmasic kartā' described as 'dīrgha-sūtrī' (procrastinator)?

An individual benumbed by tamas, slowly gathers within himself an incapacity to arrive at any firm judgement. Even if he comes to any vague decision he has not the will to consistently pursue the action determined by his judgement. Indolent as he is by nature, more often than not, he postpones the right until it is too late. This procrastinating tendency is natural to a tāmasic-kartā.

The term 'dīrgha-sūtrī' can also be interpreted as 'harbouring deep and long (dīrgha) vengeance against others (sūtra)'. (18.28)

26. In the Rāmāyaṇa epic who are the personalities that illustrate sāttvic, rājasic and tāmasic 'kartas' (doers)?

Rāvaṇa the mighty represents the rājasic kartā; Vibhīṣaṇa the devout represents the sāttvic kartā, and Kumbhakarṇa – who sleeps for six months and wakes up only to spend the rest of the six months in eating – is symbolic of tamas. (18.28)

27. After enumerating the three types of 'knowledge' (jñānam), 'action' (karma) and 'doer' (kartā) why does the Lord go on to explain the three types of 'understanding' (buddhi) and 'fortitude' (dhṛti)?

'Work' is constituted of the three factors: 'knowledge' (jñāna) 'action' (karma) and 'doer' (kartā). Each of these three factors are shown to fall under a threefold classification[5].

When a doer (kartā), guided by his knowledge (jñāna), acts in the world (karma), no doubt, manifestation of work takes place. But underlying these three are two factors that supply the fuel and the motive force in all sustained endeavours. They are 'buddhi (understanding) and 'dhṛti' (fortitude). 'Buddhi' (understanding) is the intellectual capacity in the individual to grasp what is happening around him. 'Dhṛti' (fortitude) is the faculty of constantly keeping one idea in the mind and consistently working it out to its logical end. 'Dhṛti' is thus constancy of purpose and self-application.

Since every action is thus controlled and guided by our—(1) Buddhi - intellectual capacity of understanding and (2) Dhṛti-faithful consistency of purpose or fortitude—Śrī Kṛṣṇa starts explaining the three types of 'buddhi' and 'dhṛti', considering it apt to describe these two after thoroughly explaining jñāna (knowledge), karma (action) and kartā (doer). (18.29)

5. Jñāna (knowledge) - verses 18.20-22; karma (actor) - verses 18.23-25; kartā (doer or agent) - verses 18.26-28.

28. Cite the verses that describe the three types of buddhi (understanding).

The following three verses explain the sāttvic, rājasic and tāmasic types of buddhi (understanding):

प्रवृत्तिं च निवृत्तिं च कार्याकार्ये भयाभये ।
बन्धं मोक्षं च या वेत्ति बुद्धिः सा पार्थ सात्त्विकी ॥

pravṛttiṁ ca nivṛttiṁ ca kāryākārye bhayābhaye,
bandhaṁ mokṣaṁ ca yā vetti buddhiḥ sā pārtha sāttvikī.

That which knows the paths of work and renunciation, what ought to be done and what ought not to be done, fear and fearlessness, bondage and liberation, that 'understanding' is sāttvic (pure), O Pārtha. (18.30)

यया धर्ममधर्मं च कार्यं चाकार्यमेव च ।
अयथावत्प्रजानाति बुद्धिः सा पार्थ राजसी ॥

yayā dharmamadharmaṁ ca kāryaṁ cākāryameva ca,
ayathāvatprajānāti buddhiḥ sā pārtha rājasī.

That by which one wrongly understands dharma and adharma and also what ought to be done and what ought not to be done, that intellect (understanding), O Pārtha, is rājasic (passionate). (18.31)

अधर्मं धर्ममिति या मन्यते तमसावृता ।
सर्वार्थान्विपरीतांश्च बुद्धिः सा पार्थ तामसी ॥

adharmaṁ dharmamiti yā manyate tamasāvṛtā,
sarvārthānviparītāṁśca buddhiḥ sā pārtha tāmasī.

That which, enveloped in darkness, sees adharma as dharma, and all things perverted, that intellect (understanding), O Pārtha, is tāmasic (dull). (18.32)

29. Why does Śrī Kṛṣṇa say that a true intellect (sāttvika-buddhi) is that which is capable of clearly discerning what is to be feared and what is not to be feared?

'Fools rush in where angels fear to tread'. Men of indiscrimination in their false evaluation of the sense world hug on to delusory objects and things fearing nothing from them, and yet, they fear to read and understand philosophy, to strive and to experience the Infinite! A true intellect must have the right understanding to discern between what is to be feared and what is not to be feared. (18.30)

30. Cite the verses that elaborate on the three types of dhṛti (fortitude).

The following three verses describe the sāttvic, rājasic and tāmasic dhṛti:

धृत्या यया धारयते मनःप्राणेन्द्रियक्रियाः ।
योगेनाव्यभिचारिण्या धृतिः सा पार्थ सात्त्विकी ॥

dhṛtyā yayā dhārayate manaḥprāṇendriyakriyāḥ,
yogenāvyabhicāriṇyā dhṛtiḥ sā pārtha sāttvikī.

The unwavering 'fortitude' by which, through Yoga, the functions of the mind, the prāṇa and the senses are restrained, that 'fortitude', O Pārtha, is sāttvic (pure). (18.33)

यया तु धर्मकामार्थान्धृत्या धारयतेऽर्जुन ।
प्रसङ्गेन फलाकाङ्क्षी धृतिः सा पार्थ राजसी ॥

yayā tu dharmakāmārthāndhṛtyā dhārayate'rjuna,
prasaṅgena phalākāṅkṣī dhṛtiḥ sā pārtha rājasī.

But the 'fortitude', O Arjuna, by which one holds fast to duty, pleasure and wealth, from attachment and craving for the fruits of actions, that 'fortitude', O Pārtha, is rājasic (passionate). (18.34)

यया स्वप्नं भयं शोकं विषादं मदमेव च ।
न विमुञ्चति दुर्मेधा धृतिः सा पार्थ तामसी ॥

yayā svapnaṁ bhayaṁ śokaṁ viṣādaṁ madameva ca,
na vimuñcati durmedhā dhṛtiḥ sā pārtha tāmasī.

The 'constancy' because of which a stupid man does not abandon sleep, fear, grief, depression and also arrogance (conceit), that 'fortitude', O Pārtha, is tāmasic (dull). (18.35)

31. What is the many-faceted role of dhṛti in our life?

'Dhṛti' (fortitude) is that power within us by which we constantly see the goal we want to achieve; and while striving towards it, dhṛti discovers for us the necessary constancy of purpose to pursue the path, in spite of all the mounting obstacles that rise on the way. Dhṛti also paints the idea, maintains it constantly in our vision, makes us steadily strive towards it, and when obstacles come, dhṛti mobilises secret powers within us to face them all courageously, heroically and steadily. (18.33)

32. Explain why of the four puruṣārthas (fields of self effort) – dharma, artha, kāma and Mokṣa – the one endowed with rājasic dhṛti holds on firmly only to the first three?

The constancy with which a person holds fast to duty (dharma), wealth (artha) and pleasure (kāma), encouraged by his growing desire to enjoy the fruit of each of them, is the steadiness or 'fortitude' of the rājasic type. In the enumeration of the rājasic dhṛti, Śrī Kṛṣṇa avoids Mokṣa (Liberation) and only takes the first three of the four puruṣārthas, for a rājasic man has no demand for spiritual Liberation and is satisfied with the other fields of self-effort—duty (dharma), wealth (artha) and pleasure (kāma), and he will be pursuing one or the other of them with an extreme desire to enjoy the resultant satisfactions. He follows 'dharma', only to gain the heavens; he pursues 'artha' so that he may have power in this life; and he pursues 'kāma' with a firm belief and faith that sensuous objects can give him all satisfactions in life. (18.34)

33. Explain the logic in the sequence of taking up the explanation of the three types of pleasure (sukha) after detailing the three types of jñāna (knowledge), kartā (doer), karma (action), buddhi (undertaking) and dhṛti (fortitude).

In the logical thought development in 18th chapter, the three factors that constitute the 'impulse of all actions' (karmacodanā): (1) knowledge (jñāna) (2) the doer (kartā) and (3) the action (karma) were first explained.

Afterwards, the very motive forces in all activity—which not only propel activity but intelligently control and direct it—the understanding (buddhi) and the fortitude (dhṛti) have also been explained, showing their different types. For every 'doer' (kartā) thus acts in his field (karma) guided by his 'knowledge' (jñāna), ruled by his 'understanding' (buddhi) and maintained by his 'fortitude' (dhṛti). With this dissection and observation the anatomy of work has been explained thoroughly.

Now the logical thought flow is—for what purpose does one act? Everyone acts for the same goal of gaining happiness (sukha) and a better sense of fulfilment. To explain this psychology of action the Lord takes for analysis the three types of sukha (pleasure); for in and through the variety of actions in the universe, all people—the good (sāttvic), the passionate (rājasic) and the dull (tāmasic)—seek their own sense of satisfaction (sukha) alone. (18.36)

34. Explain the Lord's declaration that sāttvic joy is poison-like at first but nectar-like at the end.

The happiness which in the beginning is like poison and very painful but when it works itself out fulfils itself in a nectarine success is the enduring happiness of the 'good' (sāttvic). In short, happiness that arises from constant effort is the happiness that can yield a greater beauty and a larger sense of fulfilment. The joy arising out of inner self-control and the consequent sense of self-perfection is no cheap gratification. In the beginning, its practice is certainly very painful and extremely arduous. Hence the description that it is poison-like in the beginning. But one who has discovered in oneself the necessary courage and heroism to walk the precipitous path of self-purification and inward balance comes to enjoy the subtlest of happiness and the all-fulfilling sense of inward peace. Hence the description that sāttvic is nectar-like in the end. (18.37)

35. Why does a true thinker not fall a prey to sense pleasures?

That happiness which arises when the desired sense object comes in contact with the sense organs is indeed a thrill that is nectarine in the beginning. But, unfortunately, it vanishes as quickly as it comes, dumping the enjoyer into a pit of exhaustion and indeed into a sense of dissipation. To explain: sense enjoyments arise only when the sense organs are actually in contact with the sense objects. This contact cannot be permanently established, for both the objects and the instruments that come in contact with the objects – the mind and intellect – are variable and changing. Also, the sense organs cannot enjoy the sense objects at all times with the same appetite, and even if they do so, the very object in the embrace of the sense organs withers and putrefies. No individual can fully enjoy even the passing glitter of joy that the sense organs give, for even at the moment of enjoyment the 'joy-possibility' in it gets unfortunately tainted by an anxiety that it may leave him. Hence, to a true thinker the temporary joys of sense objects are not at all satisfactory, since they only bury him in a tomb of sorrow. (18.38)

36. What determines a person's 'caste' (varṇa)?

The type of a man's 'actions' (karma), the quality of his 'ego' (kartā), the colour of his 'knowledge' (jñāna), the texture of his 'understanding'(buddhi), the temper of his 'fortitude' (dhṛti), and the brilliance of his 'happiness' (sukha) determine his 'caste' (varṇa). (18.41)

37. What are the duties of a 'brāhmaṇa'?

The following verse gives a list of the duties of a 'brāhmaṇa':

शमो दमस्तपः शौचं क्षान्तिरार्जवमेव च ।
ज्ञानं विज्ञानमास्तिक्यं ब्रह्मकर्म स्वभावजम् ॥

śamo damastapaḥ śaucaṁ kṣāntirārjavameva ca,
jñānaṁ vijñānamāstikyaṁ brahmakarma svabhāvajam.

Serenity, self-restraint, austerity, purity, forgiveness and also uprightness, knowledge, realisation, belief in God—are the duties of the brāhmaṇas, born of (their own) nature. (18.42)

38. Enumerate the duties of a 'kṣatriya'?

The following verse lists the various qualities of a 'kṣatriya':

शौर्यं तेजो धृतिर्दाक्ष्यं युद्धे चाप्यपलायनम् ।
दानमीश्वरभावश्च क्षात्रं कर्म स्वभावजम् ॥

śauryaṁ tejo dhṛtirdākṣyaṁ yuddhe cāpyapalāyanam,
dānamīśvarabhāvaśca kṣātraṁ karma svabhāvajam.

Prowess, splendour, firmness, dexterity, and also not fleeing from battle; generosity, lordliness—these are the duties of the kṣatriyas, born of (their own) nature. (18.43)

39. What determines the 'class' to which one belongs? Why should each individual perform the work of the 'class' to which he belongs?

The mental temperament of a man determines what class he belongs to—brāhmaṇa, kṣatriya, vaiśya or śūdra—and each class feels at home in performing particular duties. If a man who is fit temperamentally for one type of work is entrusted with a different type of activity, he will bring chaos not only into the field but also in himself. For example, if a 'kṣatriya' were asked to fan someone in a spirit of service, he may condescend to do so, but one will find him ordering somebody else, almost instinctively, to fetch a fan for him! So too, if a man of commercial temperament, a 'vaiśya', comes to serve as a temple-priest, the sacred place will soon become worse than a trading centre; and again, let him become the head of any government, he will, out of sheer instinct, begin doing profitable 'business' from the seat of government authority—which the people call corruption! (18.44)

40. Why does Śrī Kṛṣṇa explain the various 'classes' of man and their respective duties?

Each individual must analyse and discover for himself the type of vāsanās and temperaments that predominate and thus determine what type of individual he is. None belonging to the 'higher type' has any justification to look down with contempt upon others who are of the 'lower type'. Each one serves the society as best he can. Each one must work in a spirit of dedication for his own evolution and sense of fulfilment. When each one works thus according to his vāsanās and fully devotes his attention to his prescribed duties, he will develop within himself and attain, in stages, the ultimate Perfection. To explain: when a person works devotedly, in the proper field and in the environment best suited to him, he will be exhausting the existing vāsanās in him. And when the vāsanās are reduced, he will experience tranquillity and peace within and it will become possible for him to discover more and more concentration and single-pointed contemplation.

It is to thus enable an individual to determine one's temperament and the nature of work that he must choose for his self-unfoldment that Śrī Kṛṣṇa explains in detail the various classifications of men and their respective duties. (18.44)

41. Explain the logic of the Lord's declaration that an individual attains Realisation by being devoted to the duties of his 'class'.

Man can attain the highest Perfection by being devoted to the duties and functions of his own 'class' (which have been derived from his own nature) with the attitude of Karma Yoga.

The logic of this declaration is as follows: when a man does his duty according to his 'nature' (svabhāva) and station in life (svadharma), by surrendering the fruits of one's actions unto the Lord, his vāsanās get exhausted. This is verily the miracle of Karma Yoga, a unique art by which man releases himself from the binding effects of Karma and thus purifies his mind. The inner personality of such a person gets integrated, and such an integrated person grows in his meditation and evolves quickly to Realise the Self.

This idea is explained by the Lord in the following verses:

स्वे स्वे कर्मण्यभिरतः संसिद्धिं लभते नरः ।
स्वकर्मनिरतः सिद्धिं यथा विन्दति तच्छृणु ॥

sve sve karmaṇyabhirataḥ saṁsiddhiṁ labhate naraḥ,
svakarmanirataḥ siddhiṁ yathā vindati tacchṛṇu.

Devoted, each to his own duty, man attains Perfection. How, engaged in his own duty, he attains Perfection, listen. (18.45)

यतः प्रवृत्तिर्भूतानां येन सर्वमिदं ततम् ।
स्वकर्मणा तमभ्यर्च्य सिद्धिं विन्दति मानवः ॥

yataḥ pravṛttirbhūtānāṁ yena sarvamidaṁ tatam,
svakarmaṇā tamabhyarcya siddhiṁ vindati mānavaḥ.

From Whom is the evolution of all beings, by Whom all this is pervaded, worshipping Him, with one's own duty, man attains Perfection. (18.46)

42. How can work be changed into worship?

Work can be changed into worship by attuning our minds all through our activity to the consciousness of the Self. A self-dedicated man, working in the consciousness of the Supreme, pays the greatest homage to his Creator. This subtle change in attitude transforms the shape of even the most dreary situation. Even the most dreadfully unpleasant field of activity is converted into a sacred chamber of devotion—into a silent hall of prayer—into a quiet seat of meditation! (18.46)

43. Explain the excellence and importance of devoting oneself to the performance of one's duties (dharma) alone?

When an individual strives in a field contrary to the existing vāsanās, he not only fails to gain any exhaustion of the existing vāsanās, but also creates a new load of vāsanās in his temperament. The Lord therefore advises: "Better is one's own Dharma though imperfect, than the Dharma of another well-performed." To work in any field ordered by one's own vāsanās is better because, in that case, there is a chance for exhausting the existing vāsanās. By performing duties ordained by one's own nature (*svabhāva-niyatam-karma*) the individual has no chance of imprinting any new impressions (vāsanās) on his mind. (18.47)

44. What does the expression *'sahajaṁ karma'* in the following verse mean? Why does the Lord advise that *'sahajaṁ karma'* should not be abandoned even if it is occasioned by 'defects'? What is the 'defect' spoken of here?

सहजं कर्म कौन्तेय सदोषमपि न त्यजेत्।
सर्वारम्भा हि दोषेण धूमेनाग्निरिवावृताः॥

sahajaṁ karma kaunteya sadoṣamapi na tyajet,
sarvārambhā hi doṣeṇa dhūmenāgnirivāvṛtāḥ.

One should not abandon, O Kaunteya, the duty to which one is born, though faulty; for, are not all undertakings enveloped by evil, as fire by smoke?

There are two forces that control, guide, define and determine an individual's actions:

(1) The impulses from within brought forth by the pressure of the subjective vāsanās

(2) The pressure of the outside environments that could cause new temptations in an individual

One is to follow, faithfully, the subjective vāsanās. But at the same time, one must courageously renounce all the demands that the objective world makes upon us from without. The vāsanās one is born with are to be lived through, without ego and desire; while the external vāsanā-creating atmosphere into which one is born should not be allowed to contaminate one's personality. The work brought forth by the pressure of the subjective vāsanās is *'sahajaṁ karma'* and Śrī Kṛṣṇa's advice is that one should not relinquish them even if it is occasioned with 'defects'.

The defect spoken of in *'sahajaṁ karma'* is this: as action is performed by the senses and the physical organs, actions fall within the ambit of the objective world, which is conditiond by the three guṇas. Therefore, all actions are attended with some form of defect or the other. All action is 'anātmā'; it is objective; it is corrupted by the guṇas; and so all actions do partake of evil. Just as fire is enveloped by smoke and there can be no fire without the covering of smoke so too all actions are sullied by the various guṇas. Despite this inevitable defect, one should not abandon the duty to which one is born, because when duty is performed with detachment and in a spirit of surrender to the Lord, it purifies the mind and leads one to Liberation. (18.48)

45. When does one attain 'naiṣkarmya siddhi' (state of actionlessness)?

The state of 'actionlessness' (naiṣkarmya siddhi) is reached when an individual does not identify with the equipments of matter – instruments of perception, body, mind and intellect and so on – and discovers his real nature to be that of Pure Consciousness. The ego arises when one is ignorant and forgetful of one's spiritual nature. When this ignorance is ended, there is the experience of the Infinite Bliss. Such an individual feels no want and, therefore, no desire can arise. Where desires are absent, the thought-broodings end. When thoughts have dried up, actions, which are the parade of thoughts marching out through the archway of the body, are no more. This 'State of Actionlessness' attained by the destruction of ignorance is 'naiṣkarmya siddhi'. (18.49)

46. Who is a successful meditator?

A successful meditator is one who has:

(1) An intellect purified of all its extrovert desires
(2) A mind with sense organs brought well under the control of this purified intellect
(3) Sense organs that no more contact the sense objects
(4) A mind that has given up its ideas of likes and dislikes. (18.51)

47. What are the 12 necessary conditions that a seeker has to fulfil in order to Realise Brahman?

The following are the 12 necessary conditions that a seeker has to fulfil to Realise Brahman:

(1) Purity of intellect
(2) Firm control of the mind
(3) Abandoning of all sense objects
(4) Giving up attraction and hatred
(5) Dwelling in solitude
(6) Moderation in food
(7) Keeping his speech, body and mind under control
(8) Practise of intense meditation
(9) Perfect dispassion
(10) Abandoning egoism, violence, arrogance, desire, hatred and covetousness
(11) Giving up the sense of 'I' and 'mine'
(12) Being ever peaceful.

The following verses maintain these twelve requirements:

बुद्ध्या विशुद्धया युक्तो धृत्यात्मानं नियम्य च ।
शब्दादीन्विषयांस्त्यक्त्वा रागद्वेषौ व्युदस्य च ॥

buddhyā viśuddhayā yukto dhṛtyātmānaṁ niyamya ca,
śabdādīnviṣayāṁstyaktvā rāgadveṣau vyudasya ca.

Endowed with a pure intellect; controlling the self by firmness; relinquishing sound and other objects; and abandoning attraction and hatred... (18.51)

विविक्तसेवी लघ्वाशी यतवाक्कायमानसः ।
ध्यानयोगपरो नित्यं वैराग्यं समुपाश्रितः ॥

viviktasevī laghvāśī yatavākkāyamānasaḥ,
dhyānayogaparo nityaṁ vairāgyaṁ samupāśritaḥ.

Dwelling in solitude; eating but little; speech, body and mind subdued; always engaged in meditation and concentration; taking refuge in dispassion... (18.52)

अहङ्कारं बलं दर्पं कामं क्रोधं परिग्रहम् ।
विमुच्य निर्ममः शान्तो ब्रह्मभूयाय कल्पते ॥

ahaṅkāraṁ balaṁ darpaṁ kāmaṁ krodhaṁ parigraham,
vimucya nirmamaḥ śānto brahmabhūyāya kalpate.

Having abandoned egoism, power, arrogance, desire, anger and aggrandisement; freed from the notion of 'mine' and so peaceful—he is fit to become Brahman. (18.53)

48. Does the instruction of the Lord to the seeker to find a quiet place to meditate mean that he has to move out to a jungle?

The instruction that a seeker must choose a sequestered spot to meditate does not mean that he must move out of a town to the jungles. One has to choose a place wherein there is the least disturbance. Even in the midst of a market there are moments when it is deserted and quiet. If the seeker is sincere, he can discover such moments of complete solitude under his own roof. (18.52)

49. How can a seeker overcome the mind's inclination for sense enjoyments?

Seeking sense gratifications, the mind is in a constant state of agitation. To quieten such a mind, it is necessary that we must give it some point of contemplation wherein, as it engages itself more and more, it shall discover consummate happiness and get sufficiently disengaged from everything else. Diverting the mind from the world of sense objects and maintaining it in a steady flow towards contemplation of the Lord in the utter attitude of identification is called 'meditation'. To be steady in a state of such an all-consuming dedication unto a nobler and higher ideal is the method of cooling down the mind's boiling desire for sense enjoyments. (18.52)

50. Why is overcoming of the 'kartṛtvabhāvanā' without the conquest of 'bhoktṛtvabhāvanā' a futile endeavour?

Even when the 'kartṛtvabhāvanā' (the sense of "I am the doer") has been renounced, the other aspect of the ego, 'bhoktṛtvabhāvanā' (the sense of "I am the enjoyer") will assert itself and poison the mind of the meditator. To explain with an example: a worm cut into two pieces becomes very soon two separate, independent living worms. So too if one aspect of the ego, the 'kartṛtvabhāvanā' (I-do-mentality) is conquered, we must equally attend to the destruction of the other aspect of the ego, the 'bhoktṛtvabhāvanā' (I-enjoy-mentality), or else the surviving part will revive within a very short time and we shall discover a healthier ego, potentially more powerful, dangerously rising out of the seemingly dead individuality. (18.54)

51. Explain why the individual who has gained the knowledge of Brahman neither grieves nor desires (*na śocati na kāṅkṣati*)?

Once the Spiritual Truth is understood the student necessarily becomes less agitated, because all disturbances enter our life through an individual's identification with the equipments of body, senses, mind, etc. To the extent the seeker Realises the existence of the Divine and automatically withdraws his all-out clinging to the matter-realm, to that extent he is not disturbed by the objects of perception, feeling and thought. Such a seeker discovers a growing tranquillity within himself and experiences a partial liquidation of his ego-sense. This enables him to discover the courage to stand apart from both grief and desire. He grieves not (*na śocati*) because he feels no incompleteness in himself, as he used to feel in the earlier days of his arrogant ego. Since there is no sense of grief and such other imperfections, his intellect no longer spins new and novel plans for desire-based satisfactions and temporary gratifications. One who grieves not in life desires not (*na kāṅkṣati*) for the possession of anything to make his happiness complete. (18.54)

52. Cite the verse wherein the Lord declares that through devotion one gains knowledge and through knowledge one attains the union with the Lord.

The following verse declares the above mentioned idea:

भक्त्या मामभिजानाति यावान्यश्चास्मि तत्त्वतः ।
ततो मां तत्त्वतो ज्ञात्वा विशते तदनन्तरम् ॥

bhaktyā māmabhijānāti yāvānyaścāsmi tattvataḥ,
tato māṁ tattvato jñātvā viśate tadanantaram.

By devotion he knows Me in essence, what and who I am; then, having known Me in My essence, he forthwith enters into the Supreme. (18.55)

53. Explain the significance of the term 'enters' in the Lord's declaration that the seeker having known the Lord in essence, enters into the Supreme (*tato māṁ tattvato jñātvā viśate tadanantaram*).

The 'entry' (viśate) mentioned by the Lord is not like that of a man entering a structure, a house separate from himself. There is no ego to enter into the plane of God Consciousness. The term 'entry' is used here exactly in the same fashion as 'the dreamer enters the waking state'. The dreamer cannot retain his own individuality when he enters the waking world, but he himself becomes the 'waker'. Similarly, when the ego enters God Consciousness, the individuality cannot retain itself as such. The misconception that he is an individual ends, and he rediscovers, becomes, or awakens to, the Infinite Brahman-hood—the State of Kṛṣṇa-Consciousness. (18.55)

54. What is the prime contribution of the Bhagavad Gītā to the Upaniṣadic tradition?

Integral sādhanā is the core of the Gītā technique. To synthesize methods of work (karma), devotion (bhakti) and knowledge (jñāna) is at once to discipline the body, mind and intellect. To explain: all disciplines pursued at the body level in order to control the mind and turn it towards the ideal are called Karma Yoga; all methods of channelising emotions in order to discipline the mind to contemplate upon the Higher are called Bhakti Yoga; and all study, reflection, detachment and meditation practised at the intellectual level, whereby the mind is lifted to the realm of the silent experience of its own Infinitude are called Jñāna Yoga. To practise all the three during our life is to discipline all the three layers of the body, mind and intellect. Thus, the philosophy of total spiritual transformation of the perceiver, the feeler and the thinker, all at once, in an integrated fashion is the prime contribution that the Gītā has made to the timeless tradition of the Hindu culture. (18.56)

55. Who can fix his mind firmly upon the Lord?

One who has fixed the Kṛṣṇa-tattva as the goal of his life, who surrenders himself mentally at all times at this altar and serves all His creatures, who ever discriminates and avoids all undivine thoughts and egocentric self-assertions—such an individual alone can fix his mind firmly upon the Lord. (18.57)

56. Write a short note on the grace (prasāda) of the Lord.

The 'grace' (prasāda) of the Lord is the result accrued when the mind is properly tuned and peacefully settled in contemplation upon the Infinite. It does not mean any special consideration shown by the all-loving Lord to some rare persons of His own choice. The grace of the all-pervading Lord is present everywhere because 'grace' is His form. Just as the ever-present sunlight on a bright day cannot illumine the room as long as the windows are closed, so too the harmony and joy of the Infinite cannot penetrate into our life, as long as the windows of discrimination in us are tightly shut. To the extent a seeker pursues his sādhana and cultivates discrimination and the other noble traits, to that extent the 'grace' of the Self shall flood his heart. (18.58)

57. Why will Arjuna be compelled to fight in the battle inspite of his determination not to fight?

The actions we do are propelled by our own vāsanās and they shackle our personality. Arjuna is essentially of the rajoguṇa type and, therefore, he must fight. He cannot, all of a sudden, claim to have the beauties of the sāttvic nature of heart and retire to a solitary place and live a serene life of steady contemplation. Because of wrong thinking and misplaced emotions, Arjuna feels that he does not like the war and is, therefore, not ready to face it. But inspite of his determination, he will be compelled to fight by his own nature, ordered by the existing vāsanās in him.

The following verse explains this idea:

स्वभावजेन कौन्तेय निबद्धः स्वेन कर्मणा ।
कर्तुं नेच्छसि यन्मोहात्करिष्यस्यवशोऽपि तत् ॥

svabhāvajena kaunteya nibaddhaḥ svena karmaṇā,
kartuṁ necchasi yanmohātkariṣyasyavaśo'pi tat.

O son of Kuntī, bound by your own karma (action) born of your own nature, that which, through delusion you wish not to do, even that you shall do, helplessly. (18.60)

58. Who becomes a victim of circumstances and who remains unshaken by them?

He who has no control over his mind becomes a victim of circumstances. He gets thrown up and down by the whims and fancies of things around him. But he who has gained inner mastery over the mind and stands firmly rooted in the pure Light of Wisdom is unshaken by the outer circumstances. (18.60)

59. Explain the Lord's statement that He dwells in the heart of all beings making them revolve like puppets mounted on a machine.

The Lord lends His power to all living creatures and energises them to act on. Everything revolves around Him—like the unseen hand that manipulates the dolls in the marionette-play. The puppets have no existence, no vitality, no emotions of their own; they are only the expressions of the will and intention of the unseen hand behind them. Matter, in contact with the Life Principle in us, becomes vibrant and dynamic, capable of perceiving, feeling and thinking. The Spark of Life presiding over the body, the Pure Eternal Consciousness, is that which, as it were, vitalises inert matter. This Life Principle functioning in each one of us is the master, controller, director and the Lord of our individual activities. This is the significance of the Lord's statement that He dwells in the heart of all beings making them revolve like puppets mounted on a machine. (18.61)

60. Explain the importance of surrendering unto the Lord with all one's being (sarva-bhāvena).

The surrender unto the Lord should not be a temporary self-deception. We must grow into a consciousness of the Presence of the Divine in all the planes of our existence. To illustrate such a total devotion, we have the examples of Rādha, Hanumān, Prahlāda and others. Without bringing all the levels of our being and all the facets of our personality into our love for Him, we cannot drown our finite ego-sense into the joyous lap of the Infinite Lord. Thus, a true devotee must re-orient his being and surrender himself as a willing vehicle for His expression. Then and then alone do all delusions end and the mortal gains the Divine Experience and comes to live fully the State of Godhood. (18.62)

61. Why does the Lord say that His message of the Bhagavad Gītā is a 'greater secret than all secrets' (*guhyād guhyataram*)?

The Spiritual Truth and the right way of living as discussed in the Bhagavad Gītā are termed as 'the secret of all secrets' in the sense that it is not easy for one to know the Gītā way of dynamic life and the Gītā vision of Truth, unless one is initiated into them. Even a subtle intellect, very efficient in knowing the material world, both in its arrangement of things and their mutual interaction, must necessarily fail to feel the Presence of this Subtle, Eternal and Infinite Self. It is because of this reason that the Lord says that his Bhagavad Gītā message is a greater secret than all secrets. (18.63)

62. Why does the Lord after declaring the entire Gītā to Arjuna give complete freedom to Arjuna and say: "you now act as you choose" (*yathecchasi tathā kuru*)?

Śrī Kṛṣṇa ultimately leaves the decision to act, the will to live the higher life, to Arjuna's own choice. Each one must reach the Lord by his own free choice. There is no compulsion; for spontaneity is an invaluable requisite for all 'new births'. Having placed before him all the facts and figures of life, principles and methods of living, Śrī Kṛṣṇa rightly invites Arjuna to make his own independent decision after considering all the points that He has spoken to him. Spiritual teachers should never compel. And in India there has never been any form of indoctrination. (18.63)

63. What is the importance of surrender (śaraṇāgati)?

An attitude of reverence to the Supreme is necessary in order to re-incorporate into the texture of our own life, the qualities of the Supreme. Like water, knowledge also flows only from a higher to a lower level. Therefore, our minds must be in an attitude of surrender unto Him in utter reverence and devotion. (18.65)

64. Cite the verse that summarises the entire Bhagavad Gītā and explain its salient points.

The following verse is the summary of the entire Bhagavad Gītā:

सर्वधर्मान्परित्यज्य मामेकं शरणं व्रज ।
अहं त्वा सर्वपापेभ्यो मोक्षयिष्यामि मा शुचः ॥

sarvadharmānparityajya māmekaṁ śaraṇaṁ vraja,
ahaṁ tvā sarvapāpebhyo mokṣayiṣyāmi mā śucaḥ.

Abandoning all dharmas (of the body, mind and intellect) take refuge in Me alone; I will liberate thee from all sins; grieve not.

It is evident from this verse that the Lord wants the seeker to accomplish three distinct adjustments in his inner personality:

(1) Renouncing all Dharmas
(2) Surrendering unto the Lord
(3) Giving up all worries

And as a reward Lord Kṛṣṇa promises: 'I shall release you from all sins'.

(1) Renouncing all dharma (*sarvadharmān parityajya*)—As a finite ego, the seeker lives due to his identification with the matter vestures, the dharmas (qualities) of his body, mind and intellect. Because of this he exists in life as a mere ego – the perceiver, feeler and thinker. These are not our 'essential' dharmas. And since these are the 'non-essentials', 'renouncing all dharmas' means 'ending the perceiver-feeler-thinker ego'. 'Renouncing all dharmas' in essence means the giving up of extrovert tendencies and not allowing ourselves to fall again and again into this state of identification with the outer matter envelopments. Extrovert tendencies of the mind are to be renounced. 'Develop introspection diligently' is the deep suggestion of the phrase 'renouncing all dharmas' (*sarvadharmān parityajya*).

(2) Surrendering unto the Lord (*māmekaṁ śaraṇaṁ vraja*)—Self-withdrawal from our extrovert nature will be impossible unless the mind is given a positive method of developing its introvert attention. By single-pointed, steady contemplation upon the Self a seeker can successfully accomplish his total withdrawal from the misinterpreting equipments of the body, mind and intellect.

(3) Giving up all worries: (*mā śucaḥ*)—When both the above conditions are accomplished, the seeker reaches a state of growing tranquillity in meditation. But it will all be a waste if this subjective peace created after so much labour were not to form a steady and firm platform for his personality to spring into the realms of the Divine Consciousness. This 'springboard of peace' must stay firm and supply the required propulsion for the seeker's inward dive. But unfortunately, the very anxiety to reach the Infinite weakens the 'spring board'. During meditation, when the mind has been persuaded away from all its restless preoccupations with the outer vehicles and brought again and again to contemplate upon the Self, the Lord wants the seeker to renounce all his anxieties and worries in order to Realise. For even a desire to Realise is a disturbing thought that can obstruct the final achievement.

Once the Self is Realised—the disturbing, thought-gurgling, action-prompting, desire-breeding, agitation-brewing vāsanās—termed 'sins' will be destroyed. Hence the Lord's promise: "I shall release you from all sins. Grieve not."

This stanza is one of the most powerfully worded verses in the

Gītā. The Lord, the Infinite, personally undertakes to help the seeker in case the spiritual hero in him is ready to offer his ardent co-operation and put forth his best efforts. All through the days of seeking, a sādhaka can achieve steady progress in spirituality only when he is able to keep within himself a mental climate of warm optimism. To despair and to weep, to feel dejected and disappointed, is to invite restlessness of the mind and, naturally therefore, spiritual unfoldment is never in the offing. This stanza is indeed the essence in itself of the entire Bhagavad Gītā. (18.66)

65. What are the rules that should be borne in mind while imparting the knowledge of the Bhagavad Gītā to others?

The following verse gives the list of rules while imparting the Bhagavad Gītā:

इदं ते नातपस्काय नाभक्ताय कदाचन ।
न चाशुश्रूषवे वाच्यं न च मां योऽभ्यसूयति ॥

idaṁ te nātapaskāya nābhaktāya kadācana,
na cāśuśrūṣave vācyaṁ na ca māṁ yo'bhyasūyati.

This is never to be spoken by you to one who is devoid of austerities or devotion, nor to one who does not render service, nor to one who desires not to listen, nor to one who cavils at Me. (18.67)

66. Cite the relevant verses wherein the Lord delcares that those who propagate the message of the Bhagavad Gītā are most dear to him.

In the following two verses the Lord says that those who spread the message of the Bhagavad Gītā are most dear to Him and will certainly attain Him:

य इदं परमं गुह्यं मद्भक्तेष्वभिधास्यति ।
भक्तिं मयि परां कृत्वा मामेवैष्यत्यसंशयः ॥

ya idaṁ paramaṁ guhyaṁ madbhakteṣvabhidhāsyati,
bhaktiṁ mayi parāṁ kṛtvā māmevaiṣyatyasaṁśayaḥ.

He who, with supreme devotion to Me, will teach this Supreme Secret to My devotees, shall doubtless come to Me. (18.68)

न च तस्मान्मनुष्येषु कश्चिन्मे प्रियकृत्तमः ।

भविता न च मे तस्मादन्यः प्रियतरो भुवि ॥

na ca tasmānmanuṣyeṣu kaścinme priyakṛttamaḥ,
bhavitā na ca me tasmādanyaḥ priyataro bhuvi.

Nor is there any among men who does dearer service to Me, nor shall there be another on earth dearer to Me than he. (18.69)

67. Why is the study of the Bhagavad Gītā termed Jñāna Yajña (Sacrifice of Wisdom)?

In a Yajña, the Lord of Fire is invoked in the sacrificial trough and into it are offered oblations by the devotees. From this analogy, the term 'Jñāna Yajña' has been originally coined and used in the Gītā. Study of the Scriptures and regular contemplation upon their deep significances kindle the 'Fire of Knowledge' in us and into this the intelligent seeker offers as his oblation his own false values and negative tendencies. This is the significance of the metaphorical phrase 'Jñāna Yajña'.

The Bhagavad Gītā, the great philosophy of life given out as a conversation between Śrī Kṛṣṇa—the Infinite—and Arjuna—the finite—has such a compelling charm about it, that even those who read it superficially will also be slowly dragged into the very sanctifying depths of it. Such an individual is, even unconsciously, egged on to make a pilgrimage to the greater possibilities within himself and, naturally, he comes to evolve through what the Lord terms 'Jñāna Yajña'. (18.70)

68. Why is the faculty of śraddhā essential for a fruitful listening to the Bhagavad Gītā?

'Śraddhā' (faith) is the faculty in the intellect to understand, absorb, assimilate and make the student live up to the subtle import of the sacred words. This śraddhā gives the capacity to dive deep into and discover the subtler meaning of the scriptural declarations, and thus helps the seeker to absorb that understanding into the warp and the woof of his own intellect. Listening to the Lord's discourses can be fruitful only to those who have developed this essential faculty of śraddhā within themselves. (18.71)

69. Why is the student of the Bhagavad Gītā required to be 'without malice' (anasūya)?

They alone who are free from malice against the teachings of the Bhagavad Gītā can undertake, with a healthy attitude of mind, a deeper and detailed study of it. This is not to say that a student is to read and study a philosophy with an implicit and ready faith. But the human mind, as it is, will grow dull and unresponsive when it has idle prejudices against the very theme of its study. The intellect can receive the ideals preached in the Bhagavad Gītā only through the sense organs, and these ideas must reach the intellect filtered through the mind. If the mind contains any malice towards the very philosophy or the philosopher, the arguments and the goal indicated therein can never appeal to the student's intellect. No doubt, the student should bring in his own constructive criticism or an independent judgement upon what he studies, but he must be reasonably available to listen patiently to what the scripture has to say and keep an open mind and not condemn the philosophy before understanding what it has to say. (18.71)

70. How did the message of the Bhagavad Gītā benefit Arjuna?

Arjuna, with a regained self-recognition, assuredly declares that his confusions have ended—as He himself says, "I have gained a recognition of my Real Nature. The hero in me has now become awakened, and the neurotic condition that had temporarily conquered my mind has totally ended." The following verse makes this clear:

नष्टो मोहः स्मृतिर्लब्धा त्वत्प्रसादान्मयाऽच्युत ।
स्थितोऽस्मि गतसन्देहः करिष्ये वचनं तव ॥

naṣṭo mohaḥ smṛtirlabdhā tvatprasādānmayā'cyuta,
sthito'smi gatasandehaḥ kariṣye vacanaṁ tava.

Destroyed is my delusion, as I have now gained my memory (knowledge) through your grace, O Acyuta. I am firm; my doubts are gone. I will do according to your word (bidding). (18.73)

71. Cite the concluding verse of the Bhagavad Gītā and explain its import.

The following is the concluding verse of the sacred Bhagavad Gītā:

यत्र योगेश्वरः कृष्णो यत्र पार्थो धनुर्धरः ।
तत्र श्रीर्विजयो भूतिर्ध्रुवा नीतिर्मतिर्मम ॥

yatra yogeśvaraḥ kṛṣṇo yatra pārtho dhanurdharaḥ,
tatra śrīrvijayo bhūtirdhruvā nītirmatirmama.

Wherever is Kṛṣṇa, the Lord of Yoga, wherever is Pārtha, the archer, there are prosperity, victory, happiness and firm (steady or sound) policy; this is my conviction.

Lord Kṛṣṇa represents the Self, the Ātman. This Spiritual Core is the substratum upon which the entire play of happenings is staged. The Lord can be invoked within the heart of each one of us through any one of the Yoga techniques expounded in the Bhagavad Gītā.

Pārtha (Arjuna) represents the confused, limited, ordinary mortal, with all his innumerable weaknesses, agitations and fears. When he has thrown down his 'instrument' of effort and achievement, his bow (dhanus), and has reclined to impotent idleness, no doubt there is no hope for any success or prosperity. But when he is 'ready with his bow', when he is no more idle but has a willing readiness to use his faculties to brave the challenges of life, there, in that man, we recognise a 'Pārtha ready with his bow' (dhanurdhara).

Now putting these two pictures together—Lord Kṛṣṇa—the Yogeśvara and Arjuna—Dhanurdhara—the symbolism of a way-of-life gets completed, wherein, reinforced with spiritual understanding (Yogeśvara) man gets ready to exert and pour out his endeavours (Dhanurdhara) to tame life and master prosperity. (18.78)

72. What are the choices of (1) tyāga (2) jñāna (3) karma (4) kartā (5) buddhi (6) dhṛti and (7) sukham of the sāttvic, rājasic and tāmasic types of people?

Type of	Sāttvic	Rājasic	Tāmasic
Tyāga (abandonment) (18.7-10)	To abandon attachment to fruits while performing one's obligatory duties.	Abandoning obligatory duties because they are painful to do or through fear of bodily suffering.	Abandoning obligatory duties due to delusion.
Jñāna (knowledge) (18.20-22)	The Knowledge that sees the one indestructible Reality in all beings and the indivisible Truth in the manifold manifestation.	This knowledge causes the individual to perceive beings as different from one another and projects plurality on the one Reality.	This knowledge clings to one single effect, as if it were the whole, is without reason, without foundation in truth and is narrow.
Karma (action) (18.23-25)	Actions ordained by the scriptures, which is free from attachment, done without love or hatred or desire for the results.	Actions done with desire for fruit, performed with the egoistic feeling "I am the doer" and with a lot of exertion.	Actions undertaken from delusion, without regard for the consequences, injury to oneself and others and one's own ability.
Kartā (doer) (18.26-28)	One who is free from attachment, non-egoistic, endowed with firmness and enthusiasm and unaffected by success and fortune.	One who is passionate, desirous of the fruits of action, greedy, harmful, impure and moved by elation and despair.	One devoid of self-control, concentration, vulgar, stubborn, cheat, malicious, lazy, despondent and procrastinating.

Buddhi (under-standing) (18.30-32)	The intellect that understands the pattern of work and renunciation, what ought to be done and what ought not to be done, fear and fearlesness, and bondage and liberation.	The intellect that wrongly understands dharma and adharma, and also what ought to be done and what ought not to be done.	The intellect which, enveloped in darkness, thinks adharma as dharma and all things perverted.
Dhṛti (fortitude)	The unwavering fortitude by which, through Yoga, one restrains the prāṇas and senses and establishes oneself in the Self.	By which through attachment and craving for the results of actions one holds firmly to dharma, artha and kāma.	By which a stupid man does not abandon sleep, fear, grief, depression and arrogance.
Sukham (pleasure)	Poison-like at first but nectar-like in the end. Born of the purity of one's mind due to Self-Realisation.	Nectar-like at first but poison-like in the end. Born out of the contact of the sense organs with the sense objects.	Causes delusion both in the beginning and end. Arises from sleep, indolence and heedlessness.

☙❧

Selections for Reflection

1. The duty of science is to 'describe life'; it is the purpose of philosophy to 'explain life'. Science describes the natural structures and processes; philosophy attempts their explanations. Thus viewed, the Bhagavad Gītā is an enchanting impossibility; it is at once a science and a philosophy, and yet, strangely enough, it is neither a scientific philosophy nor a philosophical science. In its 18 chapters, it explains a philosophy of living and while doing so it also expounds and demonstrates the science of living. (Introduction)

2. Unless we discover in ourselves the capacity to banish from our mind its various unhealthy relationships with the world outside and re-educate it to be continuously vigilant and alert to live in a healthy, intelligent spirit of detachment (tyāga), the total withering away of the false ego and its endless desire-promptings (saṁnyāsa) can never be achieved. Abandonment (tyāga) is the true content of the state of renunciation (saṁnyāsa)—saṁnyāsa without the spirit of tyāga is but an empty show; it is a false crown with no kingdom of joy within for it to lord over! (Introduction)

3. Both saṁnyāsa and tyāga are disciplines in our activities. The Lord is never tired of emphasising the importance of work. Neither of these terms indicates that work should be ignored; on the other hand both of them insist that work we must. Work, however, can gain a total transmutation by the removal of the things that clog our efficiency, and thus every piece of work can be made to yield its fullest reward. Snapping the chains that shackle us with the past and the future and working without being hustled by anxieties or henpecked by desires, in the full freedom and inspiration of the present, is the noblest way to perform actions. (18.2)

4. Kṛṣṇa's Gītā calls upon man to make work itself the greatest homage unto the Supreme; this is spiritual 'sādhana'. (18.3)

5. A bud abandons itself to become a flower, the flower gives up its soft petals and its enchanting fragrance and gains for itself the richer status of a fruit. Real abandonment should always lead us on to the ampler fields of self-expression, push us into the fuller ways of living, and introduce us to the greater experiences of joy. (18.8)

6. The faculties of the intellect, the beauties of the heart and the vitality of the body are all vehicles for the Sacred Will of the Spirit to sing through. If the vehicles are not properly disciplined, and if they do not come to surrender totally to the Infinite, the Lord, they get broken and shattered. (18.26)

7. This chapter provides us with three beautifully framed mental pictures, bringing out in all details the sāttvic, the rājasic and the tāmasic types available in the world. Beware—these pictures are not yardsticks to classify others, but are meant for each individual seeker to observe himself. Whenever a true seeker discovers symptoms of tamas and rajas growing in him, he should take notice of them at once and consciously strive to regain his sāttvic beauty. (18.28)

8. An understanding that is capable of clearly discriminating between the right field of pursuit and the wrong field of false proposition is the highest type of understanding. The individual must have the nerve to pursue the right path and also the heroism to defect from all wrong fields of futile endeavour. In short, true understanding has a ready ability to discriminate between actions that are to be pursued and actions that are to be shunned. (18.30)

9. As every challenge reaches us and demands our response to it, no doubt the Higher in us truly guides our activities; but the lower, indolent mind seeks a compromise and tries to act, heedless of the voice of the Higher. When an individual has thus lived for some time carelessly ignoring the voice of the Higher, he becomes more and more removed from his divine perfections. He sinks lower and lower into his animal nature. (18.39)

10. Let us introspect and evaluate ourselves every day, every minute. Let us avoid the lower guṇas and steadily work ourselves up towards the achievement of the sāttvic state. Only after reaching the status of the good (sāttvic) can we be ushered into the state of Godhood—Perfection absolute. (18.40)

11. In the Kṛṣṇa-Arjuna summit talks, the Lord is only trying to make Arjuna understand that his inner equipment is such that he can be classified only as a 'kṣatriya'. Being a kṣatriya, his duty is to fight, championing the cause of the good, and thus establish righteousness. He cannot, with profit, retire to the jungle and meditate for self-unfoldment, since he will have to grow, first of all, into the status of the sāttvic personality (brāhmaṇa) before he can successfully strive on the path of total retirement and a life of rewarding contemplation. Therefore, with the available texture of mind and intellect, the only spiritual sādhana left for Arjuna is to act vigorously in the field of contention. Thereby, he can exhaust his existing vāsanās of rajas and tamas. (18.40)

12. Knowledge can be imparted, but 'Wisdom' is to be found by the individual in himself. When a student discovers in himself the enthusiasm to live the knowledge gained through his study, then from the field of his lived experience arises 'Wisdom'—Vijñānam. (18.42)

13. A man of action cannot afford to be miserly, since his success will depend upon his influence on a large number of friends and supporters. The glory of a prince is in his compassion for others who are in need of help. (18.43)

14. In no society can leaders of men and affairs claim to be at once the spiritual leaders of the people. Secular heads cannot be spiritual guides. But a true leader is one who has the subtle ability to incorporate the spiritual ideals of our culture into the work-a-day life and maintain them in the community in all its innumerable fields of activity. (18.43)

15. A vehicle that can efficiently work in one medium of transport cannot with the same efficiency work in another medium. A car is efficient on the road—but on water? The rājasic mind cannot fly into meditation and maintain its poise as easily and as beautifully as the sāttvic mind can. Similarly, in the field in which a kṣatriya can outshine everybody, a vaiśya or a śūdra cannot. To rise to the highest station in social life, all men cannot have 'identical opportunities'. A social system can only give 'equal opportunities'! (18.44)

16. A tiny Corsican boy who was asked to tend sheep refused to do so and reached Paris to become one of the greatest generals the world had ever seen—Napoleon. A Goldsmith or a Keats would rather compose his metres in a garret than take up a commercial job, courting prosperity and a life of comfort. Each one is ordered by his own svabhāva, and each can discover his fulfilment only in that self-ordered field of activity. (18.45)

17. The renunciation of the ego and its desires can never be accomplished unless there is a spirit of dedication and a total surrender to the Infinite. When unbroken awareness of the Lord becomes a constant habit of the mind, dedication becomes effective, and man's evolution starts. (18.45)

18. This intelligent classification of human beings into brāhmaṇa kṣatriya, vaiśya and śūdra on the basis of their physical behaviour, psychological structure and intellectual aptitude is applicable not in India alone. This fourfold classification is universal, both in its application in life and its implication in the cultural development of man. (18.45)

19. It is no use employing our minds in fields which are contrary to our nature. Everyone has a precise place in the scheme of created things. Each one has his own importance and none is to be despised for each can do something which the others cannot do as well. There is no redundancy in the Lord's creation; not even

a single blade of grass, anywhere, at any time, is unnecessarily created! (18.47)

20. Everything has a purpose. Not only the good but the bad also are his manifestations and serve His purpose. The Pāṇḍavas' glory is, no doubt, great, but the manifestation of the wickedness in the Kauravas is also the glory of His creation. Without the latter, the history of the former would not have been complete. Nothing is to be condemned; none to be despised. Every thing is He. And He alone is! (18.47)

21. The more an oven is ventilated in the atmospheric air, the less smoky becomes the fire burning therein. The more the mind is ventilated with the Consciousness Divine, the less will the ego assert and, therefore, no defects can pollute the actions. If there be an influx of wrong vāsanās within, the earlier we exhaust them through action—without any ego or egocentric desire of enjoying their fruits—the quicker shall the load of existing vāsanās be lifted from our personality. (18.48)

22. The State of Actionlessness cannot be gained by a cheap and ignominous escape from the fields of life's activities. Making use of the fields, we must gain in purity by getting rid of the existing vāsanās through selfless activities, which are prescribed to each one of us according to the type to which we naturally belong. (18.49)

23. In the case of Arjuna, his tall talk of detachment and renunciation were false urges of escapism paraded as an angelic urge. His saṁnyāsa arose out of his attachment to his kith and kin, while true saṁnyāsa must arise out of detachment. Arjuna being a 'kṣatriya', his duty is to fight; and by fighting alone will he exhaust his vāsanās. By the exhaustion of the vāsanās alone can one hope to reach the supreme state of pure Awareness. (18.49)

24. Detachment from matter hallucinations itself is the rediscovery of spiritual beauty. (18.50)

25. When the old interests of a person die away and when he is ordered by new intellectual visions, new interests rise up in his mind; then the old world of objects around him suddenly retires, yielding place to the new set of things that he has willed around him by his newly developed mind. As long as I was a vicious man, sensuous friends and pleasure-seekers crowded my drawing room; when I changed my way of life and took to serious social work and political activities, the group of idlers went away, yielding their places to politicians and social workers. After a time I grew in my mental make up, and so, in my spiritual interests, even these politicians with their power politics, and social workers with their unspeakable jealousies and rivalries retired, yielding their places to men of thought and spiritual benediction. This is a typical example of how, as a mind grows, it leaves its old toys behind and enters totally into a greater field of the nobler gains of life. (18.52)

26. Devotion to the Lord (Bhakti) in the Gītā is not a mere passive surrender unto the ideal, nor a mere physical ritualism. Religion, to Lord Kṛṣṇa, is not fulfilled by a mere withdrawal from the outer world of sense objects, but in a definite come-back into the world, bringing into it the fragrance of peace and joy of the yonder, to brighten and beautify the drab, inert objects that constitute the world. (18.56)

27. All activities in the world are only expressions of the Divine Consciousness flashing Its brilliance through the body. In all activities, be conscious of the Lord without Whom no action is ever possible. Keep Him as your Goal. Make your intellect constantly aware of this 'Lord of all actions'. Gradually, the mind and the body will begin to work under the command of such an inspired intellect. (18.58)

28. Most of our obstacles in life are imaginary—created by false fears and deceitful anxieties of our own confused mind. (18.58)

29. Even if Newton himself were to jump from the third-floor balcony of his house, the gravitational force would, indeed, act upon him also! There is an inevitability in nature's laws. (18.58)

30. Just as the address of a person is given in order that one may locate the individual in a busy town, so also in order to seek, discover, and identify with Him, Bhagavān Kṛṣṇa gives his 'local address'—'heart of all beings'. (18.61)

31. The one commandment that has been repeated all through the Divine Song with great insistence is: "Renounce the ego and act." The ego is the cause for all our sense of imperfections and sorrows. To the extent we liquidate this sense of separateness and individuality, to that extent we climb into an experience of greater perfection and joy within ourselves. (18.62)

32. This term 'guhyam' (secret)—that is used to describe the knowledge of the scriptures was misconstrued to mean that the spiritual knowledge, which is the core of our culture, is a great secret to be carefully preserved and zealously guarded by the privileged few against anybody else coming to learn it. This orthodox view has no sanction in the scriptures, if we read them with the same large-heartedness as that of the Ṛṣis who gave them to us. No doubt, there are persons who have not the intellectual vision nor the mental steadiness nor the physical discipline to understand correctly this great Truth in all its subtle implications and, therefore, this is kept away from them lest they should come to harm themselves by falsely living a misunderstood philosophy. (18.63)

33. The motive force behind every noble teacher coming out into the world to preach, to explain and to expound is his abundant love for mankind. (18.64)

34. Love is the correct motive force behind all spiritual teachings. Unless a teacher has infinite love for the taught there is no inspired joy in teaching. (18.65)

35. The maladjusted 'ego' in us has, by its own false concepts and imaginations, spooled us all up into cocoons of confusion and has tied us down with our own self-created shackles. Now, it is up to us to snap these cords that bind us and gain freedom from them all. The All-perfect Supreme has been as though shackled by our mind and intellect, and now the same mind and intellect must be utilised to unwind the binding cords. If we lock ourselves up in a room, it is left to us only to unlock its doors and walk out into freedom. Vāsanās are created by our egocentric activities (sakāma-karma), and by selfless work (niṣkāma-karma) alone can these vāsanās be ended. (18.65)

36. Seekers who are not able to serve others, who are selfish, who have no human qualities, who have never felt a sympathetic love for others—such persons are merely consumers and not producers of joy for others, and they invariably fail to understand or appreciate or come to live the joys of the 'Kṛṣṇa way of life'. (18.67)

37. Forceful conversion may enhance the numerical strength of a faith, but self-development and inner unfoldment cannot come that way. Religion should not be forced upon anyone. One who has mentally rejected a philosophy can never, even when one has understood it, live up to it. Therefore, those who are entertaining a secret disrespect for a philosophy should not be forced to study it. (18.67)

38. If a student feels that he cannot satisfactorily understand the Gītā, he has only to sharpen his inner nature further. Just as we cleanse a mirror to remove the dimness of the reflection, so too, by properly readjusting the mind-intellect equipment, its sensitivity to absorb the Gītā-philosophy can be increased. (18.67)

39. "Fight the evil down, whether it be within or without" is the cardinal principle that Śrī Kṛṣṇa advocates to Prince Arjuna. In order to impart such a culture, it is not enough that the teacher be a mere scholar, but he must have the Kṛṣṇa-ability. (18.68)

40. If a student who has understood even a wee bit of our cultural tradition does not convey it to others, it means that there is no mobility of intelligence or fluidity or inspiration in him. (18.68)

41. When a rusted key is heated in fire, the rust falls off and the key regains its original brightness. So too, our personality, when reacted with the knowledge of the Gītā, is chastened, since our wrong tendencies, unhealthy vāsanās and false sense of ego which have risen from false knowledge, all get burnt up in Right Knowledge. (18.70)

42. Joy is an inside job—The kingdom of joy lies within all of us. Heaven is not somewhere yonder; it is here and now. Happiness and sorrow are both within us. To the extent we learn and live the principles of right living, as enunciated in the Gītā, to that extent we shall come to gain a cultural eminence within ourselves and live an ampler life of greater achievements. (18.71)

43. The study of Vedānta broadens our vision, and we start reorganising in a new light the same old scheme of things around us, and then its previous ugliness gets lifted as though by magic. (18.72)

44. A revival within and a rediscovery of our personality are possible for all of us if only we truly understand the significance of the Gītā philosophy. The Infinite nature of Perfection is our own. It is not something that we have to gain from somewhere by the outside intervention of some agency. This Mighty Being within ourselves is now lying veiled beneath our own egocentric confusions and abject fears. Even while we are confused and confounded, and helplessly suffering the tragic sorrows of our ego, we are in reality none other than our own Self. When the dream ends, the confusions also end, and we awaken to our Real Nature. So too, in life. This awakening of the Divine in us is the ending of the beast within. (18.73)

45. When he regained his spiritual balance, which he, as it were, lost

temporarily while carrying the cross through the taunting crowd, Jesus also cried: "Thy will be done." Here Arjuna, revived by the Grace of Śrī Kṛṣṇa, similarly cries, "I shall act according to Your word" (*kariṣye vacanam tava*). In both cases we find that the statements are almost identical. (18.74)

46. The Gītā is an infinite fountain-head of inspiration and joy. It provides us with a systematic scheme of re-education whereby our mind can discover a secret power in itself to tackle intelligently the chaotic happenings around us which constitute our world of challenges. The Gītā-educated man learns to recognise a rhythm, to see a beauty, and to hear a melody in the ordinary day-to-day life—a life which was till then but a mad death-dance of appearances and disappearances of things and beings. (18.76)

47. A happy blending of the sacred and the secular is the policy for man as advised in the Bhagavad Gītā. In the vision of Śrī Veda Vyāsa, he sees a world order in which man pursues a way of life, wherein the spiritual and the material values are happily wedded to each other. Mere material production can, no doubt, bring immediately a spectacular flood of wealth into the pockets of man, but not peace and joy into his heart. Prosperity without peace within is a calamity, gruesome and terrible. (18.78)

48. To renounce the false values of life in us is at once to rediscover the Divine nature in each one of us. To discard the beast in us (saṁnyāsa) is the Liberation (mokṣa) of the Divine in us! (Epilogue)

Verses for Memorisation

काम्यानां कर्मणां न्यासं संन्यासं कवयो विदुः ।
सर्वकर्मफलत्यागं प्राहुस्त्यागं विचक्षणाः ॥

kāmyānāṁ karmaṇāṁ nyāsaṁ saṁnyāsaṁ kavayo viduḥ,
sarvakarmaphalatyāgaṁ prāhustyāgaṁ vicakṣaṇāḥ.

The sages understand saṁnyāsa to be 'the renunciation of works with desire'; the wise declare 'the abandonment of the fruits of all actions' as tyāga. (18.2)

यज्ञदानतपःकर्म न त्याज्यं कार्यमेव तत् ।
यज्ञो दानं तपश्चैव पावनानि मनीषिणाम् ॥

yajñadānatapaḥkarma na tyājyaṁ kāryameva tat,
yajño dānaṁ tapaścaiva pāvanāni manīṣiṇām.

Acts of sacrifice, charity and austerity should not be abandoned, but should be performed; worship, charity and also austerity are the purifiers of even the 'wise'. (18.5)

कार्यमित्येव यत्कर्म नियतं क्रियतेऽर्जुन ।
सङ्गं त्यक्त्वा फलं चैव स त्यागः सात्त्विको मतः ॥

kāryamityeva yatkarma niyataṁ kriyate'rjuna,
saṅgaṁ tyaktvā phalaṁ caiva sa tyāgaḥ sāttviko mataḥ.

Whatever 'obligatory action' is done, O Arjuna, merely because it ought to be done, abandoning 'attachment and also fruit', that abandonment is regarded as sāttvic (pure). (18.9)

अधिष्ठानं तथा कर्ता करणं च पृथग्विधम् ।
विविधाश्च पृथक्चेष्टा दैवं चैवात्र पञ्चमम् ॥

adhiṣṭhānaṁ tathā kartā karaṇaṁ ca pṛthagvidham,
vividhāśca pṛthakceṣṭā daivaṁ caivātra pañcamam.

The 'seat' (body), the doer (ego), the various organs of perception, the different functions of the various organs of action and also the presiding deity, the fifth. (18.14)

यस्य नाहङ्कृतो भावो बुद्धिर्यस्य न लिप्यते ।
हत्वाऽपि स इमाँल्लोकान्न हन्ति न निबध्यते ॥

yasya nāhaṅkṛto bhāvo buddhiryasya na lipyate,

hatvā'pi sa imām̐llokānna hanti na nibadhyate.

He who is free from the egoistic notion, whose intelligence is not tainted (by good or evil), though he slays these people, he slays not, nor is he bound (by the action). (18.17)

सर्वभूतेषु येनैकं भावमव्ययमीक्षते ।
अविभक्तं विभक्तेषु तज्ज्ञानं विद्धि सात्त्विकम् ॥

sarvabhūteṣu yenaikaṁ bhāvamavyayamīkṣate,
avibhaktaṁ vibhakteṣu tajjñānaṁ viddhi sāttvikam.

That by which one sees the one indestructible Reality in all beings, undivided in the divided, know that 'knowledge' as sāttvic (pure). (18.20)

अनुबन्धं क्षयं हिंसामनपेक्ष्य च पौरुषम् ।
मोहादारभ्यते कर्म यत्तत्तामसमुच्यते ॥

anubandhaṁ kṣayaṁ hiṁsāmanapekṣya ca pauruṣam,
mohādārabhyate karma yattattāmasamucyate.

That action which is undertaken from delusion, without regard for the consequence, loss, injury and ability is declared as tāmasic (dull). (18.25)

मुक्तसङ्गोऽनहंवादी धृत्युत्साहसमन्वितः ।
सिद्ध्यसिद्ध्योर्निर्विकारः कर्ता सात्त्विक उच्यते ॥

muktasaṅgo'nahaṁvādī dhṛtyutsāhasamanvitaḥ,
siddhyasiddhyornirvikāraḥ kartā sāttvika ucyate.

A 'doer' who is free from attachment, non-egoistic, endowed with firmness and enthusiasm and unaffected by success or failure is called sāttvic (pure). (18.26)

प्रवृत्तिं च निवृत्तिं च कार्याकार्ये भयाभये ।
बन्धं मोक्षं च या वेत्ति बुद्धिः सा पार्थ सात्त्विकी ॥

pravṛttiṁ ca nivṛttiṁ ca kāryākārye bhayābhaye,
bandhaṁ mokṣaṁ ca yā vetti buddhiḥ sā pārtha sāttvikī.

That which knows the paths of work and renunciation, what ought to be done and what ought not to be done, fear and fearlessness, bondage and liberation, that 'understanding' is sāttvic (pure), O Pārtha. (18.30)

यया स्वप्नं भयं शोकं विषादं मदमेव च ।
न विमुञ्चति दुर्मेधा धृतिः सा पार्थ तामसी ॥

yayā svapnaṁ bhayaṁ śokaṁ viṣādaṁ madameva ca,
na vimuñcati durmedhā dhṛtiḥ sā pārtha tāmasī.

The 'constancy' because of which a stupid man does not abandon sleep, fear, grief, depression and also arrogance (conceit), that 'fortitude', O Pārtha, is tāmasic (dull). (18.35)

यत्तदग्रे विषमिव परिणामेऽमृतोपमम् ।
तत्सुखं सात्त्विकं प्रोक्तमात्मबुद्धिप्रसादजम् ॥

yattadagre viṣamiva pariṇāme'mṛtopamam,
tatsukhaṁ sāttvikaṁ proktamātmabuddhiprasādajam.

That which is like poison at first, but in the end like nectar, that 'pleasure' is declared to be sāttvic (pure), born of the purity of one's own mind, due to Self Realisation. (18.37)

विषयेन्द्रियसंयोगाद्यत्तदग्रेऽमृतोपमम् ।
परिणामे विषमिव तत्सुखं राजसं स्मृतम् ॥

viṣayendriyasaṁyogādyattadagre'mṛtopamam,
pariṇāme viṣamiva tatsukhaṁ rājasaṁ smṛtam.

That pleasure which arises from the contact of the sense organs with the objects, (which is) at first like nectar, (but is) in the end like poison, that is declared to be rājasic (passionate). (18.38)

यदग्रे चानुबन्धे च सुखं मोहनमात्मनः ।
निद्रालस्यप्रमादोत्थं तत्तामसमुदाहृतम् ॥

yadagre cānubandhe ca sukhaṁ mohanamātmanaḥ,
nidrālasyapramādotthaṁ tattāmasamudāhṛtam.

The pleasure which at first and in the sequel deludes the Self, arising from sleep, indolence and heedlessness is declared to be tāmasic (dull). (18.39)

शमो दमस्तपः शौचं क्षान्तिरार्जवमेव च ।
ज्ञानं विज्ञानमास्तिक्यं ब्रह्मकर्म स्वभावजम् ॥

śamo damastapaḥ śaucaṁ kṣāntirārjavameva ca,
jñānaṁ vijñānamāstikyaṁ brahmakarma svabhāvajam.

Serenity, self-restraint, austerity, purity, forgiveness and also uprightness, knowledge, realisation, belief in God—are the duties of the 'brāhmaṇas', born of (their own) nature. (18.42)

शौर्यं तेजो धृतिर्दाक्ष्यं युद्धे चाप्यपलायनम्।
दानमीश्वरभावश्च क्षात्रं कर्म स्वभावजम्॥

śauryaṁ tejo dhṛtirdākṣyaṁ yuddhe cāpyapalāyanam,
dānamīśvarabhāvaśca kṣātraṁ karma svabhāvajam.
Prowess, splendour, firmness, dexterity and also not fleeing from battle; generosity, lordliness—these are the duties of the 'kṣatriyas', born of (their own) nature. (18.43)

कृषिगौरक्ष्यवाणिज्यं वैश्यकर्म स्वभावजम्।
परिचर्यात्मकं कर्म शूद्रस्यापि स्वभावजम्॥

kṛṣigaurakṣyavāṇijyaṁ vaiśyakarma svabhāvajam,
paricaryātmakaṁ karma śūdrasyāpi svabhāvajam.
Agriculture, cattle-rearing and trade are the duties of the 'vaiśyas', born of (their own) nature; and service is the duty of the 'śūdras', born of (their own) nature. (18.44)

यतः प्रवृत्तिर्भूतानां येन सर्वमिदं ततम्।
स्वकर्मणा तमभ्यर्च्य सिद्धिं विन्दति मानवः॥

yataḥ pravṛttirbhūtānāṁ yena sarvamidaṁ tatam,
svakarmaṇā tamabhyarcya siddhiṁ vindati mānavaḥ.
From whom is the evolution of all beings, by whom all this is pervaded, worshipping Him, with one's own duty, man attains Perfection. (18.46)

श्रेयान्स्वधर्मो विगुणः परधर्मात्स्वनुष्ठितात्।
स्वभावनियतं कर्म कुर्वन्नाप्नोति किल्बिषम्॥

śreyānsvadharmo viguṇaḥ paradharmātsvanuṣṭhitāt,
svabhāvaniyataṁ karma kurvannāpnoti kilbiṣam.
Better is one's own duty (though) devoid of merits than the duty of another well performed. He who does the duty ordained by his own nature incurs no sin. (18.47)

सहजं कर्म कौन्तेय सदोषमपि न त्यजेत्।
सर्वारम्भा हि दोषेण धूमेनाग्निरिवावृताः॥

sahajaṁ karma kaunteya sadoṣamapi na tyajet,
sarvārambhā hi doṣeṇa dhūmenāgnirivāvṛtāḥ.
One should not abandon, O Kaunteya, the duty to which one is born, though faulty; for, are not all undertakings enveloped by evil, as fire by smoke? (18.48)

बुद्ध्या विशुद्धया युक्तो धृत्यात्मानं नियम्य च ।
शब्दादीन्विषयांस्त्यक्त्वा रागद्वेषौ व्युदस्य च ॥
buddhyā viśuddhayā yukto dhṛtyātmānaṁ niyamya ca,
śabdādīnviṣayāṁstyaktvā rāgadveṣau vyudasya ca.
Endowed with a pure intellect; controlling the self by firmness; relinquishing sound and other objects; and abandoning attraction and hatred... (18.51)

विविक्तसेवी लघ्वाशी यतवाक्कायमानसः ।
ध्यानयोगपरो नित्यं वैराग्यं समुपाश्रितः ॥
viviktasevī laghvāśī yatavākkāyamānasaḥ,
dhyānayogaparo nityaṁ vairāgyaṁ samupāśritaḥ.
Dwelling in solitude; eating but little; speech, body and mind subdued; always engaged in meditation and concentration; taking refuge in dispassion... (18.52)

अहङ्कारं बलं दर्पं कामं क्रोधं परिग्रहम् ।
विमुच्य निर्ममः शान्तो ब्रह्मभूयाय कल्पते ॥
ahaṅkāraṁ balaṁ darpaṁ kāmaṁ krodhaṁ parigraham,
vimucya nirmamaḥ śānto brahmabhūyāya kalpate.
Having abandoned egoism, power, arrogance, desire, anger and aggrandisement, and freed from the notion of 'mine' and so peaceful——he is fit to become Brahman. (18.53)

ईश्वरः सर्वभूतानां हृद्देशेऽर्जुन तिष्ठति ।
भ्रामयन्सर्वभूतानि यन्त्रारूढानि मायया ॥
īśvaraḥ sarvabhūtānāṁ hṛddeśe'rjuna tiṣṭhati,
bhrāmayansarvabhūtāni yantrārūḍhāni māyayā.
The Lord dwells in the heart of all beings, O Arjuna, causing them, by His illusive power to revolve as if mounted on a machine. (18.61)

इति ते ज्ञानमाख्यातं गुह्याद्गुह्यतरं मया ।
विमृश्यैतदशेषेण यथेच्छसि तथा कुरु ॥

iti te jñānamākhyātaṁ guhyādguhyataraṁ mayā,
vimṛśyaitadaśeṣeṇa yathecchasi tathā kuru.

Thus the 'Wisdom' which is a greater secret than all secrets has been declared to you by Me; having reflected upon it fully, you now act as you choose. (18.63)

मन्मना भव मद्भक्तो मद्याजी मां नमस्कुरु ।
मामेवैष्यसि सत्यं ते प्रतिजाने प्रियोऽसि मे ॥

manmanā bhava madbhakto madyājī māṁ namaskuru,
māmevaiṣyasi satyaṁ te pratijāne priyo'si me.

Fix your mind upon Me; be devoted to Me; sacrifice for Me; bow down to Me; you shall come, surely then, to Me alone; truly do I promise to you, (for) you are dear to Me. (18.65)

सर्वधर्मान्परित्यज्य मामेकं शरणं व्रज ।
अहं त्वा सर्वपापेभ्यो मोक्षयिष्यामि मा शुचः ॥

sarvadharmānparityajya māmekaṁ śaraṇaṁ vraja,
ahaṁ tvā sarvapāpebhyo mokṣayiṣyāmi mā śucaḥ.

Abandoning all dharmas (of the body, mind and intellect), take refuge in Me alone; I will liberate thee from all sins; grieve not. (18.66)

इदं ते नातपस्काय नाभक्ताय कदाचन ।
न चाशुश्रूषवे वाच्यं न च मां योऽभ्यसूयति ॥

idaṁ te nātapaskāya nābhaktāya kadācana,
na cāśuśrūṣave vācyaṁ na ca māṁ yo'bhyasūyati.

This is never to be spoken by you to one who is devoid of austerities or devotion, nor to one who does not render service, nor to one who desires not to listen, nor to one who cavils at Me. (18.67)

य इदं परमं गुह्यं मद्भक्तेष्वभिधास्यति ।
भक्तिं मयि परां कृत्वा मामेवैष्यत्यसंशयः ॥

ya idaṁ paramaṁ guhyaṁ madbhakteṣvabhidhāsyati,
bhaktiṁ mayi parāṁ kṛtvā māmevaiṣyatyasaṁśayaḥ.

He who, with supreme devotion to me, will teach this supreme secret to my devotees shall doubtless come to me. (18.68)

अध्येष्यते च य इमं धर्म्यं संवादमावयोः ।
ज्ञानयज्ञेन तेनाहमिष्टः स्यामिति मे मतिः ॥
adhyeṣyate ca ya imaṁ dharmyaṁ saṁvādamāvayoḥ,
jñānayajñena tenāhamiṣṭaḥ syāmiti me matiḥ.
And he who will study this sacred dialogue of ours, by him I shall have been worshipped by the 'Sacrifice of Wisdom'. Such is my conviction. (18.70)

नष्टो मोहः स्मृतिर्लब्धा त्वत्प्रसादान्मयाऽच्युत ।
स्थितोऽस्मि गतसन्देहः करिष्ये वचनं तव ॥
naṣṭo mohaḥ smṛtirlabdhā tvatprasādānmayā'cyuta,
sthito'smi gatasandehaḥ kariṣye vacanaṁ tava.
Destroyed is my delusion, as I have now gained my memory (knowledge) through your grace, O Acyuta. I am firm; my doubts are gone. I will do according to your word (bidding). (18.73)

यत्र योगेश्वरः कृष्णो यत्र पार्थो धनुर्धरः ।
तत्र श्रीर्विजयो भूतिर्ध्रुवा नीतिर्मतिर्मम ॥
yatra yogeśvaraḥ kṛṣṇo yatra pārtho dhanurdharaḥ,
tatra śrīrvijayo bhūtirdhruvā nītirmatirmama.
Wherever is Kṛṣṇa, the Lord of Yoga, wherever is Pārtha, the archer, there are prosperity, victory, happiness and firm (steady or sound) policy; this is my conviction. (18.78)

Infobits

1. Śrīmad Bhagavad Gītā occurs in the Mahābhārata in the chapter titled ________.

Bhīṣma-parva (General Introduction)

2. The Bhagavad Gītā comprises chapters ______ to ______ of the Bhīṣma-parva of the Mahābhārata.

Chapters 25 to 42 (General Introduction)

3. The total number of chapters in Bhagavad Gītā is ________.

Eighteen (General Introduction)

4. The author of the Bhagavad Gītā is __________.

Śrī Veda Vyāsa (General Introduction)

5. The Bhagavad Gītā is a dramatic restatement of the message of the ______________.

Upaniṣads (General Introduction)

6. Who was Arjuna's charioteer?

Śrī Kṛṣṇa (General Introduction)

7. The Kaurava army's battle formation was in the shape of an __________.

Eagle[1] (General Introduction)

8. The Mahābhārata war took place in the battlefield of ________.

Kurukṣetra (1.1)

9. Who reports the Bhagavad Gītā to Dhṛtarāṣṭra?

Sañjaya (1.1)

1. The Pāṇḍava army was in the shape of a 'vajra' (thunder-bolt).

10. Who gave Sañjaya the power to witness the happenings in Kurukṣetra?

Śrī Veda Vyāsa (1.1)

11. The capital city of the Kauravas was ________.

Hastināpura (1.1)

12.What is the only verse spoken by Dhṛtarāṣṭra in the entire Bhagavad Gītā?

धर्मक्षेत्रे कुरुक्षेत्रे समवेता युयुत्सवः ।
मामकाः पाण्डवाश्चैव किमकुर्वत सञ्जय ॥

dharmakṣetre kurukṣetre samavetā yuyutsavaḥ,
māmakāḥ pāṇḍavāścaiva kimakurvata sañjaya.

What did the sons of Pāṇḍu and also my people do when, desirous to fight, they assembled together on the holy plain of Kurukṣetra, O Sañjaya? (1.1)

13. Duryodhana's teacher was ________.

Droṇa (1.2)

14. The son of Drupada and commander of the Pāṇḍava army was ________.

Dhṛṣṭadyumna (1.3)

15. Name the important warriors enumerated by Duryodhana while reviewing the strength of the Pāṇḍava army?

Yuyudhāna, Virāṭa, Drupada, Dhṛṣṭaketu, Cekitāna, Purujit (the valiant king of Kāśi), Kuntibhoja, Śaibya, Yudhāmanyu, Uttamaujas, Abhimanyu and the sons of Draupadī (1.4-6)

16.Who are the great leaders of the Kauravas mentioned by Duryodhana while reviewing his army strength.

Droṇa, Bhīṣma, Karṇa, Kṛpa, Aśvatthāman, Vikarṇa and the son of Somadatta (1.8)

17. Who is the grandfather of the Pāṇḍavas and Kauravas?

Bhīṣma (1.9)

18. Duryodhana instructs all his commanders to protect ______.

Bhīṣma (1.11)

19. Arjuna's horses were ______ in colour.

White (1.14)

20.What are the names of the conches of Kṛṣṇa, Dhanañjaya (Arjuna), Vṛkodara (Bhīma), Yudhiṣṭhira, Nakula and Sahadeva?

Kṛṣṇa - Pāñcajanya (1.15)
Dhanañjaya (Arjuna) – Devadatta (1.15)
Vṛkodara (Bhīma) - Pauṇḍra (1.15)
Yudhiṣṭhira – Anantavijaya (1.16)
Nakula - Sughoṣa (1.16)
Sahadeva - Maṇipuṣpaka (1.16)

21. Lord Kṛṣṇa's charioteer, who was also a battalion-commander in the Pāṇḍava army, was ________.

Sātyaki (1.17)

22.The ensign on Arjuna's chariot was ________.

Hanumān (1.20)

23.The only sentence spoken by Śrī Kṛṣṇa in the entire first chapter is ______.

पार्थ पश्यैतान्समवेतान्कुरूनिति ॥

pārtha paśyaitānsamavetānkurūniti.

"Behold O Pārtha! All the Kauravas gathered together" (1.25)

24. Arjuna's bow was called ______.

Gāṇḍīva (1.30)

25.What are the various terms which Arjuna uses to address Śrī Kṛṣṇa in the first chapter?

Kṛṣṇa, Keśava, Govinda, Madhusūdana, Janārdana, Mādhava and Hṛṣīkeśa are the various terms which Arjuna uses to address Śrī Kṛṣṇa in the first chapter.

26.The first chapter of the Gītā ends with the words of ______.

Sañjaya

एवमुक्त्वार्जुनः सङ्‌ख्ये रथोपस्थ उपाविशत्।
विसृज्य सशरं चापं शोकसंविग्नमानसः ॥

evamuktvārjunaḥ saṅkhye rathopastha upāviśat,
visṛjya saśaraṁ cāpaṁ śokasaṁvignamānasaḥ.

Having thus spoken in the midst of the battlefield, Arjuna sat down on the seat of the chariot, casting away his bow and arrow, with a mind distressed with sorrow. (1.47)

27.What is the Sanskrit root of the word 'yoga'?

'Yuj' – to join (Epilogue of chapter 1)

28. 'Kāmadhenu', a mythological cow from which all our desires could be milked, is said to have belonged to ________.

Sage Vasiṣṭha (3.10)

29. What is meant by 'prasthāna-traya'?

'Prasthāna-traya' refers to the following three scriptures:

(1) Upaniṣads

(2) Brahma Sūtras

(3) Bhagavad Gītā. (Epilogue of chapter 6)

30. Who are the seven great Ṛṣis?

Bhṛgu, Vivasvān, Sudāmā, Aṅgiras, Atri, Viśvāmitra and Vasiṣṭha are the sevan Ṛṣis. (10.6)

31. Who are the four Kumāras?

Sanatkumāra, Sanaka, Sanātana and Sanandana are the four Kumāras. (10.6)

32. Who are the fourteen Manus?

Svayambhuva, Svārociṣa, Uttama, Tāmasa, Raivata, Cākṣuṣa, Vaivasvata, Sāvarṇī, Rudrasāvarṇī, Devasāvarṇī, Indrasāvarṇī and Dharmasāvarṇī are the fourteen Manus. (10.6)

33. Who is 'Vāsava'?

King Indra. (10.22)

34. Who are the Vasus?

The Vasus are eight in number and are the Vedic deities presiding over the seasons. (10.23)

35. _______is the chief of the Seven Ṛṣis.

Bhṛgu (10.25)

36. Who are Gāndharvas?

'Gāndharvas' are the mythological concept of subtle entities who constitute the celestial choir, who entertain the denizens of heaven with their art and music. They are the 'stars' of entertainment in heaven. Among them, Citraratha is the most brilliant. (10.26)

37. Who are Uccaiḥśravas and Airāvata?

Uccaiḥśravas is the mighty winged-horse and Airāvata is the powerful white-elephant. Both of them were presented to the king of the gods, Indra during the churning of the ocean. (10.27)

38. Who is Vāsukī?

The serpent Vāsukī is described in our mythology as ever living on Lord Śiva's ring-finger, as an adornment. Though small enough to become a ring on the finger of the Lord, it was this Vāsukī serpent, who volunteered to serve as a rope in the churning process of the milky-ocean. (10.28)

39. Differentiate Sarpas and Nāgas?

Sarpas are single-hooded; while Nāgas are multi-hooded. (10.29)

40. What is the Gāyatrī metre?

Gāyatrī is a metre composed of three lines, each with eight syllables. (10.35)

41. What was the pen name of Kṛṣṇa Dvaipāyana?

Vyāsa. (10.37)

42. Who is Uśanas?

'Uśanas' is Śukrācārya, the guru of the Asuras. (10.37)

43. What are the total number of Ādityas, Vasus, Rudras, Aśvins and Maruts?

The Ādityas are twelve in number, the Vasus eight, the Rudras eleven, the Aśvins two and the Maruts fortynine. (11.6)

44. To whom does Pujya Gurudev Swami Chinmayanandaji dedicate the 'Holy Gītā'—his commentary on the Bhagavad Gītā?

Pujya Gurudev Swami Chinmayanandaji dedicates the Holy Gītā—his commentary on the Bhagavad Gītā at the feet of Pujya Swami Tapovanam. (Epilogue of Chapter 18)

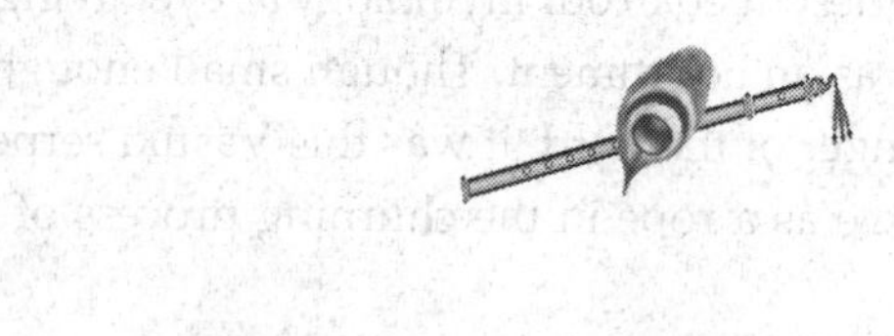

Bhagavad Gītā Pādānukramaṇikā

An alphabetical index of the pādas of the Bhagavad Gītā

Guidelines for Bhagavad Gītā Pādānukramaṇikā

1. The pādas (quarters) are arranged as per the Sanskrit alphebetical order. The pādas beginning with vowels come first. Those beginning with consonants follow.

This order can be expressed as follows:

- Vowels (अ to औ)
- क[1] followed by vowels
- क followed by क to म
- क followed by य र ल and व
- क followed by श ष and स
- क followed by ह
- क followed by anusvāra (ं)
- क followed by visarga (ः)

- का followed by vowels
- का followed by क to म
- का followed by य र ल and व
- का followed by श ष and स
- का followed by ह
- का followed by anusvāra
- का followed by visarga

The above arrangement has been followed also from कि to कौ

The consonant क् is arranged at the end of the क series (i.e., क to कौ). Refer to Pāda Nos. 975–977

2. Anusvāra (ं) within a word is retained when it is followed by semi vowels (य् र् ल् and व्), sibilants (श् ष् and स्) and aspirate (ह्).

For example refer to the words: संयाति (Pāda No. 106), संवृत्तः (Pāda No. 308), संस्मृत्य (Pāda No. 2222), सिंहनादम् (Pāda No. 2692).

3. But the anusvāra (within a word), when followed by any consonant

1. क represents any of the alphabet series — क to ह

other than semi vowels, sibilants and aspirate is converted into the nasal of the class consonant that follows the anusvāra[2]. For example refer to the words:

- धनञ्जय (Pāda No. 532) is not written as धनंजय
- सम्प्रकीर्तितः (Pāda No. 997) is not written as संप्रकीर्तितः
- साङ्ख्यैः (Pāda No. 1998) is not written as सांख्यैः

The exceptions to this rule are the two words संन्यास (Refer to Pāda No. 2068) and संज्ञा (Refer to Pāda No. 1117), the anusvāra of which has not been changed into सन्न्यास and सञ्ज्ञा respectively for ease in reading.

4. Within a pāda, the anusvāra occuring at the end of the word when followed by a word beginning with a class consonant (क् to म्) is retained as it is and not converted into the nasal of the class consonant.

Refer to Pada No. 917 - तं तं नियममास्थाय where the two anusvāras are retained as they are without joining them as तन्तन्नियममास्थाय

5. Avagraha (ऽ) and Candrabindu (ँ) have not been considered while arranging the pādas and their presence does not alter the order of the pādas.

For Avagraha refer to Pāda No. 2196. For Candrabindu refer to Pāda No. 2446.

6. When the pādas are identical, precedence is given to the chapter and verse that occur earlier.

Refer to Pāda Nos. 786–789 and Nos. 905–908

7. Whenever a compound word (samastapada) has been broken down for the arrangement of the pādas, a hyphen (-) is introduced to indicate it either at the end or beginning of the pāda as the case may be.

For example refer to Pāda Nos 430 and 936.

2. This is not the same as the arrangment in dictionaries, which retain the anusvāra not only before the semi vowels, sibilants and aspirate but also often retain them even before a class consonant. This dictionary arrangement leads to difficulty in tracking down a word containing an anusvāra.

॥ भगवद्गीतापादानुक्रमणिका ॥

अ

1.	अकर्तारं स पश्यति	13.29.4
2.	अकर्मणश्च बोद्धव्यम्	4.17.3
3.	अकर्मणि च कर्म यः	4.18.2
4.	अकीर्तिकरमर्जुन	2.2.4
5.	अकीर्तिं चापि भूतानि	2.34.1
6.	अक्लेद्योऽशोष्य एव च	2.24.2
7.	अक्षरं ब्रह्म परमम्	8.3.1
8.	अक्षराणामकारोऽस्मि	10.33.1
9.	अक्षरादपि चोत्तमः	15.18.2
10.	अग्निर्ज्योतिरहः शुक्लः	8.24.1
11.	अघायुरिन्द्रियारामः	3.16.3
12.	अचरं चरमेव च	13.15.2
13.	अचलोऽयं सनातनः	2.24.4
14.	अचिरेणाधिगच्छति	4.39.4
15.	अच्छेद्योऽयमदाह्योऽयम्	2.24.1
16.	अजानता महिमानं तवेदम्	11.41.3
17.	अजो नित्यः शाश्वतोऽयं पुराणः	2.20.3
18.	अजोऽपि सन्नव्ययात्मा	4.6.1
19.	अज्ञश्चाश्रद्दधानश्च	4.40.1
20.	अज्ञानं चाभिजातस्य	16.4.3
21.	अज्ञानं तमसः फलम्	14.16.4

22.	अज्ञानं यदतोऽन्यथा	13.11.4
23.	अज्ञानां कर्मसङ्गिनाम्	3.26.2
24.	अज्ञानेनावृतं ज्ञानम्	5.15.3
25.	अणोरणीयांसमनुस्मरेद्यः	8.9.2
26.	अत ऊर्ध्वं न संशयः	12.8.4
27.	अतत्त्वार्थवदल्पं च	18.22.3
28.	अतीतो भवति प्रभो	14.21.2
29.	अतोऽस्मि लोके वेदे च	15.18.3
30.	अत्यन्तं सुखमश्नुते	6.28.4
31.	अत्येति तत्सर्वमिदं विदित्वा	8.28.3
32.	अत्र शूरा महेष्वासाः	1.4.1
33.	अथ केन प्रयुक्तोऽयम्	3.36.1
34.	अथ चित्तं समाधातुम्	12.9.1
35.	अथ चेत्त्वमहङ्कारात्	18.58.3
36.	अथ चेत्त्वमिमं धर्म्यम्	2.33.1
37.	अथ चैनं नित्यजातम्	2.26.1
38.	अथवा बहुनैतेन	10.42.1
39.	अथवा योगिनामेव	6.42.1
40.	अथ व्यवस्थितान्दृष्ट्वा	1.20.1
41.	अथैदप्यशक्तोऽसि	12.11.1
42.	अदृष्टपूर्वं हृषितोऽस्मि दृष्ट्वा	11.45.1
43.	अदेशकाले यद्दानम्	17.22.1
44.	अद्भुतं रोमहर्षणम्	18.74.4
45.	अद्रोहो नातिमानिता	16.3.2
46.	अद्वेष्टा सर्वभूतानाम्	12.13.1
47.	अधर्मं धर्ममिति या	18.32.1
48.	अधर्माभिभवात्कृष्ण	1.41.1

184.	अश्वत्थामा विकर्णश्च	1.8.3
185.	अश्विनौ मरुतस्तथा	11.6.2
186.	असक्तबुद्धिः सर्वत्र	18.49.1
187.	असक्तं तेषु कर्मसु	9.9.4
188.	असक्तं सर्वभृच्चैव	13.14.3
189.	असक्तः स विशिष्यते	3.7.4
190.	असक्तिरनभिष्वङ्गः	13.9.1
191.	असक्तो ह्याचरन्कर्म	3.19.3
192.	असङ्गशस्त्रेण दृढेन छित्त्वा	15.3.4
193.	असत्कृतमवज्ञातम्	17.22.3
194.	असत्यमप्रतिष्ठं ते	16.8.1
195.	असदित्युच्यते पार्थ	17.28.3
196.	असम्मूढः स मर्त्येषु	10.3.3
197.	असंयतात्मना योगः	6.36.1
198.	असंशयं महाबाहो	6.35.1
199.	असंशयं समग्रं माम्	7.1.3
200.	असितो देवलो व्यासः	10.13.3
201.	असौ मया हतः शत्रुः	16.14.1
202.	अस्माकं तु विशिष्टा ये	1.7.1
203.	अस्मिन् रणसमुद्यमे	1.22.4
204.	अस्याधिष्ठानमुच्यते	3.40.2
205.	अहङ्कार इतीयं मे	7.4.3
206.	अहङ्कारविमूढात्मा	3.27.3
207.	अहङ्कारं बलं दर्पम्	16.18.1
208.	अहङ्कारं बलं दर्पम्	18.53.1
209.	अहमग्निरहं हुतम्	9.16.4

210.	अहमज्ञानजं तमः	10.11.2
211.	अहमात्मा गुडाकेश	10.20.1
212.	अहमादिर्हि देवानाम्	10.2.3
213.	अहमादिश्च मध्यं च	10.20.3
214.	अहमेवंविधोऽर्जुन	11.54.2
215.	अहमेवाक्षयः कालः	10.33.3
216.	अहर्यद्ब्रह्मणो विदुः	8.17.2
217.	अहं कृत्स्नस्य जगतः	7.6.3
218.	अहं क्रतुरहं यज्ञः	9.16.1
219.	अहं त्वा सर्वपापेभ्यः	18.66.3
220.	अहं बीजप्रदः पिता	14.4.4
221.	अहं वैश्वानरो भूत्वा	15.14.1
222.	अहं स च मम प्रियः	7.17.4
223.	अहं सर्वस्य प्रभवः	10.8.1
224.	अहं हि सर्वयज्ञानाम्	9.24.1
225.	अहिंसा क्षान्तिरार्जवम्	13.7.2
226.	अहिंसा सत्यमक्रोधः	16.2.1
227.	अहिंसा समता तुष्टिः	10.5.1
228.	अहो बत महत्पापम्	1.45.1

आ

229.	आकाशं नोपलिप्यते	13.32.2
230.	आख्याहि मे को भवानुग्ररूपः	11.31.1
231.	आगमापायिनोऽनित्याः	2.14.3
232.	आचरत्यात्मनः श्रेयः	16.22.3

259.	आदित्यानामहं विष्णुः	10.21.1
260.	आदिदेवमजं विभुम्	10.12.4
261.	आद्यन्तवन्तः कौन्तेय	5.22.3
262.	आपूर्यमाणमचलप्रतिष्ठम्	2.70.1
263.	आब्रह्मभुवनाल्लोकाः	8.16.1
264.	आयुधानामहं वज्रम्	10.28.1
265.	आयुःसत्त्वबलारोग्य-	17.8.1
266.	आरुरुक्षोर्मुनेर्योगम्	6.3.1
267.	आर्तो जिज्ञासुरर्थार्थी	7.16.3
268.	आवृतं ज्ञानमेतेन	3.39.1
269.	आवृत्तिं चैव योगिनः	8.23.2
270.	आशापाशशतैर्बद्धाः	16.12.1
271.	आश्चर्यवच्चैनमन्यः शृणोति	2.29.3
272.	आश्चर्यवत्पश्यति कश्चिदेनम्	2.29.1
273.	आश्चर्यवद्वदति तथैव चान्यः	2.29.2
274.	आश्वासयामास च भीतमेनम्	11.50.3
275.	आसुरं पार्थ मे शृणु	16.6.4
276.	आसुरं भावमाश्रिताः	7.15.4
277.	आसुरीष्वेव योनिषु	16.19.4
278.	आसुरीं योनिमापन्नाः	16.20.1
279.	आस्थितः स हि युक्तात्मा	7.18.3
280.	आस्थिता जनकादयः	3.20.2
281.	आस्थितो योगधारणाम्	8.12.4
282.	आहारस्त्वपि सर्वस्य	17.7.1
283.	आहारा राजसस्येष्टाः	17.9.3
284.	आहाराः सात्त्विकप्रियाः	17.8.4
285.	आहुस्त्वामृषयः सर्वे	10.13.1

इ

ई

उ

ए

ऐ

ख

ग

626.	गन्धर्वयक्षासुरसिद्धसङ्घाः	11.22.3
627.	गन्धर्वाणां चित्ररथः	10.26.3
628.	गरीयसे ब्रह्मणोऽप्यादिकर्त्रे	11.37.2
629.	गहना कर्मणो गतिः	4.17.4
630.	गाण्डीवं स्रंसते हस्तात्	1.30.1
631.	गामाविश्य च भूतानि	15.13.1
632.	गायत्री छन्दसामहम्	10.35.2
633.	गिरामस्म्येकमक्षरम्	10.25.2
634.	गुडाकेशः परन्तप	2.9.2
635.	गुडाकेशेन भारत	1.24.2
636.	गुणकर्मविभागयोः	3.28.2
637.	गुणकर्मविभागशः	4.13.2
638.	गुणतस्त्रिविधं श्रृणु	18.29.2
639.	गुणप्रवृद्धा विषयप्रवालाः	15.2.2
640.	गुणा गुणेषु वर्तन्ते	3.28.3
641.	गुणातीतः स उच्यते	14.25.4
642.	गुणानेतानतीत्य त्रीन्	14.20.1
643.	गुणा वर्तन्त इत्येव	14.23.3
644.	गुणाः प्रकृतिसम्भवाः	14.5.2
645.	गुणेभ्यश्च परं वेत्ति	14.19.3
646.	गुणैर्यो न विचाल्यते	14.23.2
647.	गुणैः कर्माणि सर्वशः	3.27.2
648.	गुरुणापि विचाल्यते	6.22.4
649.	गुरूनहत्वा हि महानुभावान्	2.5.1
650.	गृहीत्वैतानि संयाति	15.8.3
651.	गुह्यमध्यात्मसंज्ञितम्	11.1.2
652.	गुह्याद्गुह्यतरं मया	18.63.2

672.	छिन्नाभ्रमिव नश्यति	6.38.2
673.	छेत्ता न ह्युपपद्यते	6.39.4
674.	छेत्तुमर्हस्यशेषतः	6.39.2

ज

675.	जगतः शाश्वते मते	8.26.2
676.	जगत्प्रहृष्यत्यनुरज्यते च	11.36.2
677.	जगदव्यक्तमूर्तिना	9.4.2
678.	जगदाहुरनीश्वरम्	16.8.2
679.	जगद्भासयतेऽखिलम्	15.12.2
680.	जगद्विपरिवर्तते	9.10.4
681.	जघन्यगुणवृत्तिस्थाः	14.18.3
682.	जना न विदुरासुराः	16.7.2
683.	जनानां पुण्यकर्मणाम्	7.28.2
684.	जनाः सुकृतिनोऽर्जुन	7.16.2
685.	जन्मकर्म च मे दिव्यम्	4.9.1
686.	जन्मकर्मफलप्रदाम्	2.43.2
687.	जन्मबन्धविनिर्मुक्ताः	2.51.3
688.	जन्ममृत्युजरादुःखैः	14.20.3
689.	जन्ममृत्युजराव्याधि-	13.8.3
690.	जन्मानि तव चार्जुन	4.5.2
691.	जयोऽस्मि व्यवसायोऽस्मि	10.36.3
692.	जरामरणमोक्षाय	7.29.1
693.	जहि शत्रुं महाबाहो	3.43.3
694.	जाग्रतो नैव चार्जुन	6.16.4

722.	ज्ञानयोगव्यवस्थितिः	16.1.2
723.	ज्ञानयोगेन साङ्ख्यानाम्	3.3.3
724.	ज्ञानवान्मां प्रपद्यते	7.19.2
725.	ज्ञानविज्ञानतृप्तात्मा	6.8.1
726.	ज्ञानविज्ञाननाशनम्	3.41.4
727.	ज्ञानसङ्गेन चानघ	14.6.4
728.	ज्ञानसञ्छिन्नसंशयम्	4.41.2
729.	ज्ञानं कर्म च कर्ता च	18.19.1
730.	ज्ञानं ज्ञानवतामहम्	10.38.4
731.	ज्ञानं ज्ञेयं ज्ञानगम्यम्	13.17.3
732.	ज्ञानं ज्ञेयं परिज्ञाता	18.18.1
733.	ज्ञानं तेऽहं सविज्ञानम्	7.2.1
734.	ज्ञानं यदा तदा विद्यात्	14.11.3
735.	ज्ञानं लब्ध्वा परां शान्तिम्	4.39.3
736.	ज्ञानं विज्ञानमास्तिक्यम्	18.42.3
737.	ज्ञानं विज्ञानसहितम्	9.1.3
738.	ज्ञानाग्निदग्धकर्माणम्	4.19.3
739.	ज्ञानाग्निः सर्वकर्माणि	4.37.3
740.	ज्ञानाद्ध्यानं विशिष्यते	12.12.2
741.	ज्ञानानां ज्ञानमुत्तमम्	14.1.2
742.	ज्ञानावस्थितचेतसः	4.23.2
743.	ज्ञानिनस्तत्त्वदर्शिनः	4.34.4
744.	ज्ञानिनो नित्यवैरिणा	3.39.2
745.	ज्ञानिभ्योऽपि मतोऽधिकः	6.46.2
746.	ज्ञानी च भरतर्षभ	7.16.4
747.	ज्ञानी त्वात्मैव मे मतम्	7.18.2
748.	ज्ञानेन तु तदज्ञानम्	5.16.1

749.	ज्ञाने परिसमाप्यते	4.33.4
750.	ज्ञेयं चोक्तं समासतः	13.18.2
751.	ज्ञेयं यत्तत्प्रवक्ष्यामि	13.12.1
752.	ज्ञेयः स नित्यसंन्यासी	5.3.1
753.	ज्ञेयोऽसि नियतात्मभिः	8.2.4
754.	ज्यायसी चेत्कर्मणस्ते	3.1.1
755.	ज्योतिषामपि तज्ज्योतिः	13.17.1
756.	ज्योतिषां रविरंशुमान्	10.21.2

झ

757.	झषाणां मकरश्चास्मि	10.31.3

त

758.	त इमेऽवस्थिता युद्धे	1.33.3
759.	तच्च संस्मृत्य संस्मृत्य	18.77.1
760.	तज्ज्ञानं विद्धि राजसम्	18.21.4
761.	तज्ज्ञानं विद्धि सात्त्विकम्	18.20.4
762.	तत एव च विस्तारम्	13.30.3
763.	ततस्ततो नियम्यैतत्	6.26.3
764.	ततः कुरु यतात्मवान्	12.11.4
765.	ततः पदं तत्परिमार्गितव्यम्	15.4.1
766.	ततः शङ्खाश्च भेर्यश्च	1.13.1
767.	ततः श्वेतैर्हयैर्युक्ते	1.14.1
768.	ततः स विस्मयाविष्टः	11.14.1

796.	तत्त्वेनातश्च्यवन्ति ते	9.24.4
797.	तत्परः संयतेन्द्रियः	4.39.2
798.	तत्प्रसादात्परां शान्तिम्	18.62.3
799.	तत्र का परिदेवना	2.28.4
800.	तत्र चान्द्रमसं ज्योतिः	8.25.3
801.	तत्र तं बुद्धिसंयोगम्	6.43.1
802.	तत्र प्रयाता गच्छन्ति	8.24.3
803.	तत्र श्रीर्विजयो भूतिः	18.78.3
804.	तत्र सत्त्वं निर्मलत्वात्	14.6.1
805.	तत्रापश्यत् स्थितान् पार्थः	1.26.1
806.	तत्रैकस्थं जगत्कृत्स्नम्	11.13.1
807.	तत्रैकाग्रं मनः कृत्वा	6.12.1
808.	तत्रैवं सति कर्तारम्	18.16.1
809.	तत्रैवाव्यक्तसंज्ञके	8.18.4
810.	तत्समासेन मे शृणु	13.3.4
811.	तत्सुखं राजसं स्मृतम्	18.38.4
812.	तत्सुखं सात्त्विकं प्रोक्तम्	18.37.3
813.	तत्स्वयं योगसंसिद्धः	4.38.3
814.	तथा तवामी नरलोकवीराः	11.28.3
815.	तथा तेनेदमावृतम्	3.38.4
816.	तथात्मा नोपलिप्यते	13.32.4
817.	तथा देहान्तरप्राप्तिः	2.13.3
818.	तथान्तर्ज्योतिरेव यः	5.24.2
819.	तथापि त्वं महाबाहो	2.26.3
820.	तथाप्नोति निबोध मे	18.50.2
821.	तथा प्रलीनस्तमसि	14.15.3
822.	तथा मानापमानयोः	6.7.4

ध

ब

1667.	भक्तिरव्यभिचारिणी	13.10.2
1668.	भक्तिं मयि परां कृत्वा	18.68.3
1669.	भक्तोऽसि मे सखा चेति	4.3.3
1670.	भक्त्या त्वनन्यया शक्यः	11.54.1
1671.	भक्त्या मामभिजानाति	18.55.1
1672.	भक्त्या युक्तो योगबलेन चैव	8.10.2
1673.	भक्त्या लभ्यस्त्वनन्यया	8.22.2
1674.	भजतां प्रीतिपूर्वकम्	10.10.2
1675.	भजते मामनन्यभाक्	9.30.2
1676.	भजत्येकत्वमास्थितः	6.31.2
1677.	भजन्ते मां दृढव्रताः	7.28.4
1678.	भजन्त्यनन्यमनसः	9.13.3
1679.	भयं चाभयमेव च	10.4.4
1680.	भयाद्रणादुपरतम्	2.35.1
1681.	भयेन च प्रव्यथितं मनो मे	11.45.2
1682.	भर्ता भोक्ता महेश्वरः	13.22.2
1683.	भवतीत्यनुशुश्रुम	1.44.4
1684.	भवतोऽज्ञानमेव च	14.17.4
1685.	भवत्यत्यागिनां प्रेत्य	18.12.3
1686.	भवन्तः सर्व एव हि	1.11.4
1687.	भवन्ति भावा भूतानाम्	10.5.3
1688.	भवन्ति सम्पदं दैवीम्	16.3.3
1689.	भवान्भीष्मश्च कर्णश्च	1.8.1
1690.	भवाप्ययौ हि भूतानाम्	11.2.1
1691.	भवामि नचिरात्पार्थ	12.7.3
1692.	भविता न च मे तस्मात्	18.69.3
1693.	भविष्यति पुनर्धनम्	16.13.4

म

1931.	यच्छोकमुच्छोषणमिन्द्रियाणाम्	2.8.2
1932.	यच्छ्रेय एतयोरेकम्	5.1.3
1933.	यच्छ्रेयः स्यान्निश्चितं ब्रूहि तन्मे	2.7.3
1934.	यजन्त इह देवताः	4.12.2
1935.	यजन्ते तामसा जनाः	17.4.4
1936.	यजन्ते नामयज्ञैस्ते	16.17.3
1937.	यजन्ते श्रद्धयान्विताः	9.23.2
1938.	यजन्ते श्रद्धयान्विताः	17.1.2
1939.	यजन्ते सात्त्विका देवान्	17.4.1
1940.	यजन्तो मामुपासते	9.15.2
1941.	यजन्त्यविधिपूर्वकम्	9.23.4
1942.	यज्जुहोषि ददासि यत्	9.27.2
1943.	यज्ज्ञात्वा न पुनर्मोहम्	4.35.1
1944.	यज्ज्ञात्वा नेह भूयोऽन्यत्	7.2.3
1945.	यज्ज्ञात्वा मुनयः सर्वे	14.1.3
1946.	यज्ज्ञात्वामृतमश्नुते	13.12.2
1947.	यज्ज्ञात्वा मोक्ष्यसेऽशुभात्	4.16.4
1948.	यज्ज्ञात्वा मोक्ष्यसेऽशुभात्	9.1.4
1949.	यज्ञक्षपितकल्मषाः	4.30.4
1950.	यज्ञदानतपःकर्म	18.3.3
1951.	यज्ञदानतपःकर्म	18.5.1
1952.	यज्ञदानतपःक्रियाः	17.24.2
1953.	यज्ञशिष्टामृतभुजः	4.31.1
1954.	यज्ञशिष्टाशिनः सन्तः	3.13.1
1955.	यज्ञस्तपस्तथा दानम्	17.7.3
1956.	यज्ञः कर्मसमुद्भवः	3.14.4
1957.	यज्ञाद्भवति पर्जन्यः	3.14.3

ल

व

2691. सिद्ध्यसिद्ध्योः समो भूत्वा 2.48.3
2692. सिंहनादं विनद्योच्चैः 1.12.3
2693. सीदन्ति मम गात्राणि 1.29.1
2694. सुखदुःखे समे कृत्वा 2.38.1
2695. -सुखप्रीतिविवर्धनाः 17.8.2
2696. सुखमक्षयमश्नुते 5.21.4
2697. सुखमात्यन्तिकं यत्तत् 6.21.1
2698. सुखसङ्गेन बध्नाति 14.6.3
2699. सुखस्यैकान्तिकस्य च 14.27.4
2700. सुखं त्विदानीं त्रिविधम् 18.36.1
2701. सुखं दुःखं भवोऽभावः 10.4.3
2702. सुखं बन्धात्प्रमुच्यते 5.3.4
2703. सुखं मोहनमात्मनः 18.39.2
2704. सुखं वा यदि वा दुःखम् 6.32.3
2705. सुखिनः क्षत्रियाः पार्थ 2.32.3
2706. सुखिनः स्याम माधव 1.37.4
2707. सुखेन ब्रह्मसंस्पर्शम् 6.28.3
2708. सुखेषु विगतस्पृहः 2.56.2
2709. सुघोषमणिपुष्पकौ 1.16.4
2710. सुदुर्दर्शमिदं रूपम् 11.52.1
2711. सुसुखं कर्तुमव्ययम् 9.2.4
2712. सुहृदं सर्वभूतानाम् 5.29.3
2713. सुहृन्मित्रार्युदासीन- 6.9.1
2714. सूक्ष्मत्वात्तदविज्ञेयम् 13.15.3
2715. सूत्रे मणिगणा इव 7.7.4
2716. सूयते सचराचरम् 9.10.2

2770.	स्वाध्यायज्ञानयज्ञाश्च	4.28.3
2771.	स्वाध्यायस्तप आर्जवम्	16.1.4
2772.	स्वाध्यायाभ्यसनं चैव	17.15.3
2773.	स्वे स्वे कर्मण्यभिरतः	18.45.1

ह

2774.	हतो वा प्राप्स्यसि स्वर्गम्	2.37.1
2775.	हत्वापि स इमाँल्लोकान्	18.17.3
2776.	हत्वार्थकामांस्तु गुरूनिहैव	2.5.3
2777.	हत्वा स्वजनमाहवे	1.31.4
2778.	हत्वैतानाततायिनः	1.36.4
2779.	हनिष्ये चापरानपि	16.14.2
2780.	हन्त ते कथयिष्यामि	10.19.1
2781.	हन्तुं स्वजनमुद्यताः	1.45.4
2782.	हरन्ति प्रसभं मनः	2.60.4
2783.	हर्षशोकान्वितः कर्ता	18.27.3
2784.	हर्षामर्षभयोद्वेगैः	12.15.3
2785.	हानिरस्योपजायते	2.65.2
2786.	हित्वा पापमवाप्स्यसि	2.33.4
2787.	हृत्स्थं ज्ञानासिनात्मनः	4.42.2
2788.	हृदयानि व्यदारयत्	1.19.2
2789.	हृदि सर्वस्य विष्ठितम्	13.17.4
2790.	हृद्देशेऽर्जुन तिष्ठति	18.61.2
2791.	हृषीकेशं तदा वाक्यम्	1.21.1
2792.	हृष्टरोमा धनञ्जयः	11.14.2
2793.	हृष्यामि च पुनः पुनः	18.77.4

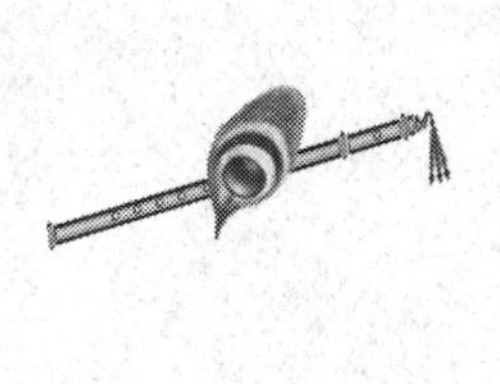

Bhagavad Gītā
Aṣṭottaraśata Nāmāvalī

108 Worshipful Glories of the Bhagavad Gītā
Composed by Pujya Swami Tejomayananda

Bhagavad Gītā Aṣṭottaraśata Nāmāvalī

1. ॐ श्रीमद्भगवद्गीतायै नमः ॥
Om śrīmadbhagavadgītāyai namaḥ.
Salutations unto Śrīmad Bhagavad Gītā.

2. ॐ श्रीकृष्णामृतवाण्यै नमः ॥
Om śrīkṛṣṇāmṛta-vāṇyai namaḥ.
Salutations unto the nectarine words of Śrī Kṛṣṇa.

3. ॐ पार्थाय प्रतिबोधितायै नमः ॥
Om pārthāya pratibodhitāyai namaḥ.
Salutations unto the Gītā imparted to Arjuna.

4. ॐ व्यासेन ग्रथितायै नमः ॥
Om vyāsena grathitāyai namaḥ.
Salutations unto the Gītā composed by Sage Vyāsa.

5. ॐ सञ्जयवर्णितायै नमः ॥
Om sañjaya-varṇitāyai namaḥ.
Salutations unto the Gītā narrated by Śrī Sañjaya.

6. ॐ महाभारतमध्यस्थितायै नमः ॥
Om mahābhārata-madhya-sthitāyai namaḥ.
Salutations unto the Gītā occupying the central place in the Mahābhārata.

7. ॐ कुरुक्षेत्रे उपदिष्टायै नमः ॥
Om kurukṣetre upadiṣṭāyai namaḥ.
Salutations unto the Gītā taught in Kurukṣetra.

8. ॐ भगवत्यै नमः ॥
Om bhagavatyai namaḥ.
Salutations unto Goddess Bhagavad Gītā.

9. ॐ अम्बारूपायै नमः
Om ambā-rūpāyai namaḥ.
Salutations unto Gītā the Mother.

10. ॐ अद्वैतामृतवर्षिण्यै नमः ॥

Om advaitāmṛta-varṣiṇyai namaḥ.

Salutations unto Gītā who showers the nectar of Advaita (non-duality).

11. ॐ भवद्वेषिण्यै नमः ॥

Om bhavadveṣiṇyai namaḥ.

Salutations unto the Ultimate Antidote to saṁsāra (sorrows of the world).

12. ॐ अष्टादशाध्याय्यै नमः ॥

Om aṣṭādaśādhyāyyai namaḥ.

Salutations unto the Gītā of Eighteen Chapters.

13. ॐ सर्वोपनिषत्सारायै नमः ॥

Om sarvopaniṣat-sārāyai namaḥ.

Salutations unto the Essence of all the Upaniṣads.

14. ॐ ब्रह्मविद्यायै नमः ॥

Om brahma-vidyāyai namaḥ.

Salutations unto Brahma Vidyā (Self-Knowledge).

15. ॐ योगशास्त्ररूपायै नमः ॥

Om yoga-śāstra-rūpāyai namaḥ.

Salutations unto the Gītā in the form of Yoga Śāstra (the practical means of yoking oneself to the Supreme Self).

16. ॐ श्रीकृष्णार्जुनसंवादरूपायै नमः ॥

Om śrīkṛṣṇārjuna-saṁvāda-rūpāyai namaḥ.

Salutations unto the Gītā who is in the form of a reverential dialogue between Lord Kṛṣṇa and Arjuna.

17. ॐ श्रीकृष्णहृदयायै नमः ॥

Om śrīkṛṣṇa-hṛdayāyai namaḥ.

Salutations unto the Gītā who is the very Heart of Lord Kṛṣṇa.

18. ॐ सुन्दर्यै नमः ॥

Om sundaryai namaḥ.

Salutations unto the Beautiful One.

19. ॐ मधुरायै नमः ॥
Om madhurāyai namaḥ.
Salutations unto the Gītā who is all sweetness.

20. ॐ पुनीतायै नमः ॥
Om punītāyai namaḥ.
Salutations unto the Sacred One.

21. ॐ कर्ममर्मप्रकाशिन्यै नमः ॥
Om karma-marma-prakāśinyai namaḥ.
Salutations unto the Gītā who reveals the secret of action.

22. ॐ कामासक्तिहरायै नमः ॥
Om kāmāsakti-harāyai namaḥ.
Salutations unto the One who destroys all attachments and desires.

23. ॐ तत्त्वज्ञानप्रकाशिन्यै नमः ॥
Om tattva-jñāna-prakāśinyai namaḥ.
Salutations unto Her who reveals the Knowledge of the Truth.

24. ॐ निश्चलभक्तिविधायिन्यै नमः ॥
Om niścala-bhakti-vidhāyinyai namaḥ.
Salutations unto the Gītā who confers unwavering devotion.

25. ॐ निर्मलायै नमः ॥
Om nirmalāyai namaḥ.
Salutations unto the Untainted One.

26. ॐ कलिमलहारिण्यै नमः ॥
Om kalimala-hāriṇyai namaḥ.
Salutations unto the Gītā who destroys the impurities of the Kali Age.

27. ॐ रागद्वेषविदारिण्यै नमः ॥
Om rāga-dveṣa-vidāriṇyai namaḥ.
Salutations unto the One who cuts asunder our likes and dislikes.

28. ॐ मोदकारिण्यै नमः ॥

Om moda-kāriṇyai namaḥ.
Salutations unto the Source of Joy.

29. ॐ भवभयहारिण्यै नमः ॥
Om bhava-bhaya-hāriṇyai namaḥ.
Salutations unto the Gītā who removes the fear of saṁsāra or 'becoming'.

30. ॐ तारिण्यै नमः ॥
Om tāriṇyai namaḥ.
Salutations unto Her who takes us across (the ocean of transmigration).

31. ॐ परमानन्दप्रदायै नमः ॥
Om paramānanda-pradāyai namaḥ.
Salutations unto the Bestower of Supreme Bliss.

32. ॐ अज्ञाननाशिन्यै नमः ॥
Om ajñāna-nāśinyai namaḥ.
Salutations unto the Dispeller of ignorance (of the Self).

33. ॐ आसुरभावविनाशिन्यै नमः ॥
Om āsura-bhāva-vināśinyai namaḥ.
Salutations unto the Gītā who eliminates (our) base tendencies.

34. ॐ दैवीसम्पत्प्रदायै नमः ॥
Om daivī-sampat-pradāyai namaḥ.
Salutations unto the One who blesses (us) with divine virtues.

35. ॐ हरिभक्तप्रियायै नमः ॥
Om hari-bhakta-priyāyai namaḥ.
Salutations unto the Beloved of the devotees of Lord Hari.

36. ॐ सर्वशास्त्रस्वामिन्यै नमः ॥
Om sarva-śāstra-svāminyai namaḥ.
Salutations unto the Queen of all Scriptures.

37. ॐ दयासुधावर्षिण्यै नमः ॥
Om dayā-sudhā-varṣiṇyai namaḥ.

Salutations unto the Gītā who showers the nectar of compassion.

38. ॐ हरिपदप्रेमदायिन्यै नमः ॥
Om hari-pada-prema-dāyinyai namaḥ.
Salutations unto the One who endows (us) with love for the Lotus Feet of Lord Hari.

39. ॐ श्रीप्रदायै नमः ॥
Om śrīpradāyai namaḥ.
Salutations unto the Bestower of (the highest) wealth.

40. ॐ विजयप्रदायै नमः ॥
Om vijaya-pradāyai namaḥ.
Salutations unto Her who grants victory.

41. ॐ भूतिदायै नमः ॥
Om bhūtidāyai namaḥ.
Salutations unto the Bestower of all well-being.

42. ॐ नीतिदायै नमः ॥
Om nītidāyai namaḥ.
Salutations unto the One who lays down the guidelines (for right living).

43. ॐ सनातन्यै नमः ॥
Om sanātanyai namaḥ.
Salutations unto the Eternal One.

44. ॐ सर्वधर्मस्वरूपिण्यै नमः ॥
Om sarva-dharma-svarūpiṇyai namaḥ.
Salutations unto the Embodiment of all dharma (righteousness).

45. ॐ समस्तसिद्धिदायै नमः ॥
Om samasta-siddhidāyai namaḥ.
Salutations unto Her who grants (us) all siddhis (accomplishments).

46. ॐ सन्मार्गदर्शिकायै नमः ॥
Om sanmārga-darśikāyai namaḥ.

Salutations unto the One who illumines the path of goodness.

47. ॐ त्रिलोकीपूज्यायै नमः ॥

Om trilokī-pūjyāyai namaḥ.

Salutations unto the Gītā who is worshipped in all the three worlds.

48. ॐ अर्जुनविषादहारिण्यै नमः ॥

Om arjuna-viṣāda-hāriṇyai namaḥ.

Salutations unto Her who quelled Arjuna's anguish.

49. ॐ प्रसादप्रदायै नमः ॥

Om prasāda-pradāyai namaḥ.

Salutations unto the Bestower of blessings.

50. ॐ नित्यात्मस्वरूपदर्शिकायै नमः ॥

Om nityātma-svarūpa-darśikāyai namaḥ.

Salutations unto the Gītā who reveals to us our Eternal Nature.

51. ॐ अनित्यदेहसंसाररूपदर्शिकायै नमः ॥

Om anitya-deha-saṁsāra-rūpa-darśikāyai namaḥ.

Salutations unto Her who reveals (to us) the ephemeral nature of the body and the world.

52. ॐ पुनर्जन्मरहस्यप्रकटिकायै नमः ॥

Om punar-janma-rahasya-prakaṭikāyai namaḥ.

Salutations unto the One who reveals the secret of transmigration (to help us go beyond it).

53. ॐ स्वधर्मप्रबोधिन्यै नमः ॥

Om svadharma-prabodhinyai namaḥ.

Salutations unto Her who grants the knowledge of svadharma (our duties).

54. ॐ स्थितप्रज्ञलक्षणदर्शिकायै नमः ॥

Om sthita-prajña-lakṣaṇa-darśikāyai namaḥ.

Salutations unto the Gītā who reveals the 'sthitaprajñalakṣaṇa' (the qualities of the Realised One).

55. ॐ कर्मयोगप्रकाशिकायै नमः ॥
Om karma-yoga-prakāśikāyai namaḥ.
Salutations unto Her who reveals Karma Yoga (the Yoga of Action).

56. ॐ यज्ञभावनाप्रकाशिन्यै नमः ॥
Om yajña-bhāvanā-prakāśinyai namaḥ.
Salutations unto Her who reveals the spirit of sacrifice and worship.

57. ॐ विविधयज्ञप्रदर्शिकायै नमः ॥
Om vividha-yajña-pradarśikāyai namaḥ.
Salutations unto the One who instructs us on different kinds of spiritual practices.

58. ॐ चित्तशुद्धिदायै नमः ॥
Om citta-śuddhi-dāyai namaḥ.
Salutations unto the Bestower of purity of mind.

59. ॐ कामनाशोपायबोधिकायै नमः ॥
Om kāma-nāśopāya-bodhikāyai namaḥ.
Salutations unto the Gītā who teaches the means to eliminate desire.

60. ॐ अवतारतत्त्वविचारिण्यै नमः ॥
Om avatāra-tattva-vicāriṇyai namaḥ.
Salutations unto Her who expounds the principle of incarnation.

61. ॐ ज्ञानप्राप्तिसाधनोपदेशिकायै नमः ॥
Om jñāna-prāpti-sādhanopadeśikāyai namaḥ.
Salutations unto the Gītā who instructs (us) about the means to Knowledge.

62. ॐ ध्यानयोगबोधिन्यै नमः ॥
Om dhyāna-yoga-bodhinyai namaḥ.
Salutations unto the Teacher of Dhyāna Yoga (the Yoga of Meditation).

63. ॐ मनोनिग्रहमार्गप्रदीपिकायै नमः ॥
Om mano-nigraha-mārga-pradīpikāyai namaḥ.
Salutations unto Her who illumines the path of mastery to the mind.

64. ॐ सर्वविधसाधकहितकारिण्यै नमः ॥
Om sarva-vidha-sādhaka-hita-kāriṇyai namaḥ.
Salutations unto the One who promotes the seeker's well-being in all ways.

65. ॐ ज्ञानविज्ञानप्रकाशिकायै नमः ॥
Om jñāna-vijñāna-prakāśikāyai namaḥ.
Salutations unto the Preceptor of Jñāna (Knowledge) and Vijñāna (Wisdom).

66. ॐ परापरप्रकृतिबोधिकायै नमः ॥
Om parāpara-prakṛti-bodhikāyai namaḥ.
Salutations unto the Teacher of the higher (sentient) and lower (insentient) aspects of the Lord.

67. ॐ सृष्टिरहस्यप्रकटिकायै नमः ॥
Om sṛṣṭi-rahasya-prakaṭikāyai namaḥ.
Salutations unto the Gītā who unearths the secret of creation.

68. ॐ चतुर्विधभक्तलक्षणदर्शिकायै नमः ॥
Om caturvidha-bhakta-lakṣaṇa-darśikāyai namaḥ.
Salutations unto the One who extols the qualities of the four kinds of devotees.

69. ॐ भुक्तिमुक्तिदायै नमः ॥
Om bhukti-muktidāyai namaḥ.
Salutations unto the Bestower of material prosperity and Liberation.

70. ॐ जीवजगदीश्वरस्वरूपबोधिकायै नमः ॥
Om jīva-jagad-īśvara-svarūpa-bodhikāyai namaḥ.
Salutations unto the Preceptor of the true Nature of the individual, the world and God.

71. ॐ प्रणवध्यानोपदेशिकायै नमः ॥
Om praṇava-dhyānopadeśikāyai namaḥ.
Salutations unto the One who initiates (us) into meditation on Omkāra.

72. ॐ कर्मोपासनफलदर्शिकायै नमः ॥
Om karmopāsana-phala-darśikāyai namaḥ.
Salutations unto the Gītā who reveals the result of work and worship.

73. ॐ राजविद्यायै नमः ॥
Om rājavidyāyai namaḥ.
Salutations unto the Regal Knowledge.

74. ॐ राजगुह्यायै नमः ॥
Om rājaguhyāyai namaḥ.
Salutations unto the Grand Secret (of Self-Knowledge).

75. ॐ प्रत्यक्षावगमायै नमः ॥
Om pratyakṣāvagamāyai namaḥ.
Salutations unto the One who is known through direct experience.

76. ॐ धर्म्यायै नमः ॥
Om dharmyāyai namaḥ.
Salutations unto Righteousness personified.

77. ॐ सुलभायै नमः ॥
Om sulabhāyai namaḥ.
Salutations unto the One who is easily attained (by the pure of heart).

78. ॐ योगक्षेमकारिण्यै नमः ॥
Om yoga-kṣema-kāriṇyai namaḥ.
Salutations unto the Source of (our) yoga (acquisitions) and kṣema (preservation).

79. ॐ भगवद्विभूतिविस्तारिकायै नमः ॥
Om bhagavadvibhūti-vistārikāyai namaḥ.

Salutations unto the One who 'word-paints' the glories of the Lord.

80. ॐ विश्वरूपदर्शनयोगयुक्तायै नमः ॥
Om viśvarūpa-darśana-yoga-yuktāyai namaḥ.
Salutations unto the Gītā who is the One who reveals the vision of the Divine Cosmic Form.

81. ॐ भगवदैश्वर्यप्रदर्शिकायै नमः ॥
Om bhagavad-aiśvarya-pradarśikāyai namaḥ.
Salutations unto the One who unveils the Sovereignty of the Lord.

82. ॐ भक्तिदायै नमः ॥
Om bhaktidāyai namaḥ.
Salutations unto Her who endows (us) with devotion.

83. ॐ भक्तिविवर्धिन्यै नमः ॥
Om bhakti-vivardhinyai namaḥ.
Salutations unto the One who increases devotion manifold.

84. ॐ भक्तलक्षणबोधिकायै नमः ॥
Om bhakta-lakṣaṇa-bodhikāyai namaḥ.
Salutations unto the Gītā who highlights the qualities of devotees.

85. ॐ सगुणनिर्गुणप्रकाशिन्यै नमः ॥
Om saguṇa-nirguṇa-prakāśinyai namaḥ.
Salutations unto Her who reveals the twofold aspect of the Lord – with attributes and beyond attributes.

86. ॐ क्षेत्रक्षेत्रज्ञविवेककारिण्यै नमः ॥
Om kṣetra-kṣetrajña-viveka-kāriṇyai namaḥ.
Salutations unto the One who grants us the power to discriminate between the 'field' and the 'Knower of the field'.

87. ॐ दृढवैराग्यकारिण्यै नमः ॥
Om dṛḍha-vairāgya-kāriṇyai namaḥ.
Salutations unto Her who grants us firm dispassion.

88. ॐ गुणत्रयविभागदर्शिकायै नमः ॥
Om guṇatraya-vibhāga-darśikāyai namaḥ.
Salutations unto the Gītā who reveals the differentiation of the three guṇas of Prakṛti (sattva, rajas and tamas).

89. ॐ गुणातीतपुरुषलक्षणदर्शिकायै नमः ॥
Om guṇātīta-puruṣa-lakṣaṇa-darśikāyai namaḥ.
Salutations unto the Gītā who reveals the qualities of the One who has transcended the three *guṇas.*

90. ॐ अश्वत्थवृक्षवर्णनकारिण्यै नमः ॥
Om aśvattha-vṛkṣa-varṇana-kāriṇyai namaḥ.
Salutations unto Her who delineates the 'tree of saṁsāra'.

91. ॐ संसारवृक्षच्छेदनोपायबोधिन्यै नमः ॥
Om saṁsāra-vṛkṣac-chedanopāya-bodhinyai namaḥ.
Salutations unto the One who imparts the technique to axe down the 'tree of saṁsāra'.

92. ॐ त्रिविधश्रद्धास्वरूपप्रकाशिकायै नमः ॥
Om trividha-śraddhā-svarūpa-prakāśikāyai namaḥ.
Salutations unto the Gītā who highlights the nature of the three kinds of faith.

93. ॐ त्यागसंन्यासतत्त्वदर्शिकायै नमः ॥
Om tyāga-saṁnyāsa-tattva-darśikāyai namaḥ.
Salutations unto the One who reveals the essence of sacrifice and renunciation.

94. ॐ यज्ञदानतपःस्वरूपबोधिन्यै नमः ॥
Om yajña-dāna-tapaḥ-svarūpa-bodhinyai namaḥ.
Salutations unto Her who instructs (us) about the nature of worship, charity and austerity.

95. ॐ ज्ञानकर्मकर्तृस्वरूपबोधिकायै नमः ॥
Om jñāna-karma-kartṛ-svarūpa-bodhikāyai namaḥ.
Salutations unto the One who conveys the true nature of Knowledge, action and the doer.

96. ॐ शरणागतिरहस्यप्रदर्शिकायै नमः ॥
Om śaraṇāgati-rahasya-pradarśikāyai namaḥ.
Salutations unto Her who transmits to us the secret of total surrender.

97. ॐ आश्चर्यरूपायै नमः ॥
Om āścarya-rūpāyai namaḥ.
Salutations unto the Wondrous One.

98. ॐ विस्मयकारिण्यै नमः ॥
Om vismaya-kāriṇyai namaḥ.
Salutations unto the Gītā who evokes wonder (in us).

99. ॐ आह्लादकारिण्यै नमः ॥
Om āhlāda-kāriṇyai namaḥ.
Salutations unto the One who inspires (in us) divine ecstasy.

100. ॐ भक्तिहीनजनागम्यायै नमः ॥
Om bhakti-hīna-janāgamyāyai namaḥ.
Salutations unto Her who is incomprehensible to those who lack devotion.

101. ॐ जगत उद्धारिण्यै नमः ॥
Om jagata uddhāriṇyai namaḥ.
Salutations unto the Saviour of the world.

102. ॐ दिव्यदृष्टिप्रदायै नमः ॥
Om divya-dṛṣṭi-pradāyai namaḥ.
Salutations unto the One who confers (upon us) the Divine Vision.

103. ॐ धर्मसंस्थापिकायै नमः ॥
Om dharma-saṁsthāpikāyai namaḥ.
Salutations unto the One who establishes *dharma* (righteousness).

104. ॐ भक्तजनसेव्यायै नमः ॥
Om bhakta-jana-sevyāyai namaḥ.
Salutations unto Her who is served by the devoted.

105. ॐ सर्वदेवस्तुतायै नमः ॥

Om sarva-deva-stutāyai namaḥ.

Salutations unto the Gītā whose is extolled by all the celestial beings.

106. ॐ ज्ञानगङ्गायै नमः ॥

Om jñāna-gaṅgāyai namaḥ.

Salutations unto Her who is jñāna-gaṅgā – the perennial flow of the highest wisdom.

107. ॐ श्रीकृष्णप्रियतमायै नमः ॥

Om śrīkṛṣṇa-priyatamāyai namaḥ.

Salutations unto the most Beloved of Lord Kṛṣṇa.

108. ॐ सर्वमङ्गलायै नमः ॥

Om sarva-maṅgalāyai namaḥ.

Salutations unto the Gītā who is all auspiciousness.

Om Tat Sat

Index of Terms and Definitions

Chapter 1 - Arjunaviṣāda Yoga

1. Who is a 'Mahāratha'? (pg. 13)
2. How does Duryodhana address his teacher? (pg. 13)
3. What are the two ways of interpreting the term 'Hṛṣīkeśa'? (pg. 13)
4. What does the word 'Pārtha' mean? (pg. 13)
5. Who is an 'Ātatāyin'? (pg.14)
6. What is 'kula-dharma' (family-dharma)? (pg.14)
7. The word 'Dharma' is derived from the Sanskrit root ____________ which means to ________. (pg.14)
8. What is the meaning of the word 'Upaniṣad'? (pg.14)
9. Define the term 'Yoga Śāstra'. (pg.14)
10. Upaniṣads teach _________. (pg.14)

Chapter 2 - Sāṅkhya Yoga

1. What does the word 'Madhusūdana' mean? (pg.25)
2. If a warrior dies fighting in battle for a righteous cause, he is said to reach _______ svarga. (pg.25)
3. What does the term 'Guḍākeśa' mean? (pg.25)
4. What does the appellation 'Govinda' mean? (pg.25)
5. Define 'unreal'. (pg.25)
6. Define 'Real'. (pg.26)
7. Enumerate the six changes common to all beings. (pg.26)
8. Differentiate between 'manifest' and 'unmanifest'. (pg.26)
9. What is the meaning of the word 'Mahābāhu'? (pg.26)
10. What are the three 'pairs of opposites'? (pg.26)
11. Define 'pratyavāya'. (pg.26)
12. What is the meaning of the word 'Kurunandana'? (pg.26)
13. What is 'śravaṇa', 'manana' and 'nididhyāsana'? (pg.26)
14. Define 'yoga' and 'kṣema'. (pg.26)
15. What is meant by 'Buddhi Yoga'? (pg.27)
16. Who is a 'buddhi-yuktaḥ'? (pg.27)

17. What are the two definitions of Yoga given by Śrī Kṛṣṇa in the second chapter? (pg.27)
18. What are the two expressions of māyā? (pg.27)
19. What does the term 'sthitaprajña' mean? (pg.28)
20. The nature of 'sthitaprajña' is described from verse _____ to verse _____ in the second chapter of the Bhagavad Gītā. (pg.28)
21. What are the three types of calamities? (pg.28)
22. What is 'pratyāhāra' in Yoga Śāstra? (pg.28)
23. What is the equivalent of 'pratyāhāra' in Vedāntic terminology? (pg.28)
24. Define 'conscience'. (pg.28)
25. What is 'prasāda'? (pg.28)
26. Define 'brāhmī-sthitiḥ'. (pg.28)

Chapter 3 - Karma Yoga

1. What is the twofold path? (pg.51)
2. Who is a 'hypocrite'? (pg.51)
3. What is meant by 'niyataṁ karma'? (pg.52)
4. Who is a 'thief'? (pg.52)
5. The appellation 'Vārṣṇeya' means___________. (pg.52)

Chapter 4 - Jñāna Karma Saṁnyāsa Yoga

1. What does the term 'Parantapa' mean? (pg.74)
2. Define 'Jñāna Tapas'. (pg.74)
3. Who is a 'kavi'? (pg.74)
4. Differentiate between 'karma' and 'vikarma'. (pg.74)
5. What is 'akarma' (unactivity)? (pg.74)
6. Who is a 'paṇḍita' (sage)? (pg.75)
7. Define the terms 'Brahman' and 'Ātman'. (pg.75)
8. What is 'ātma-saṁyama-yoga'? (pg.75)
9. Define the terms 'pūraka', 'kumbhaka' and 'recaka'. (pg.75)
10. What is prāṇa? What are the five types of prāṇa? (pg.75)
11. What are the twelve yajñas (sacrifices) mentioned in the fourth chapter? (pg.76)
12. What are three classifications of karma-phala (fruits of action)? (pg.76)

Chapter 5 - Karma Saṁnyāsa Yoga

1. What are the mantra, brāhmaṇa and āraṇyaka divisions of the Vedas? (pg.99)
2. Who is the perpetual (true) saṁnyāsī? (pg.99)
3. What do the terms 'sāṅkhya' and 'yoga' denote in the fifth chapter? (pg.100)
4. What is 'sākṣibhāva'? (pg.100)
5. What is the 'city of nine gates'? (pg.100)
6. What are the 'nine gates'? (pg.100)
7. Who lives in the 'city of nine gates'? (pg.100)
8. What is 'svabhāva'? (pg.100)
9. What does the term 'vibhu' mean? (pg.100)
10. Define desire and anger. (pg.100)

Chapter 6 - Dhyāna Yoga

1. Karma Yoga forms an ____________ to Dhyāna Yoga. (pg.121)
2. Who is a 'Yogārūḍha'? (pg.121)
3. What is 'introspection'? (pg.121)
4. Differentiate between 'jñāna' and 'vijñāna'. (pg.121)
5. What does the term 'kūṭastha' mean? (pg.122)
6. When does a meditator become a 'yukta' (united or steadfast in meditation)? (pg.122)
7. How is 'Yoga' defined in the sixth chapter of the Gītā? (pg.122)
8. Who is the highest Yogī? (pg.123)
9. What does the word 'Kṛṣṇa' mean? (pg.123)
10. Define 'abhyāsa'. (pg.123)
11. Who is a 'Yogabhraṣṭa'? (pg.123)
12. Explain the term 'śabdabrahma' in verse 6.44? (pg.123)

Chapter 7 - Jñāna Vijñāna Yoga

1. Define 'Mahāvākya'. What are the four Mahāvākyas? (pg.157)
2. Differentiate 'jñāna' from 'Vijñāna'. (pg.157)
3. Define 'jīva'. (pg.157)
4. Define parā-prakṛti and aparā-prakṛti. (pg.157)
5. What does the term 'jagat' (world) mean? (pg.158)

6. Differentiate between 'kāma' (desire) and 'rāga' (attachment). (pg.158)
7. What are the four categories of devotees? (pg.158)
8. Differentiate 'māyā' from 'avidyā'. (pg.159)
9. Define Īśvara. (pg.159)

Chapter 8 - Akṣara Brahma Yoga

1. What are the seven questions and answers with which the 8th chapter begins? (pg.174)
2. Define 'meditation'. (pg.175)
3. What is 'Bhakti'? (pg.175)
4. What does the term 'heart' (hṛd) in the Vedāntic context mean? (pg.175)
5. Explain the concept of 'krama-mukti'. (pg.175)
6. Define the term 'Mahāyuga'. (pg.176)
7. How many Mahāyugas constitute one day of Brahma? (pg.176)
8. What are the two possible paths described as being available to individuals after their death? (pg.176)
9. What are the presiding deities of the 'Path of No-return'? (pg.176)
10. What are the presiding deities of the 'Path of Return'? (pg.177)

Chapter 9 - Rājavidyā Rājaguhya Yoga

1. What is 'death'? (pg.191)
2. Subtlety of a thing is measured in terms of its __________ (pg.191)
3. Differentiate 'Īśvara' from 'jīva'. (pg.191)
4. How does Śrī Kṛṣṇa describe men of 'rākṣasic' and 'āsuric' temperaments? (pg.191)
5. Describe men of divine temperament. (pg.192)
6. What is 'Jñāna-yajña'? (pg.192)
7. What is 'svadhā'? (pg.193)
8. What is the 'Turīya-state'? (pg.193)
9. What is 'Soma'? (pg.193)
10. Differentiate 'yoga' from 'kṣema'. (pg.193)
11. What is 'Saṁnyāsa'? (pg.193)
12. Who is a 'Rājarṣi'? (pg.193)

Chapter 10 - Vibhūti Yoga

1. Distinguish 'jīva' from 'Īśvara'. (pg.215)
2. Define 'tanmātra'. (pg.215)
3. What is Avikampa Yoga (unwavering or steady)? (pg.216)
4. What is 'Buddhi Yoga'? (pg.216)
5. What does the term 'Keśava' mean? (pg.216)
6. Who are the 'Maruts'? (pg.216)
7. What is the etymology of the word 'Śaṅkara'? (pg.216)
8. What is 'jalpa', 'vitaṇḍa' and 'vāda'? (pg.216)
9. What does the term 'kavi' mean? (pg.217)
10. What do the terms 'yoga' and 'vibhūti' mean? (pg.217)

Chapter 11 - Viśvarūpa Darśana Yoga

1. What are the characteristic features of Īśvara, the God-principle? (pg.235)
2. What does the term 'Viṣṇu' signify? (pg.235)
3. Differentiate 'sat' from 'asat'. (pg.236)
4. What does the term 'viśva' mean? (pg.236)
5. What does the term 'śaśāṇka' signify? (pg.236)
6. Why does the term 'Viśva-rūpa' indicate 'Virāṭ-rūpa'? (pg.236)

Chapter 12 - Bhakti Yoga

1. What is 'śraddhā'? (pg.261)
2. What is true upāsanā (worship)? (pg.261)
3. What is the meaning of the expression 'Ananya Yoga'? (pg.261)
4. Explain the terms – rejoice, hate, grieve and desire – occurring in the verse 12.17. (pg.261)

Chapter 13 - Kṣetra Kṣetrajña Vibhāga Yoga

1. Differentiate 'prakṛti' from 'Puruṣa'. (pg.285)
2. Define 'ego' in terms of 'kṣetra' (field) and 'Kṣetrajña' (Knower of the field). (pg.286)
3. Differentiate 'kṣetra' (field) from 'Kṣetrajña' (Knower of the field). (pg.286)
4. What are the 'mahābhūtas' (five great elements)? (pg.286)
5. What is 'ahaṅkāra' (egoism)? (pg.286)

6. Define 'buddhi' (intellect). (pg.286)
7. What is the 'avyakta' (unmanifest)? (pg.287)
8. What is 'mūla-prakṛti' or 'māyā'? (pg.287)
9. Distinguish between 'Īśvara' and 'jīva'. (pg.287)
10. What are the 24 tattvas of Sāṅkhyan philosophy? (pg.287)
11. Matter and Spirit are the two aspects of ______. (pg.287)
12. The term 'Puruṣa' is used synonymously with the terms ______, ______ and ______. (pg.287)
13. What are the various appellations of Puruṣa? (pg.288)
14. What is 'meditation'? (pg.288)
15. What is 'mutual superimposition' (anyonya-adhyāsa)? (pg.288)

Chapter 14 - Guṇa Traya Vibhāga Yoga

1. Explain the term 'guṇa'. (pg.319)
2. Who is a 'muni'? (pg.320)
3. Define 'Hiraṇyagarbha'. (pg.320)
4. Define 'prakṛti'. (pg.320)
5. Differentiate 'desire' (tṛṣṇā) from 'attachment' (rāga). (pg.320)
6. What is 'greed' (lobha)? (pg.320)
7. What is 'dullness of the intellect' (aprakāśa)? (pg.320)
8. Define 'idleness' (apravṛtti). (pg.320)
9. What is death? (pg.321)

Chapter 15 - Puruṣottama Yoga

1. What is the aśvattha tree? (pg.345)
2. The metaphor of the aśvattha tree echoes the thoughts of—— Upaniṣad. (pg.345)
3. What are the leaves of saṁsāra-vṛkṣa (tree of saṁsāra)? (pg.346)
4. What are the buds of saṁsāra-vṛkṣa? (pg.346)
5. What are the roots of saṁsāra-vṛkṣa? (pg.346)
6. What is 'mysticism'? (pg.346)
7. What does the metaphor of the aśvattha tree signify? (pg.346)
8. What are the four categories into which the human diet is classified in Sanskrit literature? (pg.346)
9. What does the term 'vaiśvānara' mean? (pg.347)

10. Why is the Life Principle termed 'Puruṣa'? (pg.347)
11. What is sin? (pg.347)

Chapter 16 - Daiva Āsura Sampat Vibhāga Yoga

1. What is 'tapas' (asceticism)? (pg.369)
2. What does 'akrodha' (absence of anger) really mean? (pg.370)
3. What is 'kṣamā' (patience)? (pg.370)
4. What does the term 'śāstra' and 'prakaraṇa' mean? (pg.370)

Chapter 17 - Śraddhā Traya Vibhāga Yoga

1. What is 'yāta-yāmam food'? (pg.392)
2. What are the three categories into which the Lord divides the sāttvic tapas (austerity)? (pg.392)
3. What does the term 'dvija' (twice born) mean? (pg.392)
4. Explain the term 'brahmacarya'. (pg.393)
5. Define 'svādhyāya'. (pg.393)
6. What is 'mouna'? (pg.393)

Chapter 18 - Mokṣa Saṁnyāsa Yoga

1. Differentiate between the terms 'tyāga' (abandonment) and 'saṁnyāsa' (renunciation). (pg.415)
2. Why is Śrī Kṛṣṇa called 'Keśiniṣūdana'? (pg.416)
3. What is the mathematical definition of attachment? (pg.416)
4. What is 'attachment' (asaṅga)? (pg.416)
5. What is 'medhā śakti'? (pg.416)
6. Who is a 'medhāvī'? (pg.416)
7. What are the three types of 'results of actions' (karma-phala)? (pg.416)
8. What does the term 'guṇa' mean? What are the three guṇas? (pg.417)
9. Define 'dhṛti'. (pg.417)
10. What is 'utsāha'? (pg.417)
11. Who is a 'durmedhā' (fool)? (pg.417)
12. What is 'prasāda' (peace)? (pg.417)
13. Define 'śama'. (pg.417)
14. What is 'dama'? (pg.418)

15. Define 'tapas'. (pg.418)
16. What is 'kṣānti' (forbearance)? (pg.418)
17. Define 'ego'. (pg.418)
18. What is a 'viśuddha buddhi' (pure intellect)? (pg.418)
19. Differentiate the 'sceptic' from the 'atheist'. (pg.418)
20. What does the term 'Vāsudeva' mean? (pg.419)

Index of Thoughts and Concepts

General Introduction to Bhagavad Gītā

1. What were the causes for Arjuna's emotional repressions? (pg.7)
2. Arjuna's arguments for not wanting to fight the Kauravas reflected the earlier suggestions of ____________. (pg.7)
3. Differentiate the objective mind (manas) from the subjective mind (buddhi). (pg.8)
4. The split in the individual between the subjective and objective aspects of the mind is created by the layer of ____________. (pg.8)
5. What is the 'Yoga' pointed out in the Gītā? (pg.8)
6. How can we vitalise the mind? (pg.8)
7. ______________ would result in inner purification. (pg.8)
8. ____________ is philosophy in action. (pg.8)

Chapter 1 - Arjunaviṣāda Yoga

1. 'Duryodhana unsettled, runs to his teacher Droṇa'. How does Gurudev compare this? (pg.14)
2. Why does Duryodhana enumerate the names of the distinguished heroes in his own army? (pg.14)
3. How does Duryodhana display his vanity? (pg.15)
4. What are the two ways the verse 1.10 has been interpreted? (pg.15)
5. Why did Bhīṣma sound his conch? (pg.15)
6. Gurudev likens the 'sounding of Bhīṣma's conch' to __________ of modern warfare. (pg.16)
7. What did Arjuna see from his chariot stationed between the two armies? (pg.16)

8. The textbooks of modern psychology would label Arjuna's mental condition as ________. (pg.16)
9. What are the physical symptoms displayed by Arjuna in his neurotic condition? (pg.16)
10. What is 'sin'? (pg.16)
11. Define 'brāhmaṇa', 'kṣatriya', 'vaiśya' and 'śūdra'. (pg.17)
12. What is meant by 'varṇa-saṅkara' or 'admixture of the castes'? (pg.17)
13. What were the primary causes of Arjuna's 'anxiety-state-neurosis'? (pg.17)
14. Every chapter of the Bhagavad Gītā is called 'Upaniṣad'. Why? (pg.18)
15. The Kauravas and Pāṇḍavas represent ____________. (pg.18)
16. Dhṛtarāṣṭra represents ____________. (pg.18)
17. Gāndhārī represents ____________. (pg.18)
18. Kurukṣetra represents ____________. (pg.18)
19. On the basis of its first and last words, the contents of the Bhagavad Gītā can be summarised as ____________. (pg.18)
20. 'Dharma' can be best translated as ____________. (pg.18)
21. Explain how Arjuna's condition of dejection symbolises the seeker's mental condition. (pg.18)
22. Write a short note on 'Dharma'. (pg.20)

Chapter 2 - Sāṅkhya Yoga

1. Who is capable of living in perfect morality? (pg.29)
2. When do sentiments cloud one's understanding? (pg.29)
3. Distinguish between the functions of the mind and the intellect. (pg.29)
4. In which verse of the second chapter do we find Arjuna explicitly surrendering to Śrī Kṛṣṇa? (pg.29)
5. What is the symbolism behind the Mahābhārata battle scene? (pg.30)
6. What is the cause of Arjuna's delusory attachments? (pg.31)
7. What is the 'ego'? (pg.31)
8. From which verse of the second chapter does the teaching of the

Bhagavad Gītā actually start? (pg.31)

9. The misapprehension of Reality takes place due to_________. (pg.31)
10. The ego rises when the ______ is not recognised. (pg.31)
11. Who is fit for attaining 'Immortality'? (pg.31)
12. The Self is described as 'unknowable' (aprameya). Does that mean that the Self ever remains unknown? (pg.32)
13. Which Upaniṣad do the following verses echo? (pg.32)
14. What is the analogy used in the Bhagavad Gītā to explain 'transmigration'? (pg.33)
15. List some of the qualities of the Self as enumerated in the second chapter. (pg.33)
16. What is 'svadharma'? (pg.33)
17. Define 'sin'. (pg.34)
18. How can one live a life of inspired achievement? (pg.34)
19. What is the secret of success? What is the cause of failure? (pg.34)
20. What is the purpose of the practice of rituals? (pg.34)
21. How does one always remain established in purity (nityasattvastha)? (pg.34)
22. "Thy right is to work only, but never to its fruits." Explain. (pg.35)
23. Who is a real Karma Yogī? (pg.35)
24. What does 'giving up attachments' mean? (pg.35)
25. Briefly explain the theory of perception. (pg.35)
26. When is one said to have attained 'Yoga'? (pg.36)
27. Arjuna requests Śrī Kṛṣṇa for a description of the 'Man of steady Wisdom'. Quote the relevant verse. (pg.36)
28. Why does the 'Man of steady Wisdom' become desireless? (pg.36)
29. What is 'anger'? (pg.37)
30. The simile of a tortoise withdrawing its limbs is used to describe _______. (pg.37)
31. How does a Vedāntin gain 'sense-withdrawal' (pratyāhāra or uparati)? (pg.37)
32. Cite the verses which show the 'ladder of fall' resulting from our wrong attitude toward objects. (pg.37)
33. Elucidating which concept does Śrī Kṛṣṇa use the example of the

'wind carrying away a boat'? (pg.38)

34. Why should the senses be kept in control? (pg.38)
35. Describe an effective strategy to increase one's happiness. (pg.38)
36. Who attains peace? (pg. 39)
37. Define 'saṁnyāsa'. (pg. 39)

Chapter 3 - Karma Yoga

1. Action and renunciation are not to be practised together, but to be practised ________________. (pg. 52)
2. What prompted Arjuna to question the Lord in the beginning of the third chapter? (pg. 52)
3. Why is it not possible to prescribe a single spiritual path for all people? (pg. 53)
4. How does ignorance express itself? (pg. 53)
5. Why does the Bhagavad Gītā advise a man to act vigorously? (pg. 53)
6. Why does the Lord advise us to act without attachment? (pg. 54)
7. How does Karma Yoga become a technique of Self-Liberation? (pg. 54)
8. What is 'yajña'? (pg. 54)
9. How does Pujya Gurudev interpret the word 'deva' in the following verse? (pg. 55)
10. How does Śrī Kṛṣṇa describe those who eat the 'remnants of the sacrifices' and those who 'cook food only for their own sake'? (pg. 55)
11. How does Pujya Gurudev interpret the words 'yajña', 'rain' and 'food' in the following verse? (pg. 56)
12. What is the 'Cosmic wheel of co-operation'? (pg. 56)
13. Śrī Kṛṣṇa declares 'seekers of the senses' (indriyārāma) as 'living in sin' and 'living in vain'. Why? (pg. 57)
14. ______________ and _____________ are the two wheels of the life-chariot. (pg. 57)
15. Who is free from duties? (pg. 58)
16. How does Pujya Gurudev mathematically define attachment? (pg. 58)

17. Why does the moral rejuvenation of a society depend on the leader of the society? (pg. 58)
18. Why does the Lord work? What would be the loss if He were not to work at all? (pg. 59)
19. What is the difference between the activities of the 'wise' and the 'ignorant'? (pg. 59)
20. When does attachment become a cure for one's imperfections? (pg. 60)
21. How should a 'wise man' guide his generation? (pg.60)
22. What is the notion of the ignorant man while acting? (pg.60)
23. Explain how ignorance of the Self manifests in the intellectual and mental zones. (pg.61)
24. Why is the 'wise man' not bound by actions and their results? (pg.61)
25. What is hope? (pg.61)
26. What is the meaning of 'vigatajvara' in the following verse? (pg.61)
27. Why is the ego considered to be 'the shadow of the past'? (pg.62)
28. What is 'faith'? (pg.62)
29. How does the term 'worklessness' indicate the 'State of Self-hood'? (pg.62)
30. Who are doomed to destruction? (pg.62)
31. "Sadṛśaṁ ceṣṭate svasyāḥ prakṛterjñānavānapi—Even a 'man of knowledge' acts in accordance with his own nature." Explain. (pg.62)
32. Explain the significance of Śrī Kṛṣṇa's question 'nigrahaḥ kiṁ kariṣyati—what can restraint do'? (pg.63)
33. What are one's internal foes that prevent one from right living? (pg.63)
34. What is the relation between vāsanās, mind and ego? (pg.63)
35. Man's texture of thoughts is determined by his ______. (pg.64)
36. Distinguish 'svadharma' from 'paradharma'. (pg.64)
37. What impels man to commit sin even against his wishes? (pg.64)
38. Define 'desire'. (pg.64)

39. "Desire itself, under certain circumstances, gains expression as anger." Explain. (pg.64)
40. Śrī Kṛṣṇa uses three examples to illustrate the manner in which desire and anger veil one's reason and discrimination. What are the three examples and explain their significance. (pg.65)
41. What are the three seats of desire? (pg.65)
42. How is desire conquered? (pg.66)

Chapter 4 - Jñāna Karma Saṁnyāsa Yoga

1. What is the 'guru-śiṣya-paramparā' (lineage of teacher and taught) pointed out by Śrī Kṛṣṇa? (pg.76)
2. What is the meaning of the word 'Veda'? (pg.77)
3. Why should spiritual lessons be directly heard from a true master? (pg.77)
4. Why is the 'Science of Truth' called the 'supreme secret'? (pg.77)
5. "A jīva becomes victimised by his avidyā, while the Lord is Master of His māyā." Explain. (pg.77)
6. When does the Lord take an 'avatāra' (incarnation)? (pg.78)
7. Why does the Lord take 'avatāra'? (pg.78)
8. What are the three constituents in the technique of self-development? (pg.79)
9. Indicate how all the three paths of action, devotion and knowledge find their mention in verse 4.10. (pg.79)
10. The Lord says, "I lend my power to all without any partiality and in whatever form they invoke me, in that form I serve them." Explain. (pg.80)
11. If the Ātmic-force guides us on both the path of good and on the path of evil, then how is it that we see but a rare few who are honestly trying to travel the path of righteousness, while the majority are pursuing the road of evil? (pg.80)
12. The fourfold-castes are based on ___________and ___________. (pg.80)
13. Explain the concept of 'varṇa'. (pg.81)
14. Who is not bound by his actions? (pg.82)
15. "What is action? What is inaction? As to this even the 'wise' are

deluded." Explain. (pg.82)

16. "Physical inactivity is no criterion to call one an idler." Explain. (pg.82)
17. Who is the individual who is actionless inspite of his external action? (pg.83)
18. Who is not bound even while acting? (pg.83)
19. Explain the concept of 'yajña'. (pg.83)
20. Whose actions are 'dissolved'? (pg.83)
21. ______________makes every act a yajña. (pg.84)
22. What are the four essential factors of yajña? (pg.84)
23. What is the significance of chanting verse 4.24 before taking food? (pg.84)
24. What does the word 'deva' mean? From the subjective view-point what are the 'devas'? (pg.85)
25. What is 'dravya-yajña'? (pg.85)
26. What is 'svādhyāya-yajña'? (pg.85)
27. What is 'jñāna-yajña'? (pg.86)
28. What is meditation? (pg.86)
29. 'Jñāna-yajña' is superior to 'dravya-yajña'. Explain. (pg.86)
30. How should one approach the Guru? (pg.86)
31. What are the qualifications of a teacher? (pg.87)
32. What is true Wisdom? (pg.87)
33. "The fire of Knowledge reduces all actions to ashes." Explain. (pg.87)
34. What is the greatest purifier? (pg.88)
35. Which verses in the fourth chapter describe the glory of Knowledge? (pg.88)
36. What are the three categories of persons who get destroyed? (pg.89)
37. By what means can one destroy doubt about the Self? (pg.89)
38. What does the term 'heart' mean in spiritual literature? (pg.90)

Chapter 5 - Karma Saṁnyāsa Yoga

1. How does Arjuna's question in the third chapter differ from that of the fifth chapter? (pg.101)

2. What is Arjuna's question at the beginning of chapter five? (pg.101)
3. Renunciation of action and full participation in action are two different exercises to be practised ________ and not ________. (pg.101)
4. What are three stages in the spiritual process of self-evolution? (pg.101)
5. "To go beyond the pairs of opposites is to transcend the mind." Explain. (pg.102)
6. Why does the Lord insist that only childish minds can find Sāṅkhya and Yoga contradictory? (pg.103)
7. Explain how Karma Yoga through purification of mind makes a seeker fit for meditation and Realisation. (pg.103)
8. What is the attitude of the sage while acting? (pg.104)
9. Who is not tainted by sin? (pg.105)
10. Why does a Karma Yogi perform actions? (pg.105)
11. Who is the Observer in oneself? (pg.105)
12. Who attains eternal peace and who becomes bound? (pg.105)
13. "Knowledge reveals the supreme Brahman like the sun." Explain. (pg.106)
14. What is the hallmark of Realisation? (pg.106)
15. "Brahman is even and ever-perfect." Explain. (pg.107)
16. "The wise do not revel in sense pleasures." What is the reason? (pg.107)
17. Who is a happy man? (pg.108)
18. Who attains Nirvāṇa? (pg.108)
19. Which are the two aphoristic stanzas in the 5th chapter that give the summary of the entire sixth chapter? (pg.109)
20. What is the relationship between desire, fear and anger? (pg.109)
21. When does one discover the necessary tranquillity to start meditation? (pg.110)
22. Explain the significance of Śrī Kṛṣṇa advising the meditator to fix his gaze between the eyebrows. (pg.110)
23. Why does Śrī Kṛṣṇa advise the meditator to make the flow of breath even? (pg.110)

24. What does the term 'tapas' mean? (pg.111)
25. Why is the Self termed 'Sarva-loka-maheśvara'? (pg.111)
26. Who attains peace? (pg.111)

Chapter 6 - Dhyāna Yoga

1. How are the chapters of the Bhagavad Gītā divided on the basis of the Mahāvākya 'Tat Tvam Asi'? (pg.124)
2. Explain the thought flow and inter-connection of chapters two to six. (pg.124)
3. Explain why no achievement can be gained so long as one has not destroyed the 'unbridled saṅkalpa-śakti'. (pg.125)
4. For whom does the Gītā prescribe action as the means for spiritual progress and for whom does it prescribe inaction (śama)? (pg.126)
5. When is the Self one's friend and when is It one's enemy? (pg.127)
6. What is the test of spiritual evolution? (pg.128)
7. "A Man of Perfection regards all relationships with equal love and consideration." Explain. (pg.128)
8. Differentiate between the terms 'nirāśī' and 'aparigraha' in verse 6.10. (pg.128)
9. Śrī Kṛṣṇa enjoins on the seeker to sit in solitude (rahasi sthitaḥ) and meditate. What does 'sitting in solitude' mean? (pg.129)
10. Why should the seat of meditation be neither too high nor too low? (pg.129)
11. What is the importance of Śrī Kṛṣṇa's advice to a seeker to 'sit in a clean place' for meditation? (pg.129)
12. "The seat (āsana) for meditation is made of a cloth, a skin and kuśa-grass one over the other." Explain. (pg.130)
13. When does the mind naturally become single-pointed? (pg.130)
14. What are the initial preparations and adjustments to be made regarding the 'seat' (āsana) and 'body-posture' for meditation? (pg.130)
15. The meditator is asked to gaze at the tip of the nose. What does this instruction signify? (pg.131)
16. "Renouncing fear the seeker should meditate", is the instruction of Śrī Kṛṣṇa. What is the 'fear' spoken of here? (pg.131)

17. What is 'brahmacarya'? (pg.131)
18. "Yoga is not possible for him who eats too much nor for him who does not eat at all." Explain. (pg.132)
19. "Intelligent moderation is the golden rule for successful meditation." Quote the relevant verses and explain the importance of moderation. (pg.132)
20. Differentiate between an 'uncontrolled mind' and a 'controlled mind'? (pg.133)
21. Differentiate 'kāma' (desires) from 'spṛhā' (longing after desires)? (pg.133)
22. What is the simile used to describe a Yogī's self-controlled mind? (pg.133)
23. Cite the four verses that give a complete picture of the state of Yoga? (pg.134)
24. The Self is pointed out as being perceivable only through the pure intellect. Explain. (pg.135)
25. Explain how Śrī Kṛṣṇa defines and reinterprets Yoga? (pg.136)
26. Cite the relevant verses that explain the art of making the mind single-pointed in meditation. (pg.136)
27. "The Man of Wisdom beholds the Self in all beings and equally beholds all beings in the Self." Explain. (pg.137)
28. Should a Man of Realisation necessarily withdraw from the world to maintain his Divine Consciousness? (pg.137)
29. The mind is described by Arjuna as being ever turbulent, strong and unyielding. Explain. (pg.138)
30. How can the mind be brought under control? (pg.138)
31. Śrī Kṛṣṇa gives 'practice' (abhyāsa) and 'detachment' (vairāgya) as the twofold means to control the mind. What is the significance of listing 'practice' as the prior means of mind-control? (pg.139)
32. Cite and explain the verses wherein Arjuna questions the Lord about the fate of a Yogabhraṣṭa (fallen Yogī). (pg.140)
33. What are the two possible destinies of a Yogabhraṣṭa? (pg.141)
34. Explain the significance of Śrī Kṛṣṇa's statement—"By that very former practice the Yogabhraṣṭa is borne on inspite of himself." (pg.142)

10. What is 'Īśvara-darśana' (Vision of the Lord)? (pg. 197)
11. Cite the verses that declare the Lord's universal presence. (pg. 198)
12. What is the significance of the Lord's description of Himself being the 'immutable seed'? (pg. 199)
13. Cite the relevant verse wherein the Lord declares that He fulfils all the needs of His true devotee. (pg. 199)
14. Who is dead to the world of sorrows? (pg. 199)
15. What are the three factors that enable success in life? (pg. 199)
16. "Even those devotees who, endowed with faith, worship other devas, worship Me alone, O son of Kuntī (but) by the wrong method." What does the Lord mean by the phrase 'wrong method' (avidhipūrvakam)? (pg. 200)
17. What do the terms 'devavrata', 'pitṛvrata' and 'bhūtejya' connote in verse 9.25? (pg. 200)
18. The Lord accepts any little thing offered to Him with devotion. Cite the relevant verse. (pg. 201)
19. What are the two pre-requisites for a true offering unto the Lord? (pg. 202)
20. Cite the verse wherein the Lord goads us to offer all our actions to Him as worship? (pg. 202)
21. What would be the result of living life in the pure spirit of dedicated offering? (pg. 202)
22. If the Lord is impartial to all beings, how is it that some people show a greater manifestation of divinity? (pg. 203)
23. What is 'worship'? (pg. 203)
24. Why should even the most sinful person be regarded as 'righteous' if he has taken a strong right resolution to be good? (pg. 204)
25. Explain the terms 'strī', 'vaiśya' and 'śūdra' in verse 9.32. (pg. 204)

Chapter 10 - Vibhūti Yoga

1. Explain how the world is a projection of the Total-mind. (pg. 217)
2. What does the term 'Sapta Ṛṣi' (Seven Ṛṣis) symbolize? (pg. 217)
3. What does the term 'deva' signify? (pg. 218)

4. Who is undeluded and liberated from all sins? (pg. 218)
5. Why is the Self described as 'unborn' and 'beginningless'? (pg. 218)
6. What is 'loka'? (pg. 218)
7. Who becomes the 'Lord of the worlds' (sarva-loka-maheśvara)? (pg. 219)
8. Cite the relevant verses to elucidate that the Lord is the source of all our mental and intellectual abilities. (pg. 219)
9. What do the four 'Sanatkumāras' symbolize? (pg. 220)
10. Who becomes established in the Supreme Awareness through Avikampa Yoga (unwavering Yoga)? (pg. 220)
11. When is devotion fulfilled? (pg. 221)
12. Who is a true seeker? (pg. 221)
13. Explain the secret of successful detachment. (pg. 221)
14. Cite the relevant verses wherein the Lord declares that He bestows Ātma-jñāna (Self Knowledge) to his devotees. (pg. 221)
15. Explain the Lord's declaration that He reveals Himself to His devotees out of compassion. (pg. 222)
16. What are the four requests made by Arjuna to the Lord in the tenth chapter? (pg. 222)
17. Enumerate the 75 Vibhūtis of the Lord. (pg. 223)
18. Why is 'Śaṅkara' (Lord of destruction) respected and adored? (pg. 226)
19. What is the subjective meaning of 'Kāmadhenu'? (pg. 226)
20. Explain how annihilation is Death's creative art. (pg. 226)
21. The Lord declares that among all letters He is the letter 'A.' What is the importance of this alphabet 'A'? (pg. 226)
22. Explain why of all secret things, the Lord is the deep unbroken 'Silence'. (pg. 227)
23. What is the philosophical significance of the term 'jagat' (world)? (pg. 227)

Chapter 11 - Viśvarūpa Darśana Yoga

1. Describe briefly the concept of the Cosmic Man. (pg. 237)
2. Cite the relevant verse wherein the Lord bestows Arjuna with the

'divya-cakṣu' (divine-eye). (pg. 237)

3. Explain the term 'divya-cakṣu' (divine-eye). (pg. 237)
4. How does Sañjaya describe to Dhṛtarāṣṭra the wonderful glory of the Cosmic Form? (pg. 238)
5. What do the conch, discus, club and lotus in Lord Viṣṇu's hands symbolise? (pg. 238)
6. Explain why the Infinite is described by Arjuna as being endowed with endless arms and of having the sun and the moon as Its eyes? (pg. 239)
7. The entire human world can be brought under three heads: the 'sub-normal' the 'normal' and the 'super-normal'. Explain these three categories. (pg. 239)
8. What qualifies as 'complete philosophy'? (pg. 240)
9. Explain the following verse which uses the analogy of torrential rivers gushing towards the ocean to describe the many heroes of the war entering the Lord's flaming mouth. (pg. 240)
10. Why does Arjuna use the additional analogy of 'moths rushing hurriedly into a blazing fire' after giving the analogy of 'rivers rushing towards the ocean'? (pg. 241)
11. Why does Śrī Kṛṣṇa show Arjuna the vision of destruction of warriors? (pg. 241)
12. Explain how the perception of 'continuity of existence' is an illusion. (pg. 242)
13. In the following verse Śrī Kṛṣṇa mentions specifically that Droṇa, Bhīṣma, Karṇa and Jayadratha—as having been already killed by him. Why is a special mention made of these four warriors? (pg. 242)
14. Cite the verses of the 11th chapter that constitute the universal prayer. (pg. 243)
15. How is the Self the Primal God? (pg. 246)
16. Explain the symbolism of Lord Viṣṇu's form and his various physical attributes. (pg. 246)
17. What is the form in which Arjuna wants the Lord to appear after having the vision of the 'Universal Form'? (pg. 247)

18. What does Śrī Kṛṣṇa's declaration that His Universal Form has not been seen by anybody else other than Arjuna mean? (pg. 247)
19. Cite the relevant verse wherein Lord Kṛṣṇa declares that His Cosmic Form can be known only by those with single-minded devotion. (pg. 248)
20. What are the three stages in which Realisation dawns? (pg. 248)
21. What are the conditions required for a seeker to attain the Lord? (pg. 249)

Chapter 12 - Bhakti Yoga

1. How is chapter 12 connected with the earlier chapters? (pg. 262)
2. What is Arjuna's question at the beginning of the 12th chapter? (pg. 262)
3. What does the term 'āveśya' mean in verse 12.2? What is its importance? (pg. 263)
4. What are the three essential conditions for one to become a true devotee? (pg. 264)
5. Explain the terms (1)Akṣara (Imperishable) (2) Anirdeśya (Indefinable) (3) Sarvatraga (All-pervading) (4) Acintya (Unthinkable) (5) Kūṭastha (Unchanging) (6) Acala (Immovable) (7) Dhruva (Eternal) which are used in verse 12.3 to describe the formless Brahman. (pg. 264)
6. Why should the seeker cultivate the habit of restraining the senses? (pg. 265)
7. Explain the term 'samabuddhi' (equanimity). (pg. 266)
8. Cite the relevant verse which states the difficult nature of worshipping the unmanifest and formless Brahman. (pg. 266)
9. Śrī Kṛṣṇa says that the 'avyakta' (unmanifest) is very hard for the 'embodied' to reach. What is the meaning of the expression 'embodied' (dehavat)? (pg. 266)
10. What are the levels of spiritual practices advocated by Śrī Kṛṣṇa? (pg. 267)
11. What is the technique for controlling the mind? (pg. 268)
12. How does the Lord extol 'karma-phala-tyāga'? (pg. 268)

13. Why is 'knowledge' (jñāna) superior to 'practice' (abhyāsa)? (pg. 268)
14. Why is 'meditation' (dhyāna) superior to knowledge (jñāna)? (pg. 269)
15. Why does the Lord give greater importance to 'renunciation of fruits of action' (karma-phala-tyāga) – and place it even higher than meditation (dhyāna) – in the hierarchy of spiritual practices? (pg. 269)
16. Cite the verses that describe the attributes of a devotee and enumerate the attributes. (pg. 270)
17. A true devotee is one "by whom the world is not agitated and one who cannot be agitated by the world." Explain. (pg. 273)
18. Explain why the one who does not entertain any desire for objects is free from joy, envy, fear and anxiety. (pg. 273)
19. Why does a true devotee consider himself as only an instrument of the Lord? (pg. 274)
20. What does the description of the 'Man of Realisation' as 'Aniketa' (homeless) signify? (pg. 274)
21. Explain the deeper significance of the Lord's description that a "true devotee is equal to foe and friend, honour and dishonour and heat and cold." (pg. 274)
22. Why should one place no importance on censure and praise? (pg. 275)
23. What is the importance of contentment in spiritual life? (pg. 275)
24. Who is exceedingly dear to the Lord? (pg. 275)

Chapter 13 - Kṣetra Kṣetrajña Vibhāga Yoga

1. Cite the relevant verse wherein the Lord declares that He is the Kṣetrajña in all kṣetras. (pg. 289)
2. How does the Lord eulogise the knowledge of kṣetra and Kṣetrajña? (pg. 289)
3. What does the term 'ekam' (one) mean in the expression: 'indriyāṇi daśaikaṁ ca—the ten senses and the one'? (pg. 289)
4. Why are mental modifications such as desire, hatred, pleasure, pain, etc., also included in kṣetra (field)? (pg. 290)

5. What are the various factors that constitute the 'kṣetra'? (pg. 290)
6. What are the twenty qualities of Jñāna (Knowledge)? Cite the verses that enumerate them. (pg. 291)
7. What is the importance of perception of the evil in birth, death, old age, sickness and pain? (pg. 293)
8. What is 'concentration'? (pg. 293)
9. What is the importance of ever keeping in mind one's goal of true Knowledge? (pg. 293)
10. Why are the various attributes starting from 'humility' to 'perception of the goal' (verses 8-12) declared to be Knowledge itself when they are only attributes to be cultivated for gaining Knowledge? (pg. 294)
11. Why is Brahman neither 'sat' nor 'asat'? (pg. 294)
12. Why is the Self described as 'seeming to possess the function of all senses and yet devoid of all senses'? (pg. 294)
13. Explain why the Self is described as possessing 'incomprehensible subtlety'. (pg. 295)
14. Why is the Self described as 'far as well as near'? (pg. 295)
15. What is the nature of the 'Jñeyam' (Brahman)? (pg. 295)
16. Why is Brahman compared with light and often even called 'Light'? (pg. 297)
17. What do the terms 'jñānam', 'jñeyam' and 'jñāna-gamyam' mean? (pg. 298)
18. Cite the verse which declares that both prakṛti (matter) and Puruṣa (spirit) are beginningless. (pg. 298)
19. What are the effects of prakṛti and Puruṣa? (pg. 298)
20. What is the cause for the rebirth of the Puruṣa (Kṣetrajña)? (pg. 299)
21. The Supreme Self has been termed as Upadraṣṭā, Anumantā, Bhartā, Bhoktā and Maheśvara in the following verse. Explain these terms. (pg. 300)
22. Who becomes a 'Man of Wisdom'? (pg. 301)
23. Cite and explain the verses wherein the Lord declares that seekers attain Liberation in various ways. (pg. 301)

24. Why is the 'Ātman' described as the 'object recognised' (ātmānam) 'instrument of cognition' (ātmanā) as well as 'recognising subject' (ātmani)? (pg. 303)
25. Cite and explain the verse which asserts that every being is the union of kṣetra and Kṣetrajña. (pg. 303)
26. Explain the Lord's declaration that "he who sees the Supreme Lord existing equally in all beings, the Unperishing within the perishing, alone sees." (pg. 304)
27. Cite the two verses wherein the following expression is found: "He who sees, verily sees" (yaḥ paśyati sa paśyati). (pg. 304)
28. Who attains the Highest Goal (parāṁ gatim)? (pg. 304)
29. Explain the Lord's declaration that the person who sees that the Lord exists equally in all does not destroy the Self by the Self (na hinasti ātmanā ātmānam). (pg. 305)
30. Explain the Lord's declaration in the following verse: "he alone sees who sees the Self as actionless." (pg. 305)
31. When has one 'become' Brahman? (pg. 306)
32. Who is a person of 'True Wisdom' and 'Right Perception'? (pg. 306)
33. Cite the verse wherein the Lord declares that though dwelling in the body the Self does not act. (pg. 306)
34. What is the analogy that Śrī Kṛṣṇa uses to explain the Self's untainted nature. (pg. 307)
35. Why is the Self not contaminated by the realm of matter (prakṛti)? (pg. 307)
36. The Lord gives the example of the 'sun illumining the world' in the following verse to explain the concept of Kṣetrajña illumining the kṣetra. Explain this analogy. (pg. 307)
37. What is the 'jñānacakṣu' (eye of wisdom)? (pg. 308)

Chapter 14 - Guṇa Traya Vibhāga Yoga

1. Explain the importance of the study of the 14th chapter in one's spiritual pursuit. (pg. 321)
2. How can one explain the cause for the endless variety of individuals, if it is the one Eternal Principle alone that expresses

through all matter equipments? (pg. 321)
3. Explain how creation is a trick of the mind. (pg. 322)
4. Explain the inter-relation between 'vāsanā', 'guṇa', 'māyā', 'avidyā', 'jīva' and 'Īśvara'. (pg. 322)
5. What is the nature of the bondage produced by sattva? (pg. 322)
6. Describe the bondage caused by rajas in an individual. (pg. 323)
7. Explain the significance of 'desire' being termed 'tṛṣṇā' (thirst) in Sanskrit. (pg. 324)
8. Explain the bondage caused by tamas. (pg. 324)
9. Cite the verse which in a nutshell gives the different types of bondage produced by sattva, rajas and tamas. (pg. 325)
10. Explain how the guṇas dominate one another and cite the relevant verse. (pg. 325)
11. How can one recognise that one is under the influence of sattva? (pg. 326)
12. What are the characteristics that indicate the predominance of rajas? (pg. 326)
13. When tamas predominates what exactly are the symptoms? (pg. 327)
14. Cite the verses wherein the Lord declares the future life of an individual based on the predominance of the guṇas at the moment of death. (pg. 327)
15. Explain how the thoughts entertained during one's life time will determine the thoughts at the moment of death when one departs from the body. (pg. 328)
16. What is the fruit of sattva, rajas and tamas? (pg. 328)
17. How does one start becoming 'good'? (pg. 329)
18. What are the effects of sattva, rajas and tamas? (pg. 329)
19. Write a short note on 'evolution' as conceived in the Hindu philosophy. Explain the position that man holds in the ladder of evolution. (pg. 329)
20. How can one be free from the thraldom of thought-entanglements? (pg. 330)
21. When does one attain oneness with the Lord and gain Liberation? (pg. 331)

22. What are the three questions of Arjuna about the individual who has 'transcended the three guṇas' (guṇātīta)? (pg. 331)
23. Who is a 'Guṇātīta'? Cite the verses that describe the 'Guṇātīta'. (pg. 332)
24. Why is the 'Guṇātīta' unaffected by the play of the guṇas in his mind? (pg. 333)
25. How does the 'Guṇātīta' remain alike in pleasure and pain? (pg. 333)
26. Why is a 'Guṇātīta' free of hankering for worldly possessions? (pg. 334)
27. Why does the Lord describe the 'Guṇātīta' as 'one who is free of all enterprise' (sarvārambhaparityāgī). (pg. 334)
28. Give a bird's eye view of the three guṇas—sattva, rajas and tamas—as presented in the 14th chapter. (pg. 334)

Chapter 15 - Puruṣottama Yoga

1. Cite the verses that describe the metaphor of the aśvattha tree. (pg. 347)
2. Why has the aśvattha tree (pipal tree) been chosen to represent the entire cosmos? (pg. 348)
3. Why has saṁsāra been represented as a 'vṛkṣa' (tree)? (pg. 348)
4. Why is the 'tree of saṁsāra' described as having its roots (primary root) up? (pg. 348)
5. Explain why the leaves are compared to the Vedas themselves. (pg. 349)
6. Explain the Lord's declaration that he who knows the entire aśvattha tree is alone the 'knower of the entire Veda'—(Vedavit). (pg. 349)
7. Why are the branches of the 'tree of saṁsāra' described as growing both 'upwards and downwards'? (pg. 350)
8. Why are the secondary roots of the 'tree of saṁsāra' described as extending even downwards? (pg. 350)
9. How can one cut the 'tree of saṁsāra'? (pg. 351)
10. What is 'detachment' (asaṅga)? (pg. 351)

11. Cite the verse wherein the Lord declares the qualities that are required to attain the Paramātman. (pg. 351)
12. What are pride and delusion? (pg. 352)
13. What is the secret of cultivating 'detachment'? (pg. 352)
14. Explain why the external sources of effulgence like the sun, moon and fire cannot illumine the Supreme Self. (pg. 352)
15. Explain the logic behind the Lord's assertion that the Supreme Abode is that 'to which having gone none returns' (yad gatvā na nivartante). (pg. 353)
16. If the Infinite Consciousness, the Lord, has no parts (niraṁśa), how can it be said that the 'jīva' is a part (aṁśa) of the Lord? (pg. 353)
17. What is rebirth of the jīva (individual)? (pg. 353)
18. What is 'Jñāna Cakṣu' (Eye of Wisdom)? (pg. 354)
19. What are the two essential conditions for meditation to lead one to Liberation? (pg. 354)
20. Explain and cite the verse wherein the Lord declares that mere effort without purity of heart cannot lead one to Liberation. (pg. 355)
21. Cite the verses wherein the Immanence of the Lord as —(1) the All-illumining Light of Consciousness (2) the All-sustaining Life (3) the subjective warmth of Life in all living organisms and (4) the Self in all the hearts—is described. (pg. 355)
22. Explain the limitation of science and the pivotal role of philosophy in revealing the Absolute. (pg. 357)
23. How is the effulgence of the sun, moon, fire, etc., that of the Lord alone? (pg. 357)
24. Why is the Lord stated as being seated in the heart of all living beings? (pg. 357)
25. Define and explain the terms 'Kṣara Puruṣa' and 'Akṣara Puruṣa'. (pg. 358)
26. Define and describe the 'Uttama Puruṣa' (Puruṣottama). (pg. 359)
27. Explain how the 'Kṣara Puruṣa', 'Akṣara Puruṣa' and 'Uttama Puruṣa' are the one Consciousness alone. (pg. 360)

28. Cite the verse wherein the Lord declares that the individual who recognises Him as Uttama Puruṣa (Supreme Self) alone worships Him with pure devotion. (pg. 360)
29. Why is the knower of the Uttama Puruṣa called 'all-knower'? (pg. 360)
30. Why is Brahmavidyā termed 'secret'? (pg. 361)

Chapter 16 - Daiva Āsura Sampat Vibhāga Yoga

1. How is the 16th chapter connected with the earlier chapters? (pg. 370)
2. How can an individual attain ethical purity? (pg. 371)
3. List the qualities of the 'divine estate' (daivī sampat) and cite the relevant verses. (pg. 371)
4. In the enumeration of the qualities of the 'divine estate' 'fearlessness' has been placed upfront. Explain the importance of 'fearlessness' in one's spiritual evolution. (pg. 373)
5. What is 'dāna' (charity)? (pg. 373)
6. Explain the importance of 'dama' (sense control) in one's spiritual life. (pg. 374)
7. What is 'svādhyāya' and its importance in the seeker's life? (pg. 374)
8. What is the secret of enduring tenderness towards all beings? (pg. 374)
9. What is the importance of 'dhṛti' (fortitude) in one's life? (pg. 374)
10. What are the qualities of the 'demoniac estate' (āsurī sampat)? (pg. 375)
11. Cite the verses wherein Śrī Kṛṣṇa describes the people of demoniac traits (āsurī pravṛtti)? (pg. 375)
12. Why is the 'game of desire' an endless gamble? (pg. 378)
13. Why does the Lord declare that the individuals endowed with the diabolical qualities of 'āsurī sampat' as hating the Lord Himself in their own bodies and others? (pg. 378)
14. Cite the verses wherein the Lord declares the fate of those endowed with 'āsurī sampat'. (pg. 379)

15. What are the three gateways to hell? (pg. 379)
16. Describe the inter-relation between desire, anger and greed. (pg. 380)
17. Cite the verses that persuade an individual to live life in accordance with the declarations of the śāstras (scriptures). (pg. 380)
18. Why does the Lord advise us to follow the śāstras? (pg. 381)

Chapter 17 - Śraddhā Traya Vibhāga Yoga

1. Cite and explain the significance of Arjuna's question at the beginning of the 17th chapter. (pg. 393)
2. What is the interrelation between 'faith' (śraddhā), 'nature' (sattva or svabhāva) and 'guṇa'? (pg. 394)
3. Cite and explain the verse wherein the Lord describes the worship of the sāttvic, rājasic and tāmasic śraddhā types. (pg. 395)
4. Why does the Lord condemn the body-mortifying austerities of the āsuric type of men? (pg. 396)
5. Is there any interrelation between food and one's inner nature? (pg. 397)
6. Cite the verses wherein the Lord declares the food choice of sāttvic, rājasic and tāmasic types. (pg. 397)
7. What are the actions to be avoided and what are the actions to be performed? (pg. 398)
8. What are the yajña-types (sacrifices) that sāttvic, rājasic and tāmasic classes of men would engage themselves in? (pg. 398)
9. What is the nature and purpose of tapas? (pg. 399)
10. Cite the verse wherein the Lord describes 'austerity of speech'. (pg. 399)
11. Explain the importance of speech that is 'satyam' (true), 'priyam' (agreeable) and 'hitam' (beneficial). (pg. 399)
12. Describe austerity of the mind. (pg. 400)
13. How can one attain serenity of mind (manaḥprasāda)? (pg. 400)
14. Cite the verses that explain the nature of tapas (austerity) performed by the sāttvic, rājasic and tāmasic types of people. (pg. 400)

15. Why is the tapas (austerity) of the rājasic type of men described as 'transitory'? (pg. 401)
16. Cite the verses that enumerate the three kinds of charity. (pg. 401)
17. What is 'nirdeśa'? Why is 'Om Tat Sat' a nirdeśa? (pg. 402)
18. Explain in detail the manner in which 'Om Tat Sat' acts as a nirdeśa. (pg. 403)
19. Cite and explain the verse which explains the usage of the word 'Om'. (pg. 404)
20. Cite and explain the relevant verse wherein the Lord declares the importance of the term 'Tat'. (pg. 404)
21. Cite the verses which explain the usage of the word 'Sat'. (pg. 405)
22. Explain how even acts of sacrifice, charity and austerity which are not sāttvic in the beginning of their performance can be rendered so by the use of 'Om Tat Sat'. (pg. 405)
23. Explain how sacrifices, austerities and charity done without faith is 'asat'. (pg. 406)
24. Give an overall view of the choice of (1) altar of worship (2) āhāra (food) (3) yajña (sacrifice) (4) tapas (austerity) and dāna (charity) of the sāttvic, rājasic and tāmasic types of people. (pg. 406)

Chapter 18 - Mokṣa Saṁnyāsa Yoga

1. What is the purpose served in the 18th chapter analysing the tendencies, urges, emotions etc., of an individual? (pg. 419)
2. What is Arjuna's question at the beginning of the chapter? What is the Lord's reply? (pg. 419)
3. Why is 'tyāga' (abandonment of fruits of action) a pre-requisite for 'saṁnyāsa' (renunciation of desire-prompted actions)? (pg. 420)
4. Cite the verse wherein the Lord declares that 'yajña', 'dāna' and 'tapas' should not be given up. (pg. 421)
5. How should 'yajña' (sacrifice), 'dāna' (charity) and 'tapas' (austerity) be performed? (pg. 421)
6. Cite the verses that explain the three types of tyāga (abandonment). (pg. 422)

7. Can an individual be excused for abandoning one's duties out of ignorance? (pg. 422)
8. What is the nature of tyāga (abandonment) recommended by the Bhagavad Gītā? (pg. 423)
9. Describe the nature of the sāttvic tyāgī. (pg. 423)
10. Why does the Lord dissuade Arjuna and through Arjuna all of us from actual renunciation of all actions and recommends only the renunciation of the fruits of actions? (pg. 424)
11. What is the essence of the Gītā-technique of personality rehabilitation? (pg. 424)
12. What are the five constituent factors of all actions? Why does the Lord enumerate these five factors? (pg. 424)
13. What is the significance of the 'rāsa-krīḍā'? (pg. 426)
14. List the threefold impulse of action (karmacodanā) and the threefold basis of action (karmasaṅgraha)? (pg. 427)
15. Justify the triad of 'knower' (parijñātā), 'known' (jñeyaṁ) and 'knowledge' (jñānaṁ) together termed as the 'threefold impulse of action' (karmacodanā). (pg. 427)
16. Explain the term (1) doer (kartā) (2) instruments (karaṇa) and (3) action (karma). Why are they termed as the 'threefold basis of action (karmasaṅgraha)? (pg. 428)
17. Cite the verse that describes the three types of knowledge. (pg. 429)
18. Explain the Lord's assertion that 'to see the one undivided in the many' is 'sāttvic knowledge' (sāttvikaṁ jñānam). (pg. 429)
19. Describe the nature of rājasic knowledge (rājasaṁ jñānam). (pg. 430)
20. Briefly explain the nature of tāmasic knowledge (tāmasaṁ jñānam). (pg. 430)
21. Cite the verses which describe the three types of action. (pg. 430)
22. Why does an individual with sāttvic intellect serve the whole world with love and joy? (pg. 431)
23. Briefly describe the action of a rājasic nature. (pg. 432)
24. Why does a 'sāttvic kartā' remain non-egoistic (anahaṁvādin)? (pg. 432)

25. Why is a 'tāmasic kartā' described as 'dīrgha-sūtrī' (procrastinator)? (pg. 432)
26. In the Rāmāyaṇa epic who are the personalities that illustrate sāttvic, rājasic and tāmasic 'kartas' (doers)? (pg. 433)
27. After enumerating the three types of 'knowledge' (jñānam), 'action' (karma) and 'doer' (kartā) why does the Lord go on to explain the three types of 'understanding' (buddhi) and 'fortitude' (dhṛti)? (pg. 433)
28. Cite the verses that describe the three types of buddhi (understanding). (pg. 434)
29. Why does Śrī Kṛṣṇa say that a true intellect (sāttvika-buddhi) is that which is capable of clearly discerning what is to be feared and what is not to be feared? (pg. 434)
30. Cite the verses that elaborate on the three types of dhṛti (fortitude). (pg. 435)
31. What is the many-faceted role of dhṛti in our life? (pg. 435)
32. Explain why of the four puruṣārthas (fields of self effort) – dharma, artha, kāma and Mokṣa – the one endowed with rājasic dhṛti holds on firmly only to the first three? (pg. 436)
33. Explain the logic in the sequence of taking up the explanation of the three types of pleasure (sukha) after detailing the three types of jñāna (knowledge), kartā (doer), karma (action), buddhi (undertaking) and dhṛti (fortitude). (pg. 436)
34. Explain the Lord's declaration that sāttvic joy is poison-like at first but nectar-like at the end. (pg. 437)
35. Why does a true thinker not fall a prey to sense pleasures? (pg. 437)
36. What determines a person's 'caste' (varṇa)? (pg. 438)
37. What are the duties of a 'brāhmaṇa'? (pg. 438)
38. Enumerate the duties of a 'kṣatriya'? (pg. 438)
39. What determines the 'class' to which one belongs? Why should each individual perform the work of the 'class' to which he belongs? (pg. 439)
40. Why does Śrī Kṛṣṇa explain the various 'classes' of man and their respective duties? (pg. 439)

41. Explain the logic of the Lord's declaration that an individual attains Realisation by being devoted to the duties of his 'class'. (pg. 440)
42. How can work be changed into worship? (pg. 441)
43. Explain the excellence and importance of devoting oneself to the performance of one's duties (dharma) alone? (pg. 441)
44. What does the expression 'sahajaṁ karma' in the following verse mean? Why does the Lord advise that 'sahajaṁ karma' should not be abandoned even if it is occasioned by 'defects'? What is the 'defect' spoken of here? (pg. 441)
45. When does one attain 'naiṣkarmya siddhi' (state of actionlessness)? (pg. 442)
46. Who is a successful meditator? (pg. 443)
47. What are the 12 necessary conditions that a seeker has to fulfil in order to Realise Brahman? (pg. 443)
48. Does the instruction of the Lord to the seeker to find a quiet place to meditate mean that he has to move out to a jungle? (pg. 444)
49. How can a seeker overcome the mind's inclination for sense enjoyments? (pg. 444)
50. Why is overcoming of the 'kartṛtvabhāvanā' without the conquest of 'bhoktṛtvabhāvanā' a futile endeavour? (pg. 445)
51. Explain why the individual who has gained the knowledge of Brahman neither grieves nor desires (na śocati na kāṅkṣati)? (pg. 445)
52. Cite the verse wherein the Lord declares that through devotion one gains knowledge and through knowledge one attains the union with the Lord. (pg. 446)
53. Explain the significance of the term 'enters' in the Lord's declaration that the seeker having known the Lord in essence, enters into the Supreme (tato māṁ tattvato jñātvā viśate tadanantaram). (pg. 446)
54. What is the prime contribution of the Bhagavad Gītā to the Upaniṣadic tradition? (pg. 446)
55. Who can fix his mind firmly upon the Lord? (pg. 447)
56. Write a short note on the grace (prasāda) of the Lord. (pg. 447)

57. Why will Arjuna be compelled to fight in the battle inspite of his determination not to fight? (pg. 447)
58. Who becomes a victim of circumstances and who remains unshaken by them? (pg. 448)
59. Explain the Lord's statement that He dwells in the heart of all beings making them revolve like puppets mounted on a machine. (pg. 448)
60. Explain the importance of surrendering unto the Lord with all one's being (sarva-bhāvena). (pg. 449)
61. Why does the Lord say that His message of the Bhagavad Gītā is a 'greater secret than all secrets' (guhyād guhyataram)? (pg. 449)
62. Why does the Lord after declaring the entire Gītā to Arjuna give complete freedom to Arjuna and say: "you now act as you choose" (yathecchasi tathā kuru)? (pg. 449)
63. What is the importance of surrender (śaraṇāgati)? (pg. 450)
64. Cite the verse that summarises the entire Bhagavad Gītā and explain its salient points. (pg. 450)
65. What are the rules that should be borne in mind while imparting the knowledge of the Bhagavad Gītā to others? (pg. 452)
66. Cite the relevant verses wherein the Lord delcares that those who propagate the message of the Bhagavad Gītā are most dear to him. (pg. 452)
67. Why is the study of the Bhagavad Gītā termed Jñāna Yajña (Sacrifice of Wisdom)? (pg. 453)
68. Why is the faculty of śraddhā essential for a fruitful listening to the Bhagavad Gītā? (pg. 453)
69. Why is the student of the Bhagavad Gītā required to be 'without malice' (anasūya)? (pg. 454)
70. How did the message of the Bhagavad Gītā benefit Arjuna? (pg. 454)
71. Cite the concluding verse of the Bhagavad Gītā and explain its import. (pg. 454)
72. What are the choices of (1) tyāga (2) jñāna (3) karma (4) kartā (5) buddhi (6) dhṛti and (7) sukham of the sāttvic, rājasic and tāmasic types of people. (pg. 455)

Transliteration and Pronunciation

In the book, Devanāgarī characters are transliterated according to the scheme adopted by the International Congress of Orientalists at Athens in 1912. In it one fixed pronunciation value is given to each letter; f, q, w, x and z are not called to use. According to this scheme:

	sounds like		***sounds like***
अ	a o in s*o*n	ड्	ḍ d in *d*og
आ	ā a in m*a*ster	ढ्	ḍh dh in go*dh*hood
इ	i i in *i*f	ण्	ṇ n in u*n*der
ई	ī ee in f*ee*l	त्	t
उ	u u in f*u*ll	थ्	th th in *th*umb
ऊ	ū oo in b*oo*t	द्	d th in *th*en
ऋ	ṛ ri in *ri*m	ध्	dh theh in brea*the* *h*ere
ए	e a in ev*a*de	न्	n
ऐ	ai y in m*y*	प्	p
ओ	o	फ्	ph ph in loo*p* *h*ole
औ	au ow in n*ow*	ब्	b
क्	k	भ्	bh bh in a*bh*or
ख्	kh ckh in bloc*kh*ead	म्	m
ग्	g (hard)	य्	y
घ्	gh gh in lo*g-h*ut	र्	r
ङ्	ṅ ng	ल्	l
च्	c ch in *ch*uckle	व्	v in a*v*ert
छ्	ch chh in catc*h h*im	श्	ś sh in *sh*ut
ज्	j	ष्	ṣ s in *s*ugar
झ्	jh dgeh in he*dgeh*og	स्	s
ञ्	ñ n in ba*n*yan	ह्	h
ट्	ṭ t in *t*ank	ं	ṁ
ठ्	ṭh th in an*t-h*ill	:	ḥ (half h)

Chinmaya International Foundation
has brought out the rare and original Sanskrit
autobiography of Swami Tapovanam

ISVARADARSANAM
ATHAVA TAPOVANACARITAM

[illegible]

- Rs. [illegible] (subscriber price) [illegible]
- [illegible]
- [illegible] (including postage)
- [illegible] discount [illegible] 10 books [illegible]

[illegible]

Name [illegible]

Address [illegible]

Telephone [illegible] E-mail [illegible]

NUMBER OF COPIES [illegible]

Signature [illegible] Date [illegible]

Chinmaya International Foundation
[illegible]

cif

Chinmaya International Foundation

announces

Foundation Postal Vedanta and E-Vedanta Courses

An Introductory Course

The Chinmaya International Foundation (CIF) offers a Foundation Postal Vedanta Course and an E-Vedanta Course for those who wish to study Vedanta. The materials of study for both courses are the same, whether correspondence is via mail or e-mail.

Course Objective

The primary aim of this one-year home-study course is to introduce one to Vedanta. All important Vedantic concepts are dealt with briefly so as to give an overview of the Vedantic Philosophy and its practice.

(P.T.O.)

(P.T.O.)

REGISTRATION FORM

I would like to join (tick your choice):

Foundation Postal Vedanta Course ☐
Foundation E-Vedanta Course ☐

Full Name ....

Gender ....

Address..

....

....

E-mail..

Home Phone.. Cell Phone ....

Date of Birth..

Present Occupation ....

Educational Qualifications ....

....

....

Spoken Languages ....

Course Fee (Non-refundable)

(1) Postal Course :

Residents of India, Sri Lanka, Nepal, Bhutan, Pakistan, Bangladesh, Maldives and Afghanistan IRs. 1,000; Other Residents US$175

(2) E-Course :

Residents of India, Sri Lanka, Nepal, Bhutan, Pakistan, Bangladesh, Maldives and Afghanistan IRs. 1,000; Other Residents US$100

Registration

To register, complete the form and submit it with your draft, check or Money order, payable to 'Chinmaya International Foundation; payable at 'State Bank of Travancore'at Piravom or Ernakulam. Mail your form along with your course fee to:

Director

Chinmaya International Foundation

Adi Sankara Nilayam, Veliyanad

Ernakulam District, Pin - 682 319, Kerala, India.

If you are interested to register online for the E-course or if you seek further details about these courses visit **www.chinfo.org**

Reading/Writing Languages ....

....

Vedantic Literature studies to date ....

....

....

Are you a member of or affiliated with any spiritual/religious organization(s)? (If yes, specify.)

....

....

....

Signature Date

Chinmaya International Foundation

announces

Advanced Postal Vedanta and E-Vedanta Courses

Chinmaya International Foundation is pleased to announce its new Advanced Postal Vedanta Course and Advanced E-Vedanta Course. The materials of study for both courses are the same, whether correspondence is via mail or e-mail.

Course Objective : The primary aim of this one-year home-study course is to provide clarity and depth to your Vedantic study. All important Vedantic concepts dealt with in the prakarana granthas, such as Vivekachudamani, Atma Bodha, Tattva Bodha, Vakya Vriti and Panchadashi, are covered in a series of 24 detailed lessons.

Course Eligibility : Any individual who seeks to have an in-depth study of Vedanta is welcome to join this course. It is not required for

(P.T.O.)

REGISTRATION FORM

I would like to join (tick your option) :

Advanced Postal Vedanta Course ☐
Advanced E-Vedanta Course ☐

Full Name ....

Gender ....

Address...

....

....

E-mail...

Home Phone.. Cell Phone ....

Date of Birth..

Present Occupation ....

Educational Qualifications ....

....

....

Spoken Languages ....

students to have completed CIF's Foundation Postal or E-Vedanta Course.

Course Fee (Non-refundable)

(1) Postal Course : Residents of India, Sri Lanka, Nepal, Bhutan, Pakistan, Bangladesh, Maldives and Afghanistan IRs. 2,000; Other Residents US$175

(2) E-Course : Residents of India, Sri Lanka, Nepal, Bhutan, Pakistan, Bangladesh, Maldives and Afghanistan IRs. 2,000; Other Residents US$100

Registration : To register, complete the form and submit it with your draft, check or Money order, payable to 'Chinmaya International Foundation; payable at 'State Bank of Travancore' at Piravom or Ernakulam. Mail your form along with your course fee to:

Director
Chinmaya International Foundation
Adi Sankara Nilayam, Veliyanad
Ernakulam District, Pin - 682 319, Kerala, India.

If you are interested to register online for the E-course or if you seek further details about these courses visit **www.chinfo.org**

Reading/Writing Languages ....

....

Vedantic Literature studies to date ....

....

....

Are you a member of or affiliated with any spiritual/religious organization(s)? (If yes, specify.)

....

....

....

Have you completed the Foundation Vedanta Course?

....

Signature Date